C000176888

STREE

Cheshire

Chester, Crewe, Macclesfield, Northwich, Warrington

First published in 1995 by

Philip's, a division of
Octopus Publishing Group Ltd
2-4 Heron Quays, London E14 4JP
An Hachette Livre UK Company

Fourth colour edition 2007
First impression 2007
CHEDA

ISBN-10   0-540-09164-2 (pocket)
ISBN-13   978-0-540-09164-5 (pocket)

© Philip's 2007

Ordnance Survey®

This product includes mapping data licensed from
Ordnance Survey® with the permission of the
Controller of Her Majesty's Stationery Office.
© Crown copyright 2007. All rights reserved.
Licence number 100011710.

Data for the speed cameras provided by
PocketGPSWorld.com Ltd.

Ordnance Survey and the OS Symbol are
registered trademarks of Ordnance Survey, the
national mapping agency of Great Britain.

Printed by Toppan, China

Contents

II **List of mobile speed cameras**

III **Key to map symbols**

IV **Key to map pages**

VI **Route planning**

VIII **Administrative and Postcode boundaries**

1 **Street maps** at 2⅔ inches to 1 mile

237 **Street map of Chester city centre** at 5⅓ inches to 1 mile

238 **Index** of towns, villages, streets, hospitals, industrial estates, railway stations, schools, shopping centres, universities and places of interest

Digital Data

The exceptionally high-quality mapping found in this atlas is available as digital data in TIFF format, which is easily convertible to other bitmapped (raster) image formats.

The index is also available in digital form as a standard database table. It contains all the details found in the printed index together with the National Grid reference for the map square in which each entry is named.

For further information and to discuss your requirements, please contact james.mann@philips-maps.co.uk

Mobile speed cameras

The vast majority of speed cameras used on Britain's roads are operated by safety camera partnerships. These comprise local authorities, the police, Her Majesty's Court Service (HMCS) and the Highways Agency.

This table lists the sites where each safety camera partnership may enforce speed limits through the use of mobile cameras or detectors. These are usually set up on the roadside or a bridge spanning the road and operated by a police or civilian enforcement officer. The speed limit at each site (if available) is shown in red type, followed by the approximate location in black type.

Mike Harrington / Alamy

M6
- 70 Bradwell, northbound
- 70 Northwich, northbound
- 50 Woolston near Warrington, northbound

M62
- 70 Croft, eastbound and westbound

A50
- 30 Grappenhall, Knutsford Rd
- 30 Knutsford, Manchester/Toft Rd
- 30 Warrington, Long Lane

A54
- 60&70 Ashton, Kelsall Rd

A56
- 40 Lymm, Camsley Lane

A57
- 40 Paddington, New Manchester Rd

A523
- 30 Poynton, London Rd

A532
- 30 Crewe, West St

A533
- 40 Middlewich, Booth Lane

A537
- 50 Macclesfield, Buxton Rd nr Wildboarclough

A5019
- 30 Crewe, Mill St

A5032
- 30 Whitby, Chester Rd

A5034
- 60 Mere, Mereside Rd

A5104
- 30 Chester, Hough Green

B5071
- 30 Crewe, Gresty Rd

B5078
- 30 Alsager, Sandbach Rd North

B5082
- 30 Northwich, Middlewich Rd

B5132
- 30 Ellesmere Port, Overpool Rd

B5153
- 30 Mill Lane/Hollow Lane (speed indicator sign)

B5463
- 30 Little Sutton, Station Rd

B5470
- 30 Macclesfield, Rainow Rd

Key to map symbols

III

Motorway with junction number	Ambulance station
Primary route – dual/single carriageway	Coastguard station
A road – dual/single carriageway	Fire station
B road – dual/single carriageway	Police station
Minor road – dual/single carriageway	Accident and Emergency entrance to hospital
Other minor road – dual/single carriageway	Hospital
Road under construction	Place of worship
Tunnel, covered road	Information Centre (open all year)
Speed cameras - single, multiple	Shopping Centre
Rural track, private road or narrow road in urban area	Parking, Park and Ride
Gate or obstruction to traffic (restrictions may not apply at all times or to all vehicles)	Post Office
	Camping site, caravan site
Path, bridleway, byway open to all traffic, road used as a public path	Golf course, picnic site
Pedestrianised area	Important buildings, schools, colleges, universities and hospitals Prim Sch
Postcode boundaries	Built up area
County and unitary authority boundaries	Woods
Railway, tunnel, railway under construction	Water name River Medway
Tramway, tramway under construction	River, weir, stream
Miniature railway	Canal, lock, tunnel
Railway station Walsall	Water
Private railway station	Tidal water
Metro station South Shields	Non-Roman antiquity Church
Tram stop, tram stop under construction	Roman antiquity ROMAN FORT
Bus, coach station	Adjoining page indicators and overlap bands 87 The colour of the arrow and the band indicates the scale of the adjoining or overlapping page (see scales below) 237

Acad	Academy	Inst	Institute	Recn Gd	Recreation Ground
Allot Gdns	Allotments	Ct	Law Court		
Cemy	Cemetery	L Ctr	Leisure Centre	Resr	Reservoir
C Ctr	Civic Centre	LC	Level Crossing	Ret Pk	Retail Park
CH	Club House	Liby	Library	Sch	School
Coll	College	Mkt	Market	Sh Ctr	Shopping Centre
Crem	Crematorium	Meml	Memorial	TH	Town Hall/House
Ent	Enterprise	Mon	Monument	Trad Est	Trading Estate
Ex H	Exhibition Hall	Mus	Museum	Univ	University
Ind Est	Industrial Estate	Obsy	Observatory	W Twr	Water Tower
IRB Sta	Inshore Rescue Boat Station	Pal	Royal Palace	Wks	Works
		PH	Public House	YH	Youth Hostel

Enlarged mapping only

	Railway or bus station building
	Place of interest
	Parkland

■ The small numbers around the edges of the maps identify the 1 kilometre National Grid lines

■ The dark grey border on the inside edge of some pages indicates that the mapping does not continue onto the adjacent page

The scale of the maps on the pages numbered in blue is 4.2 cm to 1 km • 2⅔ inches to 1 mile • 1: 23810	0 ¼ ½ ¾ 1 mile
	0 250m 500m 750m 1 kilometre

The scale of the maps on pages numbered in red is 8.4 cm to 1 km • 5⅓ inches to 1 mile • 1: 11900	0 220 yards 440 yards 660 yards ½ mile
	0 125m 250m 375m ½ kilometre

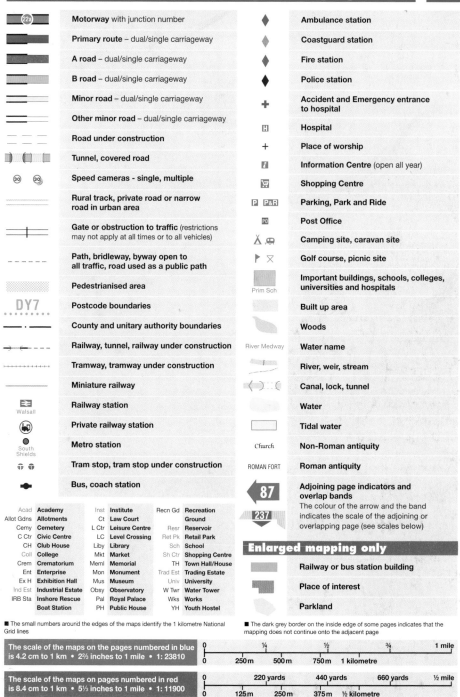

IV

Key to map pages

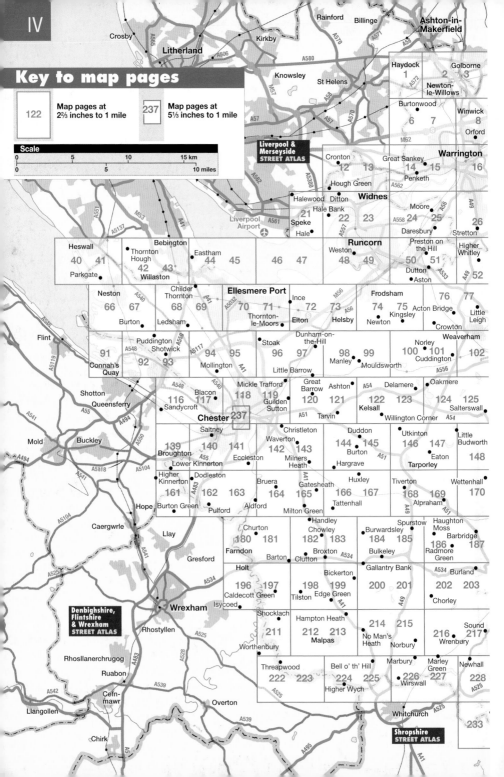

| 122 | Map pages at 2⅔ inches to 1 mile | | 237 | Map pages at 5⅓ inches to 1 mile |

Scale

0   5   10   15 km
0   5   10 miles

Liverpool & Merseyside STREET ATLAS

Denbighshire, Flintshire & Wrexham STREET ATLAS

Shropshire STREET ATLAS

Crosby · Litherland · Kirkby · Rainford · Billinge · Ashton-in-Makerfield

Knowsley · St Helens · Haydock 1 · Golborne 3

Newton-le-Willows

Burtonwood · 6 · 7 · Winwick 8 · Orford

Cronton · 12 · 13 · Great Sankey · Warrington · 14 · 15 · 16

Hough Green · Penketh

Halewood · Ditton · Widnes · Moore

Liverpool Airport · Hale Bank · 21 · 22 · 23 · 24 · 25 · 26

Speke · Hale · Daresbury · Stretton

Weston · Runcorn · Preston on the Hill · Higher Whitley

Heswall · Bebington · Eastham · 48 · 49 · 50 · 51 · 52

Thornton Hough · 44 · 45 · 46 · 47 · Dutton · Aston

Parkgate · 42 · 43 · Willaston

Neston · Childer Thornton · Ellesmere Port · Ince · Frodsham · 76 · 77

66 · 67 · 68 · 69 · 70 · 71 · 72 · 73 · 74 · 75 · Acton Bridge · Little Leigh

Burton · Ledsham · Thornton-le-Moors · Elton · Helsby · Newton · Kingsley · Crowton

Flint · Puddington · Shotwick · 94 · 95 · Stoak · Dunham-on-the-Hill · Norley · Weaverham

91 · 92 · 93 · Mollington · 96 · 97 · 98 · 99 · 100 · 101 · 102

Connah's Quay · Little Barrow · Manley · Mouldsworth · Cuddington

Shotton · Blacon · Mickle Trafford · Great Barrow · Ashton · Delamere · Oakmere

Queensferry · Sandycroft · 116 · 117 · 118 · 119 · 120 · 121 · 122 · 123 · 124 · 125

Guilden Sutton · Kelsall · Saltersswall

Chester · 237 · Tarvin · Willington Corner

Mold · Saltney · Christleton · Duddon · Utkinton · Little Budworth

Buckley · 139 · 140 · 141 · Waverton · 142 · 143 · 144 · 145 · 146 · 147 · 148

Broughton · Eccleston · Burton · Eaton · Tarporley

Lower Kinnerton · Milners Heath · Hargrave

Higher Kinnerton · Dodleston · Bruera · Huxley · Tiverton · Wettenhall

161 · 162 · 163 · 164 · 165 · 166 · 167 · 168 · 169 · 170

Hope · Burton Green · Gateshead · Alpraham

Caergwrle · Pulford · Aldford · Milton Green · Tattenhall

Llay · Churton · Handley · Chowley · Spurstow · Haughton Moss

180 · 181 · 182 · 183 · 184 · 185 · 186 · 187

Gresford · Farndon · Burwardsley · Barbridge

Holt · Barton · Broxton · Bulkeley · Radmore Green

Wrexham · Clutton · Bickerton · Gallantry Bank · Burland

196 · 197 · 198 · 199 · 200 · 201 · 202 · 203

Rhostyllen · Caldecott Green · Tilston · Edge Green · Chorley

Isycoed

Shocklach · Hampton Heath · 214 · 215 · Sound

Rhoslanerchrugog · 211 · 212 · 213 · No Man's Heath · 216 · 217

Ruabon · Worthenbury · Malpas · Norbury · Wrenbury

Cefn-mawr · Threapwood · Bell o' th' Hill · Marbury · Marley Green · Newhall

Llangollen · 222 · 223 · 224 · 225 · 226 · 227 · 228

Higher Wych · Wirswall

Chirk · Overton · Whitchurch · 233

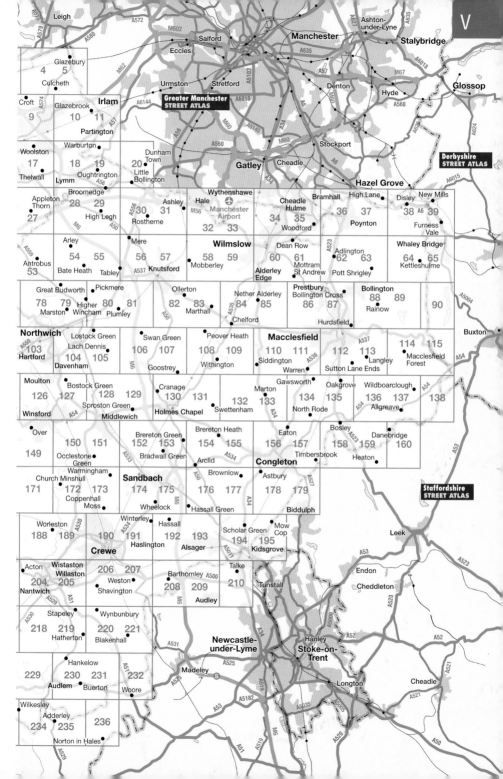

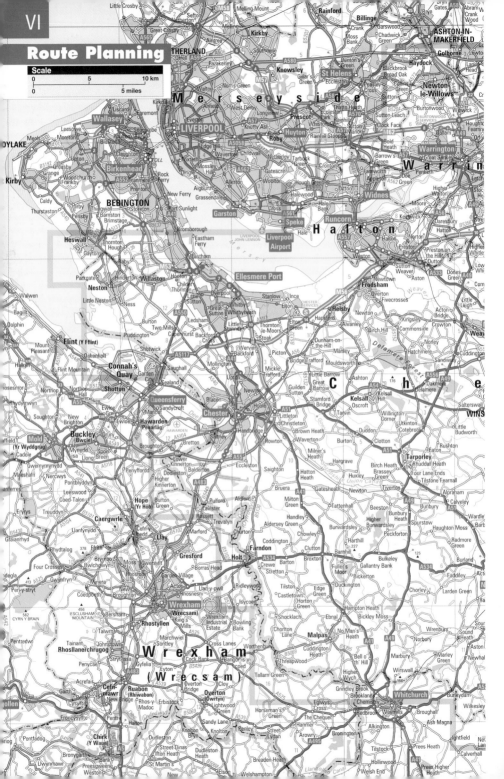

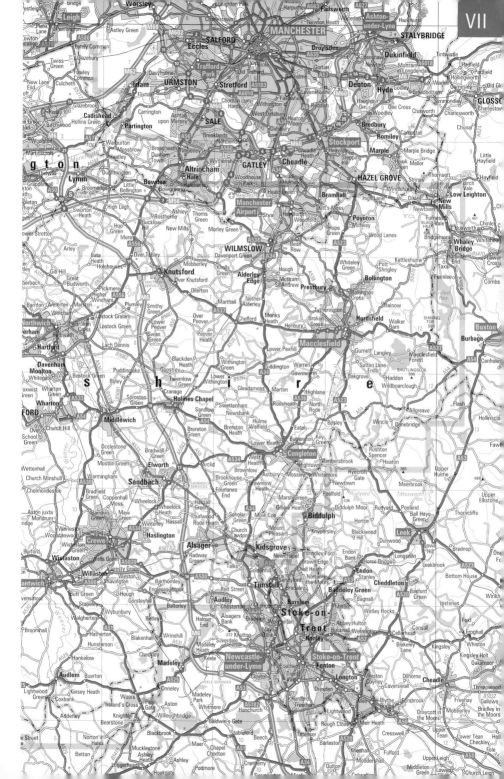

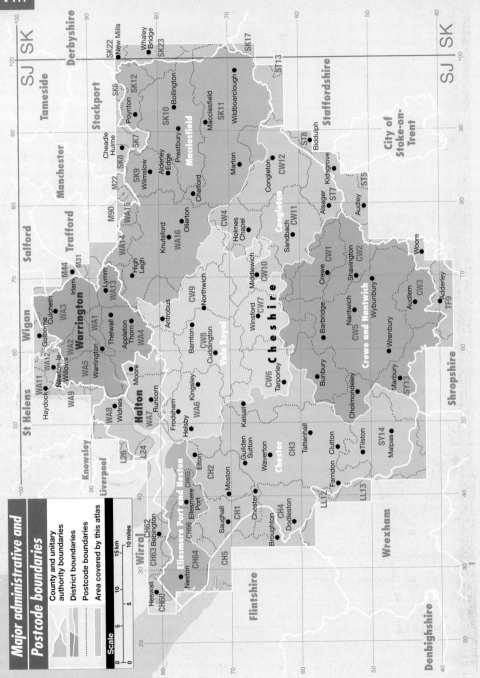

Major administrative and Postcode boundaries

County and unitary authority boundaries
District boundaries
Postcode boundaries
Area covered by this atlas

Scale

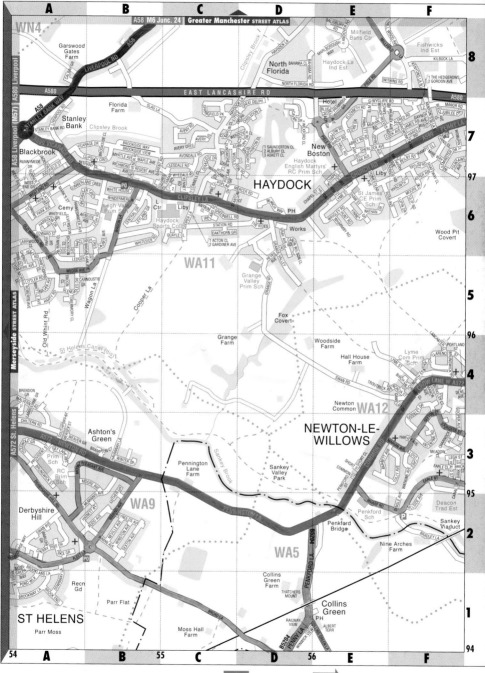

A58 M6 Junc. 24 **Greater Manchester** STREET ATLAS

WN4

Garswood Gates Farm

North Florida

Millfield Bsns Ctr

Haydock La Ind Est

Fishwicks Ind Est

KILBUCK LA

t THE HEDGEROWS
2 GORDON AVE

EAST LANCASHIRE RD

A580

A580

Florida Farm

Stanley Bank

Clipsley Brook

Hotel

New Boston

Haydock English Martyrs' RC Prim Sch

HAYDOCK

Liby

97

Blackbrook

Merseyside STREET ATLAS

PO

WHITE HOUSE

Cemy

Legh Vale Prim Sch

CLIPSLEY LA

Ctr

Liby

Haydock Sports Coll

St James CE Prim Sch

PH

1 ACTON CL
2 GARDINER AVE

STATION RD

Works

6

Wood Pit Covert

WA11

Grange Valley Prim Sch

5

Cooper La

Fox Covert

Grange Farm

Woodside Farm

Hall House Farm

96

Lyme Com Prim Sch

St Helens Canal (dis)

Old Whint Rd

Wagon La

SWAN RD

Newton Common

WA12

NEWTON-LE-WILLOWS

4

Brendon Gr

Ashton's Green

Prim Sch

RC Prim Sch

Pennington Lane Farm

Sankey Brook

Sankey Valley Park

3

Penkford Sch

MEADOW

Deacon Trad Est

95

Derbyshire Hill

WA9

PENNINGTON LA

Penkford Bridge

Sankey Viaduct

Nine Arches Farm

2

WA5

Recn Gd

Parr Flat

Collins Green Farm

THATCHERS MOUNT

Collins Green

PH

1

ST HELENS

Parr Moss

Moss Hall Farm

RAILWAY VIEW

ALBERT TERR

94

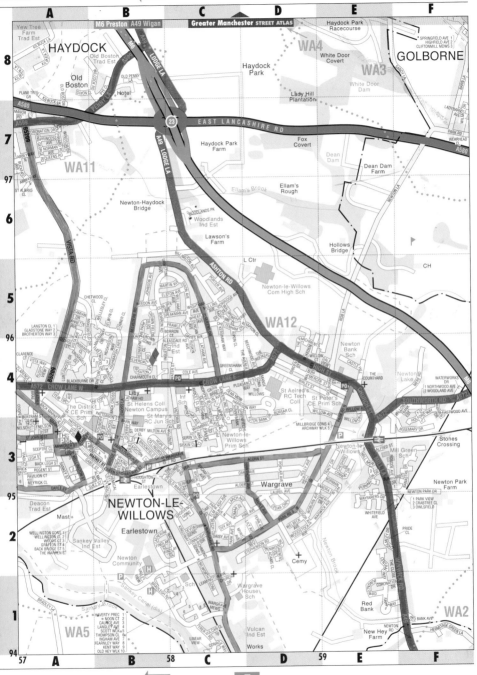

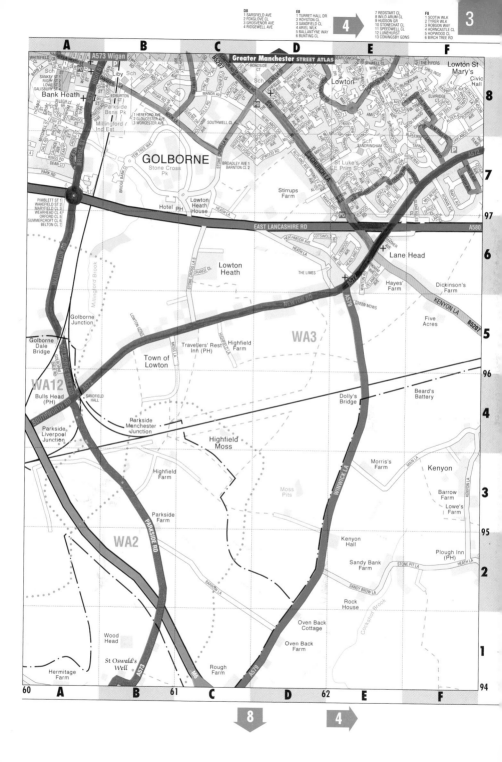

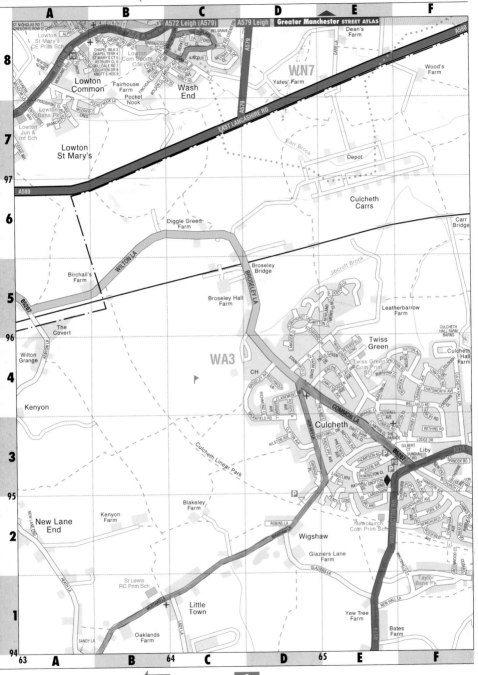

3

A572 Leigh (A579) A579 Leigh **Greater Manchester** STREET ATLAS

ST NICHOLAS RD 1
GREGORYS ROW 2
Lowton
St Mary's
CE Prim Sch

Dean's
Farm

WN7

Wood's
Farm

Lowton
St Mary's CT
CHAPEL WLK 3
CHAPEL TERR 4
ST MARY'S CT 5
ASTBURY CL 6
MILLDALE RD 7
LEIGHTON DR 8
KNOTT'S HO 9

BELGRAVE
CL
DALESFORD
CL
GREENACRES
THE POP...
ARLING...

Lowton
Com Sports
Coll

LINCOLN CL

Yates' Farm

8

Lowton
Common

Fairhouse
Farm
Pocket
Nook

**Wash
End**

STRADBROKE CL
MOORFIELD
CRES
POCKET WALK LA
BRANCASTER

EAST LANCASHIRE RD

Carr Brook

Depot

7

Lowton
Jun &
Inf Sch

Lowton
St Mary's

97 A580

Culcheth
Carrs

Diggle Green
Farm

6

Carr
Bridge

WILTON LA

Broseley
Bridge

Jibcroft Brook

5 B5207

Birchall's
Farm

Broseley Hall
Farm

BROSELEY LA

Leatherbarrow
Farm

CULCHETH
HALL FARM
BARNS

96

The
Covert

NORTHURST CL
MITTON CL

Twiss
Green

Culcheth
Hall
Farm

Wilton
Grange

WA3

TWISS GREEN CHILDREN CTR
Twiss Green
Com Prim
Sch
BURNHAM CL

CHATSWORTH AVE

4

Kenyon

CH

CLAIREMONT
AVE

COMMON LA

WELLFIELD RD

Culcheth

ROCKFIELD RD

Culcheth

THE
PARADE
LODGE DR

3 Culcheth Linear Park

RILSTON AVE

BEECHMILL DR

GILBERT
CT
SUNDIAL
HO

Liby

YARNOCK RD

A574

P B5207

Blakeley
Farm

P

THOMPSON CT
JACKSON AVE
RIMINGTON CL
RATHBRO...
LANSDOWNE
CROFTON

95 P

New Lane
End

Kenyon
Farm

ROBINS LA

Newchurch
Com Prim
Sch

NEW LANE RD

2

Wigshaw

Glaziers Lane
Farm

WARBURTON RD

Taylor
Bsns Pk

St Lewis
RC Prim Sch

GLAZIERS LA

SANDY LA

1

Little
Town

Yew Tree
Farm

NEW HALL LA

JEAN LA
LADY LA

Oaklands
Farm

A574

Bates
Farm

94 SANDY LA

63 A **B** 64 **C** **D** 65 **E** **F**

3

9

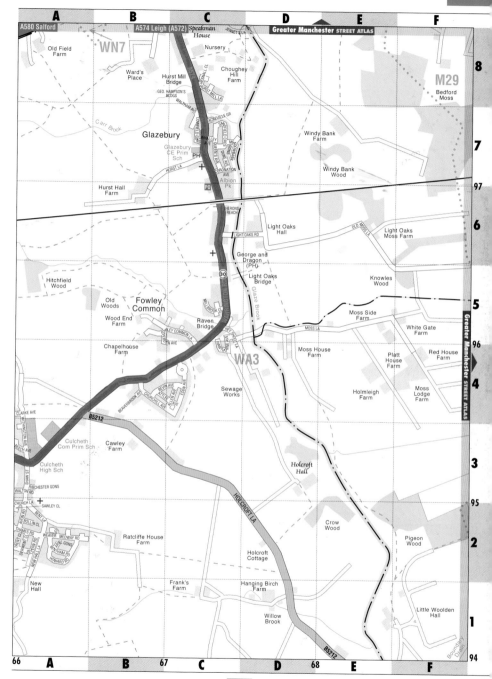

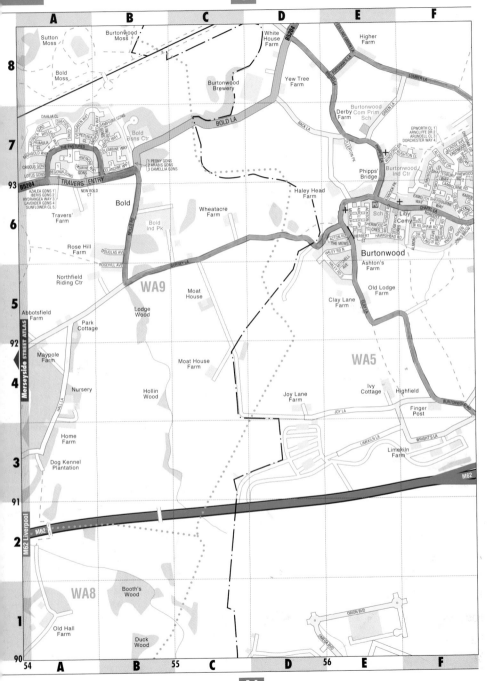

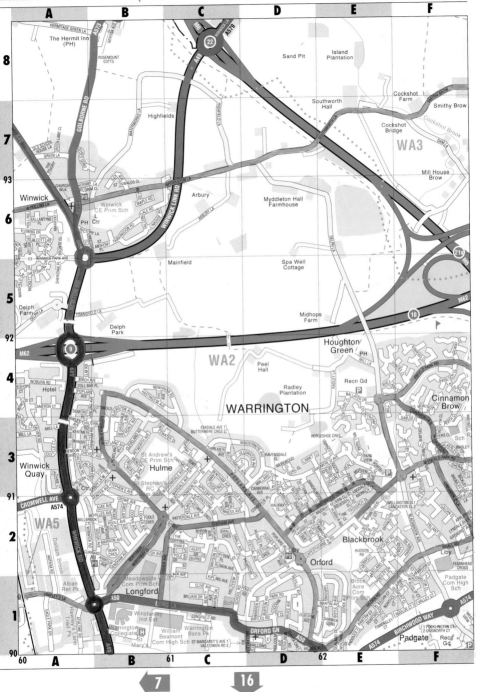

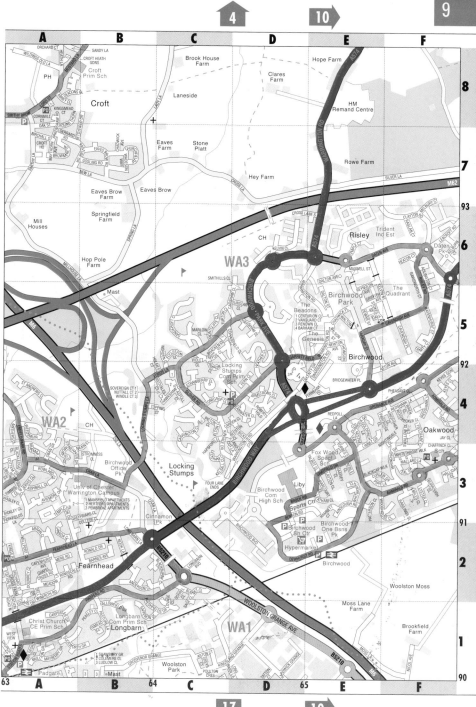

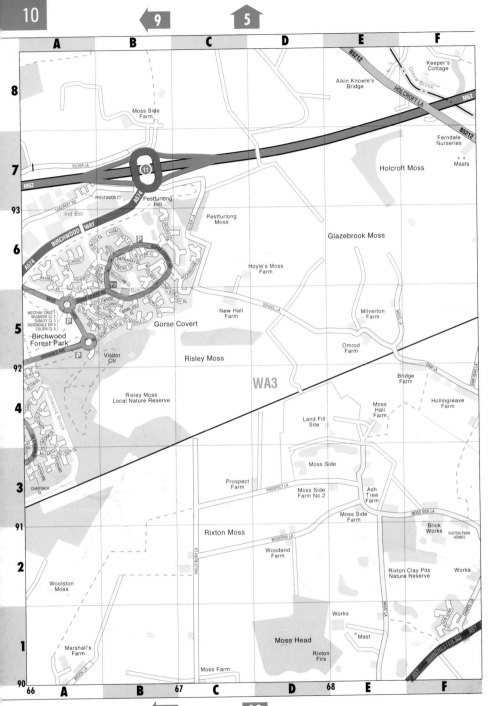

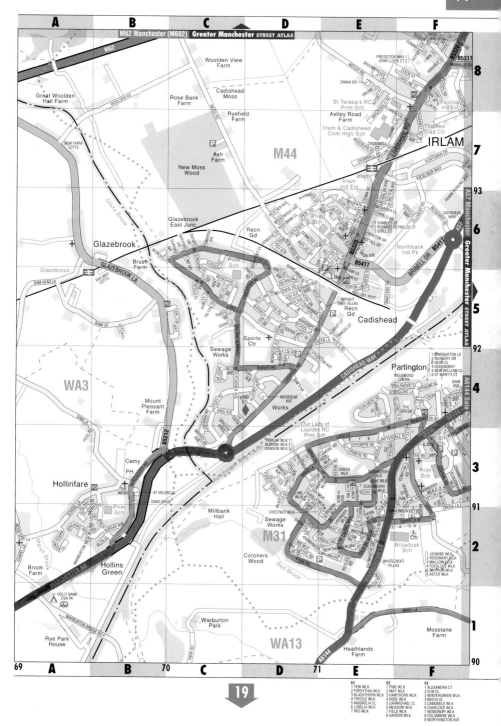

M62 Manchester (M602) **Greater Manchester** STREET ATLAS

E2
1 YEW WLK
2 FORSYTHIA WLK
3 BLACKTHORN WLK
4 THISTLE WLK
5 MAGNOLIA CL
6 LOBELIA WLK
7 IRIS WLK

E3
1 PINE WLK
2 MAY WLK
3 HAWTHORN WLK
4 ROSE WLK
5 CARMICHAEL CL
6 MEADOW WLK
7 FIELD WLK
8 GARDEN WLK

F3
1 ALEXANDRA CT
2 ELM CL
3 WINTERGREEN WLK
4 BEECH CL
5 CAMOMILE WLK
6 CHARLOCK WLK
7 WOODRUFF WLK
8 COLUMBINE WLK
9 WORTHINGTON AVE

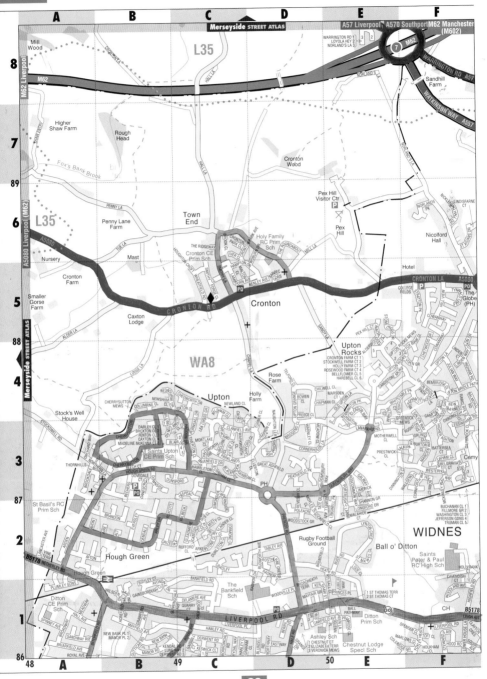

Merseyside STREET ATLAS

A57 Liverpool, A570 Southport M62 Manchester (M602)

L35

WARRINGTON RD 1
LOYOLA HEY 2
NORLAND'S LA 3

M62

WARRINGTON RD A57

M62 Liverpool

Mill Wood

Sandhill Farm

WATKINSON WAY A557

Higher Shaw Farm

Rough Head

Cronton Wood

Fox's Bank Brook

NORLANDS

LINDISFARNE CT

Pex Hill Visitor Ctr

Nicolford Hall

A5080 Liverpool (M62)

L35

Penny Lane Farm

Town End

Pex Hill

Hotel

CRONTON LA A5080

Nursery

Mast

THE RIDGEWAY

Cronton CE Prim Sch

Holy Family RC Prim Sch

COLLEGE FIELDS

The Globe (PH)

Cronton Farm

Smaller Gorse Farm

Caxton Lodge

CRONTON RD

Cronton

COWANWAY

Merseyside STREET ATLAS

Upton Rocks

CRONTON FARM CT 1
STOCKWELL FARM CT 2
HOLLY FARM CT 3
ROSEWOOD FARM CT 4
BELLFLOWER CL 5
HAREBELL CL 6

WA8

Rose Farm

Stock's Well House

Upton

Holly Farm

CHERRY SUTTON MEWS

NEWSHAM

Darley Cl
Broxton Cl
Fenton Cl
Caxton Cl
Madeline McKenna Ct

All Saints Upton CE Prim Sch

Thornhills

St Basil's RC Prim Sch

Dovedale Ct

Hough Green

Hough Green

WIDNES

Rugby Football Ground

Ball o' Ditton

Saints Peter & Paul RC High Sch

BUCHANAN CL 1
FILLMORE GR 2
WASHINGTON CL 3
JEFFERSON GDNS 4
TRUMAN CL 5

Cerny

CAVENDISH

Ditton CE Prim Sch

The Bankfield Sch

WOODVILLE PL

MAYFAIR DR

1 ST THOMAS TERR
2 ST THOMAS ST

LIVERPOOL RD

Ball Pathway

Ditton Prim Sch

CH

B5178

LIVERPOOL RD

LEIGH AVE

Ashley Sch

1 CHESTNUT CT
2 ELIZABETH TER
3 VERONICA MEWS

Chestnut Lodge Specl Sch

HOLKHAM

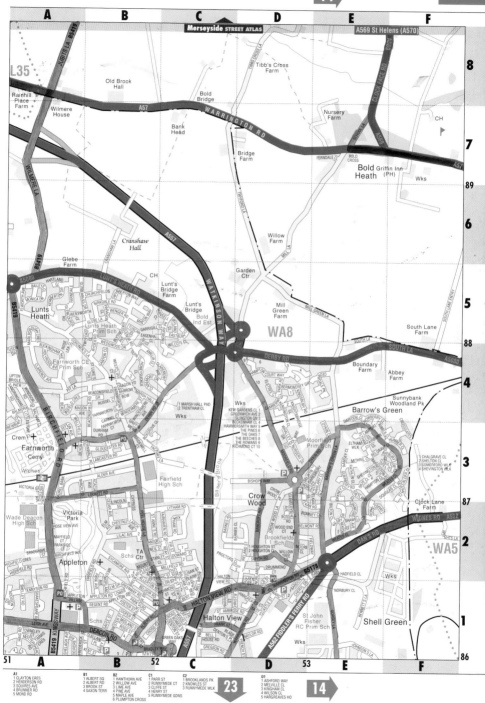

Merseyside STREET ATLAS

A1
1 CLAYTON CRES
2 HENDERSON RD
3 SQUIRES AVE
4 BRUNNER RD
5 MOND RD

B1
1 ALBERT SQ
2 ALBERT RD
3 BROOK ST
4 SAXON TERR

B2
1 HAWTHORN AVE
2 WILLOW AVE
3 LIME AVE
4 PINE AVE
5 MAPLE AVE
6 PLUMPTON CROSS

C1
1 PARR ST
2 RUNNYMEDE CT
3 CLIFFE ST
4 HENRY ST
5 RUNNYMEDE GDNS

C2
1 BROOKLANDS PK
2 KNOWLES ST
3 RUNNYMEDE WLK

D1
1 ASHFORD WAY
2 MELVILLE CL
3 KINGHAM CL
4 WILSON CL
5 HARGREAVES HO

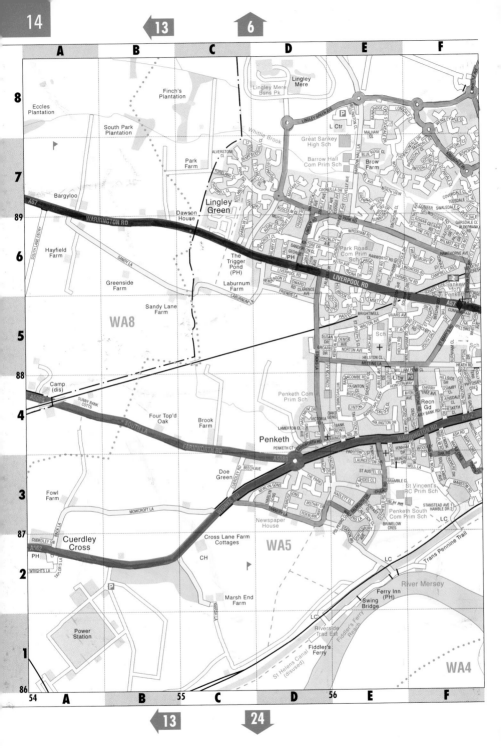

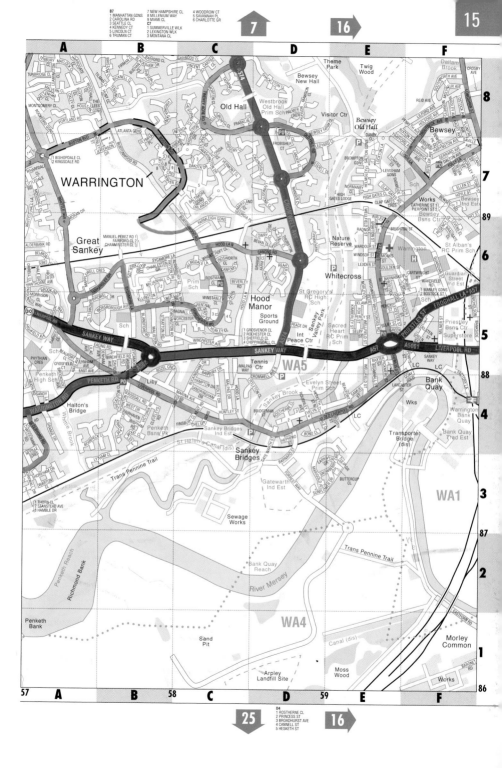

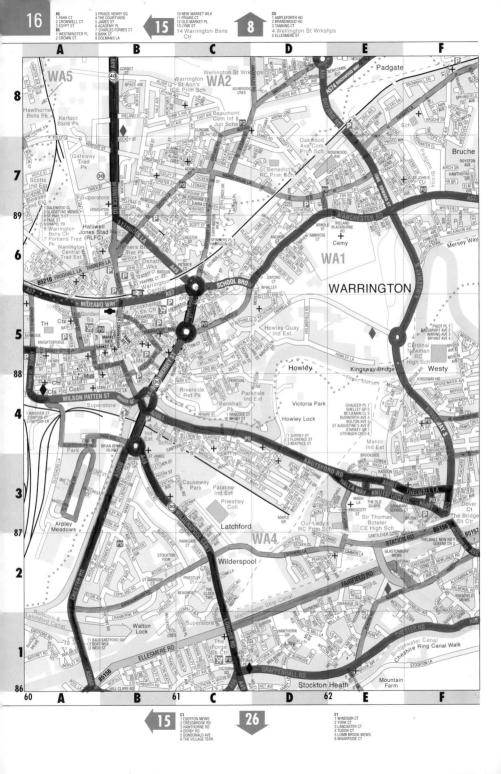

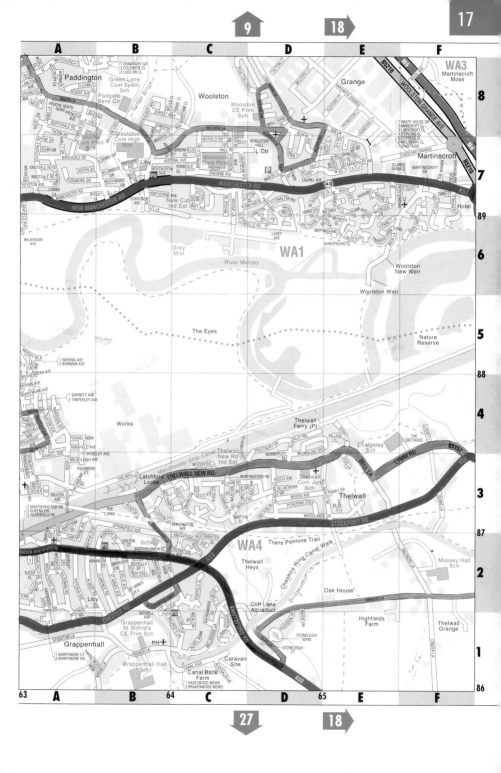

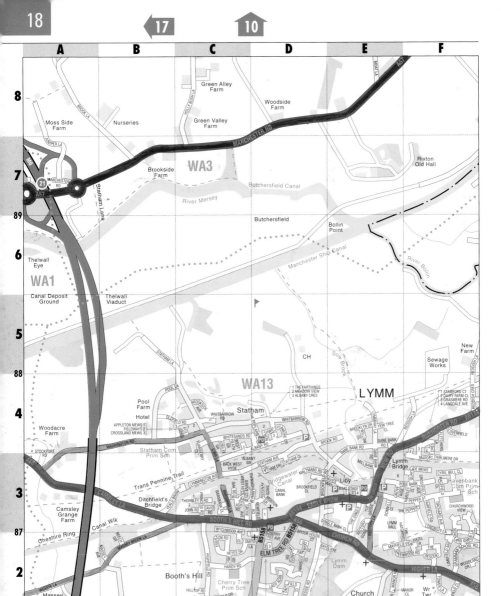

8

Green Alley
Farm

Woodside
Farm

Moss Side
Farm

Nurseries

Green Valley
Farm

Rixton
Old Hall

WA3

Brookside
Farm

MANCHESTER RD

7

Butchersfield Canal

21
MANCHESTER
RD

A57

River Mersey

89

Butchersfield

Butchersfield

Bollin
Point

River Bollin

6

Thelwall
Eye

WA1

Manchester Ship Canal

Canal Deposit
Ground

Thelwall
Viaduct

New
Farm

Sewage
Works

5

CH

Sow Brook

88

WA13

LYMM

Pool
Farm

STATHAM LA

WHITBARROW
RD

1 THE YARTHINGS
2 MEADOW VIEW
3 ALBANY CRES

1 STAMFORD CT
2 DAIRY FARM CL
3 GRASMERE RD
4 LANGDALE AVE

4

Woodacre
Farm

Hotel

Statham

WHITBARROW RD

WHITESANDS RD

SYC

P

BROOK RD

STOCKPORT
RD

WARRINGTON RD

ALBANY
GR

STATHAM AVE

Lymm
Bridge

3

Statham Com
Prim Sch

Trans Pennine Trail

BACK WEST
HYDE

Libv

Camsley
Grange
Farm

CAMSLEY LA

Ditchfield's
Bridge

Bridgewater
Canal

CANAL
BANK

BOAT STAGE

Ravenbank
Com Prim
Sch

Canal Wlk

THORNLEY RD

BROOKFIELD
CL

P

LYMM
HALL

Churchwood
View

Cheshire Ring

JOHN RD

BOOTH'S HILL RD

DINGLE BANK CL

2

Massey
Brook
Farm

WHASLE LA

MASSEY BROOK LA

WYCHWOOD AVE

OLD SMITHY

HEYES DR

HARDY RD

PO

ELM TREE RD

B5158

BROOK HOUSE LA

Lymm
Dam

Church
Green

MANOR
RD

Wr
Twr

HIGHER LA

A56

Booth's Hill

Cherry Tree
Prim Sch

HILLFOLD RD

HIGHFIELD DR

Cherrylane
Farm

1 BOOTHS HILL CL
2 HOLLY BANK
3 ELM TREE AVE

1

Booths Hill
Farm

Higher House
Farm

BOOTH'S LA

CHERRY LA

Tanners
Pool

B5158

THE AVENUE

Crosfield
Bridge

Kaylane Brook

Yewtree
Farm

86

WA4

M6

66

67

68

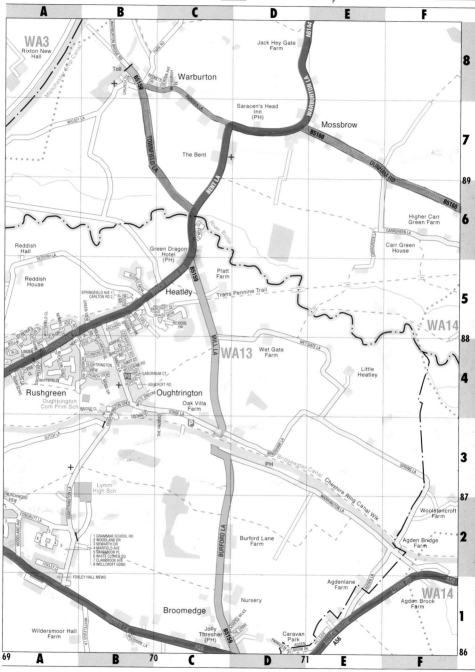

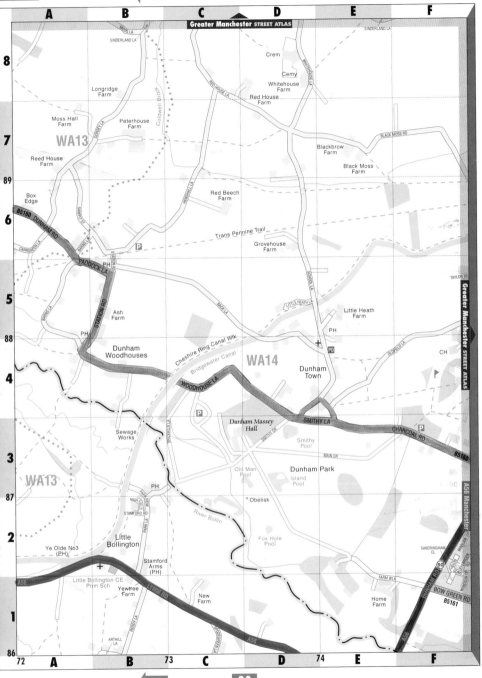

Greater Manchester STREET ATLAS

8

Crem

Cemy

Whitehouse Farm

SINDERLAND LA

MOSS LA

Longridge Farm

Red House Farm

7

WA13

Moss Hall Farm

Peterhouse Farm

Blackbrow Farm

BLACK MOSS RD

89

Reed House Farm

Black Moss Farm

Box Edge

Red Beech Farm

6

B5160 DUNHAM RD

CARROGREEN LA

PADDOCK LA

PH

Trans Pennine Trail

Grovehouse Farm

TAYLOR RD

5

BARNES LA

STATION RD

Ash Farm

BACK LA

LITTLE HEATH LA

Little Heath Farm

CH

88

PH

Dunham Woodhouses

Cheshire Ring Canal Wlk

Bridgewater Canal

WA14

PH

PO

Dunham Town

BLOREFIELD LA

4

WOODHOUSE LA

Sewage Works

BRICKKILN LA

Dunham Massey Hall

SMITHY DR

Smithy Pool

SMITHY LA

CHARCOAL RD

B5160

3

WA13

PH

HIGH FIELD

STAMFORD RD

PARK LA

Old Man Pool

Dunham Park

MAIN DR

Island Pool

90

87

River Bollin

Obelisk

A56 Manchester

2

Ye Olde No3 (PH)

Little Bollington

Stamford Arms (PH)

Fox Hole Pool

SANDRINGHAM CL

BOW GREEN RD

B5161

A56

Little Bollington CE Prim Sch

Yewtree Farm

LYMM RD

New Farm

CROSSGRETTA LA

FARM WLK

Home Farm

DUNHAM RD

1

ARTHILL LA

A56

86

72   73   74

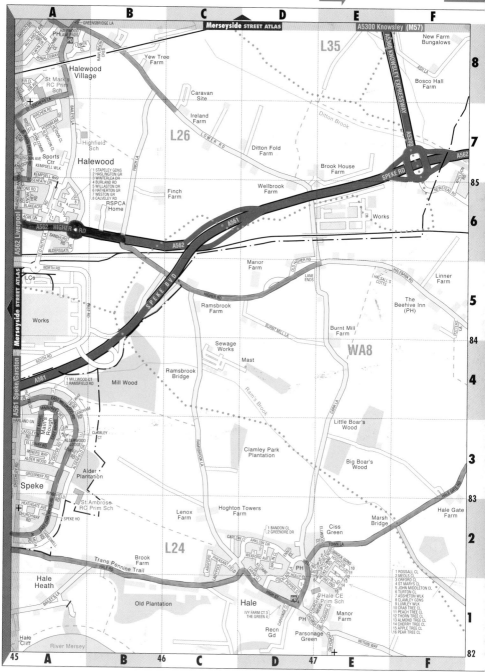

A5300 Knowsley (M57)

L35

New Farm
Bungalows

Yew Tree
Farm

Halewood
Village

Halewood

Caravan
Site

Ireland
Farm

L26

Bosco Hall
Farm

Ditton Brook

A5300 KNOWSLEY EXPRESSWAY

A5300

Highfield
Sch

Sports
Ctr

Ditton Fold
Farm

LOWER RD

A562

Brook House
Farm

SPEKE RD

85

1 STAPELEY GDNS
2 HASLINGTON GR
3 WINTERLEA DR
4 BURLAND RD
5 WILLASTON DR
6 HATHERTON GR
7 WESTON GR
8 CALVELEY RD

Finch
Farm

Wellbrook
Farm

RSPCA
Home

A562 Liverpool

HIGHER RD

A562

Works

6

A562

SPEKE BLVD

NORTH RD

Manor
Farm

OLD HIGHER RD

LANE
ENDS

HALSALL'S
COTTS

Linner
Farm

LCs

HIGHER RD

Ramsbrook
Farm

The
Beehive Inn
(PH)

5

Works

BURNT MILL LA

Burnt Mill
Farm

84

SOUTH RD

Sewage
Works

Mast

WA8

A561

Ramsbrook
Bridge

Ram's Brook

CABIN LA

4

1 MILLWOOD CT
2 RAMSFIELD RD

Mill Wood

RAMSBROOK LA

Little Boar's
Wood

Main's
Rough

CLAMLEY
CT

Alder
Plantation

Clamley Park
Plantation

Big Boar's
Wood

3

HALE GATE RD

Speke

GREENWAY RD

St Ambrose
RC Prim Sch

SPEKE HO

Lenox
Farm

Hoghton Towers
Farm

1 BANDON CL
2 GREENORE DR

Ciss
Green

Marsh
Bridge

Hale Gate
Farm

83

L24

CARLOW CL

ARKLOW DR

TOWN LA

2

Trans Pennine Trail

Brook
Farm

PHEASANT FIELD

WEXFORD AVE

PH

1 ROSSALL CL
2 MEOLS CL
3 ORFORD CL
4 ST MARY'S CL
5 JOHN MIDDLETON CL
6 TURTON CL
7 ASSHETON WLK
8 CLAMLEY GDNS
9 LUMLEY WLK
10 CRAB TREE CL
11 PEACH TREE CL
12 THORN TREE CL
13 ALMOND TREE CL
14 CHERRY TREE CL
15 APPLE TREE CL
16 PEAR TREE CL

Hale
Heath

Old Plantation

COCKSHEAD LA

HIGHER RD

Hale CE
Prim Sch

Manor
Farm

1

IVY FARM CT 3
THE GREEN 4

PH

PO

Recn
Gd

Parsonage
Green

WITHIN WAY

82

Hale
Cliff

River Mersey

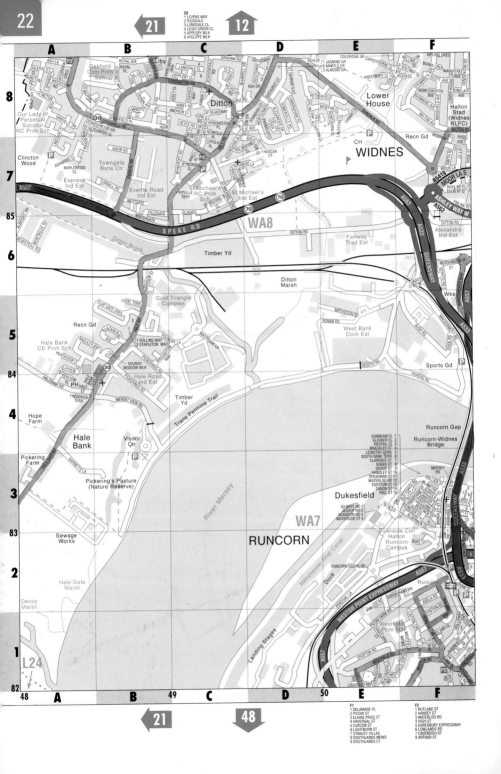

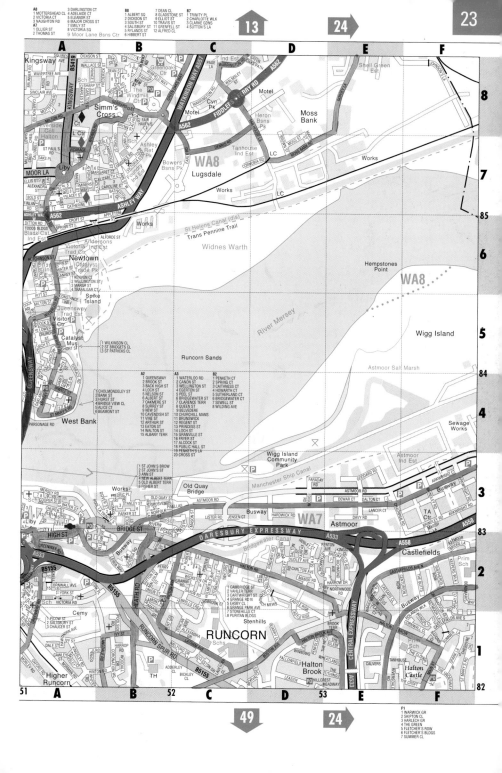

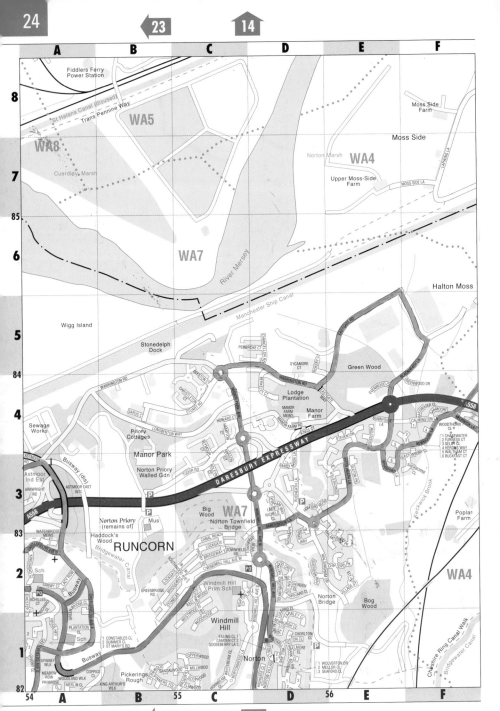

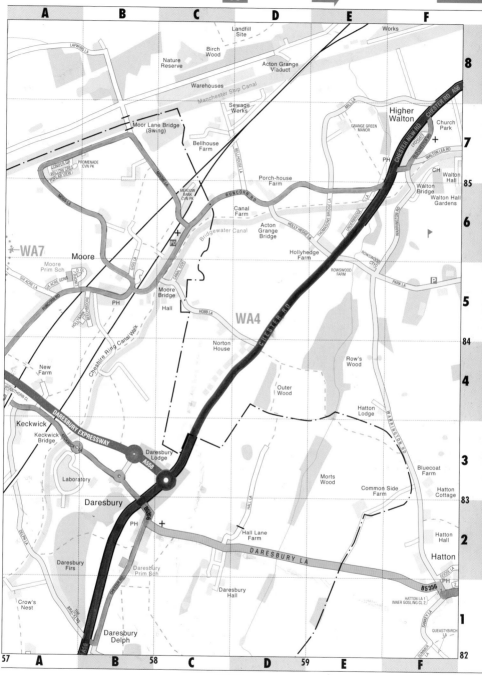

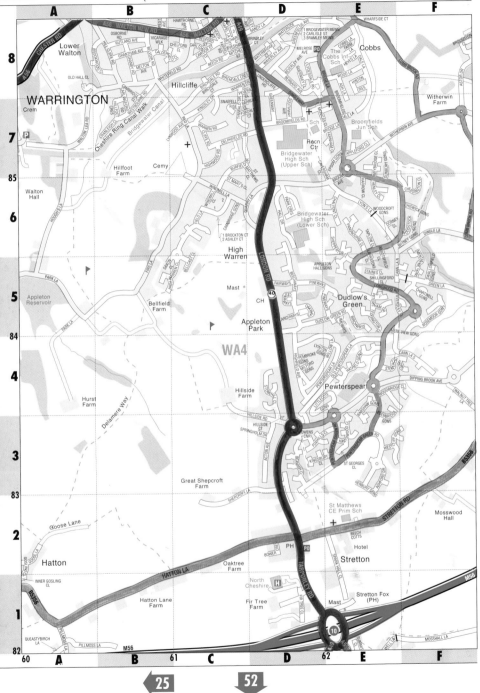

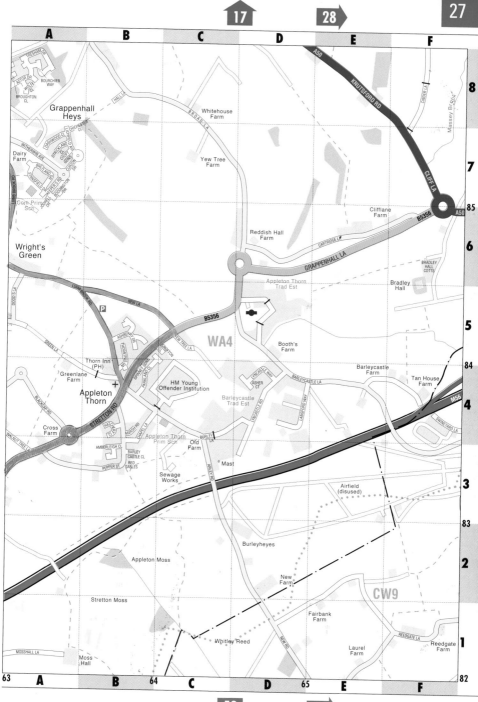

A50
KNUTSFORD RD
CLIFF LA
CHURCH LA
Massey Brook

8

Grappenhall Heys
TRECHAM RD
ASTOR DR
BOURCHIER WAY
BROUGHTON CL
HALL CL
BROAD LA
Whitehouse Farm

7
WITHERWIN AVE
DASHWOOD CL
SHIELD CL
STRELAND
CLIFTON
GORON
GORDON
Dairy Farm
BRETLAND
LANGFIELD
DELFCOTE RD
BOORINGTON DR
Corn Primary Sch
Yew Tree Farm

85
A50
B5356
Clifflane Farm

Wright's Green
6
Reddish Hall Farm
CARTRIDGE LA
GRAPPENHALL LA
BRADLEY HALL COTTS
Bradley Hall

DODD'S LA
LUMB BROOK RD
NEW LA
P
Appleton Thorn Trad Est

5
GREEN LA
ASHFIELD
THORNTREE
NEW TREE LA
B5356
WA4
Booth's Farm
Barleycastle Farm
Tan House Farm

84
Thorn Inn (PH)
Greenlane Farm
Appleton Thorn
ASHBENT
CROMPTON
SPINNEY GDNS
PARKLAND CL
LYNDCASTLE WAY
ASHER CT
LYNDCASTLE RD
Barleycastle LA
LANGFORD WAY
M56
SWINEYARD LA

4
STRETTON RD
HM Young Offender Institution
Barleycastle Trad Est

BLACKCAP RD
Cross Farm
HALL LA
MARSH RD
Appleton Thorn Prim Sch
Old Farm
BURLEY LA
HARLEY RD
Mast

3
HAZELNUT TREE LA
AMBERLEIGH CL
BARLEY CASTLE CL
RED GABLES
PEPPER ST
Sewage Works
Airfield (disused)

83
MOSSHALL LA
Appleton Moss
Burleyheyes
New Farm
CW9

2
Stretton Moss
Fairbank Farm
NEW RD
REEDGATE LA
Reedgate Farm

1
Moss Hall
Whitley Reed
Laurel Farm

63
A
B
64
C
D
65
E
F
82

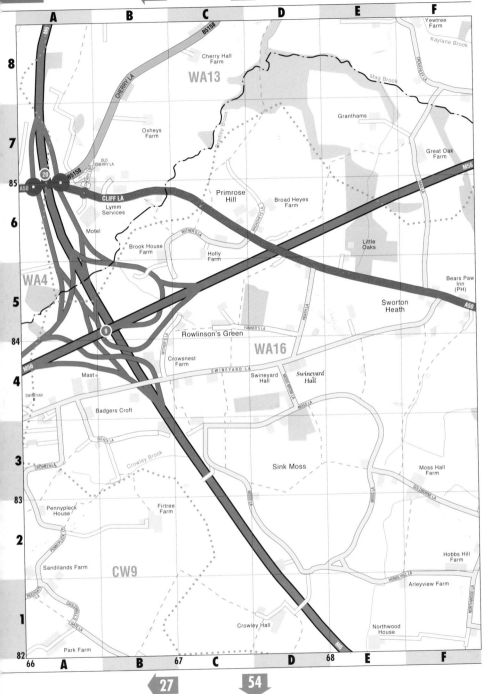

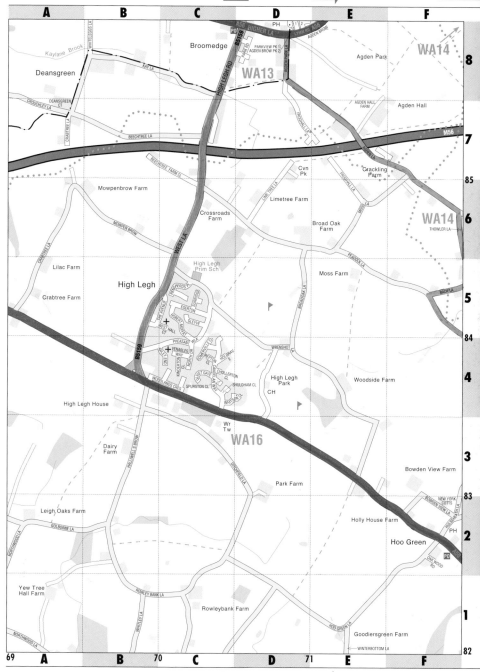

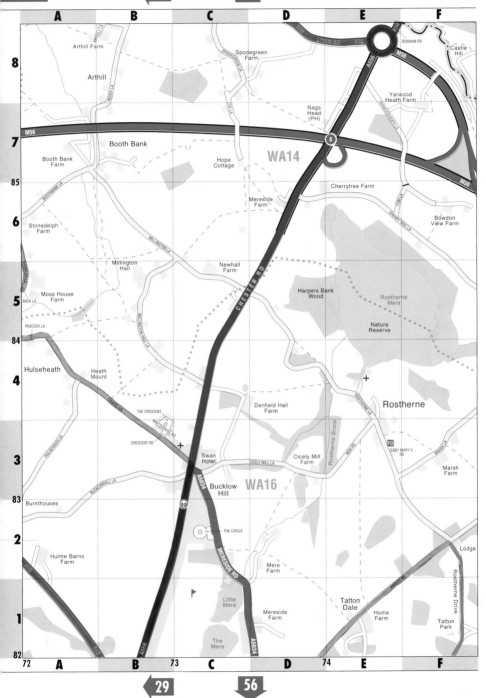

A B C D E F

8

7

85

6

5

84

4

3

83

2

1

82

72 A B 73 C D 74 E F

Arthill Farm

Arthill

ASPULL LA

PEDDY LA

Spodegreen Farm

SPODEGREEN LA

FULL LA

LYMM RD

A56

A56

Dunham Rd

Castle Hill

M56

A556

M56

Yarwood Heath Farm

EARNOCCK HILL LA

Nags Head (PH)

WA14

Booth Bank

Booth Bank Farm

M56

Hope Cottage

Mereside Farm

8

Cherrytree Farm

TAN LA

CHERRY TREE LA

Bowdon View Farm

M56

Stonedelph Farm

MILLINGTON LA

Millington Hall

Newhall Farm

CHESTER RD

Harpers Bank Wood

Rostherne Mere

Moss House Farm

BACK LA

PEACOCK LA

Nature Reserve

Hulseheath

Heath Mount

MILLINGTON HALL LA

SPENFIELD LA

HULSEHEATH LA

GRAPPLE LA

THE CRESCENT

WHITEHOUSE RD

CRESCENT RD

Denfield Hall Farm

ROSTHERNE LA

Rostherne

Cicely Mill Farm

Rostherne Brook

MERE RD

PO

LADY MARY'S SQ

MARSH LA

Marsh Farm

Swan Hotel

CICELY MILL LA

A5034

BUCKLOWHILL LA

Burnthouses

Bucklow Hill

WA16

50

A556

THE CIRCLE

Hulme Barns Farm

A50

MERESIDE RD

Mere Farm

Little Mere

Mereside Farm

Tatton Dale

Home Farm

ASH LEY RD

Lodge

Rostherne Drive

Tatton Park

A556

A5034

The Mere

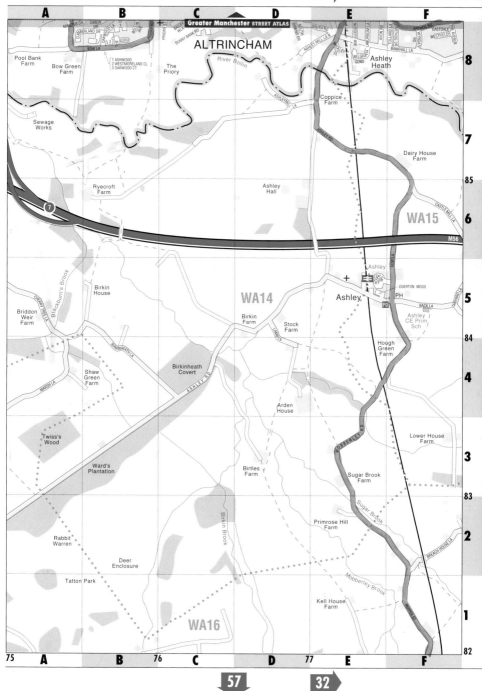

ALTRINCHAM

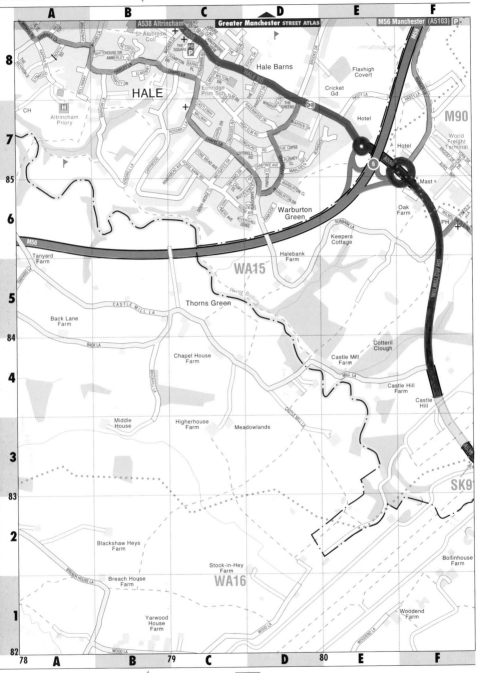

34

D8
1 ROSSETT AVE
2 WHITEFRIARS WLK
3 AUSTELL RD

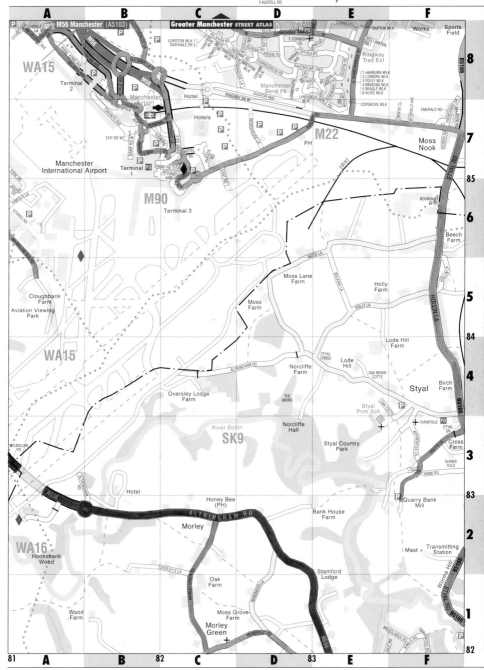

Greater Manchester STREET ATLAS

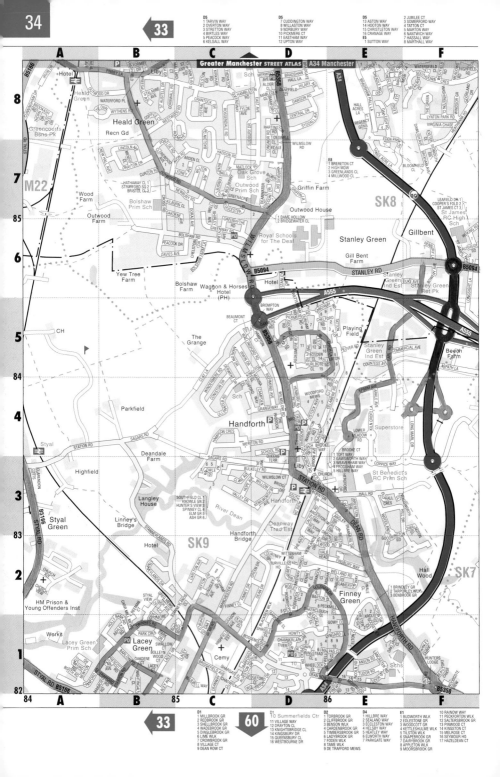

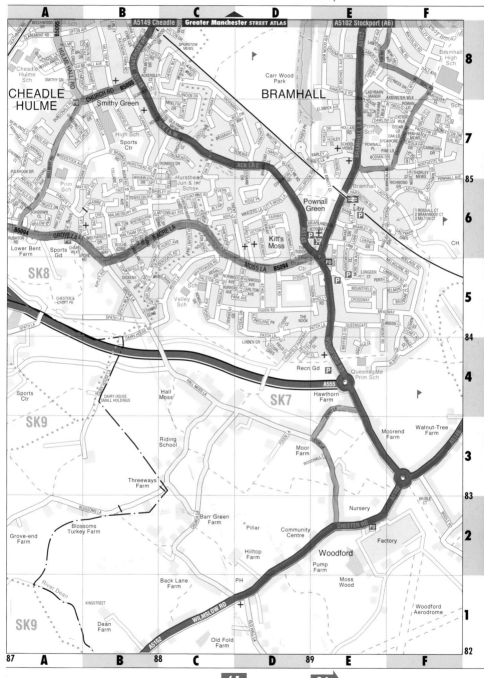

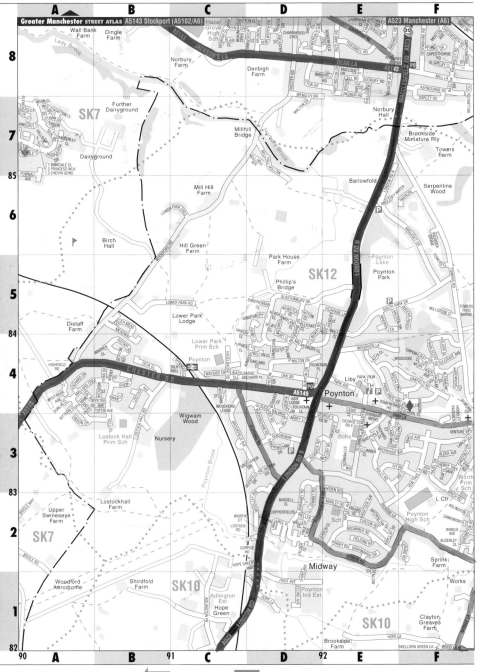

Greater Manchester STREET ATLAS A5143 Stockport (A5102/A6) A523 Manchester (A6)

8

7

85

6

5

84

4

83

3

2

82

1

A   B   91   C   D   92   E   F

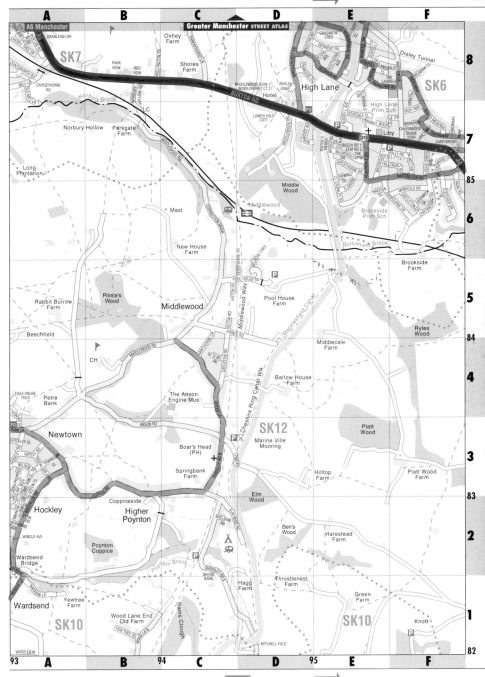

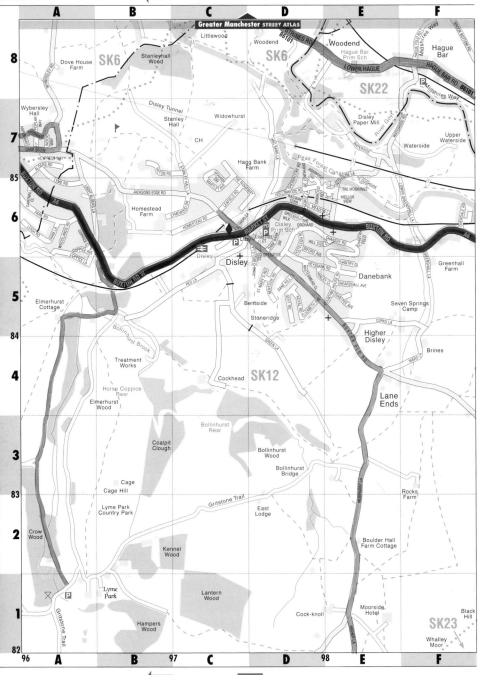

C7
1 FOUNDRY CT
2 LOWER ROCK ST
3 BACK UNION RD
4 LEES MILL

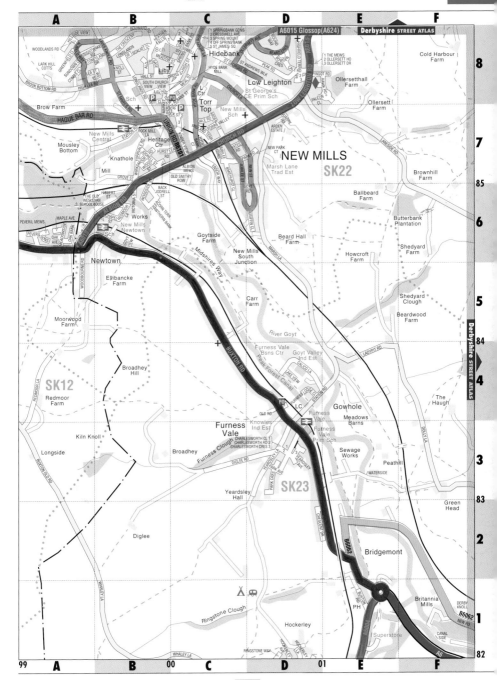

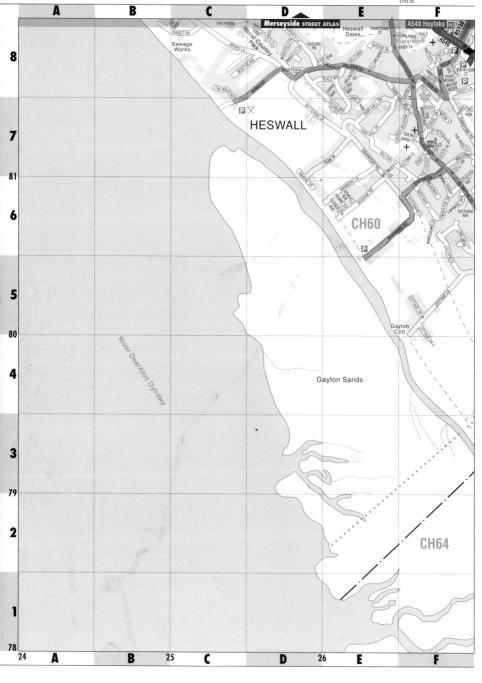

Merseyside STREET ATLAS

A540 Hoylake

HESWALL

CH60

CH64

Gayton Sands

River Dee/Afon Dyfrdwy

Sewage
Works

Wirral County
Park

Heswall
Dales

Gayton
Cott

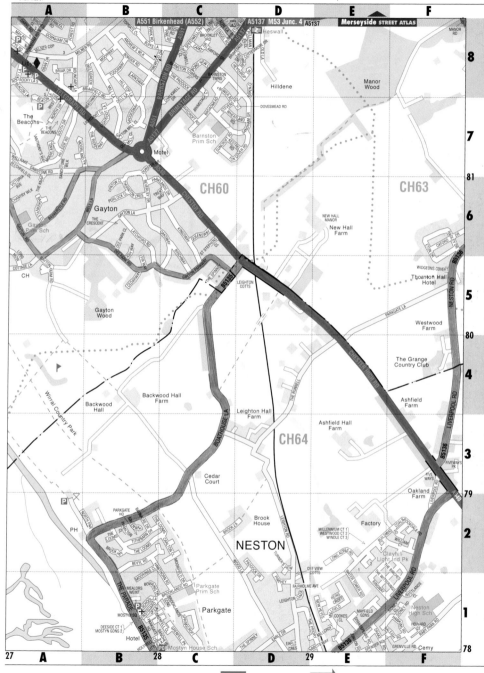

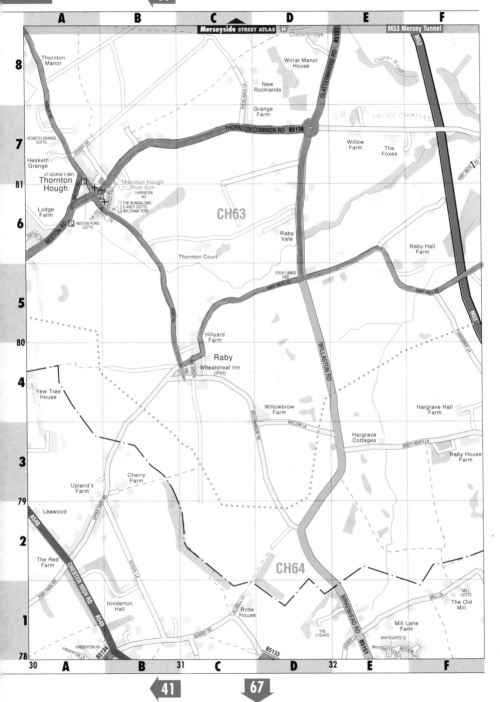

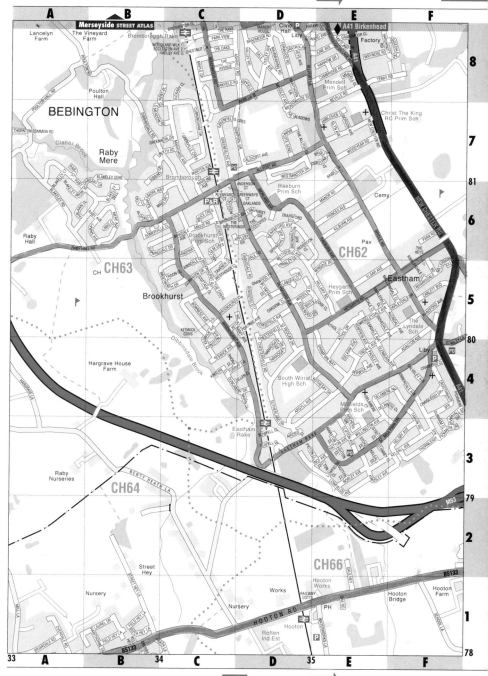

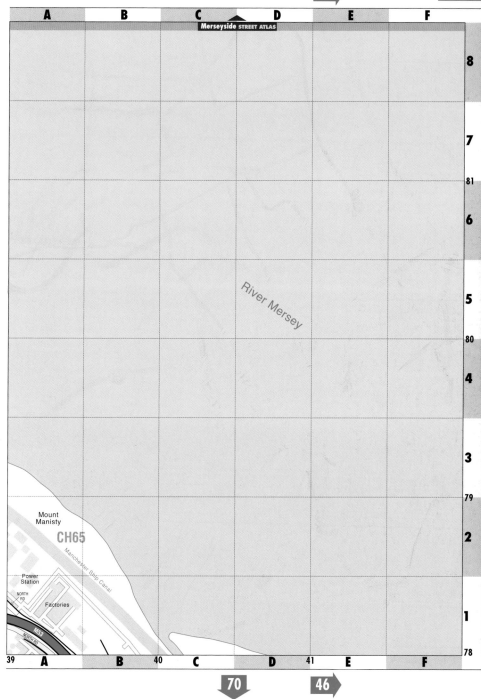

Merseyside STREET ATLAS

A B C D E F

8

7

81

6

River Mersey

5

80

4

3

79

Mount
Manisty
CH65

2

Power
Station
NORTH
RD
Factories
M53
NORTH RD

Manchester Ship Canal

1

78

39 A B 40 C D 41 E F

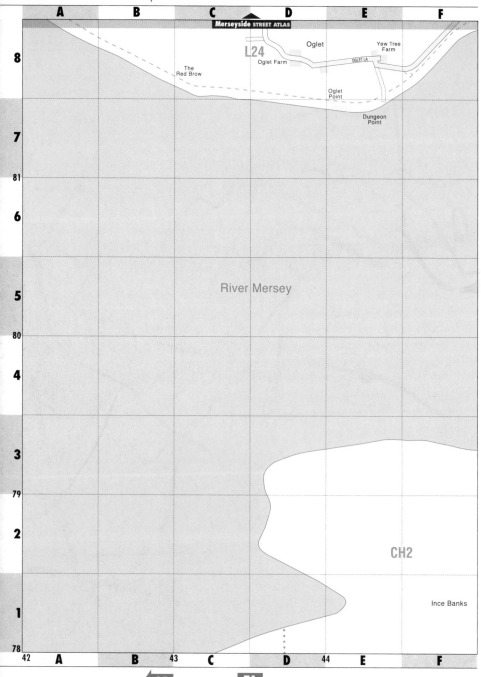

| | A | B | C | D | E | F |

Icehouse
Plantation

Hale Hall

Church Willow
Bed

WITHIN WAY

Hale Park

CHURCH RD

Willow
Bed

L24

Old Pits

LIGHTHOUSE RD

Small Ends

Hale
Head

Lighthouse
(disused)

Hale Head Shore

River Mersey

CH2

WA6

Manchester
Ship Canal

| 45 | A | B | 46 | C | D | 47 | E | F | 78 |

8
7
81
6
5
80
4
3
79
2
1
78

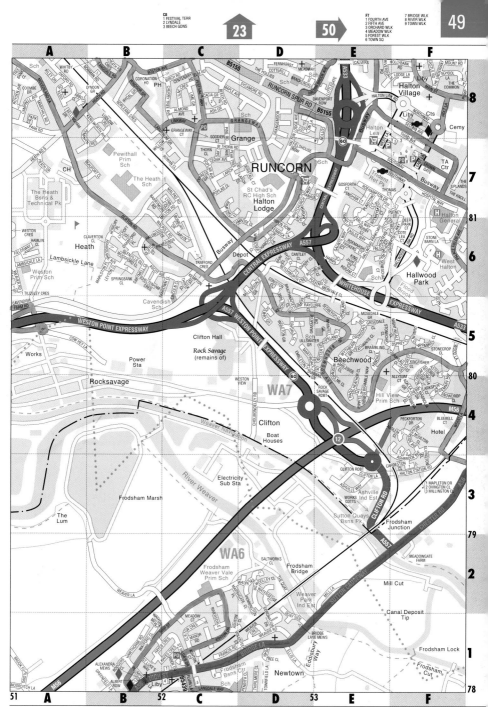

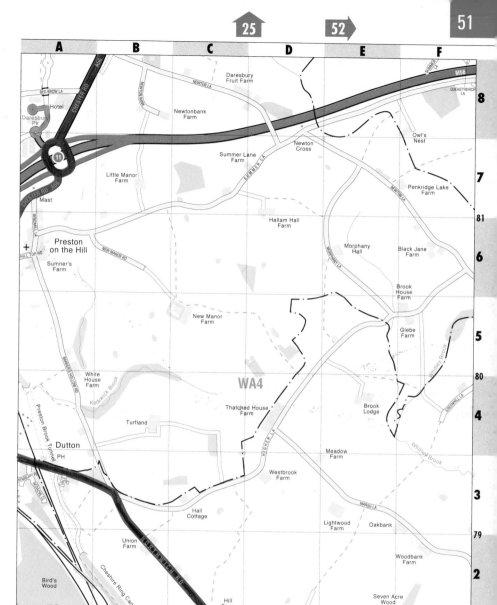

A   B   C   D   E   F

M56

SUMNER LA

QUEASTYBIRCH LA

8

RED BROW LA

NEWTON LA

Daresbury
Fruit Farm

CHESTER RD A56

Hotel

Newtonbank
Farm

Newton
Cross

Owl's
Nest

Daresbury
Pk

11

Summer Lane
Farm

SUMMER LA

Penkridge Lake
Farm

7

NEWTON LA

Little Manor
Farm

81

Mast

WINDMILL LA

Hallam Hall
Farm

CHESTER RD A56

Morphany
Hall

Black Jane
Farm

+

Preston
on the Hill

HILL TOP RD

NEW MANOR RD

6

Sumner's
Farm

Brook
House
Farm

MORPHANY LA

New Manor
Farm

Glebe
Farm

5

Whitley Brook

80

BARKERS HOLLOW RD

White
House
Farm

WA4

Keckwick Brook

Brook
Lodge

GREENALL LA

4

Thatched House
Farm

Turfland

HIGHER LA

Meadow
Farm

Whitley Brook

Preston Brook Tunnel

Dutton

PH

Westbrook
Farm

3

RUNCORN RD

ASTBURY RD

MARSH LA

Hall
Cottage

Lightwood
Farm

Oakbank

79

Union
Farm

NORTHWICH RD

Woodbank
Farm

2

Bird's
Wood

Cheshire Ring Canal Walk

Seven Acre
Wood

Hill
Farm

HILL TOP RD

Dale
Farm

Trent and Mersey Canal

Hope
Farm

1

WA7

Longacre
Wood

A533

78

57   A   58   B   C   58   59   D   E   F

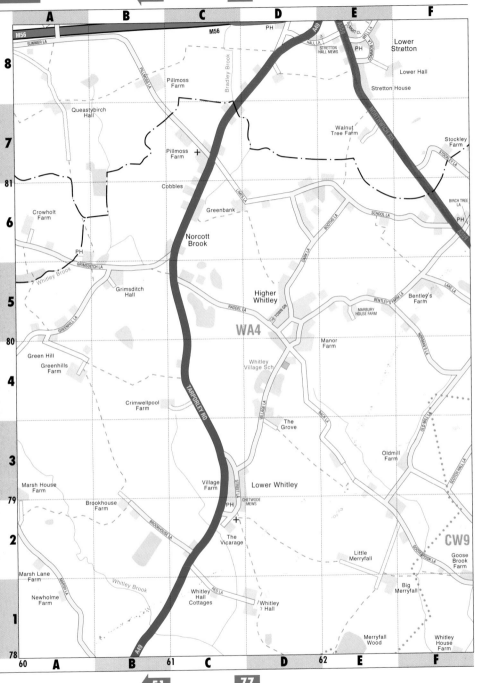

A   B   C   D   E   F

M56

SUMMER LA

M56

PH

A49

STRETTON HALL MEWS

HALL LA

SUMMIT C¹

BELL LA

PH

Lower
Stretton

Lower Hall

Stretton House

NORTHWICH RD

8

Bradley Brook

Pillmoss
Farm

PILLMOSS LA

Queastybirch
Hall

Walnut
Tree Farm

Stockley
Farm

STOCKLEY LA

7

Pillmoss
Farm

BIRCH TREE
LA

PH

81

Cobbles

LIME LA

Greenbank

SCHOOL LA

A559

6

Crowholt
Farm

Norcott
Brook

BOOTHS LA

DANK LA

LAKE LA

PH

GRIMSDITCH LA

Whitley Brook

5

Grimsditch
Hall

RADDEL LA

Higher
Whitley

THE TOWN GN

BENTLEY'S FARM LA

Bentley's
Farm

MARBURY
HOUSE FARM

GREENHILL LA

WA4

Manor
Farm

WINDMILL LA

80

Green Hill

Greenhills
Farm

Whitley
Village Sch

4

Crimwellpool
Farm

TARPORLEY RD

VILLAGE LA

The
Grove

BACK LA

Oldmill
Farm

OLD MILL LA

SCOTCHILL HALL LA

3

Marsh House
Farm

Village
Farm

STREET LA

Lower Whitley

79

Brookhouse
Farm

BROOKHOUSE LA

PH
CHETWODE
MEWS

GOOSEBROOK LA

CW9

2

Marsh Lane
Farm

BARER LA

The
Vicarage

Little
Merryfall

Goose
Brook
Farm

Whitley Brook

RED LA

Big
Merryfall

Newholme
Farm

Whitley
Hall
Cottages

Whitley
Hall

1

Merryfall
Wood

Whitley
House
Farm

78

A49

60   A   B   61   C   D   62   E   F

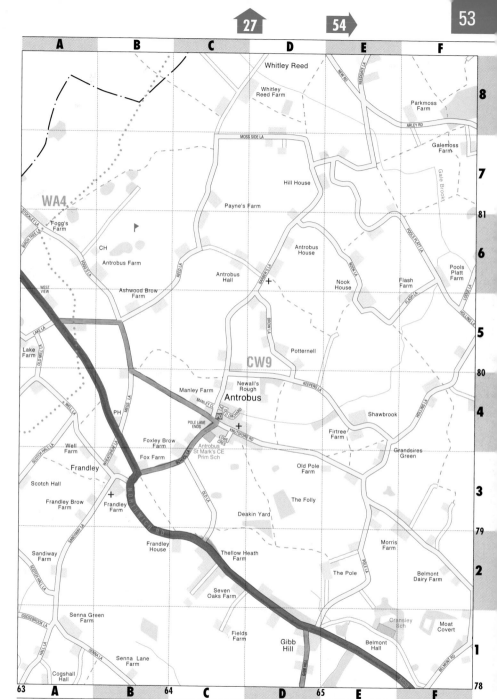

27
54

| A | B | C | D | E | F |

8

Whitley Reed

Whitley
Reed Farm

Parkmoss
Farm

ARLEY RD

Galemoss
Farm

MOSS SIDE LA

7

81

Hill House

WA4

Payne's Farm

Gale Brook

Fogg's
Farm

Antrobus
House

Pools
Platt
Farm

6

CH

Antrobus Farm

Antrobus
Hall

Flash
Farm

Nook
House

RED LA

BOBBIES LA

Ashwood Brow
Farm

WEST
VIEW

POOLS PLATT LA

HOLLINS LA

LOOMS LA

NOOK LA

FLASH LA

5

Lake
Farm

LAKE LA

OLD MILL LA

Potternell

CW9

BROW LA

Newall's
Rough

KEEPERS LA

80

Manley Farm

Antrobus

Shawbrook

PH

MESS LA

WHEATSHEAF LA

MANLEY CL

THE ORCHARD

PO

Firtree
Farm

4

Well
Farm

Foxley Brow
Farm

Antrobus
St Mark's CE
Prim Sch

KNUTSFORD RD

LOWE
CRES

Grandsires
Green

HOLLINS LA

PICK LA

Scotch Hall LA

Fox Farm

Frandley

SCHOOL LA

OLD LA

Old Pole
Farm

3

Scotch Hall

The Folly

79

Frandley Brow
Farm

Frandley
Farm

SANDIWAY LA

NORTHWICH RD

Deakin Yard

Morris
Farm

Sandiway
Farm

Frandley
House

Thellow Heath
Farm

The Pole

Belmont
Dairy Farm

2

SCOTCH HALL LA

Seven
Oaks Farm

Cransley
Sch

Moat
Covert

Senna Green
Farm

GOOSEBROOK LA

HALL LA

SENNA LA

Fields
Farm

Gibb
Hill

Belmont
Hall

BELMONT RD

1

Cogshall
Hall

Senna Lane
Farm

GIBB HILL

78

| 63 | A | B | 64 | C | D | E | 65 | F |

78
54

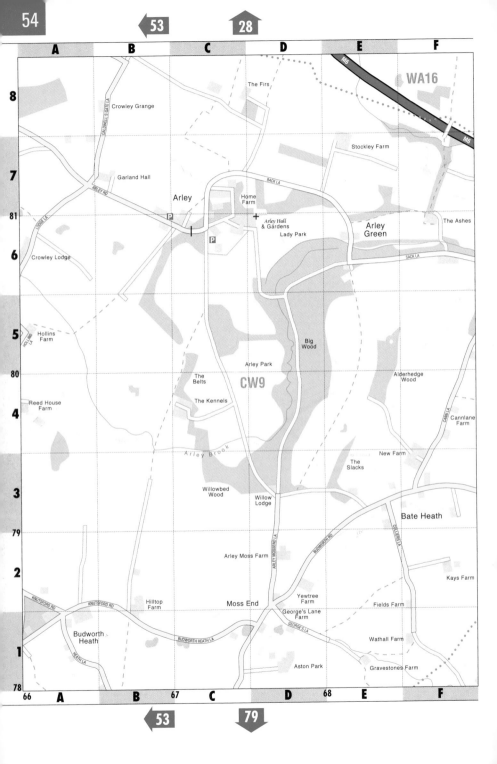

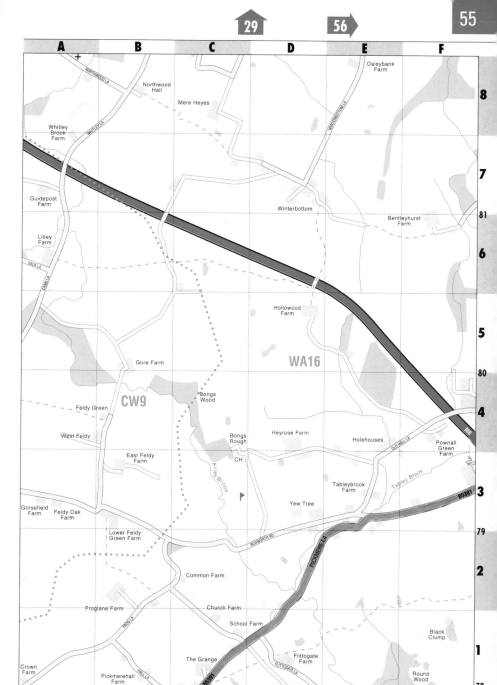

A B C D E F

8

7

81

6

80

5

4

3

79

2

1

78

Daisybank Farm

Northwood Hall

Mere Heyes

Whitley Brook Farm

Winterbottom

Bentleyhurst Farm

Guidepost Farm

Litley Farm

Hollowood Farm

Gore Farm

WA16

CW9

Bongs Wood

Feldy Green

West Feldy

Bongs Rough

Heyrose Farm

Holehouses

Pownall Green Farm

East Feldy Farm

CH

Arley Brook

Tableybrook Farm

Tabley Brook

Gorsefield Farm

Feldy Oak Farm

Yew Tree

B5391

Lower Feldy Green Farm

BUDWORTH RD

Common Farm

PICKMERE LA

Froglane Farm

FROST LA

Church Farm

School Farm

Black Clump

Crown Farm

Pickmerehall Farm

HALL LA

The Grange

B5391

Flittogate Farm

FLITTOGATE LA

Round Wood

NORTHWOOD LA

WHITLEY LA

SACK LA

CANN LA

WHITEBOTTOM LA

OLD HALL LA

HOLLY BK

M6

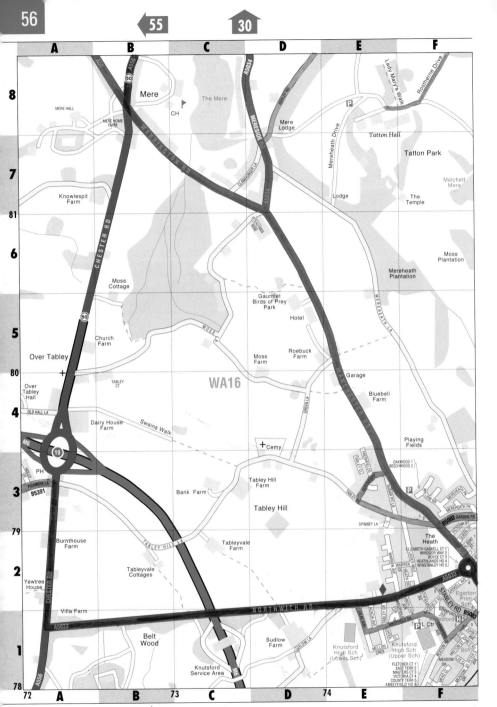

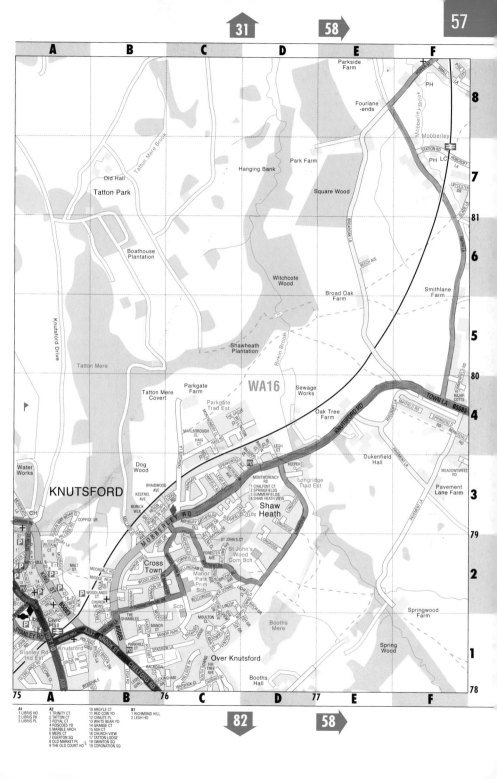

31
58
82
58

KNUTSFORD

Tatton Park

Old Hall

Hanging Bank

Park Farm

Parkside Farm

Fourlane -ends

Mobberley

PH

STATION RD

PH LC

Square Wood

Boathouse Plantation

Witchcote Wood

Broad Oak Farm

Smithlane Farm

Knutsford Drive

Tatton Mere

Shawheath Plantation

Birkin Brook

WA16

Sewage Works

Tatton Mere Covert

Parkgate Farm

Parkgate Trad Est

Oak Tree Farm

KNUTSFORD RD

TOWN LA

MAYFIELD RD

SPRINGFIELD RD

BERKSDALE RD

B5085

Dog Wood

Marlborough CL

HAIG CT

LEGH CT

Dukenfield Hall

MEADOWSWEET

Pavement Lane Farm

Water Works

BRAIDWOOD AVE

KESTREL AVE

BEWICK WLK

MONTMORENCY RD
1 CHALFONT CT
2 SPRINGFIELDS
3 SUMMERFIELD
4 SHAW HEATH VIEW

Longridge Trad Est

Shaw Heath

KEEPERS

MOBBERLEY RD

NORBURY

ST JOHN'S CT

FORESTER AVE

St John's Wood Com Sch

LONGRIDGE

Cross Town

MOORDALE RD

MIDDLE WLK

WOODLANDS

TOWNFIELD

SELLINGHAM

Manor Park Prim Sch

BEECHWOOD

MANOR PARK RD

CHURCH MEWS

THE SHAMBLES

WESTSIDE

MOULTON CL

LINDOP

Booths Mere

Springwood Farm

Spring Wood

Civic Hall

STANLEY RD

ADAMS HILL

Knutsford

A537 BROOK ST

B5085

CHELFORD RD

PARKHILL

SPARROW LA

GROVE PK

BALMORAL

KINGHAM

WOODVALE

WARWICK CL

Over Knutsford

FIR TREE AVE

CARRBROOK

Booths Hall

Libris Ho

A B C D E F

A1
1 LIBRIS HO
2 LIBRIS PK
3 LIBRIS PL

A2
1 TRINITY CT
2 TATTON CT
3 ROYAL CT
4 ROSCOES YD
5 MARBLE ARCH
6 MERE CT
7 EGERTON SQ
8 OLD MARKET PL
9 THE OLD COURT HO

10 ARGYLE CT
11 RED COW YD
12 CANUTE PL
13 WHITE BEAR YD
14 GRANGE CT
15 ASH CT
16 CHURCH VIEW
17 TATTON LODGE
18 SWINTON SQ
19 CORONATION SQ

B1
1 RICHMOND HILL
2 LEGH HO

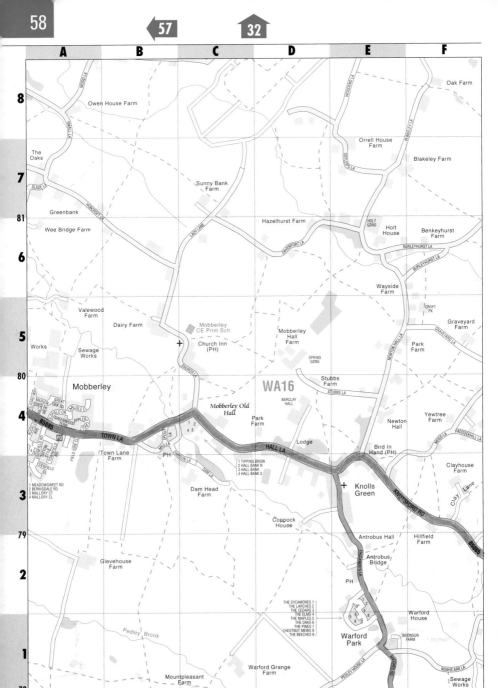

A   B   C   D   E   F

8

7

81

6

5

80

4

3

79

2

1

78

Oak Farm

Owen House Farm

Orrell House Farm

Blakeley Farm

The Oaks

SLADE LA

Greenbank

Wee Bridge Farm

HONGROFT LA

WOOD LA

SMALL LA

LADY LANE

Sunny Bank Farm

Hazelhurst Farm

DAVENPORT LA

WOODEND LA

OSTLERS LA

BLAKELEY LA

HOLT GDNS

Holt House

Benkeyhurst Farm

BURLEYHURST LA

BURLEYHURST LA

Wayside Farm

CROFT PK

Graveyard Farm

Valewood Farm

Dairy Farm

Mobberley CE Prim Sch

Church Inn (PH)

Mobberley Hall Farm

SPRING GDNS

GRAVEYARD LA

Park Farm

NEWTON HALL LA

Works

Sewage Works

Mobberley

CHURCH LA

WA16

Stubbs Farm

STUBBS LA

Mobberley Old Hall

Park Farm

BARCLAY HALL

Newton Hall

Yewtree Farm

B5085

GREENWOOD TER

GREAT OAK RD

CARLISLE CL

MARLOW

APPLE CL

TOWN LA

TOWN LANE FARM

PO

FIELD RISE

EDENFIELD CL

MALLORY CT

1 MEADOWSWEET RD
2 BERNISDALE RD
3 MALLORY CT
4 MALLORY CL

MILL LA

SPOUT LA

PH

HARGON LA

TOM LA

HALL LA

Lodge

1 TIPPING BROW
2 HALL BANK N
3 HALL BANK
4 HALL BANK S

Dam Head Farm

Coppock House

Bird In Hand (PH)

KNUTSFORD RD

MOSS LA

PADDOCKHILL LA

Clayhouse Farm

Clay Lane

Knolls Green

Antrobus Hall

Antrobus Bridge

FAULKNERS LA

PH

Hillfield Farm

B5085

Glevehouse Farm

Pedley Brook

THE SYCAMORES 1
THE LARCHES 2
THE CEDARS 3
THE ELMS 4
THE MAPLES 5
THE OAKS 6
THE PINES 7
CHESTNUT MEWS 8
THE BEECHES 9

Warford Park

Warford House

NOONSUN FARM

Mountpleasant Farm

Warford Grange Farm

PEDLEY HOUSE LA

NOAHS ARK LA

Sewage Works

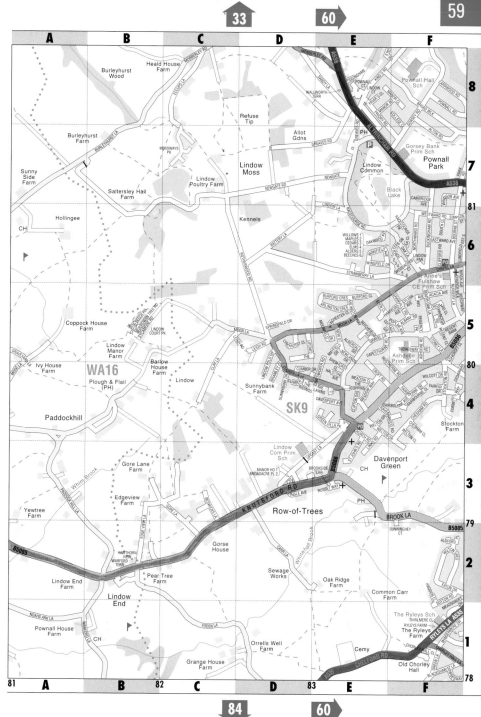

A B C D E F

8

Burleyhurst Wood

Heald House Farm

MORBERLEY RD

EDGES LA

Pownall Hall Sch

CARRWOOD RD

BIRCHINGHAM

POWNALL CT/LINDOW

KINGS RD

PAFAIT CL

ALTON RD

MANOR DR

Burleyhurst Farm

BURLEYHURST LA

Refuse Tip

WALLWORTH TERR

GREAVES RD

Allot Gdns

PH

P

Gorsey Bank Prim Sch

ALTRINGHAM RD

Pownall Park

7

Sunny Side Farm

MOSSWAYS PK

Lindow Moss

Lindow Poultry Farm

NEWGATE RD

Lindow Common

A538

BLACK Lake

Black Lake

CAMBRIDGE AVE

WINDSOR AVE

SIMPSON ST

81

Saltersley Hall Farm

Kennels

LINDOW LA

RACECOURSE RD

WILLOWS 1 MAPLES 2 CEDARS 3 ELMS 4 ALDERS 5 BEECHES 6

OAKWOOD DR

WESTWARD RD

EASTWARD RD

NORTHWARD RD

6

Hollingee

CH

BATTERY LA

ROTHERWOOD RD

Wingfield

LINDOW AVE

CHAPEL LA

St Anne's Fulshaw CE Prim Sch

ACACIA AVE

BEECHFIELD

Coppock House Farm

BEECH RD

WYCHELM RD

BROOKWAY RD

LINDOW COURT PK

Lindow Manor Farm

Ivy House Farm

GRAVEL LA

MOSS LA

WA16

Plough & Flail (PH)

Barlow House Farm

Lindow

MADOR LA

LEIGH RD

LINE RD

CLARK LA

LINDOW FOLD DR

SPRINGFIELD DR

BURFORD CRES

BURFORD CL

ARLINGTON CRES

MANCHESTER RD

MOOR LA

MOOR DR

MAPLEFIELD

ALDERLEY RD

HARTFORD

GRANGE RD

STONY LA

Thoresway RD

Ashdene Prim Sch

B5086

5

80

Paddockhill

WHIM BROOK

PADDOCKHILL LA

SK9

Sunnybank Farm

SUNNYBANK

CUMBER LA

THE BRIDGINGS

HALSTONE AVE

HALSTONE AVE

DAVENPORT AVE

THE COPPINS

MEADOW CL

FAIRBOURNE

CHESHAM CL

WILCOTT DR

FAIRFAX

Stockton Farm

4

Lindow Com Prim Sch

CLIFTON AVE

GREEN DLLA PK

WELTON CL

WELTON DR

WELTON CL

Davenport Green

CH

3

Gore Lane Farm

Edgeview Farm

GORE LA

EDGE VIEW LA

BESTWICK LA

KNUTSFORD RD

MANOR HO 1 BROADACRE PL 2

BROOKSIDE TERR

NAGLE AVE

RUSSET WAY

Row-of-Trees

B5086

CHERS WAY

PH

BROOK LA

SUNNINGHEY CT

B5085

79

Yewtree Farm

B5085

Gorse House

CABLE LA

Whitehall Brook

ALDFORD

WILTON CRES

EXTON DR

2

Lindow End Farm

HAWTHORN VIEW WARFORD TERR

Pear Tree Farm

Sewage Works

Oak Ridge Farm

Common Carr Farm

HANDGATE CL

MEADSMORE

NOAHS ARK LA

Lindow End

FODEN LA

The Ryleys Sch

THIRLMERE CL

RYLEYS FARM

The Ryleys Farm

RYLEYS LA A535

THORLEY HALL LA

1

Pownall House Farm

WARFORD LA

CH

Grange House Farm

Orrells Well Farm

CHELFORD RD

A535

Cemy

CHORLEY HALL LA

Old Chorley Hall

GREEN DR

BLACKSHAW LA

HALL LA

78

C8
1 GLADEWOOD CL
2 SANDHURST DR
3 CALVERLEY CL
4 DARESBURY CL

F1
1 CORNWELL CL
2 GAINSBOROUGH CL
3 ASHBERRY CL
4 BRACKENWOOD MEWS
5 CHERRY TREE CL
6 WARREN HEY
7 BROOMFIELD CL
8 REYNOLDS MEWS
9 LYMEWOOD DR
10 WELFORD CL

A6
1 GATCOMBE MEWS
2 HIGHGROVE MEWS
3 DENEWOOD CT
4 SANDRINGHAM WAY
5 SANDRINGHAM CT

WOODLEIGH CT 1
HURST LEA CT 2
WESTHOLME CT 3
LYNTON MEWS 4
WOODBANK 5

C2
1 WOOD GDNS
2 ELMFIELD CL
3 ANNIS CL
4 COTTAGE LAWNS

WILMSLOW

SK9

SK10

ALDERLEY EDGE

Dean Row

Hilltop

Wilmslow Park

A1
1 THE PARADE
2 ROYLES SQ
3 BROWN ST
4 BERESFORD CT
5 GREEN ST
6 MASSEY ST
7 CHAPEL ST
8 CHORLEGH GRANGE
9 HUBERT WORTHINGTON HO
10 SOUTH GR
11 WOLVERTON HO
12 ARDERNE PL
13 CARLISLE ST
14 SOUTH TERR

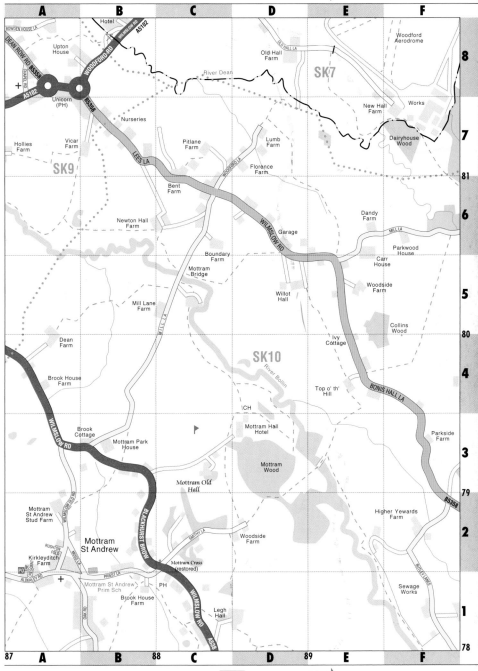

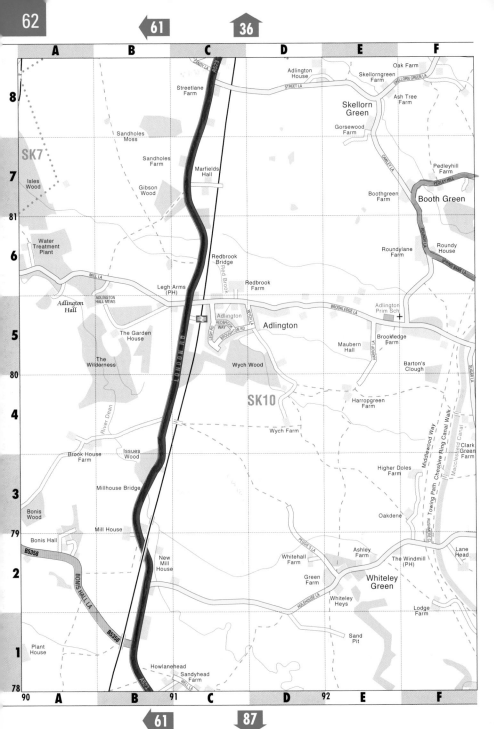

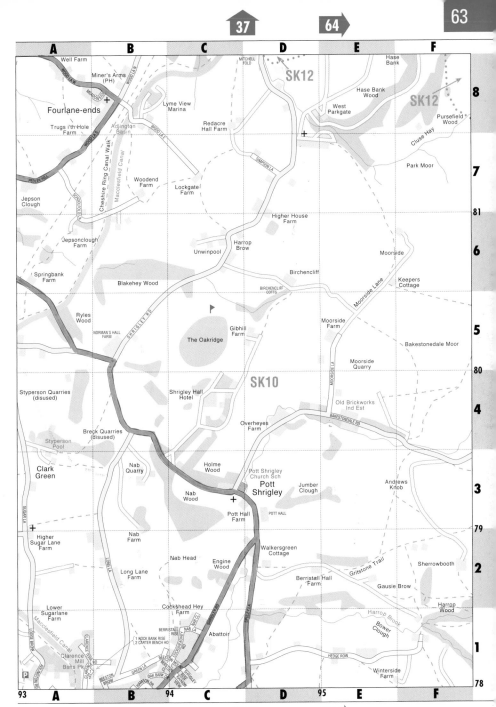

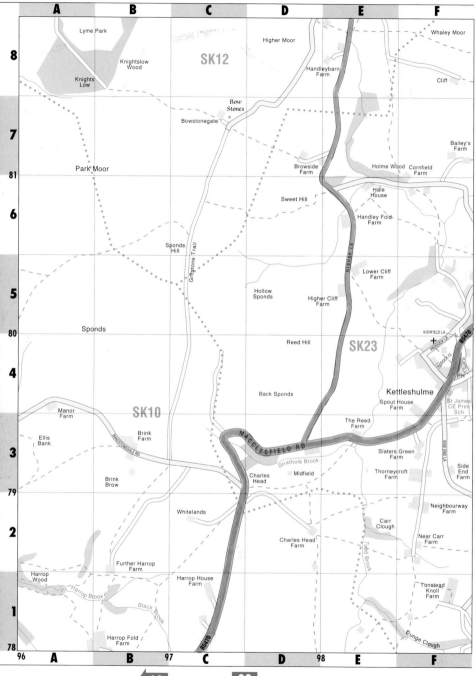

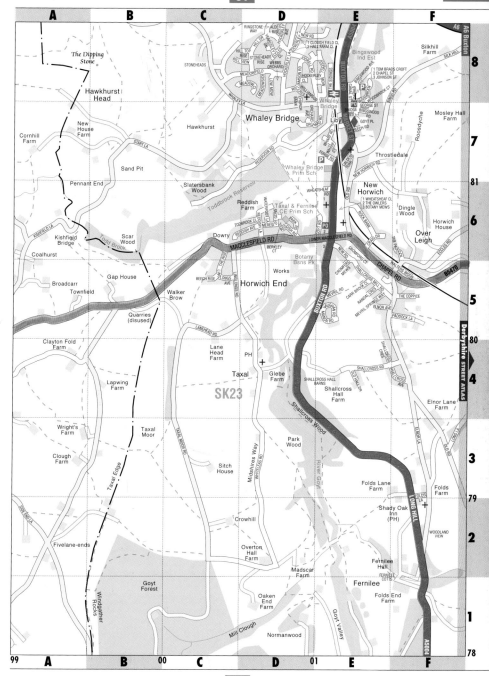

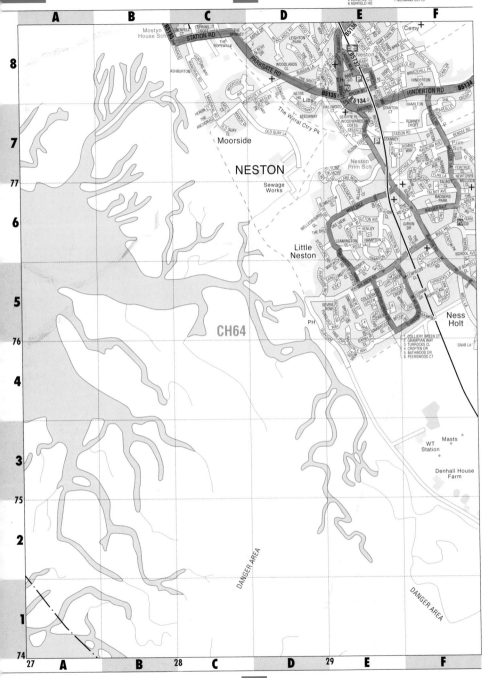

NESTON

Moorside

Little Neston

Ness Holt

CH64

Sewage Works

DANGER AREA

DANGER AREA

Masts

WT Station

Denhall House Farm

1 COLLIERY GREEN CT
2 GRAMPIAN WAY
3 TURROCKS CL
4 CROFTON DR
5 BATHWOOD DR
6 PEERSWOOD CT

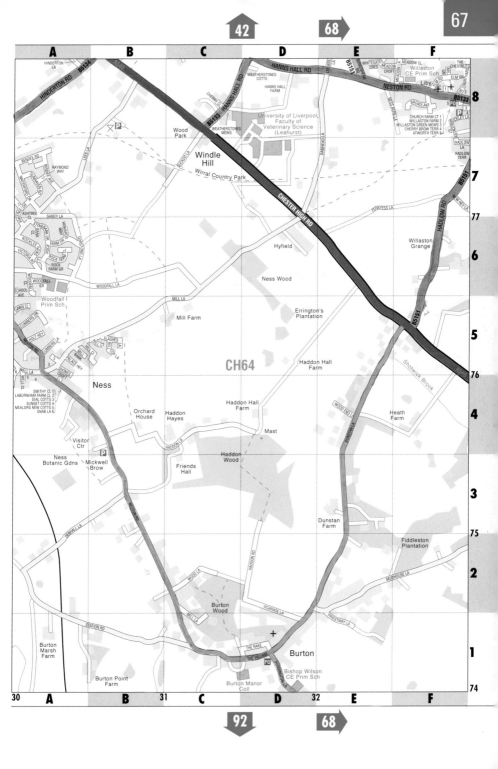

67
43

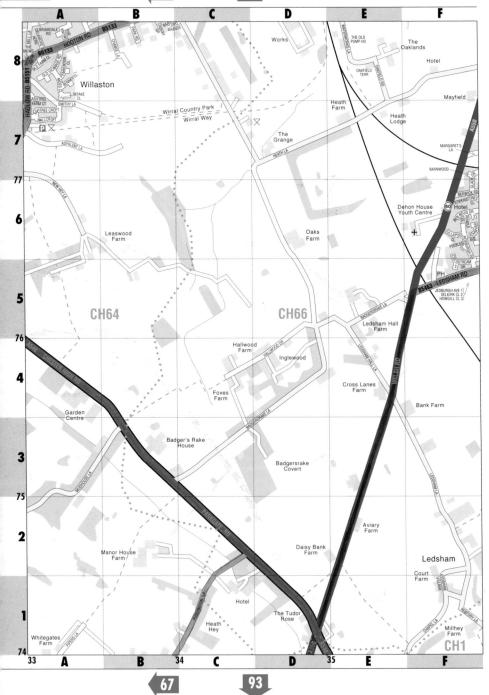

67
93

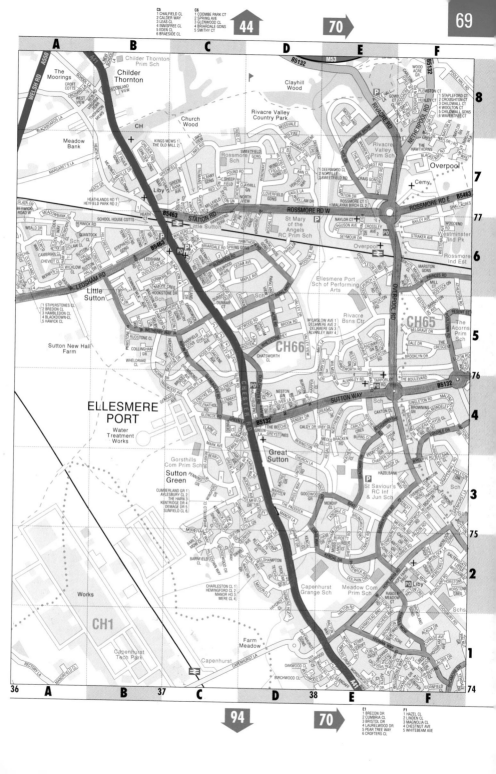

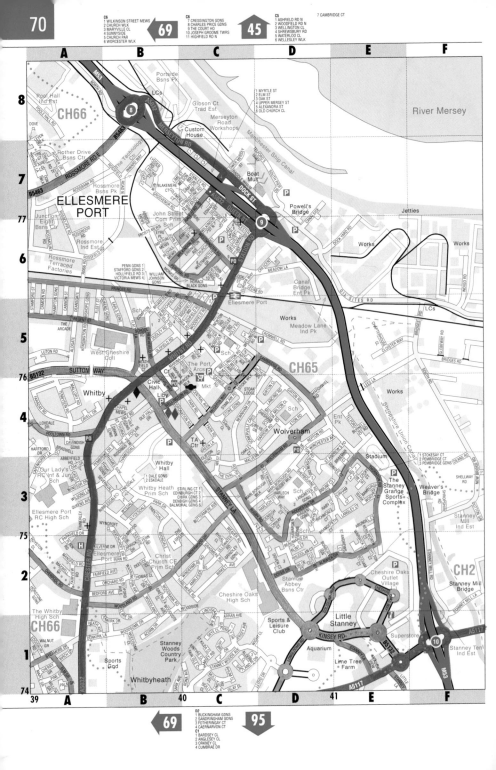

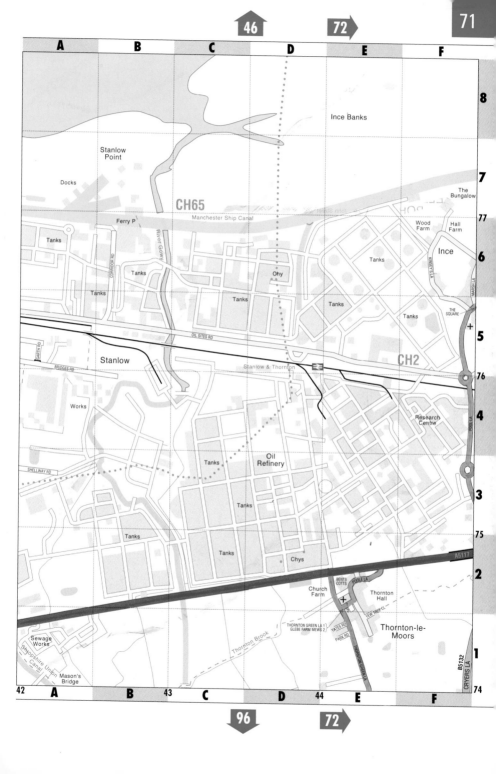

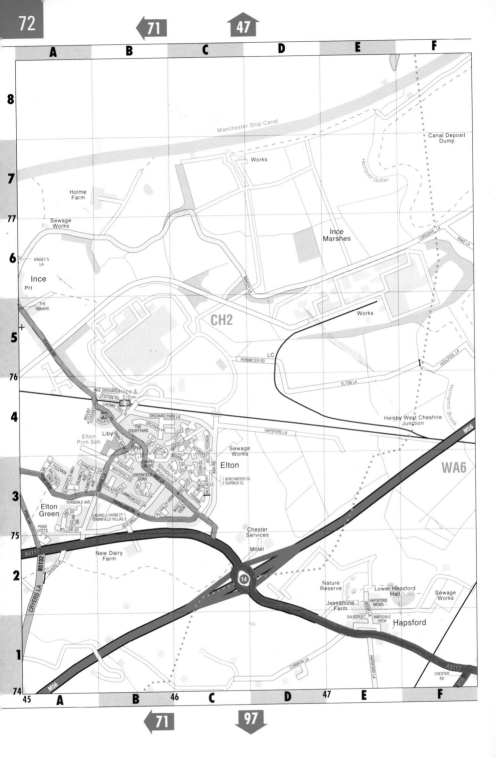

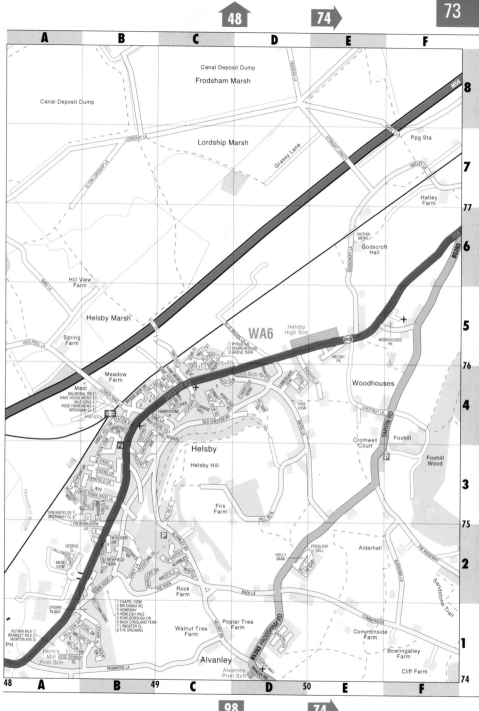

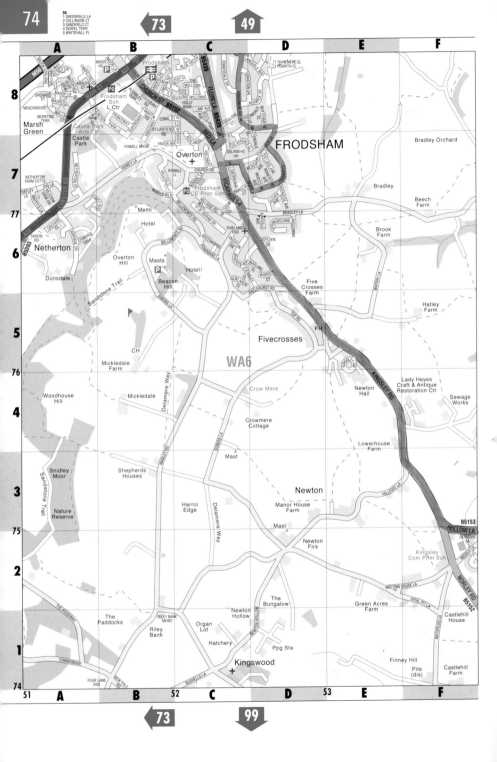

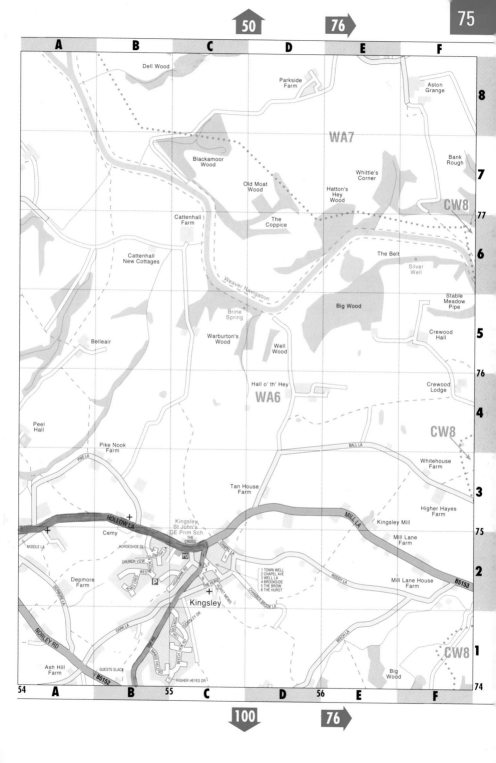

A B C D E F

8 7 77 6 5 76 4 3 75 2 1 74

Dell Wood

Parkside Farm

Aston Grange

WA7

Blackamoor Wood

Bank Rough

Old Moat Wood

Whittle's Corner

Hatton's Hey Wood

CW8

Cattenhall Farm

The Coppice

The Belt

Silver Well

Cattenhall New Cottages

Weaver Navigation

Stable Meadow Pipe

Brine Spring

Big Wood

Crewood Hall

Belleair

Warburton's Wood

Well Wood

Crewood Lodge

WA6

Hall o' th' Hey

Peel Hall

CW8

Pike Nook Farm

BALL LA

Whitehouse Farm

PIKE LA

Tan House Farm

MILL LA

Higher Hayes Farm

HOLLOW LA

Kingsley St John's CE Prim Sch

Kingsley Mill

Cemy

THE CROSS

MIDDLE LA

HORSESHOE CL

Mill Lane Farm

CHURCH VIEW

PO

CHAPEL LA

DEPMORE LA

Depmore Farm

P

1 TOWN WELL
2 CHAPEL AVE
3 WELL LA
4 BROOKSIDE
5 THE BROW
6 THE HURST

ROODY LA

Mill Lane House Farm

B5153

THE HURST

Kingsley

CHAPEL BROOK LA

NORLEY RD

DARK LA

BEECH LA

BEECH LA

CW8

Ash Hill Farm

GUESTS SLACK

B5152

HIGHER HEYES DR

Big Wood

54 A B 55 C D 56 E F

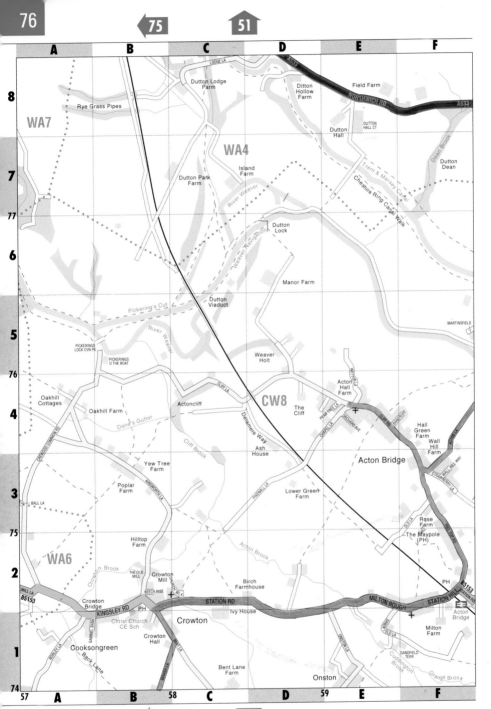

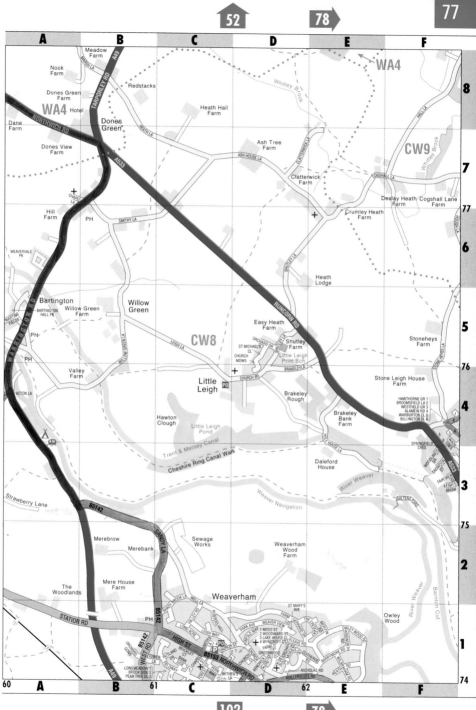

A B C D E F

8

7

77

6

5

76

4

3

75

2

1

74

WA4

Meadow Farm

Nook Farm

MARSH LA

TARPORLEY RD

A49

Dones Green Farm

Redstacks

Hotel

WA4

Dones Green

Dane Farm

NORTHWICH RD

HEATH LA

Dones View Farm

A533

Heath Hall Farm

Ash Tree Farm

ASH HOUSE LA

Whitley Brook

CLATTERWICK LA

Clatterwick Farm

Whitley Brook

CW9

LOGSHALL LA

Deslay Heath Farm

Cogshall Lane Farm

HALL LA

CHAPEL LA

Hill Farm

PH

SMITHY LA

Crumley Heath Farm

77

6

LA HOUSE LA

WEAVERVALE PK

Bartington

BARTINGTON HALL PK

Willow Green Farm

Willow Green

SHUTLEY LA

Heath Lodge

RUNCORM RD

CW8

Easy Heath Farm

Shutley Farm

Stoneheys Farm

5

WARRINGTON RD

MARTINS FIELDS

PH

PH

PH

Valley Farm

WILLOW GREEN LA

LEIGH LA

ORCHARD DR

St MICHAEL'S CL

CHURCH MDWS

Little Leigh Prim Sch

BRAKELEY LA

Stone Leigh House Farm

STONE LEIGH LA

76

Little Leigh

PO

CHURCH RD

Brakeley Rough

Brakeley Bank Farm

HAWTHORNE GR 1
BROOMSFIELD LA 2
WESTFIELD GR 3
ALAMEIN RD 4
WARBURTON CL 5
BILLINGTON CL 6

4

ACTON LA

Hawton Clough

Little Leigh Pond

Trent & Mersey Canal

Cheshire Ring Canal Walk

PIT HOUSE LA

Daleford House

River Weaver

SPRINGFIELD CRES

A533

3

Strawberry Lane

B5142

Weaver Navigation

SALTERSFORD

FAIR VIEW
LEIGH'S BROW

75

Merebrow

Merebank

SANDY LA

Sewage Works

Weaverham Wood Farm

River Weaver

Barnton Cut

Owley Wood

2

The Woodlands

STATION RD

Mere House Farm

B5142

WEST RD

A49

HIGH ST

PH

Weaverham

BRADDOCK LA

WELL CT

VALE VIEW

WHITTLE'S HILL

LEIGH WAY

ST MARY'S AVE

WEAVER VIEW

PARK AVE

1 MOSS ST
2 WOODWARD ST
3 LAKE HOUSE CL
4 WYNDROFT CT

FARM CL

MEREFIELD

OWLEY WOOD RD

1

LONG ACRE

B5142

P

CHURCH ST

B5153 NORTHWICH RD

GREENWOOD CL

CLEAVE RD

GREENFIELDS

BARRYMORE RD

NICHOLAS RD

WALLERSCOTE RD

HEATH RD

THE ROUND HILL

WITHENS

Sch

LONGMEADOW 1
BROOK SIDE 2
PEAR TREE CL 3

60 A B 61 C D 62 E F

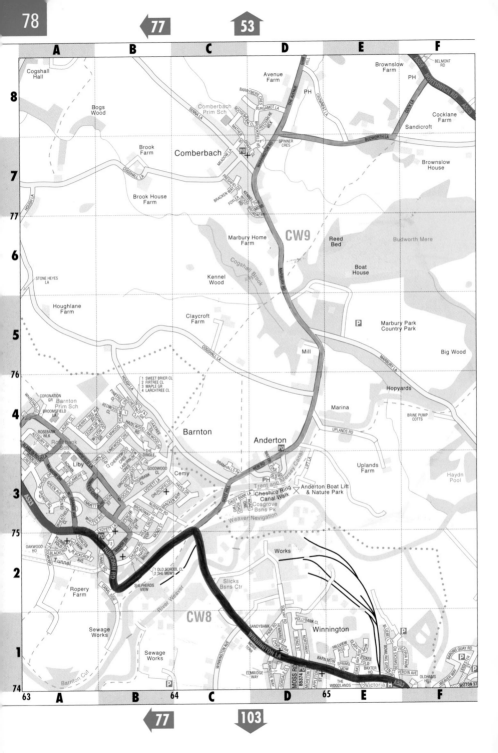

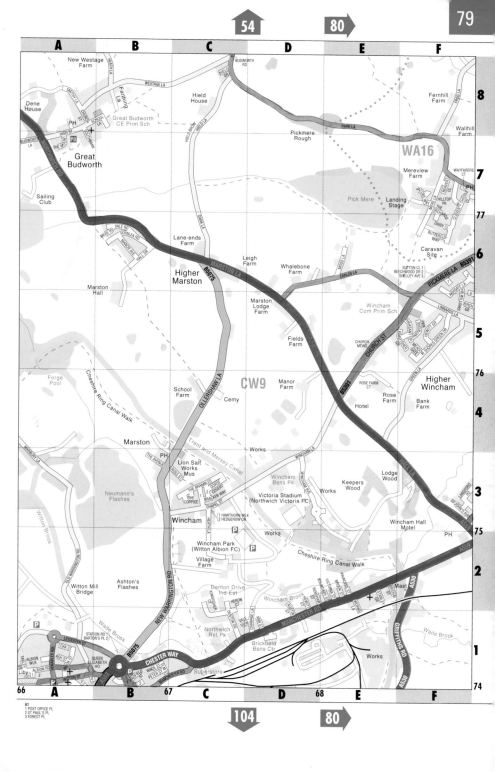

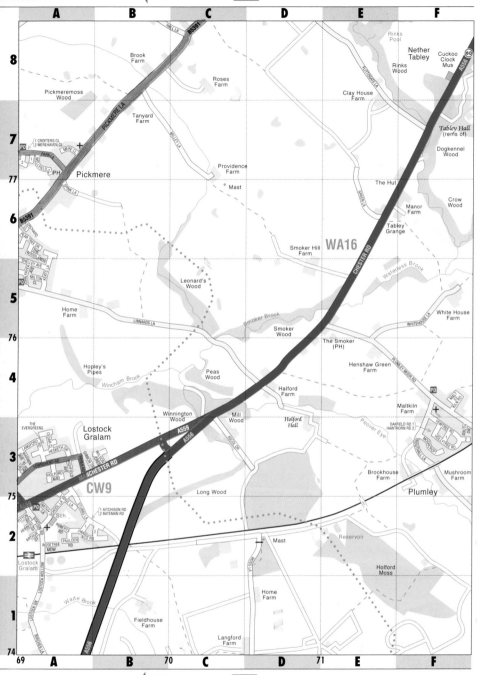

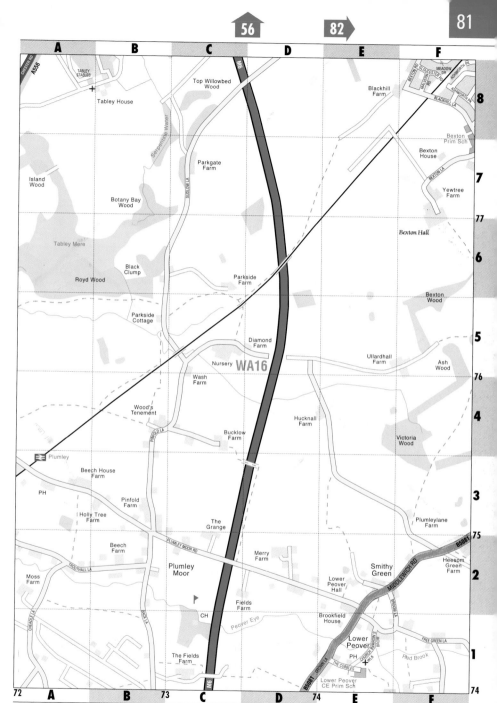

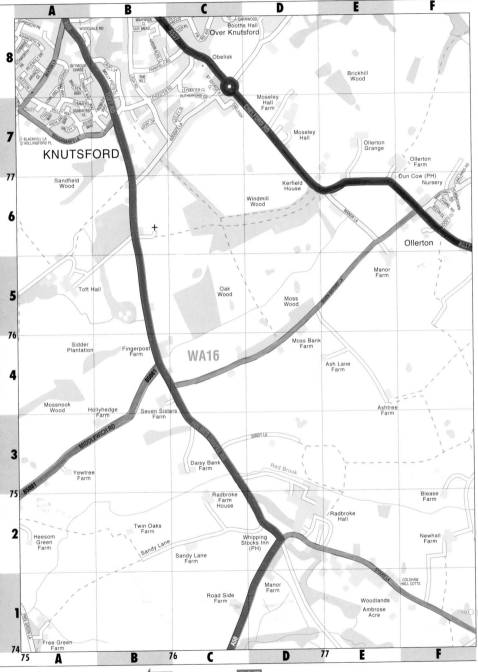

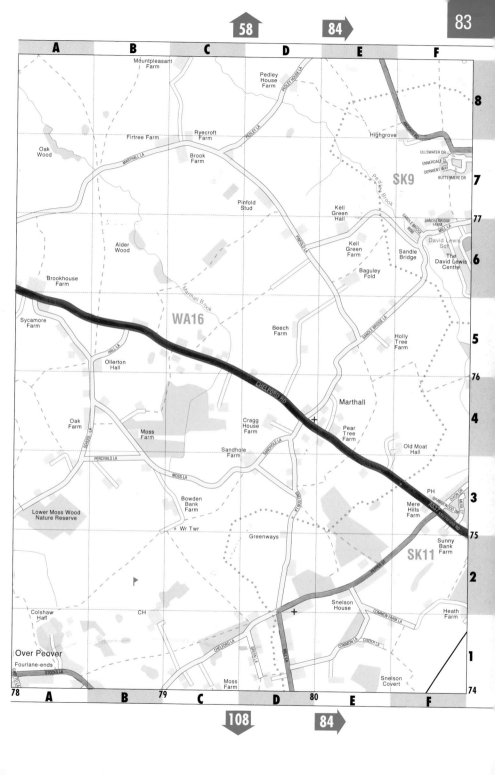

WA16

8

Tanyard Farm

FODEN LA

Oswald Farm

ABBERLEY HALL

Little Moss Farm

Field's Farm

GREEN LA

Heathgate Farm

Sandpit Farm

ANDERS RD

CONISTON CL

PH

7

Manor Farm

IVY HO

SK9

Dane Villa

MILL LA

MERIMAN LA

WARFORD CRES

Warford Hall Farm

CHELFORD RD

Walton Farm

ORCHARD CRES

77

David Lewis Sch

WARFORD HALL DR

+

Grogram Cottage

The David Lewis Centre

6

Warford Hall

Warford Hall

H

SOSSMOSS LA

WELSH ROW

Sees Moss (Mary Dendy Unit)

Stelfoxes

Dean Green

SAND LA

Gatley Green Farm

Dog Hole Wood

Sossmoss Wood

5

Peckmill Bottoms

Wyche's Farm

NURSERY LA

76

Lomas's Bottom

Peck Mill Farm

CARTER LA

Sossmoss Hall

SK10

Heawood Hall Farm

Firtree Farm

Corbishley Bridge

Corbishley

Heawood Hall

4

Callwood's Moss

Line Pits

Roadside Farm

Chandler's Farm

WOODLAND END

MILL BANK

HATCH CROFT

DRUMBER TEMP

BRANDYEN

DIXON LA

BURNT ACRE

WOODLAND

BROOM

WHINS

MOSS

HOLLY

WOODFIN CROFT

ELMSTEAD RD

CASTLE CT

CHAPEL CROFT

ALDERLEY RD

Sandle Heath

BOLLINGTON LA

Yarwoods

3

Sch

P

ROBIN CL

SK11

Mere Farm

75

A537

KNUTSFORD RD

Chelford

Bollington Pits

DIXON CT

STATION RD

STUBBS LA

2

Chelford

George's Wood

ESTELLA

Bollington Pits

Yewtree Cottages

Bloor's Pits

CHELFORD RDBT

Dumville's Farm

CHELFORD RD

A537

1

PO

A535

Willow Gaff

Knowsley Farm

Fallows Hall Farm

PEOVER LA

ADLINGTON DAVENPORT

74

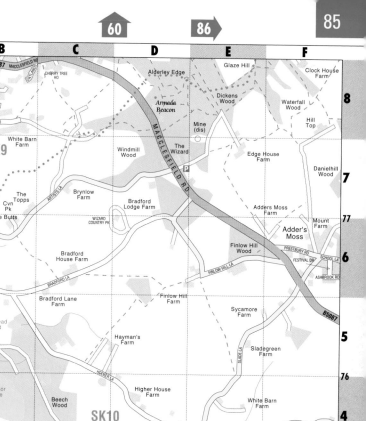

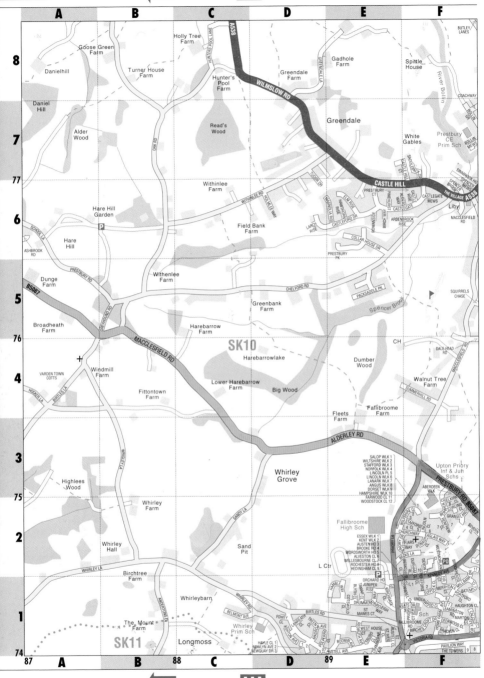

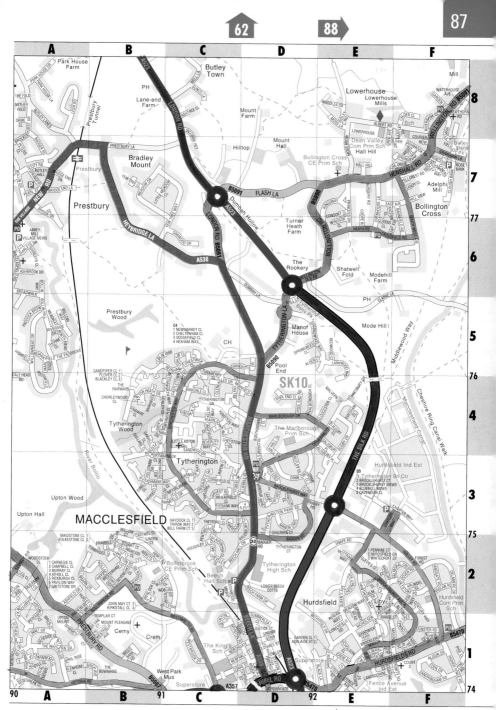

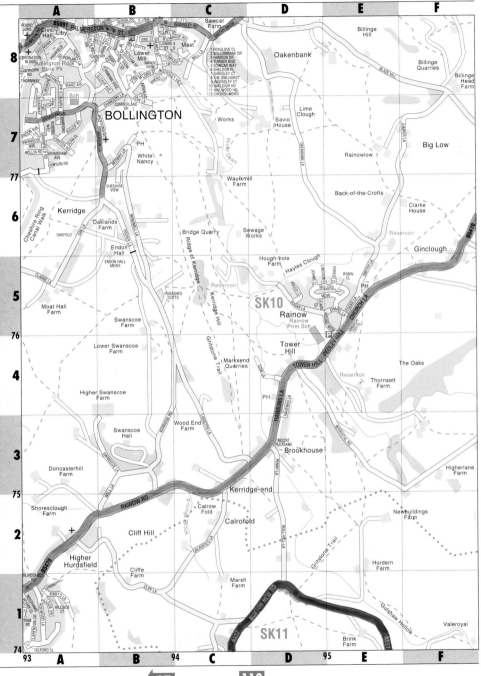

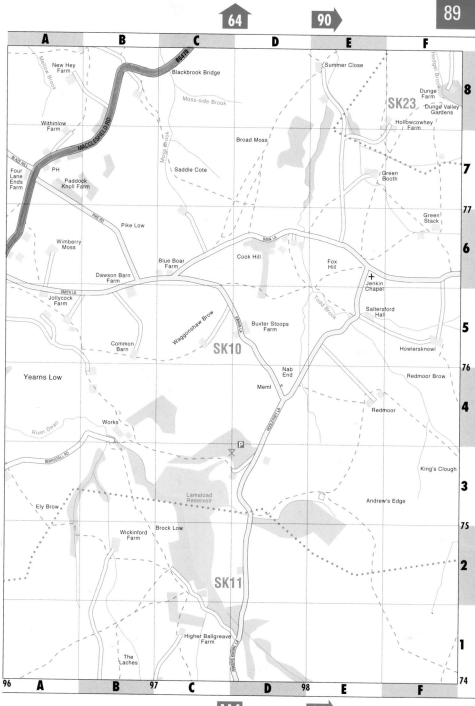

64
90

A B C D E F

New Hey Farm
Mellow Brook
B5470
Blackbrook Bridge
Moss-side Brook
Summer Close
SK23
Dunge Farm
Dunge Valley Gardens
8

Withinlow Farm
MACCLESFIELD RD
Moss Brook
Broad Moss
Hollowcowhey Farm

Four Lane Ends Farm
BLAZE HILL
PH
Paddock Knoll Farm
Saddle Cote
Green Booth
7

PIKE RD
Pike Low
Green Stack
77

Wimberry Moss
Bank La
Cook Hill
Fox Hill
Blue Boar Farm
Jenkin Chapel
6

Dawson Barn Farm
SMITH LA
Jollycock Farm
Saltersford Hall
Todd Brook

Waggonshaw Brow
Buxter Stoops Farm
Howlersknowl
5

Common Barn
SK10
BANK LA
Nab End
Redmoor Brow
76

Yearns Low
Meml
Redmoor
4

River Dean
Works
KOLDBECK LA
King's Clough

BERRISTALL RD
P
Andrew's Edge
3

Ely Brow
Lamaload Reservoir
75

Wickinford Farm
Brock Low
2

SK11

Higher Ballgreave Farm
ANKERS KNOWL LA
1

The Laches
74

96   A   B   97   C   D   98   E   F

114
90

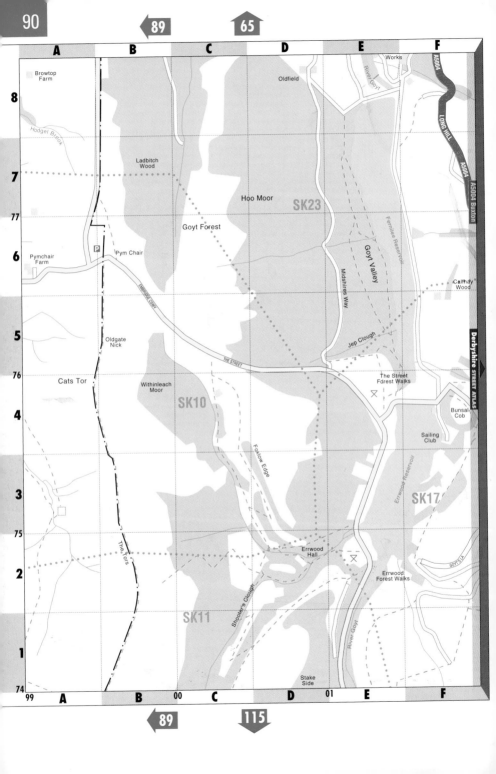

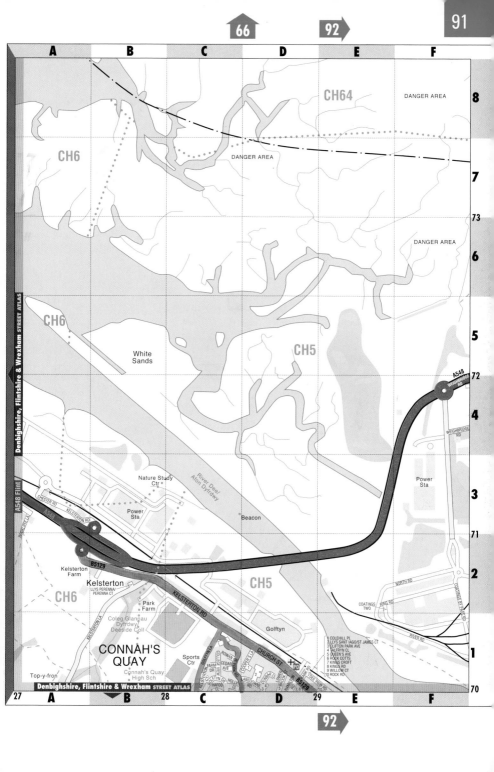

A B C D E F

8
CH64
DANGER AREA

CH6
7
DANGER AREA
73

DANGER AREA
6

5
White
Sands
CH5
72
A548
WEIGHBRIDGE RD
4
WEIGHBRIDGE
RD
Power
Sta

Nature Study
Ctr
River Dee/
Afon Dyfrdwy
3
CHESTER RD
KELSTERTON RD
A548
Power
Sta
Beacon
71
NORTH RD

B5129
Kelsterton
Farm
2
CH5
RING RD
COATINGS TWO SPUR RD
COATINGS
TWO
Kelsterton
LLYS PERENNA/
PERENNA CT
KELSTERTON RD
RIVER RD
CH6
Park
Farm
Coleg Glannau
Dyfrdwy
Deeside Coll
Golftyn
1
CHURCH ST
B5129

CONNAH'S
QUAY
Sports
Ctr
Connah's Quay
High Sch
Top-y-fron
HAFOD
1 COLEHILL PL
2 LLYS SANT IAGO/ST JAMES CT
3 CLIFTON PARK AVE
4 TALFRYN CL
5 QUEEN'S AVE
6 ROCK COTTS
7 KINGS CROFT
8 KINGS RD
9 WILLOW CT
10 ROCK RD

91
67

91

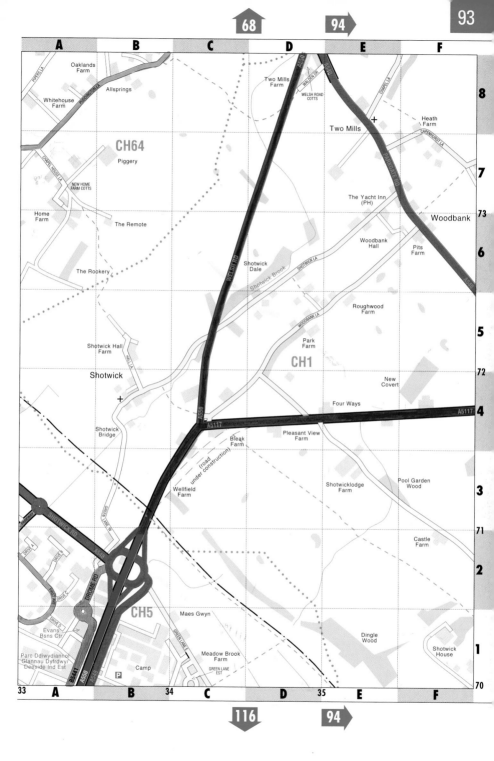

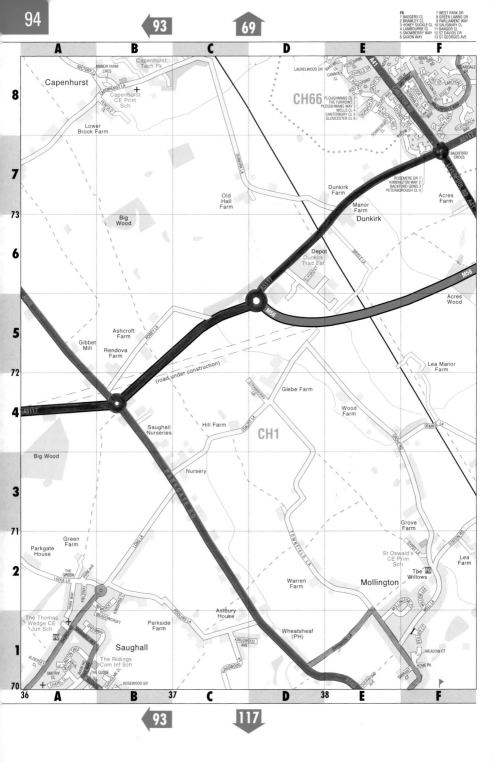

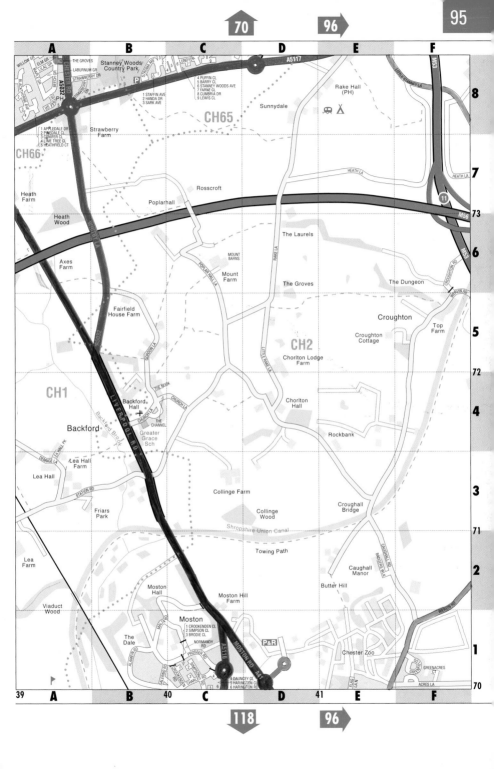

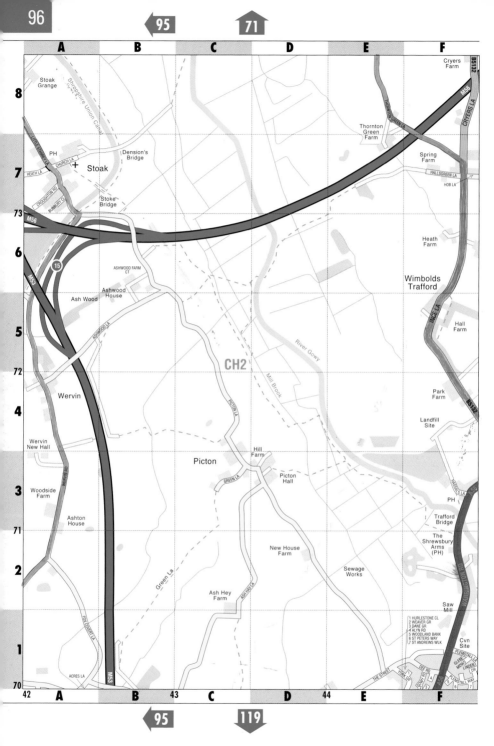

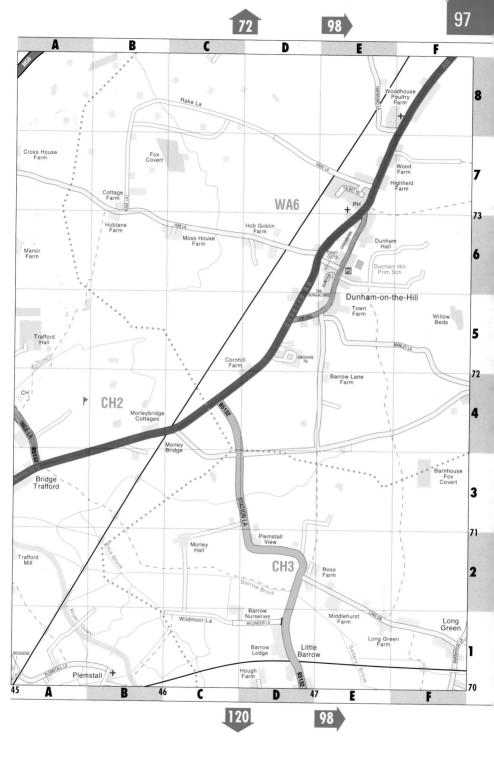

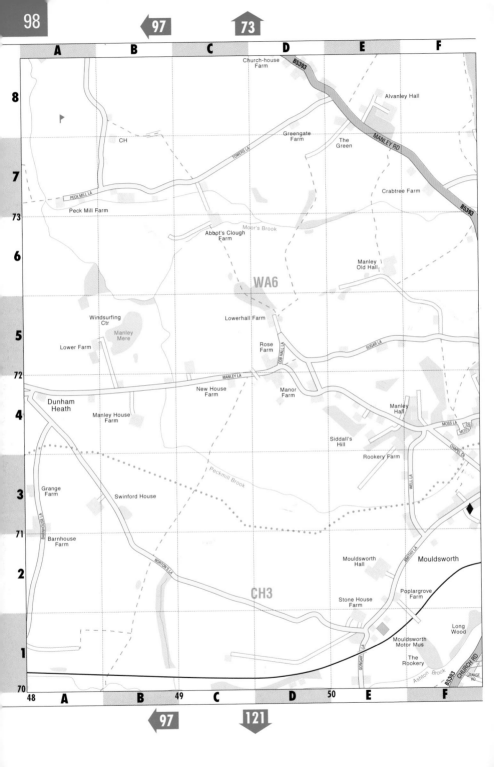

A B C D E F

8

7

73

6

5

72

4

3

71

2

1

70

Church-house Farm

B5393

Alvanley Hall

Greengate Farm

The Green

MANLEY RD

CH

TOWERS LA

PECK MILL LA

Peck Mill Farm

Crabtree Farm

B5393

Moor's Brook

Abbot's Clough Farm

Manley Old Hall

WA6

Windsurfing Ctr

Manley Mere

Lowerhall Farm

Lower Farm

Rose Farm

COB HALL LA

SUGAR LA

MANLEY LA

New House Farm

Manor Farm

Manley Hall

Dunham Heath

Manley House Farm

MOSS LA

MOSS

Siddall's Hill

CHAPEL LA

Rookery Farm

Grange Farm

Swinford House

Peckmill Brook

WELL LA

BARNHOUSE LA

Barnhouse Farm

NORTON'S LA

Mouldsworth Hall

SMITHY LA

Mouldsworth

CH3

Stone House Farm

Poplargrove Farm

Long Wood

Mouldsworth Motor Mus

The Rookery

GONSLEY LA

Ashton Brook

B5393

CHURCH RD

GRANGE RD

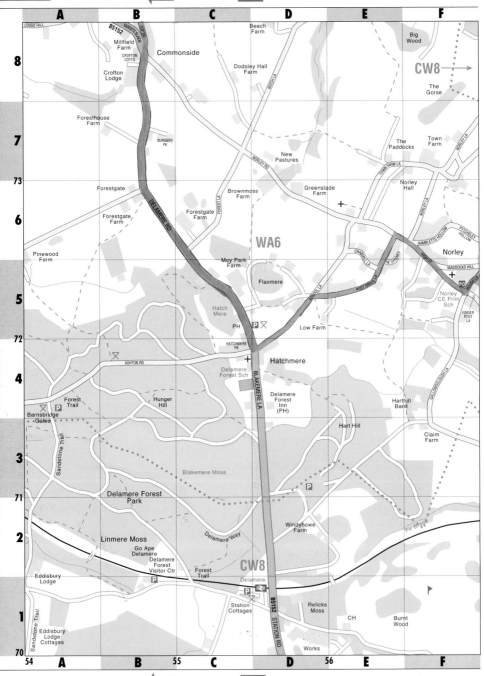

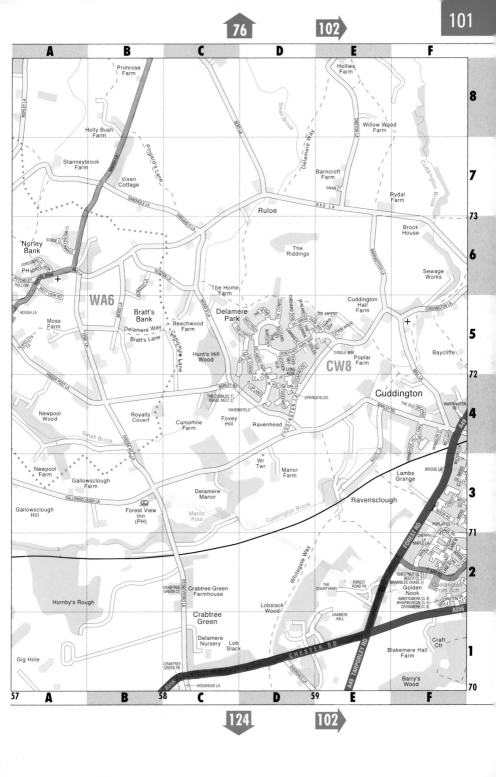

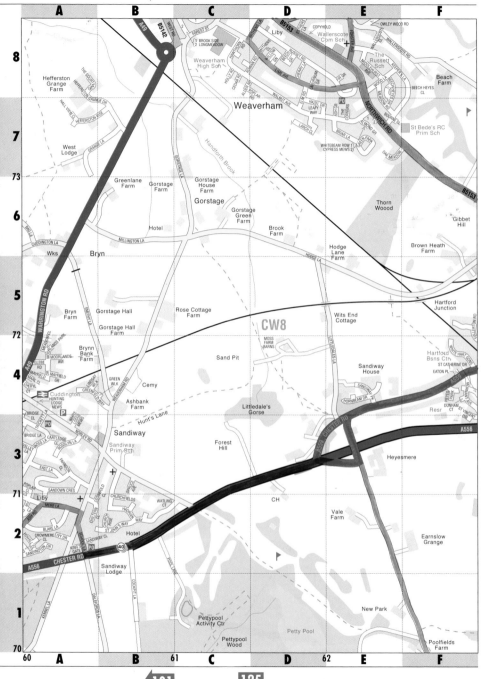

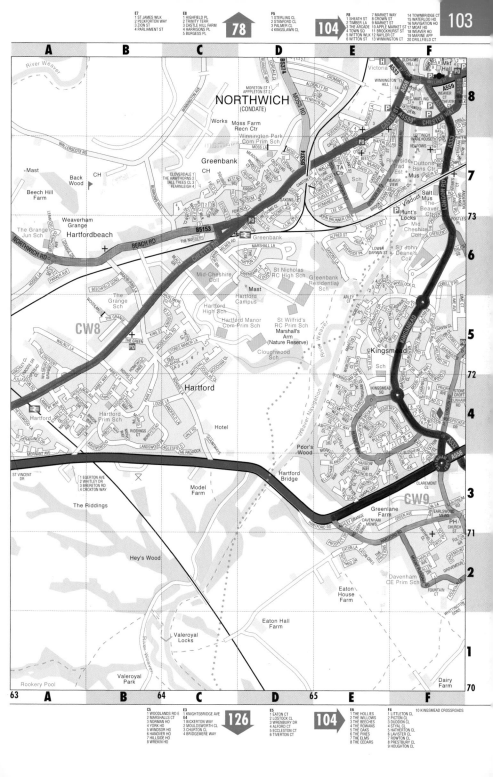

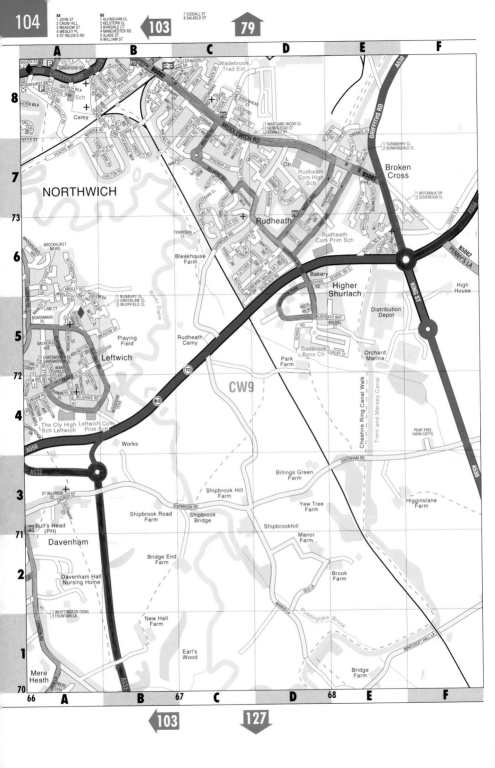

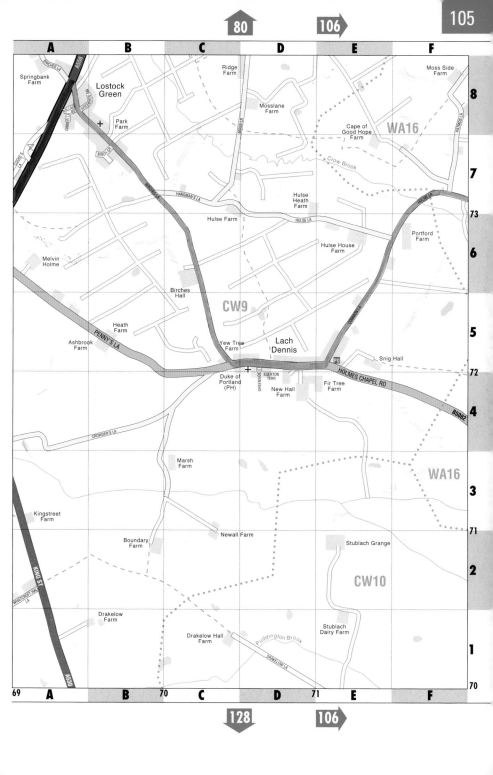

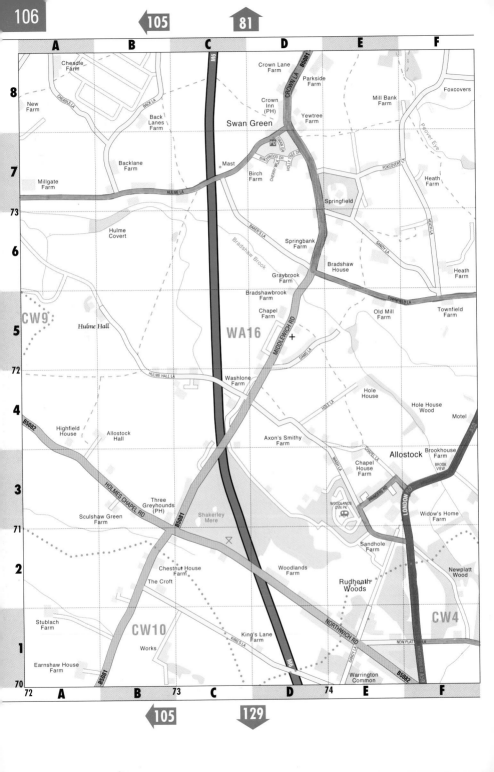

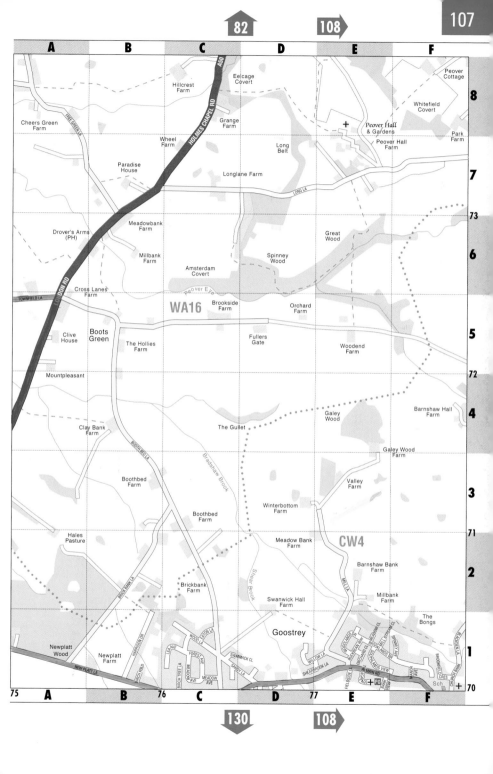

A B C D E F

8

7

73

6

5

72

4

3

71

2

1

70

A B C D E F

75 76 77

Peover Cottage

Peover Hall & Gardens

Whitefield Covert

Park Farm

Peover Hall Farm

Hillcrest Farm

Eelcage Covert

Grange Farm

Long Belt

Wheel Farm

HOLMES CHAPEL RD

A50

Cheers Green Farm

FREE GREEN LA

Paradise House

Longlane Farm

LONG LA

Meadowbank Farm

Great Wood

Drover's Arms (PH)

Millbank Farm

Spinney Wood

LONDON RD

Amsterdam Covert

Cross Lanes Farm

Peover Eye

TOWNFIELD LA

WA16

Brookside Farm

Orchard Farm

Clive House

Boots Green

The Hollies Farm

Fullers Gate

Woodend Farm

Mountpleasant

Clay Bank Farm

The Gullet

Galey Wood

Barnshaw Hall Farm

BOOTH BED LA

Bradshaw Brook

Galey Wood Farm

Boothbed Farm

Valley Farm

Boothbed Farm

Winterbottom Farm

CW4

Hales Pasture

Meadow Bank Farm

71

Barnshaw Bank Farm

BRICK BANK LA

Sheath Brook

Millbank Farm

The Bongs

Brickbank Farm

Swanwick Hall Farm

MELL LA

Newplatt Wood

HARRISON DR

Newplatt Farm

BIRCH FIELD

Goostrey

SHEARBROOK LA

NEW PLATT LA

LA LANE

WOODS LA

STATION LA

FOREST AVE

BIRCH TREE LA

MICKLOW AVE

MEADOW AVE

SWANWICK CL

GABBY LA

WILLOW LA

FIELDINGS LA

NEW MANOR RD

WILL ST PRIM AV C

SPINNEY AVE

BROOKFIELDS CRES

MEADOWS VIEW

MANOR AVE

CHURCH LANE

BLACKDEN LA

Sch

70

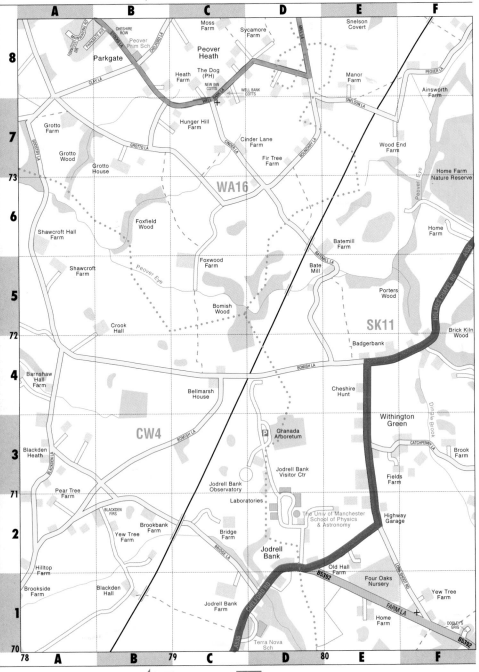

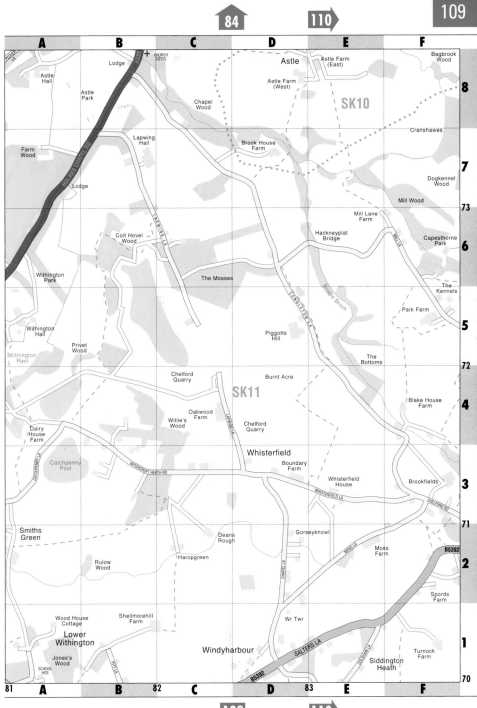

A B C D E F

Astle Hall

Astle Park

Lodge

CHURCH COTTS

Chapel Wood

Astle

Astle Farm (East)

Astle Farm (West)

Bagbrook Wood

8

SK10

Farm Wood

Lapwing Hall

Lodge

Brook House Farm

Cranshawes

7

Dogkennel Wood

Mill Wood

73

HOLMES CHAPEL RD

Colt Hovel Wood

LAPWING LA

Withington Park

The Mosses

Hackneyplat Bridge

Mill Lane Farm

MILL LA

Capesthorne Park

6

Withington Hall

Privet Wood

Withington Pool

CONGLETON LA

Shape Brook

Piggotts Hill

The Bottoms

The Kennels

Park Farm

5

72

Chelford Quarry

SK11

Burnt Acre

Blake House Farm

4

Oakwood Farm

Willie's Wood

Chelford Quarry

LAPWING LA

Dairy House Farm

CATCHPENNY LA

Catchpenny Pool

WITHCROFT HEATH RD

Whisterfield

Boundary Farm

Whisterfield House

WHISTERFIELD LA

Brookfields

CHELFORD RD

3

71

Smiths Green

Deans Rough

Haropgreen

Gorseyknowl

CHAPEL LA

MOSS LA

Moss Farm

B5392

2

Rulow Wood

Spords Farm

Wood House Cottage

Shellmorehill Farm

PITT LA

Lower Withington

Jones's Wood

SCHOOL HOS

Windyharbour

Wr Twr

SALTERS LA

B5392

DEESIDE LA

Siddington Heath

Turnock Farm

1

70

81 82 83

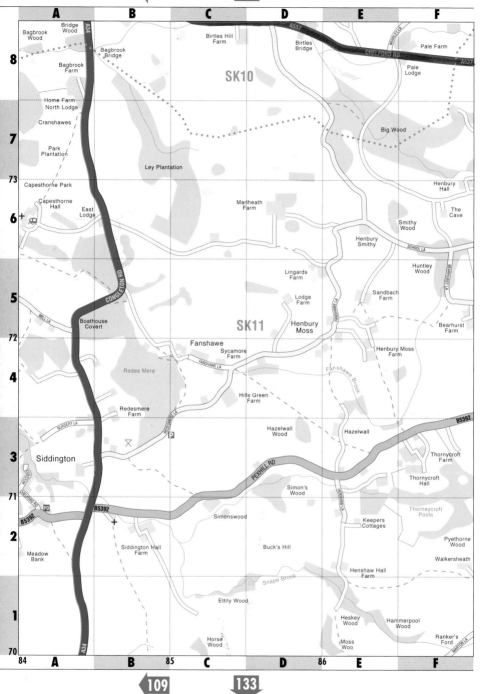

F8
1 ASHBOURNE MEWS
2 SHELBOURNE MEWS
3 ST LUKE'S HO
4 ALDERNEY CL
5 BLANDFORD DR
6 THE TOWERS

7 HEDINGHAM CL
8 MARLBOROUGH HO
9 ABINGDON CL
10 KENNET WAY
11 KENSINGTON SQ
12 WINCHESTER HO

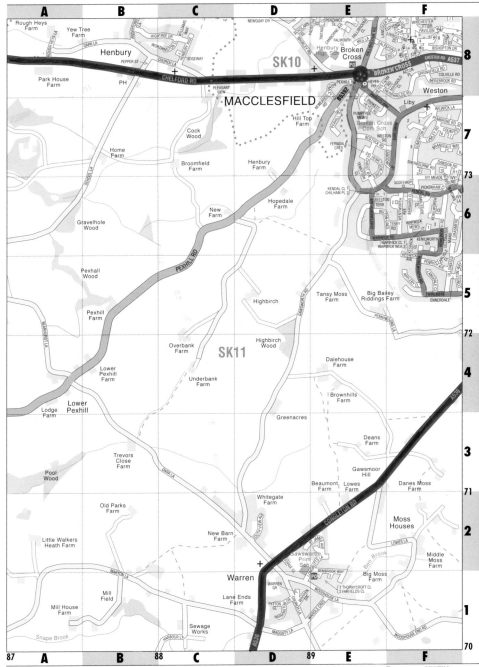

134

112

F7
1 VICARAGE WAY
2 DUDLEY WLK
3 PEVERIL WLK
4 PORTLAND WLK
5 SOMERTON CL
6 WARDOUR CL

7 COUNTESS CL
8 WAKEHAM CHASE
9 HILTON CL
10 IVY MEADE CL
11 DAWSON CL

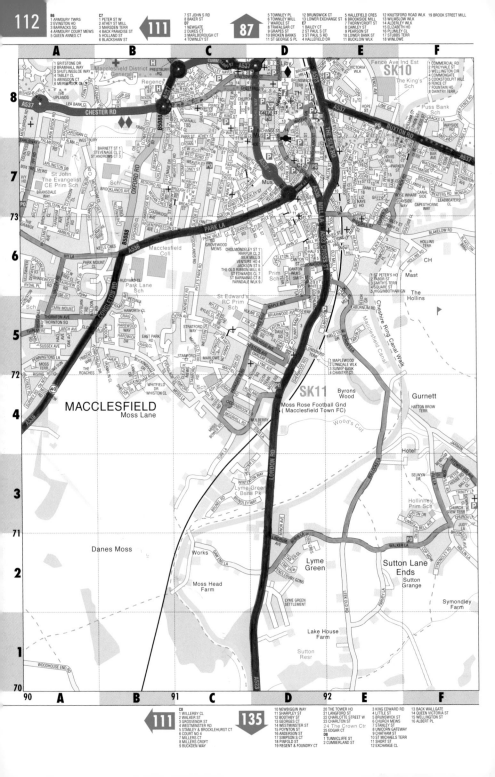

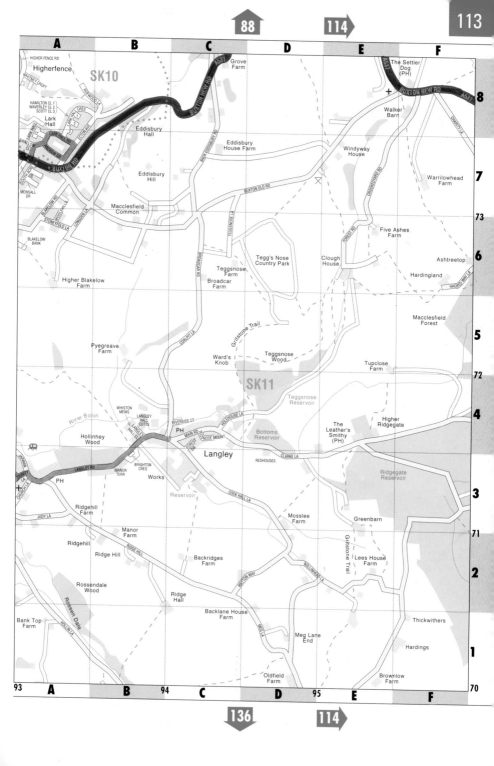

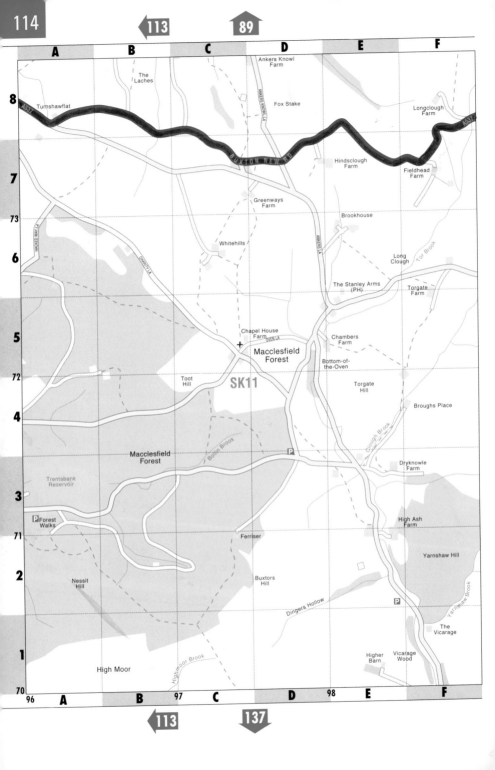

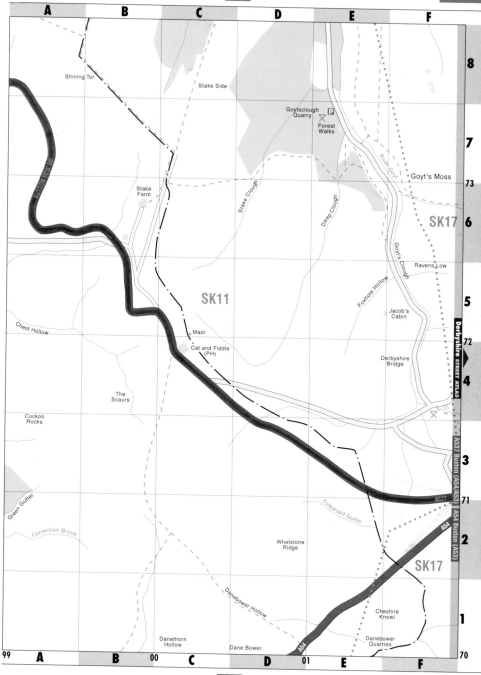

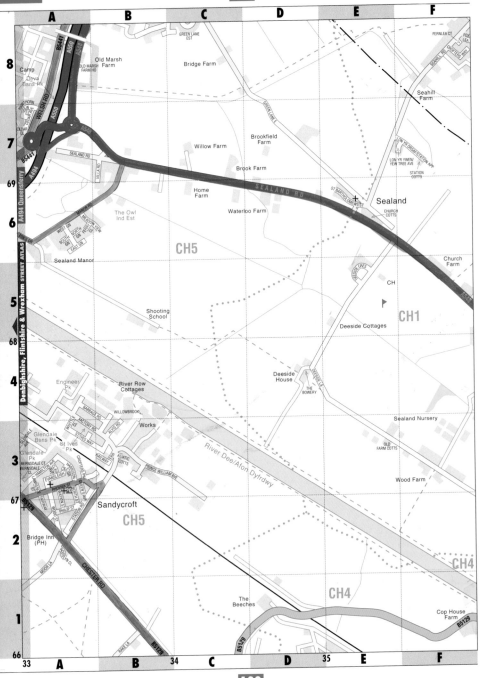

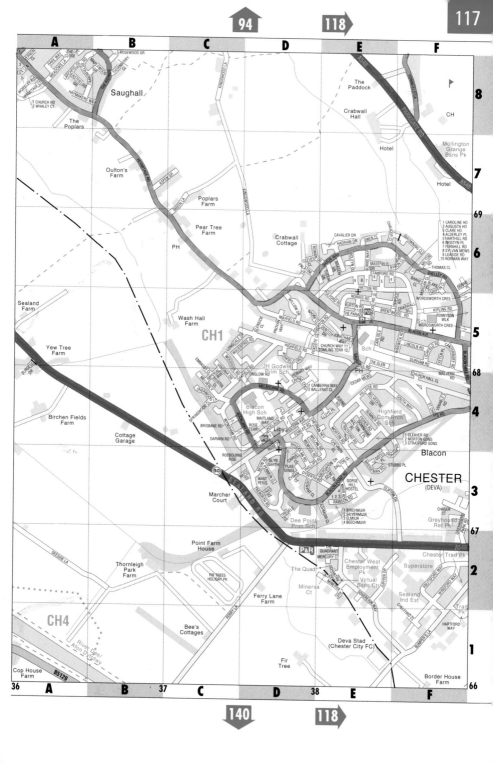

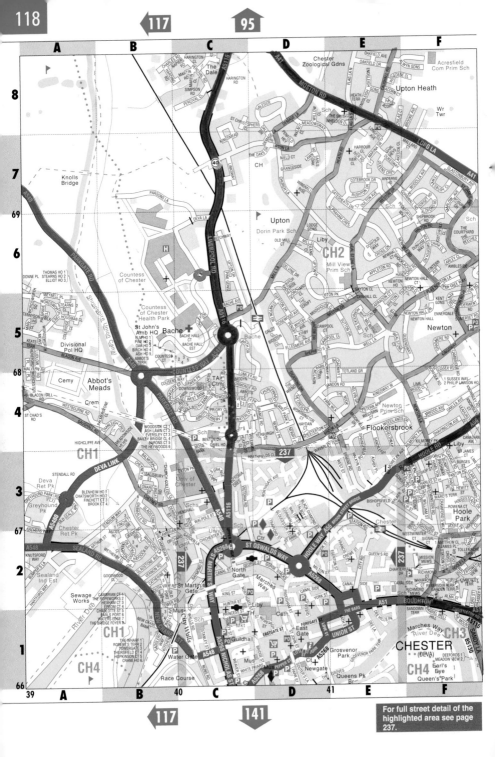

For full street detail of the highlighted area see page 237.

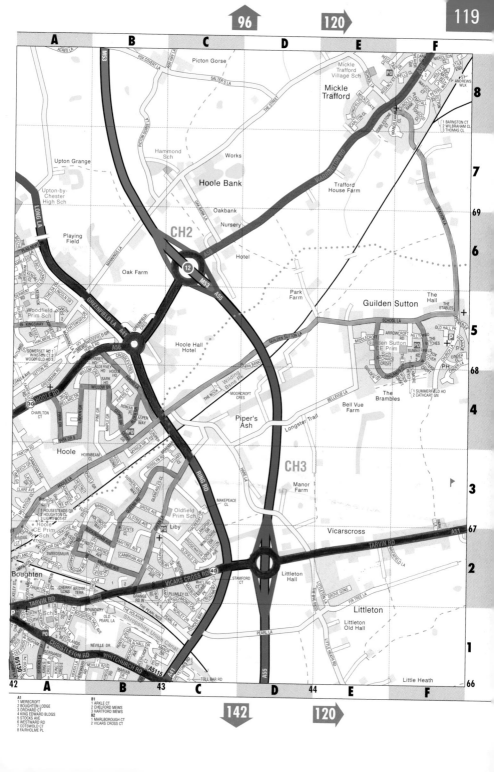

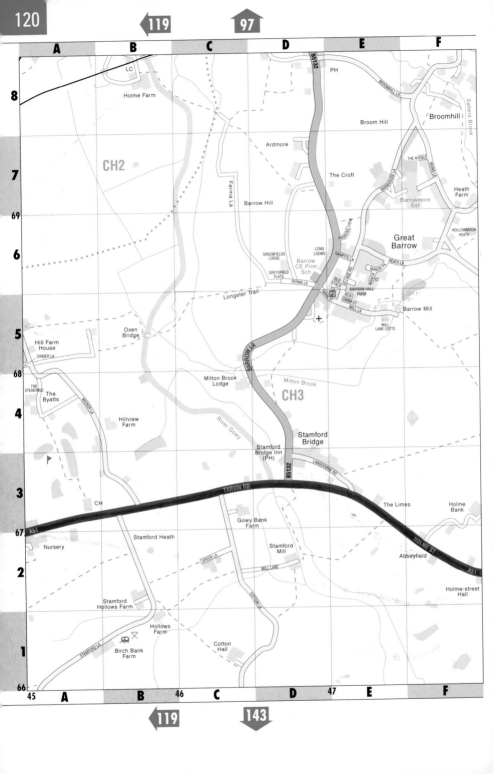

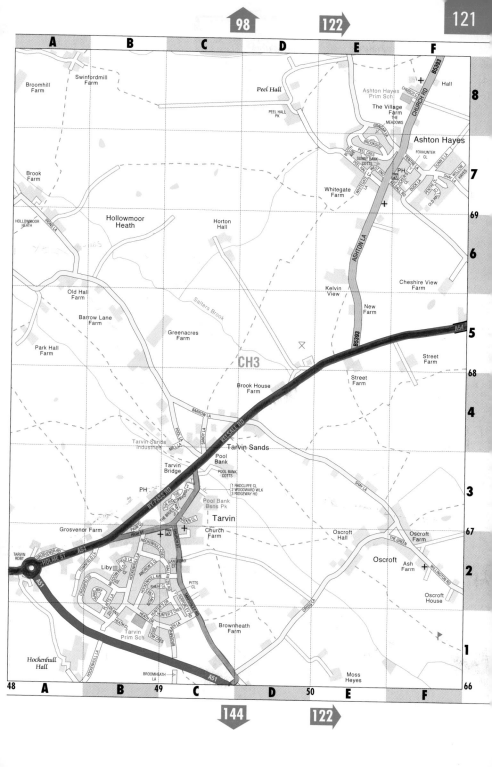

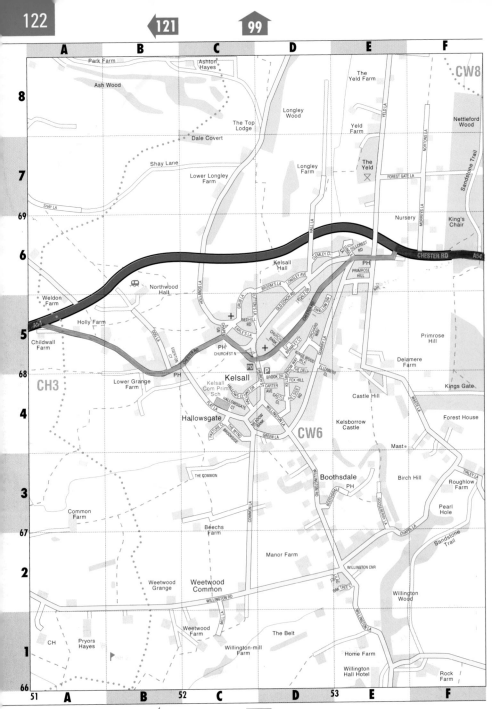

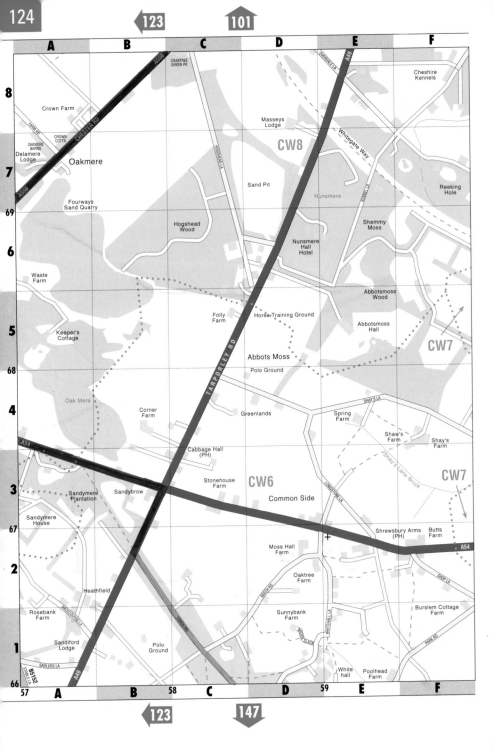

A   B   C   D   E   F

8

CRABTREE
GREEN PK

Crown Farm

Cheshire
Kennels

Masseys
Lodge

A556

CROWN
COTTS

OAKMERE
BARNS

Delamere
Lodge

Oakmere

CW8

Whitegate Way

7

CHESTER RD

A556

FARM RD

Sand Pit

Nunsmere

Reeking
Hole

69

Fourways
Sand Quarry

Hogshead
Wood

Shemmy
Moss

6

Nunsmere
Hall
Hotel

Abbotsmoss
Wood

Waste
Farm

Folly
Farm

Horse Training Ground

Abbotsmoss
Hall

5

Keeper's
Cottage

Abbots Moss

CW7

68

Polo Ground

TARPORLEY RD

4

Oak Mere

Corner
Farm

Greenlands

Spring
Farm

SHAY'S LA

Shaw's
Farm

Shay's
Farm

A54

Cabbage Hall
(PH)

Shay's Lane Brook

CW7

3

Sandymere
Plantation

Sandybrow

Stonehouse
Farm

CW6

Common Side

LONGSTONE LA

67

Sandymere
House

Shrewsbury Arms
(PH)

Butts
Farm

A54

Moss Hall
Farm

2

Heathfield

Oaktree
Farm

BEECH RD

SHOP LA

Burslem Cottage
Farm

Rosebank
Farm

Sunnybank
Farm

WHITEHALL LA

BROOK SLACK

PARK RD

1

Sandiford
Lodge

BEECONLAKE LA

Polo
Ground

GRADLINE

White
hall

Poolhead
Farm

66

B5152

SADLERS LA

STABLES LA

A49

57   A   B   58   C   D   59   E   F

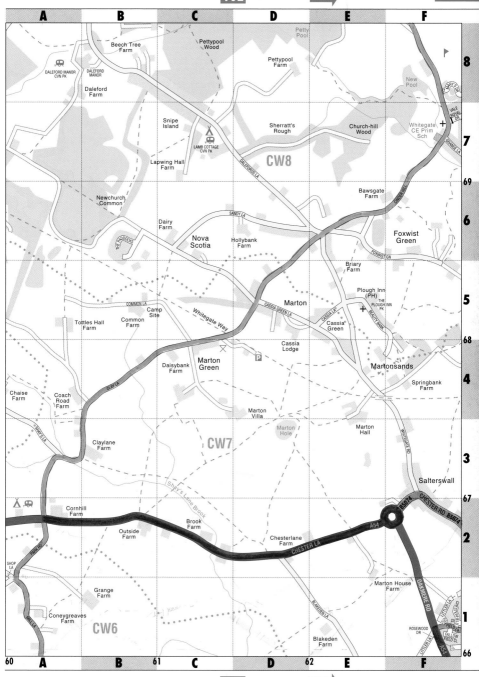

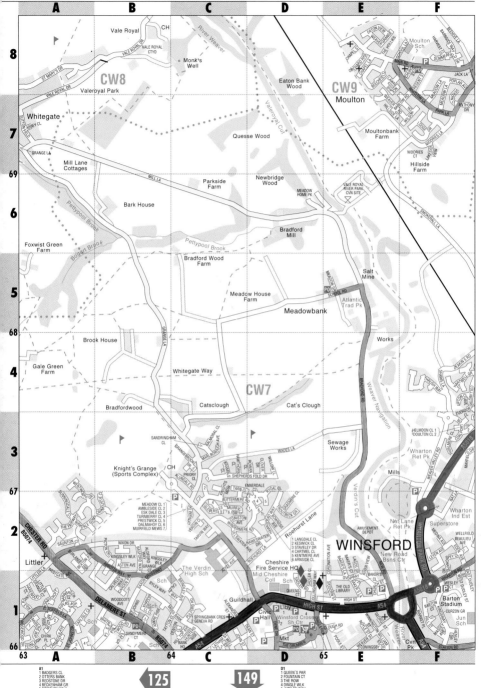

125
103

A1
1 BADGERS CL
2 OTTERS BANK
3 REDSTONE DR
4 BECKENHAM GR
5 FINSBURY WLK

D1
1 QUEEN'S PAR
2 FOUNTAIN CT
3 THE ROW
4 DINGLE WLK
5 JUBILEE WAY

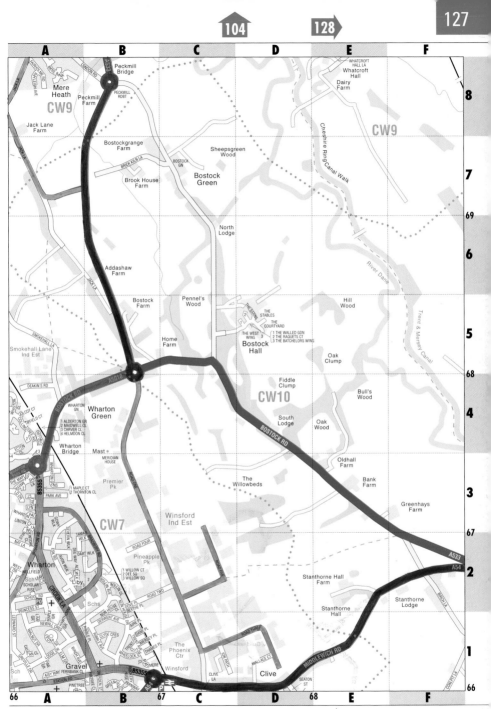

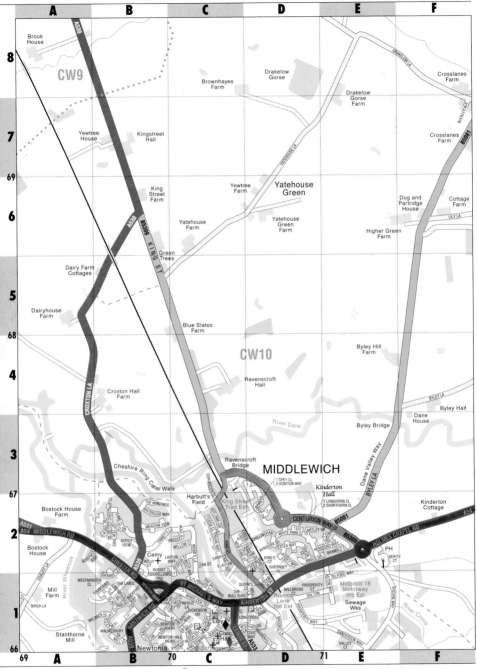

A **B** **C** **D** **E** **F**

Brook
House

CW9

8

Brownhayes
Farm

Drakelow
Gorse

Crosslanes
Farm

Yewtree
House

Kingstreet
Hall

Drakelow
Gorse
Farm

7

69

King
Street
Farm

Yewtree
Farm

Yatehouse
Green

Crosslanes
Farm

Dairy Farm
Cottages

Green
Trees

Yatehouse
Farm

Yatehouse
Green
Farm

Dog and
Partridge
House

Cottage
Farm

6

LILY LA

Dairyhouse
Farm

KING ST

Higher Green
Farm

5

68

Blue Slates
Farm

CW10

Byley Hill
Farm

4

CROXTON LA

Croxton Hall
Farm

Ravenscroft
Hall

Byley Hall

Byley Bridge

Dane
House

River Dane

Dane Valley Way

BYLEY LA

3

Cheshire Ring Canal Walk

Ravenscroft
Bridge

Ravenscroft
Bridge

MIDDLEWICH

1 SPEY CL
2 HONITON WAY

Kinderton
Hall

67

Bostock House
Farm

THE WINDINGS

WATERSIDE WAY

MEADOW VIEW

Harbutt's
Field

King Street
Trad Est

1 LONGHORN CL
2 SHORTHORN CL

CENTURION WAY

B5081

Kinderton
Cottage

A54

A533
A54 MIDDLEWICH RD

NORTH
VIEW

CHESTER RD

PHILLINGHAM

WHITE PARK CL

HARTLEY GR

HEBFORD WAY

HOLMES CHAPEL RD

B5309

PH

VERITY
CT

2

Bostock
House

River Wheelock

Mill
Farm

BIRCH LA

NANTWICH RD

ST MICHAEL'S WAY

KINDERTON ST

A533

KING'S
CT

GUERNSEY
CL

ANGUS GR

ASTON WAY

Telford WAY

DALTON

Midpoint 18
Motorway
Ind Est

Sewage
Wks

River Croco

1

Stanthorne
Mill

Newtonia

MALMESBURY

NEWTON
HEATH

NEWTON HALL
MEWS

DICKENSON
HO

PINFOLD

Lib
Hall

Civic
Hall

PO

LONGCROSS

CIVIC
WAY

SCHOOLHOUSE
LN

Brooks
Lane
Ind Est

PROSPERITY
CT

PROSPERITY WAY

SANDERSON WAY

VALLEY
CT

ROBIN WAY

66

A **B** **C** **D** **E** **F**
69 70 71

C1
1 LAMBOURNE GR
2 LAWRENCE AVE E
3 LAWRENCE AVE
4 DIERDENS TERR

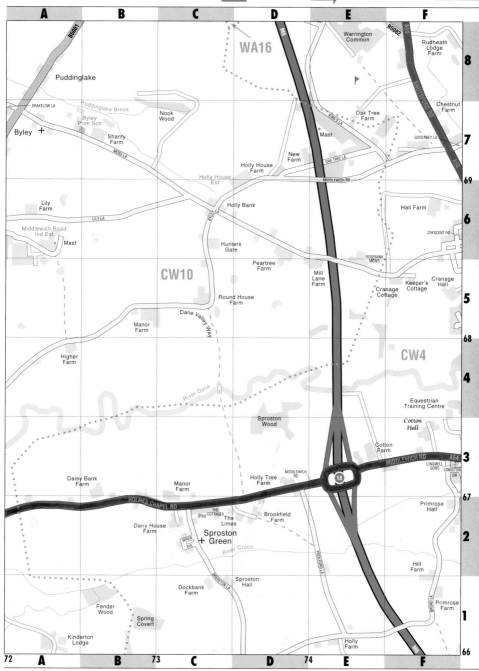

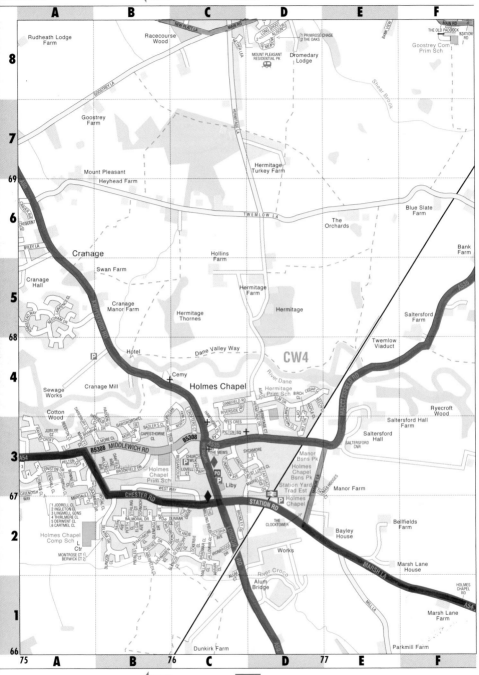

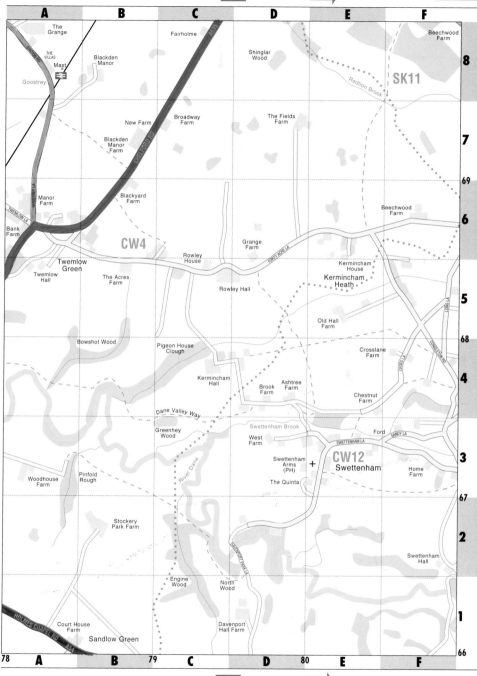

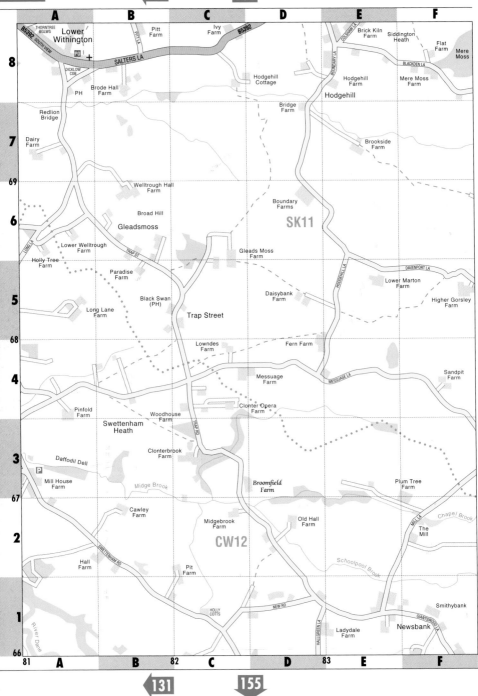

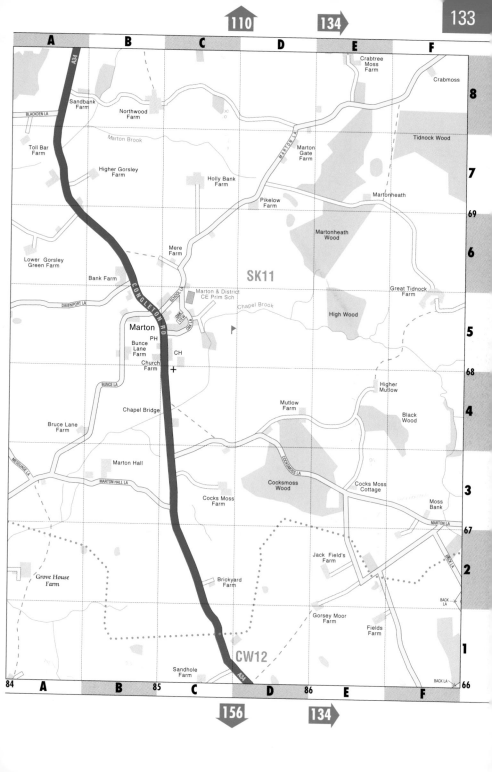

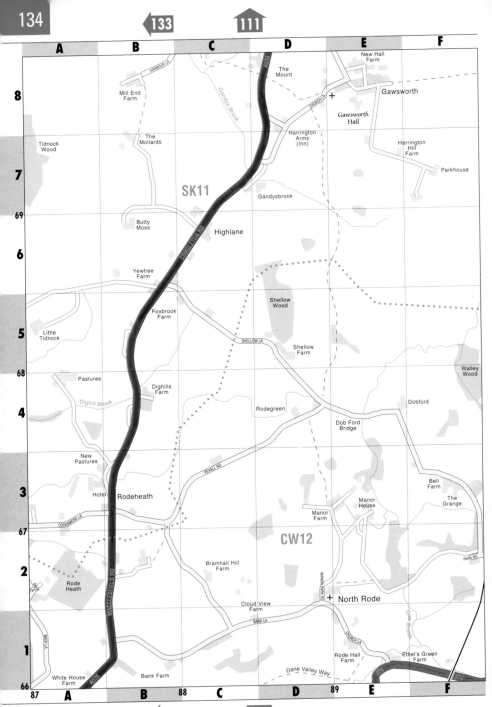

A   B   C   D   E   F

8

New Hall
Farm

Harbour La

The Mount

Mill End
Farm

Gawsworth

The
Mollards

Harrington
Arms
(Inn)

Gawsworth
Hall

Tidnock
Wood

Harrington
Hill
Farm

Parkhouse

7

SK11

Gandysbrook

69

Butty
Moss

Highlane

Congleton Rd

6

Yewtree
Farm

Shellow
Wood

Foxbrook
Farm

5

Little
Tidnock

Shellow La

Shellow
Farm

68

Pastures

Walley
Wood

Dighill Brook

Dighills
Farm

Rodegreen

Dobford

4

Dob Ford
Bridge

New
Pastures

Pexall Rd

Bell
Farm

3

Hotel

Rodeheath

Manor
House

The
Grange

Cockswoss La

Manor
Farm

67

CW12

Papa Rd

2

Bramhall Hill
Farm

Rode
Heath

Manor Park Rd

North Rode

Cow Brook

Macclesfield Rd

Cloud View
Farm

1

Bank La

Back La

Rode Hall
Farm

Ethel's Green
Farm

Church La

White House
Farm

Bank Farm

Dane Valley Way

66

87   A   B   88   C   D   89   E   F

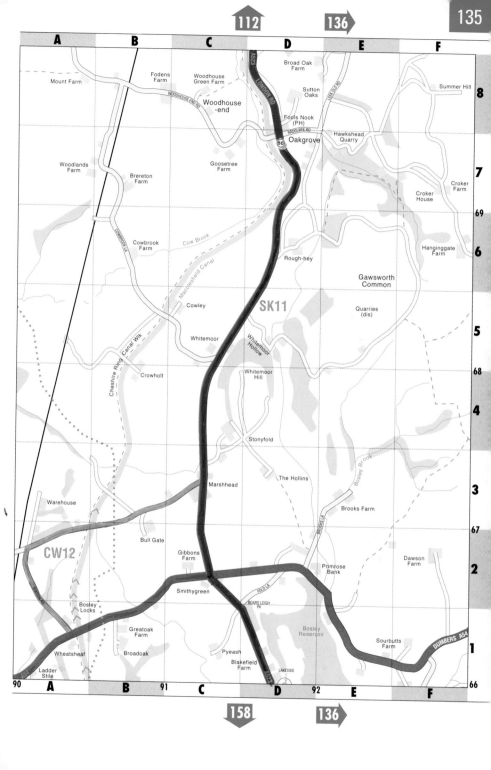

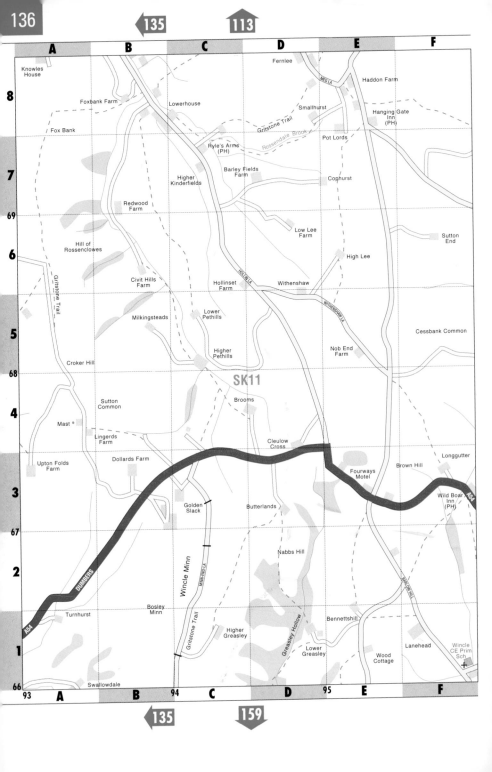

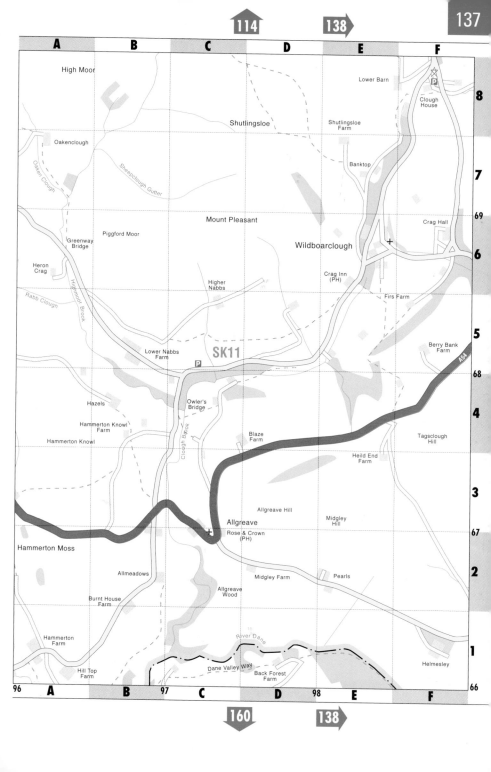

A   B   C   D   E   F

High Moor

Lower Barn

Clough House

8

Shutlingsloe

Shutlingsloe Farm

Oakenclough

Banktop

7

Oaken Clough

Sheepclough Gutter

69

Mount Pleasant

Crag Hall

Piggford Moor

Wildboarclough

6

Greenway Bridge

Heron Crag

Higher Nabbs

Crag Inn (PH)

Highmoor Brook

Rabb Clough

Firs Farm

5

Lower Nabbs Farm

SK11

Berry Bank Farm

A54

68

Hazels

Owler's Bridge

Clough Brook

4

Hammerton Knowl Farm

Blaze Farm

Tagsclough Hill

Hammerton Knowl

Heild End Farm

3

Allgreave Hill

Midgley Hill

Allgreave

67

Hammerton Moss

Rose & Crown (PH)

2

Allmeadows

Midgley Farm

Pearls

Burnt House Farm

Allgreave Wood

Hammerton Farm

River Dane

1

Hill Top Farm

Dane Valley Way

Back Forest Farm

Helmesley

66

96   A   B   97   C   D   98   E   F

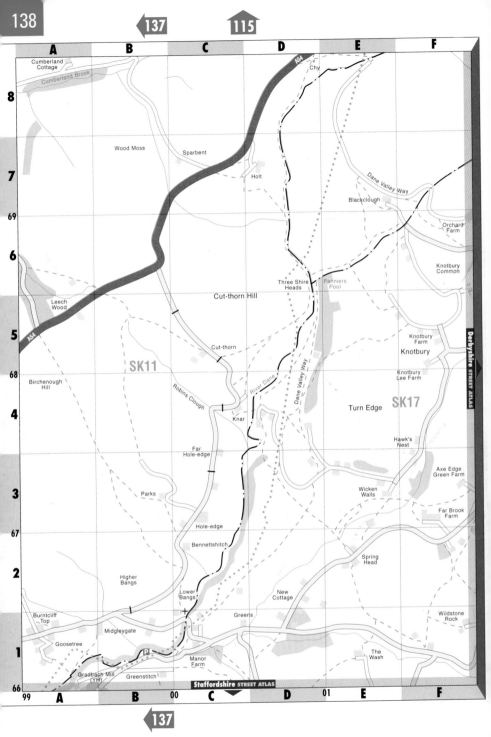

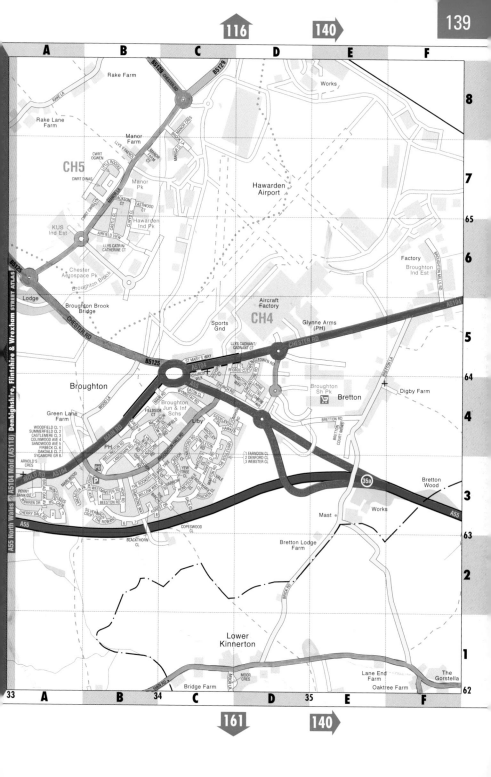

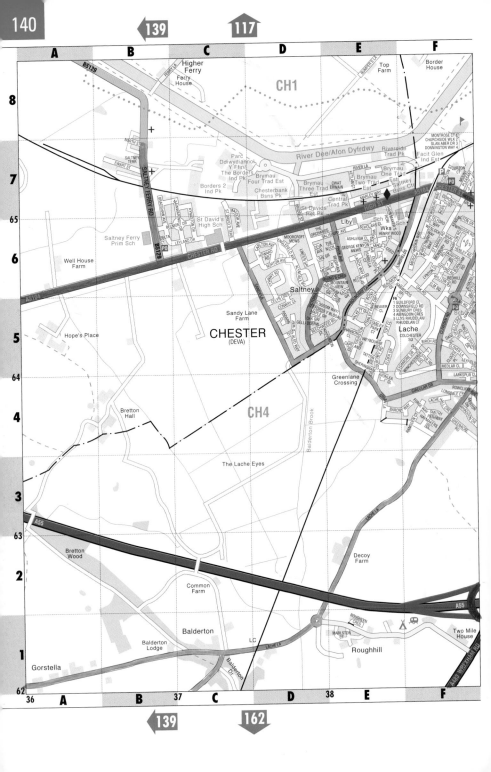

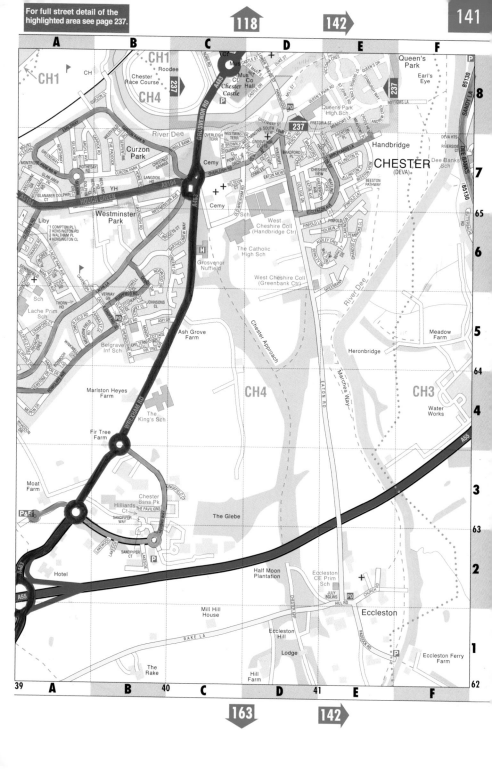

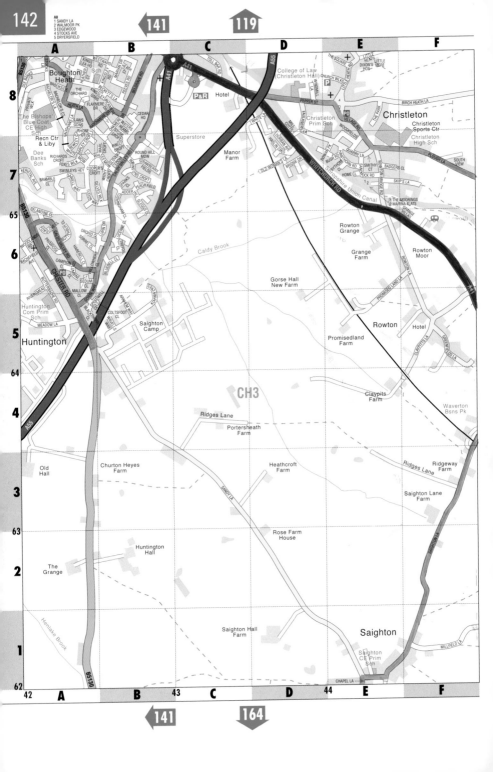

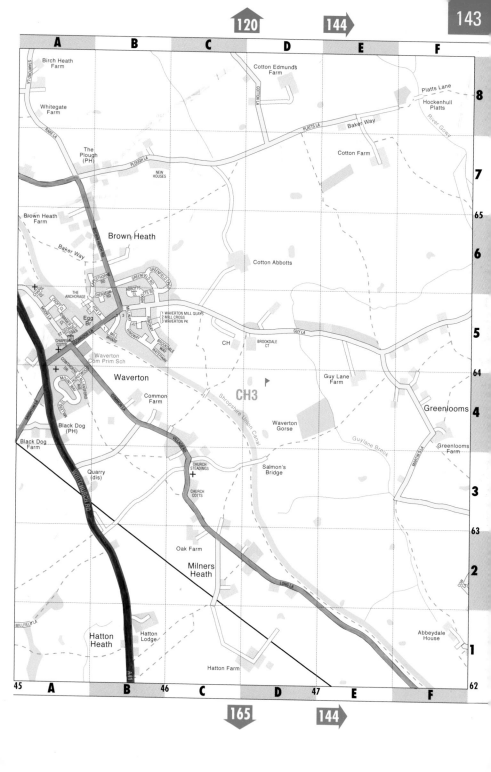

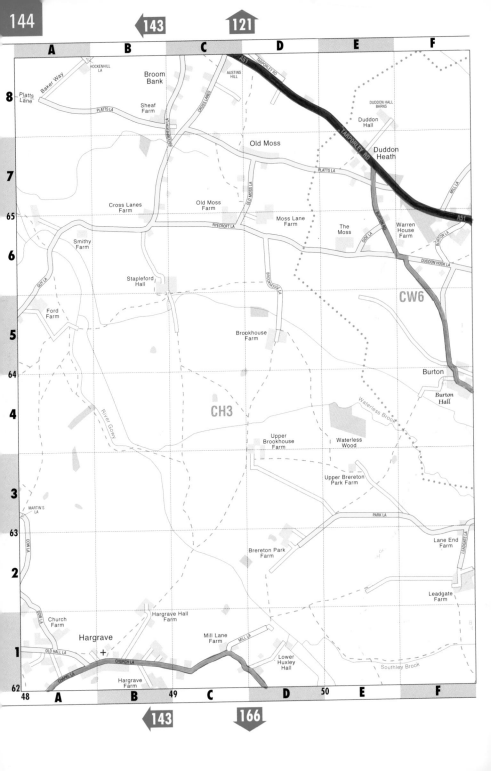

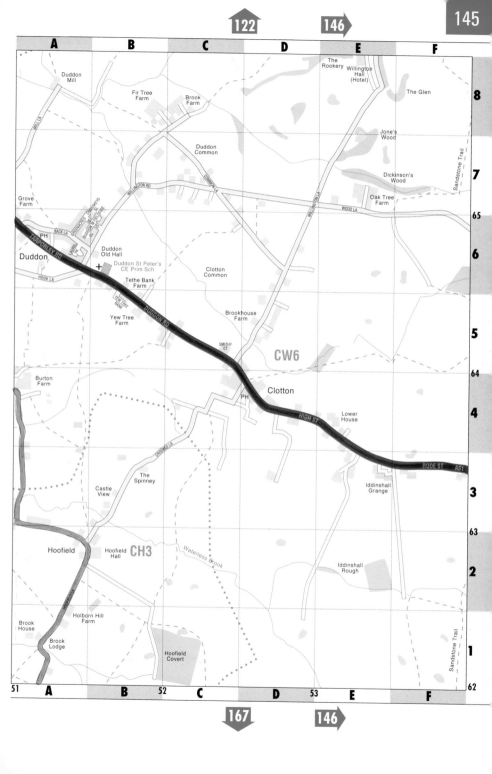

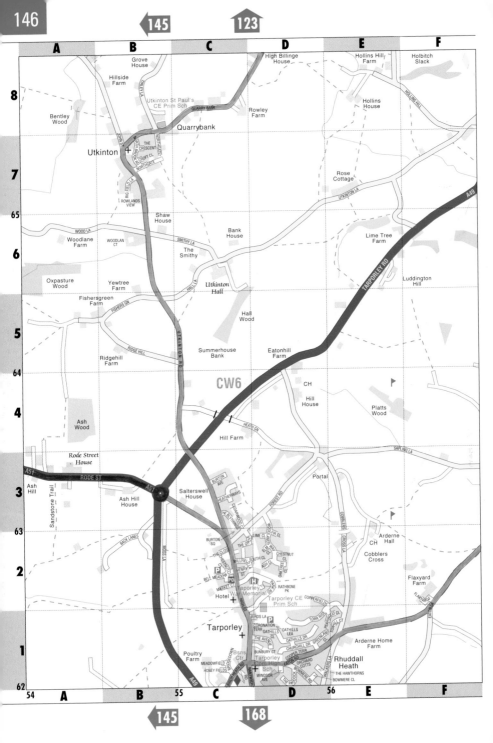

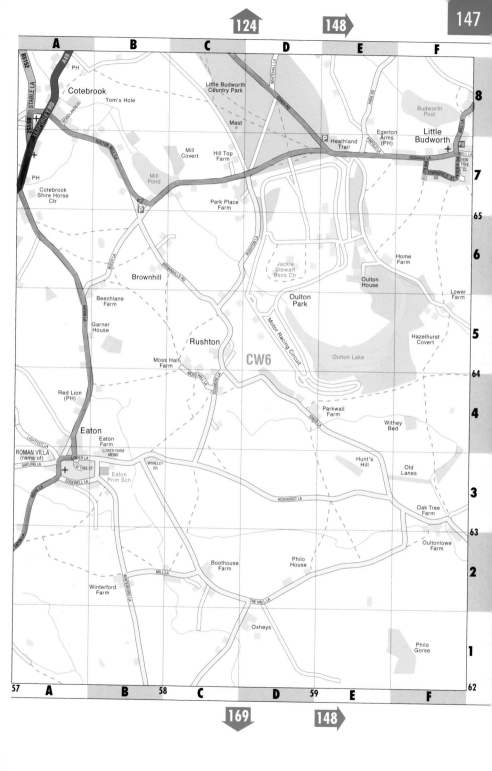

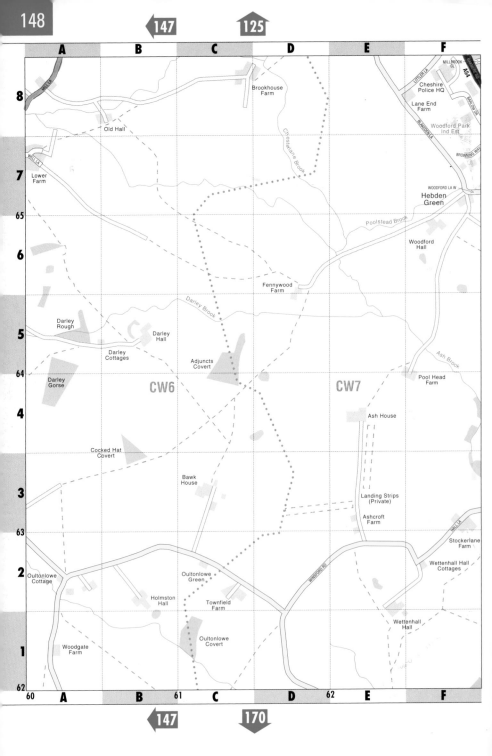

A B C D E F

8

Brookhouse Farm

Cheshire Police HQ

MILLBROOK CL

A54

LITTLER LA

MARTON DR

Lane End Farm

Woodford Park Ind Est

Old Hall

BLAKEDEN LA

BROWNING WAY

7

Lower Farm

Chesfalane Brook

WOODFORD LA W

Hebden Green

65

Poolstead Brook

6

Woodford Hall

Fennywood Farm

Darley Brook

5

Darley Rough

Darley Hall

Ash Brook

Darley Cottages

Adjuncts Covert

64

Darley Gorse

CW6

CW7

Pool Head Farm

4

Ash House

Cocked Hat Covert

3

Bawk House

Landing Strips (Private)

Ashcroft Farm

63

Stockerlane Farm

2

Oultonlowe Cottage

Oultonlowe Green

WINSFORD RD

Wettenhall Hall Cottages

Holmston Hall

Townfield Farm

WELL LA

Wettenhall Hall

1

Woodgate Farm

Oultonlowe Covert

62

60 A B 61 C D 62 E F

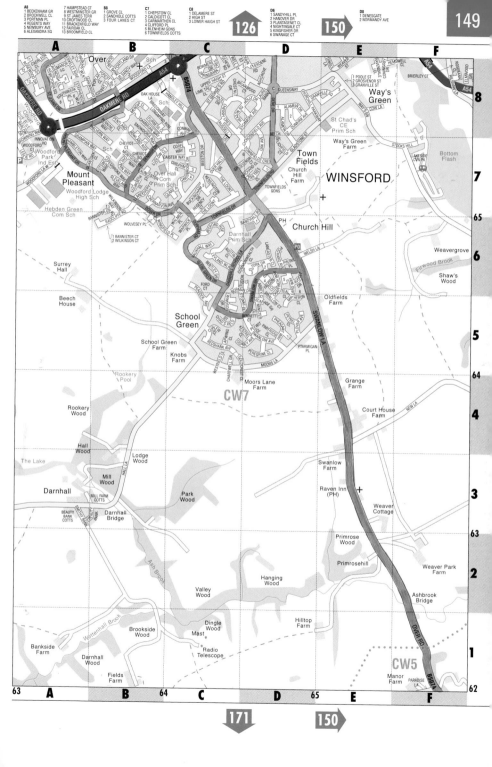

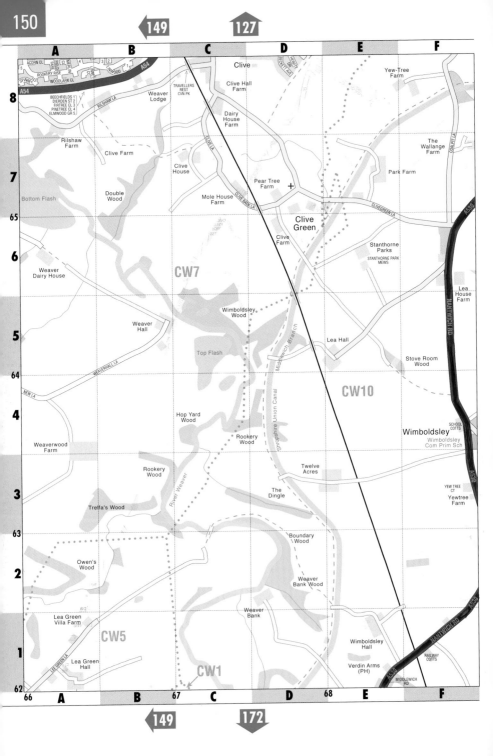

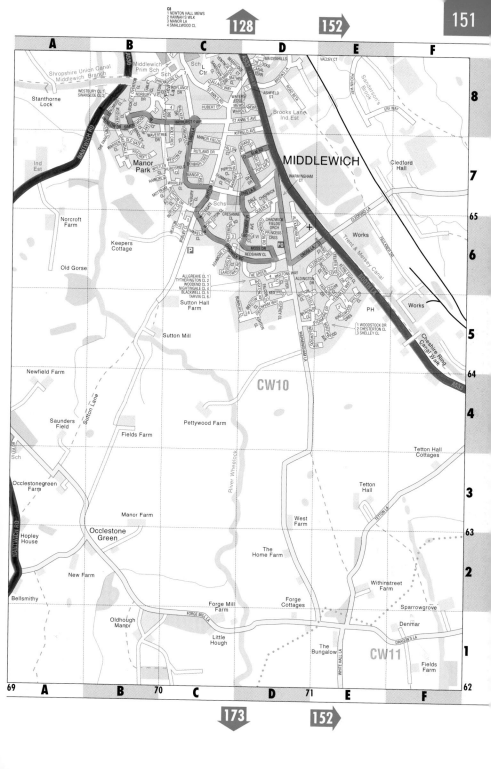

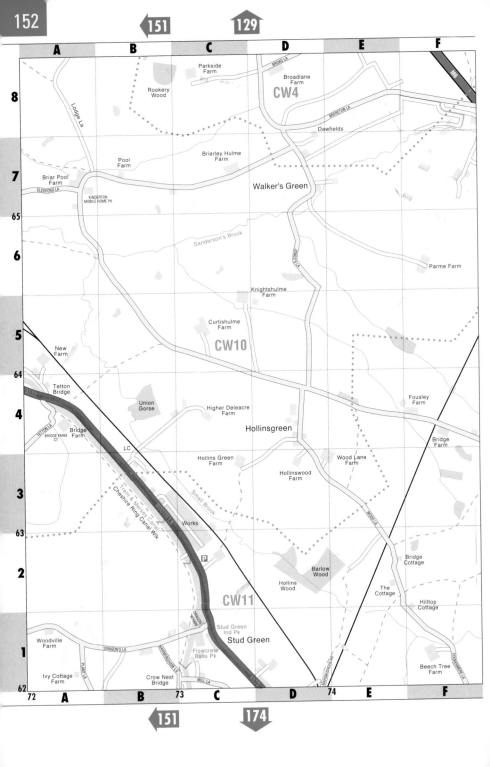

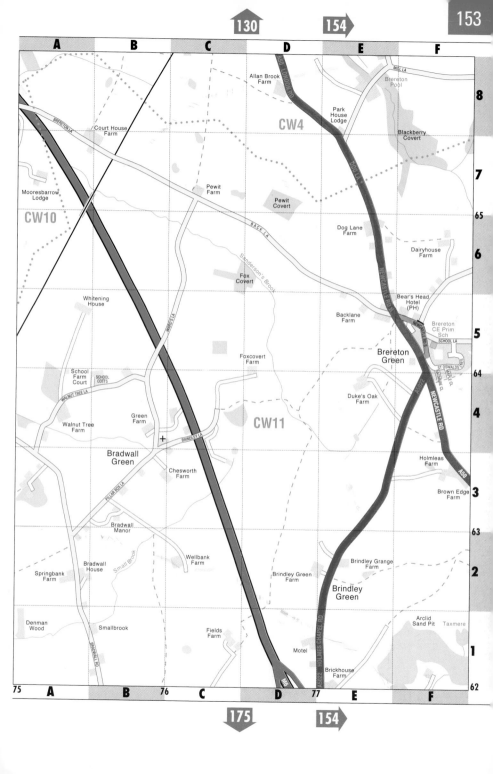

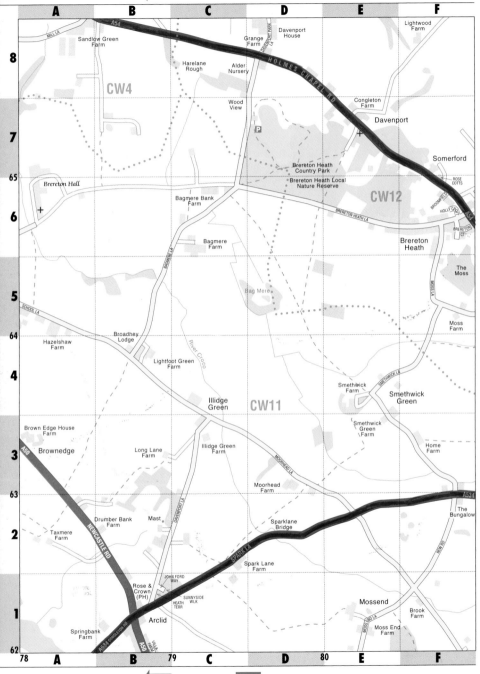

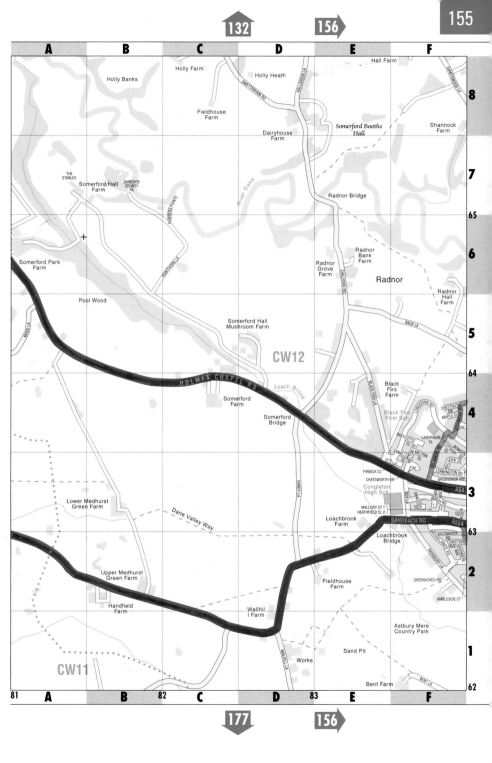

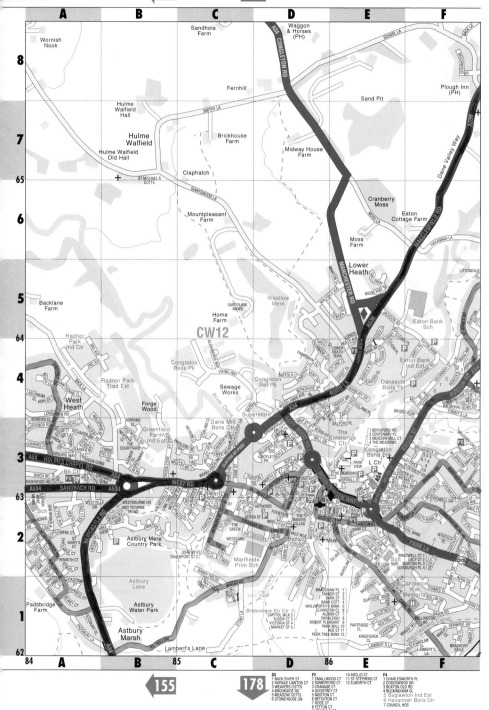

D3
1 BACK RIVER ST
2 HORACE LAWTON CT
3 WEAVERS COTTS
4 BROOKSIDE RD
5 MEADOW COTTS
6 STONEHOUSE GN

F3
1 SMALLWOOD CT
2 SOMERFORD CT
3 CRANAGE CT
4 GOOSTREY CT
5 MOSTON CT
6 BETCHTON CT
7 RODE CT
8 TETTON CT
9 NEWBOLD CT
10 ARCLID CT
11 ST STEPHENS CT
12 ELWORTH CT

F4
1 CHARLESWORTH PL
2 DODDSWOOD DR
3 BUXTON OLD RD
4 BUCKINGHAM CL
5 Buglawton Ind Est
6 Havannah Bsns Ctr
7 COUNCIL HOS

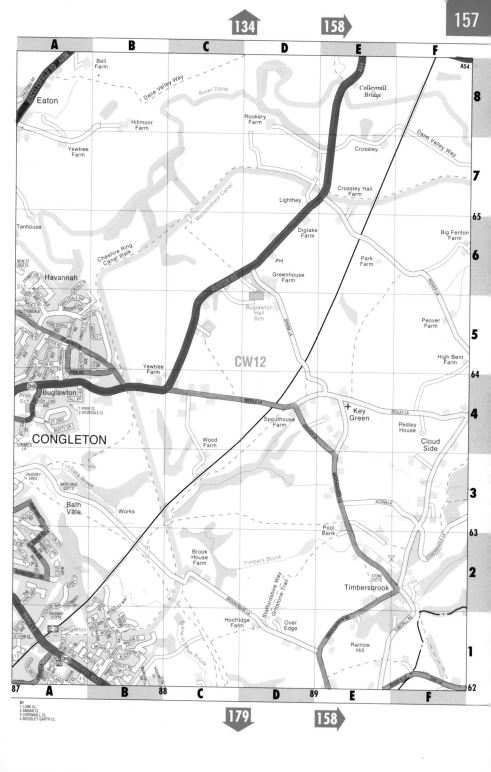

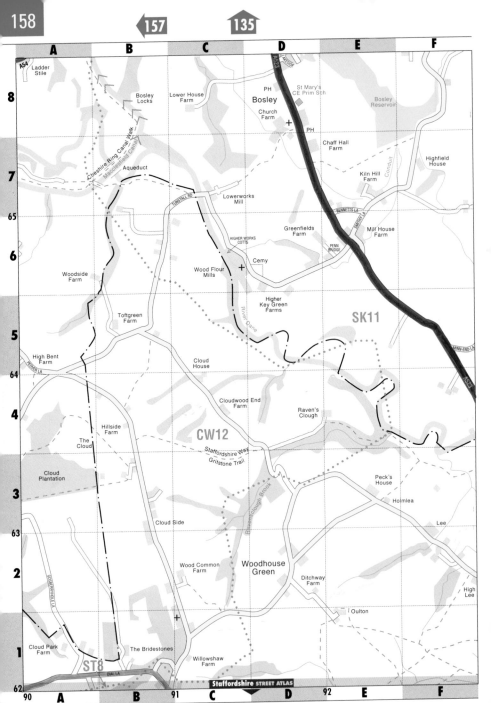

A54
Ladder
Stile

8

Bosley
Locks

Lower House
Farm

PH
Bosley

St Mary's
CE Prim Sch

Bosley
Reservoir

Church
Farm

PH

Chaff Hall
Farm

Highfield
House

Cheshire Ring Canal Walk

Macclesfield Canal

Aqueduct

7

Lowerworks
Mill

Kiln Hill
Farm

Conduit

65

TUNSTALL RD

BENNETTS LA

SMITH LA

Mill House
Farm

Greenfields
Farm

HIGHER WORKS
COTTS

PENN
BRIDGE

6

Woodside
Farm

Wood Flour
Mills

Cemy

Cemy

Higher
Key Green
Farms

SK11

Toftgreen
Farm

River Dane

5

High Bent
Farm

Cloud
House

MINN-END LA

A523

PEXER LA

64

Cloudwood End
Farm

Raven's
Clough

4

Hillside
Farm

CW12

The
Cloud

Staffordshire Way

Peck's
House

Gritstone Trail

Cloud
Plantation

Ravensclough Brook

Holmlea

3

Lee

63

Cloud Side

2

Wood Common
Farm

Woodhouse
Green

Ditchway
Farm

High
Lee

GOSBERRYHOLE LA

Oulton

1

Cloud Park
Farm

The Bridestones

ST8

DIAL LA

Willowshaw
Farm

62

90   A   B   91   C   D   92   E   F

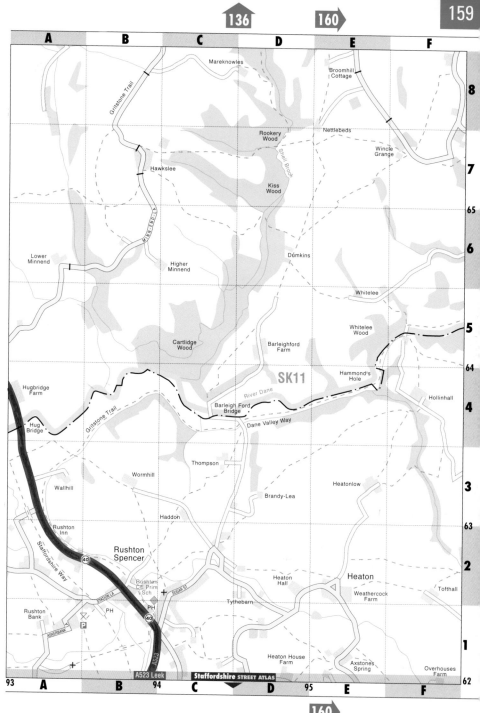

A   B   C   D   E   F

8

Mareknowles

Broomhill
Cottage

Gritstone Trail

Rookery
Wood

Nettlebeds

Shell Brook

Wincle
Grange

7

Hawkslee

Kiss
Wood

65

MINN END LA

6

Lower
Minnend

Higher
Minnend

Dumkins

Whitelee

Cartlidge
Wood

Barleighford
Farm

Whitelee
Wood

5

SK11

Hammond's
Hole

64

Hugbridge
Farm

Gritstone Trail

River Dane

Barleigh Ford
Bridge

Dane Valley Way

Hollinhall

4

Hug
Bridge

Thompson

Wormhill

Brandy-Lea

Heatonlow

3

Wallhill

Haddon

63

Rushton
Inn

Staffordshire Way

Rushton
Spencer

Heaton
Hall

Heaton

2

Rushton
CE Prim
Sch

Sugar St

Heaton
Hall

Weathercock
Farm

Tofthall

Rushton
Bank

STATION LA

PH

PH

Tythebarn

Askerbank

P

Heaton House
Farm

Axstones
Spring

Overhouses
Farm

1

A523

A523 Leek

62

93   A   B   94   C   D   95   E   F

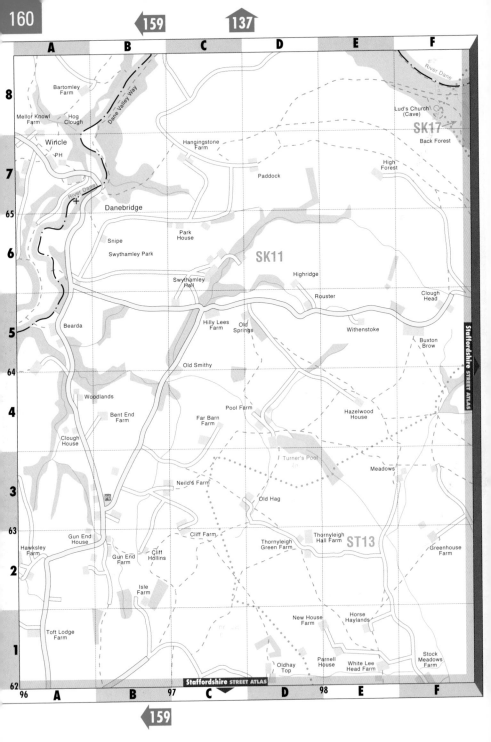

A   B   C   D   E   F

8

Bartomley
Farm

Mellor Knowl
Farm

Hog
Clough

Dane Valley Way

River Dane

Lud's Church
(Cave)

SK17

Back Forest

Wincle

PH

High
Forest

7

Hangingstone
Farm

Paddock

River Dane

Danebridge

65

Park
House

Snipe

Swythamley Park

SK11

6

Swythamley
Hall

Highridge

Rouster

Clough
Head

Bearda

Hilly Lees
Farm

Old
Springs

Withenstoke

Buxton
Brow

5

Old Smithy

64

Woodlands

Bent End
Farm

Pool Farm

Hazelwood
House

4

Far Barn
Farm

Clough
House

Turner's Pool

Meadows

Neild's Farm

3

PO

Old Hag

63

Cliff Farm

Thornyleigh
Hall Farm

ST13

Greenhouse
Farm

Hawksley
Farm

Gun End
House

Thornyleigh
Green Farm

Gun End
Farm

Cliff
Hollins

2

Isle
Farm

New House
Farm

Horse
Haylands

Toft Lodge
Farm

1

Oldhay
Top

Parnell
House

White Lee
Head Farm

Stock
Meadows
Farm

62

96   A   B   97   C   D   98   E   F

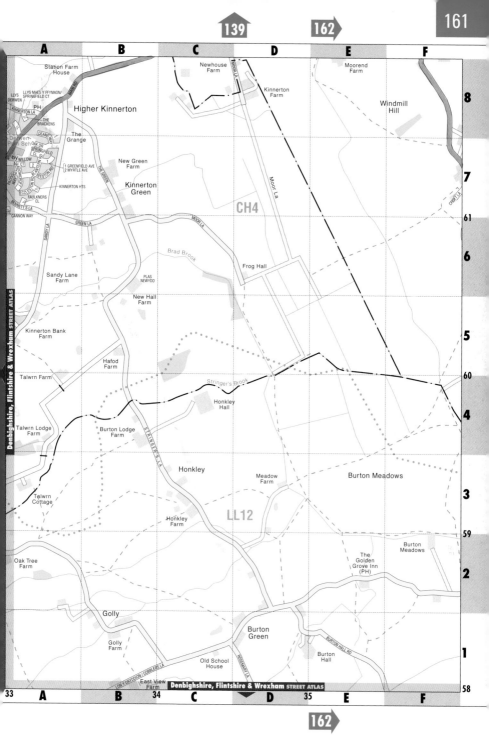

8

7

61

6

5

60

4

3

59

2

1

58

A   B   C   D   E   F

Station Farm House
Newhouse Farm
Moorend Farm
Windmill Hill
Kinnerton Farm

LLYS MAES Y FFYNNON/
SPRINGFIELD CT
LLYS
DERWEN
PH
Higher Kinnerton
The Brackens

The Grange

Derwen
Prim Sch
LIBY
WILLOW

New Green Farm

1 GREENFIELD AVE
2 MYRTLE AVE

Kinnerton Green

CH4

FAULKNERS CL
KINNERTON HTS
BENNETT'S LA
CANNON WAY

GREEN LA
SANDY LA

MOOR LA

Moor La

Brad Brook
Frog Hall

Sandy Lane Farm
PLAS NEWYDD
New Hall Farm

Kinnerton Bank Farm
Hafod Farm

Talwrn Farm

Stringer's Brook

Honkley Hall

Talwrn Lodge Farm
Burton Lodge Farm

STRINGER'S LA

Honkley
Meadow Farm
Burton Meadows

Talwrn Cottage

LL12

Honkley Farm

Burton Meadows

Oak Tree Farm

The Golden Grove Inn (PH)

Golly

Golly Farm

Burton Green

ROSEDALE LA
BURTON HALL RD

Burton Hall

Old School House

East View Farm
LON Y GRYCDION / COBBLERS LA

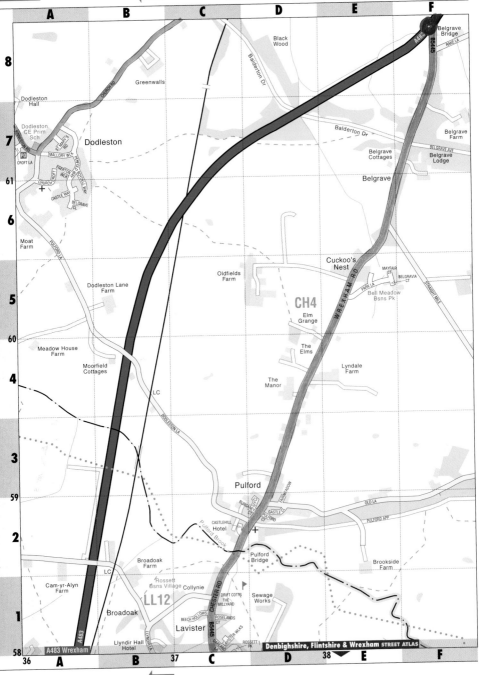

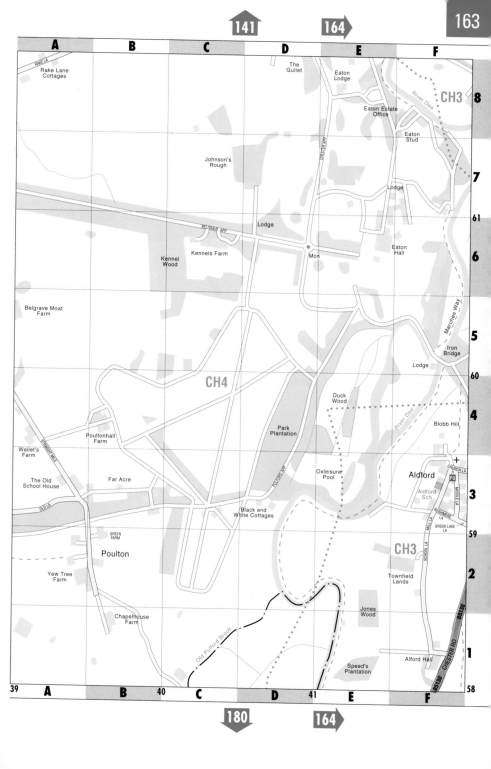

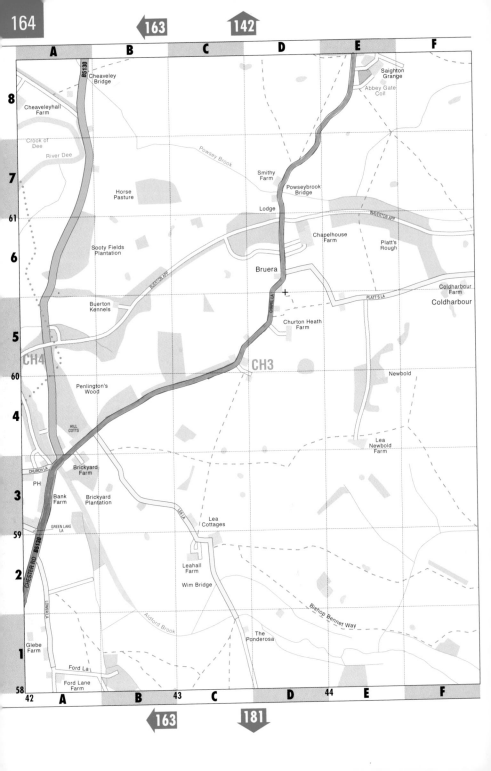

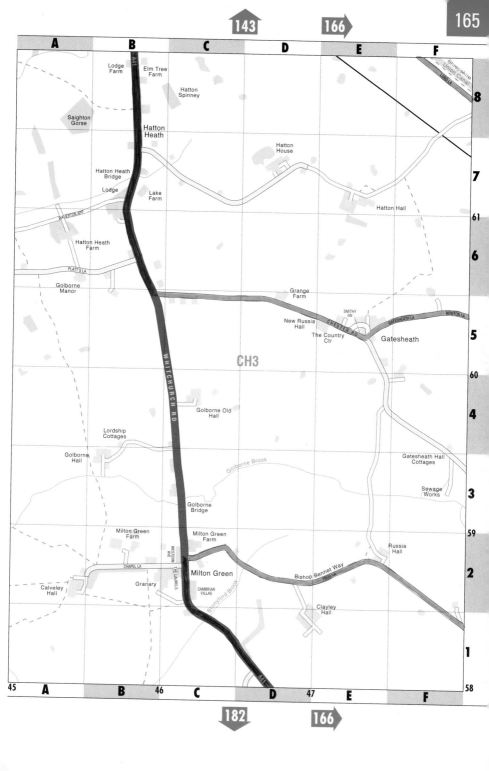

165
144

	A	B	C	D	E	F

8

Golden Nook Farm

Green Farm

The Poplars

LONG LA

Huxley Bridge

PH

7

Higher Huxley Hall

Pool Bank Farm

River Gowy

61

Nixon's Bridge

Shropshire Union Canal

6

Poplar Hall Farm

CROW'S NEST COTTS

Mast

Mill Farm

Millfields

Works

Birch Tree Farm

Crow's Nest Bridge

Dutton's Bridge

5

Manor Farm

Depot
PH

Newton Hall

NEWTON COTTS

Bishop Bennet Way

NEWTON LA

60

4

CH3

Yew Tree Farm

Ford Farm

Newton

FORD LA

TATTENHALL RD

The Cedars

Cheshire Farm Ice Cream

3

Greaves Farm

Springfield Farm

Oakfield Farm

Brook Hall

59

CHESTER RD

Keys Brook

RAVENSHOLME LA

RAVENSHOLME CT.

GREENLANDS

OAKLANDS CT

OAKLANDS AVE

CHELVELEFELDS

2

MILLBROOK

MILL BROOK

KEYSBROOK

HARDING AVE

KEYSBROOK AVE

Tattenhall Park Prim Liby Sch

The Rookery

PARK AVE

PEAR MOW

Owler Hall

TATTENHALL LA

MILLBANK COTTS

Whitehead Farm

BURWARDSLEY RD

Fox Covert

Little Owler Farm

BROOK LA

CARRS LA

GORSEFIELD

HALL VIEW

THE NINE HOS

PH

FIELD LA

Broad Oak

BROCKWAY E
BROCKWAY W

FROG LA

GOWER RD

TOWER RD

MARKET ROW

POPLARS LA

SPOUT LA

BARBOUR SQ

Bank House

1

ROSE CNR.

ROCKY LA

Tattenhall

EDGECROFT

BOLESWORTH RD

Tattenhall Hall

58

48	A		B	49	C		D	50	E		F

165
183

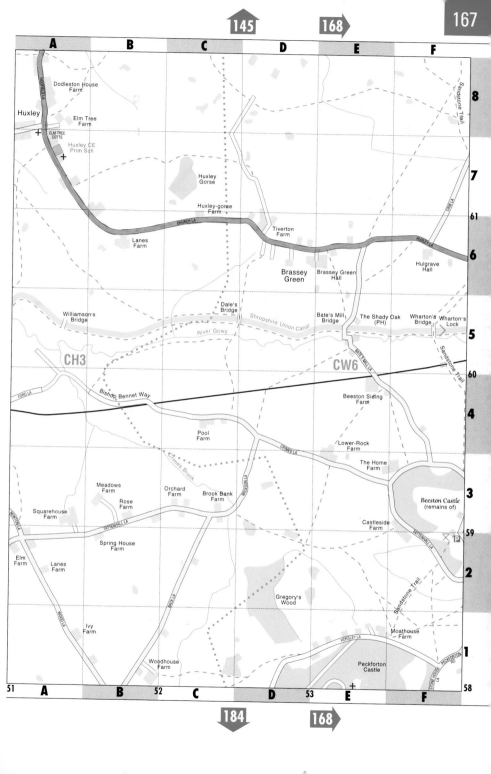

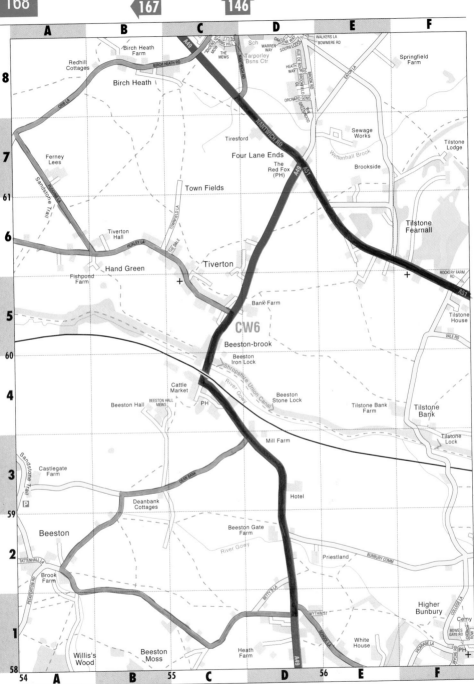

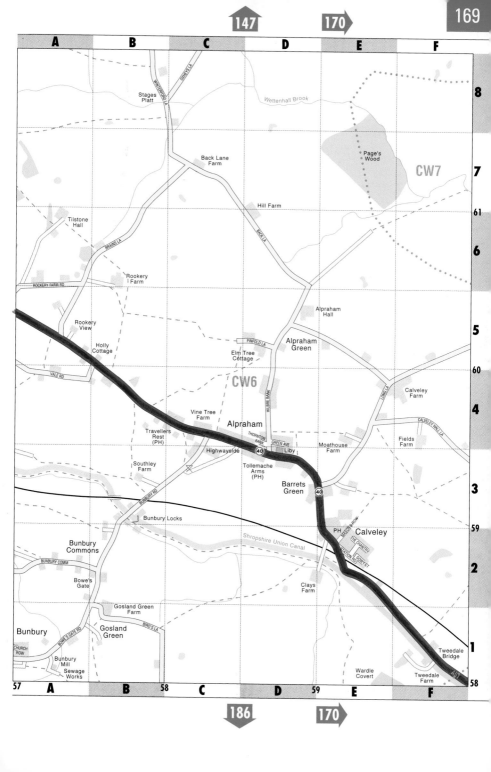

A B C D E F

8

Stages Platt

Back Lane Farm

Wettenhall Brook

Page's Wood

CW7

7

Hill Farm

61

Tilstone Hall

BRAINE LA

6

ROCKERY FARM RD

Rookery Farm

Rookery View

Holly Cottage

Alpraham Hall

5

PINFOLD LA

Elm Tree Cottage

Alpraham Green

60

VALE RD

CW6

Calveley Farm

4

Vine Tree Farm

HILBRE BANK

LONG LA

Travellers Rest (PH)

Alpraham

THORNTON BANK

GREEN AVE

Highwayside

40 Liby

Moathouse Farm

CALVELEY HALL LA

Fields Farm

Southley Farm

Tollemache Arms (PH)

BUNBURY RD

Barrets Green

40

3

Bunbury Locks

Shropshire Union Canal

PH

MAGNA RDW

Calveley

THE CHANTRY

STATION RD

GOWY CT

59

Bunbury Commons

BUNBURY COMM

2

Bowe's Gate

Clays Farm

Gosland Green Farm

BIRD'S LA

Bunbury

Gosland Green

BOWE'S GATE RD

Tweedale Bridge

1

CHURCH ROW

Bunbury Mill

Sewage Works

Wardle Covert

Tweedale Farm

A51

57 A B 58 C D 59 E F 58

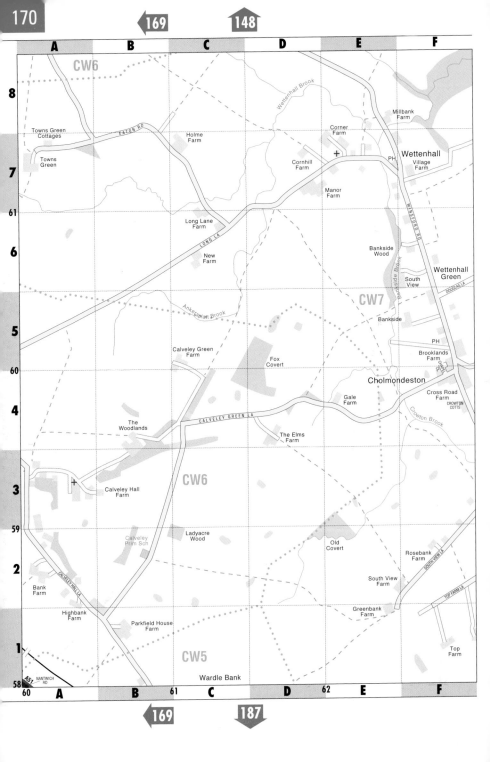

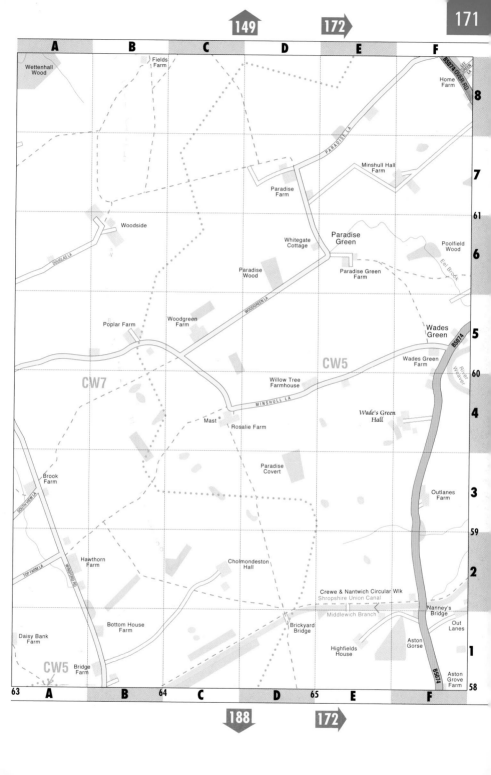

149 172

A B C D E F

8

PARADISE LA

Wettenhall Wood

Fields Farm

B5074 OVER RD
LEA
GREEN LA

Home Farm

Minshull Hall Farm

7

61

Paradise Farm

Woodside

DOUGLAS LA

Whitegate Cottage

Paradise Green

Poolfield Wood

Eel Brook

6

Paradise Wood

Paradise Green Farm

Poplar Farm

Woodgreen Farm

WOODGREEN LA

Wades Green

5

B5074

CW5

Wades Green Farm

River Weaver

60

CW7

Willow Tree Farmhouse

MINSHULL LA

Wade's Green Hall

4

Mast

Rosalie Farm

Paradise Covert

Outlanes Farm

3

Brook Farm

SOUTH VIEW LA

59

Hawthorn Farm

TOP FARM LA

WINSFORD RD

Cholmondeston Hall

2

Crewe & Nantwich Circular Wlk
Shropshire Union Canal

Nanney's Bridge

Out Lanes

Daisy Bank Farm

CW5

Bridge Farm

Bottom House Farm

Brickyard Bridge

Middlewich Branch

Highfields House

Aston Gorse

B5074

Aston Grove Farm

1

63 A B 64 C D 65 E F 58

188 172

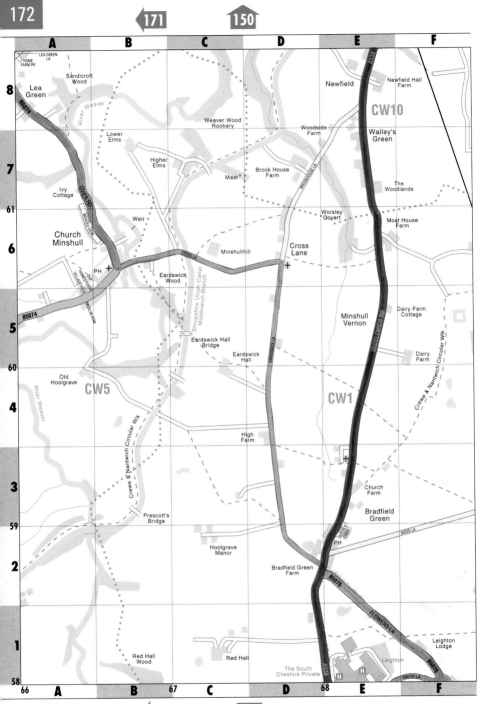

171
150

A B C D E F

8 Lea Green

HOME FARM PK
LEA GREEN LA
Sandicroft Wood

River Weaver

7 Lower Elms
Higher Elms
Weaver Wood Rookery
Mast
Brook House Farm

Newfield

Newfield Hall Farm

CW10

Walley's Green

Woodside Farm

The Woodlands

61 Ivy Cottage
OVERTON
WEAVER LDGE
Weir

6 Church Minshull
PH
THE MARKET FIELD WALK
VILLAGE WALK
Eardswick Wood
CROSS LA
Minshullhill

Cross Lane

Worsley Covert

Moat House Farm

B5074

5 Eardswick Hall Bridge
Shropshire Union Canal Middlewich Branch
Eardswick Hall

Minshull Vernon

Dairy Farm Cottage

Dairy Farm

MIDDLEWICH RD

Crewe & Nantwich Circular Wlk

60 Old Hoolgrave
CW5

4 River Weaver
Crewe & Nantwich Circular Wlk
EARDSWICK LA
High Farm

CW1

3 Church Farm
Bradfield Green

Prescott's Bridge

59 Hoolgrave Manor
Bradfield Green Farm
PH
QUEEN'S DRIVE
MOSS LA

2 B5076

Leighton Lodge

1 Red Hall Wood
Red Hall
The South Cheshire Private
A530
FLOWERS LA
Leighton
H
H
SMITHY LA
B5076

58
66 A B 67 C D 68 E F

171
189

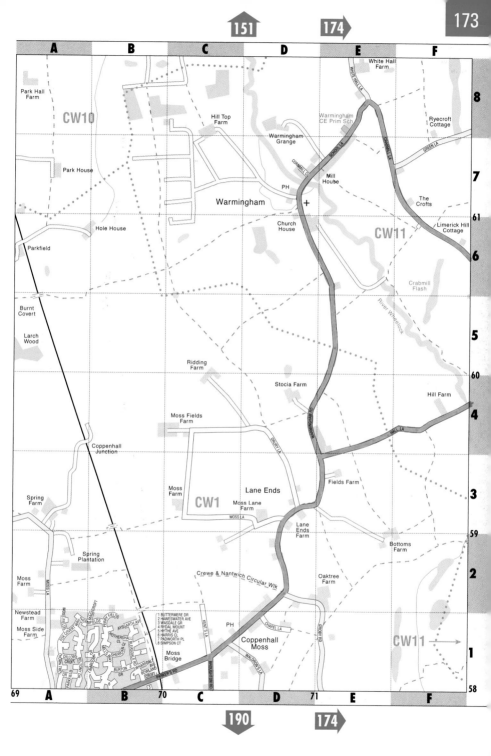

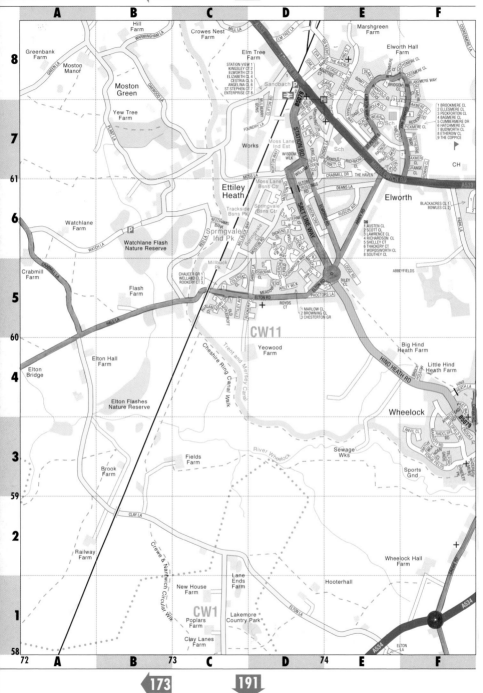

A   B   C   D   E   F

8

7

61

6

5

60

4

3

59

2

1

58

Greenbank Farm
Moston Manor
Hill Farm
Crowes Nest Farm
Elm Tree Farm
Marshgreen Farm
Elworth Hall Farm

Moston Green
Yew Tree Farm

Sandbach

STATION VIEW 1
KINGSLEY CT 2
ELWORTH CT 3
ELIZABETH CL 4
CESTRIA CL 5
ANGELINA CL 6
ST STEPHEN CT 7
ENTERPRISE CT 8

1 BROOKMERE CL
2 ELLESMERE CL
3 PECKFORTON CL
4 BAGMERE CL
5 CUMBERMERE DR
6 HATCHMERE CL
7 BUDWORTH CL
8 ETHEROW CL
9 THE COPPICE

Works

Moss Lane Ind Est

WISDOM WLK

Ettiley Heath

Moss Lane Bsns Ctr

Trackside Bsns Pk

Springvale Bsns Ctr

Elworth

BLACKACRES CL 1
BOWLES CL 2

CH

Watchlane Farm

NEEDHAMS BANK

Watchlane Flash Nature Reserve

Springvale Ind Pk

DEANS LA

SALT LINE WAY

D6
1 AUSTEN CL
2 SCOTT CL
3 LAWRENCE CL
4 RICHARDSON CL
5 SHELLEY CT
6 THACKERY CT
7 WORDSWORTH CL
8 SOUTHEY CL

Crabmill Farm

Flash Farm

Millbuck Pk

CHAUCER GR 1
WELLARD CL 2
ROOKERY CT 3

ABBEYFIELDS

CW11

ROYDS CT

1 MARLOW CL
2 BROWNING CL
3 CHESTERTON GR

Elton Hall Farm

Big Hind Heath Farm

HIND HEATH RD

Little Hind Heath Farm

Elton Bridge

Cheshire Ring Canal Walk

Trent and Mersey Canal

Yeowood Farm

Wheelock

Elton Flashes Nature Reserve

ANVIL CL

River Wheelock

Fields Farm

Sewage Wks

Sports Gnd

Brook Farm

CLAY LA

Wheelock Hall Farm

Railway Farm

Crewe & Nantwich Circular Wlk

New House Farm

Lane Ends Farm

Hooterhall

CW1

Poplars Farm

Lakemore Country Park

ELTON LA

Clay Lanes Farm

ELTON LA

A534

A534

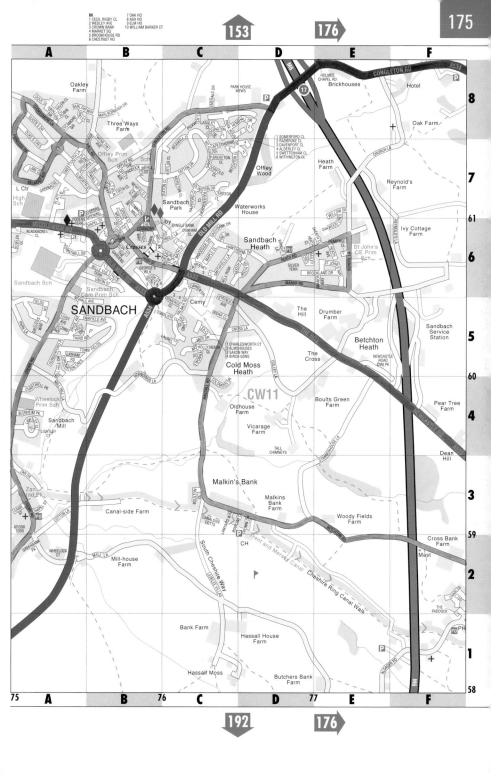

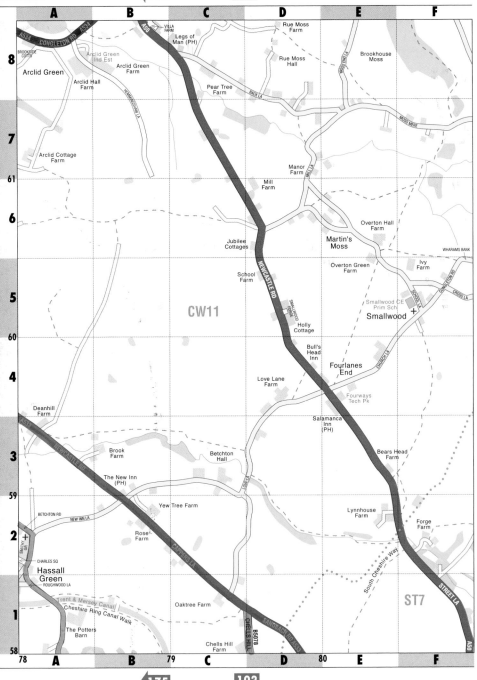

A B C D E F

8

BROOKSIDE COTTS
CONGLETON RD
A534
A534
A50
VILLA FARM
Legs of Man (PH)
Rue Moss Farm
Arclid Green Ind Est
Arclid Green
Arclid Green Farm
Arclid Hall Farm
Rue Moss Hall
Brookhouse Moss
MOSS LA

7

Pear Tree Farm
BACK LA
MOSS MERE

Arclid Cottage Farm

61

Manor Farm
MILL LA

6

Mill Farm

Jubilee Cottages

Overton Hall Farm

Martin's Moss

WHARAMS BANK

School Farm

CW11

Overton Green Farm

Ivy Farm

5

NEWCASTLE RD

SMALLWOOD
Smallwood CE Prim Sch
SCHOOL LA
CONGLETON RD
CROSS LA

Holly Cottage

Smallwood

60

Bull's Head Inn

4

Fourlanes End

Love Lane Farm

CHURCH LA

Fourways Tech Pk

Salamanca Inn (PH)

Deanhill Farm
A533
NEWCASTLE RD

Brook Farm

Betchton Hall

Bears Head Farm

3

The New Inn (PH)

CREWE LA

59

BETCHTON RD
NEW INN LA
Yew Tree Farm

Lynnhouse Farm

Forge Farm

2

SMITHY GRN
CHARLES SQ
Rose Farm

CAPPERS LA

South Cheshire Way

STREET LA

Hassall Green
ROUGHWOOD LA

ST7

1

Trent & Mersey Canal
Cheshire Ring Canal Walk
Oaktree Farm

SANDBACH RD A533

A50

58

The Potters Barn

Chells Hill Farm
CHELLS HILL
B5078

78 A B 79 C D 80 E F

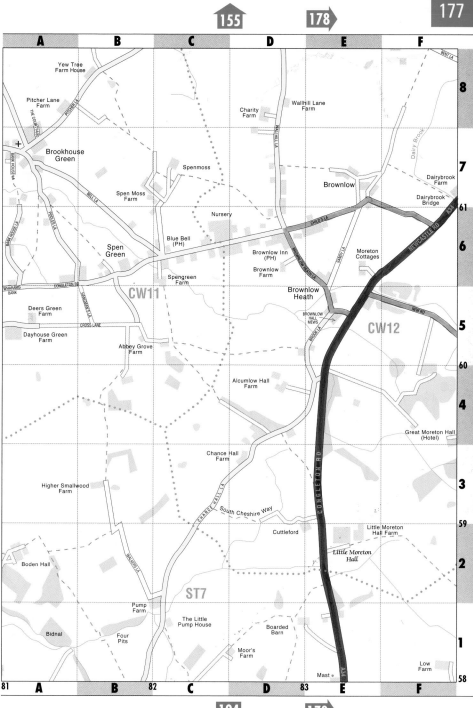

155 178

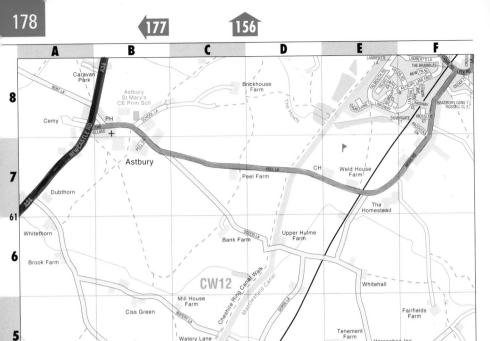

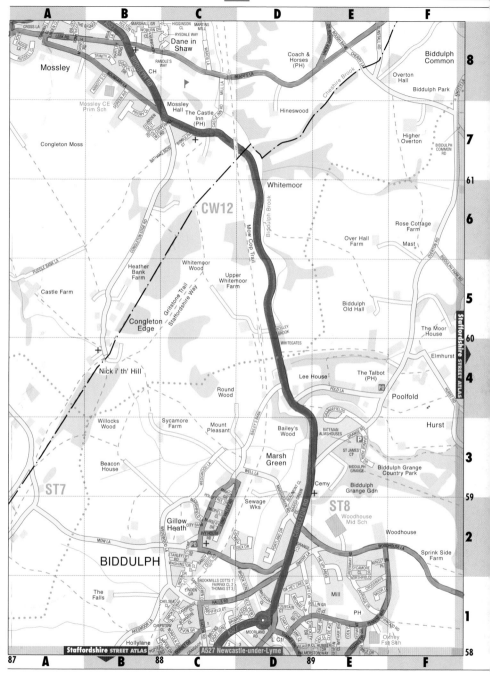

Staffordshire STREET ATLAS

A527 Newcastle-under-Lyme

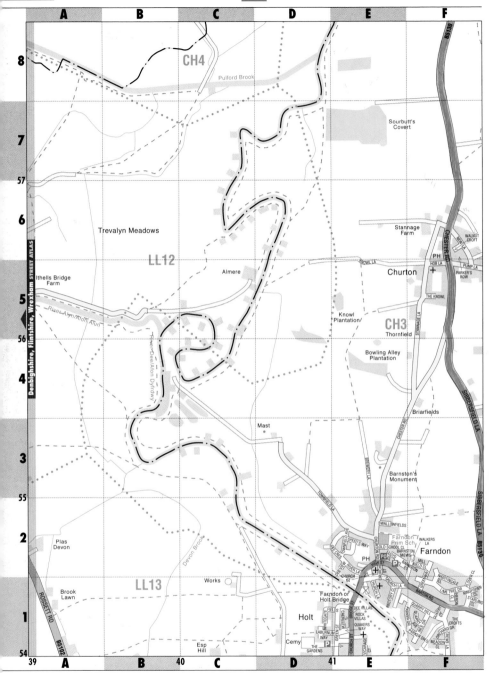

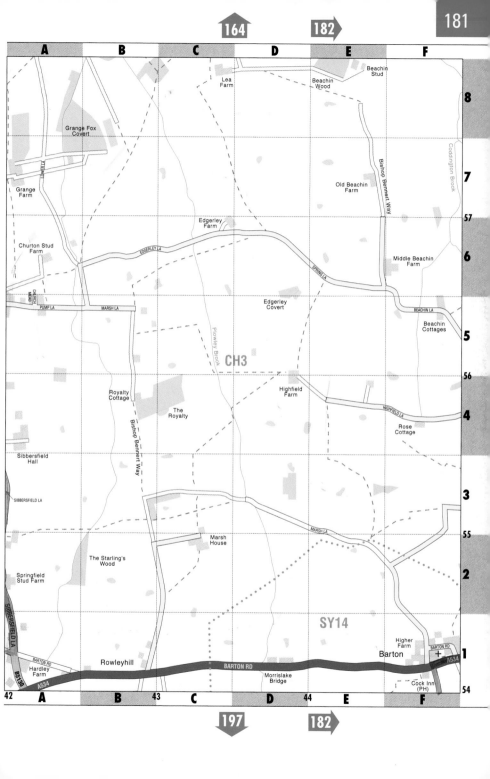

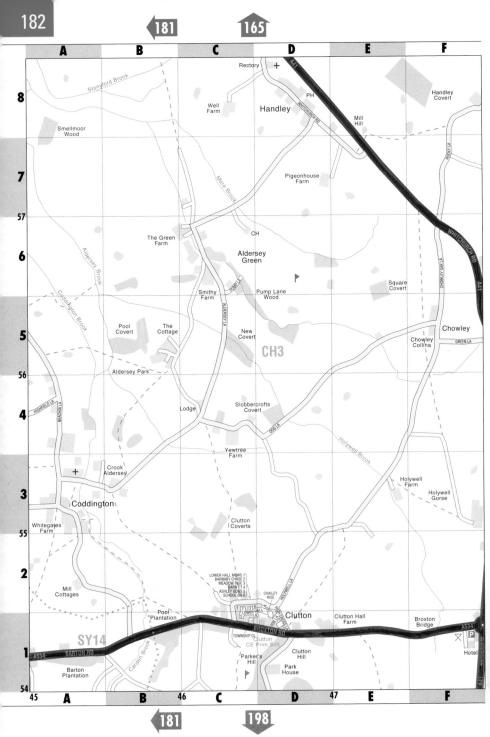

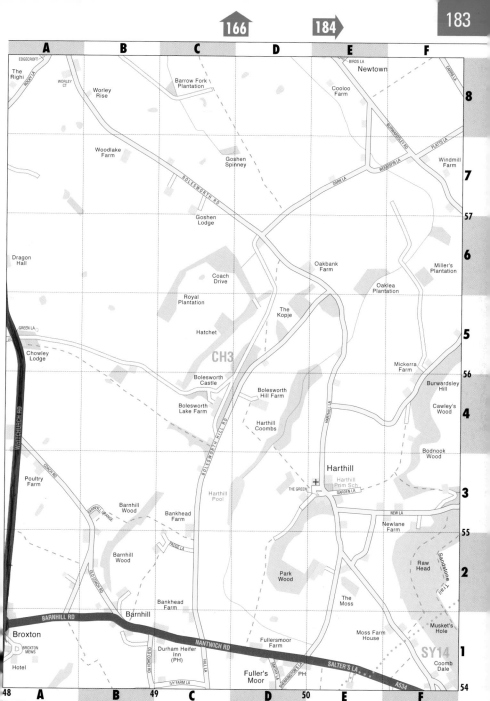

A   B   C   D   E   F

EDGECROFT

The Righi

BIRDS LA

Newtown

WORLEY CT

Worley Rise

Barrow Fork Plantation

Cooloo Farm

8

BURWARDSLEY RD

PLATTS LA

Woodlake Farm

Goshen Spinney

DARK LA

WOODFIN LA

Windmill Farm

7

BOLESWORTH RD

57

Goshen Lodge

Dragon Hall

Oakbank Farm

Miller's Plantation

6

Coach Drive

Oaklea Plantation

GREEN LA

Royal Plantation

The Kopje

Chowley Lodge

Hatchet

Mickerra Farm

5

CH3

56

Bolesworth Castle

Bolesworth Hill Farm

Burwardsley Hill

WHITCHURCH RD

Bolesworth Lake Farm

HARTHILL LA

Cawley's Wood

4

Harthill Coombs

Bodnook Wood

COACH RD

Poultry Farm

Harthill Pool

Harthill

Harthill Prim Sch

3

BARNHILL GRANGE

Barnhill Wood

Bankhead Farm

THE GREEN

GARDEN LA

BOLESWORTH HILL RD

NEW LA

Newlane Farm

55

PADGE LA

Barnhill Wood

Park Wood

Raw Head

Sandstone Trail

2

OLD COACH RD

Bankhead Farm

The Moss

BARNHILL RD

Barnhill

Moss Farm House

Musket's Hole

Broxton

NANTWICH RD

Fullersmoor Farm

SY14

BROXTON MEWS

Durham Heifer Inn (PH)

HILL LA

SHERRINGTON'S LA

PH

SALTER'S LA

Coomb Dale

Hotel

IVY FARM LA

Fuller's Moor

A534

1

48   A   B 49 C   D 50 E   F 54

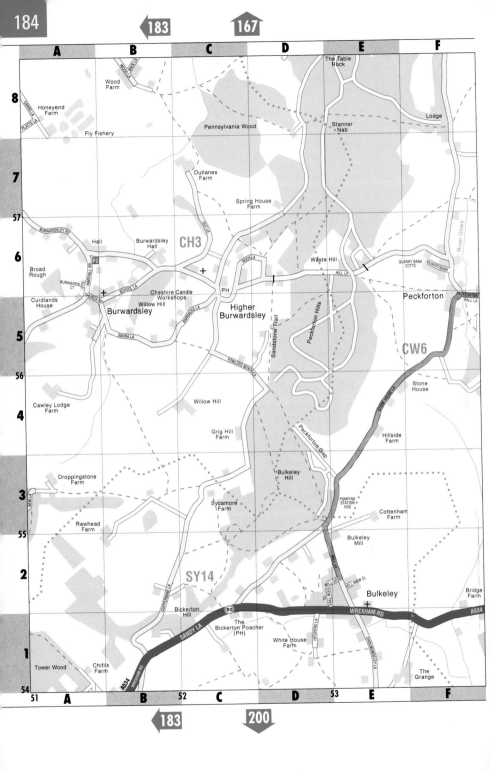

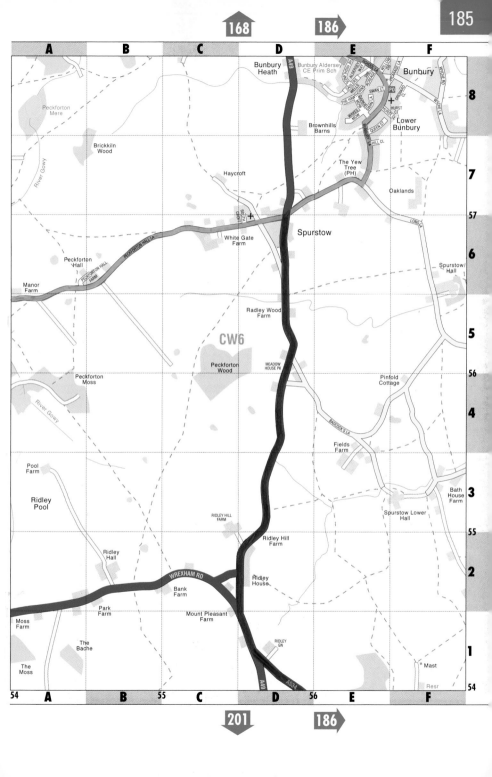

A B C D E F

8

7

57

6

56

5

4

3

55

2

1

54

Peckforton
Mere

River Gowy

Brickkiln
Wood

Peckforton
Hall

Manor
Farm

Peckforton
Moss

River Gowy

Pool
Farm

Ridley
Pool

Moss
Farm

The
Bache

The
Moss

Ridley
Hall

Park
Farm

Bank
Farm

WREXHAM RD

Mount Pleasant
Farm

RIDLEY
GN

Haycroft

SOUTH
CROFT

White Gate
Farm

PECKFORTON HALL LA

PECKFORTON HALL
FARM

CW6

Peckforton
Wood

Radley Wood
Farm

MEADOW
HOUSE PK

RIDLEY HILL
FARM

Ridley Hill
Farm

Ridley
House

A49

Bunbury
Heath

Bunbury Aldersey
CE Prim Sch

Brownhills
Barns

The Yew
Tree
(PH)

Spurstow

Oaklands

LONG LA

BADDOCK'S LA

Fields
Farm

Spurstow Lower
Hall

Bunbury

Lower
Bunbury

Spurstow
Hall

Pinfold
Cottage

Bath
House
Farm

Mast

Resr

WYCH RD

WYCH LA

SWAN CT

HURST

A49

A534

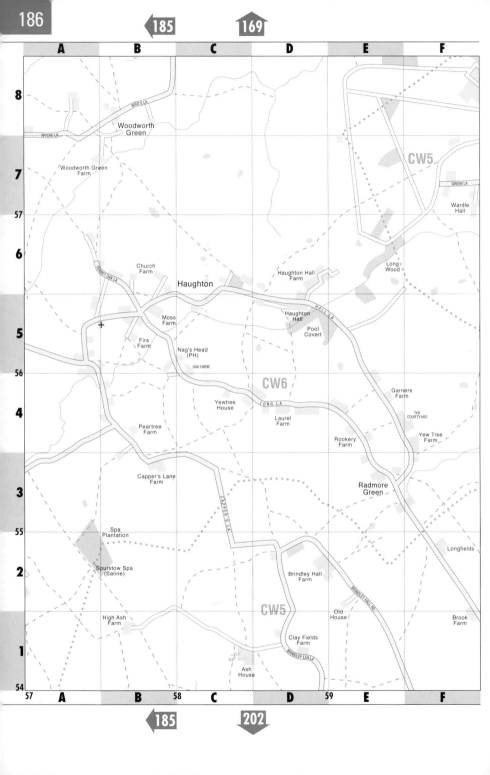

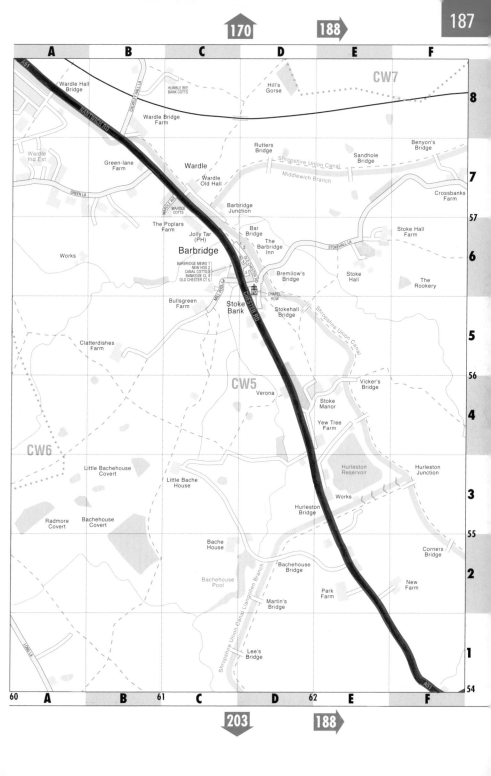

8

CW7

Middlewich Branch
Shropshire Union Canal

Aston New Farm

Cholmondeston Bridge

Marina

VENETIAN MARINA VILLAGE

WORSTON RD

Ash Villa

B5074

Firs Bank Farm

7

Aston Hall

Four Oaks Farm

57

STOKEHALL LA

Green Farm

Rose Farm

DARES LA

Aston juxta Mondrum

STATION RD

The Grange

Oak Fields Farm

Dairy House Farm

6

St Oswald's Worleston CE Prim Sch

Lower Hall Farm

CHURCH RD

Worleston

Royal Oak (PH)

Gates Farm

CW5

Crewe & Nantwich Circular Walk

BARONS RD

MAIN RD

5

Rookery Hall Farm

56

Poole Old Hall

POOLE OLD HALL LA

Hotel

Cherry Orchard Farm

Poole Farm

Poole Gorse

Rookery Bridge

4

Nursery

WETTENHALL RD

Poole Bank Farm

The Cottage

Oak Tree Farm

Pinfold Craft Ctr

Poole Hall

Park Farm

3

Poole House Farm

55

Poole Hills Farm

Mile House Farm

Mile End Farm

POOLE HILL RD

Shropshire Union Canal

2

Rease Heath

DANIEL LA

Poolehill

Reaseheath Coll

River Weaver

1

Henhullbridge Farm

Henhull Bridge

Reaseheath Old Hall

Hall Farm

Sewage Works

54

A51

A51

Sports Gd

B5074

63

64

65

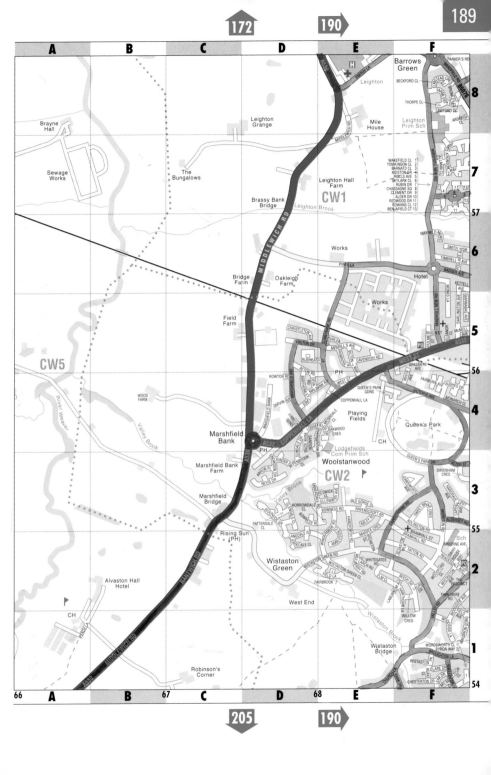

8

7

57

6

5

56

4

3

55

2

1

54

A   B   C   D   E   F

CREWE

CW1

CW2

Coppenhall
Maw Green
Sydney Bridge
Holly Tree Farm
Race Farm
Groby Farm
Stoneley Farm
Monks Coppenhall Prim Sch
Playing Field
Cumberland Sports Ctr
Loco Works
Tipkinder Park
The Valley
Superstore
Gainsborough Prim Sch
St Thomas More RC High Sch
South Cheshire Coll
Ruskin Sports Coll & Com High Sch
Grand Junction Ret Pk
Macpac Ind Est
MMU Cheshire (Crewe Campus)
Crewe Mill Bridge
Valley Brook
Crewe Bsns Pk
Crewe Gates Farm Ind Est
Gresty Road Football Gd (Crewe Alexandra FC)
The Weston Ctr
Works

BRADFIELD RD
NORTH ST
MIDDLEWICH ST
WEST ST
DUNWOODY WAY
WISTASTON RD
NANTWICH RD
CREWE RD
MACON WAY
EARLE ST
VICTORIA WAY
GRESTY RD
WESTON RD
A532   A534   A5020   A5019   B5071   B5076

B5
1 PEEL SQ
2 RAMSBOTTOM ST
3 LINCOLN ST
4 SADE CT
5 RIGG ST
6 EARDLEY CT
7 PETER PL
8 COMBERMERE PL
9 OAKMERE PL
10 ELLESMERE PL
11 LEIGHTON ST
12 GROSVENOR CT
13 GODDARD CT
14 NOVA CT

C4
1 CASTLE ST
2 STANLEY ST
3 VICTORIA ST
4 CHARLES ST
5 ROYAL ARC
6 HIGHTOWN APPTS
7 DELAMERE CT

D2
1 WAVERLEY CT
2 ABBEYFIELD HO
3 ARTHUR ST
4 LONGFORD ST
5 BROADY CT

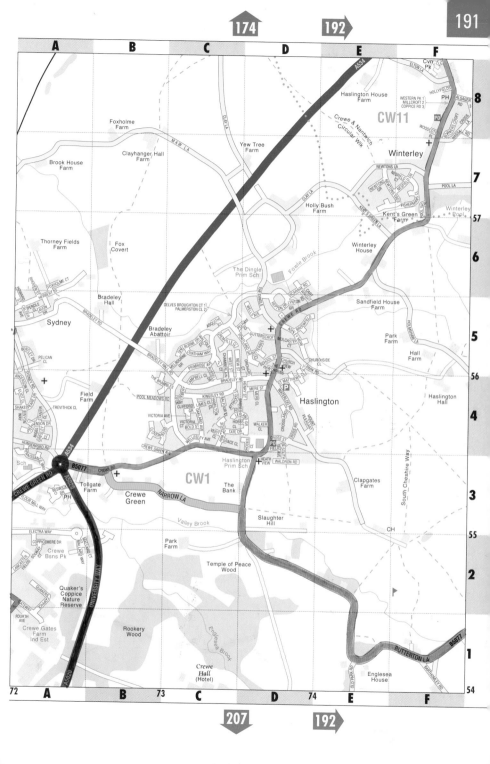

174
192

A B C D E F

8

7

57

6

5

56

4

3

55

2

1

54

CW11

Winterley

Haslington House Farm

Cvn Pk

ELTON LA

HOLLYFIELDS

ALSAGER RD

PH

PO

WESTERN PK 1
MILLCROFT 2
COPPICE RD 3

WOODCOTE PL

ROOKERY CROFT

ROOKERY RD

Foxholme Farm

Yew Tree Farm

Crewe & Nantwich Circular Wlk

MAW LA

Clayhanger Hall Farm

Brook House Farm

CLAY LA

CLAY LA

NEWTONS LA

MIDFIELD CL

NEWLANDS GR

FISHERMANS

Kent's Green Farm

KING'S GREEN LA

Holly Bush Farm

POOL LA

Winterley Pool

Thorney Fields Farm

Fox Covert

Winterley House

Sandfield House Farm

Fowle Brook

The Dingle Prim Sch

Sydney

Bradeley Hall

RHODES ST
HERBERT ST
PENDLE
ASPEN
FOXHOLME CT

Bradeley Abattoir

DELVES BROUGHTON CT 1
PALMERSTON CL 2

PALMERSTON RD

WELL LA

DELFAM

ASQUITH

CREWE RD

SCARFIELD RD

LYTTON GR

REPTON DR

ASH BROOKFIELD

CREWE RD

Park Farm

Hall Farm

HOLMEBROOK

Haslington Hall

Field Farm

BRADELEY HALL RD

BRADELEY RD

SHELBURNE DR
MILBOURNE
CHATHAM WAY

PRIMROSE AV

GLENVILLE CL

CHAMBER LA

WEST ST
ORCHARD

SCHOOL CL

GUTTERSCROFT

MULCASTER DR

ASH GR

CHURCH ST

HAWTHORNS

ST MATTHEWS CL

CHURCHSIDE

PARK RD

+

+

+

Haslington

P

THE BRAMBLES

IPOOL MEADOWS RD

ROSS WAY

CLIFFORD

LIMES CL

KINGSLEY RD

HALL GR

CAMPBELL ST

CARLTON DR

MERE ST

MERE CL

LEYLAND

MOBEL

MORRIS CL

CROSS ST

MORRELL RD

Victoria Ave

VICTORIA AVE
BOLD ST

HOBBS CL

TATE DR

VERITY CL

WALKER CL

PELICAN CL

BENTLEY DR

ANGLESEY CT
ADDISON DR
STANIER CT
MACON DR

GRESTY
SHAKESPEARE
WAY

TREVITHICK CL

CROSS ST

WELLESLEY AVE

CREWE GREEN AVE

TERRACE CL

STOCKS

Haslington Prim Sch

HEATH VIEW

WALDRON RD

CW1

Toll gate Farm

Crewe Green

The Bank

Clapgates Farm

A534

B5077

CREWE GREEN RD

CREWE RD

NARROW LA

Valley Brook

Slaughter Hill

South Cheshire Way

CH

PH

BESWICK DR

FLOUR MILL WAY

Sch

UNIVERSITY WAY

A5020

ELECTRA WAY

COPPICEMERE DR

Crewe Bsns Pk

LANCELYN
SOWERBY
DE HAVILLAND CT
MALLARD WAY

BOLTON CT

QUAKERS

LEATHERS

FOURTH AVE

Quaker's Coppice Nature Reserve

Crewe Gates Farm Ind Est

Park Farm

Rookery Wood

Temple of Peace Wood

Englesea Brook

Crewe Hall (Hotel)

Englesea House

BUTTERTON LA

BARTHOMLEY RD

B5077

72 73 74

A **B** **C** **D** **E** **F**

8

Whitehall Farm

Wheelockheath Farm

Daisy Bank House

Fingerpost Farm

MILL LA

HASSALL RD

Holly Tree Farm

Day Green

Wheelock Heath

COPPICE RD

School Farm

ALSAGER RD

Hassall Pool

7

SANDY LA

POOL LA

HASSALL RD

Walnut Tree Farm

Hassall

CW11

Hassall Hall

57

Bridgehouse Farm

Bostock House

6

South Cheshire Way

Green Bank Farm

Dunnock's Fold Farm

Moss Cottage

5

Castle Farm

56

Woodside Farm

Homeshaw Farm

Oakhanger Hall

Moss End Farm

ST7

4

Heathfield Farm

Stockton Farm

SPENCER CL

DELAMERE CT

CRANBERRY

CHELSEA

CW1

Gate Farm

Oakhanger Farm

Ashfields

3

Hall o' the Heath

HOLMSHAW LA

Mast

NURSERY RD

55

Rose Tree Farm

BUTTERTON LA

TAYLORS LA

Spartan Wood Farm

White Moss

Peartree Farm

Oakhanger Moss

White Moss Farm

Butterton Lane Farm

2

Moss Farm

CREWE RD B5077

RADWAY GREEN RD

Radway Green

Oakhanger

B5017

BUTTERTON LA

Mast

LC

1

DUNN'S COTTS

MILL LA

Works

RADWAY GREEN RD

Radway Green Bsns & Tech Ctr

CW2

54

CW2

M6

B5078

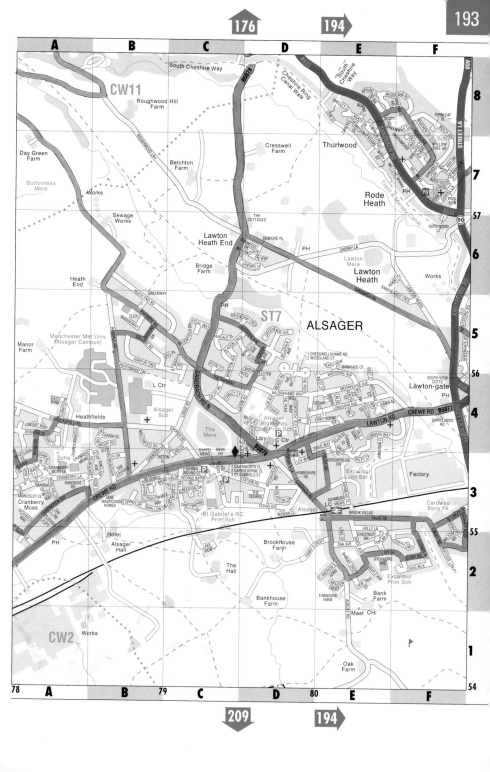

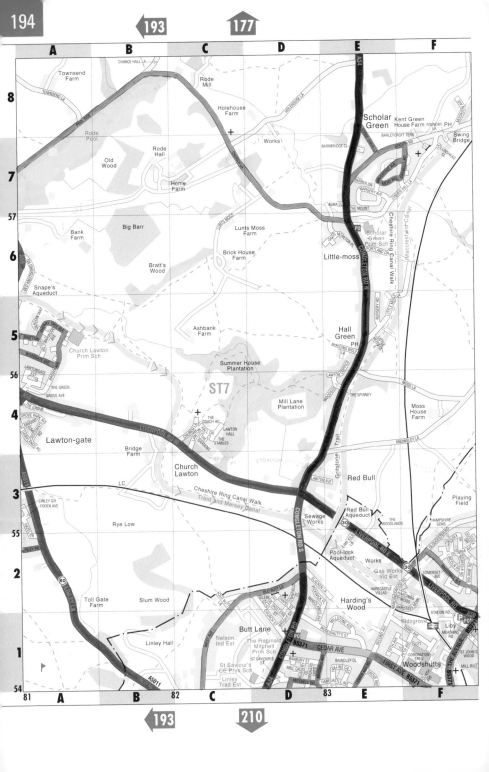

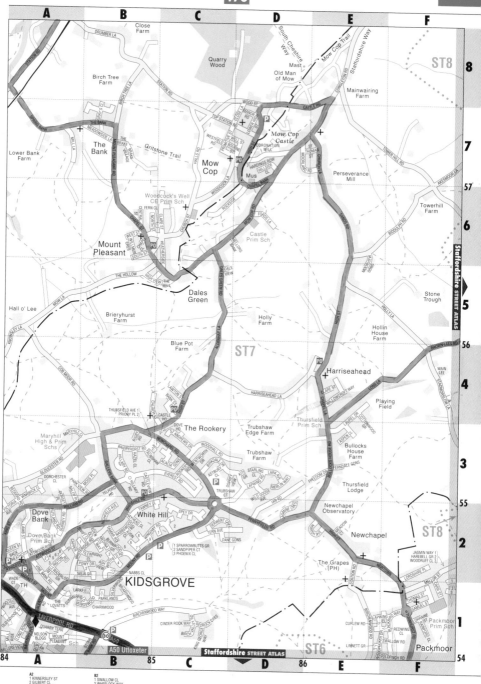

A2
1 KINNERSLEY ST
2 GILBERT CL
3 NAPIER GDNS
4 PEEL CT
5 BANK CT
6 HIGHERLAND CT
7 WESLEY GDNS
8 VICTORIA CT

B2
1 SWALLOW CL
2 WHEELOCK WAY
3 DIAMOND AVE
4 MOSSFIELD CRES
5 LITTLE ROW
6 BRIGHTS AVE
7 BIRCHES WAY
8 SILVERMINE CL
9 MAGPIE CRES

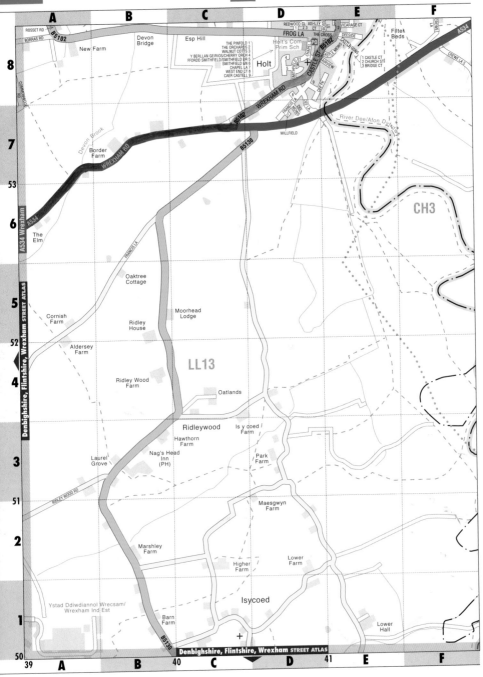

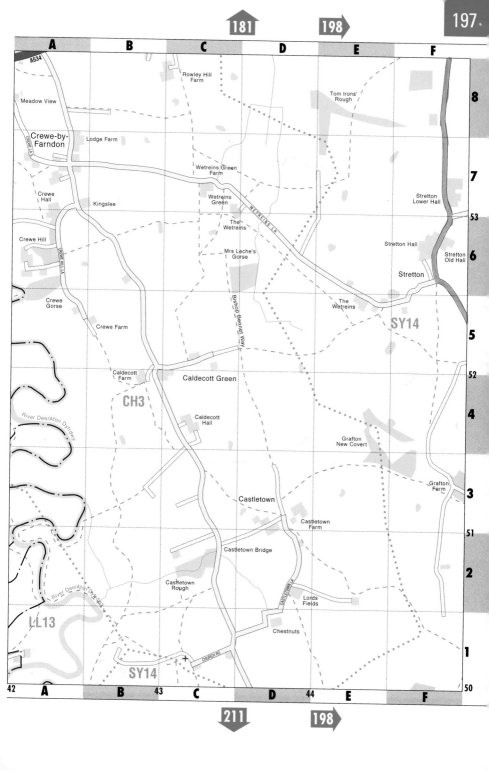

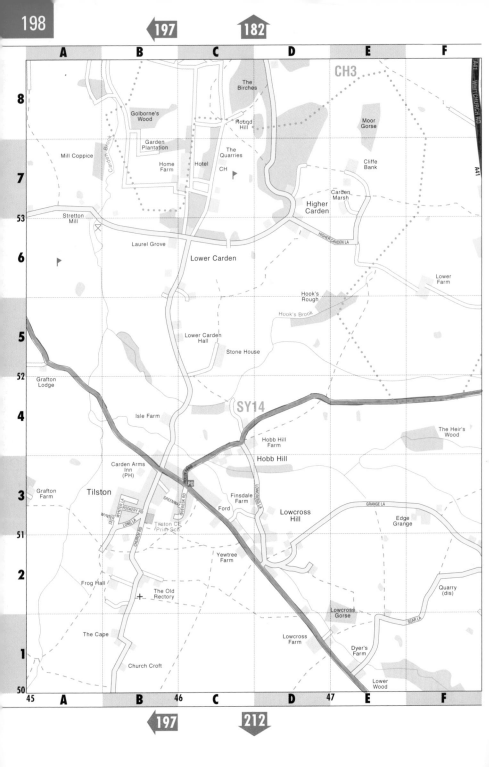

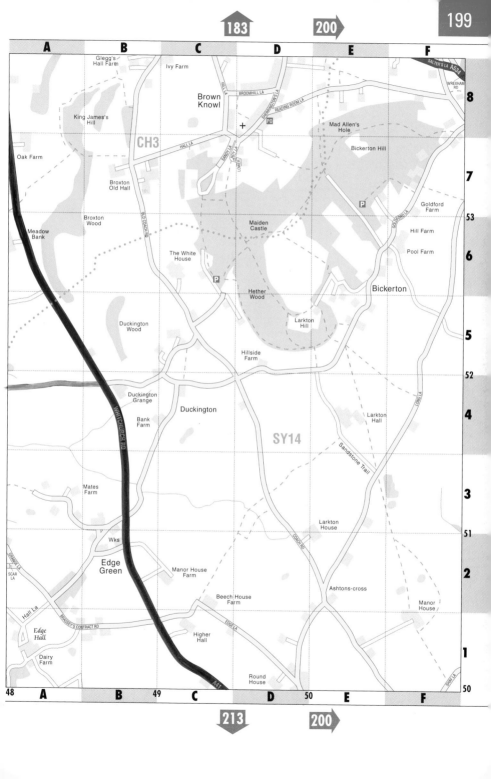

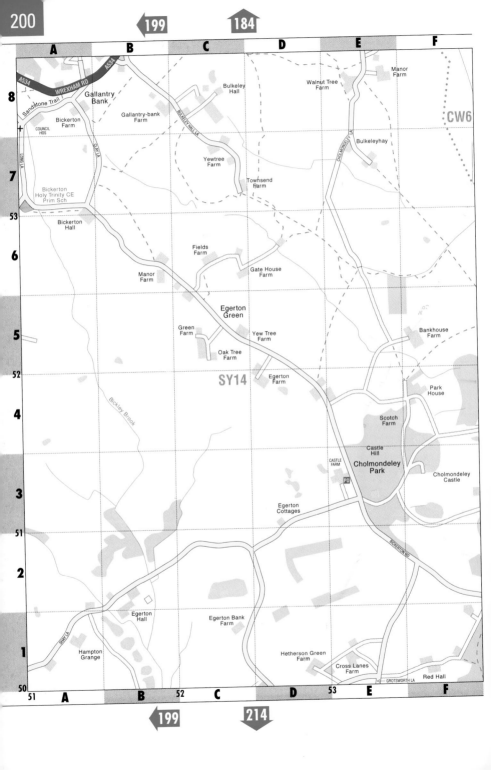

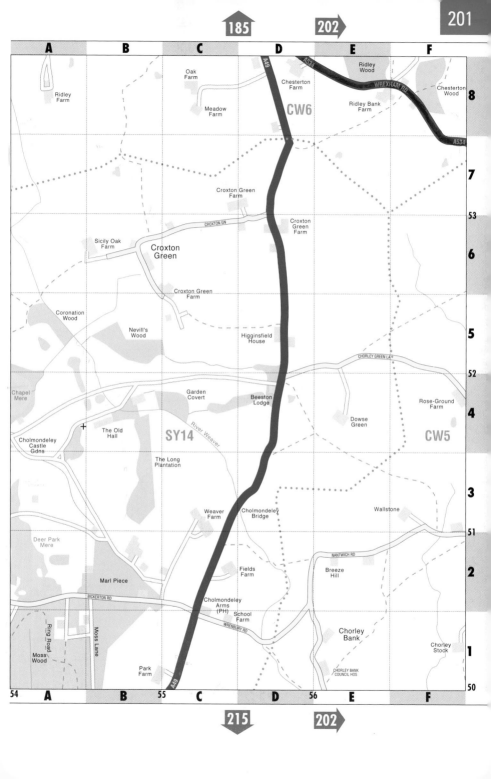

185

202

A   B   C   D   E   F

Ridley Farm

Oak Farm

Meadow Farm

Chesterton Farm

CW6

Ridley Wood

WREXHAM RD

Ridley Bank Farm

Chesterton Wood

A534

A49

A534

8

7

53

Croxton Green Farm

CROXTON GN

Croxton Green Farm

Sicily Oak Farm

Croxton Green

6

Croxton Green Farm

Coronation Wood

Nevill's Wood

Higginsfield House

5

CHORLEY GREEN LA

52

Chapel Mere

Garden Covert

Beeston Lodge

Dowse Green

Rose-Ground Farm

4

River Weaver

The Old Hall

SY14

Cholmondeley Castle Gdns

The Long Plantation

CW5

Deer Park Mere

Weaver Farm

Cholmondeley Bridge

Wallstone

3

51

NANTWICH RD

Marl Piece

BICKERTON RD

Fields Farm

Breeze Hill

2

Ring Road

Moss Lane

Moss Wood

Cholmondeley Arms (PH)

School Farm

WRENBURY RD

Chorley Bank

Chorley Stock

Park Farm

A49

CHORLEY BANK COUNCIL HOS

1

50

54   A   B   55   C   D   56   E   F

215

202

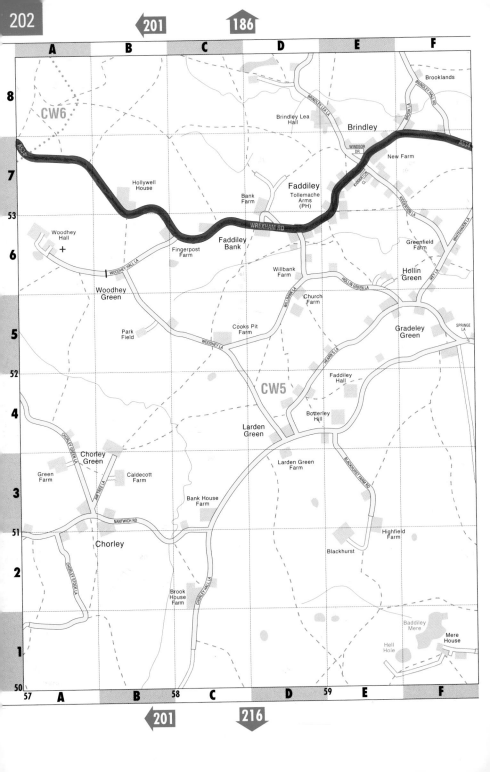

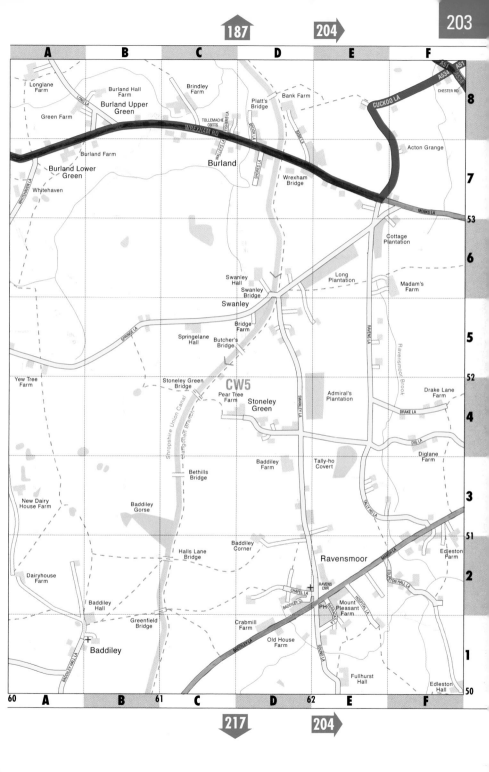

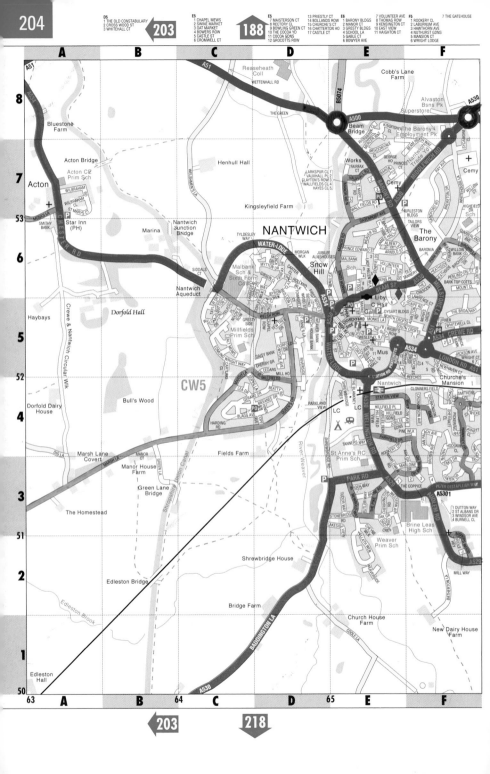

203
188
203
218

D5
1 THE OLD CONSTABULARY
2 CROSS WOOD ST
3 WHITEHALL CT

E5
1 CHAPEL MEWS
2 SWINE MARKET
3 OAT MARKET
4 BOWERS ROW
5 CASTLE ST
6 CROMWELL CT

E5
7 MAISTERSON CT
8 RECTORY CL
9 BOWLING GREEN CT
10 THE COCOA YD
11 COCOA GDNS
12 GROCOTTS ROW

13 PRIESTLY CT
14 BOLLANDS ROW
15 CHURCHE'S CT
16 CHATTERTON HO
17 CASTLE CT

E6
1 BARONY BLDGS
2 MANOR CT
3 GRESTY BLDGS
4 SCHOOL LA
5 GABLE CT
6 BOWYER AVE

7 VOLUNTEER AVE
8 THOMAS ROW
9 KENSINGTON CT
10 EAST VIEW
11 HAIGHTON CT

F5
1 ROOKERY CL
2 LABURNUM AVE
3 HAWTHORN AVE
4 NUTHURST GDNS
5 MANSION CT
6 WRIGHT LODGE

7 THE GATEHOUSE

NANTWICH

CW5

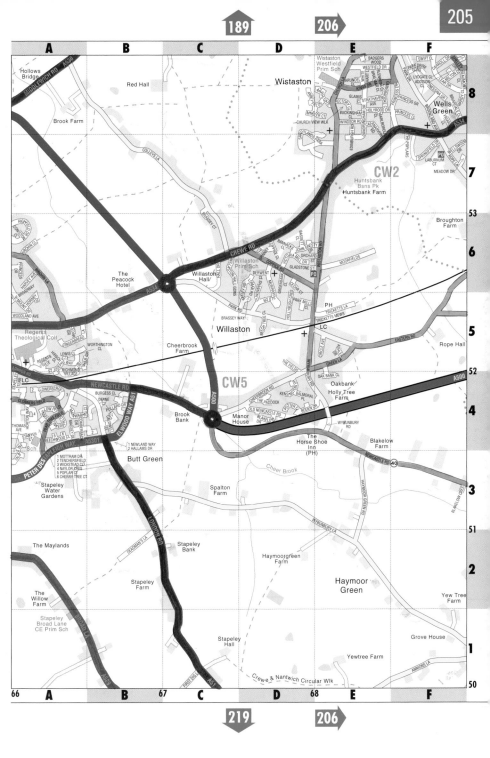

| A | B | C | D | E | F |

Hollows Bridge

MIDDLEWICH RD A540

Red Hall

Wistaston

Wistaston Westfield Prim Sch

Badgers Wood

WESTFIELD DR

8

Brook Farm

Wells Green

COLLEYS LA

CW2

7

The Peacock Hotel

A534

Huntsbank Bsns Pk
Huntsbank Farm

53

Broughton Farm

Willaston Hall

CREWE RD

Willaston Prim Sch

PO

6

HALL TERR LA

DERWENT

MOORFIELDS

Regents Theological Coll

WORTHINGTON CL

Cheerbrook Farm

PARK RD

Willaston

BRASSEY WAY

PH

TRICKETTS LA
TRICKETTS MEWS

LC

Rope Hall

EASTERN RD

A500

5

52

RICHMOND VILLAGE

NEWCASTLE RD

ELWOOD WAY A51

A6301

A500

CW5

THE FIELDS

OAK BANK CL

GREEN LA

Oakbank
Holly Tree Farm

WYBUNBURY RD

4

PETER DE STAPLEIGH WAY

Butt Green

1 NEWLAND WAY
2 HALLAMS DR

1 MOTTRAM DR
2 TENCHERSFIELD
3 WICKSTEAD CL
4 NAYLOR CRES
5 POPLAR GR
6 CHERRY TREE CT

Brook Bank

Manor House

OLD NEWCASTLE RD

THE PADDOCK

BALMORAL

The Horse Shoe Inn (PH)

Blakelow Farm

NEWCASTLE RD
40

BLAKELOW CRES

3

Stapeley Water Gardens

Cheer Brook

Spalton Farm

Haymoorgreen Farm

WYBUNBURY LA

51

The Maylands

DEADMAN'S LA

Stapeley Bank

Stapeley Farm

LONDON RD

Haymoor Green

Yew Tree Farm

2

The Willow Farm

BROAD LA

A529

Stapeley Broad Lane CE Prim Sch

Stapeley Hall

FIRST DIG LA

A51

Grove House

Yewtree Farm

ANNIORS LA

1

50

Crewe & Nantwich Circular Wlk

| 66 | A | B | 67 | C | D | 68 | E | F |

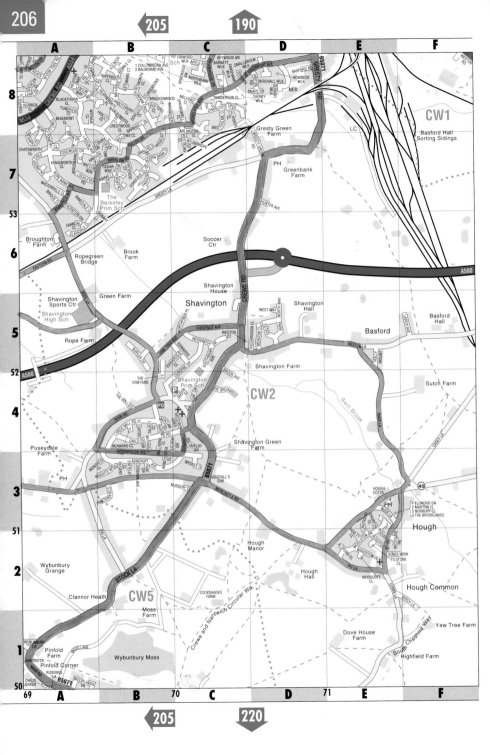

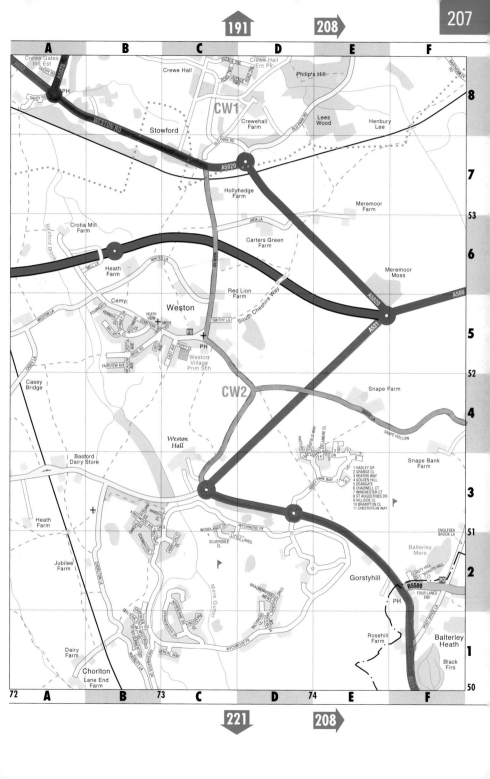

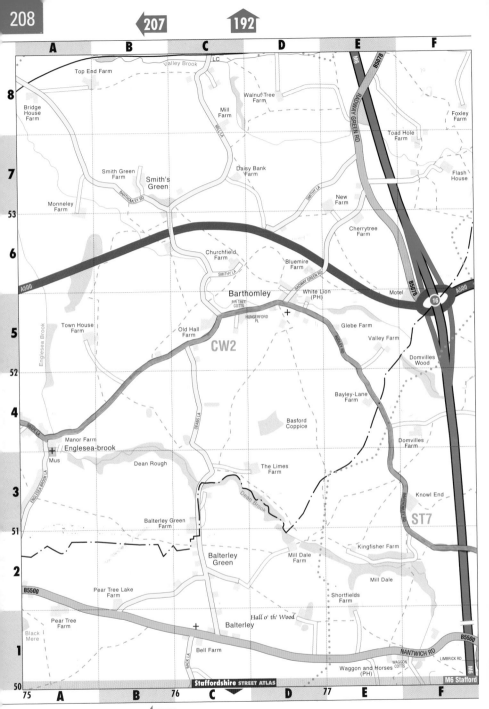

A   B   C   D   E   F

8

Top End Farm
Valley Brook   LC
Bridge
House
Farm
Walnut Tree
Farm
Mill
Farm
Foxley
Farm

7

Smith Green
Farm
Smith's
Green
Daisy Bank
Farm
Toad Hole
Farm
Flash
House

Monneley
Farm
New
Farm

53

RADWAY GREEN RD

6

Churchfield
Farm
Bluemire
Farm
Cherrytree
Farm

A500
SMITHY LA.
RADWAY GREEN RD
Motel
16
A500
Barthomley
FIR TREE
COTTS
White Lion
(PH)

5

Town House
Farm
Old Hall
Farm
HUNGERFORD
PL
Glebe Farm
Domvilles
Wood

Englesea Brook
CW2
Valley Farm

52

4

Manor Farm
Englesea-brook
Basford
Coppice
Bayley-Lane
Farm
Domvilles
Farm

Mus
Dean Rough
The Limes
Farm
Knowl End

3

Balterley Green
Farm
Dean Brook
ST7

51

Balterley
Green
Mill Dale
Farm
Kingfisher Farm

2

Pear Tree Lake
Farm
Mill Dale

B5500
Shortfields
Farm

Pear Tree
Farm
Hall o' th' Wood
Balterley
B5500

Black
Mere
Bell Farm
NANTWICH RD
LIMBRICK RD.

1

BACK LA
Waggon and Horses
(PH)
WAGGON
COTTS
M6 Stafford

50

75   A   B   76   C   D   77   E   F

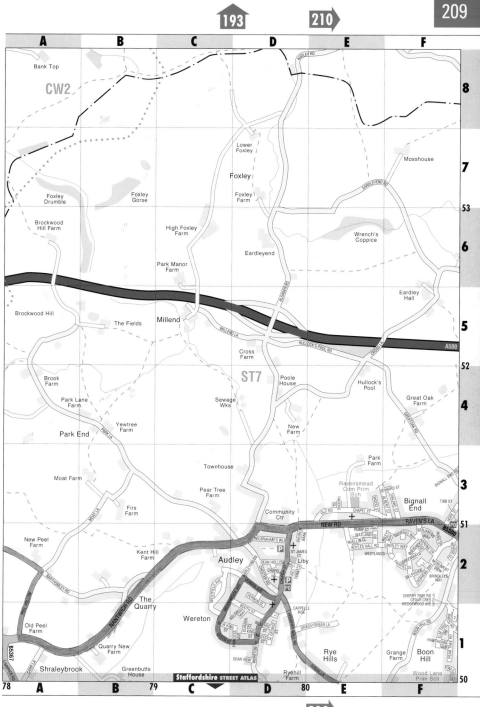

Bank Top

CW2

Lower Foxley

Foxley

Mosshouse

8

7

Foxley Drumble

Foxley Gorse

Foxley Farm

EARDLEYEND RD

Brockwood Hill Farm

High Foxley Farm

Eardleyend

Wrench's Coppice

53

6

Park Manor Farm

ALSAGER RD

Eardley Hall

Brockwood Hill

The Fields

Millend

MILLEND LA

HULLOCK'S POOL RD

A500

5

Cross Farm

52

Brook Farm

ST7

Poole House

Hullock's Pool

Great Oak Farm

GROSVENOR RD

GREATOAK RD

4

Park Lane Farm

PARK LA

Yewtree Farm

Park End

Sewage Wks

New Farm

Park Farm

Moat Farm

MOAT LA

Pear Tree Farm

Townhouse

Ravensmead Com Prim Sch

EDWARD ST

Bignall End

BIGNALL END RD

TIBB ST

3

Firs Farm

Community Ctr

OLD RD

CHAPEL ST

WOOD ST

RAVEN'S LA

PO

BS500

51

New Peel Farm

Kent Hill Farm

NEW RD

CHURCH BANK

PUMP CT

WATLANDS

McELLIN CL

BOYLES HALL RD

WESTLANDS

GRESLEY WAY

2

BARTHOMLEY RD

WILBRAHAM'S WLK

P

Audley

WESTFIELD DR

CHESTER RD

Liby

ST JAMES CT

CHAPEL

P PO

VERNON PL

DELPHSIDE

GREENWAYS

BRINDLEYS WAY

NANTWICH RD

The Quarry

Wereton

BOOTH ST

DEAN HOLLOW

CAPPELLE RISE

GRASSYGREEN LA

CHERRY TREE RD
CEDAR CRES
WEDGEWOOD AVE

RYON HILL RD

HAWTHORNE AVE

1

Old Peel Farm

PEAR TREE

Quarry New Farm

NEW KING ST

DURBER CL

KING ST

MADDOCK ST

Rye Hills

Grange Farm

Boon Hill

BS367

CRIB LA

Shraleybrook

Greenbutts House

DEAN VIEW

Ryehill Farm

RYEHILLS

Wood Lane Prim Sch

50

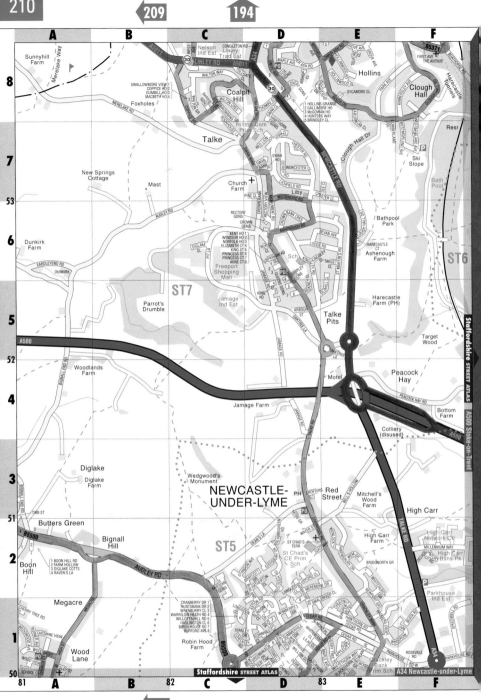

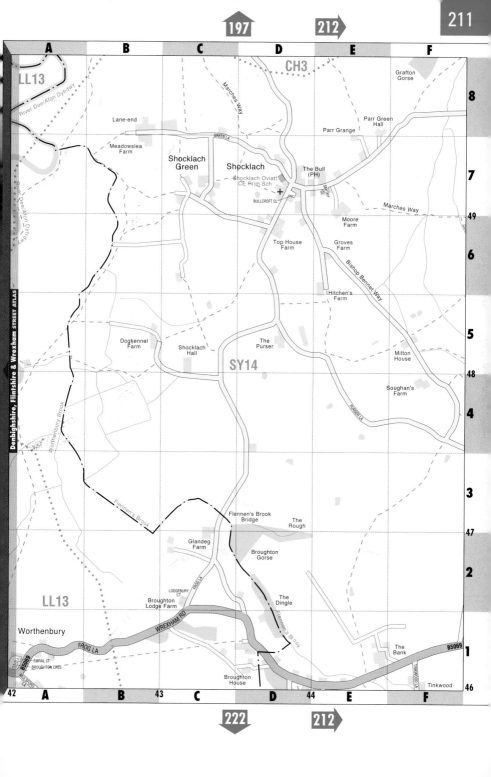

211
198

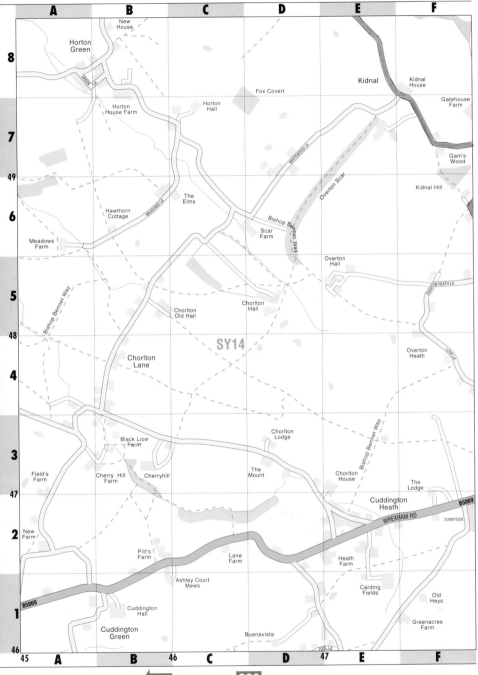

211
223

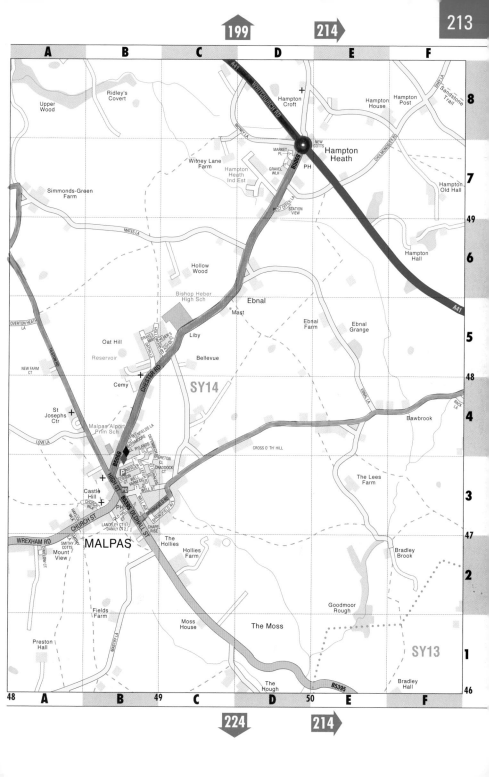

213
200

| | A | B | C | D | E | F |

8

Lower House Farm

Hetherson Green

Cross Lanes Cottage

Bret's Moss

Hampton Green

Sunnyside

SY13

Middle House

7

Broomy Bank

Pipehouse Farm

49

HETHERSON GREEN LA

CHOLMONDLEY LA

BICKLEY TOWN LA

St WENEFREDES GN

Bickley Brook

6

Robber Hill Farm

Bickley Town

BANK FARM MEWS

5

A41

SY14

Lower Bickley Wood Farm

Bickley Town Bridge

Bickley Mill

The Wheatsheaf (PH)

HAMPTON CRES

BAR PARK CT

MEADOW CT

48

No Man's Heath

CROSS O'TH HILL RD

Bickley Hall Farm

Bar Mere

BACK LA

CHOLMONDLEY RD

4

Bickleywood

Birch Pits

Steer Brook

Whitegates Farm

Sandstone Trail

3

Gorstyhill Cottage

Millmoor Farm

The Willey Farm

47

Bickley Field

2

Home Farm

Barhill Farm

Willey Moor

Marches Way

SY13

Top Farm

BARHILL DR

BARHILL FARM COTTS

A49

The Maltkiln

Moorside Farm

Quoisley Lock

1

Fox Covert

WILLEYMOOR LA

Bishop Bennet Way

Tushingham-with-Grindley CE Prim Sch

OLD CHESTER RD

A41

A49

46

| 51 | A | B | 52 | C | D | 53 | E | F |

213
225

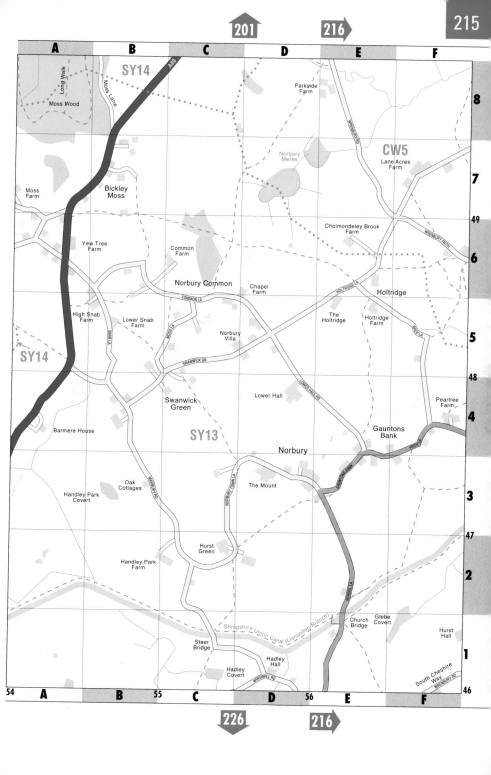

A B C D E F

SY14

Long Walk

Moss Wood

Moss Lane

A49

Parkside Farm

CW5

Norbury Meres

Lane Acres Farm

8

Moss Farm

Bickley Moss

WRENBURY RD

Cholmondeley Brook Farm

WRENBURY FRITH

49

Yew Tree Farm

Common Farm

Norbury Common

Chapel Farm

HOLTRIDGE LA

Holtridge

6

High Snab Farm

Lower Snab Farm

SNAB LA

MOSS LA

COMMON LA

Norbury Villa

The Holtridge

Holtridge Farm

BACK LA

SY14

SWANWICK GN

5

48

Swanwick Green

Lower Hall

LOWER HALL RD

Peartree Farm

4

Barmere House

SY13

Norbury

Gauntons Bank

FRITH

Handley Park Covert

Oak Cottages

MARBURY RD

The Mount

NORBURY TOWN LA

GAUNTONS BANK

3

47

Hurst Green

Church Bridge

Glebe Covert

Hurst Hall

2

Handley Park Farm

BICKLEY RD

Shropshire Union Canal (Llangollen Branch)

Steer Bridge

Hadley Hall

Hadley Covert

WIRSWALL RD

South Cheshire Way

WRENBURY RD

1

54 A B 55 C D 56 E F 46

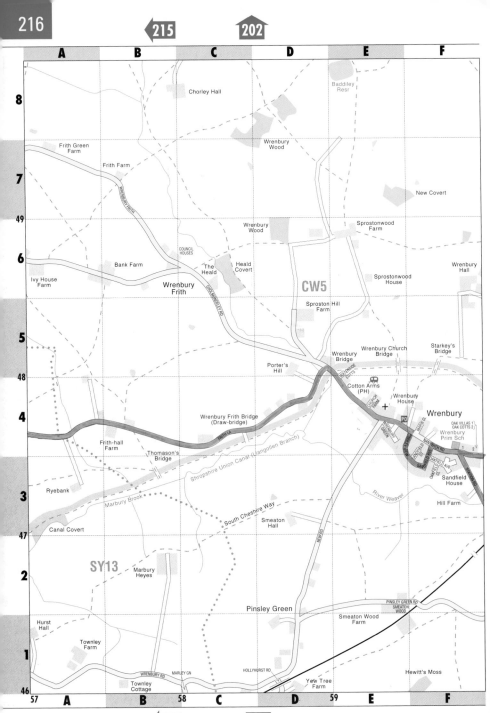

215
202

A   **B**   **C**   **D**   **E**   **F**

8

Chorley Hall

Baddiley Resr

Wrenbury Wood

7

Frith Green Farm

Frith Farm

New Covert

49

Wrenbury Wood

Sprostonwood Farm

6

COUNCIL HOUSES

Bank Farm

The Heald

Heald Covert

Wrenbury Hall

Ivy House Farm

Wrenbury Frith

Sproston Hill Farm

Sprostonwood House

CW5

5

Starkey's Bridge

Porter's Hill

Wrenbury Bridge

Wrenbury Church Bridge

48

Cotton Arms (PH)

Wrenbury House

Wrenbury

4

Wrenbury Frith Bridge (Draw-bridge)

FRITH LA

Frith-hall Farm

Thomason's Bridge

OAK VILLAS 1
OAK COTTS 2

Wrenbury Prim Sch

1
2

3

Ryebank

Marbury Brook

Shropshire Union Canal (Llangollen Branch)

River Weaver

Sandfield House

Hill Farm

47

Canal Covert

South Cheshire Way

Smeaton Hall

SY13

2

Marbury Heyes

Pinsley Green Rd

Smeaton Wood

1

Hurst Hall

Townley Farm

Pinsley Green

Smeaton Wood Farm

Hewitt's Moss

46

Wrenbury Rd

Marley Gn

Hollyhurst Rd

Townley Cottage

Yew Tree Farm

57   **A**   **B**   58   **C**   **D**   59   **E**   **F**

215
227

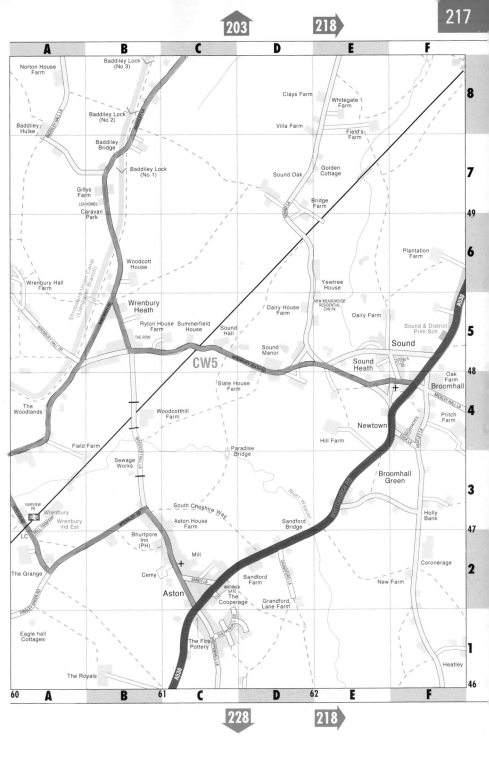

217
204

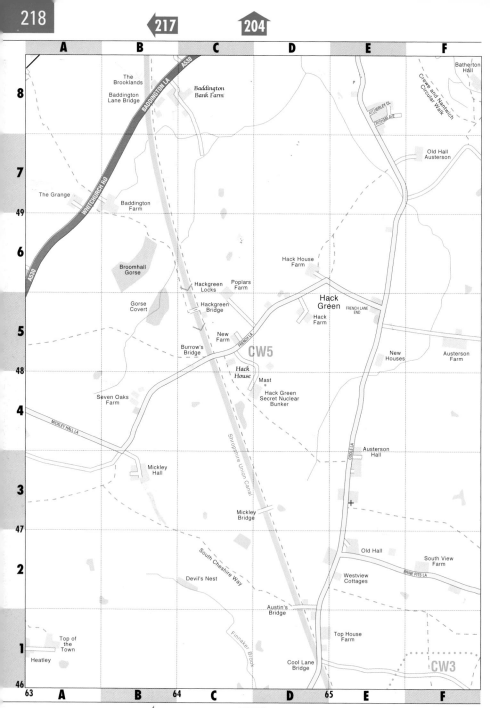

217
229

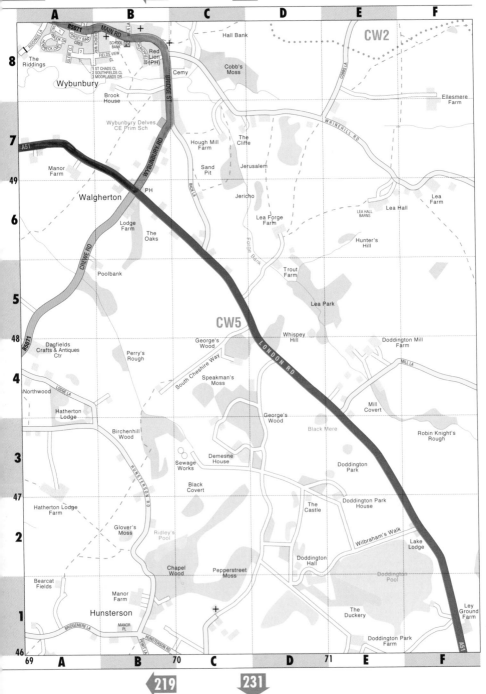

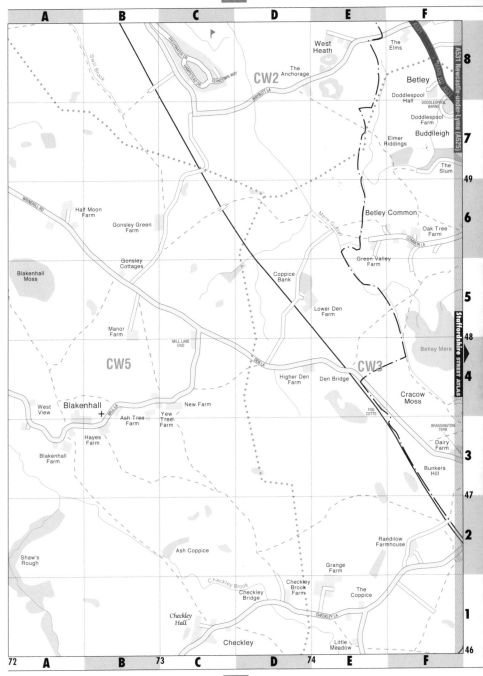

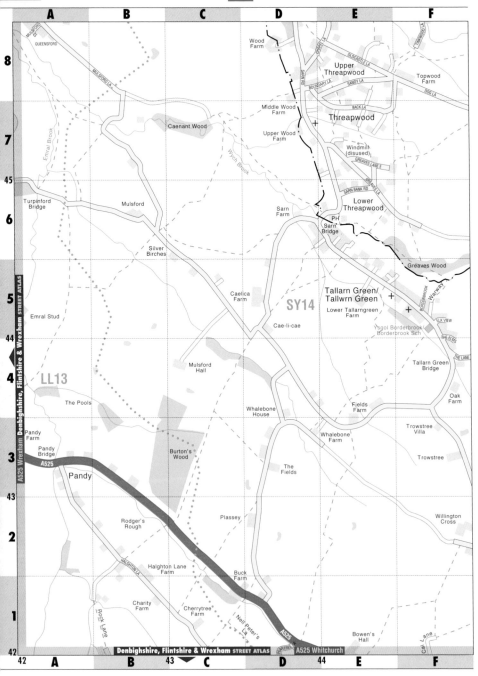

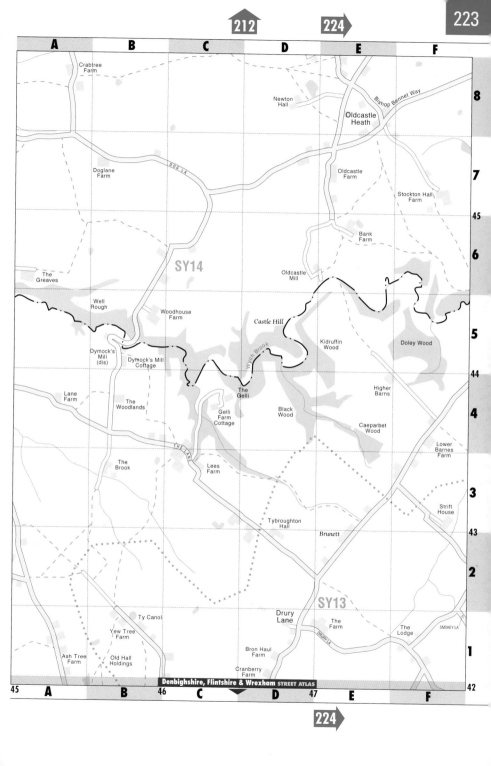

A B C D E F

8

Crabtree Farm

Newton Hall

Bishop Bennet Way

Oldcastle Heath

7

Doglane Farm

DOG LA

Oldcastle Farm

Stockton Hall Farm

45

Bank Farm

6

SY14

The Greaves

Oldcastle Mill

Well Rough

Woodhouse Farm

Castle Hill

5

Kidruffin Wood

Doley Wood

Wych Brook

Dymock's Mill (dis)

Dymock's Mill Cottage

The Gelli

44

Lane Farm

The Woodlands

Gelli Farm Cottage

Black Wood

Higher Barns

4

Caeparbet Wood

Lower Barnes Farm

The Brook

THE LANE

Lees Farm

3

Strift House

Tybroughton Hall

Brunett

43

2

SY13

Ty Canol

Drury Lane

The Farm

The Lodge

SMOKEY LA

Yew Tree Farm

DRURY LA

Ash Tree Farm

Old Hall Holdings

Bron Haul Farm

Cranberry Farm

1

45 A B 46 C D 47 E F 42

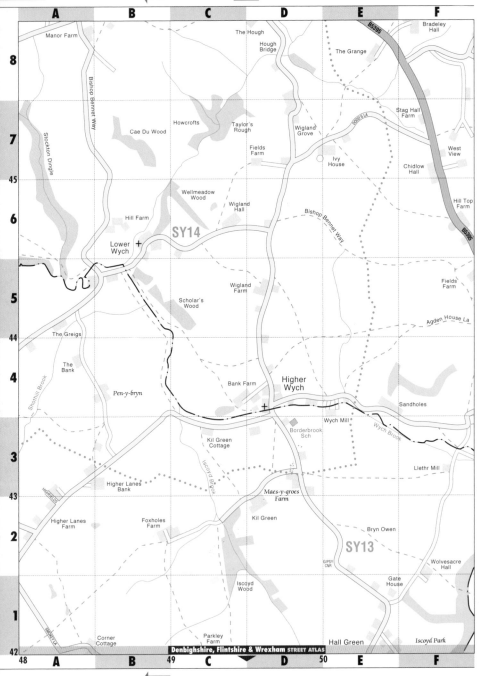

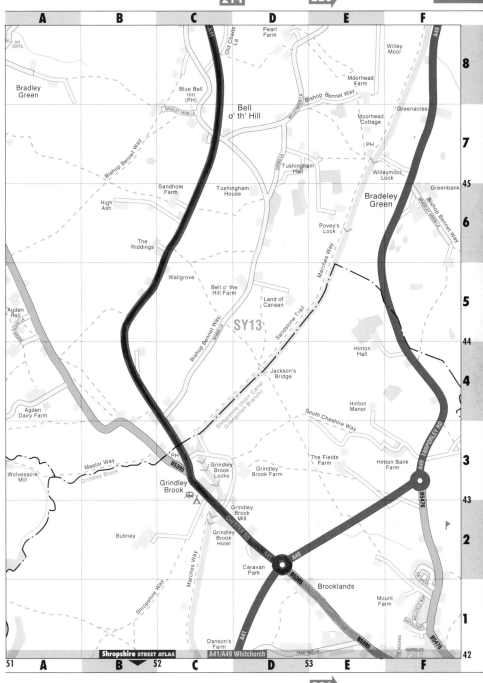

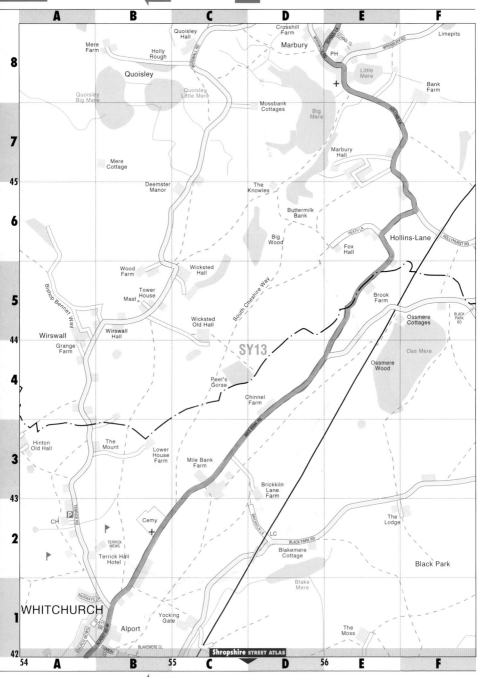

| | A | B | C | D | E | F |

8

Mere Farm
Quoisley Hall
Holly Rough
Crosshill Farm
Marbury
Limepits
PH
SCHOOL CL
WRENBURY RD
Quoisley
Little Mere
Bank Farm
Quoisley Big Mere
Quoisley Little Mere
Mossbank Cottages
Big Mere

7

Mere Cottage
Marbury Hall

45

Deemster Manor
The Knowles
Buttermilk Bank

6

Big Wood
Heath La
Hollins-Lane
HOLLYHURST RD
Fox Hall

Wood Farm
Wicksted Hall
South Cheshire Way
Brook Farm
Ossmere Cottages
BLACK PARK RD

5

Tower House
Mast.
Wicksted Old Hall
Bishop Bennet Way
Wirswall Hall

44

Wirswall
Grange Farm
SY13
Oss Mere
Ossmere Wood

4

Peel's Gorse
Chinnel Farm

Hinton Old Hall
The Mount
Lower House Farm
Mile Bank Farm

3

MILE BANK RD
Brickkiln Lane Farm

43

CH
P
TERRICK RD
Cemy
LC
Black Park Rd
The Lodge
BRICKKILN LA

2

TERRICK MEWS
Terrick Hall Hotel
Blakemere Cottage
Black Park

1

WHITCHURCH
FAIRWAYS DR
Alport
Yocking Gate
Blake Mere
The Moss

42

CLAYTON DR
ASHBY DR
OSMERE CL
BLAKEMERE CL

| 54 | A | B | 55 | C | D | 56 | E | F |

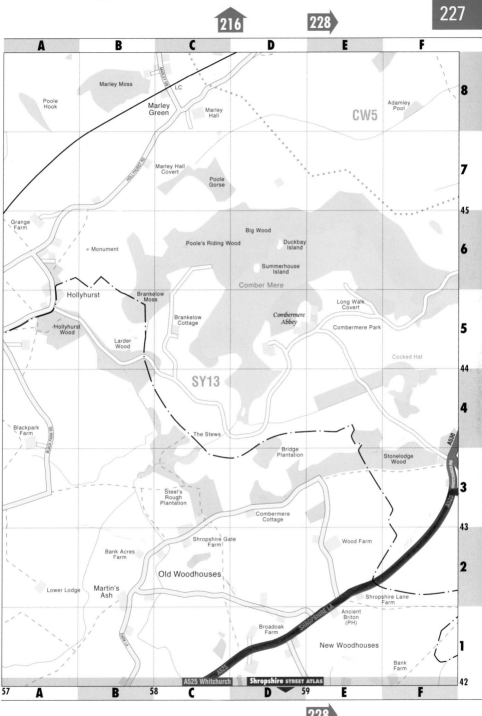

Poole Hook

Marley Moss

Marley Green

LC

Marley Hall

Adamley Pool

Marley Hall Covert

Poole Gorse

Grange Farm

Big Wood

Duckbay Island

Poole's Riding Wood

• Monument

Summerhouse Island

Comber Mere

Hollyhurst

Brankelow Moss

Long Walk Covert

Brankelow Cottage

Combermere Abbey

Combermere Park

Hollyhurst Wood

Larder Wood

Cocked Hat

SY13

The Stews

Bridge Plantation

Stonelodge Wood

Blackpark Farm

Steel's Rough Plantation

Combermere Cottage

Wood Farm

Shropshire Gate Farm

Bank Acres Farm

Old Woodhouses

Lower Lodge

Martin's Ash

Shropshire Lane Farm

Ancient Briton (PH)

Broadoak Farm

New Woodhouses

Bank Farm

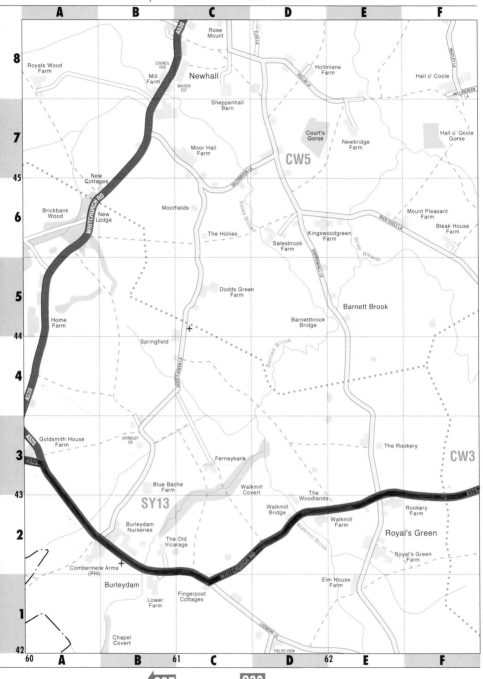

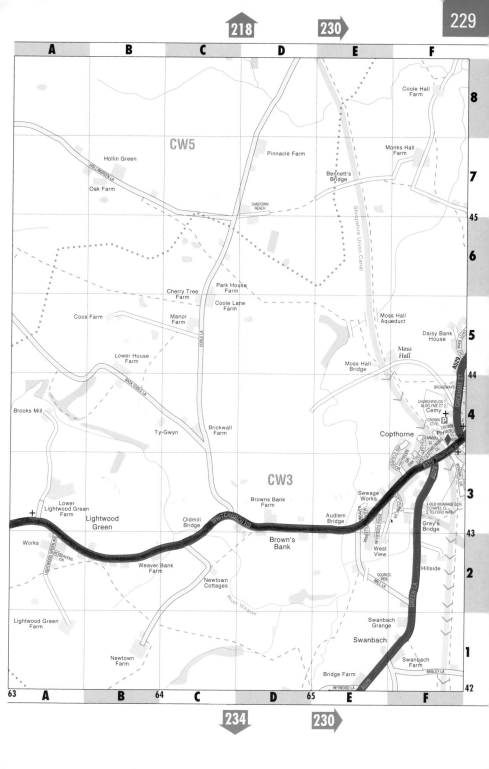

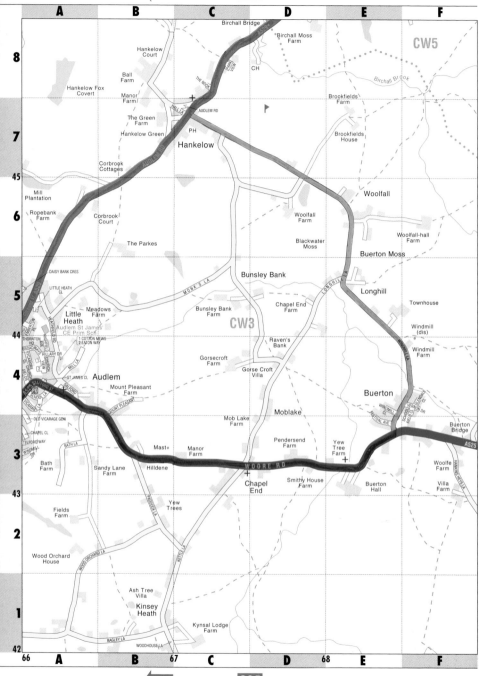

CW5

A B C D E F

8

Birchall Bridge

Hankelow
Court

Ball
Farm

Hankelow Fox
Covert

Manor
Farm

The Green
Farm

Hankelow Green

Corbrook
Cottages

Birchall Moss
Farm

CH

Brookfields
Farm

Birchall Brook

Brookfields
House

7

PH

Hankelow

AUDLEM RD

45

Mill
Plantation

Ropebank
Farm

Corbrook
Court

The Parkes

Woolfall

Woolfall
Farm

Woolfall-hall
Farm

Blackwater
Moss

Buerton Moss

6

DAISY BANK CRES

LITTLE HEATH
CL

Little
Heath

Meadows
Farm

Bunsley Bank

Bunsley Bank
Farm

CW3

Chapel End
Farm

Longhill

Townhouse

Windmill
(dis)

5

Audlem St James'
CE Prim Sch

THORNTON
HO

BROADMANS LA
HILLARY DR

MILL LA

1 COTTON MEWS
2 EATON WAY

Raven's
Bank

Gorsecroft
Farm

Gorse Croft
Villa

Windmill
Farm

44

ST JAMES CL

SALFORD

Audlem

Mount Pleasant
Farm

MOUNT PLEASANT

Mob Lake
Farm

Moblake

Buerton

WINDMILL
CL

VERNON DR

SCHOOL LA

Buerton
Bridge

4

OLD VICARAGE GDN

CHAPEL CL

TELFORD WAY

WINDMILL
DR

Bath
Farm

Sandy Lane
Farm

Mast

Hilldene

Manor
Farm

WOORE RD

Pendersend
Farm

Yew
Tree
Farm

FESTIVAL AVE

Smithy House
Farm

Buerton
Hall

A525

Woolfe
Farm

Villa
Farm

HAWKS BERRY LA

3

43

Fields
Farm

PADDOCK LA

Yew
Trees

KETTEL LA

Chapel
End

2

Wood Orchard
House

WOOD ORCHARD LA

Ash Tree
Villa

1

Kinsey
Heath

Kynsal Lodge
Farm

42

BAGLEY LA

WOODHOUSE LA

66 A B 67 C D 68 E F

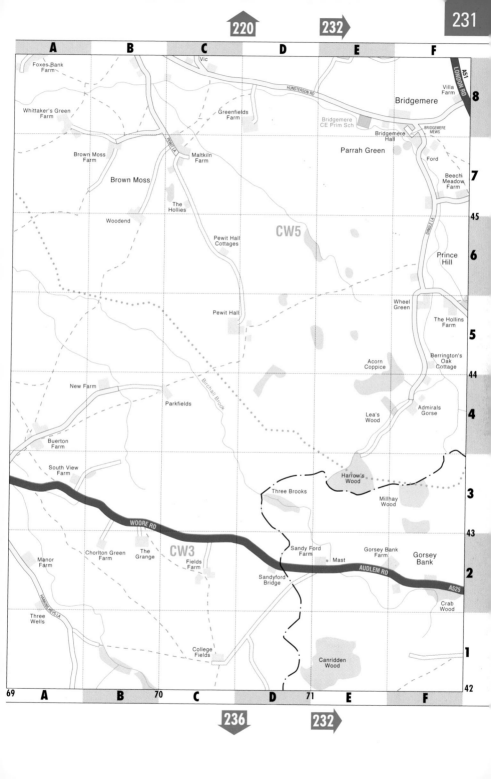

A51 LONDON RD

Foxes Bank Farm

Whittaker's Green Farm

Brown Moss Farm

Brown Moss

Woodend

The Hollies

PEWIT LA

Maltkiln Farm

Vic

HUNSTERSON RD

Greenfields Farm

Bridgemere CE Prim Sch

Bridgemere

Villa Farm

8

Bridgemere Hall

BRIDGEMERE MEWS

Parrah Green

Ford

7

Beechi Meadow Farm

45

CW5

Pewit Hall Cottages

Prince Hill

6

DINGLE LA

Wheel Green

The Hollins Farm

5

Pewit Hall

Acorn Coppice

Berrington's Oak Cottage

44

New Farm

Parkfields

Birchall Brook

Lea's Wood

Admirals Gorse

4

Buerton Farm

South View Farm

Harrow's Wood

Three Brooks

Millhay Wood

3

WOORE RD

CW3

Chorlton Green Farm

The Grange

Fields Farm

Sandy Ford Farm

Mast

Gorsey Bank Farm

Gorsey Bank

43

Manor Farm

NANTWICH RD / NAPLEY RD LA

Sandyford Bridge

AUDLEM RD

A525

2

Three Wells

Crab Wood

College Fields

Canridden Wood

1

42

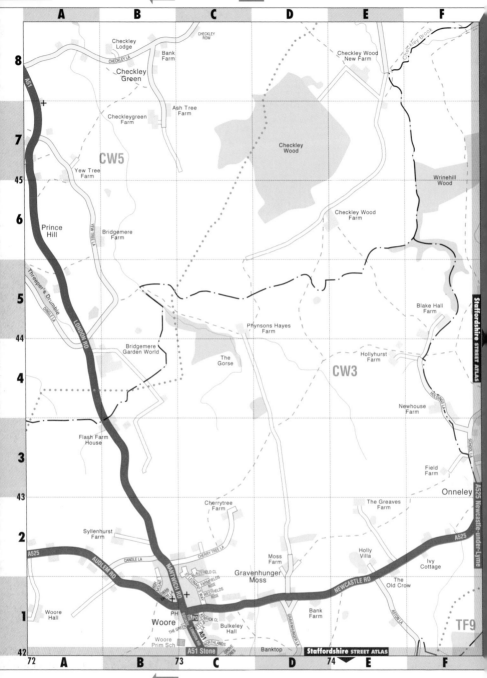

A   B   C   D   E   F

8

A51

Checkley Lodge

Checkley Green

Bank Farm

CHECKLEY LA

CHECKLEY ROW

Checkley Wood New Farm

Chetwley Brook

Ash Tree Farm

Checkleygreen Farm

7

CW5

Checkley Wood

45

Yew Tree Farm

Wrinehill Wood

6

Prince Hill

Bridgemere Farm

YEW TREE LA

Checkley Wood Farm

Threapers Drumble

5

Blake Hall Farm

BRECK LA

LONDON RD

Bridgemere Garden World

Phynsons Hayes Farm

Hollyhurst Farm

44

The Gorse

CW3

4

Newhouse Farm

HOLDING LA

Flash Farm House

3

Field Farm

SCHOOL LA

Onneley

43

Cherrytree Farm

The Greaves Farm

A525 Newcastle-under-Lyme

2

Syllenhurst Farm

CHERRY TREE LA

Moss Farm

Holly Villa

A525

Ivy Cottage

A525

AUDLEM RD

CANDLE LA

Gravenhunger Moss

NEWCASTLE RD

The Old Crow

Woore Hall

NANTWICH RD

AUDEFIELD CL

FARM FIELDS RISE

WESTFIELDS RISE

STONE LA

1

PH

Woore

PO

A51

Bulkeley Hall

Bank Farm

GRAVENHUNGER LA

THE GREENS

PATRICK CL

TF9

Woore Prim Sch

SOUTHLANDS

GROVE GDNS

42

A51 Stone

Banktop

72   A   **73**   B   C   D   **74**   E   F

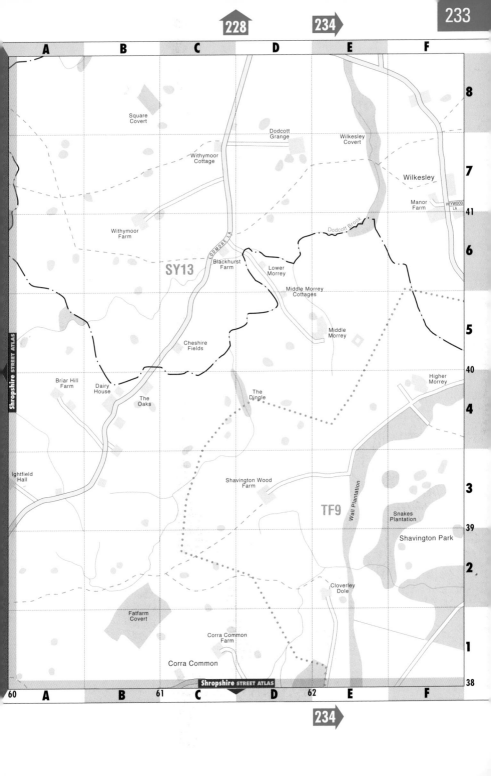

A   B   C   D   E   F

8

Square
Covert

Dodcott
Grange

Wilkesley
Covert

7

Withymoor
Cottage

Wilkesley

Manor
Farm

HEYWOOD
LA

41

Withymoor
Farm

Dodcott Brook

SY13

Blackhurst
Farm

Lower
Morrey

6

Middle Morrey
Cottages

5

Middle
Morrey

Cheshire
Fields

40

Briar Hill
Farm

Dairy
House

The
Oaks

The
Dingle

Higher
Morrey

4

Ightfield
Hall

Shavington Wood
Farm

TF9

Wall Plantation

3

Snakes
Plantation

39

Shavington Park

2

Cloverley
Dole

Fatfarm
Covert

Corra Common
Farm

1

Corra Common

38

60   A   B   61   C   D   62   E   F

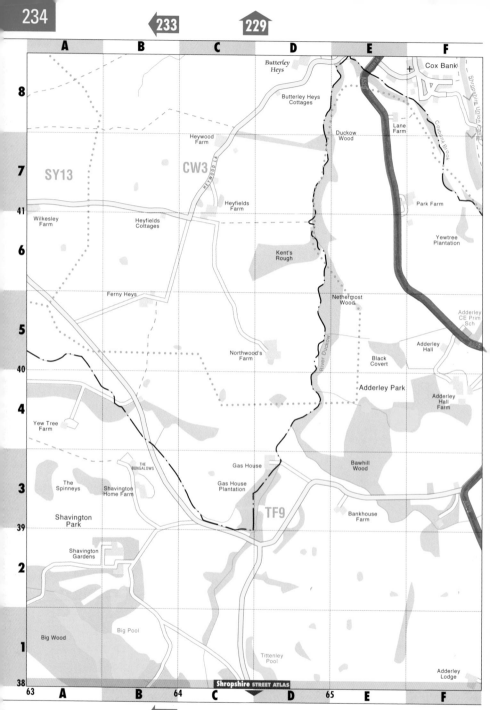

A   B   C   D   E   F

Cox Bank

8

Butterley
Heys

Butterley Heys
Cottages

Duckow
Wood

Lane
Farm

Shropshire Union Canal

Coxbank Brook

7

Heywood
Farm

SY13

CW3

HEYWOOD LA

Park Farm

41

Wilkesley
Farm

Heyfields
Farm

Heyfields
Cottages

Yewtree
Plantation

6

Kent's
Rough

Nethermost
Wood

5

Ferny Heys

River Duckow

Adderley
CE Prim
Sch

Adderley
Hall

40

Northwood's
Farm

Black
Covert

Adderley Park

Adderley
Hall
Farm

4

Yew Tree
Farm

THE
BUNGALOWS

Gas House

Bawhill
Wood

3

The
Spinneys

Shavington
Home Farm

Gas House
Plantation

TF9

Bankhouse
Farm

39

Shavington
Park

Shavington
Gardens

2

1

Big Wood

Big Pool

Tittenley
Pool

Adderley
Lodge

38

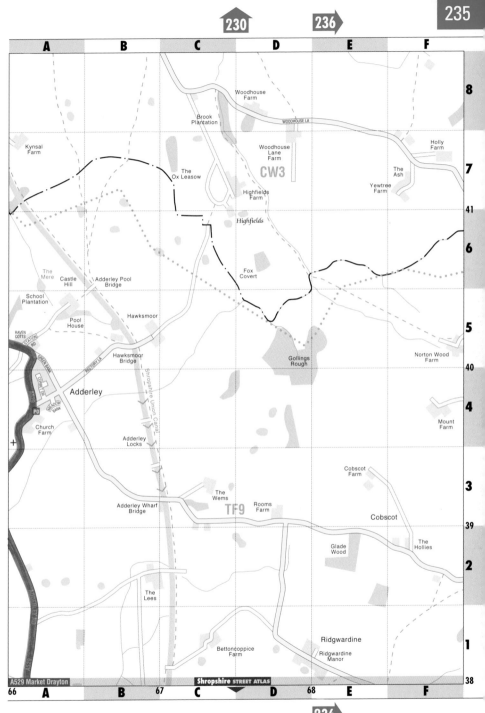

Woodhouse Farm

Brook Plantation

WOODHOUSE LA

Woodhouse Lane Farm

CW3

Holly Farm

The Ash

Kynsal Farm

The Ox Leasow

Highfields Farm

Yewtree Farm

Highfields

Fox Covert

The Mere

Castle Hill

Adderley Pool Bridge

School Plantation

Hawksmoor

Pool House

RAVEN COTTS

STATION RD

GREEN BANK

Hawksmoor Bridge

Norton Wood Farm

Gollings Rough

Shropshire Union Canal

Adderley

COBB PK

MEADOW BANK

PO

Church Farm

Mount Farm

Adderley Locks

Cobscot Farm

The Wems

Adderley Wharf Bridge

TF9

Rooms Farm

Cobscot

The Hollies

Glade Wood

The Lees

Ridgwardine

Bettoncoppice Farm

Ridgwardine Manor

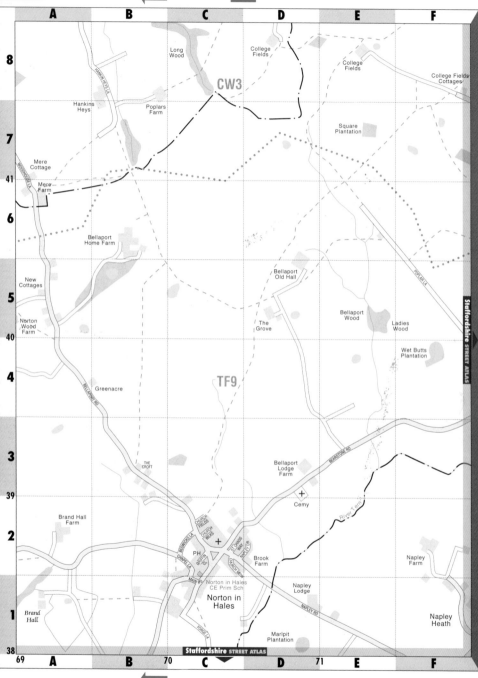

CW3

Long
Wood

College
Fields

College
Fields

College Fields
Cottages

Hankins
Heys

Poplars
Farm

Square
Plantation

Mere
Cottage

Mere
Farm

POPLAR LA

Bellaport
Home Farm

New
Cottages

Bellaport
Old Hall

Norton
Wood
Farm

The
Grove

Bellaport
Wood

Ladies
Wood

Wet Butts
Plantation

TF9

BELLAPORT RD

Greenacre

THE
CROFT

BEARSTONE RD

Bellaport
Lodge
Farm

Brand Hall
Farm

Cemy

River Tern

Napley
Farm

CHURCH
FIELDS

CHURCH
WALKS

Brook
Farm

Napley
Farm

BESTWICKS LA

PH

ST CHADS
WALK

CHAPEL NEW

Napley
Lodge

Napley
Heath

CAMPBELL

MAIN RD

GRIFFITH
RD

Brand
Hall

Norton in Hales
CE Prim Sch

Norton in
Hales

FORGE LA

Maripit
Plantation

NAPLEY RD

Staffordshire STREET ATLAS

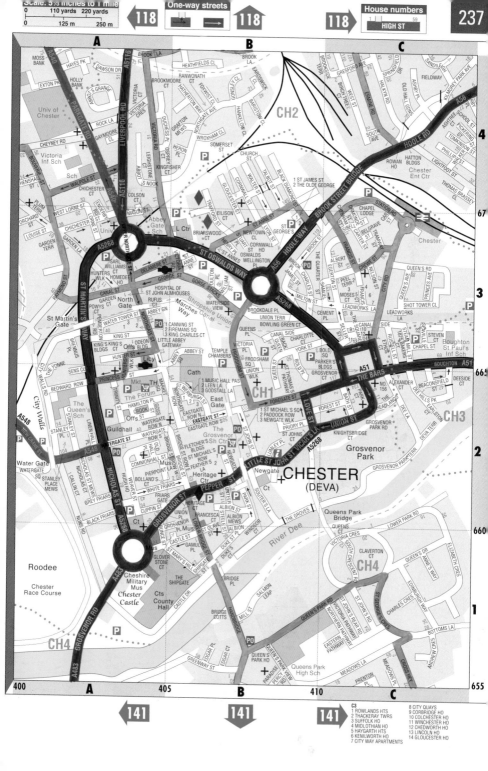

Index

Place name May be abbreviated on the map

Location number Present when a number indicates the place's position in a crowded area of mapping

Locality, town or village Shown when more than one place has the same name

Postcode district District for the indexed place

Page and grid square Page number and grid reference for the standard mapping

Church Rd 6 Beckenham BR2........53 C6

Cities, towns and villages are listed in CAPITAL LETTERS Public and commercial buildings are highlighted in magenta
Places of interest are highlighted in blue with a star★

Abbreviations used in the index

Acad	Academy	Comm	Common	Gd	Ground	L	Leisure	Prom	Promenade
App	Approach	Cott	Cottage	Gdn	Garden	La	Lane	Rd	Road
Arc	Arcade	Cres	Crescent	Gn	Green	Liby	Library	Recn	Recreation
Ave	Avenue	Cswy	Causeway	Gr	Grove	Mdw	Meadow	Ret	Retail
Bglw	Bungalow	Ct	Court	H	Hall	Meml	Memorial	Sh	Shopping
Bldg	Building	Ctr	Centre	Ho	House	Mkt	Market	Sq	Square
Bsns, Bus	Business	Ctry	Country	Hospl	Hospital	Mus	Museum	St	Street
Bvd	Boulevard	Cty	County	HQ	Headquarters	Orch	Orchard	Sta	Station
Cath	Cathedral	Dr	Drive	Hts	Heights	Pal	Palace	Terr	Terrace
Cir	Circus	Dro	Drove	Ind	Industrial	Par	Parade	TH	Town Hall
Cl	Close	Ed	Education	Inst	Institute	Pas	Passage	Univ	University
Cnr	Corner	Emb	Embankment	Int	International	Pk	Park	Wk, Wlk	Walk
Coll	College	Est	Estate	Intc	Interchange	Pl	Place	Wr	Water
Com	Community	Ex	Exhibition	Junc	Junction	Prec	Precinct	Yd	Yard

Index of towns, villages, streets, hospitals, industrial estates, railway stations, schools, shopping centres, universities and places of interest

2nd–Alb

2nd Ave CW12 .... 156 A4
3rd Ave CW12 .... 156 A4
1875 Bakers Ct CH1,
CH3 .... 237 C3

A

Aarons Dr ST7 .... 209 F2
Abberley Hall SK9 ...... 84 D7
Abbey Cl
  Croft WA3 .... 9 A8
  Whitegate CW8 .... 126 A7
  Widnes WA8 .... 22 C8
  Winsford CW7 .... 149 D5
Abbey Cl SK12 .... 36 D3
Abbeydale Cl CW2 ..... 207 C2
Abbeyfield Ho
  2 Crewe CW2 .... 190 D2
  Ellesmere Port CH65 .. 70 A3
  Knutsford WA16 .... 56 F1
Abbeyfields CW11 .... 174 F5
Abbey Gate Coll CH3 .. 164 E8
Abbey Gate Sch CH2 .. 237 A3
Abbey Gn CH1 .... 237 A3
Abbey Hey WA7 .... 50 C8
Abbey La
  Delamere CW8 .... 123 E5
  Hartford CW8 .... 103 B4
Abbey Mill SK10 .... 87 A6
Abbey Park Way CW2 . 207 E3
Abbey Pl CW1 .... 190 D6
Abbey Rd
  Golborne WA3 .... 4 C8
  Haydock WA11 .... 1 E7
  Macclesfield SK10 .... 87 B2
  Sandbach CW11 ..... 174 E6
  Widnes WA8 .... 22 C8
Abbey Sq CH1 .... 237 A3
Abbey St CH1 .... 237 A3
Abbey Way CW8 .... 103 B4
Abbeyway N WA11 ..... 2 A7
Abbeyway S WA11 ..... 2 A7
Abbotsbury Cl
  Poynton SK12 .... 36 D5
  Wistaston CW2 ...... 206 B8
Abbots Cl SK10 .... 87 B2
Abbots Ct CH2 .... 118 C4
Abbot's Dr CH2 .... 118 C4

Abbotsfield Cl WA4 ... 26 E6
Abbot's Grange CH2 .. 237 A4
Abbots Knoll CH2 ..... 118 C4
ABBOT'S MEADS 118 B5
Abbotsmere Cl CW8 .. 101 F2
Abbots Mews CH65 ... 70 B6
ABBOTS MOSS 124 D5
Abbot's Nook CH2 .... 237 A4
Abbots Pk
  Chester CH2 .... 118 C4
  Runcorn WA7 .... 50 E5
Abbot's Terr CH1 .... 118 B5
Abbots Way
  Hartford CW8 .... 103 B4
  Neston CH64 .... 41 E1
Abbotts Cl
  Runcorn WA7 .... 49 A8
  Waverton CH3 .... 143 B5
Abbotts Rd CH3 ..... 143 B5
Abbotts Way CW7 ... 126 B2
Aberdare Cl WA5 ...... 7 E1
Aberdaron Dr CH1 ... 117 C3
Aberdeen Wlk SK10 .. 86 F3
Aberfeldy Cl CW4 ... 130 B2
Abingdon Ave WA4 .. 17 E7
Abingdon Cl 9 SK11 ..111 F8
Abingdon Cres 4
  CH4 .... 140 F6
Abington Cl CW1 .... 190 B6
Abington Wlk WA7 ... 50 C5
Abstone Cl WA1 ...... 17 B7
Acacia Ave
  Knutsford WA16 ...... 56 E1
  Warrington WA1 ..... 17 D7
  Widnes WA8 .... 13 B3
  Wilmslow SK9 .... 59 F5
Acacia Cl CW2 .... 72 C3
Acacia Cres CW1 ... 190 E6
Acacia Dr
  Ellesmere Port CH66 .. 69 F1
  Sandbach CW11 .... 174 E7
Acacia Gdns ST7 .... 195 C3
Acacia Gr WA7 .... 49 C8
Acacia St WA12 .... 1 F4
Academy Pl 6 WA1 .. 16 B5
Academy St WA1 ..... 16 B5
Academy Way WA1 .. 16 B5
Acer Ave CW7 .... 190 E2
Achilles Ave WA2 .... 8 A2
Achilles Ct WA7 ...... 24 A2
Ackerley Cl WA2 ...... 8 F3
Ackers La WA4 ...... 16 E1

Ackersley Ct SK8 .... 35 B8
Ackers Rd WA4 ...... 16 E1
Ack La E SK7 .... 35 D7
Ack La W SK8 .... 35 C7
Acorn Bank Cl CW2 . 206 B7
Acorn Cl
  Cuddington CW8 .... 101 F2
  Winsford CW7 ...... 150 A8
Acorn Ct CH2 .... 118 E8
Acorn Dr CH65 .... 70 B1
Acorn La CW12 ..... 157 E3
Acorns Prim Sch The
  CH65 .... 69 E5
Acorns Sch WA12 ..... 2 D3
Acorns The CH2 .... 118 E8
Acorn Terr SK22 .... 39 B6
Acreage The
  Bunbury CW6 .... 185 E8
  Goostrey CW4 ...... 107 E1
Acrefield Rd WA8 .... 12 B1
Acre Gn 126 .... 21 A6
Acre La
  Bebington CH62 ..... 43 D8
  Cheadle SK8 .... 35 C6
  Heswall CH60 .... 41 C8
Acre Rd CH66 .... 69 D5
Acres Cres WA6 ..... 75 B2
Acresfield Com Prim Sch
  CH2 .... 118 F8
Acres La CH2 .... 119 A8
Acreville Gr WA3 ..... 5 C7
ACTON 204 A7
Acton Ave WA4 .... 26 D3
ACTON BRIDGE 76 E3
Acton Bridge Sta CW8 . 76 F1
Acton CE Prim Sch
  CW5 .... 204 A7
Acton Cl WA11 .... 1 C6
Acton La CW8 .... 76 F4
Acton Pl SK11 .... 111 F8
Acton Rd
  Burtonwood WA5 ...... 6 E6
  Crewe CW2 .... 189 D4
Acton Way ST7 ..... 193 D6
Adam Ave
  Ellesmere Port CH66 .. 69 D3
  Ellesmere Port, Great Sutton
  CH66 .... 69 C4
Adam Cl CH66 ...... 69 D4
Adams Cl
  Newton-le-W WA12 ... 2 D2
  Poynton SK12 .... 36 E2
Adams Hill WA16 ... 57 A1

Adamson Ct WA4 .... 17 B2
Adamson Ho WA7 ... 22 E3
Adamson St WA4 .... 16 B3
Adam St WA2 .... 16 C7
Adaston Ave CH62 ... 43 F4
Adder Hill CH3 ..... 142 B7
ADDERLEY 235 A4
Adderley CE Prim Sch
  TF9 .... 234 F5
Adderley Cl WA7 ..... 23 C1
Adderley Rd TF9 .... 235 A2
ADDER'S MOSS 85 F6
Addingham Ave WA8 . 22 C7
Addison Cl CW2 .... 205 F8
Addison Sq WA8 ..... 13 A1
Adelaide Ct 4 WA8 . 23 A7
Adelaide Rd
  Blacon CH1 .... 117 D4
  Bramhall SK7 .... 35 F5
  Adelaide Sch CW1 .. 190 C5
Adelaide St
  Crewe CW1 .... 190 C5
  Macclesfield SK10 .... 87 E1
Adela Rd WA7 .... 22 F2
Adey Rd WA13 ...... 19 A5
Adfalent La CH64 .... 68 A7
Adlington 62 D5
Adlington Cl SK12 .... 36 F2
Adlington Ct WA3 ..... 9 F6
Adlington Dr
  Northwich CW9 ..... 104 A5
  Sandbach CW11 .... 175 C2
Adlington Est SK10 .. 36 C1
Adlington Hall Mews
  SK10 .... 62 B5
Adlington Pk SK10 ... 36 C1
Adlington Prim Sch
  SK10 .... 62 E5
Adlington Rd
  Bollington SK10 ..... 63 A1
  Crewe CW2 .... 189 F3
  Runcorn WA7 .... 24 D2
  Wilmslow SK9 .... 60 E7
Adlington Road Bsns Pk
  SK10 .... 88 A8
Adlington St SK10 .. 112 C8
Adlington St CW1 ... 62 C5
Admirals Rd WA3 ..... 9 F3
Adshead Ct SK10 .... 88 B7
Adwell Cl WA3 .... 4 A8
Afton WA8 .... 12 A2
Agden Brow WA13 ... 19 E1

Agden Brow Pk
  Broomedge WA13 ..... 19 D1
  Lymm WA13 .... 29 D8
Agden Hall Farm
  WA13 .... 29 E7
Agden House La
  SY13 .... 225 A5
Agden La
  Broomedge WA13 ..... 19 E1
  Little Bollington WA13 .. 29 E7
Agden Park La WA13 . 29 D8
Agecroft Rd CW9 .... 104 C7
Ainley Cl WA7 .... 50 A5
Ainscough Rd WA3 ... 9 E3
Ainsdale Cl
  Bebington CH63 ..... 43 C5
  Bramhall SK7 .... 36 A7
Ainsworth La CW8 ... 76 B3
Ainsworth Rd CW8 ... 77 E1
Aintree Gr CH66 ..... 69 D3
Airdrie Cl CH62 ...... 43 D3
Aire WA8 .... 12 B2
Aire Cl CH65 .... 70 A7
Airedale Cl WA5 ..... 14 F7
Aire Pl CW7 .... 127 A1
Airfield View CH5 ... 139 B6
Aitchison Rd CW9 .... 80 A2
Ajax Ave WA2 .... 8 B2
Akesmoor La
  Biddulph ST8 .... 179 E1
  Mow Cop ST5 .... 195 F7
Alamein Cres WA2 ... 16 C7
Alamein Dr CW7 .... 149 D8
Alamein Rd
  Barnton CH8 .... 78 A4
  Chester CH2 .... 95 B1
Alan Dr WA15 .... 32 A8
Alan St CW9 .... 104 B8
Alban Ret Pk WA2 ..... 8 A1
Alban St CW1 ...... 190 C5
Albany Cres WA13 ... 18 D4
Albany Gdns CH66 ... 69 C7
Albany Gr WA13 .... 18 C4
Albany Rd
  Bramhall SK7 .... 35 F4
  Lymm WA13 .... 18 D4
  Wilmslow SK9 .... 59 F5
Albany Terr 15 WA7 .. 23 A2
Albert Dr
  Neston CH64 .... 66 D8
  Warrington WA5 ..... 14 D6

Albert Pl
Congleton CW12 . . . . .156 E2
🔟 Macclesfield SK11 . . . . 112 D8
Northwich CW9 . . . . .104 B8
Albert Rd
Bollington SK10 . . . . .87 E8
Warrington WA4 . . . . .17 A2
🛛 Widnes WA8 . . . . .13 B1
Wilmslow SK9 . . . . .60 A6
Albert Row WA6 . . . . .49 B1
Albert Sq 🛮 WA8 . . . . .23 B8
Albert St
Audley ST7 . . . . .209 F3
Chester CH1 . . . . .237 C3
Crewe CW1 . . . . .190 C5
Irlam M44 . . . . .11 E6
Knutsford WA16 . . . . .56 F2
Macclesfield SK11 . . . . . . .112 C8
Nantwich CW5 . . . . .204 E6
🔞 Runcorn WA7 . . . . .23 A2
Albert Terr WA5 . . . . .1 E1
Albion Cl CW12 . . . . .156 E2
Albion Mews
Chester CH1 . . . . .237 B2
New Mills SK22 . . . . .39 C7
Albion Pl WA3 . . . . .5 C7
Albion Pl CH1 . . . . .237 B1
Albion Rd
New Mills SK22 . . . . .39 B6
Northwich CW9 . . . . .79 A1
Albion St
Chester CH1 . . . . .237 B2
Crewe CW2 . . . . .190 A3
Albion Wlk CW9 . . . . .79 A1
Albright Rd WA8 . . . . .22 A6
Albury Cl WA11 . . . . .1 D7
Alcock St 🗠 WA7 . . . . .23 A3
Aiconbury Cl WA5 . . . . .15 B6
Alcott Pl WA2 . . . . .8 A6
Aldcliffe WA3 . . . . .3 F8
Adelyme Ct CW3 . . . . .229 F4
Alder Ave
Poynton SK12 . . . . .36 F3
Widnes WA8 . . . . .13 B3
Alderbank Rd WA5 . . . . .15 A6
Alder Cl SK8 . . . . .34 D8
Alder Cres WA2 . . . . .16 C8
Alder Ct SK10 . . . . .87 E5
Alderdale Dr SK6 . . . . .37 E2
Alderdale Gr SK9 . . . . .59 E5
Alder Dr
Crewe CW1 . . . . .189 F7
Ellesmere Port CH66 . . . . . . .69 F1
Alderfield Dr L24 . . . . .21 A3
Alder Gr CH2 . . . . .119 B4
Alderhay La ST7 . . . . .195 C4
Alder La
Burtonwood WA2, WA5 . . . . . .7 C2
Cronton WA8, L35 . . . . .12 A5
Frodsham WA6, WA7 . . . . . . .48 D3
Warrington WA2 . . . . .16 B8
Alderley Ave WA3 . . . . .3 D7
Alderley Cl
Hazel Grove SK7 . . . . .36 F8
Poynton SK12 . . . . .36 F2
Sandbach CW11 . . . . .175 D7
ALDERLEY EDGE 60 C2
Alderley Edge* SK9,
SK10 . . . . .85 D8
Alderley Edge Prim Sch
SK9 . . . . .60 A2
Alderley Edge Sch for
Girls SK9 . . . . .60 A2
Alderley Edge Sta SK9 . .60 A2
Alderley Lo SK9 . . . . .60 A5
Alderley Pl CH1 . . . . .117 E6
Alderley Rd
Alderley Edge SK10,
SK9 . . . . .60 F2
Chelford SK10 . . . . .84 C3
Northwich CW8 . . . . .103 E8
Prestbury SK10 . . . . .86 E3
Warrington WA4 . . . . .17 D4
Wilmslow SK9 . . . . .60 A6
Alderley Wlk 🗛 SK11 . . . .112 E7
Alderman Bolton Com
Prim Sch WA4 . . . . .16 F3
Aldersey Cl
Ellesmere Port CH65 . . . . . . .70 C1
🗛 Macclesfield SK11 . . . .111 F8
Aldersey Ho CH2 . . . . .119 B4
Alder Rd
Golborne WA3 . . . . .3 F8
Warrington WA1 . . . . .17 D7
Weaverham CW8 . . . . .102 D8
Alder Rise SK23 . . . . .65 D8
Alder Root La WA2 . . . . .7 D7
Alders SK9 . . . . .59 F6
Aldersey Cl
Runcorn WA7 . . . . .24 D1
Saughall CH1 . . . . .94 A1
ALDERSEY GREEN 182 C6
Aldersey La CH3 . . . . .182 C5
Aldersey Rd CW2 . . . . .190 B2
Aldersey Way CW6 . . . . . .185 E8
Aldersgate SK22 . . . . .39 B8
Aldersgate Dr L26 . . . . .21 A6
Aldersgate Rd SK8 . . . . .35 C5
Alders Green Ave SK6 . . . . . .37 F7
Alders Rd SK12 . . . . .38 A7
Alders Way SK10 . . . . .36 E6
Alderton Cl L26 . . . . .21 A7
Alderton Gr CW7 . . . . .127 A4
Alder Wood Ave L24 . . . . . . .21 A3
Alderwood Ct WA8 . . . . .12 E4
Alderwood Lo L24 . . . . .21 A3

Aldewood Dr WA3 . . . . .10 A6
ALDFORD 163 F3
Aldford Cl
Bebington CH63 . . . . .43 B6
Hough CW2 . . . . .206 E2
Aldford Pl SK9 . . . . .59 F2
Aldford Rd CH2 . . . . .118 F6
Aldford Sch CH3 . . . . .163 F3
Aldford Way CW7 . . . . . . .126 B2
Aldgate CH65. . . . . .70 A5
Aldington Dr CW10 . . . . . . .151 D5
Aldridge Dr WA5 . . . . .6 F7
Aled Way CH4 . . . . .140 D5
Alexander Cl 237 C2
Alexander Dr WA8 . . . . .22 D8
Alexandra Ct 🛮 M31 . . . . . .11 F3
Alexandra Gr
Irlam M44 . . . . .11 F8
Warrington WA4 . . . . .23 C1
Alexandra Ind Est WA8. . . .22 F7
Alexandra Mews WA6 . . . . . .49 B4
Alexandra Pl CW1 . . . . .190 B5
Alexandra St
Ellesmere Port CH65 . . . . . . .70 C7
Warrington WA1 . . . . .16 C7
Widnes WA8 . . . . .23 A7
Winsford CW7 . . . . .126 C1
Alexandria Way
CW12. . . . . .156 C4
Alford Ct 🛛 CW9 . . . . .103 E5
Alforde St WA8 . . . . .23 A7
Alfred Cl 🗠 WA8 . . . . .23 B8
Alfred Rd
Golborne WA3 . . . . .4 A8
Haydock WA11. . . . . .1 F7
Alfred St
Irlam M44 . . . . .11 E6
Newton-le-W WA12. . . . . . . .2 E3
Northwich CW9 . . . . .103 E6
Widnes WA8 . . . . .23 B8
Algernon St
Runcorn WA7 . . . . .22 F3
Warrington, Stockton Heath
WA4 . . . . .16 C1
Warrington WA1 . . . . .16 D6
Alice Ct WA8 . . . . .23 A4
Alison Dr
Goostrey CW4 . . . . .130 D8
Macclesfield SK10 . . . . .87 F1
Alistair Dr CH63 . . . . .43 C6
Allans Cl CH66 . . . . .69 E6
Allansford Ave CH3 . . . . . . .143 A4
Allans Mdw CH64 . . . . .66 E7
Allcard St WA5 . . . . .15 F7
Allen Ave WA3 . . . . .5 C4
Allenby Rd M44 . . . . .11 D4
Allendale WA7 . . . . .50 B6
Allen Dr CW9 . . . . .103 F2
Allen Pl CW1 . . . . .190 B5
Allen Rd WA7 . . . . .48 D7
Allen St
Bollington SK10 . . . . .88 B8
Macclesfield SK11 . . . . . . .112 C7
Warrington WA2 . . . . .16 A6
Allerby Way WA3 . . . . .3 E8
Allerton Rd WA8 . . . . .13 B1
ALLGREAVE 137 C3
Allgreave Cl CW10 . . . . . . .151 C6
All Hallows RC High Sch
SK11. . . . . .112 B7
Allington Cl CH4. . . . . .141 E7
Allman Cl CW1 . . . . .189 F7
ALLOSTOCK 106 E3
Allotment Rd M44 . . . . .11 D6
Allport La CH62. . . . . .43 D8
Allport Rd CH62, CH63 . . . . .43 D7
Allports The CH62 . . . . .43 D7
All Saints WA4 . . . . .17 E3
All Saints RC Prim Sch
Crewe CW1 . . . . .191 A4
Warrington WA2 . . . . .9 B2
All Saints Upton CE Prim
Sch WA8 . . . . .12 B3
Allysum Cl WA7 . . . . .49 F4
Alma Ave CW1 . . . . .190 C6
Alma Cl
Macclesfield SK11 . . . . . . .112 A7
Scholar Green ST7 . . . . . . .194 E7
Alma La SK9 . . . . .60 A7
Alma Rd SK7 . . . . .37 A8
Alma St
Chester CH2 . . . . .118 F2
Newton-le-W WA12. . . . . . . .2 B3
Almeda Rd L24 . . . . .21 A2
Almer Dr WA5 . . . . .15 C5
Almond Ave
Crewe CW1 . . . . .190 D6
Runcorn WA7 . . . . .49 C8
Almond Dr WA5 . . . . .6 F6
Almond Gr
Warrington WA1 . . . . .17 B7
Weaverham CW8 . . . . .102 E7
Widnes WA8 . . . . .22 D8
Almond Pl ST5 . . . . .210 E1
Almond Tree Cl L24 . . . . . . .21 E1
Almond Wlk M31 . . . . .11 D3
Almshouses CW11 . . . . . . .175 C6
Alnwick Dr CH65 . . . . .70 D2
Alpass Ave WA5 . . . . .16 A8
Alpine St WA12 . . . . .2 A3
ALPORT 169 C4
Alport Rd SY13 . . . . .226 B1
ALPRAHAM 169 C4

Alpraham Cres CH2. . . . . . .118 E6
Alpraham Gn CW6 . . . . .169 E5
ALPRAHAM GREEN 169 C4
Alric Wlk M22 . . . . .33 E8
ALSAGER 193 E5
Alsager Highfields Com
Prim Sch ST7 . . . . .193 D4
Alsager Rd
Audley ST7. . . . . .209 D5
Haslington CW11. . . . . .192 C7
Sandbach CW11 . . . . .193 E5
Alsager Sch ST7 . . . . .193 B4
Alsager Sta ST7 . . . . .193 E3
Alsfeld Way SK22 . . . . .39 A8
Alt WA8 . . . . .12 B2
Alton Dr SK10 . . . . .87 F1
Alton Rd SK9 . . . . .59 F7
Alton St CW2 . . . . .190 B3
ALTRINCHAM 31 C8
Altrincham Priory Hospl
WA15. . . . . .32 A7
Altrincham Rd
Styal SK9 . . . . .33 D4
Wilmslow SK9 . . . . .33 C2
Alt Wlk CW7 . . . . .127 A2
Alumbrook Ave CW4 . . . . . .130 C3
Alum Ct CW4 . . . . .130 C2
Alum Cres CH4 . . . . .141 A6
Alundale Rd CW7 . . . . .126 C3
ALVANLEY 73 C2
Alvanley Dr WA6. . . . . .73 C2
Alvanley Prim Sch
WA6. . . . . .73 D1
Alvanley Rd
Ellesmere Port CH66. . . . . . .69 E4
Helsby WA6 . . . . .73 C2
Alvanley Rise CW7 . . . . . . .104 A6
Alvanley Terr WA6 . . . . .49 B1
Alvanley View CH2 . . . . .72 B3
Alvanley Way CH66 . . . . . . .69 E4
Alvaston Bsns Pk
CW5. . . . . .204 F8
Alvaston Rd CW5 . . . . .204 F5
Alvaston Wlk CW2 . . . . .189 F2
Alverstone Ct WA5. . . . . . . .14 C7
Alverton Cl WA8 . . . . .13 A5
Alveston Dr SK10 . . . . .86 F1
Alveston Dr WA9 . . . . .1 A3
Alvingham Cl 🛛 CW9 . . . . .104 B8
Alvis Rd CH5 . . . . .116 B3
Alwyn Gdns CH2 . . . . .118 F8
Alyndale Rd CH4 . . . . .140 D6
Alyn Rd CH2. . . . . .96 F1
Amberleigh Cl WA4 . . . . . . .27 B3
Amberley Dr WA15 . . . . .32 B8
Amberley Rd SK11 . . . . . . .112 A6
Ambleside Cl
Bebington CH62. . . . . .43 E7
Crewe CW2 . . . . .189 E2
Macclesfield SK11 . . . . . . .111 F6
Runcorn WA7 . . . . .49 E5
Ambleside Cres WA2 . . . . . . .8 C3
Ambleside Cl CW12. . . . . . .156 A2
Ambleside Rd CH65 . . . . . . .70 C2
Ambrose Ct WA1 . . . . .16 D6
Ambuscade Cl CW1. . . . . . .190 E5
Amelia Cl WA8 . . . . .13 B4
Amelia St WA2 . . . . .16 C6
Amersham Cl SK10 . . . . .87 C3
America Ho 🛮 WA1. . . . . . .16 C5
Ampleforth Ho 🛮 WA1. . . .16 C5
Amusement Depot
CW7 . . . . .126 E2
Amy St CW2 . . . . .190 C3
Anchorage The
🛮 Lymm WA13 . . . . .18 D3
Neston CH64 . . . . .66 C7
Waverton CH3 . . . . .143 A5
Anchor Cl WA7 . . . . .50 D6
Anchor Ct WA1 . . . . .16 A4
Ancoats Rd WA16, SK9. . . . .83 F8
Anderson Cl
Crewe CW1 . . . . .191 A4
Warrington WA2 . . . . .9 B2
Anderson Ct CH62 . . . . .43 D6
Andersons Ind Est
WA8. . . . . .23 A6
Anderson St 🗠 SK10. . . . .112 C8
ANDERTON 78 D4
Anderton Boat Lift &
Nature Pk* CW9 . . . . .78 D3
Anderton Grange
CW9. . . . . .103 F7
Andertons La SK10,
SK11. . . . . .86 B1
Anderton Way SK9 . . . . .34 D3
Andover Cl WA2 . . . . .8 E1
Andover Rd WA11 . . . . .1 E8
Andrew Cl WA8 . . . . .22 C8
Andrew Cres CW2 . . . . .237 C1
Andrew Gr SK10 . . . . .113 A7
Andrew La SK6 . . . . .37 E6
Andrew's Cl CH3 . . . . .121 B2
Andrew's Wlk CH60. . . . . . . .41 B8
Andromeda Way WA9 . . . . . . .6 B7
Anemone Way WA9 . . . . .6 A7
Angelina Cl CW11 . . . . .174 D7
Anglers Rest M44. . . . . .11 E5
Anglesey Cl 🛛 CH65 . . . . . . .70 C1
Anglesey Dr SK12. . . . . .36 F6
Anglesey Water SK12 . . . . . .36 F6
Angus Gr CW10 . . . . .128 D2
Angus Rd CH66 . . . . .69 C5
Angus Wlk SK10 . . . . .86 F2
Ankers Knowl La
SK11. . . . . .114 D8

Ankers La SK11 . . . . .114 D6
Annable Rd M44 . . . . .11 F8
Annan Cl 🛛 CW12 . . . . . . .157 A1
Annan Ct CH66 . . . . .69 D7
Anne Ct ST7 . . . . .210 D6
Anne's Way CH4 . . . . .237 C1
Annette Ave WA12. . . . . .2 A5
Annie St WA2 . . . . .16 C6
Annions La CW5 . . . . .205 F1
Annis Rd SK9 . . . . .60 B2
Ann St W WA8 . . . . .23 B7
Ann St
Northwich CW9 . . . . .79 D1
Runcorn WA7 . . . . .23 B3
Ansdell Rd WA8 . . . . .13 C2
Anson Cl SK7. . . . . .35 F5
Anson Engine Mus The*
SK12 . . . . .37 C4
Anson Rd
Handforth SK9 . . . . .34 E1
Poynton SK12 . . . . .37 B3
Anthony Dr CW9 . . . . .126 F7
Anthony's Way CH60 . . . . . . .41 A7
Antons Cl L26 . . . . .21 A6
Antons Rd L26. . . . . .21 A6
Antony Rd WA4. . . . . .16 B1
Antrim Cl WA11 . . . . .1 C6
Antrim Dr CH66 . . . . .69 F2
Antrim Rd WA2 . . . . .8 E1
ANTROBUS 53 C4
Antrobus St CW12 . . . . . . .156 D3
Anvil Cl
Elton CH2. . . . . .72 B4
Haslington CW11. . . . . .174 F3
Saughall CH1 . . . . .94 A1
Appleby Cl
Macclesfield SK11 . . . . . . .111 F5
Widnes WA8 . . . . .22 C8
Appleby Cres WA16. . . . . . . .58 A4
Appleby Gr CH62 . . . . .43 D6
Appleby Rd WA2 . . . . .8 C3
Appleby Wlk 🛮 SK8 . . . . . .22 C8
Applecross Cl WA3 . . . . .10 A6
Appledale Dr CH66 . . . . .95 A8
Applecroft ST5 . . . . .210 E1
Appledore Cl CW8 . . . . . . .103 D7
Appleford Cl WA4 . . . . .26 E7
Apple Market St 🗠
CW9. . . . . .103 F8
APPLETON 13 A2
Appleton Cl CW12 . . . . .178 E8
Appleton Dr CH65 . . . . .69 F3
Appleton Hall Gdns
WA4. . . . . .26 E5
Appleton Mews WA15 . . . . . .18 C4
APPLETON PARK 26 D5
Appleton Rd
Chester CH2 . . . . .118 E6
Widnes WA8 . . . . .13 B1
Appleton St
Widnes WA8 . . . . .23 B7
Northwich CW9 . . . . .78 D1
APPLETON THORN 27 B4
Appleton Thorn Prim Sch
WA4. . . . . .27 C4
Appleton Thorn Trad Est
WA4. . . . . .27 C5
Appleton Village WA8 . . . . .13 B1
Appleton Wlk 🛮 SK9 . . . . . .34 E1
Appletree Gr WA2 . . . . .9 A2
Apple Tree Gr CH66 . . . . . . .94 F8
Apple Tree Gr CH64 . . . . . . .66 E8
Appleyards La CH4 . . . . . . .141 E7
Apprentice La SK9 . . . . .33 F3
April Rise SK10 . . . . .87 A1
Arabis Gdns WA9 . . . . .6 B7
Aragon Cl WA7 . . . . .24 C3
Aragon Gn CH1. . . . . .117 E6
Aran Cl L24 . . . . .21 D1
Arbour Cl
Macclesfield SK10 . . . . .87 D3
Northwich CW9 . . . . .104 C8
Arbour Cres SK10 . . . . .87 D3
Arbour Mews SK10 . . . . .87 D3
Arbour St ST7 . . . . .210 D5
Arbury La WA2 . . . . .8 C6
Arcade The
Ellesmere Port CH65 . . . . . . .70 A5
🔞 Northwich CW9 . . . . . . .103 F8
Archer Ave WA4 . . . . .16 E2
Archer Cl SK10 . . . . .87 E7
Archers Gn CH62 . . . . .43 E3
Archers Green Rd WA5 . . . . .7 B3
Archers Way
Blacon CH1 . . . . .118 A2
Ellesmere Port CH65 . . . . . . .69 E1
Arches Com Prim Sch The
CH1 . . . . .117 E5
Archway Wlk CW12 . . . . .2 E3
ARCLID 154 B1
Arclid Cl SK9 . . . . .34 E1
Arclid Ct 🔟 CW12 . . . . . . .156 F3
ARCLID GREEN 176 A8
Arclid Green Ind Est
CW11. . . . . .176 B8
Arden Wlk 12 A2
Ardenbrook Rise SK10 . . . . .86 F6
Arden Cl
Gatley SK8. . . . . .34 C7
Tarvin CH3 . . . . .121 C3
Warrington WA3 . . . . .10 B6
Arden Ct CW12 . . . . .179 B7
Arden Dr CH64. . . . . .66 E6
Ardens Ct SK22 . . . . .39 D7
Ardens Mdw CW6 . . . . .168 D8
Arden St SK22 . . . . .39 C7

Arderne Ave CW2 . . . . .190 A2
Arderne Ho CH2 . . . . .118 F7
Arderne Pl 🗠 SK9 . . . . .60 A1
Ardern Lea WA6 . . . . .73 D1
Ardleigh Cl CW1 . . . . .189 F8
Arena Gdns WA2 . . . . .9 A3
Argosy Dr M90 . . . . .32 F7
Argyle Ct 🔟 WA16 . . . . .57 A2
Argyll Ave
Bebington CH62. . . . . .43 D4
Chester CH4 . . . . .141 A7
Argyll Cl SK10 . . . . .87 A1
Ariel Gdns WA3 . . . . .5 A2
Ariel Wlk 🛮 WA3 . . . . .3 E8
Arizona Cres WA5 . . . . .15 B7
Arkenshaw Rd WA3 . . . . .9 A7
Arkenstone Cl WA8 . . . . .12 C2
Arkle Ave SK8, SK9 . . . . . . .34 B8
Arkle Ct 🛮 CH3 . . . . .119 B1
Arklow Dr L24 . . . . .21 D2
Arkwright Cl CW7 . . . . .149 A8
Arkwright Ct WA7 . . . . .23 F3
Arkwright Rd WA7 . . . . .23 F3
ARLEY 54 C7
Arley Ave WA4. . . . . .26 D8
Arley Cl
Alsager ST7. . . . . .193 C3
Chester CH2 . . . . .118 F6
Macclesfield SK11 . . . . . . .112 A7
Arley Ct CW9 . . . . .103 E5
Arley Dr WA8 . . . . .13 A3
Arley End WA16 . . . . .29 C4
ARLEY GREEN 54 A5
Arley Hall & Gdns*
CW9. . . . . .54 D6
Arley Mossend La
CW9. . . . . .54 D2
Arley Pl CW2 . . . . .206 A8
Arley Rd
Antrobus CW9 . . . . .54 B7
Appleton Thorn WA4 . . . . . . .27 C3
Northwich CW9 . . . . .104 C8
Arley Wlk CW11 . . . . .174 D5
Arlington Cres CW2 . . . . . . .206 C8
Arlington Dr
Golborne WN7 . . . . .4 C8
Macclesfield SK11 . . . . . . .112 A6
Poynton SK12 . . . . .36 D3
Warrington WA5 . . . . .14 E4
Arlington Way SK9 . . . . .59 E5
Armistead Way CW4 . . . . . .130 A5
Armitstead Rd CW11 . . . . . .174 E7
Armitt St SK11 . . . . .112 C7
Armour Ave WA2 . . . . .8 B2
Armoury Court Mews 🛮
SK11. . . . . .112 B6
Armoury Twrs 🛮
SK11. . . . . .112 B6
Armstrong Cl
Audlem CW3 . . . . .229 F4
Warrington WA5 . . . . .15 B7
Armthorpe Dr CH66 . . . . . . .69 C5
Arncliffe Dr WA5 . . . . .6 F6
Arndale WA7 . . . . .49 E5
Arnhem Cres WA2 . . . . .16 C7
Arnhem Way CH3 . . . . .142 B5
Arnold Pl WA3 . . . . .22 C7
Arnold's Cres CH4 . . . . .139 A3
Arnold St
Nantwich CW5 . . . . .204 E6
Warrington WA1 . . . . .16 D6
Arnside Ave
Congleton CW12 . . . . .156 A2
Haydock WA11. . . . . .1 B6
Arnside Cl
High Lane SK6 . . . . .37 E8
Winsford CW7 . . . . .126 D2
Arnside Gr WA4 . . . . .16 B1
Arpley Rd WA1 . . . . .16 B4
Arpley St WA1 . . . . .16 A4
Arradon Ct CH2 . . . . .118 E5
Arran Ave CH65 . . . . .70 C1
Arran Cl
Holmes Chapel CW4 . . . . . .130 C2
Warrington WA3 . . . . .9 A2
Arran Dr WA6 . . . . .73 C6
Arrivals Way M90 . . . . .33 B7
Arron Pl WA2 . . . . .189 D3
Arrowcroft Rd CH3 . . . . . . .142 E7
Arrowsmith Dr ST7 . . . . . . .193 B3
Arrowsmith Rd WA11 . . . . . . .1 F7
ARTHILL 30 B8
Arthill La
Little Bollington WA14. . . . . .20 B1
Rostherne WA16. . . . . .30 A6
Arthog Dr WA15 . . . . .31 F8
Arthog Rd
Altrincham WA14 . . . . .31 F8
Altrincham WA15. . . . . .32 A8
Arthur Ave CH65 . . . . .70 C6
Arthur St
Chester CH1 . . . . .118 A2
🛛 Crewe CW1 . . . . .190 D2
Lostock Gralam CW9 . . . . . .80 A2
🗠 Runcorn WA7 . . . . .23 A2
Warrington WA2 . . . . .16 A6
Artists La SK10 . . . . .85 C7
Artle Rd CW2 . . . . .206 C8
Arundel Ave WA3 . . . . .3 E8
Arundel Cl
Knutsford WA16 . . . . .82 A8
Macclesfield SK10 . . . . .87 F2
Wistaston CW2 . . . . .205 E8
Arundel Ct CH65 . . . . .70 E3

Arundell Cl WA5 6 F6
Arundel Rd SK8 35 A6
Ascol Dr WA16 80 C3
Ascot Ave WA7 49 B6
Ascot Cl
Congleton CW12 156 D4
Macclesfield SK10 87 C3
Warrington, Martinscroft WA1 17 E7
Warrington WA4 17 C2
Ascot Ct CW9 104 C8
Ascot Dr CH66 69 E3
Ascot Ho CH1 118 B2
Ash Ave
Irlam M44 11 D5
Newton-le-W WA12 2 C2
Ashbank CW9 104 D7
Ashberry Cl SK9 60 D8
Ashberry Dr WA4 27 B5
Ashbourne Ave WA7 49 B6
Ashbourne Cl CH66 94 E8
Ashbourne Dr
Chorlton CW2 207 C1
High Lane SK6 37 F6
Ashbourne Mews 1 SK10 111 F8
Ashbourne Rd
Hazel Grove SK7 36 F8
Warrington WA5 15 B5
Ashbrook Ave WA7 49 F3
Ashbrook Cres WA2 16 D8
Ashbrook Dr SK10 87 A6
Ashbrook Rd
Bollington SK10 87 F7
Nether Alderley SK10 85 F6
Ashburton CH64 66 C8
Ashbury Cl WA7 24 D2
Ashbury Dr WA11 1 D7
Ashby Dr CW11 174 C5
Ashby Pl CH2 237 C4
Ash Cl
Ellesmere Port CH66 69 F1
Holmes Chapel CW4 130 D4
Malpas SY14 213 C5
Tarporley CW6 146 D2
Ashcroft Ave CW2 206 B3
Ashcroft Cl SK9 59 F5
Ashcroft Ct M44 11 D5
Ashcroft Rd WA13 19 B4
Ash Ct 15 WA16 57 A2
Ashdale Cl ST7 193 C5
Ashdene Prim Sch SK9 59 F5
Ashdene Rd SK9 59 F5
Ashdown Cl SK8 35 A6
Ashdown La WA3 10 B5
Ashdown Rd WA16 82 F6
Ashenhurst Rd ST7 193 F3
Ashenough Rd ST7 210 D6
Asher Ct WA4 27 D4
Ashfield Cl WA13 19 B4
Ashfield Cres
Bebington CH62 43 D8
Blacon CH1 117 D5
Ashfield Dr SK10 87 A2
Ashfield Gdns WA4 16 F3
Ashfield Gr M44 11 E6
Ashfield Ho 6 CH64 66 E8
Ashfield Rd
Bebington CH62 43 C8
Ellesmere Port CH65 70 C5
Ashfield Rd N 1 CH65 70 C5
Ashfield St CW10 151 D8
Ashford Cl SK9 34 C4
Ashford Dr WA4 26 E3
Ashford Rd SK9 60 A4
Ashford Way 1 WA8 13 D1
Ashgate La CW9 79 F6
Ash Gr
Chester CH4 141 B5
Congleton CW12 156 A3
Ellesmere Port CH66 69 C6
Gatley SK8 34 B8
Golborne WA3 3 B8
Handforth SK9 34 C3
Knutsford WA16 57 D1
Macclesfield SK11 112 C4
Middlewich CW10 151 D7
Nantwich CW5 204 F3
Rode Heath ST7 193 F7
Runcorn WA7 49 C8
Warrington WA4 16 D3
Weaverham CW8 102 E7
Widnes WA8 22 D8
Ashgrove CW7 149 D8
Ash Grove Prim Sch SK11 112 C4
Ash Hay La
Hoole Bank CH2 119 C8
Picton CH2 96 C2
Ash Ho
Chester CH2 118 C5
8 Sandbach CW11 175 B6
Ash House La CW8 77 D7
Ash La
Warrington WA4 26 E8
Widnes WA8 22 A8
Ashlands WA6 74 C7
Ash Lawn Ct CH2 118 C4
Ashlea Dr CW5 205 E5
Ashleigh Cl CH4 140 E6
ASHLEY 31 E5
Ashley CE Prim Sch WA15 31 F5
Ashley Cl WA4 17 C3
Ashley Ct
Frodsham WA6 74 A8
Holt LL13 196 D8
Warrington WA4 26 C6
Ashley Dr
Bramhall SK7 35 C6
Hartford CW8 103 A6
Ashley Gdns
Clutton CH3 182 C1
High Lane SK6 37 D8
Ashley Gn WA8 22 D8
Ashley Grange CW9 103 E3
ASHLEY HEATH 31 E8
Ashley Mdw CW1 191 D5
Ashleymill La WA14 31 D7
Ashley Mill La N WA14 31 E8
Ashley Rd
Ashley, Ashley Heath WA14, WA15 31 E7
Ashley WA14, WA15, WA16 31 C4
Handforth SK9 34 B1
Mere WA16 56 D8
Runcorn WA7 23 D2
Ashley Ret Pk WA8 23 B7
Ashley Sch WA8 12 D1
Ashley Sta WA15 31 E5
Ashley Way WA8 23 B7
Ashley Way W WA8 22 F7
Ash Lo SK12 36 D4
Ashmead Cl ST7 193 E3
Ashmead Mews ST7 193 E3
Ashmore Cl
Middlewich CW10 151 C6
Warrington WA3 10 A3
Ashmore's La ST7 193 D3
Ash Mount CW3 232 B1
Ashmuir Cl
Blacon CH1 117 E3
Crewe CW1 190 B6
Ashness Dr SK7 35 E8
Ash Priors WA8 12 D3
Ash Rd
Crewe CW1 190 D6
Cuddington CW8 101 F2
Elton CH2 72 C3
Haydock WA11 1 E7
Hollinfare WA3 11 A2
Lymm WA13 18 C3
Partington M31 11 D3
Poynton SK12 36 F3
Warrington WA5 14 F4
Winwick WA2 8 B6
Ashridge St WA7 22 F3
Ash St CW9 79 A1
Ash Terr SK11 112 C4
Ashton Ave SK10 86 D1
Ashton Cl
Bebington CH62 43 E3
Congleton CW12 157 B1
Frodsham WA6 49 C1
Middlewich CW10 151 D5
Northwich CW9 103 E4
Runcorn WA7 48 F6
Ashton Ct WA6 49 C1
Ashton Dr WA6 49 C1
ASHTON HAYES 121 F7
Ashton Hayes Prim Sch CH3 121 F8
Ashton La CH3 121 E6
Ashton Rd
Manley WA6 99 E4
Newton-le-W WA12 2 C5
Norley WA6 100 B4
ASHTON'S GREEN 1 B3
Ashton St WA2 16 B6
Ashtree Cl
Neston CH64 67 A7
Prestbury SK10 87 C8
Ashtree Croft CH64 68 A7
Ashtree Ct CH2 237 C4
Ashtree Dr CH64 67 A7
Ashtree Farm Ct CH64 68 A7
Ash View ST7 195 B2
Ashville Ct CW2 206 B7
Ashville Ind Est WA7 49 E3
Ashville Way WA7 49 E3
Ash Way CH60 41 B6
Ashwood WA14 31 B8
Ashwood Ave
Golborne WA3 3 D8
Warrington WA1 16 E7
Ashwood Cl
Barnton CW8 78 B4
Ellesmere Port CH66 69 D1
Widnes WA8 22 A7
Ashwood Cres CW8 78 B3
Ashwood Ct CH2 119 A3
Ashwood Farm Ct CH2 96 B6
Ashwood La CH2 96 B5
Ashwood Rd SK12 38 D6
Ashworth Pk WA16 81 F8
Asiatic Cotts CH5 116 B3
Askerbank La SK11 159 A1
Askett Cl WA11 1 C7
Askrigg Ave CH66 69 B5
Aspen Cl
Ellesmere Port CH66 69 E1
Harriseahead ST7 195 E3
Heswall CH60 41 D8
Aspen Gr
Saughall CH1 117 B7
Warrington WA1 17 A7
Aspens The CW8 101 E5
Aspen Way
Chester CH2 119 B4
High Lane SK6 38 A7
Aspinall Cl WA2 9 A3
Aspull Cl WA3 9 C4
Asquith Cl CW1 191 C5
Assheton Cl WA12 2 B4
Assheton Wlk L24 21 E2
ASTBURY 178 B7
Astbury Cl
Crewe CW1 190 A7
Golborne WA3 4 B8
Kidsgrove ST7 195 C3
Astbury Dr CW8 78 A4
Astbury Lane Ends CW12 178 F8
ASTBURY MARSH 156 B1
Astbury Mere Ctry Pk* CW12 156 B2
Astbury St Mary's CE Prim Sch CW12 178 B8
Astbury St CW12 156 C2
Aster Cres WA7 49 F5
Aster Rd WA11 1 F7
Aster Wlk M31 11 F2
ASTLE 109 D8
Astle Cl CW10 151 C7
Astle Ct SK11 84 A3
Astle La SK10 84 E1
Astley Cl
Knutsford WA16 82 C7
Warrington WA4 16 B3
Widnes WA8 12 C3
Astley Ct M44 11 E8
Astley Rd M44 11 E8
ASTMOOR 23 E3
Astmoor Bridge La WA7 23 F2
Astmoor East Intc WA7 24 A3
Astmoor Ind Est WA7 23 F3
Astmoor La WA7 23 F1
Astmoor Prim Sch WA7 23 F2
Astmoor Rd
Runcorn, Astmoor WA7 23 E3
Runcorn WA7 23 C3
ASTON
Nantwich 217 C2
Runcorn 50 D1
Aston Ave
Warrington WA3 9 F4
Winsford CW7 126 B2
Aston by Sutton Prim Sch WA7 50 C2
Aston Ct WA1 9 C1
Aston Fields Rd WA7 50 E4
Aston Forge WA7 50 F5
Aston Gn WA7 50 E6
ASTON HEATH 50 E2
ASTON JUXTA MONDRUM 188 D6
Aston La
Aston WA7 50 C2
Runcorn WA7 50 F5
Woore CW3 232 E1
Aston La N WA7 50 E4
Aston La S WA7 50 E3
Aston Rd ST5 210 D1
Aston Way
13 Handforth SK9 34 D5
Middlewich CW10 128 E1
Astor Dr WA4 26 F8
Atcherley Cl CW5 218 E8
Athelbrae Cl CW8 103 F7
Atherton La M44 11 E5
Atherton Rd CH65 69 F6
Athey St Mill 2 SK11 112 C7
Athey St SK11 112 C8
Athlone Rd WA2 8 A1
Athol Cl
Bebington CH62 43 E5
Newton-le-W WA12 1 F4
Athol Dr CH62 43 E5
Atholl Ave CW2 190 C1
Atholl Cl SK10 87 A1
Athol Rd SK7 35 D5
Atkin Cl CW12 156 A3
Atlanta Ave M90 33 A8
Atlanta Gdns WA5 15 B8
Atlantic Trad Pk CW7 126 E5
Atlas Way CH66 69 F7
Atterbury Cl WA8 12 C2
Attlee Ave WA3 5 C4
Attwood Cl CW1 191 C4
Attwood Rise ST7 195 A2
Attwood St ST7 195 A2
Atworth Terr CH64 67 F8
Aubourn Cl WA8 12 C3
Auckery Ave CH66 69 D3
Auckland Rd CH1 117 D4
AUDLEM 230 B4
Audlem Cl WA7 49 F4
Audlem Dr CW9 104 A6
Audlem Rd
Hankelow CW3 230 C7
Hatherton CW5 219 D3
Nantwich CW5 204 F3
Audlem St James' CE Prim Sch CW3 230 A5
AUDLEY 209 C2
Audley Cres CH4 141 E6
Audley Rd
Alsager ST7 193 E1
Barthomley CW2 208 E5
Newcastle-u-Lyme ST7, ST5 210 B2
Talke ST7 210 B6
Audley St W CW1 190 D5
Audley St CW1 190 D5
Audre Cl WA5 14 D6
Aughton Way CH4 139 D4
Augusta Dr SK10 87 B4
Augusta Ho CH1 117 F6
Austell Rd 3 M22 33 D8
Austen Cl 1 CW11 174 D6
Austen Dr WA2 8 A6
Austen Ho SK10 86 F1
Austin Cl CW7 149 C6
Austins Hill CH3 144 C8
Austin St CW9 79 D1
Austral Ave WA1 17 C7
Australia La WA4 17 C1
Autumn Ave WA16 57 C2
Avebury Cl
Golborne WA3 3 E8
Widnes WA8 13 F3
Aveley Cl WA1 17 B7
Avens Rd M31 11 F3
Avenue One CW1 207 C8
Avenue The
Alderley Edge SK9 60 A1
Alsager ST7 193 D4
Altrincham WA15 31 F8
Bebington CH62 43 C8
Comberbach CW9 78 D8
Great Barrow CH3 120 F7
High Legh WA16 29 C5
Kidsgrove ST7 194 F1
Lymm WA13 18 D1
Marston CW9 79 B3
Newton-le-W WA12 2 D4
Sandbach CW11 174 E8
Tarporley CW6 146 D1
Avenue Two CW1 207 C8
Avery Cl WA2 8 E2
Avery Cres WA11 1 C7
Avery Rd WA11 1 C7
Avery Sq WA11 1 C7
Aviemore Dr WA2 9 A3
Avocet Cl
Newton-le-W WA12 2 C4
Warrington WA2 8 D3
Avocet Dr CW7 149 D6
Avon WA8 12 A2
Avon Ave WA5 14 F4
Avon Cl
Kidsgrove ST7 195 B2
Macclesfield SK10 87 A2
Neston CH64 66 E6
Avon Ct ST7 193 C5
Avondale CH65 70 B2
Avondale Ave CH62 43 F5
Avondale Dr WA8 12 B1
Avondale Rd WA11 1 C7
Avondale Rise SK9 60 D6
Avon Dr
Congleton CW12 156 F1
Crewe CW1 191 A5
Avonlea Cl CH4 140 E4
Avon Rd
Altrincham WA15 31 E8
Culcheth WA3 5 A2
Gatley SK8 34 C7
Avonside Way SK11 112 C5
Avon Wlk CW7 127 A2
Avro Way M90 32 F7
Axminster Wlk SK7 35 E7
Aycliffe Wlk 6 WA8 22 C8
Aylesbury Cl
Ellesmere Port CH66 69 C3
Macclesfield SK10 87 D3
Aylesby Cl WA16 57 B1
Aylsham Cl WA8 12 C4
Ayrshire Cl CW10 128 D2
Ayrshire Way CW12 157 A1
Aysgarth Ave CW1 173 B1
Azalea Gdns WA9 6 A7
Azalea Gr WA7 49 F4

B

Babbacombe Rd WA5 14 E4
Babbage Rd CH5 116 A4
BACHE 118 B5
Bache Ave CH2 118 C5
Bache Dr CH2 118 D5
Bachefield Ave CH3 142 A6
Bache Hall Ct CH2 118 C5
Bache Hall Est CH2 118 C5
Bachelor's Ct CH3 142 A8
Bachelor's La CH3 142 A8
Bache Sta CH2 118 D5
Back Bridge St WA12 2 B3
Back Brook Pl WA4 16 E3
Back Coole La CW3 229 B4
Back Crosland Terr WA6 73 B2
Back Cross La
Congleton CW12 179 A8
Newton-le-W WA12 2 B4
Back Eastford Rd WA4 16 A1
Back Eddisbury Rd SK11 113 C7
BACKFORD 95 A4
Backford Cl WA7 50 C5
Backford Cross CH66 94 F7
Backford Gdns CH1 94 F7
Back Forshaw St WA2 16 C7
Back Heathcote St ST7 195 A2
Back High St 3 WA7 23 A2
Back Jodrell St SK22 39 B7
Back La
Alpraham CW6 169 D6
Altrincham WA15 32 B4
Bate Heath CW9 54 D7
Betley CW2 208 C1
Brereton Green CW11 153 D6
Back La *continued*
Burtonwood WA5 6 D7
Congleton CW12 156 A4
Duddon CW6 145 A6
Helsby WA6 73 D2
Higher Whitley WA4 52 E4
High Legh WA14 29 F5
Marton CW12, SK11 133 F2
No Man's Heath SY14 214 A4
Norbury SY13 215 F5
Partington WA14 20 C5
Plumley WA16 81 B1
Shavington CW2 206 E4
Smallwood CW11 176 D8
Swan Green WA16 106 B8
Tattenhall CH3 167 C2
Threapwood SY14 222 E7
Warrington WA5 14 A3
Wybunbury CW5 220 C6
Backlands CW1 190 C6
Back Lanes CW6 146 B2
Back Legh St WA12 2 A3
Back Market St WA12 2 A3
Back Paradise St 4 SK11 112 C7
Back Park St CW12 156 E2
Back Queen St CH1 237 B3
Back River St 1 CW12 156 D3
Back Union Rd 3 SK22 39 C7
Back Wallgate 13 SK11 112 D8
Badbury Cl WA11 1 D7
Badcock's La CW6 185 E4
BADDILEY 203 B1
Baddiley Cl CW5 203 D2
Baddiley Hall La CW5 217 A8
Baddiley La CW5 203 D1
Baddington La CW5 204 C1
Badger Ave CW1 190 B5
Badger Bait CH64 66 F6
Badger Cl WA7 50 A6
Badger Ho SK10 87 D2
Badger Rd
Macclesfield SK10 87 D2
Prestbury SK10 87 A7
Badgers Cl
Christleton CH3 142 E7
1 Ellesmere Port CH66 94 F8
1 Winsford CW7 126 A1
Badgers Croft ST5 210 E1
Badgers Pk CH64 66 F6
Badgersrake La CH66 68 D3
Badgers Set CW8 101 D5
Badgers Wlk CH2 95 E2
Badgers Wood CW2 205 E8
Bag La
Cuddington CW8, WA6 101 E7
Norley WA6 101 A6
Bagley La CW3 230 B1
Bagmere Cl
Brereton Green CW11 153 F4
Sandbach CW11 174 F7
Bagmere La CW11 154 B5
Bagnall Cl WA5 15 C5
Bagot Ave WA5 15 F8
Bagstock Ave SK12 36 E2
Baguley Ave WA8 22 A5
Bahama Cl WA11 1 D8
Bahama Rd WA11 1 D8
Baildon Gn CH66 69 B5
Bailey Ave CH65 69 F6
Bailey Bridge Cl CH2 118 D4
Bailey Bsns Pk SK10 87 F7
Bailey Cl CW1 190 C7
Bailey Cres
Congleton CW12 157 A4
Sandbach CW11 175 D6
Bailey Ct
Alsager ST7 193 E3
1 Macclesfield SK10 112 E7
Bailey La M31 11 F3
Bailey's Bank ST8 179 D3
Baileys Cl WA8 13 A5
Baileys La L26 21 A7
Bailey's La L24 21 A1
Bailey Wlk WA14 31 C8
Bainbridge Ave WA3 3 F8
Bainbridge Cres WA5 14 E8
Baines Ave M44 11 F8
Bakehurst Cl SK22 39 C7
Baker Cl CW2 190 A2
Baker Dr CH66 69 E3
Baker Rd WA7 48 D7
Baker's Cl CW7 126 E1
Baker's Ct CW7 126 E1
Baker's La
Swan Green WA16 106 D6
Winsford CW7 126 E1
Bakers Pl WA2 16 B7
Baker St 8 SK11 112 C7
Bakers Villas The CW12 156 D2
Bakestonedale Rd SK10 63 E4
Bakewell Cl CH66 94 E8
Bakewell Rd
Burtonwood WA5 7 A7
Hazel Grove SK7 36 E8
Bala Cl WA5 7 E2
BALDERTON 140 C1
Baldock Cl WA4 17 C3
Balfour Cl CW1 191 C4
Balfour St WA7 22 F1
Balham Cl WA8 13 A4

Balharry Ave WA11 . . . . .1 E7
Ballantyne Pl WA2 . . . . .8 A6
Ballantyne Way **5** WA3 . .3 E8
Ballater Cres 119 B2
Ballater Dr WA2 . . . . .8 E4
Ballerat Cl CH1 . . . . .117 D4
Balliol Cl SK11 . . . . .112 F3
Ball La
  Bollington SK10 . . . . .87 D5
  Kingsley WA6 . . . . .75 E4
BALL O' DITTON 12 E2
Ball Pathway WA8 . . . . .12 E1
Balmoral Ave
  Crewe CW2 . . . . .190 B1
  Northwich CW9 . . . . .104 A5
Balmoral Cl
  Knutsford WA16 . . . . .57 B1
  Winsford CW7 . . . . .126 C3
Balmoral Cres SK10 . . . . . . .87 F2
Balmoral Dr
  Helsby WA6 . . . . .73 B4
  High Lane SK6 . . . . .37 E7
  Holmes Chapel CW4 . . . . .130 B2
  Poynton SK12 . . . . .36 D3
Balmoral Gdns
  Congleton CW12 . . . . .156 F4
  Ellesmere Port CH65 . . . . . .70 D3
Balmoral Pk CH1 . . . . .118 B3
Balmoral Pl CW5 . . . . .205 D4
Balmoral Rd
  Warrington WA4 . . . . .16 F2
  Widnes WA8 . . . . .13 A4
Balmoral Way SK9 . . . . .60 C8
BALTERLEY 208 C1
BALTERLEY GREEN 208 C2
BALTERLEY HEATH 207 F1
Baltimore Gdns WA15 . . . . . .15 C2
Bamburgh Ct CH65 . . . . .70 E3
Bamford Cl
  Bollington SK10 . . . . .88 A7
  Gatley SK8 . . . . .34 D8
  Runcorn WA7 . . . . .49 C7
Bamford St SK10 . . . . .87 E1
Banastre Dr WA12 . . . . .2 F3
Banbury Cl SK10 . . . . .87 E2
Banbury Dr WA5 . . . . .15 C5
Banbury St ST7 . . . . .194 D1
Bancroft CW8 . . . . .76 F4
Bancroft Rd WA8 . . . . .13 D2
Bandon Cl L24 . . . . .21 D2
Banff Ave CH63 . . . . .43 D5
Bangor Cl **11** CH66 . . . . . .94 F8
Bank Cl
  Chester CH2 . . . . .118 E5
  Macclesfield SK11 . . . . . . .112 E7
  Neston CH64 . . . . .67 A6
Bank Cott **3** ST7 . . . . . . .195 A2
Bankes' La
  Runcorn, Weston Point
    WA7 . . . . .48 E6
  Runcorn, Weston WA7 . . . . .48 F5
Bank Farm Mews
  SY14 . . . . .214 E6
Bankfield Ave
  Irlam M44 . . . . .11 D5
  Wistaston CW2 . . . . .206 A7
Bankfield Rd WA4 . . . . .12 C1
Bankfield Sch The
  WA8 . . . . .12 D1
Bankfields Dr CH62 . . . . . . .44 B5
Bank Gdns WA6 . . . . .14 E4
Bankhall La WA14,
  WA15 . . . . .31 F8
Bankhall Pk WA1 . . . . .16 C4
BANK HEATH 3 A8
Bankhey CH64 . . . . .66 F5
Bank Ho CW7 . . . . .126 C1
Bankhouse Dr CW12 . . . . . .157 A5
Bank House La
  Helsby WA6 . . . . .73 C4
  Smallwood CW11 . . . . .177 A6
Bank La
  Burland CW5 . . . . .203 D8
  Congleton CW12 . . . . .134 C1
  Rainow SK10 . . . . .89 D6
Banklands Cl M44 . . . . .11 D5
Bank Mews WA6 . . . . .73 C4
Bank Pl SK9 . . . . .60 B7
BANK QUAY 15 F4
Bank Quay Trad Est
  WA1 . . . . .15 F4
Bank Rd CH5 . . . . .91 D1
Banks Cl CW12 . . . . .156 C3
Banks Cres WA4 . . . . .16 F4
Bankside
  Altrincham WA15 . . . . .32 D6
  Runcorn WA7 . . . . .50 D7
  Warrington WA1 . . . . .16 A5
Bank Side WA8 . . . . .77 C1
Bankside Cl
  Barbridge CW5 . . . . .187 D6
  Handforth SK9 . . . . .34 D1
Bankside St ST7 . . . . .193 E5
Bank Sq SK9 . . . . .60 B7
Banks Rd CH60 . . . . .40 D8
Bank St
  Congleton CW12 . . . . .156 E2
  Macclesfield SK11 . . . . .11 B5
  Kidsgrove ST7 . . . . .195 C4
  Macclesfield SK11 . . . . . . .112 E7
  Newton-le-W WA12 . . . . .1 F3
  8 Warrington WA1 . . . . . .16 B5
  Widnes WA8 . . . . .13 D2
Bank The ST7 . . . . .195 B7
Bank Top Cotts CW5 . . . . . .204 F6
Bank View CW1 . . . . .107 E1
Banky Fields CW12 . . . . . . .156 C2

Banky Fields Cres
  CW12 . . . . .156 C1
Bannacks Cl CW5 . . . . .205 D6
Bannister Ct CW7 . . . . .149 B7
Bannister Dr CW7 . . . . .149 B6
Barbauld St WA1 . . . . .16 B5
Barber Dr ST7 . . . . .194 E7
Barberry Wlk M31 . . . . .11 F3
Barber's La
  Antrobus CW9 . . . . .53 D6
  Northwich CW8 . . . . .103 E8
Barber St SK11 . . . . .112 E6
Barbondale La WA5 . . . . . . .14 F7
Barbour Sq CH3 . . . . .166 B1
BARBRIDGE 187 C6
Barbridge Mews
  CW5 . . . . .187 D6
Barbridge Rd ST5 . . . . .210 D2
Barclay Hall WA16 . . . . .58 D4
Barclay St SK12 . . . . .36 E2
Bardell Cl SK12 . . . . .36 D2
Bardsey Cl **1** CH65 . . . . . .70 C1
Bardsley Ave WA5 . . . . .7 F1
Barford Cl WA5 . . . . .7 F1
Barford Dr
  Golborne WA3 . . . . .4 A8
  Handforth SK9 . . . . .34 C1
Barford Grange CH64 . . . . . .68 A8
Barham Ct WA3 . . . . .9 D4
Barhill Dr SY13 . . . . .214 C2
Barhill Farm Cotts
  SY13 . . . . .214 C2
Barington Dr WA7 . . . . .50 E7
Baristow Cl CH2 . . . . .237 B4
Barker's Hollow Rd
  WA4 . . . . .51 A5
Barker St
  Crewe CW2 . . . . .190 D1
  Nantwich CW5 . . . . .204 E5
Barkhill Rd CH3 . . . . .119 B3
Bark St CW12 . . . . .156 E2
Barley Castle Cl WA4 . . . . . .27 B3
Barleycastle La WA4 . . . . . .27 D4
Barleycastle Trad Est
  WA4 . . . . .27 D4
Barley Croft
  Alsager ST7 . . . . .193 E2
  Chester CH4 . . . . .142 A7
Barleycroft Terr ST7 . . . . . .194 F7
Barley Dr SK7 . . . . .35 E7
Barleyfields ST7 . . . . .209 D2
Barley Mow Cl CH66 . . . . . .69 C2
Barley Rd WA4 . . . . .17 C3
Barleywood Cl CW2 . . . . . . .206 B8
Barlow Dr CW7 . . . . .148 F8
Barlow Dr WA9 . . . . .1 A2
Barlow Hill SK11 . . . . .136 F2
Barlow Rd
  Handforth SK9 . . . . .34 B1
  Moulton CW9 . . . . .126 F7
Barlow Way CW11 . . . . .175 A8
Barmouth Cl WA5 . . . . .7 F4
Barnabas Ave CW1 . . . . . . .189 F5
Barnaby Chase CH3 . . . . . .182 C2
Barnaby Rd SK12 . . . . .36 D2
Barnacre Dr CH64 . . . . .41 B2
Barnard Cl SK11 . . . . .111 F6
Barnard St WA5 . . . . .15 D3
Barnato Cl CW1 . . . . .189 F7
Barnbridge Cl ST7 . . . . . . .194 E7
Barnbrook Cl WA3 . . . . .126 A1
Barncroft WA7 . . . . .50 D7
Barncroft Cl SK11 . . . . .84 A3
Barn Croft Rd L26 . . . . .21 A7
Barn Crt CH3 . . . . .182 C2
Barnes Ave WA2 . . . . .9 B2
Barnes Cl
  Blacon CH1 . . . . .117 F6
  Haslington CW1 . . . . .191 C4
  Warrington WA5 . . . . .15 A5
  Widnes WA8 . . . . .13 C2
Barnes Rd WA8 . . . . .13 C2
Barneston Rd WA8 . . . . .13 C3
Barnett Ave WA12 . . . . .1 E3
BARNETT BROOK 228 E5
Barnett Gr CW12 . . . . .156 A3
Barnett St SK11 . . . . .112 B7
Barnett Wlk CW2 . . . . .206 C8
Barnfield CH3 . . . . .166 A2
Barnfield Ave WA7 . . . . .50 D7
Barnfield Cl CH66 . . . . .69 C2
Barnfield Rd
  Bollington SK10 . . . . .87 F6
  Warrington WA1 . . . . .17 C7
Barnham Cl WA3 . . . . .3 A8
BARNHILL 183 B1
Barnhill Grange CH3 . . . . . .183 B3
Barnhill Rd CH3 . . . . .183 A1
Barnhouse La
  Great Barrow CH3 . . . . . . .120 E7
  Mouldsworth CH3 . . . . .98 A3
Barn La WA3 . . . . .2 F8
Barn Mdw CW8 . . . . .78 E1
Barnmoore Cl SY14 . . . . . . .213 B4
Barn Rd CW12 . . . . .156 E4
Barnside Way
  Macclesfield SK10 . . . . .87 C3
  Moulton CW9 . . . . .126 F8
Barns La
  Partington WA14 . . . . .20 A5
  Partington WA14 . . . . .20 A6
Barns Pl WA15 . . . . .32 C8
Barns The WA10 . . . . .127 D5
Barnston Ave CH65 . . . . .69 F5

Barnston Ct
  Farndon CH3 . . . . .180 E2
  Mickle Trafford CH3 . . . . . . .119 F8
Barnston Mews CH3 . . . . . .180 E2
Barnston Prim Sch
  CH60 . . . . .41 C7
Barnston Rd CH60 . . . . .41 C8
Barnston Towers Cl
  CH60 . . . . .41 C8
Barnston Twrs Cl CH60 . . . . .41 C8
Barnswood Cl WA4 . . . . .17 C1
BARNTON 78 C4
Barnton Cl WA3 . . . . .3 D7
Barnton Prim Sch
  CW8 . . . . .78 A4
Barn Way WA12 . . . . .2 B3
Barnwell Ave WA3 . . . . .4 D4
Barnwell Cl CW2 . . . . .206 B8
Barnwood CH66 . . . . .68 F7
Baron Cl WA1 . . . . .17 D7
Baronet Mews WA4 . . . . . . .16 A1
Baronet Rd WA4 . . . . .16 A1
Baron Gn SK8 . . . . .34 D7
Barons Pl CW5 . . . . .204 F6
Barons Cl WA7 . . . . .23 F1
Baron's Ct WA4 . . . . .22 C8
Barons Ct CH2 . . . . .118 C4
Barons Quay Rd CW9 . . . . . .78 F1
Barons Rd
  Shavington CW2 . . . . .206 B4
  Worleston CW5 . . . . .188 E5
Barony Bldgs **1** CW5 . . . .204 E6
Barony Ct CW5 . . . . .204 E7
Barony Employment Pk
  The CW5 . . . . .204 F8
Barony Rd CW5 . . . . .204 E8
Barony Terr CW5 . . . . .204 E6
Barony Way CW5 . . . . .140 E4
Barracks La
  Burwardsley CH3 . . . . .184 C5
  Macclesfield SK10 . . . . . . .112 F8
  Ravensmoor CW5 . . . . . . .203 E2
Barracks Sq **3** SK11 . . . . .112 B6
Barrastitch La CW8 . . . . . . .101 E6
Barratt Rd ST7 . . . . .193 F3
Barrel Well Hill CH2 . . . . . . .118 F1
BARRETS GREEN 169 D3
Barrie Gdns ST7 . . . . .210 C8
Barrie Gr CW1 . . . . .190 E4
Barrington Dr CW10 . . . . . .151 C7
Barrow Ave WA2 . . . . .8 E2
Barrow CE Prim Sch
  CH3 . . . . .120 D6
Barrowdale Rd WA3 . . . . .3 B8
Barrow Hall Com Prim Sch
  WA5 . . . . .14 E7
Barrow Hall Farm
  CH3 . . . . .120 E5
Barrow Hall La WA5 . . . . . . .14 E7
Barrow La
  Altrincham WA15 . . . . .32 B7
  Golborne WA2 . . . . .7 F7
  Great Barrow CH3 . . . . . . .120 C5
  Tarvin CH3 . . . . .121 C4
Barrow Mdw SK8 . . . . .34 E8
Barrows Green La CH3 . . . . .120 F7
Barrow's Brow WA16 . . . . . .57 E5
Barrow's Ct CW1 . . . . .190 A8
BARROWS GREEN 189 F8
BARROW'S GREEN 13 E4
Barrow's Green La 13 E3
Barrow's Row WA8 . . . . .13 A4
Barrule Cl WA4 . . . . .26 D7
Barrymore Ave WA4 . . . . . . .16 F4
Barrymore Cres CW9 . . . . . .78 D8
Barrymore Ct WA4 . . . . .17 A1
Barrymore Rd
  Runcorn WA7 . . . . .49 B7
  Warrington WA4 . . . . .17 A1
  Weaverham CW8 . . . . .77 E1
Barrymore Way CH63 . . . . . .43 B6
Barry St WA4 . . . . .16 D3
Barsbank Cl WA13 . . . . .18 C3
Barsbank La WA13 . . . . .18 C3
Barshaw Gdns WA4 . . . . . . .26 E4
Bars The CH1, CH3 . . . . . . .237 C2
Bartholomew Ct WA4 . . . . . .17 B2
Bartholomew Way
  CH4 . . . . .141 C6
BARTHOMLEY 208 C5
Barthomley Cres
  CW2 . . . . .189 D4
Barthomley Rd
  Barthomley CW2 . . . . .208 B7
  Betley ST7 . . . . .208 F3
BARTINGTON 77 A5
Bartington Hall Pk
  CW8 . . . . .77 A5
Bartlegate WA7 . . . . .50 B5
Barton Ave WA4 . . . . .17 A2
BARTON 181 F1
Barton Cl
  Handforth SK9 . . . . .34 D2
  Runcorn WA7 . . . . .50 D7
Barton Ct
  Warrington WA2 . . . . .16 B6
  Winsford CW7 . . . . .126 F1
Barton Rd
  Barton CH3, SY14 . . . . . . .181 D1
  Barton SY14 . . . . .181 F1
  Congleton CW12 . . . . .156 F3
  Farndon CH3 . . . . .180 F1
Barton's Pl CW1 . . . . .79 B1
Barton St
  Macclesfield SK11 . . . . . . .112 C7
  Barton Stad CW7 . . . . .126 F1
Barwood Ave ST7 . . . . .194 A5

Barwoods Dr CH4 . . . . .140 F6
BASFORD 206 E5
Basford Rd CW2 . . . . .206 D8
Basford Way CW7 . . . . .126 B2
Baskervyle Cl CH60 . . . . . . .41 A6
Baskervyle Rd CH60 . . . . . . .41 A6
Baslow Dr
  Gatley SK8 . . . . .34 C8
  Hazel Grove SK7 . . . . .36 F8
Bassett Cl CW5 . . . . .205 D6
Batchelors Wing The
  CW10 . . . . .127 D5
BATE HEATH 54 F3
Bateman Almshouses
  SK11 . . . . .112 C6
Bateman Cl CW1 . . . . .190 B4
Bateman Rd CW9 . . . . .80 B2
Batemans Ct CW2 . . . . .206 B8
Batemill Cl SK10 . . . . .86 F1
Batemill La WA16,
  SK11 . . . . .108 C5
Bates La WA6 . . . . .73 D4
Bate's Mill La CW6 . . . . .167 E5
Bath Cres SK8 . . . . .35 B8
Batherton Cl WA8 . . . . .23 B7
Batherton La CW5 . . . . .204 F2
Bath La CW3 . . . . .230 A3
Bath St
  Chester CH1 . . . . .237 C2
  Sandbach CW11 . . . . .175 C6
  Warrington WA1 . . . . .16 A5
BATH VALE 157 A3
Bath Vale Cotts
  CW12 . . . . .157 A3
Bathwood Dr CH64 . . . . .66 E5
Batterbee Cl CW1 . . . . .191 D5
Battersby La WA2 . . . . .16 C6
Battersea Ct WA8 . . . . .12 F3
Battery La
  Warrington WA1 . . . . .17 F7
  Wilmslow SK9 . . . . .59 D6
Bawtry Cl WA2 . . . . .8 E1
Baxter Cl WA7 . . . . .50 D7
Baxter Ho WA8 . . . . .78 E1
Baxter St WA5 . . . . .15 E5
Baycliffe WA13 . . . . .18 D2
Bayley Rd CW5 . . . . .205 D6
Bayswater Cl WA7 . . . . .24 F4
Baytree Cl CH66 . . . . .69 F1
Baymil Cl WA7 . . . . .50 E7
Beach Gr CW8 . . . . .103 C6
Beachin La CH3 . . . . .182 A4
Beach Rd CW8 . . . . .103 B6
Beacon Ct **4** CH60 . . . . . .41 A8
Beacon Hill View WA7 . . . . . .48 D7
Beacon La CH60 . . . . .41 A7
Beaconsfield Cres
  WA8 . . . . .13 A4
Beaconsfield Gr WA8 . . . . . .13 B4
Beaconsfield Rd
  Runcorn WA7 . . . . .22 E1
  Widnes WA8 . . . . .13 A4
Beaconsfield St CH3 . . . . . .237 C2
Beacons The CH60 . . . . .41 A7
Beadnell Dr WA5 . . . . .14 D3
Beagle Point CW7 . . . . .126 A1
Beagle Wlk WA3 . . . . .33 E8
Beames Ho CW1 . . . . .190 B4
Beam Heath Way
  CW5 . . . . .204 F7
Beamish Cl WA4 . . . . .26 D3
Beamont St WA8 . . . . .23 A4
Beard Cres WA12 . . . . .2 B2
Beardsmore Dr WA3 . . . . .9 B8
Bearhurst La SK11 . . . . .111 A5
Bearstone Rd TF9 . . . . .236 E3
Beasley Cl CH66 . . . . .69 D3
Beata Rd ST5 . . . . .210 F1
Beatrice St WA8 . . . . .16 D1
Beatty Ave WA2 . . . . .8 C1
Beatty Dr CW12 . . . . .157 A4
Beaty Cl CW5 . . . . .204 F6
Beaufort Chase SK9 . . . . . . .34 F1
Beaufort Cl
  Alderley Edge SK9 . . . . . . .60 B7
  Runcorn WA7 . . . . .49 B7
  Warrington WA5 . . . . .15 A5
  Widnes WA8 . . . . .22 A8
Beaufort St WA5 . . . . .16 B6
Beaulieu Ave CW7 . . . . .126 F2
Beaumaris Cres SK7 . . . . . . .36 C8
Beaumaris Dr CH65 . . . . . . .70 D2
Beaumaris Way WA7 . . . . . . .23 F2
Beaumont Cl
  Biddulph ST8 . . . . .179 D3
  Chester CH4 . . . . .140 D6
  Wistaston CW2 . . . . .205 F8
Beaumont Com Inf & Jun
  Schs WA2 . . . . .16 C7
Beaumont Ct
  Handforth SK9 . . . . .34 D3
  Warrington WA5 . . . . .16 C7
Beauty Bank
  Whitegate CW7 . . . . .125 E5
  Winsford CW7 . . . . .149 B3
Beauty Bank Cotts
  CW7 . . . . .149 A3
Beaverbrooke Ave WA3 . . . . .5 B4
Beaver Cl
  Chester CH4 . . . . .140 E6
  Pickmere WA16 . . . . .79 F7
Beaver Ctr The CW9 . . . . . .103 F7
BEBINGTON 43 A7
Bebington Rd CH66 . . . . . . .69 C3
Becconsall Cl CW1 . . . . . . .190 A8
Becconsall Dr CW1 . . . . . . .190 A8

Bechers WA8 . . . . .12 B3
Beckenham Cl WA8 . . . . . . .13 D4
Beckenham Gr **4**
  CW7 . . . . .126 A1
Beckett Ave CW7 . . . . .150 D8
Beckett Dr
  Lymm WA13 . . . . .19 B8
  Winwick WA2 . . . . .8 A5
Beckett's La CH3 . . . . .142 B8
Beckford Cl CW1 . . . . .189 F8
Becks La SK9 . . . . .60 A6
Bedalls La SK9 . . . . .60 A6
Bedder Ave CH65 . . . . .70 A2
Bedford Ave E CH65 . . . . . . .70 B2
Bedford Ct CW7 . . . . .190 C1
Bedford Gdns CW2 . . . . . . .190 C1
Bedford Gn M44 . . . . .11 B6
Bedford Gr ST7 . . . . .193 B5
Bedford Pl CW7 . . . . .190 C1
Bedford Rd
  Kidsgrove ST7 . . . . .195 A3
  Macclesfield SK11 . . . . . . .112 B7
Bedford Rise CW7 . . . . .149 C6
Bedford St
  Crewe CW2 . . . . .190 C1
  Warrington WA4 . . . . .26 C3
Bedward Row CH1 . . . . .237 A2
Beech Ave
  Culcheth WA3 . . . . .5 A3
  Frodsham WA6 . . . . .74 C8
  Golborne WA3 . . . . .2 F7
  Haydock WA11 . . . . .1 F7
  Mobberley WA16 . . . . .57 E6
  Rode Heath ST7 . . . . .193 F8
  Warrington, Thelwall
    WA4 . . . . .17 D3
  Warrington WA5 . . . . .14 C3
Beech Bank SK10 . . . . .87 D1
Beech Cl
  Alderley Edge SK9 . . . . . . .60 B3
  Congleton CW12 . . . . .156 A4
  Cuddington CW8 . . . . .101 F2
  Holmes Chapel CW4 . . . . .130 D4
  Newton-le-W WA12 . . . . .2 C2
  Ollerton M31 . . . . .82 F6
  4 Partington M31 . . . . . . .11 F3
Beech Cotts
  Alderley Edge SK9 . . . . . . .85 A8
  Stretton WA4 . . . . .26 E1
Beech Cres SK12 . . . . .36 E4
Beechcroft Ave CW2 . . . . . .206 B7
Beechcroft Dr CH65 . . . . . . .70 B2
Beech Ct WA8 . . . . .12 B3
Beech Dr
  Crewe CW2 . . . . .189 F2
  Knutsford WA16 . . . . .57 C2
  Talke ST7 . . . . .210 E8
Beeches The
  Chester CH2 . . . . .119 A6
  Ellesmere Port CH66 . . . . . .69 D4
  Helsby WA6 . . . . .73 C4
  Mobberley WA16 . . . . .58 E1
  Nantwich CW5 . . . . .204 F5
  8 Northwich CW8 . . . . . .103 E8
  Whitchurch SY13 . . . . .225 F1
  Widnes WA8 . . . . .13 D4
Beech Farm Dr SK10 . . . . . .87 D2
Beechfield
  Moulton CW9 . . . . .126 E8
  Wilmslow SK9 . . . . .60 A6
Beechfield Cl CH60 . . . . .59 F5
Beechfield Cl CH65 . . . . .41 A7
Beechfield Dr CW10 . . . . . .128 B2
Beechfield Gdns CW8 . . . . .103 B6
Beechfield Rd
  Alderley Edge SK9 . . . . . . .85 B8
  Cheadle SK8 . . . . .35 B8
  Ellesmere Port CH65 . . . . . .70 B5
  Warrington WA4 . . . . .17 A2
Beech Gdns **3** WA7 . . . . . .49 C8
Beech Gr
  Chester CH2 . . . . .119 A3
  Crewe CW2 . . . . .190 C1
  Ellesmere Port CH66 . . . . . .95 A8
  Lymm WA13 . . . . .18 B2
  Macclesfield SK11 . . . . . . .112 C5
  Sandbach CW11 . . . . .175 D6
  Warrington WA1 . . . . .17 A7
  Weaverham CW8 . . . . . . .102 D8
  Wilmslow SK9 . . . . .60 A6
  Winsford CW7 . . . . .149 D8
Beech Hall Dr SK10 . . . . . . .87 C2
Beech Hall Sch SK10 . . . . . .87 C3
Beech Heyes Cl CW8 . . . . . .102 E8
Beech Heyes Dr CW8 . . . . .102 E8
Beech Hollows LL12 . . . . . .162 C1
Beech La
  Barnton CW8 . . . . .78 A3
  Cotebrook CW6 . . . . .147 B6
  Macclesfield SK10 . . . . .87 D1
  Norley WA6 . . . . .75 E1
  Wilmslow SK9 . . . . .60 A6
Beechlands Ave CH3 . . . . . .119 A1
Beechmill Dr WA3 . . . . .4 F3
Beechmoore WA4 . . . . .25 B5
Beechmuir CH1 . . . . .117 C3
Beech Rd
  Alderley Edge SK9 . . . . . . .60 B3
  Aston WA7 . . . . .50 B4
  Heswall CH60 . . . . .41 C8

Beech Rd continued
High Lane SK6 . . . . .37 F7
Little Budworth CW6 . . . . . 124 D2
Paddockhill WA16 . . . . .59 B5
Runcorn WA7 . . . . .49 C8
Warrington WA4 . . . . .26 C8
Whaley Bridge SK23 . . . . . .65 E7
Beech Rise
Crowton CW8 . . . . .76 B2
Horwich End SK23 . . . . .65 C5
Beech St W CW1 . . . . .190 C4
Beech St CW10 . . . . .128 C1
Beech Tree Ct CW5 . . . . . .205 D5
Beechtree Farm Cl
WA16 . . . . .29 C7
Beechtree La WA13 . . . . . .29 B7
Beech View Rd WA6 . . . . . .75 C1
Beechway
Bollington SK10 . . . . .88 A7
Chester CH2 . . . . .118 C6
High Lane SK6 . . . . .37 F7
Neston CH64 . . . . .66 D7
Wilmslow SK9 . . . . .59 F5
Beechways WA4 . . . . .26 D5
Beechways Dr CH64 . . . . . .66 D7
BEECHWOOD 49 E5
Beechwood
Knutsford, Cross Town
WA16 . . . . .57 C2
Knutsford WA16 . . . . .56 F3
Beechwood Ave
Hartford CW8 . . . . .103 A6
Newton-le-W WA12 . . . . .2 D4
Runcorn WA7 . . . . .49 C5
Warrington, Padgate
WA1 . . . . .16 E7
Warrington WA5 . . . . .14 F5
Beechwood Cl CW5 . . . . . .205 A4
Beechwood Dr
Alsager ST7 . . . . .193 B4
Eaton (nr Congleton)
CW12 . . . . .156 F8
Ellesmere Port CH66 . . . . . . .69 D1
Higher Wincham CW9 . . . . . .79 F6
Wilmslow SK9 . . . . .60 E8
Beechwood Gr SK8 . . . . . .35 A8
Beechwood La WA3 . . . . . . .4 C4
Beechwood Mews
SK10 . . . . .87 C2
Beechwood Prim Sch
WA7 . . . . .49 E5
Beechwood Rd
Bebington CH62 . . . . .43 C8
Saltney CH4 . . . . .140 E5
Beechwood Sch CW1 . . . . .190 C5
Beecroft Cl WA5 . . . . .7 D1
Beechle La CW9 . . . . .126 F8
BEESTON 168 A2
BEESTON-BROOK 168 C5
Beeston Brow SK10 . . . . . . .88 B8
Beeston Castle ✱
CW6 . . . . .167 F3
Beeston Cl
Bollington SK10 . . . . .63 C1
Holmes Chapel CW4 . . . . . .130 A3
Middlewich CW10 . . . . .151 D5
Winsford CW7 . . . . .9 D4
Beeston Ct WA7 . . . . .24 C4
Beeston Dr
Alsager ST7 . . . . .193 C3
Knutsford WA16 . . . . .82 A8
Winsford CW7 . . . . .149 C7
Beeston Gn CH66 . . . . .69 E5
Beeston Hall Mews
CW6 . . . . .168 B4
BEESTON MOSS 168 B1
Beeston Mount SK10 . . . . .63 C1
Beeston Pathway
CH4 . . . . .141 E7
Beeston Rd
Broughton CH4 . . . . .139 B3
Handforth SK9 . . . . .34 D5
Higher Kinnerton CH4 . . . . .161 A7
Beeston St CW8 . . . . .103 E7
Beeston Terr SK11 . . . . . .111 E6
Beeston View CH4 . . . . . .141 E6
Beggarman's La WA16 . . . .82 A7
Begonia Gdns WA9 . . . . . . .6 A7
Beilby Rd WA11 . . . . .1 E7
Belfry Cl SK9 . . . . .60 D8
Belfry Dr SK10 . . . . .87 C4
BELGRAVE 162 E6
Belgrave App CH3 . . . . . . .163 C6
Belgrave Ave
Alsager ST7 . . . . .193 D5
Congleton CW12 . . . . .156 D3
Eccleston CH4 . . . . .162 F7
Saltney CH4 . . . . .140 E6
Warrington WA1 . . . . .17 B8
Belgrave Ct
Doddleston CH4 . . . . .162 A6
Golborne WN7 . . . . .4 A8
Widnes WA8 . . . . .13 E3
Belgrave Dr CH65 . . . . .69 F5
Belgrave Inf Sch CW4 . . . . .141 E6
Belgrave Rd
Chester CH3 . . . . .142 B8
Crewe CW2 . . . . .190 B2
Irlam M44 . . . . .11 D2
Macclesfield SK11 . . . . .112 C4
Northwich CW9 . . . . .104 A4
Belgrave St CH1 . . . . .237 C3
Belgravia Ct
Pulford CH4 . . . . .162 E5
Widnes WA8 . . . . .12 F3

Belgravia Gdns WA15 . . . . .31 E8
Bellaport Rd TF9 . . . . .236 A4
Bellard Dr CW2 . . . . .119 A4
Bell Ave SK11 . . . . .112 F3
Bellcast Cl WA4 . . . . .26 C5
Bellemonte Rd WA6 . . . . . . .74 C6
Belleville Ave WA2 . . . . .33 E8
Belleville La CH3 . . . . .119 E4
Belle Vue Terr CW11 . . . . .175 B6
Bell Farm Ct SK10 . . . . .87 C3
Bellflower Cl WA8 . . . . .12 E4
Bellhouse La
Higher Walton WA4 . . . . . . .25 D7
Warrington WA4 . . . . .17 C1
Bell House Rd WA8 . . . . . . .13 C1
Bellingham Cl WA11 . . . . . . .57 C2
Bellingham Dr WA7 . . . . . . .49 A8
Bell La
Smallwood CW11 . . . . .177 B7
Warrington WA4 . . . . .17 E3
Bell Meadow Bsns Pk
CH4 . . . . .162 E5
Bell Meadow Rd CW6 . . . . .146 C2
BELL O'TH' HILL 225 D7
Bellsfield Cl WA13 . . . . .18 F2
Bell's Hollow ST5 . . . . .210 E3
Belmont Ave
Macclesfield SK10 . . . . .86 C1
Sandbach CW11 . . . . .175 A7
Warrington WA4 . . . . .16 F3
Belmont Cres WA5 . . . . .15 A6
Belmont Dr CH4 . . . . .140 C6
Belmont Rd
Bramhall SK7 . . . . .35 F5
Great Budworth CW9 . . . . . .53 F1
Northwich CW9 . . . . .104 C7
Widnes WA8 . . . . .13 E2
Belton Cl WA3 . . . . .3 A7
Beltony Dr CW1 . . . . .173 A1
Belvedere 9 WA7 . . . . .23 A3
Belvedere Cl 8 WA4 . . . . . .16 D6
Belvedere Dr CH1 . . . . .117 E4
Belvedere Rd WA12 . . . . . . .2 B5
Belvedere Terr ST7 . . . . . . .193 F7
Belvoir Ave SK7 . . . . .36 E8
Belvoir Rd
Warrington WA4 . . . . .26 B8
Widnes WA8 . . . . .13 B1
Bembridge Cl
Warrington WA5 . . . . .14 C7
Widnes WA8 . . . . .12 F4
Bembridge Ct CW10 . . . . . .151 C8
Bembridge Dr CW10 . . . . . .151 C8
Benbrook Gr SK9 . . . . .34 E2
Benbrook Way SK11 . . . . . .111 E1
Bendee Ave CH64 . . . . .67 A7
Bendee Rd CH64 . . . . .67 A7
Benjafield Ct CW1 . . . . .189 F2
Benjamins Way ST7 . . . . . .209 F2
Bennet Cl CH64 . . . . .68 A8
Bennet Rd CW9 . . . . .104 D6
Bennett Ave WA1 . . . . .16 F6
Bennett Cl CW1 . . . . .190 E4
Bennett Ct CW7 . . . . .149 D5
Bennetts La SK11 . . . . .158 E7
Bennett's La
Higher Kinnerton CH4 . . . . .161 A7
Warrington WA8 . . . . .13 E1
Bennett St WA1 . . . . .16 B5
Ben Nevis Dr CH66 . . . . . . .68 F6
Benson Rd WA3 . . . . .9 D3
Benson Wlk 3 SK9 . . . . . . .34 D2
Bentham Ave WA2 . . . . .8 C3
Bentham Rd WA3 . . . . .5 A2
Bentinck St WA7 . . . . .22 F3
Bent La
Astbury CW12 . . . . .178 A8
Culcheth WA3 . . . . .5 A2
Lymm WA13 . . . . .19 C6
Norley CW8 . . . . .101 C8
Bentley Dr CW1 . . . . .191 A5
Bentley Gr CW7 . . . . .149 C6
Bentley's Farm La WA4 . . . .52 E5
Benton Dr CW2 . . . . .118 C4
Bents Cotts CH2 . . . . .71 E2
Bentside Rd SK12 . . . . .36 E3
Benty Heath La CH64,
CH66 . . . . .43 B3
Beresford Ct 4 SK9 . . . . . .60 A1
Beresford St WA1 . . . . .16 E7
Berisford Ho CW12 . . . . . . .156 E3
Berkeley Ave ST7 . . . . .193 D5
Berkeley Cl WN7 . . . . .4 C8
Berkeley Cres CW2 . . . . . .206 A8
Berkeley Ct
Newton-le-W WA12 . . . . .1 F4
Runcorn WA7 . . . . .24 D4
Berkeley Prim Sch The
CW2 . . . . .206 B7
Berkeley Rise CW7 . . . . . . .149 A8
Berkley Ct SK23 . . . . .65 D6
Berkley Dr CH4 . . . . .141 D6
Berkshire Cl SK10 . . . . .86 E2
Berkshire Dr
Congleton CW12 . . . . .156 D4
Irlam M44 . . . . .11 C5
Warrington WA1 . . . . .17 E7
Bermondsey Gr WA8 . . . . . .13 D4
Bernard Ave WA6 . . . . .26 D8
Bernisdale Rd WA16 . . . . . .57 F4
Bernsdale Cl CH5 . . . . .116 A3
Bernsdale Ct/Llys
Bernsdale CH5 . . . . .116 A3
Berristall Rise SK10 . . . . . .63 C1
Berristall Rd SK10 . . . . .88 E3
Berry Cl
Ellesmere Port CH66 . . . . . . .69 C3
Wilmslow SK9 . . . . .60 A5

Berry Dr CH66 . . . . .69 C3
Berry Rd WA8 . . . . .12 D1
Berrystead CW8 . . . . .103 B4
Bertram St WA12 . . . . .2 A4
Berwick Ave CH62 . . . . .43 E4
Berwick Cl
Macclesfield SK10 . . . . .86 F2
Warrington WA1 . . . . .17 E6
Berwick Ct CW4 . . . . .130 B2
Berwick Gdns CH66 . . . . . . .69 B6
Berwick Gr CH66 . . . . .69 B6
Berwick Rd CH66 . . . . .69 B6
Berwick Road W CH66 . . . . .69 A6
Bessancourt CH4 . . . . .130 C3
Bessemer Rd M44 . . . . .11 F6
Beswick Dr CW1 . . . . .191 A3
Beswicks La
Norton in Hales TF9 . . . . . .236 C2
Row-of-Trees SK9 . . . . .59 C3
Beswicks Rd CW8 . . . . .78 E1
Beswick St SK11 . . . . .112 B7
Betchton Cl CW11 . . . . .175 C7
Betchton Ct 3 CW12 . . . . .156 F3
BETCHTON HEATH 175 E5
Betchton Rd CW11 . . . . . . .175 B5
Betchworth Cres WA7 . . . . .49 D6
Betchworth Way SK10 . . . . .87 C4
Bethany Cl WA11 . . . . .1 B7
Betjeman Cl WA4 . . . . .16 F4
Betjeman Way CW1 . . . . . .190 F5
BETLEY 221 F8
Betley Cl CW9 . . . . .104 A5
Betley St CW1 . . . . .190 C4
Betsyfield Dr WA3 . . . . .9 A7
Bettisfield Ave CH62 . . . . . .43 D6
Betty's La
Beeston CW6 . . . . .168 D1
Woore CW3 . . . . .232 C1
Bevan Ave ST7 . . . . .210 E6
Bevan Cl WA5 . . . . .15 D6
Bevan Ct WA4 . . . . .16 B3
Bevan View WA5 . . . . .15 F7
Beverley Ave WA4 . . . . .26 D8
Beverley Dr CH60 . . . . .41 B6
Beverley Rd WA5 . . . . .15 C6
Beverley Way
Ellesmere Port CH66 . . . . . . .69 B7
Macclesfield SK10 . . . . .87 C4
Bevin Ave WA3 . . . . .5 B4
Bevyl Rd CH64 . . . . .41 B2
Bewick Wlk WA16 . . . . .57 B3
Bewley Ct CH3 . . . . .142 A7
BEWSEY 15 F8
Bewsey Bsns Ctr WA5 . . . . .15 F6
Bewsey Farm Cl WA5 . . . . .15 D8
Bewsey Ind Est WA5 . . . . . .16 A7
Bewsey Lodge Prim Sch
WA5 . . . . .15 F7
Bewsey Park Cl WA5 . . . . . .15 F7
Bewsey Rd WA2, WA5 . . . . .16 A6
Bexhill Ave WA2 . . . . .8 B4
Bexington Dr CW9 . . . . .190 B8
Bexton Ave CW7 . . . . .126 A2
Bexton La WA16 . . . . .82 A7
Bexton Prim Sch WA16 . . . . .81 F7
Bexton Rd WA16 . . . . .56 F1
Bibby Ave WA1 . . . . .16 E6
Bibby's La SK10 . . . . .88 A1
Bibby St ST7 . . . . .193 E7
BICKERTON 199 E6
Bickerton Ave WA6 . . . . .74 D7
Bickerton Cl WA3 . . . . .9 D4
Bickerton Holy Trinity CE
Prim Sch SY14 . . . . .200 A7
Bickerton Rd SY14 . . . . . . .201 B2
Bickerton Way 1
CW9 . . . . .103 E4
Bickley Cl
Hough CW2 . . . . .206 E2
Northwich CW9 . . . . .103 E5
Runcorn WA7 . . . . .23 C1
Warrington WA3 . . . . .9 D6
BICKLEY MOSS 215 B7
BICKLEY TOWN 214 E6
Bickley Town La SY14 . . . .214 E6
BICKLEYWOOD 214 C4
Bicknell Cl WA5 . . . . .15 B8
Bida La CW12 . . . . .179 B8
BIDDULPH 179 B2
Biddulph Common Rd
ST8 . . . . .179 F7
Biddulph Grange ST8 . . . . .179 E3
Biddulph Grange Ctry Pk✱
ST8 . . . . .179 F3
Biddulph Grange Gdn✱
ST8 . . . . .179 E3
Biddulph Park Rd
ST8 . . . . .179 F5
Biddulph Rd
Congleton CW12 . . . . .179 B8
Harriseahead ST7 . . . . .195 F6
Biddulph St CW12 . . . . .179 C7
Bideford Rd WA5 . . . . .14 E4
Bidston Cl CH2 . . . . .118 D5
Bidston Dr SK9 . . . . .34 E2
Bidvale Way CW1 . . . . .190 C8
Big Field La CW9 . . . . .78 C3
Biggin Ct WA2 . . . . .8 E1
Biggs Way CW12 . . . . .156 E5
BIGNALL END 209 F3
Bignall End Rd
Audley ST7 . . . . .210 A3
Newcastle-u-Lyme ST7 . . . .210 A4
Billington Ave WA12 . . . . . . .2 C5
Billington Cl
Barnton CW8 . . . . .77 F4

Billington Cl continued
Crewe CW2 . . . . .190 A2
Warrington WA5 . . . . .14 E8
Billington Rd WA8 . . . . .12 B3
Bilton Cl WA3 . . . . .13 E2
Bilton Way CW2 . . . . .189 E5
Bings Rd SK23 . . . . .65 F8
Bingswood Ave SK23 . . . . . .65 E8
Bingswood Ind Est
SK23 . . . . .65 E8
Binney Rd CW9 . . . . .104 B8
Binyon Way CW1 . . . . .191 A4
Birchall Ave WA3 . . . . .4 E4
BIRCHALL MOSS 219 E1
Birchall Moss La
CW5 . . . . .219 E1
Birchall St WA3 . . . . .9 A7
Birchall Wlk CW2 . . . . .206 D8
Birch Ave
Alsager ST7 . . . . .193 C2
Crewe CW1 . . . . .190 F5
Irlam M44 . . . . .11 D5
Macclesfield SK10 . . . . .87 B1
Wilmslow SK9 . . . . .59 F6
Winsford CW7 . . . . .127 A1
Birch Brook Rd WA13 . . . . .19 C5
Birch Cl
Crewe CW1 . . . . .190 F5
Holmes Chapel CW4 . . . . . .130 D3
Birch Cres WA12 . . . . .1 F4
Birch Ct CW12 . . . . .155 F3
Birchdale Cres WA4 . . . . . . .26 C8
Birchdale Ct WA4 . . . . .26 C8
Birchdale Rd
Warrington, Paddington
WA1 . . . . .17 A7
Warrington WA4 . . . . .26 C8
Birchdale Rd
Widnes WA8 . . . . .13 B5
Birkenhead Rd CH64 . . . . . .42 E1
Birkenhead St Crewe CW8 . .104 C8
Birkett Ave CH65 . . . . .70 C2
Birkin Cl WA16 . . . . .57 D4
Birkinheath La WA14 . . . . . .31 B4
Birley St WA12 . . . . .2 D4
Birstall Ct WA7 . . . . .49 D7
Birtles Cl CW11 . . . . .175 C7
Birtles Hall SK10 . . . . .85 D2
Birtles La SK10 . . . . .85 E2
Birtles Rd
Macclesfield SK10 . . . . .86 D1
Warrington WA2 . . . . .8 D1
Birtles Way 4 SK9 . . . . . . .34 D5
Birtley Ct WA8 . . . . .12 C1
Birtwistle Rd CW9 . . . . .104 D6
Bisham Pk WA7 . . . . .24 D2
Bishopdale Cl WA5 . . . . .14 F7
Bishopgates Dr CW9 . . . . . .103 E4
Bishop Heber High Sch
SY14 . . . . .213 C5
Bishop Rd SK10 . . . . .88 A7
Bishop Reeves Rd WA11 . . .1 E7
Bishops' Blue Coat CE
High Sch The CH3 . . . . . . .142 A8
Bishop's Ct SK11 . . . . .210 D8
Bishops Ct
Broughton CH4 . . . . .139 C4
Warrington WA2 . . . . .8 A4
Bishopsfield Ct CH2 . . . . . .118 F3
Bishops Gate CH2 . . . . .119 A3
Bishops Gdns CH65 . . . . . . .70 A5
Bishop St CH2 . . . . .118 F3
Bishops Way WA8 . . . . .13 D3
Bishops Wood CW5 . . . . . .204 F2
Bishopton Dr SK11 . . . . . . .111 F8
Bishop Wilson CE Prim
Sch CH64 . . . . .67 D1
Bispham Rd WA5 . . . . .15 B4
Bittern Cl
Poynton SK12 . . . . .36 A4
Runcorn WA7 . . . . .50 D8
Warrington WA2 . . . . .8 D3
Bittern Gr SK10 . . . . .87 A1
Blackacres Cl CW11 . . . . . .174 F6
Blackbird Way ST7 . . . . . . .195 F1
Blackboards La CH66 . . . . . .69 A8
BLACKBROOK
Haydock 1 A7
Warrington 8 E2
Blackbrook Ave WA2 . . . . . . .8 F2
Blackbrook Cl WA8 . . . . . . .12 C3
Blackburn Cl WA3 . . . . .3 E8
Blackburne Ave WA8 . . . . . .22 B5
Blackburne Dr WA12 . . . . . . .2 A2
Blackcap Rd WA4 . . . . .27 A4
Blackcap Wlk WA3 . . . . .9 E3
Black Cat Ind Est WA8 . . . .22 B6
Blackcroft Ave CW8 . . . . . . .78 A2
Blackden Firs CW4 . . . . . . .108 B2
Blackden La
Goostrey CW4 . . . . .108 A3
Siddington SK11 . . . . .132 F8
Black Denton's Pl WA8 . . . .13 C1
Black Diamond St
CH1 . . . . .237 B4
Blackdown Cl CH66 . . . . . . .69 A5
Blackeys La CH64 . . . . .66 E8
Black Firs La CW12 . . . . . .155 E4
Black Firs Prim Sch
CW12 . . . . .155 F4
Black Friars CH1 . . . . .237 A2
Blackhill La WA4 . . . . .24 F5
Blackhill La WA16 . . . . .31 E8
Blackhurst Brow SK10 . . . . .61 B2
Blackhurst Farm Rd
CW5 . . . . .202 E3

Blackhurst St WA1 . . . . .16 B5
Black La SK10 . . . . .87 E1
Blackledge Cl WA2 . . . . 9 A3
Blackley Cl
 Macclesfield SK10 . . . . .87 B4
 Warrington WA4 . . . . .16 D3
Black Lion La CH66 . . . . . . .69 C6
Black Moss Rd WA14 . . . . .20 F7
BLACK PARK 226 F2
Black Park Rd SY13 . . . . . .226 D2
Black Rd SK11 . . . . .112 F7
Blackshaw Cl CW12 . . . . . .157 B1
Blackshaw Dr WA5 . . . . .7 B1
Blackshaw La WA9 . . . . . . .59 F1
Blackshaw St **6**
 SK11 . . . . .112 C7
Blackstairs Rd CH66 . . . . . .69 F7
Blackthorn Cl
 Broughton CH4 . . . . .139 B3
 Huntington CH3 . . . . .142 A5
 Wistaston CW2 . . . . .206 B8
Blackthorne Ave CH66 . . . .95 A8
Blackthorn Pl ST5 . . . . . . .210 C1
Blackthorn Wlk **3**
 M31 . . . . .11 E2
Blackwell Cl CW10 . . . . . .151 D6
BLACON 117 F3
Blacon Ave CH1 . . . . .118 A5
Blacon Hall Rd CH1 . . . . . .117 F5
Blacon High Sch CH1 . . . . .117 D4
Blacon Point Rd CH1 . . . . .117 E3
Bladon Cres ST7 . . . . .193 C5
Blagg Ave CW5 . . . . .204 C4
Blair Cl SK7 . . . . .36 C8
Blair Dr WA8 . . . . .12 C3
Blairgowrie Dr SK10 . . . . . .87 B4
Blaizefield Cl CW3 . . . . . . .232 C2
Blakeacre Rd L26 . . . . .21 A6
Blake Cl
 Blacon CH1 . . . . .117 F6
 Crewe CW2 . . . . .189 F1
Blakeden La CW7 . . . . . . .148 F8
Blake La CW8 . . . . .102 A2
Blakeley Brow CH63 . . . . . .43 A6
Blakeley Cl CH63 . . . . .43 A7
Blakeley Dell CH63 . . . . . . .43 B6
Blakeley Dene CH63 . . . . . .43 B7
Blakeley La WA16 . . . . .58 F8
Blakeley Rd CH63 . . . . .43 A6
Blakelow Bank SK11 . . . . .112 F6
Blakelow Cl CW10 . . . . . . .151 B8
Blakelow Cres CW5 . . . . . .205 F3
Blakelow Dr CW5 . . . . .205 D4
Blakelow Rd SK11 . . . . . . .112 F6
Blakemere Ct SY13 . . . . . .226 B1
Blakemere Dr CW9 . . . . . .103 E5
Blakemere La WA6 . . . . . .100 D4
Blakemere Way CW11 . . . .174 F8
BLAKENHALL 221 A4
Blake St CW12 . . . . .156 C3
Blandford Dr
5 Macclesfield SK11 . . . . . .111 F8
 Northwich CW9 . . . . .103 E3
Blandford Rd WA5 . . . . . . .15 B5
Blankney The CW5 . . . . . .204 E4
Blantern Rd CH4 . . . . .161 A7
Blantyre St WA7 . . . . .22 F3
Blaze Hill SK10 . . . . .88 E8
Bleadale Cl SK9 . . . . .34 D1
Bleasdale Rd
 Crewe CW1 . . . . .173 B1
 Newton-le-W WA12 . . . . 2 C4
Bleeding Wolf La ST7 . . . . .194 E5
Blenheim Cl
 Macclesfield SK10 . . . . .87 A1
 Northwich CW9 . . . . .103 F4
 Poynton SK12 . . . . .36 F4
 Warrington WA2 . . . . .9 B3
 Wilmslow SK9 . . . . .60 D7
 Wistaston CW2 . . . . .205 E8
Blenheim Ct ST7 . . . . .193 D5
Blenheim Gdns **5**
 CW7 . . . . .149 C7
Blenheim Ho CH1 . . . . . . .118 B3
Blenheim Pk CW11 . . . . . .175 A4
Bloomfield Cl SK8 . . . . .34 E7
Bloomsbury Way WA8 . . . .12 D3
Blossom Hts CW8 . . . . . . .103 D7
Blossom La M31 . . . . .11 E2
Blossoms La SK7 . . . . .37 A7
Blossom Way/Ffordd Y
Blodau CH4 . . . . .140 D5
Blount Cl CW1 . . . . .190 B4
Bluebell La CH64 . . . . .42 C1
Bluebell Ave WA11 . . . . .1 E7
Bluebell Cl
 Huntington CH3 . . . . .142 B6
 Macclesfield SK10 . . . . .87 D3
 Winnington CW8 . . . . .78 E1
Bluebell Ct WA7 . . . . .49 F4
Bluebell Ct SK10 . . . . .87 C3
Bluebell Mews **4**
 SK10 . . . . .87 D3
Bluebell Way
 Alsager ST7 . . . . .193 B3
 Handforth SK9 . . . . .34 C1
Blue Bridge La WA6 . . . . . .73 C5
Bluecoat St WA2 . . . . .16 B7
Blue Hatch WA6 . . . . .74 C8
Blue Planet Aquarium *
 CH65 . . . . .70 F6
Blue Ridge Cl WA5 . . . . . . .14 E7
Blundell Rd WA8 . . . . .22 D8
Blunstone Cl CW2 . . . . . . .190 A2
Blyth Cl
 Macclesfield SK10 . . . . .86 E1
 Runcorn WA7 . . . . .50 D5

Blythe Ave
 Bramhall SK7 . . . . .35 C6
 Congleton CW12 . . . . .156 A2
 Widnes WA8 . . . . .13 B5
Blythe Pl CW7 . . . . .127 B2
Blythings The CW6 . . . . . . .146 C3
Blyth Rd CH63 . . . . .43 C7
Boardmans Pl CH4 . . . . . . .104 A5
Boars Leigh Pk SK11 . . . . .135 D1
Boathorse Rd ST7 . . . . . . .210 F8
Boathouse La CH64 . . . . . . .41 C3
Boat Mus The * CH65 . . . . .70 C7
Boat Stage WA13 . . . . .18 E3
Boat Wlk WA4 . . . . .16 A1
Bob's La M44 . . . . .11 D4
Boddington Dr WA4 . . . . . .27 A7
Boden Dr CW5 . . . . .205 D4
Boden St SK11 . . . . .112 D8
Bodiam Cl CH65 . . . . .70 E2
Bodmin Ave SK10 . . . . .86 E1
Bodmin Dr SK7 . . . . .35 E7
Bodnant Cl CW1 . . . . .190 A8
BOLD 6 B6
Bold Bsns Ctr WA9 . . . . .6 B7
Bold Cross WA8 . . . . .13 E7
BOLD HEATH 13 E7
Bold Ind Est WA8 . . . . .13 C5
Bold Ind Park WA9 . . . . .6 B6
Bold La WA5, WA9 . . . . .6 C7
Bold Pl CH1 . . . . .237 B3
Bold Sq CH1 . . . . .237 C3
Bold St
 Haslington CW1 . . . . .191 C4
 Runcorn WA7 . . . . .23 B3
 Sandbach CW11 . . . . .175 B6
 Warrington WA1 . . . . .16 A5
 Widnes WA8 . . . . .23 A7
Bolesworth Hill Rd
 CH3 . . . . .183 C4
Bolesworth Rd
 Chester CH2 . . . . .118 F6
 Tattenhall CH3 . . . . .183 C7
Boleyn Cl CH1 . . . . .117 E6
Boleyn Ct WA7 . . . . .24 C3
Bolland's Ct CH1 . . . . .237 A2
Bollands Row **14** CW5 . . .204 E5
Bolleyn Wood Ct SK9 . . . . .34 B1
Bollin Ave
 Altrincham WA14 . . . . .31 B8
 Winsford CW7 . . . . .127 B2
Bollinbarn SK10 . . . . .87 B2
Bollinbarn Dr SK10 . . . . . . .87 A2
Bollinbrook CE Prim Sch
 SK10 . . . . .87 B2
Bollinbrook Rd SK10 . . . . . .87 B2
Bollin Cl
 Alsager ST7 . . . . .192 F3
 Culcheth WA3 . . . . .5 A2
 Lymm WA13 . . . . .19 A4
 Sandbach CW11 . . . . .174 E7
 Winsford CW7 . . . . .127 B2
Bollin Ct SK9 . . . . .60 C6
Bollin Dr
 Congleton CW12 . . . . .156 F1
 Lymm WA13 . . . . .19 A4
Bollin Gr
 Biddulph ST8 . . . . .179 C1
 Prestbury SK10 . . . . .87 A7
BOLLINGTON 88 B7
Bollington Ave CW5 . . . . . .104 A5
Bollington Cross CE Prim
 Sch SK10 . . . . .87 E7
Bollington Ho CW12 . . . . . .156 F1
Bollington La SK10 . . . . . . .84 E2
Bollington Old Rd
 SK10 . . . . .87 D6
Bollington Rd SK10 . . . . . . .87 E6
Bollinhead La SK11 . . . . . .113 D2
Bollin Hill
 Prestbury SK10 . . . . .87 A5
 Wilmslow SK9 . . . . .60 B8
Bollin Mews SK10 . . . . .86 F7
Bollinway WA15 . . . . .32 A8
Bollin Way SK10 . . . . .87 A8
Bollin Wlk SK9 . . . . .60 C7
Bollinwood Chase SK9 . . . .60 D7
Bolshaw Cl CW1 . . . . .190 A7
Bolshaw Farm La SK8 . . . . .34 C6
Bolshaw Prim Sch SK8 . . . .34 B7
Bolshaw Rd SK8 . . . . .34 C6
Bolton Ave
 Cheadle SK8 . . . . .35 B6
 Warrington WA4 . . . . .16 F4
Bolton Cl
 Golborne WA3 . . . . .4 B8
 Poynton SK12 . . . . .36 D4
Bomish La CW4, SK11 . . . .108 C3
Bond Cl WA5 . . . . .15 D4
Bond St
 Macclesfield SK11 . . . . . . .112 C7
 Winnington CW8 . . . . .78 D1
Bonis Hall La SK10 . . . . . . .61 F4
BOON HILL 210 A2
Boon Hill Rd ST7 . . . . .209 F1
Booth Ave
 Ashton Hayes CH3 . . . . . . .121 E7
 Little Budworth CW6 . . . . . .147 F7
 Sandbach CW11 . . . . .175 C6
BOOTH BANK 30 B7
Boothbank La WA14 . . . . . .30 A6
Booth Bed La WA16,
 .107 A4
Boothby St **12** SK10 . . . .112 C8
Boothfields WA16 . . . . .57 C2
BOOTH GREEN 62 F7

Booth La
 Middlewich CW10 . . . . . . .151 E6
 Middlewich, Stud Green CW10,
 CW11 . . . . .152 B3
Booth Rd
 Handforth SK9 . . . . .34 A1
 Hartford CW8 . . . . .103 A4
BOOTHSDALE 122 D3
Boothsdale CW6 . . . . .122 D3
BOOTH'S HILL 18 C2
Booths Hill Cl WA13 . . . . . .18 C2
Booths Hill Ho **3**
 WA13 . . . . .18 D3
Booth's Hill Rd WA13 . . . . .18 C2
Booths La WA4 . . . . .52 E6
Booth's La WA13 . . . . .18 B1
Boothsmere Cl CW11 . . . . .174 F8
Booth St
 Audley ST7 . . . . .209 D1
 Congleton CW12 . . . . .156 C2
 Warrington WA5 . . . . .15 E4
BOOTS GREEN 107 B5
Borderbrook Sch
 Higher Wych SY14 . . . . . . .224 D3
 Tallarn Green/Tallwrn Green
 SY14 . . . . .222 F5
Border Rd CH60 . . . . .41 B8
Border Way CH3 . . . . .119 C1
Borough Rd CW12 . . . . . . .156 F3
Borras Rd CH13 . . . . .196 A8
Borron Ct WA12 . . . . .2 B4
Borron Rd WA12 . . . . .2 B5
Borron Road Ind Est
 WA12 . . . . .2 A5
Borrowdale Ave WA2 . . . . . .8 C3
Borrowdale Cl
 Crewe CW2 . . . . .189 E3
 Frodsham WA6 . . . . .74 D8
Borrowdale Rd WA8 . . . . . .22 C8
Bosden Cl SK9 . . . . .34 D5
BOSLEY 158 D8
Bosley Brook CW12 . . . . . .179 D5
Bosley Cl
 Handforth SK9 . . . . .34 D2
 Middlewich CW10 . . . . . . .151 C6
Bosley Dr SK12 . . . . .37 A3
Bosley View CW12 . . . . . . .157 B1
Bostock Gn
 Bostock Green CW9 . . . . . .127 C7
 Ellesmere Port CH65 . . . . . .69 F6
BOSTOCK HALL 127 D5
Bostock Rd
 Macclesfield SK11 . . . . . . .111 E7
 Winsford CW7 . . . . .126 F1
Bostock St WA5 . . . . .15 E6
Boston Ave WA7 . . . . .23 D1
Boston Bvd
 Warrington WA5 . . . . .15 A7
 Warrington WA5 . . . . .15 B7
Boston Cl
 Bramhall SK7 . . . . .35 D7
 Warrington WA5 . . . . .15 A7
Boswell Ave WA4 . . . . .16 B2
Botany Bsns Pk SK23 . . . . .65 D6
Botany Mews SK23 . . . . . . .65 E6
Boteler Ave WA5 . . . . .15 F7
Bottoms La CH64 . . . . .141 F8
Boughey Rd ST7 . . . . .209 F2
BOUGHTON 119 A2
Boughton CH2, CH3 . . . . . .118 F2
Boughton Hall Ave
 CH3 . . . . .119 A1
Boughton Hall Dr
 CH3 . . . . .119 A1
BOUGHTON HEATH 142 A8
Boughton Heath Prim Sch
 CH3 . . . . .119 B8
Boughton Lo **2** CH3 . . . .119 A1
Boughton St Paul's Inf Sch
 CH3 . . . . .237 C3
Boulevard The
 Broughton CH4 . . . . .139 C3
 Ellesmere Port CH65 . . . . . .69 F4
Boulting Ave WA5 . . . . .7 F1
Boulton Cl CW11 . . . . .175 C6
Boundary Ct CH3 . . . . .119 B1
Boundary La
 Chester CH4 . . . . .140 E5
 Congleton CW12 . . . . .179 B8
 Heswall CH60 . . . . .41 A8
 Over Peover WA16,
 SK11 . . . . .108 D7
 Siddington SK11 . . . . .132 E8
 Threapwood SY14 . . . . . . .222 F2
Boundary Lane N
 CW8 . . . . .101 F2
Boundary Lane S
 CW8 . . . . .101 F2
Boundary Pk CH64 . . . . . . .66 D7
Boundary St
 Northwich CW9 . . . . .79 E2
 Warrington WA1 . . . . .16 E7
Boundary Terr WA13 . . . . . .18 D1
Bourchier Way WA4 . . . . . .27 A8
Bourne Ave CW3 . . . . .143 C1
Bourne Cl WA7 . . . . .102 E7
Bournemouth Cl WA7 . . . . .50 D6
Bourne St ST7 . . . . .194 F2
Bourne St
 Mow Cop ST7 . . . . .195 C7
 Wilmslow SK9 . . . . .59 F6
Bouverie St CH1 . . . . .237 A4

Boverton Cl WA5 . . . . .7 E1
Bowden Cl
 Congleton CW12 . . . . .156 A3
 Culcheth WA3 . . . . .4 F4
Bowden Cres CW2 . . . . . . .239 D8
Bowden House La SK9 . . . . .61 A8
Bowden View La WA16 . . . .29 F2
Bowdon Cl WA1 . . . . .16 F8
Bowen Cl
 Bramhall SK7 . . . . .35 F5
 Widnes WA8 . . . . .12 D4
Bowen Cooke Ave
 CW1 . . . . .190 A5
Bowen St CW2 . . . . .190 A3
Bower Cres WA4 . . . . .26 D2
Bowerfield Ave SK7 . . . . . . .36 D8
Bowerfield Cres SK7 . . . . . .36 E8
Bower Rd CH60 . . . . .41 C8
Bowers Bsns Pk **4** 23 B7
Bowers Row **4** CW5 . . . .204 E5
Bowery Ave SK8 . . . . .34 F6
Bowery The CH1 . . . . .116 D4
Bowe's Gate Rd CW6 . . . . .169 A1
Bowfell Cl CH62 . . . . .43 E8
Bowfell Dr SK6 . . . . .37 E8
Bow Green Rd WA14 . . . . . .20 F1
Bowkers Croft CW11 . . . . .191 F8
Bowland Cl
 Runcorn WA7 . . . . .49 C5
 Warrington WA3 . . . . .10 B5
Bowland Croft CW1 . . . . . .173 B1
Bowland Rise CW7 . . . . . . .149 B7
Bowles Cl CW1 . . . . .175 A6
Bowland View CW11 . . . . .175 D3
Bowling Green Ct
 Chester CH1 . . . . .237 B3
8 Nantwich CW5 . . . . . .204 E5
 Winnington CW8 . . . . .78 E1
Bowman Ave WA4 . . . . .17 A5
Bowmans The SK10 . . . . . .87 B1
Bowmere Cl
 Biddulph ST8 . . . . .179 C1
 Tarporley CW6 . . . . .146 D1
Bowmere Dr CW7 . . . . . . .149 C8
Bowmere Rd CW6 . . . . . . .146 D1
Bowness Ave
 Bebington CH63 . . . . .43 C5
 Irlam M44 . . . . .11 D4
 Warrington WA2 . . . . .8 C2
 Winsford CW7 . . . . .126 D2
Bowness Cl CW4 . . . . .130 A3
Bowness Cl CW12 . . . . . . .156 A1
Bowness Rd CW2 . . . . .189 E3
Bowood Ct WA2 . . . . .8 A4
Bowring Dr CH64 . . . . .41 B1
Bowyer Ave **6** CW5 . . . . .204 E6
Boxgrove Cl WA8 . . . . .13 B3
Box La CW12 . . . . .155 F3
Box Tree Mews SK11 . . . . .112 A7
Box Wlk M31 . . . . .11 E3
Boydell Ave
 Warrington WA4 . . . . .17 B2
Boydell Way CH4 . . . . .162 A6
Boyle Ave WA2 . . . . .8 E1
Boyles Hall Rd ST7 . . . . . .209 E2
Bracken Cl
 Broughton CH4 . . . . .139 C3
 Macclesfield SK10 . . . . .86 F1
 Rode Heath ST7 . . . . .193 F8
 Warrington WA3 . . . . .9 C5
Brackendale
 Elton CH2 . . . . .72 B3
 Runcorn WA7 . . . . .49 D8
Brackendale Mews
 Chorlton CW2 . . . . .207 D2
 Wilmslow SK9 . . . . .60 E8
Bracken Way
 Barnton CW8 . . . . .78 B3
 Comberbach CW9 . . . . .78 C7
 Frodsham WA6 . . . . .74 C6
 Knutsford WA16 . . . . .82 A8
 Wincham CW9 . . . . .79 C3
Brackenwood Cl CW2 . . . . .206 B8
Brackenwood Dr WA8 . . . . .22 A8
Brackenwood Mews
 Chorlton CW2 . . . . .207 D2
 Wilmslow SK9 . . . . .60 E8
Brackley Ave M44 . . . . .11 D6
Brackley St
 Runcorn WA7 . . . . .22 F3
 Warrington WA4 . . . . .16 C1
Bradburn Rd M44 . . . . .11 E7
Bradburns La CW8 . . . . . . .103 B6
Bradbury Gdns CW12 . . . . .156 F1
Bradbury Rd CW7 . . . . .127 B2
Bradbury Wik **7** 155 B7
Braddon Cl CW9 . . . . .103 F3
BRADELEY GREEN 225 E6
Bradeley Green La
 SY13 . . . . .225 E6
Bradeley Hall Rd
 CW1 . . . . .191 B5
BRADFIELD GREEN 172 E3
Bradfield Rd CW1 . . . . .190 B8
Bradford La SK10 . . . . .85 C6
Bradford Pl CH4 . . . . .141 D7
Bradford St CW1 . . . . .141 D7
Bradgate Sk8 . . . . .34 D8
Bradgate Cl WA5 . . . . .15 F6

Brading Wlk M22 . . . . .33 E8
Bradlegh Rd WA12 . . . . .2 B1
Bradley Cl CW10 . . . . .151 B7
Bradley Farm La
 SY13 . . . . .225 C2
BRADLEY GREEN 225 A8
Bradley Hall Cotts
 WA4 . . . . .27 F6
Bradley La
 Frodsham WA6 . . . . .74 D7
 Newton-le-W WA5, WA12 . . . .2 A1
BRADLEY MOUNT 87 B7
Bradley St SK11 . . . . .112 E6
Bradley Way WA8 . . . . .13 A2
Bradmoor Rd CH62 . . . . . . .43 D8
Bradshaw Ave CH4 . . . . . . .140 B7
Bradshaw Com Prim Sch
 WA4 . . . . .17 B2
Bradshaw La
 Lymm WA13 . . . . .19 D3
 Warrington WA4 . . . . .17 B3
Bradshaw Pl CW12 . . . . . .156 E2
Bradshaw St WA3 . . . . .13 A2
BRADWALL GREEN 153 B3
Bradwall Rd CW11 . . . . . . .175 B7
Bradwall St CW11 . . . . . . .175 B7
Bradwall Cl CH65 . . . . .70 A4
Bradwell Cl CW12 . . . . . . .156 F2
Bradwell Dr SK8 . . . . .34 C7
Bradwell Gr CW12 . . . . . . .156 F2
Bradwell Rd
 Golborne WA3 . . . . .3 E7
 Hazel Grove SK7 . . . . .36 E8
Braemar Ave CW9 . . . . . . .104 C7
Braemar Cl
 Chester CH3 . . . . .119 C3
 Holmes Chapel CW4 . . . . . .130 C2
 Warrington WA2 . . . . .9 A3
 Wistaston CW2 . . . . .205 E8
Braemar Ct CH65 . . . . .70 E3
Braeside Cl
6 Ellesmere Port
 CH66 . . . . .69 C5
 Macclesfield SK11 . . . . . . .112 F6
Braidwood Ave WA16 . . . . .57 C3
Brains La CW6 . . . . .169 B6
Braintree Rd M22 . . . . .33 E8
Braithwaite Cl WA7 . . . . . . .49 D6
Braithwaite Rd WA3 . . . . . . .3 D8
Brakeley La CW8 . . . . .77 D4
Brakenwood
 WA7 . . . . .17 C1
Brake The ST7 . . . . .195 B7
Brake Village ST7 . . . . .195 B7
Bramall Cl CW11 . . . . .175 C7
Bramble Cl
 Chester CH3 . . . . .142 A7
 Macclesfield SK10 . . . . .87 B2
 Middlewich CW10 . . . . . . .128 E2
 Warrington WA3 . . . . .14 E3
 Winsford CW7 . . . . .126 C3
Brambles Chase CW8 . . . .101 F2
Brambles The
 Burtonwood WA5 . . . . .7 A7
 Congleton CW12 . . . . .178 F8
 Wincham CW9 . . . . .79 C3
Bramble Way WA7 . . . . .49 E4
Brambling Cl WA7 . . . . .49 F5
Brambling Way WA3 . . . . . . .3 E7
BRAMHALL 35 D8
Bramhall Cl CW7 . . . . .126 B1
Bramhall Cl CW2 . . . . .189 F2
Bramhall Ctr The SK7 . . . . .35 E6
Bramhall Dr
 Bebington CH62 . . . . .43 F4
 Holmes Chapel CW4 . . . . . .130 A3
Bramhall High Sch
 SK7 . . . . .35 F8
Bramhall La S SK7 . . . . .35 E7
Bramhall Rd CW2 . . . . .189 F2
Bramhalls Pk CW9 . . . . .78 C3
Bramhall St WA5 . . . . .15 E5
Bramhall Sta SK7 . . . . .35 E6
Bramhall Way SK10 . . . . . .112 A8
Bramley Cl
 Bramhall SK7 . . . . .35 E6
2 Ellesmere Port CH66 . . .94 F8
 Wilmslow SK9 . . . . .59 D4
Bramley Ct CW6 . . . . .122 D5
Bramley Dr SK7 . . . . .35 E6
Bramley Mews WA4 . . . . . . .26 C8
Bramley Rd SK7 . . . . .35 E6
Bramley Wlk WA6 . . . . .73 A1
Brampton Ave SK10 . . . . . .87 A2
Brampton Cl CW2 . . . . .207 E3
Brampton Ct WA9 . . . . .1 B3
Bramshill Cl WA3 . . . . .10 A6
Bramway
 Bramhall SK7 . . . . .35 C7
 High Lane SK6 . . . . .37 F7
Bramwood Ct SK7 . . . . .35 E6
Brancaster Dr WA3 . . . . .4 F7
Brancepeth Ct CH65 . . . . . .70 E3
Branch Way WA11 . . . . .1 D6
Brancote Gdns CH62 . . . . . .43 D7
Brandon Dr WA6 . . . . .57 B1
Brandon Hall WA3 . . . . .4 D2
Brandon Cl SK9 . . . . .34 D2
Brandreth Dr WA3 . . . . .4 B2
Brandwood Ho **2**
 WA1 . . . . .16 C5

Bransdale Cl WA5 . . . . .14 F7
Bransdale Way SK11 . . . . . . .111 F7
Brantfield Ct WA2 . . . . .8 E2
Brassey Ct CW5 . . . . .205 C6
BRASSEY GREEN 167 D6
Brassey's Contract Rd
SY14 . . . . .199 A1
Brassey St CH3 . . . . .118 F1
Brassey Way CW5 . . . . .205 D5
Brassington Terr
CW3 . . . . .221 F3
Brathay Cl WA2. . . . . .8 C3
BRATT'S BANK 101 B5
Brattswood Dr ST7 . . . . . . .194 A5
Bray Cl
Crewe CW1 . . . . .190 E5
Runcorn WA7 . . . . .49 D6
Bray Rd CH4 . . . . .140 F6
Breach House La
WA16 . . . . .32 A1
Bread St SK11 . . . . .112 C7
Breck Rd WA8 . . . . .13 B1
Breck The CH66 . . . . .69 E7
Brecon Cl SK12 . . . . .36 F4
Brecon Ct WA5 . . . . .7 E2
Brecon Dr **1** CH66 . . . . . . .69 E1
Breconway CW7 . . . . .149 B8
Brecon Way CW2 . . . . .206 A4
Bredon Cl CH66 . . . . .69 A6
Breen Cl CH3 . . . . .166 B1
Breezehill Cl CH64 . . . . .66 F8
Breezehill Pk CH64 . . . . .66 F8
Breezehill Rd CH64 . . . . .66 F8
Brendon Ave WA2 . . . . .8 A3
Brendon Gr WA9 . . . . .1 A4
Brennus Pl CH1 . . . . .237 A3
Brent Cl SK12 . . . . .36 B4
Brentfield WA8 . . . . .12 D2
Brentnall Cl WA5 . . . . .15 C5
Brentwood Ave M44 . . . . . . .11 D6
Brentwood Rd CH1 . . . . . . .117 E5
Brereton CE Prim Sch
CW11 . . . . .153 F5
Brereton Cl
Crewe CW2 . . . . .189 E2
Malpas SY14 . . . . .213 B3
Runcorn WA7 . . . . .50 A8
Sandbach CW11 . . . . .175 C7
Brereton Ct
Brereton Green
CW12 . . . . .154 F6
1 Cheadle SK8 . . . . .34 E8
Brereton Dr CW5 . . . . .204 F7
Brereton Gr M44 . . . . .11 E6
BRERETON GREEN 153 E5
BRERETON HEATH 154 F6
Brereton Heath Ctry Pk*
CW12 . . . . .154 D7
Brereton Heath La CW11,
CW12 . . . . .154 G6
Brereton Heath Local
Nature Reserve*
CW12 . . . . .154 D6
Brereton La CW4 . . . . .152 E8
Brereton Rd
Handforth SK9 . . . . .34 E3
Hartford CW8 . . . . .103 A4
Bretland Dr WA4 . . . . .27 A7
Breton Cl CH2 . . . . .118 E5
BRETTON 139 E4
Bretton Court Mews
CH4 . . . . .139 E4
Bretton Dr CH4 . . . . .139 B3
Bretton La CH4 . . . . .139 F5
Bretton Rd CH4. . . . . .139 E4
Bretton Wlk M22 . . . . .33 D8
Brewery La ST7 . . . . .180 E3
Brian Ave
Warrington WA4, Stockton Heath
WA4 . . . . .16 E1
Warrington WA4 . . . . .16 D8
Brian Bevan Island
WA1 . . . . .16 B4
Briar Ave WA3 . . . . .11 B2
Briar Cl WA16 . . . . .57 A3
Briardale Cl CW2 . . . . .205 F8
Briardale Gdns **4**
CH66 . . . . .69 C6
Briardale Rd
Ellesmere Port CH66 . . . . . .69 C6
Willaston CH64 . . . . .43 A1
Briar Dr CH60 . . . . .41 A8
Briarfield Ave WA8 . . . . .12 A1
Briarfield Rd
Ellesmere Port CH65 . . . . . .70 B5
Heswall CH60 . . . . .41 B8
Briar La CW8 . . . . .102 E7
Briarlands Cl SK7 . . . . .35 D6
Briar Rd WA3 . . . . .3 B8
Briarstead Cl SK7 . . . . .35 D7
Briarswood
Biddulph ST8 . . . . .179 D1
Kidsgrove ST7 . . . . .195 B1
Briarswood Ct CH1 . . . . . . .237 B3
Briar Wlk WA3 . . . . .3 B8
Briarwood
Runcorn WA7 . . . . .50 B8
Wilmslow SK9 . . . . .60 C7
Briarwood Ave
Macclesfield SK11 . . . . . . .112 D5
Warrington WA1 . . . . .16 E7
Briarwood Ct CW7 . . . . .149 C8
Brick Bank CW5 . . . . .204 F5
Brick Bank La WA16,
CW4 . . . . .107 B2

Brickfield Bsns Ctr
CW9 . . . . .79 D1
Brickfield La CH3 . . . . .119 F2
Brickhill La WA15 . . . . .32 B4
Brickhurst Way WA11 . . . . . . .17 B8
Brickkiln La
Little Bollington WA14 . . . . . .20 C3
Whitchurch SY13 . . . . .226 D2
Brick Kiln La CW10 . . . . . . .127 B7
Brickley Ct CW8 . . . . .77 C1
Brick Rd CH4 . . . . .139 D2
Brick St
Newton-le-W WA12 . . . . .1 F3
Warrington WA1 . . . . .16 C5
Bridestone Sh Ctr
CW12 . . . . .156 D2
Bridewell Ct WA8 . . . . .13 B3
Bridge Ave WA4 . . . . .16 F4
Bridge Ave E WA4 . . . . .16 F5
Bridge Bank Cl WA3 . . . . .3 B7
Bridge Cl
Audley ST7 . . . . .209 F2
Cuddington CW8 . . . . .102 A3
Lymm WA13 . . . . .19 B4
Wistaston CW2 . . . . .206 A7
Bridge Cotts CH4 . . . . .237 B1
Bridge Ct
Chester CH2 . . . . .119 A2
Holt LL13 . . . . .196 E8
Neston CH64 . . . . .66 E7
Bridgedown CW6 . . . . .146 C1
Bridge Dr
Christleton CH3 . . . . .142 D7
Handforth SK9 . . . . .34 D3
Bridge End Dr SK10 . . . . .87 A7
Bridge End La SK10 . . . . .87 A7
Bridge Farm Ct CW10 . . . . .152 A4
Bridgefield Ave SK9 . . . . .34 C1
Bridgefoot Ind Est
WA4 . . . . .16 B4
Bridge Foyer The
CH1 . . . . .118 B2
Bridge Gn SK10 . . . . .87 A7
Bridge La
Cuddington CW8 . . . . .101 F3
Frodsham WA6 . . . . .49 D1
Goostrey CW4 . . . . .108 C2
Warrington WA4 . . . . .26 E7
Warrington WA4 . . . . .26 E8
Warrington, Woolston
WA1 . . . . .17 C7
Bridge Lane Mews
WA6 . . . . .49 D1
Bridgeman Rd CH1 . . . . . . .117 E3
Bridgeman St WA5 . . . . .15 D4
Bridge Mdw CH66 . . . . .69 F2
BRIDGEMERE 231 F8
Bridgemere CE Prim Sch
CW5 . . . . .231 E8
Bridgemere Ct CW11 . . . . . .174 F8
Bridgemere Garden
World* CW5 . . . . .232 B4
Bridgemere La CW5 . . . . . . .219 E1
Bridgemere Mews
CW5 . . . . .231 F8
Bridgemere Way **4**
CW9 . . . . .103 E4
BRIDGEMONT 39 E2
Bridgend CH2 . . . . .97 A2
Bridgend Cl WA8 . . . . .12 D3
Bridge Pl CH1 . . . . .237 B1
Bridge Rd WA1 . . . . .17 C7
Bridge Row CW12 . . . . .156 F4
Bridge St Row E CH1 . . . . . .237 B2
Bridge St Row W CH1 . . . . .237 B2
Bridge Sh Ctr The
WA6 . . . . .16 F3
Bridge Side Dr WA6 . . . . .73 B4
Bridges Rd CH65 . . . . .70 F5
Bridge St
Chester CH1 . . . . .237 B2
Congleton CW12 . . . . .156 D2
Golborne WA3 . . . . .3 A7
Holt LL13 . . . . .180 E1
Macclesfield SK11 . . . . . . .112 C7
Neston CH64 . . . . .66 E7
Newton-le-W WA12 . . . . .2 B3
Northwich CW9 . . . . .79 E2
Runcorn WA7 . . . . .23 B2
Saltney CH4 . . . . .140 D7
Warrington WA1 . . . . .16 B4
Warrington WA1 . . . . .16 B5
Whaley Bridge SK23 . . . . . . .65 E7
Wybunbury CW5 . . . . .220 B8
Bridge Terr CH3 . . . . .119 F2
BRIDGE TRAFFORD 97 A3
Bridge View Cl WA8 . . . . .23 A4
Bridgewater Ave WA4 . . . . . .16 F4
Bridgewater Cl
Congleton CW12 . . . . .157 B1
6 Frodsham WA6 . . . . . . .49 C1
Gatley SK8 . . . . .34 D7
Bridgewater Ct
5 Lymm WA13 . . . . .18 C3
6 Runcorn WA7 . . . . .23 B2
Bridgewater Dr CH3 . . . . . . .119 C2
Bridgewater Grange
WA7 . . . . .50 F5
Bridgewater High Sch
(Lower Sch) WA4 . . . . . . .26 D6
Bridgewater High Sch
(Upper Sch) WA4 . . . . . . .26 D7
Bridgewater Mews
WA4 . . . . .26 C8
Bridgewater Pl WA3 . . . . .9 E4
Bridgewater St
4 Lymm WA13 . . . . .18 E3
6 Runcorn WA7 . . . . .23 A3

Bridgeway E WA7 . . . . .24 C2
Bridgeway W WA7 . . . . .24 C2
Bridge Wlk **7** WA7 . . . . . . .24 C2
Bridgewood Dr CH66 . . . . . . .69 C2
Bridgfield Cl SK6 . . . . .37 E7
Bridgnorth Gr ST5 . . . . .210 E2
Bridle Cl CH62 . . . . .43 E7
Bridle Ct
Bramhall SK7 . . . . .35 F2
Crewe CW2 . . . . .190 B4
Bridle Hey CW5 . . . . .204 F2
Bridle La CH1 . . . . .94 E6
Bridlemere Ct WA1 . . . . .16 E8
Bridle Pk CH62 . . . . .43 E7
Bridle Rd
Bebington CH62 . . . . .43 E6
Crewe CW2 . . . . .190 B4
Woodford SK7 . . . . .35 F2
Bridle Way
Ellesmere Port CH66 . . . . . .69 D3
Woodford SK7 . . . . .36 A2
Briedden Way CH66 . . . . .69 A6
Brierley Bsns Ctr
CW1 . . . . .190 D4
Brierley Prim Sch
CW1 . . . . .190 D4
Brierley Rd CW12 . . . . .157 B1
Brierley St CW1 . . . . .190 D4
Briers Cl WA2 . . . . .8 F3
Brieryhurst Rd ST7 . . . . .195 B3
Briggs Ave CW2 . . . . .190 D1
Brighton Cres SK11 . . . . . . .113 B3
Brighton St WA5 . . . . .15 E6
Brights Ave **8** ST7 . . . . . . .195 B2
Bright St CW1 . . . . .190 B5
Brightwell Cl WA5 . . . . .14 E5
Brimelow Cres WA5 . . . . .14 E3
Brimstage Cl CH60 . . . . .41 C8
Brimstage Gn CH60 . . . . .41 C8
Brimstage Rd CH60 . . . . .41 C7
BRINDLEY 186 E8
Brindley Ave
Warrington WA4 . . . . .17 A3
Winsford CW7 . . . . .126 C1
Brindley Cl
Kidsgrove ST7 . . . . .194 E1
Talke ST7 . . . . .210 E8
Brindley Ct WA4 . . . . .26 D8
Brindley Gr SK9 . . . . .34 E2
BRINDLEY GREEN 153 E2
Brindley Hall Rd CW5 . . . . . .186 E2
Brindley La CW11 . . . . .153 E4
Brindley Lea La CW5 . . . . . . .186 D1
Brindley Pk CW11 . . . . .174 F3
Brindley Rd WA7 . . . . .23 F3
Brindley St WA7 . . . . .22 F3
Brindleys Way ST7 . . . . .209 F2
Brindley Way
Congleton CW12 . . . . .157 B1
Macclesfield SK11 . . . . . . .112 C3
Brindley Wharf WA4 . . . . .50 F6
Brine Leas High Sch
CW5 . . . . .204 F3
Brinell Dr M44 . . . . .11 F6
Brine Pits La CW5 . . . . .218 F2
Brine Pump Cotts CW9 . . . . .78 F4
Brine Rd CW5 . . . . .204 E3
Brines Brow La CH3 . . . . .99 C2
Brinley Cl CH62 . . . . .43 D5
Brinton Cl WA8 . . . . .22 E8
Brisbane Cl SK7 . . . . .35 F5
Brisbane Rd CH1 . . . . .117 C4
Bristol Ave WA7 . . . . .50 E6
Bristol Cl
Blacon CH1 . . . . .117 C4
Gatley SK8 . . . . .34 C7
Bristol Dr **3** CH66 . . . . . . .69 E1
Bristow Cl WA5 . . . . .15 B8
Britannia Dr CW9 . . . . .104 E7
Britannia Rd WA6 . . . . .73 B2
Brittania Gdns WA6 . . . . .73 B1
Brixham Ave SK8 . . . . .34 F7
Brixham Wlk SK7 . . . . .35 E7
Broadacre CW9 . . . . .78 D6
Broadacre Dr CH3 . . . . .59 D3
Broadacres CW5 . . . . .217 F4
Broadbent Ave WA4 . . . . .16 F4
Broadcar Rd SK11 . . . . .113 C6
Broad Ct SK9 . . . . .85 B8
Broadfields WA7 . . . . .50 C8
Broadheath Terr WA8 . . . . . .12 D1
Broadheys La WA16 . . . . .28 D6
Broadhurst Ave
Culcheth WA3 . . . . .4 F2
3 Warrington WA5 . . . . . .15 D4
Broadhurst La CW12 . . . . . .156 C3
Broad La
Altrincham WA15 . . . . .32 B8
Appleton Thorn WA4 . . . . . .27 C8
Burtonwood WA5 . . . . .6 E8
Haydock WA5, WA9 . . . . .1 C1
Heswall CH60 . . . . .40 C8
Holmes Chapel CW4 . . . . . .129 F1
Stapeley CW5 . . . . .205 A1
Broadlake CH64 . . . . .67 F8
Broadland Gdns CH66 . . . . . .69 F2
Broadland Rd CH66 . . . . .69 F2
Broadleigh Way CW2 . . . . . .206 C8
Broadley Ave WA3 . . . . .3 C7
Broadmead
Chester CH3 . . . . .119 C2
Heswall CH60 . . . . .41 C7
BROADOAK 162 B1
Broad Oak Ave
Broughton CH4 . . . . .139 A3
Haydock WA11 . . . . .1 A6
Warrington WA5 . . . . .14 E4

Broad Oak Com Prim Sch
WA9 . . . . .1 A3
Broadoak La
High Legh WA16 . . . . .29 D5
Mobberley WA16 . . . . .57 E6
Broadoak Sch M31 . . . . .11 F2
Broad St CW1 . . . . .190 C6
Broadwalk SK10 . . . . .87 A5
Broadway
Altrincham WA15 . . . . .32 A8
Barnton CW8 . . . . .78 B3
Widnes WA8 . . . . .12 A1
Wilmslow SK9 . . . . .60 B6
Broadway E CH2 . . . . .118 C5
Broadways CW3 . . . . .230 A4
Broadway The CW5 . . . . . . .204 F5
Broadway W CH2 . . . . .118 D5
Broad Wlk SK9 . . . . .59 F8
Broadwood Ct CH66 . . . . .37 F7
Broady Ct **5** CW2 . . . . . . .190 D2
Brock Dr SK8 . . . . .35 B8
Brock Gdns L24 . . . . .21 E2
Brock Hollow CW11 . . . . . . .174 F4
Brockhurst Mews
CW9 . . . . .104 A6
Brockhurst St CW9 . . . . .104 A8
Brockhurst Way CW9 . . . . . .104 A6
Brocklebank Dr CW8 . . . . . .103 E7
Brocklehurst Ave SK10 . . . . .87 F2
Brocklehurst Ct **2**
SK10 . . . . .87 D3
Brocklehurst Dr SK10 . . . . . .87 A7
Brocklehurst Manor
SK10 . . . . .87 E1
Brocklehurst Mews **3**
SK10 . . . . .87 D3
Brocklehurst Way
SK10 . . . . .87 D3
Brock Rd WA3 . . . . .9 D3
Brocks Croft Gdns
ST8 . . . . .179 C1
Brock St
Macclesfield SK10 . . . . .87 D1
Macclesfield SK10 . . . . . . .112 D8
Brockton Ct WA4 . . . . .26 C6
Brockway E CH3 . . . . .166 A1
Brockway W CH3 . . . . .166 A1
Brockwell Cl CW7 **2** 149 A8
Brodie Cl CH2 . . . . .95 C1
Brogden Ave WA3 . . . . .4 E4
Broken Banks **10**
SK11 . . . . .112 D7
BROKEN CROSS 111 E8
Broken Cross SK11 . . . . . . .111 F8
BROKEN CROSS 104 E7
Broken Cross Com Sch
SK11 . . . . .111 E7
Brokencross Pl CW9 . . . . . .104 E7
Bromborough Rake Sta
CH62 . . . . .43 C8
Bromborough Sta
CH63 . . . . .43 C7
Bromborough Village Rd
CH62 . . . . .43 E8
Bromley Ave WA3 . . . . .3 D7
Bromley Cl
Crewe CW1 . . . . .189 F8
Heswall CH60 . . . . .40 E7
Warrington WA2 . . . . .8 F3
Bromley Dr CW4 . . . . .130 C2
Bromley Rd
Congleton CW12 . . . . .156 F3
Macclesfield SK10 . . . . . . .111 E8
Brompton Gdns WA5 . . . . . .15 E7
Brompton Way
Ellesmere Port CH66 . . . . . .69 E1
Handforth SK9 . . . . .34 C5
Bronington Ave CH62 . . . . . .43 D6
Bronte Cl WA2 . . . . .8 E1
Brook Acre Com Prim Sch
WA2 . . . . .8 E1
Brookash Rd M22 . . . . .34 A8
Brook Ave
Handforth SK9 . . . . .34 D4
Shavington CW2 . . . . .206 C5
Warrington, Westy WA4 . . . . .16 F5
Brook Bank SK12 . . . . .36 E2
Brook Bottom Rd SK22 . . . . .39 A8
Brook Cl
Crewe CW1 . . . . .190 F4
Cronton WA8 . . . . .12 C6
Brook Ct
Chester CH1 . . . . .118 B3
Sandbach CW11 . . . . .175 B6
Brookdale WA8 . . . . .12 A3
Brookdale Ave WA16 . . . . . . .57 C2
Brookdale Ct CH3 . . . . .143 D5
Brookdale Pk CW2 . . . . .190 A3
Brookdale Pl CH1 . . . . .237 B3
Brookdale Way CH3 . . . . . . .143 B5
Brook Dr
Kelsall CW6 . . . . .122 D4
Warrington WA5 . . . . .15 A5
Brooke Ave CH2 . . . . .118 F8
Brooke Cl SK9 . . . . .34 E4
Brooke Dr SK9 . . . . .34 D4
Brooke Ho SK10 . . . . .86 F1
Brook End WA9 . . . . .1 A1
Brookes Ave CH4 . . . . .139 B3
Brooke Way SK9 . . . . .34 D4
Brook Farm Cl M31 . . . . .11 E2
Brookfield CW1 . . . . .191 D5
Brookfield Ave
Poynton SK12 . . . . .36 C3
Runcorn WA7 . . . . .23 E2

Brookfield Cl
Lymm WA13 . . . . .18 D3
Tarporley CW6 . . . . .168 D8
Brookfield Cotts **2**
WA13 . . . . .18 D3
Brookfield Cres CW4 . . . . . .107 F1
Brookfield Ct CW1 . . . . .190 B5
Brookfield Dr
Alsager ST7 . . . . .193 C5
Chester CH2 . . . . .118 E4
Holmes Chapel CW4 . . . . . .130 B3
Brookfield La CW1 . . . . .112 F7
Brookfield Pk WA4 . . . . .17 A2
Brookfield Rd
Comberbach CW9 . . . . .78 D8
Culcheth WA3 . . . . .4 D3
Ellesmere Port CH66 . . . . . .69 E3
Brookfields Sch WA8 . . . . . . .13 D2
Brookfield St WA12 . . . . .2 B3
Brook Furlong WA6 . . . . .48 F2
Brook Gdns ST8 . . . . .179 D1
Brook Hey CH64 . . . . .41 B2
Brook Ho WA4 . . . . .16 F3
BROOKHOUSE 88 D3
Brookhouse Cl SK10 . . . . .86 F1
Brook House Ct WA13 . . . . . .18 D2
Brookhouse Dr CW2 . . . . . . .206 C8
BROOKHOUSE GREEN 177 A7
Brookhouse La
Church Minshull CW1,
CW10 . . . . .172 D7
Congleton CW12 . . . . .157 C2
Duddon CH3 . . . . .144 D6
Lower Whitley WA4 . . . . .52 B2
Brookhouse Rd
Alsager ST7 . . . . .193 D3
5 Sandbach CW11 . . . . .175 B6
BROOKHURST 43 C5
Brookhurst Ave CH63 . . . . . .43 C5
Brookhurst Cl CH63 . . . . .43 C5
Brookhurst Prim Sch
CH63 . . . . .43 C6
Brookhurst Rd CH63 . . . . . . .43 C5
Brook La
Alderley Edge SK9 . . . . .59 F3
Astbury CW12 . . . . .177 E5
Broughton CH5 . . . . .139 C7
Burland CW5 . . . . .203 D8
Chester CH2 . . . . .118 E4
Faddiley CW5 . . . . .202 F8
Knutsford WA16 . . . . .57 B1
Neston CH64 . . . . .41 C2
Northwich CW9 . . . . .104 D7
Warrington WA3 . . . . .18 A8
Brookland Ave CW2 . . . . . . .205 F8
Brookland Dr CW11 . . . . . . .175 C6
Brookland La WA9 . . . . .1 A1
BROOKLANDS 225 C1
Brooklands Ave SK11 . . . . . .112 B7
Brooklands Dr
Goostrey CW4 . . . . .107 F1
Northwich CW9 . . . . .104 A4
Brooklands Gr CW1 . . . . . . .190 A6
Brooklands Pk **1** WA8 . . . .13 C2
Brooklands Rd
Congleton CW12 . . . . .155 F2
Neston CH64 . . . . .41 C1
Brookland St WA1 . . . . .16 E7
Brooklands The CW2 . . . . . .206 E3
Brookledge La SK10 . . . . . . .62 E5
Brooklet Rd CH60 . . . . .41 C8
Brooklyn Dr
Ellesmere Port CH65 . . . . . .69 F5
Lymm WA13 . . . . .18 E4
Brooklyn St CW2 . . . . .190 C2
Brookmere Cl CW11 . . . . . . .174 E8
Brookmills Cotts ST8 . . . . . .179 C1
Brookmoore Ct CH2 . . . . . . .237 A4
Brook Pl
Chester CH1 . . . . .237 B3
Warrington WA4 . . . . .16 E3
Brook Rd
Ellesmere Port CH66 . . . . . .69 D5
Lymm WA13 . . . . .18 E4
Tarporley CW6 . . . . .168 D8
Brooks Dr WA15 . . . . .32 D8
Brookside
Ashton Hayes CH3 . . . . . . .121 F7
Chester CH3 . . . . .142 A8
Cuddington CW8 . . . . .101 F3
Kelsall CW6 . . . . .122 C4
Kingsley WA6 . . . . .75 C2
Warrington WA4 . . . . .16 E3
Brook Side CH3 . . . . .120 C8
Brook Side **8** WA11 . . . . . . .1 B7
Brookside Ave
Lymm WA13 . . . . .18 C4
Poynton SK12 . . . . .36 E3
Sutton Lane Ends SK11 . . . .112 F2
Warrington, Stockton Heath
WA4 . . . . .16 D1
Warrington WA5 . . . . .14 E4
Brookside Cl WA11 . . . . .1 B7
Brookside Cotts
CW11 . . . . .176 A8
Brookside Cl SK10 . . . . .87 A1
Brookside Gn **2** CW2 . . . .206 C8
Brookside La SK6 . . . . .37 E7
Brookside Mill **6**
SK11 . . . . .112 E7
Brookside Miniature Rly*
SK12 . . . . .37 A3
Brookside Prim Sch
Ellesmere Port CH66 . . . . . .69 E4
High Lane SK6 . . . . .37 E6
Brookside Rd
4 Congleton CW12 . . . . .156 D3

Brookside Rd
Frodsham WA6 . . . . .74 A8
Brookside Terr
Chester CH2 . . . . .237 C4
Wilmslow SK9 . . . . .59 E3
Brookside View WA11 . . . . .1 B7
Brookside Way WA11 . . . . . .1 B7
Brooks La
Bosley SK11 . . . . .135 E2
Brook Slack CW6 . . . . .124 D1
Brooks Lane Ind Est
Middlewich CW10 . . . . . . .128 D1
Middlewich CW10 . . . . . . .151 D8
Brook St
Chester CH1 . . . . .237 B3
Congleton CW12 . . . . .156 F3
Crewe CW2 . . . . .190 D3
Golborne, Bank Heath
WA3 . . . . .3 A8
Knutsford WA16 . . . . .57 B1
Macclesfield SK11 . . . . . . .112 E7
Neston CH64 . . . . .66 E8
Northwich CW9 . . . . .79 A1
Northwich, Lostock Gralam
CW9 . . . . .79 E2
2 Runcorn WA7 . . . . .23 A2
3 Widnes WA8 . . . . .13 B1
Brook Street Bridge CH1,
CH2 . . . . .237 C4
Brook Street Mill **15**
SK11 . . . . .112 E7
Brook Terr
Runcorn WA7 . . . . .23 E1
Sandbach CW11 . . . . .175 A3
BROOKVALE 50 B5
Brookvale Ave N WA7 . . . . .50 B6
Brookvale Ave S WA7 . . . . .50 B6
Brookvale CI WA5 . . . . .7 E6
Brookvale Prim Sch
WA7 . . . . .50 B5
Brook View
Alderley Edge SK9 . . . . . . .60 A3
Allostock WA16 . . . . .106 F3
Brookwood CI CW2 . . . . . .206 C8
Brook Villas ST7 . . . . .193 E3
Brook Way
Hartford CW8 . . . . .103 B4
Nantwich CW5 . . . . .204 E3
Warrington WA5 . . . . .15 A5
Brookway La WA9 . . . . .1 A1
Brook Well CH64 . . . . .66 F5
Brookwood CI WA4 . . . . . . .26 B8
Broom Ave WA4 . . . . .26 E6
BROOM BANK 144 B8
Broom Cres CH3 . . . . .121 B1
Broome Ct WA7 . . . . .50 B5
BROOMEDGE 29 C8
Broomehouse Ave
M44 . . . . .11 E8
Broomfield CW12 . . . . . . .154 F6
Broomfield CI
Chelford SK11 . . . . .84 A3
Wilmslow SK9 . . . . .60 E8
13 Winsford CW7 . . . . .149 A8
Broomfields WA4 . . . . .26 E7
Broomfields Jun Sch
WA4 . . . . .26 E7
Broomfields La CW8 . . . . . .77 F4
Broomfields Rd WA4 . . . . . .26 D7
BROOMHALL 217 F4
BROOMHALL GREEN 217 F3
Broomheath La
Tarvin, Broom Bank
CH3 . . . . .144 C7
Tarvin CH3 . . . . .121 C1
Broomhill La
Brown Knowl CH3 . . . . . . .199 D8
Great Barrow CH3 . . . . . . .120 E8
Broom La WA16 . . . . .81 F2
Broomlands CH60 . . . . . . .40 E8
Broomlands Cots
CW5 . . . . .219 E1
Broom Rd M31 . . . . .11 F2
Broomsfield La CW8 . . . . . .78 A4
Broom's La CW6 . . . . .122 D6
Broom St CW1 . . . . .190 A6
Broseley Ave WA3 . . . . .4 D5
Brotherton La WA12 . . . . . .2 A4
Brotherton Way CH62 . . . . .43 C8
Brough St W SK11 . . . . . . .112 C7
BROUGHTON 139 A4
Broughton Ave WA3 . . . . . . .3 D7
Broughton CI WA4 . . . . . . .26 F8
Broughton Cres SY14 . . . . .211 A1
Broughton Hall Rd
CH4 . . . . .139 C4
Broughton Ind Est
CH4 . . . . .139 F4
Broughton Inf Sch
CH4 . . . . .139 C4
Broughton Jun Sch
CH4 . . . . .139 C4
Broughton La CW2 . . . . . .189 F1
Broughton Mills Rd
CH4 . . . . .139 F6
Broughton Rd
Adlington SK10 . . . . .62 C5
Crewe CW1 . . . . .190 C8
1 Broughton Sh Pk CH4 .139 E4
Broughton Way WA8 . . . . . .22 B5
Brow Com Prim Sch The
CH4 . . . . .139 F1
Brow La
Antrobus CW9 . . . . .53 D5
Heswall CH60 . . . . .40 F7
Browmere Dr WA3 . . . . .9 A7

Brown Ave
Lawton-gate ST7 . . . . .194 A5
Nantwich CW5 . . . . .204 F4
BROWNEDGE 154 A3
BROWN HEATH 143 B6
Brown Heath Rd CH3 . . . . .143 B6
BROWNHILL 147 B6
Brownhill Dr WA1 . . . . .16 F8
Brownhills Rd CW6 . . . . . .147 C6
Browning Ave WA8 . . . . . . .22 F8
Browning CI
Blacon CH1 . . . . .117 F6
Macclesfield SK11 . . . . . . .174 D5
Browning Dr
Ellesmere Port CH65 . . . . . .69 F4
Winwick WA2 . . . . .8 A6
Browning Gn CH65 . . . . . . .69 F4
Browning Gr ST7 . . . . .210 C8
Browning St CW1 . . . . .190 C4
Browning Way CW7 . . . . . .149 A7
BROWN KNOWL 199 C8
Brown Lees CI CW12 . . . . .156 E3
Brown Lees Rd ST7 . . . . . . .95 F4
BROWNLOW 177 E7
Brownlow CI SK12 . . . . .36 E2
Brownlow Hall Mews
CW12 . . . . .177 E5
BROWNLOW HEATH 177 D5
Brownlow Heath
CW12 . . . . .177 E5
Brownlow Heath La
CW12 . . . . .177 D6
BROWN MOSS 231 B7
BROWN'S BANK 229 D2
Brown's La
Chester CH4 . . . . .141 C7
Widnes WA8 . . . . .60 E8
Brown St
3 Alderley Edge SK9 . . . .60 A1
Congleton CW12 . . . . .156 E3
Macclesfield SK11 . . . . . . .112 C7
Widnes WA8 . . . . .23 D7
Brow The WA6 . . . . .75 C2
BROXTON 183 A1
Broxton Ave CW10 . . . . . .151 D6
Broxton CI WA8 . . . . .12 C3
Broxton Mews CH3 . . . . . .183 A1
Broxton Rd
Clutton CH3 . . . . .182 D1
Ellesmere Port CH66 . . . . . .69 E5
Bruce Ave WA2 . . . . .8 D1
Bruce Cres CH63 . . . . .43 C6
Bruce Dr CH66 . . . . .69 C4
BRUCHE 16 F7
Bruche Ave WA1 . . . . .16 F7
Bruche Com Prim Sch
WA1 . . . . .17 A7
Bruche Dr WA1 . . . . .16 F8
Bruche Heath Gdns
WA1 . . . . .17 A8
Bruen The CH3 . . . . .121 C3
BRUERA 164 D6
Bruera Rd CH65 . . . . .69 F4
Brunel Ct CW9 . . . . .104 E5
Brunel Rd SK11 . . . . .112 C3
Brunner Gr CW5 . . . . .205 A5
Brunner Rd WA8 . . . . .23 A8
Brunsborough CI CH62 . . . .43 C6
Brunswick **11** WA7 . . . . . .23 A3
Brunswick Cres CH66 . . . . .69 E3
Brunswick Ct **12**
SK11 . . . . .112 D7
Brunswick Hill SK10 . . . . .112 D8
Brunswick Rd WA12 . . . . . . .1 F4
Brunswick St
Congleton CW12 . . . . .156 F3
5 Macclesfield SK10 . . .112 D8
St Helens WA9 . . . . .1 A3
Brunswick Terr SK10 . . . . .112 D8
Bruntleigh Ave WA4 . . . . . .17 A3
Bryant Ave WA4 . . . . .16 F5
Brymau Four Trad Est
CH4 . . . . .140 D7
Brymau One Trad Est
CH4 . . . . .140 E7
Brymau Three Trad Est
CH4 . . . . .140 D7
Brymau Two Trad Est
CH4 . . . . .140 E7
BRYN 102 A6
Brynlow Dr CW10 . . . . .151 B8
Brynmore Dr SK11 . . . . . . .112 F7
Brynn St WA8 . . . . .23 B8
Brynton CI SK10 . . . . .87 C1
Brynton Rd SK10 . . . . .87 C1
Buchanan CI WA8 . . . . .12 F3
Buchan CI WA5 . . . . .15 B8
Buchan Gr CW2 . . . . .190 B3
Buckbean Way CW4 . . . . . .107 E1
Buckden Way **9**
SK10 . . . . .112 C8
Buckfast CI WA11 . . . . .2 A7
Buckfast Ct
Cheadle SK8 . . . . .35 B6
Macclesfield SK10 . . . . .87 C2
Poynton SK12 . . . . .36 D5
Buckfast Way CW10 . . . . . .128 B1
Buckfast St WA7 . . . . .24 E3
Buckingham Ave
Chester CH3 . . . . .119 B2
Widnes WA8 . . . . .13 A4
Buckingham CI
4 Congleton CW12 . . . . .156 F4
Wistaston CW2 . . . . .205 E8
Buckingham Dr
Knutsford WA16 . . . . .57 B1
Macclesfield SK11 . . . . . . .112 B5

Buckingham Dr continued
Northwich CW9 . . . . .103 E4
Warrington WA5 . . . . .15 C4
Winsford CW7 . . . . .149 C7
Buckingham Gdns **1**
CH65 . . . . .70 D2
Buckingham Rd
Irlam M44 . . . . .11 C6
Poynton SK12 . . . . .36 D3
Wilmslow SK9 . . . . .59 F6
Buckingham Rise
SK11 . . . . .112 B4
Buck La CW2 . . . . .206 E3
Buckland CI WA8 . . . . .22 D7
Buckley Ave CW10 . . . . . . .128 F7
Buckley CI CW10 . . . . .151 B8
Buckley Ct CH64 . . . . .67 F8
Buckley St
Macclesfield SK11 . . . . . . .112 D7
Warrington WA2 . . . . .16 B6
Bucklow Ave
Mobberley WA16 . . . . .58 A4
Warrington WA1 . . . . .16 E6
Bucklow Gdns WA13 . . . . . .19 A3
BUCKLOW HILL 30 C3
Bucklowhill La WA16 . . . . . .30 B3
Bucklow Wlk **11** SK11 . . .112 E7
BUCKOAK 99 A5
Buckton St WA1 . . . . .16 D7
BUDDILEIGH 221 F7
Bude CI
Alsager ST7 . . . . .193 B3
Bramhall SK7 . . . . .35 F7
Crewe CW1 . . . . .190 B8
Bude Rd WA8 . . . . .12 E2
Budworth Ave
Warrington WA4 . . . . .16 F4
Widnes WA8 . . . . .12 D2
Budworth CI
Runcorn WA7 . . . . .49 D7
Sandbach CW11 . . . . .174 F7
BUDWORTH HEATH 54 A1
Budworth Heath La
CW9 . . . . .54 C1
Budworth La CW9 . . . . .78 E7
Budworth Rd
Bate Heath CW9 . . . . .54 E2
Ellesmere Port CH66 . . . . . .69 E2
Over Tabley WA16 . . . . .55 C2
Budworth Wlk **1** SK9 . . . .34 E1
BUERTON 230 E4
Buerton App CH3 . . . . .164 B6
BUERTON MOSS 230 E6
Buffs La CH60 . . . . .41 B8
Buggen La CH64 . . . . .66 D8
BUGLAWTON 157 A4
Buglawton Hall Sch
CW12 . . . . .157 D5
Buglawton Ind Est **5**
CW12 . . . . .156 F4
Buglawton Prim Sch
CW12 . . . . .157 D5
Buildwas Rd CH64 . . . . .41 F2
BULKELEY 184 E2
Bulkeley Hall La SY14 . . . .200 C8
Bulkeley Rd
Handforth SK9 . . . . .34 D3
Poynton SK12 . . . . .36 E3
Bulkeley St
Chester CH3 . . . . .119 A1
Crewe CW1 . . . . .190 E3
Bullcroft Ct SY14 . . . . .211 D7
Bull Hill CH64 . . . . .66 F6
Bull-Hill-La SK10, SK11 . . .88 D7
Bullocks House Rd
ST7 . . . . .195 E3
Bullocks La SK11 . . . . .112 E3
Bull Ring CW9 . . . . .103 F8
Bull Ring The CW10 . . . . . .128 C1
Bumper's La CH1 . . . . .117 F1
BUNBURY 185 F8
Bunbury Aldersey CE Prim
Sch CW6 . . . . .185 E8
Bunbury CI
Middlewich CW10 . . . . . . .151 D5
Northwich CW9 . . . . .104 A5
Stoak CH2 . . . . .94 A1
Bunbury Comm CW6 . . . . .168 E2
BUNBURY COMMONS . . .169 A2
Bunbury Dr CW9 . . . . .146 D1
Bunbury Dr WA7 . . . . .49 C6
Bunbury Gn CH65 . . . . .70 D2
BUNBURY HEATH 185 D8
Bunbury La CW6 . . . . .185 E8
Bunbury Mill* CW6 . . . . . .169 B1
Bunbury Rd CW6 . . . . .169 B3
Bunce La SK11 . . . . .133 B4
Bunce St CH1 . . . . .237 A1
Bungalow Rd WA12 . . . . . . .2 E1
Bungalows The
Alderley TF9 . . . . .234 B3
Dunham-on-t-H WA6 . . . . . .97 E6
Thornton Hough CH63 . . . . .42 B6
BUNSLEY BANK 230 D5
Bunting CI **6** WA3 . . . . . . .3 E8
Buntingford Rd WA4 . . . . . .17 A2
Bunts La CW12 . . . . .156 E1
Burdett Rd CH66 . . . . .69 E2
Burfield Dr WA4 . . . . .26 D7
Burford Ave
Bramhall SK7 . . . . .35 F5
Newcastle-u-Lyme ST5 . . .210 D1
Burford CI SK9 . . . . .59 E5
Burford Cres SK9 . . . . .59 E5
Burford La WA13 . . . . .19 C2
Burgamot La CW9 . . . . .78 D8
Burganey Ct CH4 . . . . .162 D2

Burgess Ave WA4 . . . . .16 B2
Burgess CI CW5 . . . . .205 B4
Burgess Dr CH1 . . . . .117 A5
Burgess La WA3 . . . . .101 B6
Burgess PI **5** CW8 . . . . .103 E8
Burgess St CW10 . . . . .112 F8
Burges St CH2 . . . . .118 F3
Burjen Way CW1 . . . . .190 B6
Burkhardt Dr WA12 . . . . . . .2 E1
BURLAND 203 C7
Burland CI WA7 . . . . .22 F1
Burland Gr CW7 . . . . .126 A2
BURLAND LOWER GREEN
. . . . .203 A7
Burland Rd
Halewood L26 . . . . .21 A6
Newcastle-u-Lyme ST5 . . .210 D2
BURLAND UPPER GREEN
. . . . .203 B8
Burlea CI CW2 . . . . .189 C5
Burlea Dr CW2 . . . . .206 B5
BURLEYDAM 228 B1
Burleyhurst La SK9,
WA16 . . . . .59 B7
Burley La WA4 . . . . .27 C4
Burnell CI CW5 . . . . .204 F3
Burnell Rd CH65 . . . . .70 E4
Burnet CI WA2 . . . . .9 C2
Burnfell WA3 . . . . .3 E7
Burnham CI
Culcheth WA3 . . . . .4 E4
Warrington WA5 . . . . .14 F5
Widnes WA8 . . . . .12 C5
Burnham Rd CH4 . . . . .140 F6
Burnsall Ave WA3 . . . . .3 F8
Burnsall Dr WA8 . . . . .12 C2
Burns CI
Ellesmere Port CH66 . . . . . .69 E3
Rode Heath ST7 . . . . .193 E8
Burns Cres WA8 . . . . .22 F8
Burns Dr CW1 . . . . .190 F4
Burns Gr WA2 . . . . .8 C2
Burnside WA15 . . . . .32 D7
Burnside Ave WA4 . . . . .16 D1
Burnside CI SK9 . . . . .60 C6
Burnside Way
Northwich CW8 . . . . .103 D8
Winnington CW8 . . . . .78 D1
Burns Rd CW12 . . . . .157 A2
Burns St WA11 . . . . .1 A6
Burns Way CW8 . . . . .101 D5
Burnt Acre SK11 . . . . .117 E6
Burnt Mill La WA8 . . . . .21 D5
Burnwood Gr ST7 . . . . . . .195 B2
Burran Rd M22 . . . . .33 D8
Burrough CI WA3 . . . . .9 F3
Burrows Hill WA8 . . . . .103 B7
Burrows La WA6 . . . . .73 F2
Burrows St WA11 . . . . .1 A6
Burrows The CW8 . . . . . . .101 D5
Bursar CI WA12 . . . . .2 D4
Burslam St CW12 . . . . .156 E2
BURTON
Duddon 144 F4
Neston 67 D1
Burton Ave CW6 . . . . .146 C3
Burton CI
Culcheth WA3 . . . . .4 F3
Widnes WA8 . . . . .12 F3
Burton Dr SK12 . . . . .36 D4
Burton Gn CH66 . . . . .69 D4
Burton Gr CW1 . . . . .173 B1
BURTON GREEN 161 D1
Burton Hall Rd LL12 . . . . .161 E1
Burton La CW6 . . . . .144 F6
Burton Manor Coll
. . . . .67 D1
Burton Rd
Blacon CH1 . . . . .117 E5
Duddon CW6 . . . . .144 E6
Neston CH64 . . . . .66 F6
Warrington WA2 . . . . .8 D1
Burton Sq CW6 . . . . .146 C2
BURTONWOOD 6 E6
Burtonwood Com Prim
Sch WA5 . . . . .6 E7
Burtonwood Ind Ctr
WA5 . . . . .6 E7
Burtonwood Rd
Warrington, Great Sankey
WA5 . . . . .15 C6
Warrington, Kingswood
WA5 . . . . .7 A2
BURWARDSLEY 184 B5
Burwardsley Ct CH3 . . . . .184 A6
Burwardsley Rd CH3 . . . . .166 D1
Burwardsley Way
CW9 . . . . .103 E4
Bushell CI CH64 . . . . .66 F7
Bushell Rd CH64 . . . . .66 F7
Bushells La WA6 . . . . .99 B8
Bush Rd
Christleton CH3 . . . . .142 E7
Widnes WA8 . . . . .22 E5
Bush Way CH60 . . . . .40 D8
Butler Way CW5 . . . . .204 E3
Butley CI
Macclesfield SK10 . . . . .87 D3
Middlewich CW10 . . . . . . .151 C7
Butley Hall SK10 . . . . .87 A7
Butley Lanes SK10 . . . . . . .61 F1
BUTLEY TOWN 87 C8
Butterbache Rd CH3 . . . . .142 A6
Butterbur CI CH3 . . . . .142 A6
Buttercup CI WA5 . . . . .15 E3
Buttercup Way WA16 . . . . . .79 F6
Buttermarket St WA1 . . . . .16 B5
Buttermere Ave
Ellesmere Port CH65 . . . . . .70 C3

Bro-Cal **245**

Buttermere Ave continued
Warrington WA2 . . . . .8 C3
Buttermere CI WA6 . . . . . . .74 D8
Buttermere Cres WA2 . . . . . .8 C3
Buttermere Ct CW12 . . . . .156 A2
Buttermere Dr
Alderley Edge SK9 . . . . . . .83 F7
Altrincham WA15 . . . . .32 D6
Crewe CW1 . . . . .173 B1
Buttermere Gr WA7 . . . . . . .49 D5
Buttermere Rd
Partington M31 . . . . .11 E3
Winsford CW7 . . . . .126 C2
BUTTERS GREEN 210 A2
Butterton La
Oakhanger CW1 . . . . .192 B2
Oakhanger CW1 . . . . .192 C1
BUTT GREEN 205 B3
BUTT LANE 194 D1
Butts Gn WA5 . . . . .7 A3
Butts The
Alsager ST7 . . . . .193 D4
Runcorn WA7 . . . . .23 F2
Buxton Ave CW1 . . . . .190 E4
Buxton CI WA5 . . . . .15 A8
Buxton New Rd
Buxton SK11 . . . . .115 A6
Macclesfield Forest
SK11 . . . . .114 D7
Macclesfield SK11 . . . . .88 E1
Buxton Old Rd
Congleton CW12 . . . . .157 A4
Disley SK12 . . . . .38 E4
Macclesfield SK11 . . . . . . .113 D7
Buxton Rd
Congleton CW12 . . . . .157 C6
High Lane SK6, SK7,
SK12 . . . . .37 D8
Horwich End, New Horwich
SK23 . . . . .65 C6
Macclesfield SK10,
SK11 . . . . .113 A7
New Mills SK2, SK23 . . . . .39 C4
Whaley Bridge SK23 . . . . . .39 E1
Buxton Rd W SK12 . . . . . . .38 B5
Bye Pass The CH3 . . . . . . .119 E2
Byland Ave SK8 . . . . .35 B6
Byland CI WA8 . . . . .13 C5
Bylands CI SK12 . . . . .36 D4
BYLEY 129 A7
Byley La
Cranage CW4, CW10 . . . . .129 C6
Middlewich CW10 . . . . . . .128 E3
Byley Prim Sch CW10 . . . .129 B7
Byley Way CW7 . . . . .126 B1
Byng Ave M44 . . . . .11 D4
By-Pass Rd CH3 . . . . .121 B3
Byron CI
Blacon CH1 . . . . .117 F6
Crewe CW2 . . . . .190 A4
Middlewich CW10 . . . . . . .151 D5
Rode Heath ST7 . . . . .193 E7
Sandbach CW11 . . . . .174 D6
Byron Ct WA2 . . . . .8 C2
Byron's La SK11 . . . . .112 E5
Byrons St SK11 . . . . .112 D6
Byron St WA7 . . . . .2 A1
Byron Way CW2 . . . . .190 A1
Byron Wlk CW5 . . . . .204 D6
Bythom CI CH3 . . . . .142 E7

C

Cabot CI WA5 . . . . .7 C1
Cabul CI WA7 . . . . .16 D7
CADISHEAD 11 E5
Cadishead Prim Sch
M44 . . . . .11 E6
Cadishead Way M44 . . . . . .11 F6
Cadnant CI CH1 . . . . .117 D3
Cadnant Ct/Llys Cadnant
CH4 . . . . .139 D5
Cadshaw CI WA3 . . . . .9 D5
Caer Castell LL13 . . . . . . .196 D8
Caerleon CI CW7 . . . . .149 A8
Caerllew LL13 . . . . .180 E1
Caernarvon Ave CW7 . . . . .149 B7
Caernarvon Ct **4**
CH65 . . . . .70 D2
Caernarvon Rd CW2 . . . . .205 E8
Caesars CI WA7 . . . . .23 E2
Cairn Brae WA12 . . . . .2 C4
Cairns Cres CH1 . . . . .117 D4
Cairo St WA1 . . . . .16 B5
Caister Way CW7 . . . . .149 C7
Caithness Ct **3** WA7 . . . .23 B2
Calamine St SK11 . . . . .112 E6
Calday Gr WA11 . . . . .1 A8
Caldbeck Ave WA2 . . . . .8 D3
CALDECOTT GREEN 197 C4
Caldene Terr SK23 . . . . .65 E7
Calder Ave CW1 . . . . .191 A5
Calder CI
Bollington SK10 . . . . .87 F8
Poynton SK12 . . . . .36 D2
Widnes WA8 . . . . .13 F3
Calderfield CI WA4 . . . . . . .26 B8
Calder Way **3** CW8 . . . . . .69 C5
Caldicott Ave CH62 . . . . . . .43 D7
Caldicott CI **2** CW7 . . . . .149 C7
Caldwell Ave WA5 . . . . .7 E2
Caldwell CI CW5 . . . . .205 B4
Caldwell Rd WA8 . . . . .23 A7

Caldwell's Gate La
CW9 . . . . .54 B8
Caldy Cl CH2 . . . . 118 D5
Caldy Dr CH66 . . . . .69 D4
Caldy Rd
Alsager ST7 . . . . 193 C4
Handforth SK9 . . . . .34 D3
Caldy Valley Rd
Chester CH3 . . . . 142 B7
Huntington CH3 . . . . 142 A6
Caldy Way CW7 . . . . 126 C1
Cale Rd SK22 . . . . .39 D8
Calico La SK23 . . . . .39 D4
California Cl WA5 . . . . .15 C8
Callands Prim Sch WA5 . . .7 E2
Callands Rd WA5 . . . . .7 D2
Callender Gdns WA6 . . . . .73 A2
Callin Ct CH1 . . . . 237 A2
Calmington La WA7 . . . . . .24 F4
CALROFOLD 88 C2
Calrofold Dr ST5 . . . . 210 D1
Calrofold La SK10 . . . . . . .88 C2
Calstock Cl WA5 . . . . .14 E3
CALVELEY 169 E2
Calveley Ave CH62 . . . . . .43 F4
Calveley Cl CW9 . . . . 103 E5
Calveley Green La CW6,
CW7 . . . . 170 C4
Calveley Hall La CW5,
CW6 . . . . 170 A2
Calveley Prim Sch
CW6 . . . . 170 B2
Calveley Rd
Halewood L26 . . . . .21 A6
Macclesfield SK10 . . . . . . .86 F1
Calveley Way CW7 . . . . . 126 B1
Calverley Cl 3 SK9 . . . . . .60 C8
Calverly Cl WA7 . . . . .50 C5
Calver Rd WA2 . . . . .8 A3
Calvers WA7 . . . . .23 D3
Camberley Cl SK7 . . . . . . .36 A7
Camberwell Park Rd
WA8 . . . . .13 D4
Camborne Ave SK10 . . . 111 E8
Camborne Cl
Congleton CW12 . . . . 178 E8
Runcorn WA7 . . . . .50 C6
Cambourne Rd WA5 . . . . .6 F6
Cambrai Ave WA4 . . . . . . .16 C2
Cambrian Ave CH3 . . . . . 119 B2
Cambrian Cl CH66 . . . . . . .69 A6
Cambrian Ct CH1 . . . . 118 B2
Cambrian Rd CH1 . . . . . . 118 B2
Cambrian Villas CH3 . . . 165 C2
Cambrian Way CW7 . . . . 149 B8
Cambridge Ave
Macclesfield SK11 . . . . . . 112 B7
Wilmslow SK9 . . . . .59 F7
Winsford CW7 . . . . 126 A1
Cambridge Cl
Biddulph ST8 . . . . 179 C1
Warrington WA4 . . . . .26 B7
Cambridge Ct 7 CH65 . .70 C5
Cambridge Gdns
Helsby WA6 . . . . .73 D4
Warrington WA4 . . . . .26 C6
Cambridge Rd
Bebington CH62 . . . . .43 E8
Chester CH2 . . . . 118 F5
Ellesmere Port CH65 . . . . .70 D5
Macclesfield SK11 . . . . . . 112 B7
Cambridge Road Com
Prim Sch CH65 . . . . .70 C5
Cambridge St
Runcorn WA7 . . . . .23 C2
Widnes WA8 . . . . .23 B1
Camden Cl WA7 . . . . .24 D1
Camden Rd CH65 . . . . .70 A5
Camden St CW1 . . . . 190 D4
Camellia Gdns WA9 . . . . . .6 B7
Camelot Cl WA12 . . . . .1 F4
Camelot Gr CW2 . . . . 206 C4
Camelot Way WA7 . . . . . . .50 A8
Cameron Ave
Runcorn WA7 . . . . .48 E8
Shavington CW2 . . . . 206 B3
Cameron Ct WA4 . . . . .8 A4
Cameron Rd WA8 . . . . .23 A8
Camm St CW2 . . . . 190 D2
Camomile Wlk 5 M31 . . .11 F3
Campbell Ave WA7 . . . . . .49 A8
Campbell Cl
Congleton CW12 . . . . 157 A4
Haslington CW1 . . . . 191 C4
Macclesfield SK10 . . . . . . .87 A1
Northwich CW9 . . . . 103 F4
Campbell Cres WA5 . . . . .14 F6
Campden Way SK9 . . . . . .34 D4
Campion Cl
Huntington CH3 . . . . 142 A6
Warrington WA3 . . . . .9 C4
Campsey Ash WA8 . . . . . .12 F4
Camrose Cl WA7 . . . . .50 C7
Camsley La WA13 . . . . . . .18 B3
Canaan WA3 . . . . .4 C8
Canada Cl WA2 . . . . .9 A2
Canadian Ave CH2 . . . . . 119 A3
Canal Bank WA13 . . . . . . .18 D3
Canal Bridge Ent Pk
CH65 . . . . .70 D6
Canal Cotts CW5 . . . . 187 D6
Canal Rd CW12 . . . . 156 F1
Canal Reach WA7 . . . . . . .24 C2
Canalside CH65 . . . . .70 D6

Canal Side
Barnton CW8 . . . . .78 B2
Chester CH1 . . . . 237 C3
Macclesfield SK11 . . . . . . 112 F7
Moore WA4 . . . . .25 C5
Runcorn WA7 . . . . .48 D7
Warrington WA4 . . . . .17 C1
Whaley Bridge SK23 . . . . .39 F1
Canalside Cotts
CW11 . . . . 175 C3
Canal Side Cotts WA7 . . .50 F6
Canal St
Chester CH1 . . . . 237 A3
Congleton CW12 . . . . 156 E2
Macclesfield SK10 . . . . . . 112 E8
Newton-le-W WA12 . . . . . .1 F3
Runcorn WA7 . . . . .23 B2
Whaley Bridge SK23 . . . . .65 E8
Candy La SK10 . . . . .62 C8
Canford Cl
Crewe CW1 . . . . 190 B8
Warrington WA5 . . . . .15 C6
Cannell Ct WA7 . . . . .50 A6
Cannell St 4 WA5 . . . . . . .15 D4
Canning St CH1 . . . . 237 A3
Canniswood Rd WA11 . . . .1 A6
Cann La CW9 . . . . .55 A6
Cann La N WA4 . . . . .26 E5
Cann La S WA4 . . . . .26 F4
Cannock Cl CH66 . . . . .94 E8
Cannonbury Cl WA7 . . . . .50 A8
Cannon St CH65 . . . . .70 A5
Cannon Way WA14 . . . . . .31 A8
Canons Rd WA5 . . . . .15 D6
Canon St WA7 . . . . .22 F3
Canon Wilson Cl WA11 . . .1 D6
Canterbury Cl CH66 . . . . .94 E8
Canterbury Rd
Blacon CH1 . . . . 117 F5
Widnes WA8 . . . . .22 C8
Canterbury St WA4 . . . . . .16 E2
Cantilever Gdns WA4 . . . .16 E2
Cantley Cl WA7 . . . . .49 D6
Canton Pl CW8 . . . . 103 D7
Canton St SK11 . . . . 112 D6
Canton Wlks SK11 . . . . . . 112 D6
Canute Pl 12 WA16 . . . . . .57 A2
Capeland Cl CH4 . . . . 140 E5
Capel Way CW5 . . . . 204 D6
CAPENHURST 94 A8
Capenhurst Ave
Crewe CW2 . . . . 190 A3
Warrington WA2 . . . . .9 A2
Capenhurst CE Prim Sch
CH1 . . . . .94 B8
Capenhurst Ct 12 CH65 . .36 F4
Capenhurst Gdns
CH66 . . . . .69 D1
Capenhurst Grange Sch
CH66 . . . . .69 E2
Capenhurst La
Capenhurst CH1 . . . . .94 B8
Ellesmere Port CH65 . . . . .70 A3
Woodbank CH1 . . . . .93 F7
Capenhurst Sta CH1 . . . . .69 C1
Capenhurst Tech Pk
Capenhurst CH1 . . . . .69 B1
Capenhurst CH1 . . . . .94 B8
Capesthorne Cl
Alsager ST7 . . . . 193 C3
Hazel Grove SK7 . . . . .36 F8
Holmes Chapel CW4 . . . . 130 B3
Northwich CW9 . . . . 103 F4
Sandbach CW11 . . . . 175 C7
Widnes WA8 . . . . .12 F4
Capesthorne Hall*
SK11 . . . . 110 A6
Capesthorne Rd
Crewe CW2 . . . . 189 F3
Hazel Grove SK7 . . . . .36 F8
High Lane SK6 . . . . .37 E7
Warrington WA2 . . . . .8 D2
Waverton CH3 . . . . 143 B6
Wilmslow SK9 . . . . .59 E5
Capesthorne Way 10
SK11 . . . . 112 F7
Capitol Wlk CW12 . . . . . . 156 D2
Cappelle Rise ST7 . . . . . . 209 D1
Capper Cl ST7 . . . . 195 A2
Cappers La CW11 . . . . . . 176 C2
Capper's La CW5,
CW6 . . . . 186 C3
Carden Ave CW7 . . . . 126 D2
Cardenbrook Gr 4
SK9 . . . . .34 D2
Carden Cl WA3 . . . . .9 D4
Cardeston Cl WA7 . . . . . . .49 F3
Cardiff Cl CH66 . . . . .94 E8
Cardigan Cl
Macclesfield SK11 . . . . . . 112 A8
Warrington WA5 . . . . .7 D2
Cardinal Newman RC High
Sch WA4 . . . . .17 A1
Cardway Bsns Ctr ST7 . . 193 F3
Carey St WA8 . . . . .13 B1
Carisbrook Ave SK10 . . . .87 E2
Carisbrook Dr CW7 . . . . . 149 C7
Carisbrooke Cl CW2 . . . . 205 E8
Carleton Rd SK12 . . . . . . .37 C4

Carlett Bvd CH62 . . . . . . .43 F5
Carlingford Rd WA4 . . . . .26 B7
Carlisle Cl
Macclesfield SK11 . . . . . . 111 F5
Mobberley WA16 . . . . .58 A4
Winsford CW7 . . . . 126 A1
Carlisle Rd CH1 . . . . 117 F5
Carlisle St
13 Alderley Edge SK9 . . . . .60 A1
Crewe CW2 . . . . 190 B2
Warrington WA4 . . . . .26 C8
Carlow Cl L24 . . . . .21 D2
Carlton Ave
Bramhall SK7 . . . . .35 D5
Handforth SK9 . . . . .34 C2
Warrington WA4 . . . . .23 D2
Saltney CH4 . . . . 140 D6
Carlton Cl
Mickle Trafford CH2 . . . . . 119 E8
Neston CH64 . . . . .41 C2
Carlton Cres CH66 . . . . . .69 F8
Carlton Pl CH2 . . . . 119 A4
Carlton Rd
Lymm WA13 . . . . .19 B5
Northwich CW9 . . . . 104 B7
Carlton St
Warrington WA4 . . . . .26 C8
Widnes WA8 . . . . .23 A8
Carlton Way M44 . . . . .11 C5
Carlyle Cl ST7 . . . . 193 E8
Carlyle Cres CH66 . . . . . .69 E4
Carmarthen Cl
Warrington WA5 . . . . .7 D2
3 Winsford CW7 . . . . 149 C7
Carmel Cl CH1 . . . . 117 D3
Carmel Ct WA4 . . . . .13 B4
Carmenna Dr SK7 . . . . . . .35 F7
Carmichael Cl 6 M31 . . . .11 E3
Carnegie Cl SK10 . . . . . . .87 A1
Carnoustie Cl
Wilmslow SK9 . . . . .60 D8
Winsford CW7 . . . . 126 B2
Carnoustie Dr SK10 . . . . .87 D5
Carnoustie Gr WA11 . . . . .1 A5
Carol Dr CH60 . . . . .41 C8
Carolina Rd 2 WA5 . . . . . .15 B7
Caroline Ho CH1 . . . . 117 F6
Caroline St
Irlam M44 . . . . .11 F8
Widnes WA8 . . . . .23 B7
Carol St WA4 . . . . .16 D4
Carpenter Gr WA2 . . . . . . .9 A1
Carpenters Ct SK9 . . . . . .60 A1
Carr Brook Cl SK23 . . . . . .65 E5
Carr Brow SK6 . . . . .38 A7
Carrgreen La WA13 . . . . . .19 F6
Carriage Cl L24 . . . . .21 D1
Carriage Dr
Biddulph ST8 . . . . 179 E1
Frodsham WA6 . . . . .74 A6
Carriage Ho CW1 . . . . . . 190 A5
Carrick Dr CH65 . . . . .70 B2
Carrick Rd CH4 . . . . 141 B7
Carrington Cl WA3 . . . . . . .9 C4
Carrington Way CW1 . . . . 190 B8
Carrington Wlk WA1 . . . . .16 C6
Carr La
Alderley Edge SK9 . . . . . . .59 D2
Audley ST7 . . . . 209 A1
Golborne WA3 . . . . .4 A7
Golborne, Wash End WN7 . . .4 A8
Hale L24, WA8 . . . . .21 E4
Carr Mill Mews SK9 . . . . .34 B1
Carroll Dr CW2 . . . . 205 F8
Carr St CH5 . . . . .60 B7
Carrs La CH3 . . . . 166 F1
Carr St ST7 . . . . 195 F1
Carrwood
Altrincham WA15 . . . . .32 B7
Knutsford WA16 . . . . .57 C1
Carr Wood Ave SK7 . . . . .35 E8
Carrwood Cl WA11 . . . . . . .1 A6
Carrwood Rd SK9 . . . . . . .59 F8
Carsdale Rd M22 . . . . .33 E8
Car St CH1 . . . . 237 C3
Carter Ave CW6 . . . . 122 D4
Carter Bench Ho SK9 . . . .63 A1
Carter Cl CW2 . . . . 205 D6
Carter La SK11 . . . . .84 B4
Carter St CH1 . . . . 237 C3
Cartier Cl
Warrington, Old Hall
WA5 . . . . .7 C1
Warrington WA5 . . . . .15 C8
Cartlake Cl CW5 . . . . 204 C5
Cartledge Cl CW8 . . . . . . 102 A3
Cartmel Ave WA2 . . . . .8 C3
Cartmel Cl
Holmes Chapel CW4 . . . . 130 A3
Macclesfield SK10 . . . . . . .87 B2
Warrington WA5 . . . . .14 E2
Winsford CW7 . . . . 126 D2
Carter CH66 . . . . .69 F2
Cartmell Cl WA7 . . . . .49 B6
Cartridge La WA4 . . . . . . .27 E6
Cartwright Rd CW1 . . . . . 191 D5
Cartwright St
Runcorn WA7 . . . . .23 C2
Warrington WA5 . . . . .15 E6
Carver Ave CW4 . . . . 130 A3
Carver Cl CW7 . . . . 127 A4
Case Rd WA11 . . . . .1 C6
Casey La CW2 . . . . 206 F4
Cassia Green La CW7 . . . 125 C3
Cassia La CW7, CW8 . . . 125 C5
Cassley Rd L24 . . . . .21 A2
Casson St CW1 . . . . 190 B5
Castle Bank CW8 . . . . 103 E7

Castle Cl
Broughton CH5 . . . . 139 B6
Kelsall CW6 . . . . 122 D4
Pulford CH4 . . . . 162 D2
Castle Croft Rd CH4 . . . . 141 B5
Castle Ct
Holt LL13 . . . . 196 E8
11 Nantwich CW5 . . . . . . 204 E5
Northwich CW8 . . . . 103 E7
Castle Dr
Chester CH1 . . . . 237 B1
Ellesmere Port CH65 . . . . .70 A3
Heswall CH60 . . . . .40 F8
Castle Farm ST4 . . . . 200 E3
Castlefields 24 A2
Castlefields CH3 . . . . 166 C3
Castlefields Ave E
WA7 . . . . .24 A2
Castlefields Ave N
WA7 . . . . .23 F2
Castlefields Ave S
WA7 . . . . .24 A2
Castleford Dr SK10 . . . . . .86 E6
Castlegate SK10 . . . . .86 E6
Castlegate Mews SK10 . .86 F6
Castle Gdns LL13 . . . . 196 E8
Castle Gn WA5 . . . . .7 B2
Castlehill CH4 . . . . 162 C2
Castle Hill
Newton-le-W WA12 . . . . . .2 E4
Prestbury SK10 . . . . .86 E6
Castle Hill Ct SK10 . . . . . .86 F6
Castle Hill Farm 8
CW8 . . . . 103 E8
Castle Ho ST7 . . . . 195 C3
Castle Inn Rd CW12 . . . . 179 C7
Castlemead Wlk CW9 . . . 103 E4
Castlemere Cl CH4 . . . . . 139 A3
Castlemere Dr CW1 . . . . . 190 C7
Castle Mews LL13 . . . . . . 196 E8
Castle Mill La WA15 . . . . .32 B5
Castle Park Arts Ctr
WA6 . . . . .74 A8
Castle Prim Sch ST7 . . . . 195 D6
Castle Rd
Mow Cop ST7 . . . . 195 D7
Runcorn WA7 . . . . .49 F8
Castle Rise
Prestbury SK10 . . . . .86 F6
Runcorn WA7 . . . . .23 D2
Castle St
Chester CH1 . . . . 237 B1
1 Crewe CW1 . . . . 190 C4
Holt LL13 . . . . 196 D8
Macclesfield SK11 . . . . . . 112 D8
5 Nantwich CW5 . . . . 204 E5
Northwich CW8 . . . . 103 F8
Widnes WA8 . . . . .13 D1
Castleton Dr SK6 . . . . .37 F6
CASTLETOWN 197 D3
Castletown Cl SK10 . . . . . .87 C4
Castletown La CH3 . . . . . 197 D2
Castle View Prim Sch
WA7 . . . . .49 D8
Castleview Rd ST7 . . . . . . 195 B3
Castleway SK11 . . . . .32 C7
Castle Way CH4 . . . . 162 A6
Castner Ave WA7 . . . . .48 E7
Catalan Cl CW7 . . . . 127 A1
Catalyst Mus* WA8 . . . . . .23 A5
Catalyst Trade Pk WA8 . .23 A6
Catchpenny La SK11 . . . . 108 F3
Catford Cl WA8 . . . . .12 C2
Catfoss Cl WA7 . . . . .8 E1
Cathcart Gn CH3 . . . . 119 F5
Cathedral Church of
Christ & the Blessed
Virgin Mary* CH1 . . . . . 237 B2
Catherine Ct/Llys Catrin
CH5 . . . . 139 B6
Catherine St
Chester CH1 . . . . 118 B2
Crewe CW2 . . . . 190 D2
Macclesfield SK11 . . . . . . 112 C8
Warrington WA5 . . . . .15 F7
Widnes WA8 . . . . .23 A7
Catherine Way WA12 . . . . .2 B2
Catholic High Sch The
CH4 . . . . 141 D6
Catterall Ave WA2 . . . . . . .8 D2
Caughall Rd CH2 . . . . .95 E2
Caunce Ave
Golborne WA3 . . . . .3 A7
Haydock WA11 . . . . .1 B6
Newton-le-W WA12 . . . . . .2 C1
Causeway Ave WA4 . . . . .16 C3
Causeway Pk WA4 . . . . . .16 C3
Cavalier Dr CH1 . . . . 117 E6
Cavan Dr WA11 . . . . .1 B6
Cavell Dr CH65 . . . . .70 A4
Cavendish Ave WA3 . . . . . .9 F5
Cavendish Cl
5 Macclesfield SK10 . . . . .87 D3
Warrington WA5 . . . . .15 D7
Winsford CW7 . . . . 149 A8
Cavendish Cres ST7 . . . . 193 D5
Cavendish Ct
Chester CH4 . . . . 141 A5
Widnes WA8 . . . . .12 F1
Cavendish Farm Rd
WA7 . . . . .49 A5
Cavendish Gdns CH65 . . .70 A4
Cavendish Mews SK9 . . . .60 A6
Cavendish Pl WA3 . . . . . . .9 F5
Cavendish Rd
Chester CH4 . . . . 141 B6
Crewe CW2 . . . . 189 E5

Cavendish Rd continued
Hazel Grove SK7 . . . . .36 E8
Cavendish Sch CH4 . . . . .49 C5
Cavendish St 7 WA7 . . . .22 F2
Cavendish Way CW4 . . . . 130 A3
Caversham Cl WA4 . . . . . .26 E6
Cawdor Dr CH3 . . . . 119 A2
Cawdor St
Runcorn WA7 . . . . .22 F3
Warrington WA4 . . . . .26 C8
Cawfield Ave WA8 . . . . . . .12 D1
Cawley Ave WA3 . . . . .4 E4
Cawley La SK10 . . . . .62 E7
Cawley St
8 Macclesfield SK11 . . . . 112 E7
Runcorn WA7 . . . . .23 A1
Cawood Cl CH66 . . . . .69 B5
Cawthorne Ave WA4 . . . . .17 A2
Caxton Cl
Ellesmere Port CH66 . . . . .69 E4
Widnes WA8 . . . . .12 C3
Cecil Rd ST8 . . . . 179 C2
Cecil Rigby Cl 1
CW11 . . . . 175 B6
Cecil St CH3 . . . . 119 A1
Cedab Rd CH65 . . . . .70 C6
Cedar Ave
Alsager ST7 . . . . 193 D3
Aston WA7 . . . . .50 B4
Widnes WA8 . . . . .12 C3
Connah's Quay, Garden City
CH5 . . . . 116 A7
Ellesmere Port CH66 . . . . .69 D6
Golborne WA3 . . . . .3 F7
Kidsgrove ST7 . . . . 194 D1
Runcorn WA7 . . . . .49 C7
Warrington WA8 . . . . .13 B2
Cedar Cl
Connah's Quay CH5 . . . . . 116 A7
Holmes Chapel CW4 . . . . 130 D4
Lostock Gralam CW9 . . . . .80 A3
Middlewich CW10 . . . . . . 151 E6
Poynton SK12 . . . . .36 E3
Sandbach CW11 . . . . 175 C5
Cedar Cres
Audley ST7 . . . . 209 F1
Newton-le-W WA12 . . . . . .2 D2
Cedar Ct
Alsager ST7 . . . . 193 E4
Congleton CW12 . . . . 178 E8
Culcheth WA3 . . . . .4 F1
Willaston CW5 . . . . 205 D6
Cedardale Dr CH66 . . . . . .94 F8
Cedardale Pk WA8 . . . . . .13 E4
Cedar Dr
Barnton CW8 . . . . .78 A4
Chester CH2 . . . . 119 B4
Cedarfield Rd WA13 . . . . .19 B4
Cedar Gr
Chester CH2 . . . . 119 B4
Haydock WA11 . . . . .1 E7
Macclesfield SK11 . . . . . . 112 D5
Nantwich CW5 . . . . 205 A5
Neston CH64 . . . . .66 F8
Warrington, Latchford
WA4 . . . . .16 D3
Warrington WA4 . . . . .17 A7
Winsford CW7 . . . . 127 A1
Cedar Ho CH3 . . . . 142 B8
Cedar Lo CH3 . . . . .35 F7
Cedar Mews CH1 . . . . 117 E4
Cedar Pk CH3 . . . . 119 C2
Cedar Rd
Newcastle-u-Lyme
ST5 . . . . 210 D1
Partington M31 . . . . .11 E3
Warrington WA5 . . . . .14 F6
Weaverham CW8 . . . . 102 C8
Cedars SK9 . . . . .59 F6
Cedar St WA12 . . . . .2 C2
Cedars The
Alsager ST7 . . . . 193 E3
Mobberley WA16 . . . . .58 E2
Nantwich CW5 . . . . 204 D5
8 Northwich CW9 . . . . . . 103 E6
Cedarway
Bollington SK10 . . . . .88 A7
Heswall CH60 . . . . .41 B5
Wilmslow SK9 . . . . .59 F5
Cedar Way CW7 . . . . 206 B7
Cedarways WA4 . . . . .26 D5
Cedarwood Cl WA8 . . . . . 101 D5
Cedarwood Ct CW6 . . . . . 146 C3
Celandine Cl CH3 . . . . . . 142 A7
Celandine Way WA9 . . . . . .6 B7
Celyn Cres CH4 . . . . 140 D5
Cement Pl CH1 . . . . 237 B3
Cemetery Rd CW2 . . . . . . 207 B5
Cemlyn Cl CH1 . . . . 117 E3
Centenary Ho WA7 . . . . . .49 C8
Centenary Pl WA12 . . . . . 156 E3
Central Ave
Alsager ST7 . . . . 192 F1
Ellesmere Port CH65 . . . . .70 C4
Warrington, Latchford
WA4 . . . . .16 B3
Central Dr
Barnton CW8 . . . . .78 A3
Gatley SK8 . . . . .34 D8
Haydock WA11 . . . . .1 B6
Central Expressway
WA7 . . . . .49 D6
Central Gr CW7 . . . . 104 D6
Central Pl SK9 . . . . .60 B7
Central Rd
Northwich CW9 . . . . 104 D7
Partington M31 . . . . .11 D5

Central Rd continued
Warrington WA4 . . . . .16 C3
Central St ST7. . . . . .195 B6
Central Trad Pk CH4 . . . . . .140 E7

Central Way
Newton-le-W WA12. . . . . .2 E2
Warrington WA3 . . . . .18 B6
Centre Ct ST7 . . . . .193 E4
Centre Park Sq WA1. . . . . . .16 A4
Centre Pk WA1 . . . . .16 A4
Centurion Cl WA3 . . . . .9 D4
Centurion Row WA4 . . . . . . .23 F2
Centurion Way CW10 . . . . . 128 C2
Century Rd ST5. . . . . .210 F2
Century Way SK10 . . . . .87 F2
Cestria Cl CW11 . . . . .174 D7
Chads Gn CW5 . . . . .206 A1
Chadwell Ct CW2 . . . . .207 E4

Chadwick Ave
Croft WA3 . . . . .9 B7
Warrington WA4 . . . . .16 E1
Chadwick Cl SK9 . . . . .34 C1
Chadwick Ct CW10 . . . . . . .151 D7
Chadwick Cl CW5 . . . . .204 D5

Chadwick Fields Orch
CW10. . . . . .151 D6
Chadwick Pl WA3 . . . . .9 E5

Chadwick Rd
Middlewich CW10 . . . . .151 C6
Runcorn WA7. . . . . .23 E3
Chadwick Terr SK10. . . . . . .87 E1
Chaffinch Cl
Congleton CW12 . . . . .156 E1
Warrington WA3 . . . . .9 F3
Chaffinch Way CW7 . . . . . .149 D6
Chaigeley Sch WA4 . . . . . . .17 E4
Chailey Rise CH3 . . . . .182 D1

Chain Maker's Row
WA6. . . . . .75 D2
Chaise Mdw WA13 . . . . .19 C5
Chalfield Ave CH66 . . . . . . .69 C5
Chalfield Cl
❶ Ellesmere Port
CH66. . . . . .69 C5
Wistaston CW2 . . . . .206 B2
Chalfont Cl WA4 . . . . .26 E6
Chalfont Cres CW2 . . . . . . .207 B2
Chalfont Cl WA16. . . . . .57 C3
Chalgrave Cl WA8 . . . . .13 F3
Chalkwell Dr CH60. . . . . . . .41 C7
Challinor St CH3 . . . . .119 A1

Chamber Brook La
WA6. . . . . .75 D2
Chamberlain Ct CW1 . . . . .191 C4
Chamberlain Dr SK9 . . . . . .34 D1
Chambers St CW2 . . . . . . .190 D2
Chance Hall La CW12,
ST7. . . . . .177 C3
Chancel La SK9. . . . . .60 B8
Chancellor Rd WA7 . . . . . . .24 D5

Chancery La
Alsager ST7 . . . . .193 B3
Bollington SK10. . . . . .88 B7
Chandlers Ct WA7 . . . . .22 E1
Chandler Way WA3 . . . . .3 E8
Chandos Cl CH4 . . . . .141 E6
Change La CH64 . . . . .68 B8
Channel The CH1 . . . . .95 B4
Chantler Ave WA4 . . . . .16 E4
Chantry Ave CW8 . . . . .103 B4
Chantry Cl SK12 . . . . .38 E5

Chantry Ct
Chester CH1 . . . . .117 C2
Crewe CW1 . . . . .190 D4
Macclesfield SK11 . . . . .112 D5
Chantry Fold SK12 . . . . . . .38 E6
Chantry Rd SK12. . . . . .38 E6
Chantry The CW6 . . . . .169 E2
Chantry Wlk CH60 . . . . .41 A6
Chapel Ave WA6. . . . . .75 C2
Chapel Bank ST7 . . . . .195 D6

Chapel Cl
Audlem CW3 . . . . .229 F3
Cholmondeston CW7 . . . . . .170 F4
Comberbach CW9 . . . . .78 D7
Ellesmere Port CH65. . . . . . .70 C7
Mount Pleasant ST7 . . . . . . .195 B6
Saughall CH1. . . . . .94 A1
Waverton CH3 . . . . .143 A5
Chapel Cotts CH3. . . . . . . .143 A5
Chapel Croft SK11 . . . . .84 B7
Chapel Cross Rd WA2 . . . . . .9 A2

Chapel Ct
Northwich CW9 . . . . .103 F7
Wilmslow SK9 . . . . .60 A6
Chapel Dr WA15. . . . . .32 C7
Chapelfields WA6. . . . . .74 A8
Chapel Gn CW6. . . . . .122 C4
Chapel House La CH64. . . . .93 A7

Chapel La
Acton Bridge CW8 . . . . .76 E4
Aldford CH3 . . . . .164 D5
Alsotock WA16 . . . . .106 E3
Altrincham WA15. . . . . .32 C7
Appleton Thorn WA4 . . . . . . .27 B4
Audley ST7. . . . . .209 D2
Burtonwood WA5. . . . . .6 F6
Chester CH3 . . . . .119 A1
Crewe CW1 . . . . .173 D1
Dutton WA4 . . . . .77 B7
Harriseahead CH3 . . . . .195 E1
Hargrave CW2 . . . . .144 A1
Hartford CW8 . . . . .103 C5
Hollins Green WA3 . . . . .10 F1
Holt LL13 . . . . .196 D8
Kelsall CW6 . . . . .122 E2
Kingsley WA6. . . . . .75 C2
Ledsham CH66. . . . . .68 F1
Manley WA6, CH3 . . . . .98 F3

Chapel La continued
Mere WA16 . . . . .30 B4
Milton Green CH3 . . . . .165 B2
Moulton CW9. . . . . .126 E8
Norton in Hales TF9. . . . . . .236 C2
Partington M31. . . . . .11 F2
Rainow SK10 . . . . .88 E5
Ravensmoor CW5 . . . . .203 D2
Rode Heath ST7 . . . . .193 F7
Saighton CH3. . . . . .142 E1
Threapwood SY14 . . . . .222 E8
Warrington WA4 . . . . .26 C8
Widnes WA8 . . . . .12 C4
Wilmslow SK9 . . . . .60 A6
Windyharbour SK11. . . . . . .109 D2
Winsford CW7 . . . . .149 D1
Wistaston CW2 . . . . .206 A1
Chapel Lo CH1 . . . . .237 C2
Chapelmere Cl CW11 . . . . .174 E7
Chapelmere St CW1 . . . . . .190 C7

Chapel Mews
Alsager ST7 . . . . .193 C3
Ellesmere Port CH65. . . . . . .70 B4
Elton CH2 . . . . .72 B3
❶ Nantwich CW5. . . . . . . .204 E5
Wilmslow SK9 . . . . .61 A8
Winsford CW7 . . . . .126 F1

Chapel Rd
Alderley Edge SK9 . . . . .60 A1
Horwich End SK23 . . . . .65 E5
Ollerton WA16. . . . . .82 F6
Warrington WA5 . . . . .14 E3
Wilmslow SK9 . . . . .61 A8
Winsford CW7 . . . . .126 F1
Chapel Rise SY14 . . . . .213 B3
Chapel Row
Barbridge CW5 . . . . .187 D6
Nantwich CW5. . . . . .204 D5
Chapel St
❼ Alderley Edge SK9. . . . . .60 A1
Audley ST7. . . . . .209 E3
Bollington SK10. . . . . .88 B8
Chester CH3 . . . . .237 C3
Congleton CW12 . . . . .156 D2
Crewe CW2 . . . . .190 D3
Haydock WA11. . . . . .1 A6
Holt LL13 . . . . .196 D8
Kidsgrove ST7 . . . . .194 D2
Macclesfield SK11 . . . . .112 D6
Moulton CW9. . . . . .126 E8
Mount Pleasant ST7 . . . . . . .195 B6
New Mills SK22 . . . . .39 B6
Newton-le-W WA12. . . . . .2 B3
Northwich CW8 . . . . .103 E7
Sandbach CW11 . . . . .175 B6
Sandbach, Wheelock
CW11. . . . . .175 A3
Weaverham CW8. . . . . .77 C1
Whaley Bridge SK23 . . . . . . .65 E8
Widnes WA8 . . . . .23 A7
Wincham CW9 . . . . .79 C3

Chapel Terr WA3. . . . . .4 B8
Chapel View
Bebington CH62. . . . . .44 A6
Helsby WA6. . . . . .73 B2
Chapel Wlk WA3 . . . . .4 B8

Chapel Wlks
Broomedge WA13 . . . . .19 D1
Cheadle SK8 . . . . .35 B6
Chapel Yd WA12 . . . . .16 A6
Chapman Cl WA8 . . . . .12 D4
Chapterhouse Cl CH65. . . . .70 C5
Charcoal Rd WA14. . . . . . . .20 F3

Charity La
Macclesfield Forest
SK11. . . . . .114 B6
Macclesfield SK11 . . . . .113 F8

Charles Ave
Davenham CW9 . . . . .103 F2
Warrington WA5 . . . . .14 F6
Charles Cres CH4 . . . . .237 C1
Charles Ct CW2 . . . . .190 C3
Charles Darwin Prim Sch
WA1. . . . . .16 B5
Charles Forbes Ct ❼
CH65. . . . . .70 C6
Charles Price Gdns ❽
CH65. . . . . .70 C6
Charles Rd CH2 . . . . .95 C1
Charles Sq CW7 . . . . .175 F2

Charles St
Chester CH1 . . . . .237 B3
Chester, Hoole Park
CH2. . . . . .118 F3
Crewe CW1 . . . . .190 C4
Irlam M44 . . . . .11 E6
Widnes WA8 . . . . .23 A8
Charleston Cl CH66 . . . . . . .69 D2
Charleston Gr WA5 . . . . . . .15 B6
Charlesworth SK23 . . . . . . .39 D3
Charlesworth Cres
SK23. . . . . .39 D3
Charlesworth Ct
CW11. . . . . .175 C6
Charlesworth Pl ❶
CW12. . . . . .156 F4
Charlesworth Rd SK23 . . . . .39 D3
Charlesworth St CW1 . . . . .190 D6
Charlock Wlk ❻ M31 . . . . .11 F3
Charlotte Cl CH11 . . . . .237 B3
Charlotte Gr ❻ WA5 . . . . . .15 C7
Charlotte St W ❷
SK11. . . . . .112 C8
Charlotte St
Chester CH1 . . . . .118 B2
Macclesfield SK11 . . . . .112 D7
Charlotte Wlk ❷ WA8 . . . . .23 B7
Charlton Cl WA7. . . . . .50 A7

Charlton Ct CH2. . . . . .119 A4
Charlton St
❷ Macclesfield SK11 . . . . .112 C8
Warrington WA4 . . . . .16 F3
Charminster Cl WA5 . . . . . .15 B5
Charmouth Cl WA12 . . . . . . .2 B4
Charnock Ave WA12 . . . . . . .1 F3
Charnock Rd WA3 . . . . .4 F3

Charnwood
High Lane SK6 . . . . .37 F7
Kidsgrove ST7 . . . . .195 B1

Charnwood Cl
Macclesfield SK10 . . . . .87 A1
Warrington WA3 . . . . .10 B5
Charnwood Cres SK7 . . . . . .36 D8
Charon Way WA5 . . . . .7 B3
Charter Ave WA5. . . . . .16 A8
Charter Cres CH66. . . . . . . .69 E2
Charterhall Dr CH2 . . . . . . .118 F2
Charter Rd SK10. . . . . .88 A7
Charter Way CW10 . . . . .87 F3
Chartley Gr CW10. . . . . . . .128 D2
Chartwell Gdns WA4. . . . . . .26 F5
Chartwell Cl CW7 . . . . .149 C5
Chartwell Pk CW11 . . . . . . .175 A4
Chase Dr CH66 . . . . .69 E2
Chaser Ct CH1. . . . . .117 F3
Chase The
Bebington CH63. . . . . .43 C5
❺ Heswall CH60. . . . . .41 A8
Warrington WA1 . . . . .17 D8
Chasewater WA7 . . . . .24 F4
Chase Way CH66. . . . . .69 E2
Chassange Sq CW1 . . . . . .189 F7
Chatburn Cl WA3 . . . . .4 F2
Chater Dr CW5 . . . . .204 F3
Chatfield Dr WA3 . . . . .9 E3
Chatham St ❾ SK11 . . . . . .112 D8
Chatham Way CW1 . . . . . . .191 C5

Chatsworth Ave
Culcheth WA3 . . . . .4 F4
Macclesfield SK11 . . . . .111 E6

Chatsworth Cl
Ellesmere Port CH66. . . . . . .69 C5
Northwich CW9 . . . . .104 A5
Wistaston CW2 . . . . .206 A7

Chatsworth Dr
Chester CH2 . . . . .119 A5
Congleton CW12 . . . . .155 F3
Widnes WA8 . . . . .12 C3
Chatsworth Ho CH1. . . . . . .118 B3

Chatsworth Rd
Hazel Grove SK7 . . . . .36 F8
High Lane SK6. . . . . .37 F6
Wilmslow SK9 . . . . .59 E4
Chatteris Pk WA7. . . . . .24 E2
Chatterton Dr WA7 . . . . .50 E8
Chatterton Ho ❶❻
CW5. . . . . .204 E5
Chaucer Cl CH1 . . . . .117 E6
Chaucer Gr CW11 . . . . .174 C5
Chaucer Pl WA4. . . . . .16 C4
Chaucer St WA7 . . . . .23 A1
CHEADLE HULME 35 A8
Cheadle Hulme High Sch
SK8. . . . . .35 B7
Cheadle Hulme Sch
SK8. . . . . .35 A8
Cheadle La WA16. . . . . .30 F1
Cheadle Wood SK8 . . . . . . .34 E8
CHECKLEY 221 C1
Checkley Dr ST8. . . . . .179 D1
CHECKLEY GREEN 232 B8
Checkley La CW3,
CW5. . . . . .221 E1
Checkley Rd ST5 . . . . .210 C1
Checkley Row CW5 . . . . . . .232 C8
Cheddar Gr WA5. . . . . .7 B2
Cheddington Cl SK8 . . . . . . .35 A7
Chedle Dr SK8 . . . . .34 E8
Chedworth Dr WA4. . . . . . . .12 C4
Chedworth Ho ❶❷
CH1 . . . . .237 B3
Cheerbrook Rd CW5 . . . . . .205 D4
Cheese Hill La WA6,
CW8. . . . . .101 B4
CHELFORD 84 B2
Chelford Ave WA3 . . . . .3 D8
Chelford CE Prim Sch
SK11. . . . . .84 A3

Chelford Cl
Chester CH11 . . . . .117 F1
Warrington WA4 . . . . .26 C8
Chelford Dr CW9 . . . . .103 F5
Chelford La WA16 . . . . .83 C1
Chelford Mews ❷
CH3 . . . . .119 B1

Chelford Rd
Chelford, Marthall WA16,
SK11. . . . . .83 D4
Chelford SK10, SK11. . . . . . .84 F2
Congleton CW12 . . . . .155 E6
Goostrey CW4 . . . . .131 B7
Handforth SK9. . . . . .34 D5
Macclesfield SK10,
SK11. . . . . .111 C8
Monks Heath SK10 . . . . .85 B1
Nether Alderley SK9 . . . . . . .84 C7
Ollerton WA16. . . . . .82 D7
Prestbury SK10 . . . . .86 D5
Whisterfield SK11. . . . . .109 F3
Chelford Rdbt SK11. . . . . . .84 B1
Chelford Sta SK11 . . . . .84 A2
Chells Hill CW11 . . . . .176 C1
Chell St CW1 . . . . .190 B5
Chelsea Cl ST8 . . . . .179 C1
Chelsea Gdns WA5 . . . . . . .15 C4
Chelston Dr SK8 . . . . .34 C6

Cheltenham Cl
❷ Macclesfield SK10 . . . . .87 C4
Warrington WA5 . . . . .15 A8
Cheltenham Cres
Crewe CW1 . . . . .190 B7
Runcorn WA7. . . . . .49 B6
Cheltenham Dr WA12 . . . . . .2 C5
Cheltenham Rd CH65 . . . . . .70 D3
Chemical St WA12 . . . . .2 B3
Cheney Wlk CW2 . . . . .206 D8

Chepstow Cl
Biddulph ST8 . . . . .179 C1
Macclesfield SK10 . . . . .87 C4
Warrington WA5 . . . . .7 E3
❶ Winsford CW7 . . . . .149 C7
Cherington Cl SK9. . . . . . . .34 F3

Cherington Cres
SK11. . . . . .112 B7
Cheriton Way CW2 . . . . . . .206 A8
Cherrington Rd CW5. . . . . .204 E3

Cherry Blossom Rd
WA7. . . . . .49 F4
Cherry Brow Terr
CH64 . . . . .67 F8

Cherry Cl
Nantwich-u-Lyme
ST5. . . . . .210 D1
Newton-le-W WA12 . . . . .1 F4
Willaston CH64 . . . . .67 C8
Cherry Cnr WA13. . . . . .28 A7
Cherry Cres CW7 . . . . .149 C8
Cherry Dale Rd CW4 . . . . . .139 A3
Cherryfields Rd SK11 . . . . .111 F8
Cherry Gdns CH3 . . . . .119 A1
Cherry Gr
Ellesmere Port CH66. . . . . . .70 A1
Nantwich CW5. . . . . .204 D5
Cherry Grove Prim Sch
CH3 . . . . .119 A1
Cherry Grove Rd CH3 . . . . .119 A1

Cherry La
Congleton CW12 . . . . .179 E8
Cuddington CW8 . . . . .101 F2
Lawton Heath ST7 . . . . .193 E6
Lymm WA13 . . . . .18 C1
Weaverham CW8 . . . . .102 D8
Cherry Orch/Y Berllan
Geirios LL13 . . . . .196 D8
Cherry Rd CH3 . . . . .119 A1
Cherrysutton WA8 . . . . .12 B3

Cherrysutton Mews
WA8 . . . . .97 D5
Cherry Tree Ave
Barnton CW8 . . . . .78 A4
Lawton-gate ST7 . . . . .194 A5
Lymm WA13 . . . . .18 D2
Poynton SK12 . . . . .36 F3
Runcorn WA7. . . . . .49 C8
Warrington WA5 . . . . .14 F4

Cherry Tree Cl
Elton CH2 . . . . .72 B4
Hale L24 . . . . .21 E1
Haydock WA11. . . . . .1 A5
Wilmslow SK9 . . . . .60 E8
Cherry Tree Ct SK8 . . . . . . .205 A4
Cherry Tree Dr
Hazel Grove SK7 . . . . .37 A8
St Helens WA9 . . . . .1 A2
Cherry Tree Ho SK9 . . . . . . .85 C8

Cherry Tree La
Rostherne WA14 . . . . .30 E6
Woore CW3 . . . . .232 C2
Cherry Tree Mews ❸
CH60 . . . . .41 A8
Cherry Tree Prim Sch
WA13. . . . . .18 C2

Cherry Tree Rd
Audley ST7. . . . . .209 F1
Crewe CW1 . . . . .190 E6
Golborne WA3 . . . . .3 F8
Newcastle-u-Lyme ST5 . . . . .210 E1

Cherry Tree Way
CW12. . . . . .156 E2

Cherry Wlk
Cheadle SK8 . . . . .35 C8
Partington M31. . . . . .11 D2
Swan Green WA16. . . . . . . .106 D7
Cherrywood Cres CW8 . . . . .78 B4

Cherwell Cl
Cheadle SK8 . . . . .35 A7
Warrington WA2 . . . . .8 E2
Cheryl Ct CW8. . . . . .102 A4
Cheryl Dr WA8 . . . . .13 D1
Chesford Grange WA1 . . . . .17 F7
Chesham Cl SK9 . . . . .59 F4
Chesham Ct CH65 . . . . .70 D4
Chesham Rd SK9 . . . . .59 C8
Chesham St CW1 . . . . .237 C3
Cheshire Acad CW1. . . . . . .190 E2
Cheshire Candle
Workshops* CH3 . . . . . .184 C5
Cheshire Cl WA12 . . . . .2 C5
Cheshire Farm Ice
Cream* CH3. . . . . .166 D4
Cheshire Military Mus*
CH1 . . . . .237 A1
Cheshire Oaks High Sch
CH65 . . . . .70 C2
Cheshire Oaks Outlet
Village CH65 . . . . .70 E2
Cheshire Oaks Way
CH65 . . . . .70 C2
Cheshire Pk WA6. . . . . .97 D5
Cheshire Rd M31 . . . . .11 D2
Cheshire Row WA16 . . . . . .108 B8
Cheshire St CW3 . . . . .229 F4
Cheshire View
Audley ST7. . . . . .210 A1

Cheshire View continued
Bollington SK10. . . . . .88 B6
Chester CH4 . . . . .141 E7
Cheshyre Dr WA1 . . . . .23 F1
Cheshyre's La WA7 . . . . . . .48 E7
Chessington Cl WA4 . . . . . .26 F6
CHESTER 237 B2
Chester Aerospace Pk
CH5 . . . . .139 B6
Chester App
Aldford CH3. . . . . .163 E7
Eccleston CH4 . . . . .141 D2
Chester Ave WA3 . . . . .3 D8
Chesterbank Bsns Pk
CH4 . . . . .140 D7
Chester Bsns Pk CH4 . . . . .141 B3
Chester Castle* CH1 . . . . . .237 A1

Chester Cl
Handforth SK9. . . . . .34 E2
Irlam M44 . . . . .11 D5
Runcorn WA7. . . . . .24 A2
Talke ST7 . . . . .210 E7
Chester Ent Ctr CH2 . . . . . .237 C4
Chesterfield Cl CW7 . . . . . .125 F1
Chesterfield Rd CH62 . . . . . .43 D4
Chestergate SK10,
SK11. . . . . .112 D8
Chester Heritage Ctr*
CH1 . . . . .237 B2
Chester High Rd
Neston CH64, CH64 . . . . . . .41 E4
Willaston CH64 . . . . .67 D7
Chester New Rd WA4 . . . . . .25 F7
Chester Race Course*
CH1 . . . . .237 A1

Chester Rd
Acton CW5 . . . . .204 A6
Aston WA7. . . . . .50 B4
Audley ST7. . . . . .209 D2
Barbridge CW5 . . . . .187 D5
Broughton CH4 . . . . .139 D5
Churton CH3 . . . . .180 F6
Connah's Quay CH6. . . . . . . .91 A3
Cuddington CW8 . . . . .101 D1
Daresbury WA4 . . . . .25 B1
Delamere CW6, CW8. . . . . . .123 C5
Dunham-on-t-H CH2,
WA6 . . . . .97 D5
Ellesmere Port, Great Sutton
CH66. . . . . .69 D4
Ellesmere Port, Whitby CH65,
CH66. . . . . .70 A2
Frodsham WA6 . . . . .74 A7
Gatesheath CH3 . . . . .165 C3
Grappenhall WA4. . . . . .17 B1
Hartford CW8 . . . . .102 E3
Hartford, Greenbank
CW8 . . . . .103 C3
Hazel Grove SK7 . . . . .36 D8
Helsby WA6. . . . . .73 C4
Heswall CH60, CH64. . . . . . .41 C6
Higher Walton WA4 . . . . . . .25 D5
Holmes Chapel CW4 . . . . . .130 B2
Huntington CH3 . . . . .142 A6
Kelsall CW6 . . . . .122 D5
Lavister LL12 . . . . .162 C1
Macclesfield SK11 . . . . .112 B8
Malpas SY14 . . . . .213 B4
Mere WA16 . . . . .56 B6
Middlewich CW10 . . . . .128 B2
Neston CH64 . . . . .66 E7
Over Tabley WA16 . . . . .56 A3
Plumley WA16 . . . . .80 E5
Poynton SK12 . . . . .36 B4
Rostherne WA14, WA16 . . . .30 D7
Runcorn WA7. . . . . .50 E5
Saltney CH4. . . . . .140 C6
Sandycroft CH5 . . . . .116 A2
Talke ST7 . . . . .210 D7
Warrington WA4 . . . . .16 A2
Whitchurch SY13 . . . . .225 D2
Winsford CW7 . . . . .125 F2
Woodford SK7 . . . . .35 E2

Chester St
Chester CH4 . . . . .140 F7
Crewe CW1 . . . . .190 C4
Warrington WA2 . . . . .16 B1
Widnes WA8 . . . . .13 B1
Chester Sta CH1. . . . . .237 C3
Chesterton Cl CW10 . . . . . .151 E5
Chesterton Ct CH2. . . . . . . .118 D4
Chesterton Dr
Crewe CW2 . . . . .189 F1
Winwick WA2 . . . . .8 A5
Chesterton Gr CW11 . . . . . .174 D5
Chesterton Way CW2 . . . . .207 B3
Chester Toy & Doll Mus*
CH1 . . . . .237 B2
Chester Trad Pk CH1 . . . . . .117 F2
Chester Way CW7 . . . . .104 A8
Chester West Employment
Pk CH1 . . . . .117 C2
Chester Zoo* CH2 . . . . .95 E1
Chester Zoological Gdns*
CH2 . . . . .118 D8

Chestnut Ave
❹ Ellesmere Port
CH66. . . . . .69 F1
Irlam M44 . . . . .11 D5
Macclesfield SK10 . . . . .87 E2

Chestnut Ave continued
Rode Heath SK7 . . . .**193** F7
Shavington CW2 . . . . **206** C5
Warrington WA5 . . . . **14** F6
Widnes WA8 . . . .**13** B2
Chestnut Cl
Chester CH2 . . . .**119** A3
Cuddington CW8 . . . .**101** F2
Middlewich CW10 . . . .**128** B2
Tarporley CW6 . . . .**146** D2
Wilmslow SK9 . . . .**60** E8
Chestnut Ct
Tarporley CW6 . . . .**146** C2
Widnes WA8 . . . .**12** D1
Chestnut Dr
Alsager ST7 . . . .**193** E2
Congleton CW12 . . . .**156** A4
Holmes Chapel CW4 . . . . .**130** D3
Poynton SK12 . . . .**36** F3
Chestnut Gr
Barnton CW8 . . . .**78** B4
Bebington CH62 . . . .**43** C8
Crewe CW1 . . . .**190** E5
Golborne WA3 . . . .**3** F8
Newcastle-u-Lyme ST5 . . .**210** E1
Winsford CW7 . . . .**149** C8
Chestnut Grange CH4 . . .**141** B7
Chestnut Ho [6] CW11 . .**175** B6
Chestnut La WA4 . . . .**26** E1
Chestnut Lodge Specl Sch
WA8 . . . .**12** E1
Chestnut Mews WA16 . . . .**58** E1
Chestnut The CH4 . . . .**67** F8
Chestnut Wlk M31 . . . .**11** D2
Chetham Ct WA2 . . . .**8** A3
Chetton Dr WA7 . . . .**50** E7
Chetwode Mews WA4 . . . .**52** C2
Chetwode St CW1 . . . . . .**190** C5
Chetwood Dr WA8 . . . .**22** B5
Chetwood Dr WA8 . . . .**12** F4
Cheveley Cl SK10 . . . .**87** C2
Chevin Gdns SK7 . . . .**36** A2
Cheviot Ave WA2 . . . .**8** A3
Cheviot Cl CH66 . . . .**69** A6
Cheviot Ct CW7 . . . .**149** B7
Cheviot Sq CW7 . . . .**149** B7
Chevron Cl CH1 . . . .**117** E4
Chevron Hey CH1 . . . .**117** E4
Cheyne Wlk CW5 . . . .**204** E3
Cheyney Rd CH1 . . . .**118** B3
Chicago Ave M90 . . . .**33** B7
Chichester Cl
Grappenhall Heys WA4 . . . .**27** A7
Runcorn WA7 . . . .**50** D6
Chichester Ct CH1 . . . . . .**237** A3
Chichester St CH1 . . . . . .**237** A3
Chidlow Cl
Hough CW2 . . . .**206** E2
Widnes WA8 . . . .**23** A5
Childer Cres CH66 . . . .**69** B7
Childer Gdns CH66 . . . .**69** B7
CHILDER THORNTON . . .**69** B8
Childer Thornton Prim
Sch CH66 . . . .**69** B8
Child's La CW12 . . . .**177** E6
Childwall Ct CH66 . . . .**69** F8
Childwall Gdns CH66 . . . . .**69** F8
Childwall Rd CH66 . . . .**69** F8
Chilham Cl CW7 . . . .**149** C7
Chilham Pl SK11 . . . .**111** F6
Chilington Ave WA8 . . . .**22** D8
Chillingham Cl CW10 . . . .**128** D2
Chiltern Ave SK11 . . . .**112** A7
Chiltern Cl
Chester CH4 . . . .**141** B5
Chorlton CW2 . . . .**207** B1
Cuddington CW8 . . . .**102** A2
Chiltern Cres WA2 . . . .**8** A3
Chiltern Cl SK10 . . . .**87** D3
Chiltern Pl WA2 . . . .**8** A3
Chiltern Rd
Culcheth WA3 . . . .**4** E4
St Helens WA9 . . . .**1** A3
Warrington WA2 . . . .**8** A3
Chiltern Way CW7 . . . .**149** B7
Chilton Dr CH66 . . . .**69** F2
Chilwell Cl WA8 . . . .**12** D4
Chilworth Ct CW2 . . . .**206** C8
China La WA4 . . . .**16** C2
Chines The CW8 . . . .**101** D5
Chippingdall Cl WA5 . . . . . .**15** C5
Chipstead Cl CW8 . . . .**103** A4
Chirk Cl CH2 . . . .**118** F6
Chirk Gdns CH65 . . . .**70** D3
Chirk Pl CW7 . . . .**126** A1
Chirton Cl WA11 . . . .**1** D7
Chisledon Cl WA11 . . . .**1** D7
Chislet Ct WA8 . . . .**12** E4
Chiswick Cl WA7 . . . .**50** D7
Chiswick Gdns WA4 . . . .**26** F6
Chollerton Cl WA16 . . . .**29** C4
Cholmley Dr WA12 . . . .**2** E2
Cholmondeley Castle
Gdns * SK14 . . . .**201** A4
Cholmondeley La
SK14 . . . .**200** E2
Cholmondeley Rd
Ellesmere Port CH65 . . . . . .**69** F4
Hampton Heath SY14 . . . . .**213** E2
Runcorn WA7 . . . .**49** D4
Wrenbury CW5 . . . .**216** C5
Cholmondeley St
Macclesfield SK11 . . . .**112** D6
Widnes WA8 . . . .**23** A4
CHOLMONDESTON **170** E4

Cholmondley Rise
SY14 . . . .**214** B4
Chorlegh Grange [8]
SK9 . . . .**60** A1
CHORLEY **202** B2
CHORLEY BANK **201** E1
Chorley Bank Council Hos
CW5 . . . .**201** E1
CHORLEY GREEN **202** A3
Chorley Green La CW5,
SY14 . . . .**201** E1
Chorley Hall Cl SK9 . . . .**59** F1
Chorley Hall La
Alderley Edge SK9 . . . .**60** A1
Faddiley CW5 . . . .**202** C2
Chorley's La WA8 . . . .**13** E3
Chorley St
Warrington WA2 . . . .**16** B6
Warrington WA2 . . . .**16** C6
Chorley Stock La
CW5 . . . .**202** A2
Chorleywood Cl SK10 . . . . . .**87** B4
CHORLTON **207** B1
Chorlton Cl WA7 . . . .**24** D1
Chorlton La CW7 . . . .**207** B2
CHORLTON LANE **212** B4
CHOWLEY **182** F5
Chowley Oak La CH3 . . . . .**182** F6
Chrimes Dr CW8 . . . .**123** F6
Christchurch Ave
CW2 . . . .**190** A1
Christ Church CE Prim
Sch
Ellesmere Port CH65 . . . . . .**70** B2
Warrington WA2 . . . .**9** A1
Christ Church CE Sch
CW8 . . . .**76** B1
Christie Cl CH66 . . . .**44** A2
Christie St WA8 . . . .**13** D1
CHRISTLETON **142** E8
Christleton Ave
Crewe CW2 . . . .**189** D5
Northwich CW9 . . . .**104** A4
Christleton Ct WA7 . . . .**24** C4
Christleton Dr CH66 . . . .**69** E6
Christleton High Sch
CH3 . . . .**142** F7
Christleton Prim Sch
CH3 . . . .**142** E8
Christleton Rd CH3 . . . . . .**119** A1
Christleton Sports Ctr
CH3 . . . .**142** F8
Christleton Way [15]
SK9 . . . .**34** D5
Christopher Dr CH62 . . . . . .**44** A5
Christ The King RC Prim
Sch CH22 . . . .**43** E7
Church Ave SK9 . . . .**34** A5
Church Bank
Audley ST7 . . . .**209** D2
Goostrey CW4 . . . .**107** F1
Kelsall CW6 . . . .**122** D5
Tattenhall CH3 . . . .**166** B2
Church Bk SK23 . . . .**65** D7
Church Cl
Handforth SK9 . . . .**34** D3
Weaverham CW8 . . . .**77** D1
Church College Cl
CH1 . . . .**118** B3
Church Cotts
Astle SK11 . . . .**109** B8
Rainow SK10 . . . .**88** E5
Sealand CH1 . . . .**116** E6
Waverton CH3 . . . .**143** C3
Church Croft CH4 . . . .**162** A6
Church Ct
Ashton Hayes CH3 . . . . . .**121** F8
Farndon CH3 . . . .**180** E2
Church Dr
Newton-le-W WA12 . . . .**2** C1
Warrington WA1 . . . .**9** A1
Church End L24 . . . .**21** D1
Church End Mews L24 . . . . .**21** D1
Churche's Ct [15] CW5 . . .**204** E5
Churches Mansion*
CW5 . . . .**204** F5
Church Farm CW5 . . . .**216** E4
Church Farm Ct
Heswall CH60 . . . .**40** F7
Willaston CH64 . . . .**67** F8
Churchfield Rd WA6 . . . .**74** C8
Churchfields
Audlem CW3 . . . .**230** A4
Barnton CW8 . . . .**78** B3
Croft WA3 . . . .**9** B7
Cuddington CW8 . . . .**102** B2
Helsby WA6 . . . .**73** C4
Knutsford WA16 . . . .**57** C2
Widnes WA8 . . . .**13** B5
Wybunbury CW5 . . . .**220** B8
Church Fields TF9 . . . .**236** C2
Church Gn WA13 . . . .**19** B8
CHURCH GREEN **18** E2
Church Hall Cl CH1 . . . . . .**117** F7
CHURCH HILL **149** D6
Church Hill WA16 . . . .**57** A2
Churchill Ave WA3 . . . .**5** B4
Churchill Cl CW12 . . . .**156** A3
Churchill Dr CW6 . . . .**146** D1
Churchill Mans [10]
WA7 . . . .**23** A3
Churchill Parkway
CW7 . . . .**149** D8
Churchill Way
Macclesfield SK11 . . . .**112** D6
Neston CH64 . . . .**66** E8
Church La
Alderley Edge SK9 . . . .**60** A2

Church La continued
Aldford CH3 . . . .**163** F3
Backford CH1 . . . .**95** B4
Bebington CH62 . . . .**44** A4
Bramhall SK7 . . . .**35** C2
Chester CH2 . . . .**118** D7
Congleton CW12 . . . .**134** E1
Culcheth WA3 . . . .**4** E3
Ellesmere Port CH66 . . . . . .**69** D3
Farndon CH3 . . . .**180** E1
Golborne WA3 . . . .**3** D7
Guilden Sutton CH3 . . . . . .**119** F5
Hargrave CH3 . . . .**144** B1
Henbury SK11 . . . .**111** C8
Huxley CH3, CW6 . . . .**167** C6
Lawton-gate ST7 . . . .**194** C4
Mobberley WA16 . . . .**58** C5
Mow Cop ST7 . . . .**195** E7
Nantwich CW5 . . . .**204** E5
Neston CH64 . . . .**66** E7
New Mills SK22 . . . .**39** C8
Rainow SK10 . . . .**88** E5
Sandbach CW11 . . . .**175** E7
Scholar Green ST7 . . . .**194** C7
Smallwood CW11 . . . .**176** E4
Stoak CH2 . . . .**96** A7
Sutton Lane Ends SK11 . . .**112** F3
Warren SK11 . . . .**134** D8
Warrington WA4 . . . .**17** B1
Weaverham CW8 . . . .**77** D1
Wistaston CW2 . . . .**205** E8
CHURCH LAWTON **194** C3
Church Lawton Prim Sch
ST7 . . . .**194** A5
Church Mdw TF9 . . . .**236** C2
Church Mdws
Little Leigh CW8 . . . .**77** D5
Whitchurch SY13 . . . .**226** A1
Church Mead CH3 . . . .**181** A5
Church Meadow La
CH60 . . . .**40** F7
Church Meadow Wlk
WA8 . . . .**22** B5
Churchmere Cl CW1 . . . . .**190** C7
Church Mews
Bollington SK10 . . . .**88** B8
Higher Wincham CW9 . . . . .**79** E5
Knutsford WA16 . . . .**57** B2
[6] Macclesfield SK11 . . .**112** D8
CHURCH MINSHULL . . .**172** A6
Church Par [5] CH65 . . . . . .**70** C6
Church Rd
Alsager ST7 . . . .**193** C4
Ashton Hayes CH3 . . . . . .**121** F8
Barnton CW8 . . . .**78** B2
Broughton CH4 . . . .**139** C4
Burwardsley CH3 . . . .**184** A5
Cheadle SK8 . . . .**35** B8
Dodleston CH4 . . . .**162** B8
Eccleston CH4 . . . .**141** E6
Frodsham WA6 . . . .**74** C7
Hale L24 . . . .**47** E8
Handforth SK9 . . . .**34** D3
Haydock WA11 . . . .**1** E7
Little Leigh CW8 . . . .**77** D4
Lymm WA13 . . . .**18** E2
Mouldsworth CH3 . . . .**98** F1
New Mills SK22 . . . .**39** C7
Northwich CW9 . . . .**104** A8
Saughall CH1 . . . .**94** A1
Shocklach CH3 . . . .**197** C1
Thornton Hough CH63 . . . . .**42** B6
Tilston SY14 . . . .**198** B2
Wilmslow SK9 . . . .**59** E4
Worleston CW5 . . . .**188** D6
Church Rise CW8 . . . .**102** B2
Church Row CW6 . . . .**168** F1
Church St N CW6 . . . .**122** C5
Church St W SK11 . . . .**112** C8
Churchside SK10 . . . .**112** D8
Churchside Cl CW1 . . . . . .**191** D5
Churchside Wlk CH4 . . . . .**140** F7
Church St
Audlem ST7 . . . .**209** D2
Audley, Wood Lane ST7 . . .**210** A1
Bollington SK10 . . . .**88** B8
Chester CH1 . . . .**237** B4
Connah's Quay CH5 . . . .**91** D1
Davenham CW9 . . . .**104** A3
Ellesmere Port CH65 . . . . . .**70** C6
Farndon LL13 . . . .**180** E2
Frodsham WA6 . . . .**74** B8
Great Budworth CW9 . . . . . .**79** A8
Higher Wincham CW9 . . . . .**79** E5
Kelsall CW6 . . . .**122** D4
Kidsgrove, Butt Lane
ST7 . . . .**194** D1
Kidsgrove, The Rookery
ST7 . . . .**195** C4
Macclesfield SK10,
SK11 . . . .**112** D8
Malpas SY14 . . . .**213** B3
Moulton CW9 . . . .**126** F8
Mount Pleasant ST7 . . . . . .**195** C6
Newton-le-W WA12 . . . .**2** E4
Runcorn WA7 . . . .**23** B2
Sandbach CW11 . . . .**175** B6
Tarvin CH3 . . . .**121** C2
Warrington WA1 . . . .**16** C5
Weaverham CW8 . . . .**77** D1
Widnes WA8 . . . .**23** A5
Wilmslow SK9 . . . .**60** B7
Church Steadings
CH3 . . . .**143** C3
Church Terr SK9 . . . .**34** D4
Church View
Audlem CW3 . . . .**230** A4

Church View continued
Handforth SK9 . . . .**34** A2
Haslington CW1 . . . .**191** D5
Kingsley WA6 . . . .**75** B2
[18] Knutsford WA16 . . . . . .**57** A2
Lymm WA13 . . . .**19** B4
New Mills SK22 . . . .**39** C8
Church View Terr
SK11 . . . .**112** F3
Church View Wlk
CW2 . . . .**205** E8
Churchward Cl CH2 . . . . .**118** D4
Churchway SK10 . . . .**86** F2
Church Way
Alvanley WA6 . . . .**73** A1
Blacon CH1 . . . .**117** E5
Wybunbury CW5 . . . .**220** B8
Churchway Rd L24 . . . .**21** A2
Church Wlk
Broughton CH4 . . . .**139** C5
Crowton CW8 . . . .**76** C2
[2] Ellesmere Port CH65 .**70** C6
Holmes Chapel CW4 . . . . .**130** C3
Knutsford WA16 . . . .**57** A2
Lower Peover WA16 . . . .**81** C1
Malpas SY14 . . . .**213** B3
Northwich CW9 . . . .**104** A8
Wilmslow SK9 . . . .**59** F6
Winwick WA2 . . . .**8** A6
Church Wlks
Christleton CH3 . . . .**142** E8
Norton in Hales TF9 . . . . . .**236** C2
Churchwood View
WA13 . . . .**18** F3
Churchyard Side
CW5 . . . .**204** E5
CHURTON **180** E5
Churton Cl
Hough CW2 . . . .**206** E3
[3] Northwich CW9 . . . . . .**103** E4
Churton Rd
Chester CH3 . . . .**119** A2
Farndon CH3 . . . .**180** E2
Churton St CH3 . . . .**119** A2
Cicely Mill La WA16 . . . .**30** D3
Cinder Cl CH3 . . . .**119** F5
Cinder Hill CW7 . . . .**125** F6
Cinder-hill La ST7 . . . .**194** F7
Cinder La
Chelford SK11 . . . .**83** E1
Guilden Sutton CH3 . . . . . .**119** F5
Lostock Green CW9 . . . . . .**105** A8
Nantwich CW5 . . . .**188** C2
Over Peover WA16 . . . .**108** C2
Warrington WA4 . . . .**17** F1
Cinder Rock Way ST7 . . . .**195** C1
CINNAMON BROW **8** F4
Cinnamon Brow CE Prim
Sch WA2 . . . .**8** F3
Cinnamon La WA2 . . . .**8** F3
Cinnamon La N WA2 . . . .**8** F3
Cinnamon Pk WA2 . . . .**9** B3
Circle Ave CW5 . . . .**205** E5
Circle The
Crewe CW2 . . . .**190** D1
Mere WA16 . . . .**30** C2
Circuit The
Alderley Edge SK9 . . . .**60** B3
Cheadle SK8 . . . .**35** A7
Wilmslow SK9 . . . .**59** D5
Circular Dr CH4 . . . .**140** F4
City Bank ST8 . . . .**179** C2
City Quays [8] CH1 . . . . . .**237** C3
City Rd CH1 . . . .**237** C3
City Walls Rd CH1 . . . .**237** A2
City Way Apartments [7]
CH **237** C3
Civic Way
Ellesmere Port CH65 . . . . . .**70** B4
Middlewich CW10 . . . .**128** C1
Clair Ave CH5 . . . .**116** A3
Clamhanger La WA16 . . . . . .**56** D7
Clamley Ct L24 . . . .**21** A3
Clamley Gdns L24 . . . .**21** E2
Clanbrook Ave WA13 . . . . . .**19** A2
Clanfield Ave WA8 . . . .**12** E4
Clap Gate Cres WA8 . . . . . .**22** B5
Clap Gates Cres WA5 . . . . .**15** E7
Clap Gates Rd WA5 . . . .**15** E7
Clare Ave
Chester CH2 . . . .**119** A3
Handforth SK9 . . . .**34** C3
Clare Dr
Crewe CW2 . . . .**189** F1
Ellesmere Port CH65 . . . . . .**70** B1
Macclesfield SK10 . . . .**87** C3
Clare Ho CH1 . . . .**117** F6
Claremont Ave WA8 . . . .**13** C4
Claremont Cl CW9 . . . .**103** F3
Claremont Dr WA8 . . . .**13** B4
Claremont Rd
Cheadle SK8 . . . .**35** A8
Crewe CW2 . . . .**190** B2
Culcheth WA3 . . . .**4** D4
Runcorn WA7 . . . .**23** B2
Clarence Ave
Chester CH3 . . . .**119** B2
Warrington WA5 . . . .**14** D6
Widnes WA8 . . . .**13** A4
Clarence Ct
Newton-le-W WA12 . . . .**2** A4
Wilmslow SK9 . . . .**60** A6
Clarence Gr CW1 . . . .**190** B5
Clarence Mill Bsns Pk
SK10 . . . .**63** A1
Clarence Rd
Bollington SK10 . . . .**63** A1
Warrington WA4 . . . .**17** B2

Clarence St
Newton-le-W WA12 . . . .**1** F4
Runcorn WA7 . . . .**22** F3
Warrington WA1 . . . .**16** E7
Clarence Terr
Bollington SK10 . . . .**63** A1
[7] Runcorn WA7 . . . .**23** A3
Clarendon Cl
Chester CH4 . . . .**141** E6
Runcorn WA7 . . . .**50** D7
Clarendon Cotts SK9 . . . . . .**34** A3
Clarendon Ct WA2 . . . .**7** F4
Clarendon Dr SK10 . . . .**88** A1
Clarendon Rd M44 . . . .**11** F7
Clare Pl CW7 . . . .**149** C7
Clares Farm Cl WA1 . . . .**17** F7
Clare St
Harrisehead ST7 . . . .**195** E4
Mount Pleasant ST7 . . . . .**195** C6
Clarke Ave
Culcheth WA3 . . . .**5** A4
Warrington WA4 . . . .**16** C3
Clarke Gdns [3] WA8 . . . . .**23** B7
Clarke La
Bollington SK10 . . . .**87** E5
Langley SK11 . . . .**113** D3
Clarke Terr SK11 . . . .**112** D6
CLARK GREEN **63** A3
Clarks Terr WA7 . . . .**48** D8
Clary Mdw CW8 . . . .**78** E1
Clatterbridge Hospl
CH63 . . . .**42** D8
Clatterbridge Rd CH63 . . . .**42** D8
Clatterwick La CW8 . . . .**77** D7
Claude St WA1 . . . .**16** C6
Claughton Ave CW2 . . . . . .**190** C1
Claverton Cl WA7 . . . .**49** B6
Claverton Ct CH4 . . . .**237** C1
Claydon Gdns WA3 . . . .**10** F1
Clay Heyes SK11 . . . .**84** A3
Clayhall Gn CH66 . . . .**69** D7
Clayhill Gr WA3 . . . .**4** B8
Clayhill Light Ind Pk
CH64 . . . .**41** F2
Clay La
Bickerton SY14 . . . .**200** B7
Burtonwood WA5 . . . .**6** E5
Handforth SK9 . . . .**34** C5
Haslington CW1, CW11 . . .**191** D7
Over Peover WA16 . . . .**108** B8
Sandbach CW11, CW1 . . . .**174** B2
Wilmslow SK9 . . . .**59** C4
Winsford CW7 . . . .**125** B4
Claypit Rd CH4 . . . .**141** B5
Claypits La CH3 . . . .**142** F5
Clayton Ave
Congleton CW12 . . . .**157** A5
Golborne WA3 . . . .**3** E8
Clayton-By-Pass
CW12 . . . .**156** C3
Clayton Cl CW1 . . . .**190** A7
Clayton Cres
Runcorn WA7 . . . .**22** F1
Widnes WA8 . . . .**12** F1
Clayton Dr SY13 . . . .**226** B1
Clayton Rd WA3 . . . .**9** F6
Clayton's Row CW5 . . . . . .**204** E7
Cleadon Way WA8 . . . .**12** E4
Cleaver Mews SK11 . . . . . .**112** C5
Cleaver Rd CH1 . . . .**117** E4
Cledford Cres CW10 . . . . . .**151** E6
Cledford Inf Sch
CW10 . . . .**151** D7
Cledford Jun Sch
CW10 . . . .**151** D7
Cledford La CW10 . . . .**151** E7
Cledwen Rd/Ffordd
Cledwen CH4 . . . .**139** D5
Cleethorpes Rd WA7 . . . . . .**50** C7
Cleeves Cl WA1 . . . .**16** C5
Cleeve Way SK8 . . . .**35** B6
Clegge St WA2 . . . .**16** B7
Clelland St WA4 . . . .**16** C3
Clement Dr CW1 . . . .**189** F7
Clemley Cl CW6 . . . .**122** D6
Clerewood Ave WA8 . . . .**34** B7
Clevedon Cl SK11 . . . .**112** A7
Cleveland Dr CH66 . . . .**69** A6
Cleveland Rd WA2 . . . .**8** A3
Cleveland Way CW7 . . . . . .**149** B7
Cleveleys Ave WA8 . . . .**13** D2
Cleveleys Rd WA5 . . . .**15** B4
Cliff Dr CW8 . . . .**77** D6
Cliffbrook Gr [2] SK9 . . . . . .**34** D2
Cliffe Rd
Crewe CW1 . . . .**190** B7
Neston CH64 . . . .**66** F5
Warrington WA4 . . . .**26** C7
Cliffe St [3] WA8 . . . .**13** C1
Cliff La
Acton Bridge CW8 . . . .**76** C4
Lymm WA13 . . . .**28** C6
Macclesfield SK10, SK11 . . .**88** B1
Warrington WA4 . . . .**17** D1
Clifford Dr CH4 . . . .**140** F5
Clifford Gr CW1 . . . .**191** C4
Clifford Pl [4] CW7 . . . .**149** C7
Clifford Rd
Macclesfield SK11 . . . .**112** A8
Poynton SK12 . . . .**36** D3
Warrington WA5 . . . .**15** A4
Wilmslow SK9 . . . .**59** E6
Cliff Rd
Acton Bridge CW8 . . . .**76** E4
Wilmslow SK9 . . . .**60** B8
Cliff Side SK9 . . . .**60** B8
Cliff View WA6 . . . .**74** A8
CLIFTON **49** D4

Clifton Ave
 Bebington CH62.........43 E3
 Crewe CW2...........190 B3
 Culcheth WA3............4 D3
Clifton Cl WA1.........17 C7
Clifton Cres WA6.......49 C1
Clifton Ct WA7.........49 B6
Clifton Dr
 Blacon CH1..........117 E3
 Northwich CW9.......104 A5
 Wilmslow SK9..........59 E4
Clifton Gdns CH65......70 C3
Clifton La WA7.........49 E3
Cliftonmill Mdws WA3...91 D4
Clifton Park Ave CH5...91 D1
Clifton Rd
 Runcorn, Clifton WA7...49 B5
 Runcorn, Heath WA7....49 B6
 Sandbach CW11.......174 D7
Clifton Rdbt..........49 E3
Clifton St
 Alderley Edge SK9.....60 A1
 Crewe CW2...........190 B3
 Warrington WA4.......16 C4
Cliftonville Rd WA1....17 D6
Clincton Cl WA8........22 A8
Clincton View WA8......22 A8
Clipsley Cres WA11......1 B7
Clipsley La WA11........1 C6
Clitheroe Rd CW8.......77 E1
CLIVE...............127 D1
Clive Ave WA2..........8 C1
Clive Back La CW7.....150 D7
Cliveden Rd CH4.......140 F5
CLIVE GREEN..........150 D6
Clivegreen La CW10....150 E7
Clive La CW7..........150 C8
Clock Face Rd WA8.....13 E8
Clocktower The CW4....130 D7
Clock Twr The WA4......16 C2
Cloister Way CH65......70 E5
Clonners Field CW5....205 A4
Closeburn Ave CH60....40 E6
Close La
 Alsager ST7.........192 F3
 Mow Cop ST7.........195 D7
Close The
 Alsager ST7.........193 A3
 Hartford CW8........103 D6
 Newton-le-W WA12......2 E1
 Saughall CH1.........94 A1
 Tarporley CW6.......146 C2
CLOTTON............145 D4
Cloudberry Wlk M31.....11 F3
CLOUD SIDE.........157 F4
Cloud The* CW12......158 A4
Cloud View CW12......157 A2
Clough Ave
 Handforth SK9........34 B2
 Warrington WA2........8 B2
Clough Bank SK10......87 F7
Clough Field Cl SK23...65 D8
CLOUGH HALL........210 F8
Clough Hall Dr ST7....210 E6
Clough Hall Rd ST7....210 F8
Clough Hall Tech Sch
 ST7...............194 F1
Clough La CW8........103 D6
Clough Rd CW7........126 E1
Cloughside SK12........38 E6
Clough The WA7........23 F1
Clough Wlk CW2.......206 D8
Cloughwood Sch
 CW8...............103 D5
Clovelly Ave WA6.......14 E7
Clovelly Gr WA7........50 C5
Clover Ave WA6........74 D7
Clover Ct WA7.........50 B5
Cloverdale CW8.......103 C7
Cloverdale Rd SK11...113 C5
Clover Dr
 Pickmere WA16........79 F7
 Winsford CW7........126 D3
Cloverfield
 Lymm WA13...........18 F4
 Runcorn WA7.........50 C7
Cloverfield Gdns CH66..69 D7
Cloverfields CW1.....191 B4
Clover La CH4.........140 F5
Clover Pl CH4.........140 F5
Clowes Ave CW7.......193 F2
Clowes St SK11.......112 B8
Clumber Cl SK12........36 E3
Clumber Rd SK12........36 E3
CLUTTON............182 D1
Clutton CE Prim Sch
 CH3...............182 D1
Clwyd Cl CH5.........139 B6
Clwyd Way CH66........69 A6
Clyde Ave ST8........179 C1
Clyde Cres CW7.......127 B1
Clyde Gr CW2.........190 A3
Clydesdale CH65........70 B3
Clydesdale Ave CW4...190 B3
Clydesdale Rd WA4......26 D8
Coach Ho The ST7.....194 C4
Coach Rd
 Broxton CH3.........183 A3
 Clyde Green SY14....199 D2
 Little Budworth CW6..147 D8
Coachway SK10.........86 F7
Coalbrookdale Rd
 CH64...............41 F2
COALPIT HILL........210 C8
Coalpit Hill ST7.....210 D8
Coalpit La
 Clive Green CW10....150 F7
 Langley SK11........113 C5

Coalpit La continued
 Mollington CH1.......94 D4
Coalport Dr CW7......126 F3
Coare St SK10.........87 D1
Coastguard La CH64....41 B1
Coatings By Pass Rd
 CH5................91 F2
Coatings Two CH5......91 E2
Cobal Ct WA6.........74 B8
Cobbett's Way SK9.....59 F4
Cobblers Cross La
 CW6...............146 E2
Cobblers La / Lon Y
 Cryddion LL12......161 B1
Cobbles The
 Chester CH4.........141 D7
 Cuddington SK8......101 D4
 Lower Peover WA16....81 C1
Cobblestone Ct CH2...119 E8
COBBS..............26 E8
Cobbs Inf Sch The
 WA4...............26 E8
Cobbs La
 Hough CW2..........206 E2
 Warrington WA4......26 E8
Cobden St
 Newton-le-W WA12......2 D4
 Warrington WA2......16 B6
Cob Hall La WA6.......98 D5
Cob Moor Rd ST7......195 A4
COBSCOT............235 E3
Cock Hall La SK11....113 D3
Cockhedge La WA1.....16 C5
Cockhedge Sh Ctr
 WA1...............16 B5
Cockhedge Way WA1....16 B5
Cockington Cl CW9....104 A4
Cock La
 Great Budworth CW9...78 F8
 Sound CW5..........217 F4
Cocklade La L24.......21 D1
Cock Lane Ends WA8....22 B4
Cockpit La SK8.......102 B1
Cockshades farm
 CW5...............206 C2
Cocksheadhey Rd
 SK10...............63 C1
Cocksmoss La
 Congleton SK11......134 A3
 Marton SK11.........133 D3
Cocoa Gdns CW5......204 E5
Cocoa Yd The [10]
CODDINGTON.........182 A3
Coe La WA14..........30 C7
Cogshall La
 Anderton CW9........78 C5
 Comberbach CW9......78 B7
Colchester Ho [10]
 CH1...............237 C3
Colchester Sq CH4....140 F5
COLDHARBOUR........164 F5
Coldmoss Dr CW11....175 C4
COLD MOSS HEATH.....175 C5
Coldstream Cl WA3......8 E3
Coldstream Dr CH66....68 F5
Cole Ave WA12..........2 C4
Colebrook Cl WA3......10 A4
Coleclough Pl WA3......4 F4
Coleg Glannau Dyfrdwy/
 Deeside Coll CH5....91 B1
Colehill Bank CW8....156 E2
Colehill Pl CH5.......91 D1
Colemere Cl WA1.......17 A8
Colemere Ct CH65......70 C7
Coleridge Cl
 Blacon CH1.........118 A5
 Sandbach CW11.......174 C5
Coleridge Gr WA8......12 E1
Coleridge Way CW7....190 F5
Colinwood Ave CH4....139 B3
Coliseum Way CH5......70 D2
Collar House Dr SK10..86 E6
College Cl
 Warrington, Fearnhead
 WA2................9 B2
 Wilmslow SK9........59 F8
College Fields
 Crewe CW2..........190 A1
 Widnes WA8..........12 F5
College Gn CH4.......141 D7
College La CW6.......168 F1
College of Law
 (Christleton Hall)
 CH3...............142 D8
College Rd ST7.......193 B5
College View CH5......91 C1
Colley La CW11.......175 D5
Colliers La CW5......205 B7
Colliers Row WA3......48 E7
Collier St WA7........22 F3
Colliery Green Cl CH64.66 E5
Colliery Green Ct CH64.66 E5
Colliery Green Dr
 CH64..............66 E5
Collinbrook Ave CW2..190 B1
Collingham Gn CH66....69 B5
Collingham Way CW7...126 D1
Collingtree Ave CW7..127 A3
Collingwood Cl
 Macclesfield SK10....87 B2
 Poynton SK12........37 A3
Collingwood Rd WA12...2 B3
COLLINS GREEN.........1 E1
Collins Green La WA5...1 E1
Collinson Ct [2] WA6..74 B8

Collins St CW2.......190 A3
Collin St WA5.........15 F5
Colne Rd WA5..........6 F6
Colorado Cl WA5......15 C7
Colshaw Dr SK9........34 D2
Colshaw Hall Cotts
 WA16...............82 F1
Colshaw La SK11......109 E1
Colson Ct CH2........237 A4
Coltsfoot Cl CH3.....142 B5
Columbine Cl
 Huntington CH3......142 A4
 Widnes WA8..........12 B4
Columbine Way WA4.....6 B7
Columbine Wlk [8] M31.11 F3
Colville Cl WA3........8 A3
Colville Rd SK11.....111 F8
Colwyn Cl
 Ellesmere Port CH65..70 D3
 Warrington WA5.......7 E2
Colwyn Rd SK7.........35 F8
COMBERBACH..........78 C7
Comberbach Dr CW5...205 A4
Comberbach Prim Sch
 CW9...............78 C8
Combermere Pl [8]
 CW1...............190 B5
Comber Way WA16......82 A8
Comboy Dr CW9........104 C6
Combs Cl SK22.........39 A8
Commercial Ave SK8....34 F5
Commercial Rd SK10...112 E8
Common Farm La
 SK11..............83 E1
Commongate SK10.....112 E8
Commonhall St CH1...237 A2
Common La
 Betley CW3.........221 F6
 Chelford SK11.......83 E1
 Culcheth WA3.........4 F4
 Duddon CW6.........145 C7
 Hapsford WA6........72 D1
 Kelsall CW6........122 C3
 Lach Dennis CW9....105 E5
 Norbury SY13.......215 C5
 Stretton WA4........52 E8
 Warrington WA4......16 E2
 Warrington WA3.....143 B4
 Winsford CW7.......143 E5
Common Rd WA12,WA5....1 E3
COMMONSIDE.........100 B8
Commonside WA6.......73 E1
COMMON SIDE........124 D3
Commons Mill CW11...175 B7
Commons The WA12......1 A2
Commons The CW11....175 B6
Common The
 Kelsall CW6........122 C3
 Runcorn WA7.........49 F8
Commonwealth Cl
 CW7...............149 D6
Commonwood Rd
 LL13..............196 A8
Company's Cl WA7......49 A6
Compass Cl WA7.......50 D5
Compstall Gr WA11....1 C7
Compton Pl
 Chester CH4........141 A6
 Ellesmere Port CH65..70 B5
Concorde Pl WA2.......8 D2
Concourse Way WA9.....1 A2
Condliffe Cl CW11....175 C5
Conery Cl WA6........73 C4
Coney Gr WA7.........50 B5
CONGLETON..........157 A3
Congleton Bsns Ctr
 CW12..............156 C4
Congleton Bsns Pk
 CW12..............156 C4
Congleton Cl SK9.....85 A8
CONGLETON EDGE.....179 B5
Congleton Edge Rd
 CW12..............179 B6
Congleton High Sch
 CW12..............155 F3
Congleton La SK11....109 D5
Congleton Mus*
 CW12..............156 E2
Congleton Rd
 Alderley Edge SK9...60 A1
 Biddulph ST8.......179 D2
 Broughton CH4......139 C4
 Kidsgrove ST7......194 D1
 Macclesfield SK11..112 B5
 Marton SK11........133 B5
 Mow Cop ST7........178 F1
 North Rode SK11....134 C6
 Sandbach, Arclid Green
 CW11.............175 E8
 Sandbach CW11......175 B8
 Scholar Green CW12,
 ST7..............177 E3
 Siddington SK11.....84 F2
 Smallwood CW11.....177 A6
 Swettenham CW12....131 F4
 Warren SK11........111 E2
Congleton Rd N ST7..194 D3
Congleton Rd S ST7..194 D3
Congleton Ret Pk
 CW12..............156 D4
Congleton Sta CW12..157 A1
Congleton War Meml
 Hospl CW12........156 F1
Conifer Cl CH66......95 A8
Conifer Gr
 Moore WA4..........25 F8
 Warrington WA5......14 F7
Conifers The ST7....193 B3

Conifer Wlk M31......11 E3
Coningsby Dr CW7....126 E1
Coningsby Gdns [13] WA3.3 E8
Coniston Ave
 Bebington CH63......43 C4
 Congleton CW12.....155 F2
 Warrington WA5......14 D4
 Winsford CW7.......126 C2
Coniston Cl
 Alderley Edge SK9...84 A7
 Hooton CH66.........44 B2
 Nantwich CW5.......205 A6
 Runcorn WA7.........49 D6
Coniston Dr
 Frodsham WA6.......74 D8
 Handforth SK9.......34 C4
 Holmes Chapel CW4..130 A3
Coniston Rd
 Chester CH2........118 F5
 High Lane SK6.......37 D8
 Neston CH64.........66 E6
 Partington M31......11 E4
Coniston Way SK11...111 F5
CONNAH'S QUAY.......91 B1
Connah's Quay High Sch
 CH5...............91 C1
Connaught Ave WA1....16 E7
Connaught Cl SK9.....60 C8
Connaught Dr WA12....2 C2
Conrad Cl CW1.......190 E4
Conroy Way WA12......7 C8
Consort Cl SK10......87 E7
Constable Dr SK9.....60 E8
Constables Cl WA7....24 A1
Constance Rd M31....11 F3
Constance Way WA8...23 A5
Convamore Rd SK7.....35 D7
Conway Ave
 Irlam M44...........11 F8
 Warrington WA5.......7 F2
 Winsford CW7.......149 C7
Conway Cl
 Crewe CW1..........190 C8
 Knutsford WA16......82 A8
 Saltney CH4........140 D5
 Warrington WA5......14 F6
Conway Cres SK10.....87 F1
Conway Ct CH65.......70 D3
Conway Gr CW2........36 E3
Conwy Ct WA7.........24 A2
Coogee Ave WA5......14 E7
Cook Ave WA11........1 F7
Cookes Cl CH64.......41 E1
Cookes Ct CH65......166 B1
Cooke's La CW9......104 F6
Cookesmere La
 CW11.............175 A8
Cookes La WA8........99 F8
Cooks La SY13.......225 D7
COOKSONGREEN.......76 A1
Cook St CH65.........70 C6
Coole La
 Hack Green CW5.....218 E3
 Newhall CW3........229 C5
Coombe Park Ct [1]
 CH66..............69 C6
Coombe Pk CH64.......69 C6
Co-operative St SK12..38 D6
Cooper Ave
 Newton-le-W WA12.....1 F3
 Warrington WA2.......8 A5
Coope Rd SK10........87 E6
Cooperis Fold SK8....34 F6
Cooper's Croft CH3..142 A7
Cooper's La CH5......91 D1
Coopers Opening
 CW11.............175 B7
Coopers Pl WA4.......16 C1
Cooper St
 Congleton CW12.....156 E3
 Runcorn WA7........23 A3
 Widnes WA8.........13 B1
Copper Terr CW6....146 D1
Cope Ave CW5.......204 D4
Copeland Gr WA7.....49 E5
Copeland Rd WA4.....16 B2
Copes La CW5.......204 C4
Copeswood Cl CH4...139 C3
Copgrove Wlk M22....33 E7
Copley Wlk CW5.....204 D5
Cop Mdw SK11.......112 F2
COPPENHALL........190 D7
Coppenhall Gr CW2..190 A4
Coppenhall Heyes
 CW2..............190 A4
Coppenhall La CW2..189 D4
COPPENHALL MOSS
 ....173 D1
Copper Beech CH4...139 C3
Copperfield Cl WA3...9 C3
Copperfield Rd
 Cheadle SK8.........35 B5
 Poynton SK12........36 F2
Copperfields
 Poynton SK12........36 D2
 Tarporley CW6......146 D2
 Wilmslow SK9........60 C8
Copperhill Rd CW12..179 B7
Coppermine La SY14..184 B2
Copper St SK11......112 E6
Copperwood WA7.....24 C1
Copper Wood CW8...101 E5
Coppice Ave SK12.....38 A6
Coppice Cl
 High Lane SK12.......38 A6
 Runcorn WA7.........24 A1

Coppice Cl continued
 Willaston CW5......205 D6
Coppice Ct SK8.......34 B8
Coppice Dr CW10....151 E6
Coppice Gn
 Elton CH2...........72 C4
 Warrington WA5.......7 A1
Coppice Gr WA16.....57 A3
Coppice Ho
 Poynton SK12........36 D2
 Talke ST7..........210 C8
Coppice La SK12......38 A5
Coppicemere Dr CW1..191 A2
Coppice Rd
 Haslington CW11....192 A8
 Poynton SK12........37 B3
 Talke ST7..........210 C8
 Willaston CW5......205 D6
Coppice Rise SK11...112 D5
Coppice The
 Altrincham WA15.....32 B8
 Cuddington CW8.....101 D5
 Horwich End SK23....65 F5
 Nantwich CW5.......204 F3
 Sandbach CW11......174 E7
 Wincham CW9.........79 C3
Coppice Way SK9.....34 E3
Coppins Cl
 Chester CH3........119 A2
 Helsby WA6..........73 B4
Coppins The
 Warrington WA2.......8 C2
 Wilmslow SK9........59 E4
Copse The
 Altrincham WA15.....32 D7
 High Lane SK6.......37 E7
 Newton-le-W WA12.....2 B4
 Warrington WA5......50 A6
COPTHORNE.........229 F4
Copthorne Cl CW12..156 F2
Copthorne Dr CW3...229 F3
Copyhold CW8........102 D8
Corbet Ave WA2......16 B8
Corbet Dr TF9.......235 A4
Corbet St WA2.......16 B8
Corbridge Ho [2] CH1.237 C3
Corfe Way CW7......126 E1
Coriander Cl CW10..128 C3
Corks La SK12........38 E5
CORLTON...........207 B1
Cormorant Cl CW1...190 F4
Cormorant Dr WA7....22 E2
Cornbrook Rd SK11..112 C4
Corner Croft SK9.....60 A4
Cornerhouse La WA8..12 D3
Corners The CW6....102 E7
Cornfield Cl
 Ellesmere Port CH66..69 F1
 Macclesfield SK10....87 C3
Cornforth Way WA8...12 F3
Cornhill Cl ST5.....210 D1
Cornish Cl M22.......33 D8
Cornishway Ind Est
 M22...............33 D8
Cornmill Cl CH1.....173 D7
Cornmill Ct WA3......9 A8
Cornubia Rd WA8.....23 D7
Cornwall Ave WA7....23 A2
Cornwall Cl
 [3] Congleton CW12.157 A1
 High Lane SK6.......37 E7
 Macclesfield SK10...86 E1
 Warrington WA3......23 F1
Cornwall Gr CW1....190 B5
Cornwall Ho CH1....237 B3
Cornwall Rd
 Chester CH2........118 F7
 Gatley SK8..........34 B8
 Irlam M44...........11 D5
 Widnes WA8.........13 B3
Cornwall St
 Chester CH1........237 B4
 Warrington WA1......16 E7
Cornwell Cl WA7.....60 D8
Coronation Ave
 Alsager ST7........193 A3
 Glazebury WA3........5 C7
 Warrington WA1......17 C2
 Winsford CW7.......126 E1
Coronation Bldgs
 SK10..............88 A8
Coronation Cres
 Crewe CW2..........190 E6
 Kidsgrove ST7......194 E1
 Sandbach CW11......175 A5
Coronation Dr
 Frodsham WA6.......49 D1
 Haydock WA11........2 E1
 Newton-le-W WA12.....2 E1
 Warrington WA5......14 F4
 Widnes WA8.........22 C8
Coronation Gr CW8...78 A4
Coronation Ho CW7...49 C8
Coronation Mill ST7.195 D7
Coronation Rd
 Broughton CH4......139 B3
 Congleton CW12.....156 F3
 Ellesmere Port CH65..70 C4
 Middlewich CW10....151 D6
 Runcorn, Higher Runcorn
 WA7..............23 B1
 Runcorn, Preston Brook
 WA7..............50 F6

Coronation Sq 🔟
WA16 . . . . .57 A2
Coronation St
  Chester CH4 . . . . 140 F7
  Crewe CW1 . . . . 190 D5
  Macclesfield SK11 . . . . 112 D6
Coronation Terr CW6 . . 146 D1
Coroner's La WA8 . . . . . . 13 A4
Coronet Ave CW9 . . . . 103 F3
Coronet Way WA8 . . . . . 22 B8
CORRA COMMON 233 C1
Correction Brow SK12 . . 37 C6
Corridor Rd CH65 . . . . . 71 B6
Corwen Cl WA5 . . . . 7 E1
Cosgrove Bsns Pk
  CW9 . . . . 78 D3
Cossack Ave WA2 . . . . . . 8 C1
COTEBROOK 147 A8
Cotebrook Dr CH2 . . . . 118 E7
Cotebrook Rd CW9 . . . . 104 C8
Cotebrook Shire Horse
  Ctr* CW6 . . . . 147 A7
Cote Lea Ct WA7 . . . . . . 49 F6
Cotes Pl CH1 . . . . 117 E3
Cotgreaves Cl CH4 . . . . 141 B5
Cotswold Ave WA3 . . . . . . 3 D6
Cotswold Cl
  Chester CH2 . . . . 118 F6
  Cuddington CW8 . . . . . 102 A2
  Macclesfield SK10 . . . . . 86 C1
Cotswold Ct 🔳 CH3 . . . 119 A1
Cotswold Gr WA9 . . . . . . 1 A3
Cotswold Pl WA3 . . . . . . 8 B4
Cotswold Rd WA2 . . . . . . 8 B3
Cotswold Way CW7 . . . 149 B7
Cottage Cl
  Bebington CH63 . . . . . . 43 C5
  Neston CH64 . . . . 66 F7
  Rudheath CW9 . . . . . . 104 E8
Cottage Dr E CH60 . . . . 40 F5
Cottage Dr W CH60 . . . . 40 F5
Cottage Gr SK9 . . . . 59 F5
Cottage La
  Heswall CH60 . . . . 40 F5
  Macclesfield SK10 . . . . 112 F7
Cottage Lawns SK9 . . . . 60 B2
Cottage Rd CH4 . . . . . 141 B5
Cottage St SK11 . . . . . 112 B8
Cottages The
  Lawton Heath ST7 . . . . 193 D6
  Sproston Green CW4 . . . 129 C2
  Warrington WA4 . . . . . . 17 F4
Cottam Dr WA2 . . . . 9 A3
Cotterdale Cl WA5 . . . . . 14 F7
Cotterill Dr WA1 . . . . . . 17 C7
Cotterill St CW2 . . . . . 190 D2
Cottesmore Dr CH60 . . . 41 D8
Cottesmore Gdns
  WA15 . . . . .32 C8
Cotton La
  Christleton CH3 . . . . . 120 D2
  Runcorn WA7 . . . . 49 D8
  Sandbach CW11 . . . . . 175 A3
Cotton Mews CW3 . . . . 230 A4
Cottons Bridge WA4 . . . . 50 F5
Cottonwood Gr ST7 . . . 195 E4
Cottrell Rd WA15 . . . . . 32 C7
Coulton Rd WA8 . . . . . . 13 F3
Council Hos
  Audlem CW3 . . . . 229 E2
  Bickerton SY14 . . . . . 200 A8
  Congleton CW12 . . . . . 156 F4
  Newhall CW5 . . . . 228 B8
Council Houses CW5 . . 216 B6
Countess Ave SK8 . . . . . 34 E5
Countess Ct 🔸 SK11 . . 111 F7
Countess Ct CH1 . . . . . 118 B5
Countess of Chester
  Health Pk CH2 . . . . . 118 B6
Countess Rd SK11 . . . . 111 F7
Countess Way CH2 . . . . 118 C5
Counting House Rd
  SK12 . . . . .38 E5
Country Ctr The*
  CH3 . . . . 165 E5
County Terr WA16 . . . . . 56 F1
Courier Row SK10 . . . . . 87 F7
Court 2 SK10 . . . . 87 F1
Court Ho The 🔳 CH65 . . 70 C6
Courtney Gn SK9 . . . . . 34 D2
Courtney Rd CH4 . . . . . 140 E5
Court No 4 🔳 SK10 . . . 112 C8
Court The CH64 . . . . . . 66 F6
Courtyard The
  Bostock Green CW10 . . . 127 D5
  Chester CH2 . . . . 118 F6
  Congleton CW12 . . . . . 156 B3
  Cuddington CW8 . . . . . 101 E2
  Elton CH2 . . . . 72 B4
  Haughton CW6 . . . . . . 186 F4
  Newton-le-W WA12 . . . . . 2 E4
  Smallwood CW11 . . . . . 177 A7
  🔺 Warrington WA1 . . . . 16 B5
  Weaverham CW8 . . . . . 102 A2
Cousens Way CH1 . . . . 118 B4
Covell Rd SK12 . . . . . . 36 D5
Coventry Ave CH4 . . . . . 94 E8
Coverdale Cl WA5 . . . . . 14 F7
Coverdale Fold CW11 . . 174 D5
Covert Cl WA3 . . . . . . 149 B8
Covert Gdns ST7 . . . . . 210 D8

Covert Rise CH3 . . . . . 166 A2
Covington Pl SK9 . . . . . 60 B6
Cowanway WA8 . . . . . . 12 F5
Cowbrook La SK11 . . . . 135 B6
Cowdell St WA2 . . . . . . 16 B7
Cowfields CW5 . . . . . . 204 E6
Cowhey Cl CH4 . . . . . . 141 B5
Cow Hey La WA6, WA7 . . 49 A5
Cow La
  Ashley WA15 . . . . 31 F6
  Bollington SK10 . . . . . . 88 B7
  Hargrave CH3 . . . . . . 144 A2
  Macclesfield SK11 . . . . 112 D6
  Norley WA6 . . . . 101 A5
  Rainow SK10 . . . . 88 D4
  Winslow SK9 . . . . 60 C7
  Winsford CW7 . . . . . . 149 E8
Cowley Way CW1 . . . . . 190 E1
Cowper Cl CW2 . . . . . . 206 A8
Cowthorne Dr CH3 . . . . 143 A4
COX BANK 234 F8
Crab La WA2 . . . . 9 B3
Crabbrook Dr CW11 . . . 174 E7
Crabmill La
  Norley WA6 . . . . 100 C6
  Warmingham CW11 . . . 173 E7
Crabtree Ave
  Altrincham WA15 . . . . . 32 D7
  Disley SK12 . . . . 38 E5
Crabtree Cl
  Crab Tree Cl L24 . . . . . 21 E2
Crabtree Ct SK12 . . . . . 38 D6
Crabtree Fold WA7 . . . . 50 C8
Crabtree Gr CW1 . . . . . 190 E6
CRABTREE GREEN 101 C1
Crabtree Green Ct
  CW8 . . . . 101 C2
Crabtree Green Pk 124 C8
Crabtree La WA13 . . . . . 29 A7
Crabwall Pl CH1 . . . . . 117 F5
Crackley Bank ST5 . . . . 210 E1
Crackley Bank Prim Sch
  ST5 . . . . 210 E1
Craddock Ct SY14 . . . . 213 B3
Cradley WA8 . . . . 12 C2
Cragside Way SK9 . . . . . 60 C6
Craig Cl SK11 . . . . 112 B5
Craig Dr SK23 . . . . 65 E8
Craig Gdns CH66 . . . . . 69 E7
Craigleigh Gr CH62 . . . . 43 F4
Craig Rd
  Congleton CW12 . . . . . 156 F4
  Macclesfield SK11 . . . . 112 B5
Craigside ST8 . . . . 179 C1
Craig Wlk ST7 . . . . . . 193 F2
Craithie Rd CH3 . . . . . 119 A2
Crampton Dr WA15 . . . . 32 C8
CRANAGE 130 A6
Cranage Cl WA7 . . . . . . 49 D7
Cranage Ct 🔳 CW12 . . 156 F3
Cranage La CW9 . . . . . . 79 D1
Cranage Rd CW2 . . . . . 190 A3
Cranage Way 🔟 SK9 . . 34 D5
Cranberry Dr ST5 . . . . . 210 D1
Cranberry Inf Sch
  ST7 . . . . 193 A3
Cranberry Jun Sch
  ST7 . . . . 193 A3
Cranberry La ST7 . . . . 193 A3
Cranberry Moss La
  ST7 . . . . 193 A3
Cranberry Rd M31 . . . . . 11 F3
Cranborne Ave WA4 . . . . 16 B1
Cranborne Rd CW1 . . . . 190 D6
Cranbrook Cl CW1 . . . . 190 A8
Crane Ho CH1 . . . . . . 118 B1
Cranfield Dr ST7 . . . . . 193 A3
Cranford Ave
  Knutsford WA16 . . . . . . 56 F1
  Macclesfield SK11 . . . . 112 F7
Cranford Cl CH62 . . . . . 43 F4
Cranford Ct
  Chester CH4 . . . . 141 A5
  🔸 Warrington WA1 . . . . 17 E8
Cranford Mews ST7 . . . 193 A3
Cranford Rd SK9 . . . . . . 34 A6
Cranford Sq WA16 . . . . . 56 F1
Cranham Ave WA3 . . . . . 3 E7
Cranleigh Cl WA4 . . . . . 26 B7
Cranleigh Cres CH1 . . . 118 B4
Cranleigh Dr SK7 . . . . . 37 A8
Cranmere Cl CW9 . . . . 104 A4
Cranshaw La WA8 . . . . . 13 B6
Cransley Sch CW9 . . . . . 53 E1
Cranswick Gn CH66 . . . . 69 C5
Crantock Dr SK8 . . . . . . 34 C8
Cranwell Ave WA3 . . . . . 4 F4
Craufurd Rd CW12 . . . . 157 A8
Craven Ave WA3 . . . . . . 3 E7
Craven Ct WA2 . . . . 7 F4
Crawford Ave WA8 . . . . . 12 B1
Crawford Pl WA7 . . . . . . 49 A8
Crawford's Wlk CH2 . . . 118 F3
Crawley Ave WA2 . . . . . . 8 A3
Crayford Ave CW7 . . . . 157 A5
Cresanne Cl CW10 . . . . 151 C7
Crescent Dr
  Furness Vale SK23 . . . . . 39 D2
  Helsby WA6 . . . . 73 B3
Crescent Rd
  Alderley Edge SK9 . . . . . 60 B2
  Congleton CW12 . . . . . 156 C2
  Cranage CW4 . . . . . . 129 F6
  Ellesmere Port CH65 . . . 70 D6
  Rostherne WA16 . . . . . . 30 B3
Crescent The
  Chester CH2 . . . . 118 D4

Crescent The continued
  Congleton CW12 . . . . . 156 C2
  Ellesmere Port CH65 . . . 69 F5
  Hartford CW8 . . . . . . 103 A5
  Heswall, Gayton CH60 . . . 41 B6
  Heswall WA13 . . . . 18 F2
  Macclesfield SK10 . . . . . 87 E1
  Middlewich CW10 . . . . 128 B1
  Mottram St Andrew
    SK10 . . . . .61 A1
  Nantwich CW5 . . . . . . 204 F6
  New Mills SK22 . . . . . . 39 B8
  Northwich CW9 . . . . . 103 F6
  Rostherne WA16 . . . . . . 30 B3
  Utkinton CW6 . . . . . . 146 B7
  Weaverham CW8 . . . . . . 77 E1
Cressbrook Rd 🔼 WA4 . . 16 C1
Cressingham Gdns 🔸
  CH65 . . . . .70 C6
Cresswell Ave
  Newcastle-u-Lyme
    ST5 . . . . 210 D1
  New Mills SK22 . . . . . . 39 C8
Cresswell Cl WA5 . . . . . . 7 D2
Cresswellshawe Rd
  ST7 . . . . 193 D4
Cresswell St SK22 . . . . . 39 C8
Cresta Dr WA7 . . . . 48 F6
Crestwood Cl CW2 . . . . . 66 C0
Crew Ave SK10 . . . . 87 E1
CREWE 190 E5
Crewe Bsns Pk CW1 . . . 190 F2
CREWE-BY-FARNDON
  . . . . 197 A7
Crewe Gates Farm Ind Est
  CW1 . . . . 190 F2
Crewe Gates Ind Est
  CW1 . . . . 207 A8
Crewe Green Ave
  CW1 . . . . 191 B4
Crewe Green Rd CW1 . . 191 A3
Crewe Hall Ent Pk
  CW1 . . . . 207 D8
Crewe Hill La CH3 . . . . 197 A6
Crewe La CH3 . . . . 180 F1
Crewe La S CH3 . . . . . 197 A7
Crewe Rd
  Alsager ST7 . . . . 193 B3
  Crewe, Crewe Green
    CW1 . . . . 191 B3
  Haslington CW1, CW11 . . 191 D5
  Hatherton CW5 . . . . . . 219 F3
  Lawton-gate ST7 . . . . . 193 F4
  Nantwich CW2, CW5 . . . 205 D6
  Sandbach CW11 . . . . . 175 A5
  Shavington CW2 . . . . . 206 C6
Crewe St
  Chester CH1 . . . . 237 C3
  Crewe CW1 . . . . 190 D4
Crewe Sta CW1 . . . . . . 190 E2
Crewood Common Rd
  CW8 . . . . .76 A3
Crib La CW6 . . . . 168 A8
Criccieth Ct CH65 . . . . . 70 D2
Criftin Cl CH66 . . . . . . 69 C2
Crimes La CH3, CW6 . . . 167 D4
Crisham Ave CW5 . . . . 218 E8
Crispin Rd M22 . . . . . . 33 E8
Critchley Rd CH4 . . . . . 21 A3
Croasdale Dr WA7 . . . . . 49 E5
Crocus Gdns WA9 . . . . . . 6 A7
Crocus St CW8 . . . . 78 B3
Croesmere Dr CH66 . . . . 69 D2
CROFT 9 B8
Croft Cl
  Altrincham WA15 . . . . . 32 C6
  Congleton CW12 . . . . . 156 F2
  Utkinton CW6 . . . . . . 146 B7
  Waverton CH3 . . . . . . 143 A5
Croft Cotts
  Dunham-on-t-H WA6 . . . 97 E6
  Ellesmere Port CH65 . . . 69 A8
Croft Ct CH65 . . . . 70 E3
Croften Dr CH64 . . . . . . 66 E5
Crofters Cl
  🔶 Ellesmere Port
    CH66 . . . . .69 E1
  Penketh WA16 . . . . 80 A7
Crofters Ct
  Holmes Chapel CW4 . . . 130 C3
  Newcastle-u-Lyme ST5 . . 210 D3
Crofters Gn SK9 . . . . . . 59 F6
Crofters Heath CH66 . . . 69 E1
Crofters Lea CH3 . . . . . 103 D7
Crofters Pk CH5 . . . . . 116 A3
Crofters Way CH1 . . . . . 116 F8
Croft Gdns WA4 . . . . . . 27 A7
Croft Heath Gdns WA3 . . . 9 A8
Croft Ho WA3 . . . . 9 A7
Croft La
  Dodleston CH4 . . . . . . 162 A4
  Knutsford WA16 . . . . . . 82 B8
Crofton Cl WA4 . . . . . . 27 C5
Crofton Cotts WA6 . . . . 100 B8
Crofton Gdns WA3 . . . . . 4 E3
Crofton Rd WA7 . . . . . . 22 E1
Croft Pk WA16 . . . . 58 F5
Croft Prim Sch WA3 . . . . 9 A8
Croft Rd SK9 . . . . 59 E4
Croftside WA1 . . . . 17 F7
Croftside Way SK9 . . . . . 60 E8
Croft St
  Golborne WA3 . . . . 3 A8
  Widnes WA8 . . . . 23 A6
Crofts The CH3 . . . . . . 180 F1

Croftsway CH60 . . . . . . 40 D8
Croft The
  Chester CH2 . . . . 118 D5
  Norton in Hales TF9 . . . 236 B3
  Runcorn WA7 . . . . 23 F1
Croftwood Cl 🔟 CW7 . . 149 A8
Cromdale Way WA5 . . . . 14 E6
Cromer Dr CW1 . . . . . . 190 B8
Cromford Cl CW8 . . . . . 65 E6
Cromford Mews SK23 . . . 65 E5
Cromley Rd SK6 . . . . . . 37 E6
Crompton Cl CW12 . . . . 157 A6
Crompton Dr WA2 . . . . . 8 A6
Crompton Rd SK11 . . . . 112 C7
Crompton Way WA3 . . . . 4 A8
Cromwell Ave WA5 . . . . 15 D6
Cromwell Ave S WA5 . . . 15 D4
Cromwell Cl 2 A4
Cromwell Ct
  Irlam M44 . . . . 11 E7
  🔼 Nantwich CW5 . . . . 204 E5
  🔼 Warrington WA1 . . . . 16 A5
Cromwell Dr CW2 . . . . 206 C4
Cromwell Rd
  Bramhall SK7 . . . . 35 D5
  Ellesmere Port CH65 . . . 70 D5
  Irlam M44 . . . . 11 E7
  Northwich CW8 . . . . . 103 E8
Cromwell St 🔳 SK10 . . . 87 E1
Cronkinson Ave CW5 . . 204 F4
Cronkinson Oak CW5 . . 204 F4
CRONTON 12 D5
Cronton CE Prim Sch
  WA8 . . . . 12 C6
Cronton Farm Ct WA8 . . 12 C6
Cronton La
  Cronton L35 . . . . 12 B8
  Widnes WA8 . . . . 12 C5
Cronton Park Ave WA8 . . 12 C6
Cronton Park Cl WA8 . . . 12 C6
Cronton Rd L35, WA8 . . . 12 C5
Cronulla Dr WA5 . . . . . 14 E7
Crooked La CH3, CW6 . . 145 C4
Crookedyard Rd SK11 . . 113 E7
Crookenden Cl CW2 . . . . 95 C1
Crookenden Rd CH2 . . . . 95 C1
Crook La CW7 . . . . . . 127 A2
Crook St CH1 . . . . 237 A2
Croppers Rd WA2 . . . . . 8 F3
Crosby Ave WA5 . . . . . . 16 A8
Crosby Gr CH64 . . . . . . 43 B1
Crosfield Ct WA5 . . . . . 15 A5
Crosfield St WA1 . . . . . 16 A5
Crossall St 🔼 SK11 . . . 112 C7
Crossdale Rd CH62 . . . . 43 D5
Cross Farm WA2 . . . . . . 9 A2
Crossfield Ave
  Culcheth WA3 . . . . 4 F2
  Lymm WA13 . . . . 18 D3
  Winsford CW7 . . . . . . 149 D7
Crossfield Rd
  Bollington SK10 . . . . . . 87 E6
  Handforth SK9 . . . . . . 34 D4
Crossfields CH3 . . . . . . 121 B2
Crossgates WA8 . . . . . . 13 F3
Cross Gn CH2 . . . . 118 E6
Cross Hey CH4 . . . . . . 237 C1
Crossings Ho CW1 . . . . 190 A5
Crossings The WA12 . . . . 2 C3
Crosskeys Cl CW5 . . . . 145 A6
Cross La
  Audley ST7 . . . . 209 E5
  Church Minshull CW1,
    CW5 . . . . 172 C6
  Congleton CW12 . . . . . 157 A1
  Croft WA3 . . . . 9 B7
  Haslington CW11 . . . . . 191 F8
  Neston CH64 . . . . 66 E5
  Newton-le-W WA12 . . . . . 2 B3
  Sandbach CW11 . . . . . 175 D5
  Smallwood CW11 . . . . . 176 F5
  Smallwood CW11 . . . . . 177 B5
  Swettenham CW12 . . . . 131 F4
  Tarvin CH3 . . . . 121 E2
  Warrington WA4 . . . . . . 17 A3
  Wilmslow SK9 . . . . 60 F8
Cross La E M31 . . . . . . 11 F3
Crossland Mews WA13 . . 18 C4
Crosslands
  Congleton CW12 . . . . . 157 A1
  Haslington CW1 . . . . . 191 D4
Crossland Terr WA6 . . . . 73 B2
CROSS LANE 172 D6
Cross Lanes CH3 . . . . . 144 C8
Cross Lane S WA3 . . . . . 9 B6
Cross La W WA11 . . . . . 1 F2
Crossledge CW12 . . . . . 156 B3
Crossley Ave CH66 . . . . . 69 E6
Crossley Cres CH2 . . . . 119 B5
Crossley Dr CH60 . . . . . 40 D8
Crossley Pk WA6 . . . . . . 99 C7
Crossley St WA1 . . . . . . 16 C5
Cross o' th' Hill SY14 . . 213 D4
Cross O'Th' Hill Rd
  SY14 . . . . 214 A4
Cross Rd
  Gatley SK8 . . . . 34 B7
  Haslington CW1 . . . . . 191 D4
Cross St
  Alsager ST7 . . . . 193 C3
  Barnton CW8 . . . . 78 B3
  Chester CH2 . . . . 118 F3
  Congleton CW12 . . . . . 156 D3
  Crewe CW1 . . . . 190 D3
  Golborne WA3 . . . . 3 A7
  Haslington CW1 . . . . . 191 D4
  Holt LL13 . . . . 196 E8

Cross St continued
  Macclesfield SK11 . . . . 112 C6
  Marston CW9 . . . . 79 C3
  Neston CH64 . . . . 66 E8
  New Mills SK22 . . . . . . 39 C8
  🔟 Runcorn WA7 . . . . . 23 A3
  Warrington WA2 . . . . . . 16 B7
  Widnes WA8 . . . . 13 C1
Cross The
  Holt LL13 . . . . 196 E8
  Kingsley WA6 . . . . 75 C2
  Lymm WA13 . . . . 18 E3
  🔸 Neston CH64 . . . . . . 66 E8
CROSS TOWN 57 B2
Crossway
  Bramhall SK7 . . . . 35 E5
  Crewe CW1 . . . . 190 D6
  Widnes WA8 . . . . 22 D8
Crossways ST8 . . . . . . 179 E1
Crossways Rd ST7 . . . . 194 A4
Crossway The CH63 . . . . 42 C4
Cross Wood St 🔼
  WA5 . . . . 204 D5
Crosthwaite Ave CH62 . . 43 F4
Croston Cl
  Alderley Edge SK9 . . . . . 60 C1
  Widnes WA8 . . . . 12 C3
Crotia Ave CW2 . . . . . . 207 B5
Crouch La CW12 . . . . . 157 D4
Crouchley Hall Mews
  WA13 . . . . 18 F1
Crouchley La WA13 . . . . 18 F1
CROUGHTON 95 F5
Croughton Ct CH66 . . . . 69 F8
Croughton Rd
  Ellesmere Port CH66 . . . 69 F8
  Stoak CH2 . . . . 96 A7
  Stoak, Croughton CH2 . . 95 F6
Crowbrook Gr 🔸 SK9 . . 34 D1
Crowder's La CW9 . . . . 105 B4
Crowe Ave WA2 . . . . 8 B2
Crowland Gdns SK8 . . . . 35 B6
Crow Lane E WA12 . . . . . 2 C2
Crow Lane W WA12 . . . . . 2 A4
Crowley La CW9, WA16 . . 28 A3
Crowmere Cl CW8 . . . . 102 A2
Crown Ave WA8 . . . . . . 22 B8
Crown Bank
  🔳 Sandbach CW11 . . . 175 B6
  Talke ST7 . . . . 210 D6
Crown Bank Cres
  ST7 . . . . 210 D6
Crown Bldgs WA8 . . . . . 73 B1
Crown Cotts CW8 . . . . . 124 A7
Crown Ctr The 🔼
  SK11 . . . . 112 C8
Crown Ctyd CW3 . . . . . 229 F4
Crown Dr CW1 . . . . . . 175 D3
Crownest La CW9 . . . . . 78 E8
Crown Fields Cl WA12 . . . 2 B5
Crown Gate WA7 . . . . . . 49 F7
Crown Gdns
  Newton-le-W WA12 . . . . . 2 A3
  Talke ST7 . . . . 210 D6
Crown Gn WA13 . . . . . . 19 B4
Crown La WA16 . . . . . . 106 D8
Crown Mews CW9 . . . . . 78 E8
Crown Park Dr WA12 . . . 2 B5
Crown St W SK11 . . . . . 112 C7
Crown St
  Newton-le-W WA12 . . . . . 2 A3
  🔳 Northwich CW8 . . . 103 F8
  🔼 Warrington WA1 . . . . 16 B5
Crow's Nest Cotts
  CH3 . . . . 166 C6
CROWTON 76 C1
Crowton Cotts CW7 . . . 170 F4
CROW WOOD 13 D3
Crow Wood La WA8 . . . . 13 D2
Crow Wood Pl WA8 . . . . 13 D3
Croxton Gn SY14 . . . . . 201 C6
Croxton La CW10 . . . . . 128 A4
Croxton Way CW8 . . . . 103 A4
Croyde Cl M22 . . . . 33 F7
Croyde Rd L24 . . . . 21 A3
Cryers La
  Elton CH2 . . . . 72 A2
  Thornton-le-M CH2 . . . . 96 F8
Cty High Sch Leftwich The
  CW9 . . . . 104 A4
Cuckoo Clock Mus*
  WA16 . . . . 57 A2
Cuckoo La
  Acton CW5 . . . . 203 E8
  Neston CH64 . . . . 67 C7
CUCKOO'S NEST 162 E5
Cuckstoolpit Hill
  SK10 . . . . 112 E8
CUDDINGTON 101 F4
CUDDINGTON GREEN
  . . . . 212 B1
CUDDINGTON HEATH
  . . . . 212 B2
Cuddington La
  Cuddington CW8 . . . . . 101 C4
  Sandiway CW8 . . . . . . 102 A6
Cuddington Prim Sch
  CW8 . . . . 101 F2
Cuddington Sta CW8 . . 102 A4
Cuddington Way 🔸
  SK9 . . . . .34 D5
CUERDLEY CROSS 13 A2
Cuerdley Gn WA5 . . . . . 14 C2
Cuerdley Rd WA5 . . . . . 14 C2
Cuerdon Dr WA4 . . . . . . 17 D1
Culbin Cl WA3 . . . . 3 E8

CULCETH 4 E3
Culcheth Com Prim Sch
  WA3 . . . . .5 A3
Culcheth Hall Dr WA3 . . . .4 F4
Culcheth Hall Farm Barns
  WA3 . . . . .4 F4
Culcheth High Sch WA3. . .5 A3
Culford Cl WA7 . . . . .24 D1
Culland St CW2 . . . . .190 C2
Cullen Cl CW63 . . . . .43 C4
Cullen Rd WA7 . . . . .48 D7
Cumber Cl SK9 . . . . .59 D4
Cumber Dr SK9 . . . . .59 D4
Cumber La SK9 . . . . .59 D4
Cumberland Ave
  Irlam M44 . . . . .11 C5
  Nantwich CW5 . . . . .204 F6
Cumberland Cl
  Crewe CW1 . . . . .190 D5
  Talke ST7 . . . . .210 E7
Cumberland Cres WA11. . . .1 A6
Cumberland Dr
  Altrincham WA14 . . . . . . .31 B8
  Bollington SK10. . . . . .88 B8
Cumberland Gr CH66 . . . .69 C3
Cumberland Rd
  Congleton CW12 . . . . . .156 A3
  Partington M31 . . . . .11 E2
Cumberland St
  2 Macclesfield SK10 . . .112 D8
  Warrington WA4 . . . . .16 C3
Cumbermere Dr
  CW11 . . . . .174 E7
Cumbers Dr CH64 . . . . . . .67 A5
Cumbers La CH64 . . . . . . .67 A5
Cumbrae Dr **4** CH65. . . .70 C1
Cumbria Cl **2** CH66 . . . .69 E1
Cundiff Cl SK11. . . . . .112 E6
Cunliffe Ave WA12 . . . . . . .2 B5
Cunliffe Cl WA7 . . . . .50 A7
Cunningham Cl
  Warrington Cl WA5 . . . .14 F5
Cunningham Dr
  Bebington CH63 . . . . .43 C7
  Gatley M22 . . . . .34 A8
  Runcorn WA7 . . . . .22 E1
Cunningham Ho WA7 . . . .48 E8
Cunningham Rd WA8 . . . .22 D8
Cuppin St CH1 . . . . .237 B2
Curlender Way L24 . . . . . .21 E2
Curlew Cl
  Golborne WA3 . . . . .3 C8
  Macclesfield SK10 . . . . . .87 C5
  Winsford CW7 . . . . .149 C5
Curlew Gr WA3 . . . . .9 E3
Curlew Rd CH7 . . . . .195 E1
Currans Rd WA2 . . . . .8 B2
Curzon Cl CW41 . . . . .141 B8
Curzon Ct CH4 . . . . .140 F7
Curzon Dr WA4 . . . . .27 A7
Curzon Gr CW7 . . . . .126 F1
Curzon Mews SK9 . . . . . . .60 A5
CURZON PARK. 141 B7
Curzon Pk N CH4 . . . . . . .141 B7
Curzon Pk S CH4 . . . . . . .141 B7
Curzon Rd
  Gatley SK8 . . . . .34 B7
  Poynton SK12 . . . . .36 E2
Curzon St
  5 Chester CH4 . . . . . . .140 F7
  Runcorn WA7 . . . . .22 F1
Cwat Erwain CH4 . . . . . .140 E7
Cwrt Cwellyn CH5 . . . . . .139 B7
Cwrt Dinas CH5 . . . . .139 B7
Cwrt Ogwen CH5 . . . . . . .139 B7
Cygnet Cl CH66 . . . . .69 D4
Cygnet Ct WA1 . . . . .16 A3
Cyman Cl CH1 . . . . .117 D3
Cynthia Ave WA1 . . . . . . .17 B7
Cynthia Rd WA7 . . . . .22 F1
Cypress Ave
  Ellesmere Port CH66 . . . . .69 F1
  Widnes WA8 . . . . .13 B2
Cypress Cl WA1 . . . . .17 E7
Cypress Gr WA7 . . . . .49 C7
Cypress Mews CW8 . . . . .102 E7
Cypress Way SK6 . . . . .38 A7
Cyril Bell Cl WA13 . . . . . .18 F3
Cyril St WA2 . . . . .16 B7

D

Daffodil Cl WA8 . . . . .13 E4
Daffodil Gdns WA9 . . . . . . .6 A7
Dagfields Crafts &
  Antiques Ctr* CW5 . .220 A4
Dagnall Ave WA5 . . . . .7 F2
Dahlia Cl WA9 . . . . .6 A7
Daintry St SK11 . . . . .112 E7
Dainty Terr SK10 . . . . .88 B8
Dairy Bank CH2 . . . . .72 B4
Dairybrook Gr **7** SK9 . . .34 E1
Dairy Farm Cl WA3 . . . . . .18 F4
Dairyground Rd SK7 . . . . .35 F7
Dairy House La SK7 . . . . . .35 B4
Dairy House Rd SK7 . . . . .35 B5
Dairy House Small
  Holdings SK7 . . . . .35 B5
Dairy House Way
  CW2 . . . . .189 F2
Daisy La CW5 . . . . .188 D6
Dairylands Rd ST7 . . . . . .193 F4
Daisy Ave WA12 . . . . .2 C2
Daisy Bank
  Alsager ST7 . . . . .193 A4
  Nantwich CW5 . . . . .204 D5
Daisy Bank Cres CW3 . . .229 F5

Daisybank Dr
  Congleton CW12 . . . . . .156 D4
  Sandbach CW11 . . . . . . .175 C6
Daisy Bank La CW9 . . . . . .78 C3
Daisy Bank Mill Cl WA3 . . .4 E3
Daisy Bank Rd
  Lymm WA13 . . . . .18 C3
  Warrington WA5 . . . . .14 F4
Daisy Cl WA16 . . . . .79 F6
Daisy Way SK6 . . . . .37 F7
Dakota Dr WA5 . . . . .15 C7
Dalby Cl WA3 . . . . .10 B5
Dalby Ct CW9 . . . . .104 E5
Dale Ave
  Bebington CH62 . . . . .43 D8
  Bramhall SK7 . . . . .35 F8
  Ellesmere Port CH66 . . . .69 C6
Dale Cl
  Warrington WA5 . . . . .15 D4
  Widnes WA8 . . . . .22 A8
Dale Cres CW12 . . . . . . .156 F2
Dalecroft WA6 . . . . .72 E1
Dale Dr
  Chester CH2 . . . . .118 D8
  Ellesmere Port CH65 . . . .69 F5
Daleford Manor CW8 . .125 B8
Daleford Manor Cvn Pk
  CW8 . . . . .125 A8
Dalefords La
  Cuddington CW8 . . . . . . .102 A1
  Whitegate CW8 . . . . .125 D7
Dale Gdns CH65 . . . . .70 B3
Dale Gr
  Congleton CW12 . . . . . .157 A2
  Irlam M44 . . . . .11 E6
Dale Head Rd SK10 . . . . . .86 F4
Dale Hey CH66 . . . . .43 E2
Dale House Fold SK12 . . .37 A4
Dale La WA4 . . . . .26 E7
Dale Pl CW12 . . . . .156 F2
Dale Rd
  Bebington CH62 . . . . .43 D6
  Golborne WA3 . . . . .3 A7
  New Mills SK22 . . . . .39 C7
Dalesford Cl WN7 . . . . .4 C8
Dalesford Cres SK10 . . . .111 E8
DALES GREEN 195 C5
Dales Green Rd ST7 . . . .195 C5
Daleside CH2 . . . . .118 D8
Dale's Sq CW9 . . . . .103 F6
Dale St
  Chester CH1 . . . . .119 A1
  Macclesfield SK10 . . . . . .112 E8
  Runcorn WA7 . . . . .23 A1
Dalesway CH60 . . . . .40 E8
Dale The
  Neston CH64 . . . . .66 E6
  Tiverton CW6 . . . . .168 C6
  Warrington WA5 . . . . .14 F5
Dale View
  Kidsgrove ST7 . . . . .195 C5
  Newton-le-W WA12 . . . . . .2 E4
Dale Way CW1 . . . . .190 A5
Dalewood Cl WA2 . . . . . . .16 A6
Dalewood Cres CW2 . . . . .72 A3
DALLAM 7 F1
Dallam Com Prim Sch
  WA5 . . . . .7 F1
Dallam La WA2 . . . . .16 A7
Dalmahoy Cl CW7 . . . . . .126 C2
Dalston Dr SK7 . . . . .35 C5
Dalton Ave
  Warrington, Birchwood
    WA3 . . . . .9 E6
  Warrington WA5 . . . . .15 F7
Dalton Bank WA1 . . . . . . .16 C6
Dalton Cl CH1 . . . . .117 E3
Dalton Ct
  Runcorn WA7 . . . . .23 E3
  Sandbach CW11 . . . . . . .174 E7
Dalton St
  Runcorn WA7 . . . . .23 D2
  Warrington WA3 . . . . .9 E5
Dalton Way WA10 . . . . . .128 D1
Dalwood Cl WA7 . . . . .50 E7
Dame Hollow SK8 . . . . . . .34 D7
Damery Ct SK7 . . . . .35 E8
Damery Rd SK7 . . . . .35 E8
Damhead La CH64 . . . . . .67 E7
Dam Head La WA3 . . . . . . .11 A5
Damian Dr WA12 . . . . .2 A5
Dam La
  Hollinfare WA3 . . . . .11 A4
  Mobberley WA16 . . . . .58 C3
  Warrington WA1 . . . . .17 D7
  Winwick WA3 . . . . .8 F7
Dams La WA16 . . . . .106 D5
Damson La WA16 . . . . . . .58 C5
Damson Wlk M31 . . . . . . .11 D3
Danby Cl
  Runcorn WA7 . . . . .49 D6
  Warrington WA5 . . . . .15 E7
Dane Ave M31 . . . . .11 F4
DANEBANK 38 E5
Dane Bank Ave
  Congleton CW12 . . . . . .156 E4
  Crewe CW2 . . . . .190 A2
Dane Bank Dr SK12 . . . . .38 D6
Dane Bank Rd
  Lymm WA13 . . . . .18 E4
  Northwich CW9 . . . . .104 B7
Dane Bank Rd E WA13 . . .18 E4
Dane Ct
  Alsager ST7 . . . . .193 A3
  Chester CH4 . . . . .140 F5

Dane Cl continued
  Sandbach CW11 . . . . . . .174 E7
Dane Dr
  Biddulph ST8 . . . . .179 E1
  Wilmslow SK9 . . . . .60 D6
Danefield Ct SK8 . . . . .34 D8
Danefield Rd
  Holmes Chapel CW4 . . . .130 C4
  Northwich CW9 . . . . .104 B7
Dane Gdns ST7 . . . . .195 C2
Dane Gr CH2 . . . . .119 F8
Dane Hill Cl SK12 . . . . . . .38 D5
DANE IN SHAW 179 C8
Dane Mill Bsns Ctr
  CW12 . . . . .156 C3
Dane Pl
  Crewe CW1 . . . . .190 D6
  Winsford CW7 . . . . .127 B1
Danescroft WA8 . . . . .12 B3
Daneside Bsns Pk
  CW12 . . . . .156 C4
Daneside County Pk
  CW12 . . . . .155 B7
Danes Sq SK11 . . . . .112 D5
Dane St
  Congleton CW12 . . . . . .156 C3
  Middlewich CW10 . . . . . .128 D2
  Northwich CW9 . . . . .103 F8
Daneswell Rd L24 . . . . . . .21 A2
Daniel Adamson Ave
  M31 . . . . .11 D3
Daniel Cl WA1 . . . . .10 A4
Daniel Ct M31 . . . . .11 F4
Daniell Way CH1 . . . . . . .142 A7
Danily Ct SY14 . . . . .213 B3
Dan's Rd WA8 . . . . .13 E2
Dappleheath Rd CW2 . . .190 A1
Darby Cl CH64 . . . . .66 E4
D'Arcy Cotts CH63 . . . . . .42 B6
Darent Rd WA11 . . . . .1 B7
DARESBURY 25 B2
Daresbury Cl
  Holmes Chapel CW4 . . . .130 A3
  4 Wilmslow SK9 . . . . . .60 C8
Daresbury Ct WA8 . . . . . . .13 E3
DARESBURY DELPH . . .25 B1
Daresbury Expressway
  Daresbury WA4 . . . . .25 A3
  Runcorn WA7 . . . . .23 C2
  Warrington WA4 . . . . .25 D2
  Daresbury Pk WA4. . . . . . .51 A8
Daresbury Prim Sch
  WA4 . . . . .25 B2
Darian Ave M22 . . . . .33 D8
Dario Gradi Dr CW2 . . . .190 D1
Dark Ark La CH3, WA6 . . .99 B3
Darkie Mdw CW5 . . . . . . .185 E8
Dark La
  Henbury SK11 . . . . .111 B8
  Higher Whitley WA4 . . . . . .52 D6
  Kingsley WA6 . . . . .75 B1
  Marston CW9 . . . . .79 C6
  Tattenhall CH3 . . . . .183 E7
  Warren SK11 . . . . .111 C3
  Whitchurch SY13 . . . . . . .227 B1
Darley Ave
  Crewe CW2 . . . . .190 A3
  Warrington WA2 . . . . .8 E3
Darley Cl WA8 . . . . .12 B3
Darleydale Dr CH62 . . . . .43 F5
Darley Rd SK7 . . . . .36 F7
Darlington Ave CW1 . . . .189 F5
Darlington Cres WA1 . . . .94 A1
Darlington Ct **3** WA8 . . .23 A4
Darlington St CW10 . . . . .128 C1
Darnaway Cl WA3 . . . . . . .10 B6
DARNHALL 149 A3
Darnhall Prim Sch
  CW7 . . . . .149 D6
Darnhall School La
  CW7 . . . . .149 D6
Dart Cl
  Alsager ST7 . . . . .193 A4
  Biddulph ST8 . . . . .179 D1
Dartnall Cl SK12 . . . . .38 A6
Dart Wlk CW7 . . . . .127 B2
Darwen Gdns WA9 . . . . . . .8 E1
Darwin Gr SK7 . . . . .35 E6
Darwin Rd CH1 . . . . .117 C4
Darwin St CW8 . . . . .103 E7
Daryl Rd CH60 . . . . .41 A8
Dashwood Cl WA4 . . . . . . .22 A7
Daten Ave WA3 . . . . .9 E6
Daten Pk WA3 . . . . .9 F6
Dauncey Cl CH2 . . . . .95 C1
Davehall Ave SK9 . . . . . . .60 A7
DAVENHAM 104 A2
Davenham CE Prim Sch
  CW9 . . . . .103 F2
Davenham Cres CW2 . . .190 A3
Davenham Ct CW9 . . . . . .104 A3
Davenham Mdws
  CW9 . . . . .103 E3
Davenham Rd
  Davenham CW9 . . . . .104 A2
  Handforth SK9 . . . . .34 D4
  Widnes WA8 . . . . .23 B8
Davenham Way
  CW10 . . . . .151 D5
DAVENPORT 154 E7
Davenport Ave
  Crewe CW2 . . . . .206 D8
  Nantwich CW5 . . . . .204 E7
  Warrington WA4 . . . . .16 F5
  Wilmslow SK9 . . . . .59 E4
Davenport Cl CW11 . . . . .175 D8

DAVENPORT GREEN . . .59 F3
Davenport La
  Brereton Green
    CW11 . . . . .154 C2
  Marton SK11 . . . . .132 F5
  Mobberley WA16 . . . . .58 D6
Davenport Park La
  CW12 . . . . .131 D2
Davenport Rd CH60 . . . . .40 E7
Davenport Row WA7 . . . . .49 D8
Davenport St
  Congleton CW12 . . . . . .156 C2
  Crewe CW1 . . . . .190 C6
  Macclesfield SK10 . . . . . .112 E8
Daven Prim Sch
  CW12 . . . . .156 E2
Daven Rd CW12 . . . . .156 F1
Davey La SK9 . . . . .60 B2
Daveylands CW8 . . . . .60 D7
David Lewis Sch SK9 . . . .83 F6
David Rd WA13 . . . . .18 C2
David's Ave WA5 . . . . .15 B5
Davidson Ave CW12 . . . .157 A5
David's Cl WA5 . . . . .103 E7
Davies Ave
  Gatley SK8 . . . . .34 B6
  Newton-le-W WA12 . . . . . .2 C4
  Warrington WA4 . . . . .16 F4
Davies Cl WA8 . . . . .23 A4
Davies St SK10 . . . . .112 E8
Davies Way WA13 . . . . . . .18 E3
Davy Ave
  Crewe CW1 ST7 . . . . . . .193 E3
  9 Sandbach CW11 . . . .9 E5
Davy Ave WA3 . . . . .9 E5
Davy Rd WA7 . . . . .23 E3
Dawlish Ave SK8 . . . . .34 F7
Dawlish Cl
  Bramhall SK7 . . . . .35 C7
  Hollinfare WA3 . . . . .11 B3
Dawn Cl CH64 . . . . .67 A5
Dawn Gdns CH65 . . . . . . .70 B4
Dawpool Cl CH2 . . . . .118 D5
Dawpool Ct CW2 . . . . . . .118 D5
Dawpool Dr CH62 . . . . . . .43 C7
Dawson Cl **11** SK11 . . . .111 F7
Dawson Dr CH2 . . . . .237 A4
Dawson Rd
  Bollington SK10 . . . . .88 A7
  Gatley SK8 . . . . .34 D8
  Macclesfield SK11 . . . . . .111 F7
Dawstone Ct CH60 . . . . . .40 F8
Dawstone Rd CH60 . . . . . .41 A7
Dawstone Rise CH60 . . . .40 F7
DAY GREEN 192 F8
Deacon Rd WA8 . . . . .13 B1
Deacons Cl WA3 . . . . .9 A8
Deacon Trad Est WA12 . . .2 A2
Deadman's La CW5 . . . . .205 B2
Deakin's Rd
  Winsford CW7 . . . . .126 F4
  Winsford, Wharton Green
    CW7 . . . . .127 A4
Dean Bank CW6 . . . . . .168 C3
Dean Cl
  Bollington SK10 . . . . .88 A7
  Handforth SK9 . . . . .34 C1
  Partington M31 . . . . .11 F4
  Sandbach CW11 . . . . . . .174 E8
  Widnes WA8 . . . . .12 B3
Dean Cres WA2 . . . . .8 B2
Dean Ct
  Bollington SK10 . . . . .88 B8
  Golborne WA3 . . . . .3 A7
Dean Dr SK9 . . . . .34 D2
Deane Ct CW5 . . . . .205 B4
Deanery Cl CH2 . . . . .118 C4
Deangate CW2 . . . . .207 E3
Dean Hollow ST7 . . . . . . .209 D2
Dean La CW7 . . . . .36 E8
Dean Mdw WA12 . . . . .2 C4
Dean Pk SY14 . . . . .214 A5
Dean Rd
  Golborne WA3 . . . . .3 A7
  Handforth SK9 . . . . .34 E3
  Irlam M44 . . . . .11 E6
Dean Row Ct SK9 . . . . . . .61 A8
DEAN ROW 60 F8
Dean Row Ct **8** SK9 . . .34 C1
Dean Row Run Sch
  SK9 . . . . .34 C1
Dean Row Rd SK9 . . . . . . .61 A8
Deans Cl
  Chester CH2 . . . . .118 D6
  Tarvin CH3 . . . . .121 B1
Dean's La
  Barthomley CW2 . . . . . . .208 D8
  Newcastle-u-Lyme ST5 . . .210 D2
  Dean Rd CH65 . . . . .70 F3
Dean St
  Middlewich CW10 . . . . . .128 C2
  Northwich CW9 . . . . .104 C8
  Winsford CW7 . . . . .126 D1
Deansway WA8 . . . . .13 A2
Dean Valley Com Prim Sch
  SK10 . . . . .87 E8
Dean View SK10 . . . . .209 D1
Deanwater Cl WA3 . . . . . . .9 A4
Deanwater Ct SK8 . . . . . . .34 D7
Deanway SK9 . . . . .34 C1

Deanway Trad Est SK9 . . .34 D3
Dearnford Ave CH62 . . . . .43 D6
Dearnford Cl CH62 . . . . . .43 D6
Debra Cl CH66 . . . . .69 C4
Debra Rd CH66 . . . . .69 C4
Decade Cl ST5 . . . . .210 F2
Dee Banks
  Chester CH3 . . . . .142 A8
  Huntington CH3 . . . . .141 F7
Dee Banks Sch CH3 . . . . .142 A7
Dee Cl
  Biddulph ST8 . . . . .179 E1
  Sandbach CW11 . . . . . . .174 E8
  Talke ST7 . . . . .210 E7
Dee Cres CH3 . . . . .180 E2
Deefords CH3 . . . . .118 F1
Dee Fords Ave CH3 . . . . .119 A1
Dee Hills Pk CH3 . . . . . . .237 C2
Dee La
  Chester CH1, CH3 . . . . . .237 C2
  Holt LL13 . . . . .196 D7
Dee Mdws LL13 . . . . .196 D7
Dee Park Rd CH60 . . . . . .41 B6
Dee Park Rd CH60 . . . . . .41 B5
Deepdale WA8 . . . . .12 C3
Deep Dale WA5 . . . . .14 F6
Dee Rd LL13 . . . . .196 D8
Dee Point Prim Sch
  CH1 . . . . .117 D3
Deer Park Ct CH2 . . . . . . .96 F1
Deer Park Ct **4** WA7 . . .49 F6
Deerwood Cl
  Ellesmere Port CH66 . . . .69 D7
  Macclesfield SK10 . . . . . .86 F1
Deerwood Cres CH66 . . . .69 D7
Deeside
  Ellesmere Port CH65 . . . .70 B2
  Neston CH64 . . . . .66 F7
Dee Side CH60 . . . . .40 C8
Deeside Cl CH65 . . . . .70 B2
Deeside Coll/Coleg
  Glannau Dyfrdwy
    CH5 . . . . .91 B1
Deeside Cres CH1 . . . . . .116 E5
Deeside Ct
  Chester CH2 . . . . .237 C2
  Neston CH64 . . . . .41 B1
Deeside Ind Pk/Parc
  Ddiwydiannol Glannau
    Dyfrdwy CH5 . . . . .92 C2
Deeside La CH1 . . . . .116 C4
Dee Side CW7 . . . . .127 B2
Dee View SK10 . . . . .180 E2
Dee View Cotts CH64 . . . .41 D1
Dee View Rd CH1 . . . . . . .66 F5
Dee View Rd
  Connah's Quay CH5 . . . . .91 E1
  Heswall CH60 . . . . .40 F8
Dee Villas LL13 . . . . .180 E1
Dee Way CW7 . . . . .127 A2
Deirdre Ave WA8 . . . . .13 A1
De Lacy Row WA7 . . . . . . .24 A2
Delafield Cl WA2 . . . . .8 F3
Delaisy Way CW7 . . . . . . .127 A1
Delamar Pl **1** WA7 . . . .123 D6
DELAMERE 123 D6
Delamere Ave
  Bebington CH62 . . . . .43 E4
  Ellesmere Port CH66 . . . .69 E5
  Golborne WA3 . . . . .3 E6
  Widnes WA8 . . . . .12 C3
Delamere CE Prim Sch
  CW6 . . . . .123 C5
Delamere Cl
  Barnton CW8 . . . . .78 A3
  Bebington CH62 . . . . .43 E4
  Chorlton CW2 . . . . .207 E4
  Sandbach CW11 . . . . . . .174 F8
Delamere Ct
  Alsager ST7 . . . . .192 F4
  Bebington CH62 . . . . .43 E4
  7 Crewe CW1 . . . . . . .190 C4
Delamere Dr
  Ellesmere Port CH66 . . . .69 E5
  Macclesfield SK10 . . . . . .87 F2
Delamere Forest Sch
  WA6 . . . . .100 C4
Delamere Forest Trail*
  WA6 . . . . .100 A4
Delamere Forest Visitor
  Ctr* CW8 . . . . .100 D3
Delamere Gn CH66 . . . . . .69 E5
Delamere Gr **2** WA7 . . .123 D7
Delamere Ho WA6 . . . . . . .74 C7
Delamere La CH3 . . . . . . .99 B2
DELAMERE PARK 101 C5
Delamere Park Way E
  CW8 . . . . .101 D5
Delamere Park Way W
  CW8 . . . . .101 D5
Delamere Rd
  Congleton CW12 . . . . . .155 F3
  Handforth SK9 . . . . .34 C4
  Norley WA6 . . . . .100 B6
  Warrington WA5 . . . . .15 C5
  Winsford CW7 . . . . .127 A2
Delamere St
  Chester CH1 . . . . .237 A3
  5 Crewe CW1 . . . . . . .190 C4
  Warrington WA5 . . . . .15 E5
  Winsford CW7 . . . . .127 A2
Delamere Sta CW8 . . . . .100 D1
Delamore's Acre CH64 . . .68 A8
Delavor Cl CH60 . . . . .40 E8
Delavor Rd CH60 . . . . . . .40 E8

Delenty Dr WA3 . . . . .9 E4
Delery Dr WA1 . . . . 16 E8
Delfur Rd SK7 . . . . .35 F7
Delhi Rd M44 . . . . .11 F8
Dell Cl CH63 . . . . .43 B6
Dell Dr WA2 . . . . .9 A2
Dell La CH60 . . . . .41 B7
Dell The
Cuddington CW8 . . . . 101 D5
Guilden Sutton CH3 . . . . 119 F5
Kelsall CW6 . . . . 122 D5
Delmar Rd WA16 . . . . .57 C1
Delphfields Rd WA4 . . . . .26 C7
Delphield WA7 . . . . .50 D8
Delph La
Daresbury WA4 . . . . .25 A2
Warrington, Houghton Gn
WA4 . . . . .8 E6
Winwick WA2. . . . . .8 A5
Delphside ST7 . . . . 209 F2
Delta Cres WA5 . . . . .7 C2
Delta Ct CH4 . . . . 140 B6
Delves Ave WA5 . . . . .15 F7
Delves Broughton Ct
CW1 . . . . 191 D5
Delves Cl CW2 . . . . 206 B4
Delves Wlk CH3 . . . . 142 B7
Delvine Dr CH2 . . . . 118 D6
Demage Dr CH66 . . . . .69 D3
Demage La
Backford CH1 . . . . .94 F4
Chester CH2 . . . . 118 D8
Demage La S CH2 . . . . 118 D7
Denbigh Cl
Hazel Grove SK7 . . . . .36 C8
Helsby WA6 . . . . .73 A1
Denbigh Cres CW10 . . . . 151 C7
Denbigh Ct CH65 . . . . .70 D3
Denbigh Dr CW7 . . . . 149 B7
Denbigh Gdns CH65 . . . . .70 C3
Denbigh St CH1 . . . . 118 B3
Denbury Ave WA4 . . . . .16 F7
Dene Ave WA12 . . . . .1 F4
Dene Dr CW7 . . . . 149 D8
Denehurst Cl WA5 . . . . .14 F4
Denehurst Park Way
CW8 . . . . 101 D5
Denesgate 1 CW7 . . . . 149 D8
Deneside Ave CW1 . . . . 190 C6
Deneway
Bramhall SK7 . . . . .35 D7
High Lane SK6 . . . . .37 F8
Denewood Ct 3 SK9 . . . . . . .60 A6
Denford Cl CH4 . . . . 139 C4
Denford Pl ST7 . . . . 193 D6
Denhall Cl CH2 . . . . 118 E5
Denhall La CH64 . . . . .67 A3
Denham Ave WA5 . . . . .15 B5
Denison Rd SK7 . . . . .35 D7
Denise Ave WA5 . . . . .14 E5
Dennison Rd SK8 . . . . .35 B8
Dennis Rd WA8. . . . . .23 C7
Dennis Round Ct ST7 . . . . . . 193 C3
Denstone Ave WA2 . . . . .8 B2
Denston Cl CW2 . . . . 190 B1
Denstone Dr CH4 . . . . 141 A4
Dentdale Wlk M22 . . . . .33 C8
Dentith Dr CH1 . . . . 117 E5
Denton Cl CW1 . . . . 126 C1
Denton Dr CW9 . . . . .79 C1
Denton Drive Ind Est
CW9 . . . . .79 C2
Denton St WA8 . . . . .13 C1
Denver Ave CW2 . . . . 190 B3
Denver Dr WA5 . . . . .15 B7
Denver Rd WA4 . . . . .17 A3
Denwall Ho 5 CH64 . . . . .66 E8
Depenbech Cl SY14 . . . . 213 B4
Depmore La WA6 . . . . .75 A2
Derby Cl
Irlam M44 . . . . .11 C5
Newton-le-W WA12 . . . . .2 B3
Derby Dr WA1 . . . . .16 F7
Derby Knoll SK23 . . . . .39 F1
Derby St
Golborne WA3 . . . . .3 D8
Talke ST7 . . . . 210 D7
4 Warrington WA4 . . . . .16 C1
Widnes, Barrow's Green
WA8 . . . . .13 D4
Widnes, Lunts Heath
WA8 . . . . .13 B4
Derby Row WA12 . . . . .7 D8
DERBYSHIRE HILL 1 A2
Derbyshire Hill Rd WA9 . . . . . .1 A2
Derbyshire Rd
Partington M31 . . . . .11 E2
Poynton SK12 . . . . .37 D5
Dereham Way
Congleton CW12 . . . . 156 D3
Crewe CW1 . . . . 190 B5
Newton-le-W WA12 . . . . .2 B3
Dereham Way WA7 . . . . .24 D3
Derek Ave WA2 . . . . .8 E1
Derfel Terr 4 WA6 . . . . .74 B8
Derrington Ave CW2 . . . . 190 C3
Derwen Prim Sch
CH4 . . . . 161 A4
Derwent Ave CW7 . . . . 127 B1
Derwent Cl
Alsager ST7 . . . . 193 A4

Derwent Cl continued
Culcheth WA3 . . . . .5 A2
Holmes Chapel CW4 . . . . 130 A3
Macclesfield SK11 . . . . 112 A6
Partington M31 . . . . .11 F4
Willaston CW5 . . . . 205 D6
Derwent Dr
Biddulph ST8 . . . . 179 E1
Bramhall SK7. . . . . .35 C5
Congleton CW12 . . . . 156 F1
Handforth SK9 . . . . .34 C5
Hooton CH66 . . . . .44 B2
Derwent Rd
Chester CH2 . . . . 119 A5
High Lane SK6 . . . . .37 E8
Warrington WA4 . . . . .16 B2
Widnes WA8 . . . . .12 C1
Derwent Way
Alderley Edge SK9 . . . . .83 F7
Neston CH64 . . . . .66 F7
Desoto Rd WA8 . . . . .22 E5
Desoto Rd E WA8 . . . . .22 F6
Desoto Rd W WA8 . . . . .22 F6
De Trafford Mews 9
SK9. . . . . .34 D2
Deva Ave CH4 . . . . 140 D6
Deva Bsns Pk CH5 . . . . 116 A8
Deva Cl SK12 . . . . .36 B4
Deva Ct CH2 . . . . 118 F2
Deva Hts CH3 . . . . 141 F7
Deva La CH2 . . . . 118 C6
Deva Rd CW2. . . . . 189 D4
Deva Ret Pk CH1 . . . . 118 A3
**Deva Roman Experience
Mus*** CH1 . . . . 237 B2
Deva Stad (Chester City
FC) CH1 . . . . 117 E1
Deva Terr CH3 . . . . 237 C2
Devon Cl
Macclesfield SK10 . . . . .86 F2
Northwich CW10 . . . . 128 D2
Devon Gr ST8 . . . . 179 C1
Devon Pl
Congleton CW12 . . . . 156 E4
Widnes WA8 . . . . .13 B3
Devon Rd
Chester CH2 . . . . 118 F5
Irlam M44 . . . . .11 D5
Partington M31 . . . . .11 E2
Devonshire Dr SK10 . . . . . . .86 F2
Devonshire Gdns WA12 . . . . . .2 C2
Devonshire Pl CH4 . . . . 141 E7
Devonshire Rd
Broughton CH4 . . . . 139 C4
Hazel Grove SK7 . . . . .36 F8
Warrington WA4 . . . . .16 F8
Dewar Ct WA7 . . . . .23 E3
Dewar St WA3 . . . . .9 E5
Dewes St CW1 . . . . 190 B5
Dewhurst Rd WA3 . . . . .4 B1
Dexter Way CW10 . . . . 128 D2
Dial Cotts CH64 . . . . .67 A5
Dial La CW12, SK11 . . . . 158 B1
Dial Rd WA15 . . . . .32 C8
Dial St WA1 . . . . .16 C5
Diamond Ave 3 ST7 . . . . 195 B2
Dibbinsdale Rd CH63 . . . . . . .43 B7
Dibbins Gn CH63 . . . . .43 B7
Dickens Cl
Cheadle SK8 . . . . .35 B5
Sandbach CW11 . . . . 174 D6
Dickens La SK12 . . . . .36 E2
Dickenson Ho CW10 . . . . 128 C1
Dickenson St WA2 . . . . .16 C7
Dickinson Cl WA11 . . . . .1 A6
Dickinson Way ST7 . . . . 193 A3
Dickson Cl SK11 . . . . 132 A8
Dickson Cl WA8 . . . . .22 A5
Dicksons Dr CH2 . . . . 118 D4
Dickson St
Widnes, Kingsway
WA8 . . . . .23 A8
2 Widnes WA8 . . . . .23 B8
Dierden St CW7 . . . . 127 B1
Dierdens Terr 4
CW10 . . . . 128 C1
Dig La
Acton CW5 . . . . 203 F4
Frodsham WA6 . . . . .74 A7
Shavington CW5 . . . . 206 B2
Warrington WA2 . . . . .9 B3
Diglake Cl ST7 . . . . 210 C6
Diglake Cotts ST7 . . . . 210 A2
Diglake St ST7 . . . . 209 F3
Diglee Rd SK23 . . . . .39 C3
Dillors Croft CW1 . . . . 173 A1
Dimelow Ct SY14 . . . . 213 A2
Dinas Cl CH1 . . . . 117 D3
Dingle Ave
Newton-le-W WA12 . . . . .1 F2
Row-of-Trees SK9 . . . . .59 D3
Dingle Bank
Chester CH4 . . . . 141 C7
Sandbach CW11 . . . . 175 C6
Dingle Bank Cl WA13 . . . . .18 E3
Dinglebrook Gr 5 SK9 . . . . . . .34 D1
Dingle Cl SK10 . . . . .87 B3
Dingle La
Bridgemere CW5 . . . . 231 F6
Kelsall CW6 . . . . 122 E6
Sandbach CW11 . . . . 175 C6
Warrington WA4 . . . . 126 F1
Winsford CW7 . . . . 126 F1
Dingle Prim Sch The
CW1 . . . . 191 D6

Dingle The
Barnton CW8 . . . . .78 B4
Haslington CW1 . . . . 191 D5
Lymm WA13 . . . . .18 E3
Dingleway WA4 . . . . .26 D8
Dingle Way CW8 . . . . 101 E5
Dingle Wlk 4 CW7 . . . . 126 D1
Dinnington Ct WA8 . . . . .12 E3
Diploma Dr CW10 . . . . 128 C2
Dipping Brook Ave
WA4 . . . . .26 F4
DISLEY 38 C5
Disley Prim Sch SK12 . . . . . . .38 D6
Disley Sta SK12 . . . . .38 C6
Distaff Rd SK12 . . . . .36 B4
District CE Prim Sch The
WA12. . . . . .2 A4
Ditchfield La WA16 . . . . .29 D3
Ditchfield Pl WA8 . . . . .22 B8
Ditchfield Rd
Warrington WA5 . . . . .14 E3
Widnes WA8 . . . . .22 B8
DITTON 22 B5
Ditton CE Prim Sch
WA8 . . . . .12 A1
Ditton Prim Sch WA8 . . . . . . .12 E1
Ditton Rd WA8 . . . . .22 D6
Dixon Ave WA12 . . . . .2 C5
Dixon Cl WA11 . . . . .2 A8
Dixon Ct SK11 . . . . .84 A2
Dixon Dr SK11 . . . . .84 B3
Dixon Rd CW12 . . . . 157 A5
Dixon's Hos CH3 . . . . 142 E8
Dixon St
Irlam M44 . . . . .11 F8
Warrington WA1 . . . . .16 A5
Dobb Hedge Cl WA15 . . . . . . .32 C6
Dobell's Rd CW9 . . . . 103 F5
Dobers La WA6 . . . . .74 C4
Dobson St SY14 . . . . 213 B3
Dock Rd
Northwich CW9 . . . . 103 F7
Widnes WA8 . . . . .22 F5
Widnes WA8 . . . . .23 A5
**Dock Road Edwardian
Pumping Station The***
CW9 . . . . 103 F7
Dock St
Ellesmere Port CH65 . . . . .70 C7
Widnes WA8 . . . . .23 A5
Dock Yard Rd CH65 . . . . .70 E6
Doddington Dr CW11 . . . . . . 175 C8
Doddington Rd CW2 . . . . 190 A3
Doddlespool Barns
CW3 . . . . 221 F7
Dodd's Green La CW5,
SY13. . . . . 228 C4
Dodds La CW12 . . . . 178 C6
Dodd's La SY13, SY14 . . . . . . 224 E7
Doddswood Dr 2
CW12. . . . . 156 F4
Dodgsley Dr WA6 . . . . .75 C1
DODLESTON 162 B7
Dodleston CE Prim Sch
CH4 . . . . 162 A7
Dodleston La CH4 . . . . 162 C3
Doeford Cl WA3 . . . . .4 E5
Doe's Meadow Rd
CH63 . . . . .43 B7
Dog La
Brereton Green CW4,
CW11 . . . . 153 E7
Kelsall CW6 . . . . 122 B5
Nantwich CW5 . . . . 204 E6
Tattenhall CH3 . . . . 182 D4
Threapwood SY14 . . . . 223 C7
Dogmore La CH3 . . . . 147 C4
Dolly La SK23 . . . . .39 F3
Dolmans La 3 WA1 . . . . .16 B5
Dolphin Cres CH66 . . . . .69 E2
Dolphin Ct CH1 . . . . 141 A7
Dombey Rd SK12 . . . . .36 D2
Domestic App M90 . . . . .33 C6
Domville Cl WA13 . . . . .18 E3
Donagh Cl SK10 . . . . .86 F1
Donne Pl CH1 . . . . 117 F6
Donnington Way CH4 . . . . . . 140 F7
Don Wlk CH65 . . . . .70 A7
Dood's La WA4 . . . . .27 A5
Dooley's Grig SK11 . . . . 108 F1
Dooley's La SK9 . . . . .33 C2
Dorac Ave SK8 . . . . .34 C7
Dorchester Cl
Kidsgrove ST7 . . . . 195 A3
Willmslow SK9 . . . . .60 D8
Dorchester Pk WA7 . . . . .24 E3
Dorchester Rd
Chester CH4 . . . . 140 F5
Warrington WA5 . . . . .15 C5
Dorchester Way
Burtonwood WA5 . . . . .6 F6
Macclesfield SK10 . . . . .87 C4
Doreen Ave CW12 . . . . 179 B8
Dorfold Cl CW11 . . . . 175 C7
Dorfold Dr CH65 . . . . 204 D5
Dorfold Hall* CW5 . . . . 204 B5
Dorfold St CW1 . . . . 190 C4
Dorfold Way CH2 . . . . 118 E6
Doric Ave WA6 . . . . .74 D7
Dorin Park Sch CH2 . . . . 118 D6
Dormer Cl CH3 . . . . 143 A5
Dorney Cl WA4 . . . . .26 E6
Dornoch Ct CW4 . . . . 130 B2
Dorothea St WA2 . . . . .16 C7
Dorric Way CW1 . . . . 190 C7
Dorrington Cl WA7 . . . . .50 E8

Drury La continued
Warmingham CW1 . . . . 173 D4
DRURY LANE 223 D1
Dryden Cl CW2 . . . . 190 A1
Dryden Pl WA2 . . . . .8 C2
Dryersfield 5 CH3 . . . . 142 A8
Dryhurst Dr SK12 . . . . .38 D6
Dryhurst La SK12 . . . . .38 D6
Dublin Croft CH66 . . . . .69 E1
Duchess Pl CH2 . . . . 237 A4
Duchy Rd CW1 . . . . 207 A8
DUCKINGTON 199 C4
Duck La CH3 . . . . 121 F7
Duckworth Gr WA2 . . . . .9 A1
DUDDON 145 A6
Duddon Cl
Duddon CW6 . . . . 145 B6
3 Northwich CW9 . . . . 103 F4
Duddon Ct
CW6 . . . . 144 E8
DUDDON HEATH 144 E7
Duddon Hook La
CW6 . . . . 144 F6
Duddon Rd CW6 . . . . 145 B5
**Duddon St Peter's CE Prim
Sch** CW6 . . . . 145 B6
Dudlestone Rd CH66 . . . . .69 B6
Dudley Ave WA7 . . . . .23 D2
Dudley Cres CH65 . . . . .44 B3
Dudley Rd
Ellesmere Port CH65 . . . . .70 B5
Irlam M44 . . . . .11 D4
Dudley St WA2 . . . . .16 B7
Dudley Wlk 2 SK11 . . . . 111 F7
Dudlow Green Rd WA4 . . . . . .26 E5
DUDLOW'S GREEN 26 E5
Dufton Wlk M22 . . . . .33 E8
Duke Cl
Cheadle SK8 . . . . .34 F6
Glazebury WA3 . . . . .5 C7
Duke Cl WA7 . . . . .22 F2
Dukesbridge Ct 7
WA13 . . . . .18 E3
Duke's Cres CW11 . . . . 175 A7
Duke's Ct 2 SK11 . . . . 112 D7
Duke's Ct CH1 . . . . 237 B1
DUKESFIELD 22 E3
Duke St
Alderley Edge SK9 . . . . .60 B2
Chester CH1 . . . . 237 B1
Congleton CW12 . . . . 156 D2
Crewe CW2 . . . . 190 C3
Macclesfield SK11 . . . . 112 D7
Newton-le-W WA12 . . . . .2 B3
Dukesway CH2 . . . . 118 E7
Dukes Way CW9 . . . . 103 E5
Dukes Wharf WA7 . . . . .50 C6
Dulas Cl CW2 . . . . 118 E8
Dulverton Ave CH3 . . . . 119 C2
Dumbah La SK10 . . . . .87 D6
Dumbers SK11 . . . . 136 A2
Dumbill Ho ST7 . . . . 210 C8
Dunbar Cl
Connah's Quay CH5 . . . . .91 D1
Ellesmere Port CH66 . . . . .69 C5
Holmes Chapel CW4 . . . . 130 C2
Ellesmere Port CH66 . . . . .69 C5
Duncan Ave
Newton-le-W WA12 . . . . .2 C5
Runcorn WA7 . . . . .23 C1
Duncansby Cres WA5 . . . . . . .14 E6
Duncansby Dr CH63 . . . . .43 C4
Duncan St WA2 . . . . .16 C7
Dundalk Rd WA8 . . . . .22 E8
Dundee Cl WA2 . . . . .8 F4
Dundee Ct CH65 . . . . .70 E3
Dundonald Ave 5
WA4 . . . . .16 C1
Dundonald Rd SK8 . . . . .35 A7
Dundrennan Cl SK12 . . . . .36 D5
Dunge Valley Gdns*
SK23 . . . . .89 F8
Dunham Cl
Alsager ST7 . . . . 193 C3
Bebington CH62 . . . . .43 F3
Sandbach CW11 . . . . 175 C6
Dunham Cres CW2 . . . . 206 B8
Dunham Ct
Dunham-on-t-H WA6 . . . . .97 E6
Hartford CW8 . . . . 102 F4
DUNHAM HEATH 97 E6
Dunham Hill Prim Sch
WA6 . . . . .97 E6
Dunham Massey Hall*
WA14 . . . . .20 D3
DUNHAM-ON-THE-HILL
 . . . . .97 E6
Dunham Pk (Deer Pk)*
WA14 . . . . .20 D3
Dunham Rd
Altrincham, Bowgreen
WA14 . . . . .20 F1
Handforth SK9 . . . . .34 D5
Mossbrow WA13 . . . . .19 E7
Northwich CW9 . . . . 104 A4
Dunham Way CH2 . . . . 118 F6
DUNHAM WOODHOUSES
 . . . . .20 D3
DUNKIRK 94 E6
Dunkirk ST7 . . . . 210 A6
Dunkirk Ave CW7 . . . . 149 D8
Dunkirk Dr CH65 . . . . .70 B1
Dunkirk La
Capenhurst CH1 . . . . .94 C2
Ellesmere Port CH65 . . . . .70 A1
Dunkirk Trad Est CH1 . . . . . . .94 D2
Dunley Cl WA3 . . . . .10 A5
Dunlin Ave WA12 . . . . .2 C4

Dunlin Cl
  Poynton SK12 . . . . .36 A4
  Runcorn WA7 . . . . .49 F5
  Warrington WA2 . . . . .8 E3
Dunlin Rise SK10 . . . . .87 B5
Dunlop St WA4 . . . . .16 B3
Dunmail Gr WA7 . . . . .49 E5
Dunmore Cl CW10 . . . . . .151 C7
Dunmore Cres CH66 . . . . . .69 B6
Dunmore Rd CH66 . . . . . . .69 B6
Dunmow Rd WA4 . . . . .17 C3
Dunnilow Field CW5 . . . .205 A4
Dunnock Cl WA2 . . . . .8 E3
Dunnock Ct WA3 . . . . .9 E4
Dunnocksfold Rd ST7 . . .193 A4
Dunnockswood ST7 . . . . .193 A4
Dunn's Cotts CW1 . . . . . .192 C1
Dunn's La CH3 . . . . .121 F7
Dunoon Cl CW4 . . . . .130 B2
Dunraven Rd CH64 . . . . . . .67 A7
Dunscar Cl WA3 . . . . .9 D5
Dunsford CW8 . . . . .12 B3
Dunsmore Cl WA11 . . . . . . .1 C7
Dunstan La CH64 . . . . .67 E3
Dunster Cl CW9 . . . . .104 A4
Dunster Gr CH60 . . . . .41 B7
Dunster Rd SK10 . . . . .87 F1
Dunwood Dr ST7 . . . . . . .193 D6
Dunwoody Way CW1,
  CW2 . . . . .190 B4
Durber Ave CH3 . . . . .142 D7
Durber Cl ST7 . . . . .209 D1
Durham Cl
  Macclesfield SK10 . . . . . . .86 F2
  Warrington WA1 . . . . .17 E2
Durham Ct CH65 . . . . .70 E3
Durham Dr CW7 . . . . .149 C6
Durham Gr M44 . . . . .11 C6
Durham Rd
  Blacon CH1 . . . . .117 F5
  Widnes WA8 . . . . .13 B3
Durston Cl WA8 . . . . .12 C2
Durrell Way WA3 . . . . .3 E8
DUTTON 51 A4
Dutton Ct WA1 . . . . .16 C5
Dutton Gn CH2 . . . . .70 F3
Dutton Hall Ct WA4 . . . . . .76 E8
Dutton La CW8, WA6 . . . .101 B6
Duttons Bsns Ctr
  CW9 . . . . .103 F7
Dutton's La CW6 . . . . .122 C5
Dutton Way
  Crewe CW1 . . . . .190 B6
  Nantwich CW5 . . . . .204 E3
Duxford Ct WA2 . . . . .8 E1
Dyar Terr 78 D1
Dye House La SK22 . . . . . .39 C8
Dyers Cl WA13 . . . . .19 A4
Dyers Ct SK10 . . . . .88 B8
Dyers La WA13 . . . . .19 A4
Dykin Cl WA8 . . . . .13 E3
Dykin Rd WA8 . . . . .13 E3
Dysart Bldgs CW5 . . . . . .204 E5
Dyserth Rd CH1 . . . . .117 D3
Dystelegh Rd SK12 . . . . . .38 D6

E

Eadie Gr CW1 . . . . .190 A7
Eaglais Way SK10 . . . . . . .86 F2
Eagland Pl CW12 . . . . . . .156 E4
Eagle Brow WA13 . . . . . . .18 D3
Eagle La CH66 . . . . .69 D7
Eagle Mount WA4 . . . . . . .16 C2
Eagle Park Dr WA2 . . . . . . .8 A1
Eaglesfield CW8 . . . . .103 C4
Eagles Way WA7 . . . . .49 E6
Ealing Cl WA7 . . . . .24 D1
Ealing Rd WA5 . . . . .15 B5
Eanleywood Farm Cl
  WA7 . . . . .50 C7
Eanleywood La WA7 . . . . .50 C7
Eardley Cres CW12 . . . . . .156 E4
Eardley Ct **6** CW1 . . . . . .190 B5
Eardleyend Rd ST7 . . . . . .209 E7
Eardswick Cl CH2 . . . . . . .237 B4
Eardswick La CW7 . . . . . .172 D5
Eardswick Rd CW10 . . . . .151 C6
Earle Cl WA12 . . . . .1 F3
Earle Cres CH64 . . . . .41 D1
Earle Dr CH64 . . . . .41 D1
Earle Rd WA8 . . . . .23 C7
Earles La CW9 . . . . .79 E6
Earle's La CW6 . . . . .122 C5
Earle St
  Crewe CW1 . . . . .190 D4
  Newton-le-W WA12 . . . . . .2 A3
EARLESTOWN 2 B2
Earlestown Sta WA12 . . . .2 B3
Earl Rd SK8, SK9 . . . . .34 E5
Earls Gdns CH65 . . . . .70 B5
Earls Oak CH2 . . . . .118 D7
Earl's Port CH1 . . . . .118 B2
Earls Rd CW2 . . . . .206 B4
Earl St WA2 . . . . .16 B7
Earlston Ct CH3 . . . . .237 C2
Earlsway
  Chester CH4 . . . . .141 A8
  Macclesfield SK11 . . . . . . .111 F7
Earls Way
  Northwich CW9 . . . . .103 E4
  Runcorn WA7 . . . . .49 E6
Earlswood Mews
  CW9 . . . . .103 F3
Easby Cl
  Cheadle SK8 . . . . .35 B6
  Poynton SK12 . . . . .36 D4

Easby Cl continued
  Runcorn WA7 . . . . .23 C2
Easenhall Cl WA8 . . . . . . .13 C5
East Ave
  Bollington SK10 . . . . .87 F7
  Gatley SK8 . . . . .34 D8
  Northwich CW9 . . . . .104 D6
  Warrington, Great Sankey
  WA5 . . . . .15 A4
  Warrington, Stockton Heath
  WA4 . . . . .16 D1
  Warrington WA2 . . . . .16 C8
  Weston CW2 . . . . .207 C5
Eastbury Cl WA8 . . . . .13 C5
Eastcott Cl CW12 . . . . . . .155 F4
East Ct ST7 . . . . .193 E4
Eastdale WA5 . . . . .31 F8
Eastdale Rd WA1 . . . . .17 A7
East Dam Wood Rd
  L24 . . . . .21 A2
East Dudley St CW7 . . . .126 F1
East Ct WA5 . . . . .7 B2
Eastern Pathway CH4 . . .237 B2
Eastern Rd CW5 . . . . .205 F5
Eastfields Gr CH1 . . . . . . .117 A8
Eastford Rd WA4 . . . . .16 A1
Eastgate SK10 . . . . .112 E8
Eastgate Rd
  Holmes Chapel CW4 . . . . .130 D3
  Runcorn WA7 . . . . .24 E5
Eastgate Row N CH1 . . . .237 B2
Eastgate Row S CH1 . . . .237 B2
Eastgate St CH1 . . . . .237 B2
Eastgate Way WA7 . . . . . .24 D4
East Gn CH5 . . . . .116 A6
East Lancashire Rd WA11,
  WA12, WA3 . . . . .2 C7
East Mains L24 . . . . .21 A3
East Millwood Rd L24 . . . .21 A4
East Park Rd SK11 . . . . . .112 B5
East Rd
  Halewood L24, L26 . . . . . . .21 A5
  Middlewich CW10 . . . . . . .128 B1
  Wythenshawe M90 . . . . . . .33 C7
East St WA8 . . . . .13 D1
East Terr WA16 . . . . .56 F1
East View
  10 Nantwich CW5 . . . . . .204 E6
  Warrington WA4 . . . . .17 B2
Eastward Ave SK9 . . . . . . .59 F6
Eastway
  Ellesmere Port CH66 . . . . .69 D7
  Widnes WA8 . . . . .12 D1
Eastwood WA7 . . . . .24 C2
Eastwood Ave 2 F3
Eastwood Ct CH5 . . . . . . .139 B7
Eastwood Rd WA5 . . . . .6 F7

Eccles Cl SK23 . . . . .65 D8
Eccles Rd SK23 . . . . .65 F6
ECCLESTON 141 E1
Eccleston Ave
  Bebington CH62 . . . . .43 C8
  Chester CH4 . . . . .141 D6
  Ellesmere Port CH66 . . . . .69 E5
Eccleston CE Prim Sch
  CH4 . . . . .141 E2
Eccleston Cl WA3 . . . . .9 C5
Eccleston Ct **5** CW9 . . . .103 E5
Eccleston Dr WA7 . . . . . . .23 C1
Eccleston Rd CH4 . . . . . . .161 A7
Eccleston Way **3** SK9 . . . .34 E1
Eccups La SK9 . . . . .59 C8
Echo Cl CH4 . . . . .140 E5
Ecton Ave WA16 . . . . .113 A7
Ecton Cl CW7 . . . . .127 A4
Edale Cl
  Bebington CH62 . . . . .43 E5
  Gatley SK8 . . . . .34 D7
Edale Dr CW6 . . . . .122 D5
Edburton CW4 . . . . .3 A8
Edisbury Cl CH3 . . . . .112 F7
Edisbury Dr ST5 . . . . .210 D2
Edisbury Hill CW6,
  CW8 . . . . .123 D7
Edisbury Hill Pk
  CW8 . . . . .123 D7
Edisbury Rd CH66 . . . . . . .69 F1
Edisbury Sq WA6 . . . . .74 B8
Edisbury Terr SK11 . . . . . .112 F7
Edisbury Way CW9 . . . . . .103 E3
Eddisford Dr WA3 . . . . .4 D1
Edelsten St WA5 . . . . .15 F5
Eden Ave
  Fowley Common WA3 . . . . . .5 C4
  High Lane SK6 . . . . .37 E7
  Winsford CW7 . . . . .126 F2
Edenbridge Cl CW2 . . . . .207 B2
Edenbridge Gdns WA4 . . .26 E3
Eden Cl
  Biddulph ST8 . . . . .179 E1
  5 Ellesmere Port CH66 . . .69 C5
  Kidsgrove ST7 . . . . .195 B2
  Wilmslow SK9 . . . . .59 E5
Edendale WA8 . . . . .12 B2
Edenfield Cl WA16 . . . . . . .58 A3
Edenfield Rd WA16 . . . . . .58 A4
Edenhall Cl CW4 . . . . .130 A3
Eden Park Rd SK8 . . . . . . .34 E8
Edgar Ct
  Chester CH4 . . . . .237 B1
  2 Macclesfield SK11 . . . .112 C8
Edgar Pl CH4 . . . . .237 B1
Edgecroft CH3 . . . . .166 A1
Edge Gr CH2 . . . . .118 F2
EDGE GREEN 199 B2
Edgehill Chase SK9 . . . . . .60 E7
Edge La SY14 . . . . .199 C1
Edgerley La CH3 . . . . .181 B6
Edgerton Rd WA3 . . . . .3 F8
Edge View La SK9 . . . . . . .59 B2
Edgeway
  Henbury SK11 . . . . .111 C8
  Wilmslow SK9 . . . . .60 B8
Edgewell La CW6 . . . . . . .147 A3
Edgewood **3** CH3 . . . . . .142 A8
Edgewood Dr
  Bebington CH62 . . . . .43 D5
  Wistaston CW2 . . . . .206 A7
Edgworth St WA2 . . . . .16 A6
Edinburgh Ct CH65 . . . . . .70 D3
Edinburgh Dr SK10 . . . . . .87 A1
Edinburgh Pl CW12 . . . . .156 F2
Edinburgh Rd
  Congleton CW12 . . . . .156 F2
  Widnes WA8 . . . . .22 A8
  Wistaston CW2 . . . . .206 A7
Edinburgh Way CH4 . . . . .237 C1
Edison Rd WA7 . . . . .23 D3
Edith St WA7 . . . . .22 F3
Edlestone Gr **2** SK9 . . . . .34 E1
Edleston Hall La CW5 . . .203 F2
Edleston Prim Sch
  CW2 . . . . .190 D3
Edleston Rd CW2 . . . . . . .190 D3
Edmund Wright Way
  CW5 . . . . .204 C5
Edna St CH2 . . . . .118 F3
Edward Gdns WA1 . . . . . .17 F6
Edward Rd WA5 . . . . .14 D6
Edwards Ave CW2 . . . . . .206 C5
Edwards Cl CW2 . . . . .206 C5
Edwards Rd CH4 . . . . .141 A6
Edward St
  Audley ST7 . . . . .209 F3
  Crewe CW2 . . . . .190 D2
  Ellesmere Port CH65 . . . . .70 C7
  Haydock WA11 . . . . .1 A6
  Macclesfield SK11 . . . . . . .112 B7
  Northwich CW9 . . . . .104 C8
  Widnes WA8 . . . . .13 D1
Edwards Way
  Alsager ST7 . . . . .193 D4
  Widnes WA8 . . . . .22 C8
Edwin St WA8 . . . . .13 C1
Egdon Cl WA8 . . . . .13 E2
Egerton Ave CH66 . . . . . . .69 C5
Egerton Ct WA6 . . . . .122 B5
Egerton Dr CH2 . . . . .118 D5

EGERTON GREEN 200 C5
Egerton Mews **1** WA4 . . .16 C1
Egerton Moss WA15 . . . . .31 E5
Egerton Prim Sch
  WA16 . . . . .56 F2
Egerton Rd
  Blacon CH1 . . . . .117 C5
  Handforth SK9 . . . . .34 B1
  Lymm WA13 . . . . .18 C2
Egerton St **7** WA16 . . . . .57 A2
Egerton St
  Chester CH1 . . . . .237 C3
  Congleton CW12 . . . . .156 C2
  Ellesmere Port CH65 . . . . .70 C6
  Runcorn WA7 . . . . .22 F3
  Warrington, Howley
  WA1 . . . . .16 D5
  Warrington, Stockton Heath
  WA4 . . . . .16 C1
Egerton Terr CW9 . . . . . . .105 D4
Egerton Wlk CH4 . . . . . . .162 A7
Eggbridge La CH3 . . . . . .143 A5
Egypt St
  3 Warrington WA1 . . . . . .16 A5
  Widnes WA8 . . . . .22 F7
Eilison Ct CH1 . . . . .237 B3
Elaine Cl
  Ellesmere Port CH66 . . . . .69 C4
  Widnes WA8 . . . . .13 C1
Elaine Price Ct **3** WA7 . . .23 F1
Elan Way 16 D7
Elanor Rd CW11 . . . . .174 D7
Elcombe Ave WA3 . . . . .3 E7
Elderberry Way SK9 . . . . . .60 E8
Elderberry Wlk M31 . . . . . .11 E3
Elder Dr CH4 . . . . .140 E5
Eldon Cl WA16 . . . . .57 A1
Eldon St WA1 . . . . .16 D5
Eldon Terr CH64 . . . . .66 E7
Eleanor Cl CW1 . . . . .189 F5
Eleanor St
  Ellesmere Port CH65 . . . . .70 C6
  6 Warrington WA8 . . . . . .23 A7
Electra Way CW1 . . . . . . .191 A2
Electricity St CW1 . . . . . . .190 E4
Electricity St CW7 . . . . . . .190 C3
Elgar Ave CH62 . . . . .43 E5
Elgar Cl CH66 . . . . .69 F3
Elgin Ave
  Holmes Chapel CW4 . . . . .130 B2
  Macclesfield SK10 . . . . . . .87 A2
  Warrington WA5 . . . . .14 F4
Elgin Cl CH3 . . . . .119 B3
Eliot Cl CW1 . . . . .191 A4
Elizabethan Way CW9 . . .104 E6
Elizabeth Ave SK12 . . . . . .38 D5
Elizabeth Cl
  Kelsall CW6 . . . . .122 D5
  Sandbach CW11 . . . . .174 D7
Elizabeth Cres CH4 . . . . .237 C1
Elizabeth Ct
  Talke ST7 . . . . .210 D5
  Widnes WA8 . . . . .23 B7
Elizabeth Dr WA1 . . . . . . .17 E5
Elizabeth Gaskell Ct
  WA16 . . . . .56 F2
Elizabeth Rd
  Haydock WA11 . . . . .1 E7
  Partington M31 . . . . .11 F4
Elizabeth St
  Congleton CW12 . . . . .156 C2
  Crewe CW1 . . . . .190 B5
  Macclesfield SK11 . . . . . . .112 D7
Elizabeth Terr WA8 . . . . . .12 D1
Elkan Cl WA8 . . . . .13 E2
Elkan Rd WA8 . . . . .13 E2
Elk View SY14 . . . . .222 F5
Ella Gr WA16 . . . . .57 B2
Elland Dr CH66 . . . . .69 A2
Ellen Brook Rd M22 . . . . . .33 D8
Ellen St WA5 . . . . .15 F7
Ellerby Cl WA7 . . . . .50 E7
Ellerton Ave CH66 . . . . . . .69 C5
Ellerton Cl WA8 . . . . .12 D3
Ellesmere Ave
  Broughton CH4 . . . . .139 D4
  Chester CH2 . . . . .118 D5
Ellesmere Cl CW11 . . . . . .174 D8
Ellesmere Pl **10** CW1 . . .190 B5
ELLESMERE PORT 70 A2
Ellesmere Port Hosp
  CH65 . . . . .70 A2
Ellesmere Port RC High
  Sch CH65 . . . . .70 A3
Ellesmere Port Sch of
  Performing Arts
  CH66 . . . . .69 E6
Ellesmere Port Sta
  CH65 . . . . .70 C5
Ellesmere Port Stadium
  The CH65 . . . . .70 E3
Ellesmere Rd
  Culcheth WA3 . . . . .4 E3
  Northwich CW9 . . . . .104 A4
  Warrington WA4 . . . . .16 B1
Ellesmere St
  Runcorn WA7 . . . . .16 C5
  6 Warrington WA1 . . . . . .16 C5
Ellesworth Cl WA5 . . . . . . .15 C8
Ellingham Way CW7 . . . . .126 A1
Ellington Dr WA5 . . . . .15 B5
Elliot Ho CW1 . . . . .118 A5
Elliot St **9** WA8 . . . . .23 B8
Elliott Ave WA1 . . . . .16 D7
Ellis La CW6 . . . . .49 D1

Ellison St
  Warrington, Howley
  WA1 . . . . .16 C5
  Warrington, Stockton Heath
  WA4 . . . . .16 D1
Ellis St
  Crewe CW1 . . . . .190 B6
  Widnes WA8 . . . . .22 F7
Elloway Rd L24 . . . . .21 A3
Ellwood Cl L24 . . . . .21 E2
Ellwood Gn CW2 . . . . . . .206 E3
Elm Ave
  Newton-le-W WA12 . . . . . . .2 C1
  Warrington WA8 . . . . .13 B2
Elm Beds Rd SK12 . . . . . .37 C2
Elm Cl
  Crewe CW2 . . . . .189 E3
  2 Poynton M31 . . . . .11 F3
  Poynton SK12 . . . . .36 F3
  Tarporley CW6 . . . . .146 D2
Elm Cres SK9 . . . . .60 B3
Elm Ct CW1 . . . . .190 D6
Elm Dr
  Crewe CW1 . . . . .190 E6
  Holmes Chapel CW4 . . . . .130 D4
  Macclesfield SK10 . . . . . . .87 C2
Elmfield Cl SK9 . . . . .60 B2
Elmfield Rd SK9 . . . . .60 B2
Elm Gdns CH64 . . . . .67 F8
Elm Gr
  Alderley Edge SK9 . . . . . . .60 B2
  Alsager ST7 . . . . .193 E4
  Ellesmere Port CH66 . . . . .70 A1
  Handforth SK9 . . . . .34 C3
  Saltney CH4 . . . . .140 E5
  Warrington WA1 . . . . .16 F7
  Warrington WA5 . . . . .13 B1
  Winsford CW7 . . . . .127 A1
Elm Ho
  Chester CH2 . . . . .118 C5
  3 Sandbach CW11 . . . . .175 B6
Elmore Cl
  Holmes Chapel CW4 . . . . .130 B3
  Runcorn WA7 . . . . .24 D1
Elm Rd
  Congleton CW12 . . . . .156 B3
  Haydock WA11 . . . . .1 E7
  High Lane SK6 . . . . .37 F7
  Hollinfare WA3 . . . . .11 A2
  Middlewich CW10 . . . . . . .151 D7
  Runcorn WA7 . . . . .49 C8
  Warrington WA5 . . . . .14 F4
  Weaverham CW8 . . . . . . .102 D7
  Willaston CH64 . . . . .67 F8
Elmridge Ct WA3 . . . . .8 B4
Elmridge Cl WA3 . . . . .3 F8
Elmridge Dr WA15 . . . . . . .32 C8
Elmridge Prim Sch
  WA15 . . . . .32 C8
Elmridge Way CW8 . . . . . .78 D1
Elm Rise
  Frodsham WA6 . . . . .74 C7
  Prestbury SK10 . . . . .86 E6
Elms SK9 . . . . .59 F6
Elmsett Cl WA5 . . . . .14 E5
Elm Sq CH4 . . . . .140 F6
Elm St
  Ellesmere Port CH65 . . . . .70 C7
  Northwich CW9 . . . . .79 B1
Elmstead Cres CW1 . . . . .189 F8
Elmstead Rd SK11 . . . . . .84 A3
Elms The
  Golborne WA3 . . . . .3 F7
  Mobberley WA16 . . . . .58 E2
  7 Northwich CW9 . . . . . .103 E6
  Runcorn WA7 . . . . .22 F1
  Tallarn Green/Tallwrn Green
  SY14 . . . . .222 F5
Elmsway
  Altrincham WA15 . . . . .32 C8
  Bollington SK10 . . . . .88 A8
  Bramhall SK7 . . . . .35 C7
  High Lane SK6 . . . . .37 E6
Elm Terr CW1 . . . . .190 E6
Elm Tree Ave
  Lymm WA13 . . . . .18 D2
  Warrington WA1 . . . . .16 F8
Elm Tree Cotts CH3 . . . . .167 A7
Elm Tree Ct CH66 . . . . . . .147 A3
Elm Tree Dr ST7 . . . . .209 F1
Elm Tree La CW11 . . . . . .174 D8
Elm Tree Rd
  Golborne WA3 . . . . .3 F8
  Lymm WA13 . . . . .18 D2
Elmuir CH1 . . . . .117 E3
Elmwood CW7 . . . . .24 C1
Elmwood Ave
  Chester CH2 . . . . .118 F4
  Warrington WA1 . . . . .16 F7
Elmwood Cl ST7 . . . . .194 A4
Elmwood Gr CW7 . . . . . . .149 F8
Elmwood Rd CW8 . . . . . . .78 B4
Elnor Ave SK23 . . . . .65 E5
Elnor La SK23 . . . . .65 F4
Elphins Dr WA4 . . . . .16 C1
Elsby Rd ST7 . . . . .193 F2
Elston Ave WA12 . . . . .2 C5
Elstree Ave CH3 . . . . .119 B3
Elstree Ct WA8 . . . . .13 D4
Elswick Ave SK7 . . . . .35 E5
Eltham Cl WA3 . . . . .3 E8
Eltham Wlk WA8 . . . . .13 E3
ELTON 72 C3

Elton Cl
Bebington CH62..........43 E3
Golborne WA3.............3 E7
Handforth SK9............34 E1
Warrington WA3............9 C4
Elton Crossings Rd
CW11..................174 D6
Elton Dr SK7...........36 D8
ELTON GREEN..........72 A3
Elton La
Elton CH2...............72 E4
Haslington CW11, CW1..174 D1
Winterley CW11.........191 F8
Elton Lordship La WA6...73 B7
Elton Prim Sch CH2......72 B4
Elton Rd CW11.........174 D5
Elvington Cl
Congleton CW12.........156 E2
Runcorn WA7.............49 F4
Elwood Way CW5........205 B4
ELWORTH..............174 E6
Elworth Ave WA8........13 A5
Elworth CE Prim Sch
CW11..................174 E7
Elworth Ct
 12 Congleton CW12....156 F3
 Sandbach CW11.........174 D7
Elworth Hall Prim Sch
CW11..................174 E6
Elworth Rd CW11........174 E6
Elworth St CW11........175 A7
Elworth Way 6 SK9......34 D4
Elwyn Dr L26...........21 A8
Ely Cl CH66.............94 E8
Ely Pk WA7.............24 E2
Embassy Cl CH1.........117 C4
Emberton Pl CW3........230 A5
Embleton Cl WA7........49 D5
Embridge Cswy SK10.....90 B5
Emerald Dr CW11........175 C8
Emerald Rd M22.........33 F7
Emily St 7 WA8..........23 A7
Emmett St CW8..........78 A3
Empire Ct WA1..........16 A4
Empress Dr CW2........190 B3
Emral Ct SY14..........211 A1
Emslie Ct CH64..........66 C7
Enderby Rd CH1.........237 A3
Endon Ave SK10..........88 A7
Endon Hall Mews SK10....88 B5
Endsleigh Cl CH2.......118 E8
Endsleigh Gdns CH2.....118 E8
Enfield Cl CW2.........206 B3
Enfield Park Rd WA2......9 A3
Enfield Rd CH65.........70 B5
Engineer Pk CH5.......116 A4
Englefield Ave CH4.....140 D6
Englefield Cl CW1......190 A8
ENGLESEA-BROOK.....208 A4
Englesea Brook La
CW2..................208 A3
Englesea Brook Mus of
 Primitive Methodism*
CW2..................208 A3
Englesea Gr CW2.......190 B1
Ennerdale
Chester CH2............118 F5
Macclesfield SK11......111 F5
Ennerdale Ave
Bebington CH62..........43 F4
Warrington WA2...........8 B3
Ennerdale Cl
Alderley Edge SK9........83 F7
Winsford CW7..........126 D3
Ennerdale Dr
Congleton CW12.........156 B2
Frodsham WA6............74 C8
Ennerdale Rd
Crewe CW2.............189 D3
Partington M31..........11 E3
Ennis Cl L24............21 D2
Ensor Way SK22..........39 C7
Enterprise Ct CW11.....174 D7
Enterprise Ctr The
CW12..................156 E3
Enterprise Way WA3......4 A7
Enticott Rd M44.........11 C5
Enville St WA4..........16 C4
Epping Dr WA1...........17 D8
Epsom Ave SK8, SK9......34 E4
Epsom Ct CH1..........118 B2
Epsom Gdns WA4..........26 E2
Epworth Cl WA5...........6 F7
ERF Way CW10..........151 E8
Eric Ave WA1............16 E8
Eric Dr CW11...........174 D7
Eric Fountain Rd CH65...44 D3
Eric St WA8.............13 C2
Erindale Cres WA6.......74 A6
Ermine Rd CH2..........237 C4
Ernest St CW2..........190 C1
Ernley Cl CW5..........204 D6
Errington Ave CH65......70 C6
Errwood Forest Walks*
SK17...................90 E2
Erskine Rd M31.........11 F3
Erwood St WA2..........16 B6
Eskdale CH65............70 B3
Eskdale Ave
Bebington CH62..........43 E5
Bramhall SK7............35 C5
Warrington WA2...........8 C3
Eskdale Cl WA7..........49 D5
Esk Dale Cl CW7.........126 C2
Esk Rd CW7.............127 A2

Essex Cl CW12..........156 E5
Essex Dr
Biddulph ST8...........179 D2
Kidsgrove ST7..........194 F2
Essex Gdns M44..........11 C4
Essex Rd CH2...........119 A5
Essex Wlk SK10..........86 F1
Esthers La CW8.........102 D8
Etchells Prim Sch SK8...34 C8
Ethelda Dr CW2.........119 A5
Etherow Cl CW11.......174 E7
Ethos Ct CH1...........237 C3
Eton Dr CH63............41 F6
Eton Rd CH65............70 D4
Ettiley Ave CW11.......174 C5
ETTILEY HEATH........174 C6
Ettrick Pk CH3.........119 A2
Euclid Ave WA4..........17 B2
Europa Bvd WA5..........7 D3
Europa Way CH65.........70 C6
Eustace St WA4..........16 A5
Evans Bsns Ctr CH5......93 A1
Evans Cl WA11............1 F7
Evansleigh Dr CH5......116 A3
Evans Pl WA4............16 D3
Evans St CW1...........190 C6
Eva St CW11............174 D8
Evelyn St WA5...........15 D4
Evelyn Street Com Prim
Sch WA5................15 D4
Evenwood Cl WA7.........24 E4
Everdon Cl CW7.........126 F4
Everest Cl CH66.........69 F3
Everest Rd ST7.........195 C3
Everglade Cl WA11......112 B5
Evergreens The CW9......80 A3
Evergreen Way WA9.......6 A7
Everite Rd WA8..........22 B7
Everite Road Ind Est
WA8...................22 B7
Eversley WA8............12 B2
Eversley Cl
Frodsham WA6...........74 C6
Warrington WA4..........26 F5
Eversley Ct CH2.........118 C4
Eversley Pk CH2........118 C4
Evesham Cl
Macclesfield SK10........87 E4
Warrington WA4..........26 C8
Evesham Dr SK9..........34 C2
Evington Ho 2 SK11....112 B6
Ewart St CH4...........140 B7
Ewloe Ct CH65...........70 D2
Ewrin La SK10...........89 D5
Excalibur Ind Est ST7..193 E3
Excalibur Prim Sch
ST7...................193 E2
Excalibur Way M44.......11 F7
Exchange Cl 12 SK11...112 D8
Exchange St SK11.......112 D8
Exeter Cl SK8............34 F8
Exeter Pl CH1...........117 F5
Exeter Rd CH65..........70 C5
Exeter Wlk SK7..........35 F7
Exit Rd W M90...........33 B7
Exmouth Cres WA7........50 E6
Exmouth Way WA5.........6 F7
Express Ind Est WA8.....22 A7
Exton Pk CH1...........237 A4
Eyam Rd SK7............36 E8
Eyebrook Rd WA14.......20 F2
Eyre Pl CH65............70 B6
Eyston Cl CW9..........103 E5

F

Facit Glen Ind Est
CH4...................140 F7
Factory La
Warrington WA1, WA5.....15 F4
Widnes WA8.............13 B3
Factory Rd CH5.........116 A3
FADDILEY..............202 D7
FADDILEY BANK........202 C6
Fairacre Dr CW10......151 E6
Fairacres Rd SK8........37 E8
Fairbourne Ave
Alderley Edge SK9........60 B3
Wilmslow SK9............59 F4
Fairbourne Cl
Warrington WA5...........7 E3
Wilmslow SK9............59 F4
Fairbourne Dr SK9.......59 F4
Fairbrook CW2..........189 E2
Fairbrother Cres WA2.....8 D2
Fairburn Ave CW2.......189 F4
Fairburn Cl WA8.........13 E3
Fairclough Ave WA1......16 C4
Fairclough Cres WA11....1 A6
Fairclough St
Burtonwood WA5..........6 E6
Newton-le-W WA12........2 B3
Fairfax Cl ST8.........179 C1
Fairfax Ct CW5.........204 E7
Fairfax Dr
Nantwich CW5...........204 D6
Runcorn WA7.............23 D2
Wilmslow SK9............59 F4
Fairfield Ave
Bollington SK10..........88 A8
Ellesmere Port CH65.....70 C2
Sandbach CW11..........175 B5
Fairfield Gdns WA4......16 E2
Fairfield High Sch
WA8...................13 B3
Fairfield Inf Sch WA8...13 B2
Fairfield Jun Sch WA8...13 B2

Fairfield Rd
Broughton CH4..........139 B4
Chester CH2............119 A4
Irlam M44...............11 C5
Lymm WA13..............18 F3
Northwich CW9..........104 A4
Warrington WA4..........16 E2
Widnes WA8.............13 B2
Fairfields
Audley ST7.............209 F2
Whitchurch SY13........225 F1
Fairfield St WA1.........16 D6
Fairford Cl WA5..........15 B6
Fairford Rd CH4.........140 F6
Fairford Way SK9........60 D7
Fairhaven CW2..........207 B1
Fairhaven Cl
Bramhall SK7............35 F8
Macclesfield SK10.......87 B4
Warrington WA5..........15 A4
Fairhaven Rd CH63.......43 C5
Fairhaven Rd WA8........13 C2
Fair Haven's Ct WA8.....23 B8
Fairhills Ind Est M44....11 F8
Fairhills Rd M44.........11 F8
Fairholme Ave CH4.......41 D1
Fairholme Cl CH1........94 B1
Fairholme Rd CW9.......127 A8
Fair Isle Cl CH65........70 C1
Fair Mead WA16..........82 B8
Fairmeadow CH4.........162 D2
Fairoak Cl 12 CW2......149 A8
Fairoak Ct WA7..........50 F3
Fairoak La WA7..........50 F3
Fair Oak Rd ST5.........210 D1
Fairview LL13..........196 E8
Fairview Ave
Alsager ST7.............193 D4
Weston CW2.............207 B5
Fair View Cl CW8.........77 F3
Fairview Rd
Ellesmere Port CH65.....70 A2
Macclesfield SK11......112 A6
Fairway
Bramhall SK7............35 D6
Sandycroft CH5.........116 A2
Fairways
Frodsham WA6...........74 D7
Warrington WA4..........26 D5
Fairways Dr
Ellesmere Port CH66.....69 D7
Whitchurch SY13........226 A1
Fairways The
Macclesfield SK10.......87 B4
Winsford CW7..........126 A2
Fairway The ST7........193 C4
Fairway Trad Est WA8....22 E6
Fairywell Cl SK9.........34 D1
Falcon Cl
Middlewich CW10........151 D5
New Mills SK22..........39 D8
Winsford CW7..........149 D6
Falcondale Rd WA2........8 B4
Falcon Dr CW1..........190 B8
Falconers Gn WA5........7 F2
Falcon Rd CH66..........69 F3
Falcons Way WA7.........49 E6
Falkirk Ave WA8.........12 F3
Fallbrook Cl SK11......111 E8
Fallibroome High Sch
SK10....................86 E2
Fallon Ct CW10.........151 C7
Fallowfield WA7.........23 D1
Fallowfield Cl CW7.....125 F1
Fallowfield Ct CW1.....190 A6
Fallowfield Gr WA2.......9 B1
Falmouth Cl SK10.......111 E8
Falmouth Dr WA5........14 E3
Falmouth Pl WA7.........50 E6
Falmouth Rd
Congleton CW12.........178 E8
Crewe CW1.............190 A6
Falstone Cl WA3.........10 B6
Falstone Dr WA7.........50 E7
Fanner's La WA16.......28 D5
Fanny's Croft ST7......193 D2
FANSHAWE.............110 C4
Fanshawe La SK11......110 E5
Faraday Rd
Ellesmere Port CH65.....70 A4
Runcorn WA7............23 D3
Farams Rd ST7..........193 E7
Farbailey Cl CH4........141 B5
Farcroft Cl WA13........19 C5
Farfields Cl SK11.......111 E1
Farley Cl CW10.........151 B8
Farm Cl ST8.............77 D1
Farmdale Dr CH2.........72 A3
Farm Dr CH5.............91 C1
Farmer Cl CW2..........190 A4
Farmers Heath CH66......69 D2
Farmer's La WA5..........7 A6
Farmfield Dr SK10........87 C3
Farmfields Rise CW3.....232 C1
Farmfold SK9............33 F3
Farm Hollow ST7........210 A2
Farm La
High Lane SK6...........38 A6
Warrington WA4..........26 E8
Withington Green SK11..108 A1
Farmleigh Dr CW1.......189 F8
Farmleigh Gdns WA5.....15 C6

Farm Rd
Northwich CW9..........104 E7
Oakmere CW8...........124 A8
Weaverham CW8..........77 D1
Farmside Cl WA5.........15 F7
Farmstead Way CH66......69 E1
Farm Way WA12...........2 E1
Farm Wlk WA14..........20 E1
Farndale WA8............13 A5
Farndale Cl
Warrington WA5..........14 F7
Wistaston CW2..........206 A6
Farndale Wlk SK11......112 D6
FARNDON..............180 F2
Farndon Cl
Broughton CH4..........139 C4
Cuddington CW8.........102 A3
Farndon Prim Sch
CH3...................180 E2
Farndon Rd CH66.........69 E6
Farne Cl CH65...........95 C8
Farnham Ave SK11......112 A6
Farnham Cl
Cheadle SK8.............35 A7
Warrington WA4..........26 E7
Farnhill Cl WA7.........50 D8
Farnley Cl WA7..........24 D1
FARNWORTH............13 A3
Farnworth CE Prim Sch
WA8...................13 A4
Farnworth Cl WA8........13 A4
Farnworth Ct WA8........13 B3
Farnworth Rd WA5.......14 C8
Farnworth St WA8........13 B4
Farrant St WA8..........23 B8
Farrell Rd WA4..........26 C8
Farrell St WA1...........16 D5
Farr Hall Dr CH60........40 E7
Farr Hall Rd CH60.......40 F8
Farrier Ct CW1.........190 D7
Farriers Way CW7.......126 A1
Farringdon Rd WA2........8 D5
Farthing La CW9.........79 B8
Farthings The WA13......18 D4
Farwood Cl SK10.........86 F2
Faulkner Dr CW10.......151 E6
Faulkners La CH3........142 D8
Faulkner's Cl CH4......161 A7
Faulkner's La WA16......58 E2
Fawns Keep SK9..........60 D7
Fawns Leap CW8.........101 E5
Fearndown Way SK10......87 C4
FEARNHEAD..............9 B2
Fearnhead Cross WA2......8 F2
Fearnhead La WA2.........9 A2
Fearnleigh CW9.........103 C7
Fearnley Way WA12.......2 C1
Feather La CH60.........40 F8
Feather's La CH1........237 B2
Feilden Ct CH1..........94 F1
Felix Rd CW8...........103 E8
Felskirk Rd M22.........33 C8
Felton Ave SK10........112 E8
Fence Ave Ind Est
SK10..................112 E8
Fence Ct SK10..........112 E8
Fence La CW12.........178 D4
Fenham Dr WA5..........14 F4
Fennel St WA1...........16 C5
Fenton Cl
Congleton CW12.........157 A1
Widnes WA8.............12 C3
Fenwick La WA7..........49 D6
Fenwick Rd CH66.........69 E2
Ferguson Ave CH66.......69 E6
Ferguson Dr WA2.........8 D1
Ferma La CH3...........120 D6
Fern Ave WA12...........2 D2
Fernbank Cl
Crewe CW1.............190 F3
Warrington WA3..........9 E4
Winsford CW7..........127 B1
Fernbank Rise SK10......88 B8
Fern Cl
Mount Pleasant ST7.....195 C6
Warrington WA3..........9 E4
Fern Cres CW12.........157 A3
Fern Ct CW1...........190 E3
Ferndale Ave CH2........72 A3
Ferndale Cl
Bold Heath WA8..........13 E7
Sandbach CW11.........175 C5
Warrington WA1.........17 C7
Weston CW2.............207 B5
Ferndale Cres SK11......111 E7
Ferndale Gdns ST7......195 E3
Ferndown Way CW2......221 C8
Fernhill Rd CH1.........117 E6
Fernhurst WA7...........49 D8
FERNILEE...............65 E1
Fernilee Cotts SK23......65 E1
Fernlea Ct CH1..........116 F8
Fern Lea Dr SK11.......112 A8
Fernleigh Cl ST7.......193 F8
Fernlea Rd
Heswall CH60............41 A8
Marston CW9............79 B6
Fernleigh Cl ST7
Widnes WA8.............13 C2
Fern Rd CH65............70 B2
Fernway CW7...........127 B1
Fern Way CW8...........77 C1
Fernwood WA7...........24 B1
Fernwood Gr SK9.........60 C8
Fernyess La CW6.........67 E7
Ferret Oak La CW6......186 B6

Ferrous Way M44.........11 F6
Ferry Cl CH5...........116 A6
Ferry La
Sealand CH1............117 C1
Warrington WA4..........17 E4
Ferry Rd CH62...........44 A6
Festival Ave
Buerton CW3............230 E3
Warrington WA2...........8 D2
Festival Cres WA2........8 D2
Festival Dr SK10.........85 F6
Festival Hill CW12......156 F2
Festival Rd CH65.........69 F5
Festival Terr 1 WA7.....49 C8
Festival Way WA7........49 C8
Ffordd Cledwen/Cledwen
Rd CH4.................139 D5
Ffordd Smithfield/
 Smithfield Dr LL13....196 D8
Ffordd Y Blodau/Blossom
Way CH4................140 D5
Fiddlers Ferry Rd WA5...23 C8
Fiddler's Ferry Rd
WA8...................13 D1
Fiddlers La CH1..........94 C1
Field Ave CW7..........189 F1
Fieldbank Rd SK11......112 B8
Field Cl
Bollington SK10..........87 F7
Bramhall SK7............35 D4
Northwich CW8..........103 C7
Tarvin CH3.............121 B2
Fielders Cl CH4.........150 A8
Fieldfare Cl
Golborne WA3............3 D8
Warrington WA3...........9 F4
Fieldgate WA8...........22 D8
Field Hey La CH64........43 B1
Fieldhouse Row WA7......49 D7
Fielding Ave SK22........36 E2
Field La
Crewe CW2.............189 E2
Tarvin CH3.............121 B2
Tattenhall CH3.........166 B1
Warrington WA4..........26 C6
Fields Cl ST7..........193 E4
Fields Dr CW11.........175 A5
Fieldsend Dr WN7........4 C8
Fieldside CH6..........145 B6
Fieldside Cl
Bramhall SK7............35 D4
Goostrey CW4...........107 E1
Field Side Cl WA16.......58 A4
Fieldside Ct CH4........139 B4
Fields Rd
Alsager ST7............193 E3
Congleton CW12.........178 F8
Haslington CW1.........191 D4
Fields The CW5.........205 D5
Fields View CY13........228 D1
Fields View Cl CW5......220 B8
Fieldsway WA7...........49 A6
Field View ST8.........179 D1
Fieldview Dr WA2.........8 C1
Field View Dr SK11......112 E5
Fifth Ave
Kidsgrove ST7..........194 F1
 2 Runcorn WA7.........49 F7
Fildes Cl WA5............15 C5
Filkin's La CH3.........119 A1
Fillmore Gr WA8.........13 A1
Finchdale Gdns WA3.......4 B8
Finchett Ct CH1.........118 B3
Finchett Dr CH1........118 B3
Finch La L26............21 B7
Findlay Cl WA12..........2 C2
Finger Post La WA6.....101 A4
Finlan Rd WA8...........22 F7
Finlay Ave WA5..........14 E3
Finlow Hill La SK10......85 E6
Finney Cl SK9...........34 C2
Finney Dr SK9...........34 C2
Finney Gr WA11...........1 F7
FINNEY GREEN..........34 E2
Finney La SK8...........34 E2
Finney's La CW10.......128 B2
Finningley Ct WA2........8 E1
Finsbury Cl WA5..........7 E3
Finsbury Pk WA8.........12 F3
Finsbury Way SK9........34 E2
Finsbury Wlk CW7......149 A8
Fir Ave
Bramhall SK7............35 E8
Halewood L26............21 A8
Firbank CH2.............72 C3
Firbank Cl WA7..........49 D7
Firbeck Cl
Broughton CH4..........139 B3
Congleton CW12.........155 F3
Firbeck Gdns CW2.......189 D4
Fir Cl
Halewood L26............21 A8
Poynton SK12...........36 F3
Tarporley CW6..........146 D2
Fir Ct SK10.............86 E7

Firdale Rd CW8.........103 D7
Firecrest Ct WA1.........16 A3
Firemans Sq CH1.........237 A3
Fir Gr
　Macclesfield SK11.........112 D5
　Warrington WA1.........16 F7
　Weaverham CW8.........102 E8
Fir La CW8.........102 A2
Firman Cl WA5.........15 B8
Fir Rd SK7.........35 E8
Firrview Pk CW5.........217 A3
Firs La WA4.........26 B6
Firs Pottery The*
　WA5.........217 C1
Firs Sch CH2.........118 E5
Fir St
　Irlam M44.........11 D6
　Widnes WA8.........13 C2
First Ave
　Connah's Quay CH5.........93 A2
　Crewe CW1.........190 F2
　Kidsgrove ST7.........194 E1
　Poynton SK12.........36 D1
　Sandbach CW11.........175 A5
First Dig La CW5.........219 C8
Firs The SK9.........60 A5
First Wood St CW5.........204 D5
Firs View WA6.........73 D4
Firth Bvd WA2.........16 C7
Firth Cl CW11.........175 B7
Firth Fields CW9.........103 F2
Firthfields Ct CW9.........103 F2
Firtree Ave WA1.........17 A8
Fir Tree Ave
　Chester CH4.........141 B5
　Golborne WA3.........3 F8
　Knutsford WA16.........82 C8
Firtree Cl
　Barnton CW8.........78 B4
　Winsford CW7.........127 B1
Fir Tree Cl WA4.........26 D1
Fir Tree Cotts CW2.........208 C5
Firtree Gr CH66.........95 A8
Fir Tree La
　Burtonwood WA5.........7 A7
　Chester CH3.........119 E2
　Faddiley CW5.........202 B3
Fir Trees Holiday Pk
　CH1.........117 C2
Fir Tree Wlk WA3.........3 F8
Fir Way CH60.........41 B5
Firwood Rd ST8.........179 E1
Firwood Wlk CW2.........190 C1
Fisher Ave WA2.........8 B2
Fisherfield Dr WA3.........10 A6
Fishermans Cl CW11.........191 F7
Fishers Cl WA7.........117 E4
Fishers Gn CW6.........146 A5
Fishers La CW5.........203 C8
Fisher St WA7.........23 B3
Fishpool Rd GB.........123 F3
Fishwicks Ind Est WA11.........1 F8
Fistral Ave SK8.........34 C8
Fitton's Cl CW5.........217 F5
Fitton St CW9.........80 A2
Fitz Cl SK10.........87 D3
Fitz Cres SK10.........87 D3
Fitzherbert St WA2.........16 C7
Fitzwalter Rd WA1.........17 D7
Fitzwilliam Ave WA1.........112 F3
Fiveashes Cotts SK10.........88 B5
Five Ashes Rd CW4.........141 B5
FIVECROSSES.........74 D5
Fiveways End WA6.........74 C6
Five Ways CH64.........4 C3
Fiveways Par SK7.........36 E8
Fiveways Pk CH64.........41 F3
Flacca Ct CH3.........166 B1
Flag La
　Crewe CW1, CW2.........190 C4
　Neston CH64.........66 F7
　Newhall CW5.........228 D8
Flag La N CH2.........118 E8
Flag La S CW2.........118 E8
Flander Cl WA8.........12 C2
Flashes La CH64.........67 B5
Flash La
　Antrobus SK9.........53 F5
　Bollington SK10.........87 D7
Flat La
　Kelsall CW6.........122 C4
　Sandbach CW11.........175 B6
Flatt La CH65.........70 B5
Flatts La SK23.........64 F4
Flavian Cl CW10.........128 C2
Flavian Ct WA7.........23 E2
Flaxley Cl WA3.........10 A5
Flaxmere Dr CH3.........142 B8
Flaxyards Cl CW9.........146 F2
Fleet La WA9.........1 A2
Fleet St CH65.........70 A5
Fleetwood Cl WA5.........15 B4
Fleetwood Dr WA12.........2 B4
Fleetwood Wlk WA7.........50 C6
Fleming Dr WA2.........8 A6
Fleming St CH65.........70 C6
Flers Ave WA4.........16 C3
Fletcher Ct WA16.........56 F1
Fletcher Gr SK12.........37 F6
Fletcher Gr CW9.........104 C6
Fletcher's Bldgs
　Chester CH1.........237 B2
　[6] Runcorn WA7.........23 F1
Fletchers La WA13.........18 F4
Fletcher's Row [5] WA8.........13 C1
Fletcher St
　Crewe CW1.........190 B5
　Warrington WA4.........16 B3

Fletsand Rd SK9.........60 D6
Flint Cl CH64.........66 E6
Flint Ct CH65.........70 D2
Flint Dr CH64.........66 E6
Flint M44.........11 C6
Flint Mdw CH64.........66 E7
Flint St SK10.........112 E8
Flittogate La WA16.........80 E8
Flixton Dr CW2.........190 A2
FLOOKERSBROOK.........118 E4
Florence St WA4.........16 D3
Florida Cl WA5.........15 C7
Flour Mill Way CW1.........191 A3
Flowcrete Bsns Pk
　CW11.........152 C1
Flowerscroft CW5.........205 A4
Flowers La CW1.........172 E1
Flower St CW8.........103 E7
Fluin La WA6.........74 C8
Flying Fields Dr SK11.........112 A5
Foden Ave ST7.........194 A3
Foden La
　Alderley Edge SK9.........59 C1
　Bramhall SK7.........35 D3
Foden St SK10.........87 D1
Fodens Terr CW11.........175 A6
Foden Wlk [7] SK9.........34 D2
Fog Cotts CW3.........221 E4
Fogg's La CW9, WA4.........53 A6
Fold La
　Biddulph ST8.........179 E4
　Bosley SK11.........135 D2
Folds La SK23.........65 F3
Folds The CH63.........42 A6
Fold The SK10.........87 A8
Foley Wlk M22.........33 E8
Fol Hollow CW12.........156 B1
Folkestone Cl SK10.........87 B2
Folkstone Way WA7.........50 C7
Folly La WA5.........15 F7
Forbes Cl WA3.........9 E3
Forbes Pk SK7.........35 D7
Ford Cl CW1.........190 B5
Ford Ct CW7.........149 C6
Fordington Rd WA5.........15 B5
Ford La
　Crewe CW1.........190 B6
　Tattenhall CH3.........166 F4
Ford's La SK7.........35 D6
Ford St WA1.........16 D6
Foregate St CH1.........237 B2
Foreland Cl WA5.........14 C7
Forest Ave CW4.........107 C1
Forest Cl
　Cuddington CW8.........101 F3
　Rainow SK10.........88 E5
Forest Dr
　Broughton CH4.........139 C3
　Langley SK11.........113 C4
Forester Ave WA16.........57 C2
Foresters Cl WA5.........101 A6
Forest Gate Com Prim Sch
　M31.........11 D3
Forest Gate La CW6.........122 E7
Forest Gdns M31.........11 D3
Forest Ho SK10.........87 F2
Forest La WA6.........100 A6
Forest Pl [3] CW9.........79 A1
Forest Rd
　Cuddington CW8.........101 F2
　Delamere CW6.........124 B1
　Ellesmere Port CH66.........69 E7
　Heswall CH60.........41 A8
　Macclesfield SK11.........113 C6
　Tarporley CW6.........146 D3
　Winsford CW7.........149 B8
Forest Road Pk CW8.........101 E2
Forest St
　Chester CH1.........237 C2
　Weaverham CW8.........102 C8
Forest Wlk [5] WA7.........49 F7
Forge Cl
　Cronton WA8.........12 C5
　Warren SK11.........111 D2
Forge Fields CW11.........174 F3
Forge La
　Congleton CW12.........156 B3
　Norton in Hales TF9.........236 C1
Forge Mill La WA10.........151 C1
Forge Rd
　Ellesmere Port CH66.........69 C6
　Warrington WA5.........14 F5
　Whaley Bridge SK23.........65 F7
Forge Sh Ctr The WA4.........16 C1
Forge St CW1.........190 D4
Forge Way CH4.........140 F4
Formby Cl WA5.........14 F4
Formby Dr SK8.........34 B8
Forrest Way WA5.........15 D3
Forshaw's La WA4.........6 E8
Forshaw St WA2.........16 C7
Forster Ave WA8.........102 E8
Forster St WA2.........16 B7
Forsythia Wlk [2] M31.........11 E1
Forty Acre La CW4,.........131 D6
Forum The CH1.........237 A2
Forwood Rd CH62.........43 D8
Fossa Cl CW10.........128 C2
Foster Ct CW10.........157 A5
Foster St WA8.........13 B1
Fothergill St WA1.........16 D7
Fotheringay Ct [3]
　CH65.........70 D2
Foulkes Ave CW1.........189 F6
Foundry Bank CW12.........156 E3
Foundry Ct [1] SK22.........39 C7

Foundry Ind Est WA8.........23 B7
Foundry La
　Sandbach CW11.........174 D7
　Scholar Green ST7.........194 F7
　Widnes WA8.........22 C5
Foundry St
　Bollington SK10.........88 B8
　Newton-le-W WA12.........2 B3
　Warrington WA2.........16 B6
Fountain Cl
　Biddulph ST8.........179 D1
　Davenham CW9.........103 F2
　[2] Winsford CW7.........126 D1
Fountain Ho SK10.........112 E8
Fountain La
　Davenham CW9.........103 F2
　Frodsham WA6.........74 B8
Fountain Pl WA12.........36 D4
Fountains Ave WA11.........1 F7
Fountains Cl
　Middlewich CW10.........128 B1
　Runcorn WA7.........50 C5
Fountain Sq SK10.........38 D6
Fountains Rd SK8.........35 C6
Fountains Wlk WA3.........74 B8
Fouracres Cl CW12.........156 D2
　Macclesfield SK10.........112 E8
Fountains Wlk WA3.........74 B8
FOURLANE-ENDS.........63 A8
FOUR LANE ENDS.........168 D7
Four Lane Ends
　Alvanley WA6.........74 B1
　Warrington WA3.........9 D3
Four Lanes Ct [3]
　CW7.........149 B8
FOURLANES END.........176 E4
Four Lanes End
　Betley CW3.........207 F2
　Thornton Hough CH63.........42 D5
Fourseasons Cl CW2.........206 B8
Fourth Ave
　Connah's Quay CH5.........92 E2
　Crewe CW1.........190 F1
　Kidsgrove ST7.........194 F1
　[1] Runcorn WA7.........49 F7
Fourways Tech Pk
　CW11.........176 E4
Fowey Cl SK10.........86 D1
Fowler Rd CH1.........117 D4
Fowlers Bench La
　CH3.........184 C5
Fowler St SK10.........87 D1
FOWLEY COMMON.........5 B5
Fowley Common La
　WA3.........5 C5
Foxall Way CH66.........69 D2
Fox Bank Cl WA8.........12 F4
Fox Bench Cl SK7.........35 C6
Foxcote WA8.........12 B2
Foxcote Cl CH1.........117 D5
Fox Cover CW3.........119 F5
Fox Cover Rd CH60.........41 D7
Foxcovert La WA16.........106 E7
Fox Covert La
　Hoole Bank CH2.........119 B8
　Picton CH2.........96 A1
Fox Covert Way CW1.........173 A1
Foxdale Ct WA4.........26 D7
Foxdene CH65.........69 D5
Foxendale Cl CW8.........103 D7
Foxes Fold CW8.........78 E1
Foxes Hey WA6.........101 D5
Foxes Hollow CW1.........190 E7
Foxes Wlk WA4.........142 A7
Foxfield Cl WA2.........8 F3
Foxfield La CW7.........126 A1
Fox Gdns
　Lymm WA13.........18 C4
　Talke ST7.........210 D8
Foxglove Cl
　Bollington SK10.........88 C8
　[2] Golborne WA3.........3 D8
　Huntington CH3.........142 A6
　Wistaston CW2.........206 B7
Foxglove Ct WA6.........74 D8
Foxglove Dell WA6.........73 D2
Foxglove Way CH64.........66 E5
Foxglove Wlk M31.........11 F2
Fox Gr WA16.........57 F2
Fox Hill WA6.........122 D4
Foxhill Cl CW8.........102 A2
Foxhill Ct WA6.........146 E1
Foxhill Gr WA6.........73 D4
Foxhills Cl WA4.........26 D3
Foxholme Ct WA1.........16 A3
Foxhunter Cl CH3.........121 F7
Fox La
　Clutton CH3.........182 D1
　Waverton CH3.........143 B5
Foxlea CW9.........78 C7
Fox Lea CH1.........117 A8
FOXLEY.........209 D7
Foxley Cl WA13.........19 A2
Foxley Hall Mews
　WA13.........19 A2
Foxley Heath WA8.........22 E8
Fox's Dr CH5.........116 A6
Fox St
　Congleton CW12.........156 F3
　Runcorn WA7.........22 F2
　Warrington WA5.........15 E5
Foxwist Cl CH2.........237 B4
Foxwist Gn CW8.........125 E6
FOXWIST GREEN.........125 F6
Foxwood Dr WA16.........108 A8

Fox Wood Specl Sch
　WA3.........9 E3
Francesca Ct CH1.........237 B2
Frances St
　Crewe CW2.........190 D2
　Irlam M44.........11 E5
　Macclesfield SK11.........112 B8
Francis Cl SK12.........36 D4
Francis Ct CH1.........237 C3
Francis La
　Holt LL13.........196 D7
　Holt, Ridleywood LL13.........196 B6
Francis Rd
　Frodsham WA6.........49 C1
　Irlam M44.........11 F8
　Warrington WA4.........16 B1
Francis St CH1.........237 C3
FRANDLEY.........53 A3
Frank Bott Ave CW1.........190 A7
Franklin Cl
　Macclesfield SK11.........112 B5
　Warrington WA5.........15 C8
　Winsford CW7.........149 B8
Franklyn Ave CW2.........190 B3
Frank Perkins Way
　M44.........11 F7
Frank St WA8.........13 C1
Frank Webb Ave CW1.........190 A6
Frappel Cl WA2.........16 B6
Fraser Ct CH4.........141 D7
Fraser Rd WA3.........14 D6
Frawley Ave WA2.........2 C5
Freckleton Cl WA5.........15 B4
Frederick St
　Warrington WA4.........16 E3
　Widnes WA8.........23 B8
Frederick Terr WA8.........22 A4
Fredric Pl WA7.........23 B3
Freedom Dr ST7.........195 E3
Free Green La WA16.........107 A8
Freeport Shopping Mall
　ST7.........210 C3
French La CW5.........218 C5
French Lane End
　CW5.........218 E5
French St WA8.........13 D1
Freshfield SK8.........34 B8
Freshfield Dr SK10.........87 C3
Freshfields
　Comberbach CW9.........78 C7
　Knutsford WA16.........56 E3
　Wistaston CW2.........206 A7
Freshfields Dr WA2.........9 C1
Freshmeadow La WA6.........73 B2
Freshwater Ct WA6.........73 B2
Freshwater Dr CW2.........221 C8
Freshwater View
　CW8.........103 F8
Friars Ave WA5.........14 E5
Friars Cl
　Rainow SK10.........88 D5
　Wistaston CW2.........205 F8
Friar's Ct SK9.........59 E8
Friar's Ct [1] WA1.........16 B4
Friars Gate
　Chester CH1.........237 B2
　Warrington WA1.........16 B4
Friars La WA1.........16 B4
Friars Way SK10.........86 F2
Frida Cres CW9.........103 E6
Friends La WA5.........14 D6
Friesian Gdns ST5.........210 C2
Frith Ave CW9.........123 D8
Frith La CW9.........123 D8
Frith Terr SK11.........112 D4
Frobisher Cl WA5.........15 D8
Frobisher Rd CH64.........66 E8
Froda Ave WA6.........74 B7
FRODSHAM.........74 C7
Frodsham Bsns Ctr
　WA6.........49 C1
Frodsham CE Prim Sch
　WA6.........74 C7
Frodsham Manor House
　Prim Sch WA6.........49 C1
FRODSHAM MARSH.........48 E2
Frodsham Rd WA6.........73 D1
Frodsham Sq CH1.........237 B3
Frodsham St
　Chester CH1.........237 B3
　Frodsham Sta WA6.........74 B8
　Warrington WA2, WA5.........34 E4
Frodsham Weaver Vale
　Prim Sch WA6.........49 C2
Froghall La
　High Legh WA16.........29 D7
　High Legh WA16.........29 E6
　Warrington WA2, WA5.........15 F5
Frog La
　Holt LL13.........196 D8
　Milton Green CH3.........165 E2
　Pickmere WA16.........55 B1
　Worthenbury LL13,
　　SY14.........211 B1
　Worthenbury SY14.........211 C2
Frome Ct CH65.........70 B7
Frost St CW1.........175 C6
Frosts Mews CH65.........70 B6
Fryer Rd CW9.........80 A3
Fryer St [6] WA7.........23 A3
Fuchsia Cl CH66.........69 F1
Fulbeck WA8.........12 B2
Fulbeck Cl CW2.........206 B8
Fulbeck Ave WA5.........35 A6
Fuller Dr CW2.........206 B7
FULLER'S MOOR.........183 D1
Fullerton Rd CW8.........103 A4
Fulmar Cl SK12.........36 A4

Fulmards Cl SK9.........60 C7
Fulshaw Ave SK9.........60 A6
Fulshaw Cross SK9.........60 A5
Fulshaw Ct SK9.........60 B5
FULSHAW PARK.........60 B5
Fulshaw Pk SK9.........60 A5
Fulshaw Pk S SK9.........60 A4
Fulton Gr CW9.........103 F2
Fulwood Gdns CH66.........69 C6
Fulwood Mews CH66.........69 C6
Fulwood Rd
　Ellesmere Port CH66.........69 C5
　Golborne WA3.........3 E7
Furber St CW1.........190 C5
Furne Rd CH1.........117 E4
Furness Cl
　Holmes Chapel CW4.........130 A3
　Poynton SK12.........36 D4
　Winsford CW7.........149 B8
Furness Ct WA7.........24 F4
Furness Lodge Cl
　SK23.........39 D4
Furness Rd SK8.........35 C6
FURNESS VALE.........39 C3
Furness Vale Bsns Ctr
　SK23.........39 D4
Furness Vale Prim Sch
　SK23.........39 D3
Furnival St SK23.........39 D4
Furnival St CW2.........190 C2
Furrocks Cl CH64.........66 F5
Furrocks La CH64.........66 F5
Furrows The CH66.........94 E8
Fylde Ave SK8.........34 C8
Fytton Cl SK11.........111 D1

G

Gable Ave SK9.........60 A7
Gable Ct [5] CW5.........204 E6
Gables Cl WA2.........8 F3
Gables La WA12.........2 B3
Gables The ST7.........193 C3
Gabriel Bank CW8.........76 A1
Gadbrook Bsns Ctr
　CW9.........104 D5
Gadbrook Pk CW9.........104 D6
Gadbrook Rd CW9.........104 D6
Gail Cl SK9.........60 B2
Gainford Cl WA8.........12 C3
Gainsborough Ct [5].........60 D8
Gainsborough Ct WA5.........15 C8
Gainsborough Prim Sch
　CW2.........190 B2
Gainsborough Rd
　Crewe CW2.........190 B3
　Warrington WA4.........16 B2
Gairloch Cl WA2.........8 F4
Gaisgill Ct WA8.........12 C1
Galbraith Cl CW12.........156 D2
Gale Ave WA5.........7 F1
Galion Way WA8.........12 F4
GALLANTRY BANK.........200 B8
Galleys Bank ST7.........195 B3
Gallimore Ho ST7.........210 D8
Galloway Cl
　Holmes Chapel CW4.........130 C2
　Middlewich CW10.........128 E2
Galloway Gn CW2.........156 C5
Gallowsclough La
　WA6.........100 F4
Galway Ave WA8.........12 E3
Galway Gr CW2.........206 B4
Game St CW11.........175 A3
Gamul Pl CH1.........237 B1
Ganton Cl WA8.........13 A4
Garden Cl SK10.........87 E1
Garden Ct CH1.........237 A3
Garden La
　Chester CH1.........237 A3
　Harthill CH3.........183 E3
Garden Rd WA16.........56 F3
Garden St
　Bollington SK10.........87 F8
　Congleton CW12.........156 C3
　Macclesfield SK10.........87 E1
Gardens The
　Holt LL13.........180 E1
　Lawton-gate ST7.........194 C4
　Sandbach CW11.........175 B6
Garden Terr
　Chester, Boughton
　　CH2.........118 F2
　Chester CH1.........237 A3
Garden Wlk [8] M31.........11 E3
Gardiner Ave WA11.........1 C6
Garfit St CW10.........128 C2
Garner St WA2.........16 C7
Garnett Ave WA4.........17 A4
Garnett Cl CW5.........204 F4
Garnetts La WA8.........22 A3
Garrett Field WA3.........9 D3
Garrigill Cl WA8.........13 C5
Garsdale Cl WA5.........14 F7
Garside Ave WA3.........3 F8
Garth Dr CH2.........118 C5
Garth Hts CH65.........60 C7
Garth Rd CH65.........71 A5
Garton Dr WA3.........3 E8
Garven Pl WA1.........16 A5
Garwood Cl WA5.........15 C8

Gaskell Ave
  Knutsford WA16 . . . . . 56 F2
  Warrington WA4 . . . . . 17 A3
Gaskell St WA4 . . . . . 16 C1
Gas Rd SK11 . . . . . 112 D8
Gas Works Ind Est ST7 . . . . . 194 E2
Gatcombe Mews 🔲 SK9 . . . . . 60 A6
Gateacre Ct CH66 . . . . . 69 F8
Gatefield St WA1 . . . . . 190 C4
Gatehouse The 🔲 CW5 . . . . . 204 F5
Gateley Cl WA4 . . . . . 17 E3
GATESHEATH 165 E5
Gatesheath Dr CH2 . . . . . 118 E7
Gatesheath La CH3 . . . . . 165 F5
Gatewarth Ind Est WA5 . . . . . 15 D3
Gate Warth St WA5 . . . . . 15 D4
Gateway
  Crewe CW1 . . . . . 190 F2
  Newcastle-u-Lyme ST5 . . . . . 210 D2
Gateway Trad Pk WA5 . . . . . 16 A7
Gathurst Ct WA8 . . . . . 22 D8
Gauntlet Birds of Prey Pk* WA16 . . . . . 56 D5
GAUNTONS BANK 215 E4
Gauntons Bank SY13 . . . . . 215 E3
Gaunts Way WA7 . . . . . 49 E6
Gavin Rd WA8 . . . . . 22 B7
Gaw End La SK11 . . . . . 112 C2
Gawer Pk CH2 . . . . . 118 C4
GAWSWORTH 135 E8
Gawsworth Ave CW2 . . . . . 189 F3
Gawsworth Cl
  Alsager ST7 . . . . . 193 C3
  Bramhall SK7 . . . . . 35 E8
  Holmes Chapel CW4 . . . . . 130 B3
  Northwich CW9 . . . . . 104 A4
  Poynton SK12 . . . . . 36 F2
Gawsworth Ct WA3 . . . . . 9 F5
Gawsworth Dr CW11 . . . . . 175 C7
Gawsworth Hall* SK11 . . . . . 134 E8
Gawsworth Prim Sch SK11 . . . . . 111 D2
Gawsworth Rd
  Ellesmere Port CH66 . . . . . 69 E5
  Macclesfield SK11 . . . . . 111 D5
Gawsworth Way SK9 . . . . . 34 E4
Gayhurst Ave WA2 . . . . . 8 F2
Gaymoore Cl CH2 . . . . . 237 A4
Gaynor Ave WA11 . . . . . 1 F7
GAYTON 41 B6
Gayton Cl CH2 . . . . . 118 E5
Gayton Farm Rd CH60 . . . . . 41 A5
Gayton La CH60 . . . . . 41 B6
Gayton Mill Cl CH60 . . . . . 41 B7
Gayton Parkway CH60 . . . . . 41 A5
Gayton Prim Sch CH60 . . . . . 41 A6
Gayton Rd CH60 . . . . . 41 A6
Gelli Dderw/Oak Gr CH4 . . . . . 140 D5
GEMINI 7 D3
Gemini Bsns Pk WA5 . . . . . 7 E3
Gemmull Cl CW3 . . . . . 229 F4
General St WA1 . . . . . 16 C5
Genesis Ctr The WA3 . . . . . 9 E5
Geneva Rd CW7 . . . . . 126 C1
Geo Hampson's Bldgs WA3 . . . . . 5 C8
George Bates Cl ST7 . . . . . 193 C3
George Cl WA6 . . . . . 73 A2
George Ho CW5 . . . . . 204 E7
George Kenyon Mews CH4 . . . . . 140 E6
George Rd WA5 . . . . . 15 C4
George St W SK11 . . . . . 112 C8
George's Cl SK12 . . . . . 36 E3
Georges Cres WA4 . . . . . 17 C1
George's Ct 🔲 SK10 . . . . . 112 C8
George's La CW9 . . . . . 54 D1
George's Prec WA5 . . . . . 14 D6
George's Rd E SK12 . . . . . 36 E3
George's Rd W SK12 . . . . . 36 E3
George St
  Alderley Edge SK9 . . . . . 60 A1
  Audley ST7 . . . . . 209 D1
  Barnton CW8 . . . . . 78 B3
  Chester CH1 . . . . . 237 A3
  Ellesmere Port CH65 . . . . . 70 C7
  Knutsford WA16 . . . . . 57 A2
  Macclesfield SK11 . . . . . 112 D7
  Newton-le-W WA12 . . . . . 2 A4
  Sandbach CW11 . . . . . 174 E8
  Whaley Bridge SK23 . . . . . 65 E7
  Winsford CW7 . . . . . 126 E1
Georges Way ST7 . . . . . 209 D2
George's Wlk CW10 . . . . . 175 B6
George VI Ave CW10 . . . . . 151 D6
George VI Ct CW10 . . . . . 151 D6
Georgia Pl WA5 . . . . . 15 C7
Gerard Dr CW5 . . . . . 204 C4
Gerosa Ave WA2 . . . . . 8 B8
Gerrard Ave
  Ellesmere Port CH66 . . . . . 69 C4
  Warrington WA5 . . . . . 15 F7
Gerrard Dr CW8 . . . . . 77 D1
Gerrard Rd WA3 . . . . . 9 A7
Gerrards Ave CH3 . . . . . 119 A1
Gerrard St WA8 . . . . . 23 B8
Giantswood La
  Congleton CW12 . . . . . 156 C6
  Marton CW12 . . . . . 132 F1

GIBB HILL 53 D1
Gibb Hill CW9 . . . . . 53 D1
Gibbon Dr CW9 . . . . . 80 B3
Gibson Cl CW5 . . . . . 204 D6
Gibson Cres CW11 . . . . . 174 D6
Gibson Cl Trad Est CH65 . . . . . 70 C8
Gibson St
  Warrington, Howley WA1 . . . . . 16 C5
  Warrington, Stockton Heath WA4 . . . . . 16 D1
Gigg La
  Moore WA4 . . . . . 25 B5
  Warrington WA4 . . . . . 17 E3
Gig La WA1 . . . . . 17 E8
Gilbert Cl 🔲 ST7 . . . . . 195 A2
Gilbert Ct CH3 . . . . . 4 F3
Gilbert Ho WA7 . . . . . 22 E3
Gilchrist Ave SK11 . . . . . 111 E7
Gilchrist Rd WA4 . . . . . 11 F6
Gilderdale Cl WA3 . . . . . 10 B5
Gillan Cl WA7 . . . . . 50 C5
GILLBENT 34 F6
Gillbent Rd SK8 . . . . . 35 A7
Gillow Cl CW1 . . . . . 190 A8
GILLOW HEATH 179 C2
Giltbrook Cl WA8 . . . . . 12 F3
Gilwell Cl WA4 . . . . . 17 C2
Gilwern Cl CH2 . . . . . 118 C4
GINCLOUGH 88 F6
Gingerbread La CW5 . . . . . 205 A5
Gipsy Cnr SY13 . . . . . 224 E2
Girton Cl CH65 . . . . . 70 D4
Girton Rd CH65 . . . . . 70 D4
Girvin Dr CH64 . . . . . 66 F6
Glade Dr CH66 . . . . . 68 F6
Gladewood Cl 🔲 SK9 . . . . . 60 C8
Gladstone Ave CH1 . . . . . 118 B2
Gladstone Mews CW2 . . . . . 16 A6
Gladstone Rd
  Broughton CH4 . . . . . 139 B3
  Chester CH1 . . . . . 118 B3
  Neston CH64 . . . . . 66 E8
Gladstone St
  Crewe CW1 . . . . . 190 C4
  Northwich CW8 . . . . . 103 E7
  Warrington WA2 . . . . . 16 A6
  🔲 Widnes WA8 . . . . . 23 B8
  Wilmslow CW5 . . . . . 205 D6
  Winsford CW7 . . . . . 149 D8
Gladstone Way WA12 . . . . . 2 B4
Glaisdale Cl CW2 . . . . . 206 A6
Glamis Cl
  Chester CH3 . . . . . 119 A2
  Wistaston CW2 . . . . . 206 A8
Glan Aber Dr CH4 . . . . . 141 A7
Glan Aber Pk CH4 . . . . . 140 F7
Glandon Dr SK8 . . . . . 35 C8
Glastonbury Ave
  Cheadle SK8 . . . . . 35 C6
  Chester CH2 . . . . . 118 F7
  Golborne WA3 . . . . . 3 A8
Glastonbury Cl WA7 . . . . . 24 F3
Glastonbury Dr
  Middlewich CW10 . . . . . 128 B1
  Poynton SK12 . . . . . 36 D5
Glastonbury Mews WA4 . . . . . 16 E2
GLAZEBROOK 11 B6
Glazebrook La WA3 . . . . . 11 B5
Glazebrook St WA1 . . . . . 16 D6
Glazebrook Sta WA3 . . . . . 11 A5
GLAZEBURY 5 B7
Glazebury CE Prim Sch WA3 . . . . . 5 C7
Glaziers La WA3 . . . . . 4 D2
Gleadmere WA8 . . . . . 12 C2
GLEADSMOSS 132 B6
Gleaner Cl WA7 . . . . . 22 F3
Gleave Ave SK10 . . . . . 88 B8
Gleave Rd
  Burtonwood WA5 . . . . . 6 F6
  Weaverham CW8 . . . . . 77 D1
Glebe Ave WA4 . . . . . 17 C1
Glebe Cl CW5 . . . . . 220 A8
Glebecroft Ave CH2 . . . . . 72 A3
Glebe Ct ST7 . . . . . 194 D2
Glebe Farm Mews CH2 . . . . . 71 E2
Glebe Green Dr CW7 . . . . . 149 C6
Glebe La WA8 . . . . . 13 B5
Glebeland WA3 . . . . . 4 E2
Glebelands Rd WA16 . . . . . 57 A1
Glebe Mdws CW7 . . . . . 96 F1
Glebe Rd CW8 . . . . . 102 A4
Glebe St ST7 . . . . . 194 D2
Glebe The WA7 . . . . . 23 C1
Glebeway Rd CH65 . . . . . 70 F5
Gleggs Cl CH3 . . . . . 142 B7
Glegg St SK11 . . . . . 112 C7
Glenathol Rd CH66 . . . . . 69 C4
Glenbourne Pk SK7 . . . . . 35 D5
Glenburn Ave CH62 . . . . . 43 E4
Glen Cl WA3 . . . . . 3 D8
Glencoe Cl CW4 . . . . . 130 C2
Glencoe Rd CH66 . . . . . 69 E3
Glencourse Rd WA8 . . . . . 13 A5
Glendale Ave
  Chester CH3 . . . . . 72 A3
  Sandycroft CH5 . . . . . 116 A3
Glendale Bsns Pk CH5 . . . . . 116 A3
Glendale Cl
  Buerton CW3 . . . . . 230 F4
  Crewe CW2 . . . . . 189 D3
Glendale Pk CH5 . . . . . 116 A3
Glendene Ave SK7 . . . . . 35 D5

Glendyke Rd CH66 . . . . . 69 C4
Gleneagles Cl
  Bramhall SK7 . . . . . 36 A7
  Chester CH3 . . . . . 119 B3
  Golborne WA3 . . . . . 3 F7
  Wilmslow SK9 . . . . . 60 D8
Gleneagles Dr
  Haydock WA11 . . . . . 1 A5
  Holmes Chapel CW4 . . . . . 130 B2
  Macclesfield SK10 . . . . . 87 C4
  Widnes WA8 . . . . . 13 B5
  Winsford CW7 . . . . . 126 C2
Gleneagles Rd CH66 . . . . . 69 C4
Glenesk Rd CH66 . . . . . 69 C4
Glenfield Dr SK12 . . . . . 36 D3
Glenholme Rd SK7 . . . . . 35 D7
Glenmaye Rd CH66 . . . . . 69 C4
Glenn Pl WA8 . . . . . 12 E1
Glenorchy Cl CW4 . . . . . 130 C2
Glen Rd CH66 . . . . . 69 C4
Glenside CH1 . . . . . 117 D5
Glenside Dr SK9 . . . . . 60 C6
Glen The
  Blacon CH1 . . . . . 117 C6
  Runcorn WA7 . . . . . 49 F5
Glenton Pk CH64 . . . . . 66 F6
Glenville Cl WA7 . . . . . 49 B6
Glenwood WA7 . . . . . 24 C1
Glenwood Cl 🔲 CH66 . . . . . 69 C6
Glenwood Gdns CH66 . . . . . 69 C6
Glenwood Rd CH66 . . . . . 69 C6
Gleyve WA16 . . . . . 29 C5
Gloucester Ave 🔲 3 . . . . . 3 B8
Gloucester Cl
  Ellesmere Port CH66 . . . . . 94 E8
  Macclesfield SK10 . . . . . 87 E4
  Warrington WA1 . . . . . 17 D7
Gloucester Ho 🔲 CH1 . . . . . 237 C3
Gloucester Rd
  Gatley SK8 . . . . . 34 C7
  Kidsgrove ST7 . . . . . 195 A3
  Knutsford WA16 . . . . . 81 F8
  Poynton SK12 . . . . . 36 D3
  Widnes WA8 . . . . . 13 B3
Gloucester St CH1 . . . . . 237 B4
Glover Rd WA3 . . . . . 9 C4
Glovers Loom CH3 . . . . . 142 B7
Glover St
  Crewe CW1 . . . . . 190 A5
  Newton-le-W WA12 . . . . . 2 C3
Gloverstone Ct CH1 . . . . . 237 B1
Glyn Ave CH62 . . . . . 43 D8
Glyn Garth CH1 . . . . . 117 D3
Go Ape Delamere* 100 B2
Goathland Way CW11 . . . . . 112 D6
Goddard Ct 🔲 CW1 . . . . . 190 B5
Goddard Rd WA7 . . . . . 23 E3
Goddard St CW1 . . . . . 190 B5
Godfrey St WA2 . . . . . 16 D7
Godscroft La WA6 . . . . . 73 E6
Godshill Cl WA5 . . . . . 14 C8
Godstall La CH1 . . . . . 237 B2
Godstow WA7 . . . . . 24 E4
Godward Rd SK22 . . . . . 39 B8
GOLBORNE 3 B7
Golborne Dale Rd WA3, WA12 . . . . . 3 A8
Golborne Jun & Inf Sch WA3 . . . . . 3 A8
Golborne La WA16 . . . . . 28 F3
Golborne Rd
  Golborne WA3 . . . . . 3 C8
  Winwick WA12, WA2 . . . . . 8 A7
Golborne St WA12 . . . . . 2 E4
Goldcrest Cl
  Runcorn WA7 . . . . . 49 F5
  Winsford CW7 . . . . . 149 C5
Golden Hill CW2 . . . . . 207 E3
Golden Sq WA1 . . . . . 16 B5
Goldfinch Cl SK10 . . . . . 156 E1
Goldfinch Dr ST7 . . . . . 193 B3
Goldfinch La WA3 . . . . . 9 E4
Goldfinch Rd WA3 . . . . . 195 F1
Goldford La SY14 . . . . . 199 F6
Goldsmith Dr CW11 . . . . . 174 D6
Gold Triangle Complex WA8 . . . . . 22 C5
Golftyn Dr CH5 . . . . . 91 C1
Golftyn La CH5 . . . . . 91 C1
GOLLY 161 B1
Gongar La
  Ashton Hayes CH3 . . . . . 121 E8
  Mouldsworth CH3 . . . . . 98 E1
Gonsley Ct CH2 . . . . . 237 B4
Gonville Ave SK11 . . . . . 112 F3
Gooch Dr WA12 . . . . . 2 D2
Goodall's Cnr CW2 . . . . . 206 C3
Goodall St SK11 . . . . . 112 E7
Goode Way CW7 . . . . . 190 D1
Goodier Ct WA7 . . . . . 49 C7
Goodrington Rd SK9 . . . . . 34 E3
Goodwin Cres CW2 . . . . . 206 C4
Goodwood Cl
  Barnton CW8 . . . . . 78 B3
  Chester CH2 . . . . . 118 B2
Goodwood Ct ST7 . . . . . 193 F6
Goodwood Gr CH66 . . . . . 69 D3
Goodwood Rise CW10 . . . . . 128 A2
Gooseberry La
  Kelsall CH3 . . . . . 122 E3
  Runcorn WA7 . . . . . 24 D1
Goosebrook La CW9 . . . . . 78 D8
Goosebrook La WA4, CW9 . . . . . 52 F2

Goose La WA4 . . . . . 26 A2
Goostrey Cl SK9 . . . . . 34 E1
GOOSTREY 107 D1
Goostrey Com Prim Sch CW4 . . . . . 130 F8
Goostrey Com Prim Sch (The Annexe) CW4 . . . . . 107 F1
Goostrey Ct 🔲 CW12 . . . . . 156 F3
Goostrey Dr
  Goostrey CW4 . . . . . 130 B8
  Macclesfield SK10 . . . . . 131 A6
Goostrey Sta CW4 . . . . . 131 A8
Goostry La WA16 . . . . . 108 A7
Gordale Cl
  Congleton CW12 . . . . . 157 A5
  Northwich CW8 . . . . . 103 D8
  Warrington WA5 . . . . . 14 F7
  Winnington CW8 . . . . . 78 D1
Gordon Ave
  Bebington CH62 . . . . . 43 E7
  Haydock WA11 . . . . . 1 F7
  Warrington WA1 . . . . . 17 B7
Gordon La CH1 . . . . . 95 B5
Gore La SK9 . . . . . 59 C3
Gorran Haven WA7 . . . . . 50 C5
Gorse Bank Rd WA13 . . . . . 32 C7
Gorse Cl CH66 . . . . . 94 E8
GORSE COVERT 10 A5
Gorse Covert CW9 . . . . . 79 C3
Gorse Covert Prim Sch WA3 . . . . . 10 B6
Gorse Covert Rd WA3 . . . . . 10 B6
Gorsefield CH3 . . . . . 166 A1
Gorsefield Ave CH62 . . . . . 43 D5
Gorsefield Cl CH62 . . . . . 43 D5
Gorsehill Rd SK9 . . . . . 60 F8
Gorse Hill Hostel CH1 . . . . . 117 E3
Gorse La CW12 . . . . . 178 D5
Gorselands SK8 . . . . . 35 B5
Gorse Sq WA3 . . . . . 11 D3
Gorse Stacks CH1 . . . . . 237 B3
Gorse The WA14 . . . . . 31 B8
Gorse Way CH3 . . . . . 142 A5
Gorsewood Prim Sch WA7 . . . . . 50 D7
Gorsewood Rd WA7 . . . . . 50 D6
GORSEY BANK 231 F2
Gorsey Bank Cres CW5 . . . . . 220 A8
Gorsey Bank Prim Sch SK9 . . . . . 59 F7
Gorsey La
  Partington WA13 . . . . . 20 B7
  St Helens WA5, WA9 . . . . . 6 C5
  Warrington WA1, WA2 . . . . . 16 D7
  Widnes WA8 . . . . . 13 C4
Gorsey Rd SK9 . . . . . 59 F8
Gorseywell La WA7 . . . . . 50 F6
Gorsley Cl CW10 . . . . . 151 C6
GORSTAGE 102 C6
Gorstage La CW8 . . . . . 102 C7
GORSTELLA 140 A1
Gorsthills Com Prim Sch CH66 . . . . . 69 C3
Gorstons La CH64 . . . . . 67 A6
Gorston Wlk M22 . . . . . 33 C8
GORSTYHILL 207 E2
Gorsty Hill Cl CW7 . . . . . 207 F2
Gorsty Hill Ct CW7 . . . . . 207 F2
Gosberryhole La CW12 . . . . . 158 A2
Gosforth Cl WA7 . . . . . 49 E7
Gosforth Pl CH2 . . . . . 118 F3
GOSLAND GREEN 169 B1
Gosling Cl WA4 . . . . . 26 A1
Gosling Rd WA3 . . . . . 9 F3
Gosling Way CW12 . . . . . 156 A3
Gosport Cl WA7 . . . . . 50 D7
Goss St CH1 . . . . . 237 A2
Gough Ave WA2 . . . . . 8 B2
Gough's La WA16 . . . . . 82 C7
Goulden St
  Crewe CW1 . . . . . 190 A5
  Warrington WA5 . . . . . 15 E6
Goulders Ct WA7 . . . . . 50 B6
GOWHOLE 39 E4
Gowy Cl
  Alsager ST7 . . . . . 192 F3
  Handforth SK9 . . . . . 34 E1
  Sandbach CW11 . . . . . 174 E8
Gowy Cres CW11 . . . . . 121 B2
Gowy Ct
  Calveley CW6 . . . . . 169 E2
  Ellesmere Port CH66 . . . . . 69 E8
Gowy Rd CH2 . . . . . 96 F1
Gowy Wlk CW7 . . . . . 127 A3
Goyt Forest Walks* 115 E7
Goyt Pl SK23 . . . . . 65 E7
Goyt Rd
  Disley SK12 . . . . . 38 D5
  Horwich End SK23 . . . . . 65 E6
  New Mills SK22 . . . . . 39 D6
Goyt's La SK17 . . . . . 90 F2
Goyt View Ind Est SK23 . . . . . 39 D4
Goyt Way SK22 . . . . . 39 B6
Grace Ave WA3 . . . . . 16 B8
Grace Cl CW1 . . . . . 191 C4
Gradbach Mill (YH)* SK17 . . . . . 138 A1
GRADELEY GREEN 202 F5
Grafton Mews CW2 . . . . . 237 B4
Grafton Rd CH65 . . . . . 70 C7
Grafton St
  Newton-le-W WA12 . . . . . 2 B3
  Warrington WA5 . . . . . 15 E6

Graham Ave CH66 . . . . . 69 D5
Graham Cl WA8 . . . . . 12 C1
Graham Cres M44 . . . . . 11 C3
Graham Dr
  Disley SK12 . . . . . 38 C6
  Halewood L26 . . . . . 21 A8
Graham Rd
  Blacon CH1 . . . . . 117 F3
  Widnes WA8 . . . . . 22 C8
Grainger's Rd CW9 . . . . . 103 F5
Grammar School Ct 16 F3
Grammar School Rd
  Lymm WA13 . . . . . 18 F2
  Warrington WA4 . . . . . 16 F3
Grampian Way
  Bebington CH62 . . . . . 43 E4
  Neston CH64 . . . . . 66 E5
  Winsford CW7 . . . . . 149 A7
Granary Mews SK12 . . . . . 36 E3
Granary Mill WA7 . . . . . 50 F6
Granby Cl WA7 . . . . . 50 C5
Granby Rd
  Cheadle SK8 . . . . . 35 B8
  Warrington WA4 . . . . . 26 B8
Grandford La CW5 . . . . . 217 D2
Grand Junction Ret Pk CW1 . . . . . 190 D3
GRANGE 49 D7
  Warrington 17 E8
Grange Ave
  Barnton CW8 . . . . . 78 A3
  Warrington WA4 . . . . . 16 E4
Grangebrook Dr CW7 . . . . . 126 C3
Grange Cl
  Chorlton CW2 . . . . . 207 E4
  Crewe CW1 . . . . . 190 E3
  Golborne WA3 . . . . . 3 C6
  Sandbach CW11 . . . . . 174 F7
Grange Com Prim Sch CW7 . . . . . 126 B1
Grange Comp Sch WA7 . . . . . 23 C1
Grange Cres CH66 . . . . . 44 A1
Grange Ct
  Biddulph ST8 . . . . . 179 D2
  🔲 Knutsford WA16 . . . . . 57 A2
  Warrington CW7 . . . . . 126 B2
Grange Dr
  Hartford CW8 . . . . . 103 A6
  Thornton Hough CH63 . . . . . 42 A7
  Warrington WA5 . . . . . 15 A4
  Widnes WA8 . . . . . 13 A1
Grange Farm Cl WA5 . . . . . 15 D6
Grangefields ST8 . . . . . 179 E4
Grange Green Manor WA3 . . . . . 28 E7
Grange Inf Sch The WA7 . . . . . 23 C1
Grange Jun Sch The
  Hartford CW8 . . . . . 103 A6
  Runcorn WA7 . . . . . 23 C2
Grange La
  Tilston SY14 . . . . . 198 E3
  Weaverham CW8 . . . . . 102 A7
  Whitegate CW8 . . . . . 125 F7
  Winsford CW7 . . . . . 126 B3
Grange Lea SK10 . . . . . 86 F2
Grange Lea CW10 . . . . . 128 B1
Grangemoor WA7 . . . . . 49 D8
Grange Park Ave
  Runcorn WA7 . . . . . 23 C2
  Wilmslow SK9 . . . . . 60 A8
Grange Park Dr ST8 . . . . . 179 E3
Grange Pl M44 . . . . . 11 E5
Grange Rd
  Barnton CW8 . . . . . 78 A3
  Biddulph ST8 . . . . . 179 E3
  Chester CH2 . . . . . 118 D4
  Chester, Vicarscross CH3 . . . . . 119 C2
  Cuddington SK8 . . . . . 101 F3
  Ellesmere Port CH65 . . . . . 70 C4
  Haydock WA11 . . . . . 1 B7
  Macclesfield SK11 . . . . . 112 C6
  Mouldsworth CH3 . . . . . 99 B1
  Northwich, Rudheath CW9 . . . . . 104 D6
  Runcorn WA7 . . . . . 23 C2
Grange Rd N WA7 . . . . . 23 C2
Grange Rd W CH3 . . . . . 119 C2
Grange Sch The CW8 . . . . . 103 B6
Grangeside CH2 . . . . . 118 D7
Grange The
  Congleton CW12 . . . . . 179 B8
  Hartford CW8 . . . . . 103 B5
  Macclesfield SK11 . . . . . 112 A6
Grange Valley WA11 . . . . . 1 D5
Grange Valley Prim Sch WA11 . . . . . 1 D5
Grange Villas CH3 . . . . . 142 F6
Grangeway
  Handforth SK9 . . . . . 34 D4
  Runcorn WA7 . . . . . 49 C8
Grangeway Ct WA7 . . . . . 49 C8
Grangewood Dr SK11 . . . . . 83 F3
Granston Cl WA5 . . . . . 7 D1
Grant Cl WA5 . . . . . 7 D1
Grantham Ave
  WA1 . . . . . 16 F1
  Warrington WA4 . . . . . 26 B8
Grantham Cl CW9 . . . . . 104 C7
Granville Dr CH66 . . . . . 69 B7
Granville Rd
  Chester CH1 . . . . . 118 B3

Granville Rd continued
Northwich CW9 . . . . . 104 A5
Wilmslow SK9 . . . . 59 F5
Granville Sq CW7 . . . . 149 E8
Granville St
[15] Runcorn WA7 . . . . . 23 A3
Warrington WA1 . . . . . . 16 D6
Winsford CW7 . . . . . . 149 E8
Grapes St [9] SK11 . . . 112 D7
GRAPPENHALL 17 A1
Grappenhall Hall Sch
WA4 . . . . 17 B1
GRAPPENHALL HEYS . . 27 A4
Grappenhall Heys Com
Prim Sch WA4 . . . . . . 27 A4
Grappenhall La WA4 . . 27 A5
Grappenhall Rd
Ellesmere Port CH65 . . 69 F3
Warrington WA6 . . . . . 16 D1
Grappenhall St Wilfrid's
CE Prim Sch WA4 . . . 17 B1
Grasmere CH1 . . . . . 112 A6
Grasmere Ave
Congleton CW12 . . . . 155 F2
Crewe CW2 . . . . 189 F5
Warrington WA3 . . . . . . 8 E3
Grasmere Cl CW7 . . . 126 D2
Grasmere Cres
Bramhall SK7 . . . . 35 E8
High Lane SK12 . . . . . . 37 E8
Grasmere Dr
Holmes Chapel CW4 . . 130 A3
Runcorn WA7 . . . . 49 D5
Grasmere Rd
Alderley Edge SK9 . . . . 60 A1
Chester CH2 . . . . 118 F5
Ellesmere Port CH65 . . 70 C2
Frodsham WA6 . . . . . . 74 C8
Lymm WA13 . . . . 18 F4
Neston CH64 . . . . 66 E6
Partington M31 . . . . . . 11 E3
Grason Ave SK9 . . . . . 34 C1
Grassfield Way WA16 . . 82 A8
Grassmoor Cl CH62 . . . 43 E8
Grassygreen La ST7 . . 209 E1
Gratrix Rd CH62 . . . . . 43 D8
GRAVEL 127 A1
Gravel La SK9 . . . . 59 E5
Gravel Wlk SY14 . . . . 213 D7
Gravenhunger La
CW3 . . . . 232 E1
GRAVENHUNGER MOSS
. . . . 232 D2
Graveyard La WA16 . . . 58 F5
Gray Ave WA11 . . . . 1 D6
Graylag Cl WA7 . . . . . . 49 F5
Graymarsh Dr SK12 . . . 36 E2
Gray's Ct ST7 . . . . . . 195 B7
Greasby Dr CH66 . . . . 69 E4
Great Ashfield WA8 . . 12 D3
GREAT BARROW 120 E6
Great Budworth CE Prim
Sch CW9 . . . . 79 B8
Great Delph WA11 . . . . 1 D7
Greater Grace Sch
CH1 . . . . 95 B4
Great King St SK11 . . 112 C8
Greatoak Rd ST7 . . . . 209 F4
Great Oak Sq SK11 . . . 58 A4
Great Queen St SK11 . 112 C8
Great Riding WA7 . . . . 50 C7
GREAT SANKEY 15 A6
Great Sankey High Sch
WA5 . . . . 14 E7
Great Sankey Prim Sch
WA5 . . . . 15 A5
Greaves La SY14 . . . . 222 E6
Greaves La E SY14 . . . 222 E7
Greaves Rd SK9 . . . . . 59 E7
Grebe Cl
Knutsford WA16 . . . . . 57 B3
Poynton SK12 . . . . 36 B4
Greeba Ave WA4 . . . . 16 B3
Greek St WA7 . . . . 22 F3
Greenacre SK8 . . . . . . 34 C7
Green Acre Cl WA16 . . 82 B8
Greenacre Dr CH63 . . . 43 C7
Greenacre Rd CH4 . . . 140 F4
Greenacres
Crewe CW1 . . . . 190 D6
Duddon CW6 . . . . 145 A6
Frodsham WA6 . . . . . . 74 C6
Sandbach CW11 . . . . 175 A7
Greenacres Cl WA3 . . . 4 B8
Greenacres Ct CW2 . . . 95 F1
Greenacres Rd CW12 . 155 F2
Greenacres The WA13 . 19 A4
Greenall Ave WA4 . . . 14 D4
Greenall Rd CW9 . . . 104 B8
Greenall's Ave WA4 . . 16 C2
Green Ave
Alpraham CW6 . . . . . 169 D4
Barnton CW8 . . . . 78 A3
Davenham CW9 . . . . 103 E3
GREENBANK 103 C7
Greenbank
Chester CH4 . . . . 141 E6
Handforth / New Mill WA6 . 97 E6
Green Bank
Adderley TF9 . . . . . . 235 A5
Chester CH4 . . . . 141 E6
Greenbank Ave CH66 . 69 C7
Greenbank Cl CW5 . . 205 D6
Greenbank Dr SK10 . . 88 A8
Greenbank Gdns WA4 . 16 F2
Greenbank La CW8 . . 103 D6

Greenbank Pk CW11 . . 175 A2
Greenbank Rd
Chester CH2 . . . . 119 A4
Warrington WA4 . . . . . 16 F2
Greenbank Residential
Sch CW8. . . . . 103 D6
Greenbank St WA4 . . . 16 C2
Greenbank Sta CW8 . . 103 D6
Green Bridge Cl WA4 . . 24 A2
Greenbridge Rd WA7 . . 24 B2
Green Coppice WA7 . . 50 C8
Greencourts Bsns Pk
M22 . . . . 34 A8
GREENDALE 86 E7
Greendale Dr
Middlewich CW10 . . . 151 B7
Newcastle-u-Lyme ST5 . 210 D1
Greendale Gdns CW1 . 190 E5
Greendale La SK10 . . . 86 D8
Green Dr
Alsager ST7 . . . . 193 D4
Handforth SK9 . . . . . . 34 D2
Green Farm CH4 . . . . 163 B2
Greenfield Ave CH4 . . 161 A7
Greenfield Cl SK22 . . . 39 A8
Greenfield Cres
Chester CH2 . . . . 119 B5
Waverton CH3 . . . . . . 143 B6
Greenfield Farm Ind Est
CW12 . . . . 156 B3
Greenfield Gdns CH2 . 72 B3
Greenfield La
Chester CH2 . . . . 119 B5
Frodsham WA6 . . . . . . 49 B1
Greenfield Rd
Bollington SK10 . . . . . 88 A7
Broughton CH4 . . . . . 139 C4
Congleton CW12 . . . . 156 B3
Ellesmere Port CH66 . 69 B7
Waverton CH3 . . . . . . 143 B6
Greenfields
Chester CH2 . . . . 95 F1
Winsford CW7 . . . . . . 127 B1
Greenfields Ave
Bebington CH62 . . . . . 43 C7
Shavington CW2 . . . . 206 B4
Warrington WA4 . . . . . 26 D8
Greenfields Cl
Neston CH64 . . . . 66 F5
Newton-le-W WA12 . . . 2 C4
Warrington WA1 . . . . . 17 C7
Greenfields Cres CH62 43 C7
Greenfields Croft
CH64 . . . . 66 E5
Greenfields Dr
Alsager ST7 . . . . 193 E3
Neston CH64 . . . . 66 F5
Greenfields La
Malpas SY14 . . . . . . 213 B4
Rowton CH3 . . . . 143 B4
Greenfields Lo CH3 . . 120 D6
Greenfields Prim Sch
CW7 . . . . 126 A1
Greenfield Way CW8 . 102 A4
Greengate SK10 . . . . . 32 D7
Greengate Rd ST7 . . . 193 F5
Greengates Cres CH64 . 66 E5
Green Hall Mews WA6 . 60 B6
Greenhaven Ct CW5 . 219 E5
Greenhill La WA4 . . . . 17 D1
Greenhills Cl SK11 . . . 112 E7
Greenhill Wlk SK12 . . . 38 D6
Greenhouse Farm Rd
WA7 . . . . 50 B6
Greenhythe Rd SK8 . . 34 C6
Green Jones Brow WA5 . 6 F6
Green La
Acton CW5 . . . . 204 A3
Alderley Edge SK9 . . . 59 F1
Audlem CW3 . . . . 229 F2
Barbridge CW5 . . . . . 187 A7
Bollington SK10 . . . . . 63 B1
Burtonwood WA5 . . . . . 6 C7
Chester CH4 . . . . 140 E4
Chester, Vicarscross
CH3. . . . . 119 B3
Christleton CH3 . . . . 120 C2
Davenham CW9 . . . . 103 F3
Disley SK12 . . . . 38 D4
Ellesmere Port, Great Sutton
CH66 . . . . 69 C4
Ellesmere Port, Great Sutton
CH66 . . . . 69 D4
Ellesmere Port, Wolverham
CH65 . . . . 70 C4
Higher Kinnerton CH4 . 161 B6
Higher Walton CW9 . . . 79 F4
Irlam M44 . . . . 11 E5
Kelsall CW6 . . . . 122 D4
Knutsford WA16 . . . . . 56 D4
Lindow End SK9 . . . . . 84 F8
Over Peover WA16 . . . 83 D1
Picton CH2 . . . . 96 C3
Plumley WA16 . . . . . . 80 E6
Poynton SK12 . . . . 36 F4
Sandbach CW11 . . . . 173 F7
Saughall CH1 . . . . . . 117 C7
Shocklach SY14 . . . . 211 C7
Tattenhall CH3 . . . . . 182 F5
Tilston SY14 . . . . 212 B8
Warrington, Dudlow's Green
WA4 . . . . 17 A8
Warrington, Paddington
WA1 . . . . 17 A8
Widnes WA8 . . . . 12 E1
Willaston CW5 . . . . . 205 E5
Wilmslow SK9 . . . . . . 60 B1
Winwick WA2 . . . . 8 A7

Green Lake La CH3 . . . 163 F3
Greenland Cl CW6 . . . 146 D1
Greenlands CH3 . . . . . 166 B1
Greenlands Cl [3] SK8 . 34 E8
Green Lane Cl WA2 . . . . 8 A7
Green Lane Com Specl
Sch WA1 . . . . 17 B8
Green Lane E
Connah's Quay CH5 . . . 93 C1
Sealand CH5 . . . . 116 D7
Green Lane Est
Connah's Quay CH5 . . . 93 C1
Sealand CH5 . . . . 116 C8
Green Lane W CW5 . . . 93 B3
Greenlaw CW9 . . . . . 104 A5
Green Lawns Dr [8]
CH66 . . . . 94 F8
Greenlea Cl CH65 . . . . 70 B2
Greenleighs ST7 . . . . 194 E3
Greenlooms
Green Mdws
Golborne WA3 . . . . 3 E5
Macclesfield SK11 . . . 111 F6
Greenoaks Ctr WA8 . . 23 B8
Greenoaks Farm Ind Est
WA8 . . . . 23 C8
Green Oaks Path WA8 . 23 C8
Green Oaks Way WA8 . 23 C8
Green Mdws WA8 . . . 12 E3
Grenore Dr L24 . . . . . . 21 D2
Green Pk CW5 . . . . . . 102 E7
Green Rd M31 . . . . 11 E3
Greensbridge La L26 . . 21 A8
Greenshall La SK12 . . . 38 F5
Greenshank WA12 . . . . 2 C4
Greenside Ave CH66 . . 74 D7
Greenside Ct CW9 . . . 105 D5
Greenside Dr CW9 . . . 105 D5
Green St
[5] Alderley Edge SK9 . 60 A1
Holt LL13 . . . . 180 E1
Knutsford WA16 . . . . . 57 A2
Macclesfield SK10 . . . 112 E7
Sandbach CW11 . . . . 175 B6
Warrington WA5 . . . . . 15 F5
Warrington WA5 . . . . . 15 F5
Greens The WA15 . . . . 32 D7
Greensway CH4 . . . . . 141 A7
Green The
Cheadle SK8 . . . . 34 F8
Congleton CW12 . . . . 156 C2
Ellesmere Port CH65 . . 70 B2
Hale L24 . . . . 21 D1
Hartford CW8 . . . . 34 E3
Hartford CH3 . . . . 183 E3
Higher Kinnerton CH4 . 161 B7
Lawton-gate ST7 . . . . 194 A4
Middlewich CW10 . . . 151 D6
Nantwich CW5 . . . . . 204 D8
Neston CH64 . . . . 41 B2
Neston, Little Neston
CH64 . . . . 66 F6
Partington M31 . . . . . . 11 F3
[4] Runcorn WA7 . . . . 23 F1
Saughall CH1 . . . . . . 94 A2
Tarvin CH3 . . . . 121 F2
Thornton Hough CH63 . 42 C4
Woore CW3 . . . . 232 C1
Green View WA13 . . . . 19 B5
Green Villa Pk SK9 . . . 59 E4
Greenway
Alsager ST7 . . . . 193 B5
Bramhall SK7 . . . . 35 D5
Congleton CW12 . . . . 156 B3
Crewe CW1 . . . . 190 D7
Farndon CH3 . . . . 180 F1
Neston CH64 . . . . 41 B2
Saughall CH1 . . . . . . 94 A1
Tilston SY14 . . . . 198 C3
Warrington, Great Sankey
WA5 . . . . 14 E7
Warrington, Paddington
WA1 . . . . 17 F7
Greenway Cl
Helsby WA6 . . . . 73 B3
Rode Heath ST7 . . . . 193 F8
Greenway Dr CW7 . . . 104 C7
Greenway Rd
Biddulph ST8 . . . . . . 179 E2
Gatley SK8 . . . . 34 C6
Runcorn WA7 . . . . 23 A1
Speke L24 . . . . 21 A3
Widnes WA8 . . . . 13 B1
Greenways ST7 . . . . . 209 F2
Greenways Ct CH62 . . 43 C6
Greenways Dr CW8 . . 237 B1
Greenway Wlk CW7 . . 104 C7
Greenwell Rd WA11 . . . 1 C6
Greenwich Ave WA8 . . 13 D4
Green Wlk
Cuddington CW8 . . . . 102 B4
Partington M31 . . . . . . 11 E3
Greenwood Ave
Chester CH4 . . . . 141 D7
Congleton CW12 . . . . 156 F3
Greenwood Cl WA8 . . . 77 D1
Greenwood Cres WA2 . . 8 E2
Greenwood Ct WA3 . . . 4 F1
Greenwood Dr
Newton-le-W WA12 . . . 2 D2
Runcorn WA7 . . . . 24 F4
Wilmslow SK9 . . . . . . 60 B7
Greenwood Terr WA16 . 58 A4
Greenwood The CW6 . 168 D8
Greg Ave SK10 . . . . . . 87 E8

Greg Mews SK9 . . . . . 34 B2
Gregory Cl WA5 . . . . . 15 C7
Gregorys Row WA3 . . . 4 A8
Gregson Rd WA8 . . . . 13 C1
Grenfell Cl CH4 . . . . . 41 C1
Grenfell Ct CH64 . . . . 66 C8
Grenfell Pk CH64 . . . . 41 C1
Grenfell St [11] WA8 . . 23 B8
Grenville Cl CW1 . . . . 191 C5
Grenville Cres CH64 . . 43 C7
Grenville Rd CH64 . . . 41 F1
Gresford Ave CH2 . . . 237 C4
Gresford Cl WA5 . . . . 7 E1
Gresley Way ST7 . . . . 209 F2
Gresty Bldgs [3] CW5 . 204 E6
Gresty Green Rd
CW2 . . . . 206 D7
Gresty La CW2 . . . . . 206 B7
Gresty Rd CW2 . . . . . 190 D1
Gresty Road Football Gd (
Crewe Alexandra FC)
CW2 . . . . 190 D2
Gresty Terr CW1 . . . . 190 E4
Greta Ave SK8 . . . . . . 34 C6
Greville Dr CW7 . . . . . 127 A1
Grey Friars CH1 . . . . 237 A2
Greyfriars Cl WA2 . . . . 9 A3
Greyhound Park Rd
CH1 . . . . 118 A3
Greyhound Pk CH1 . . 118 A3
Greyhound Rd SK10 . . 86 B5
Greymist Ave WA1 . . . 17 C7
Greys CH1 . . . . 9 C1
Greysfield Flats CH3 . 120 D6
Grey St WA1 . . . . 16 C6
Greystoke Dr SK9 . . . . 60 A2
Greystoke Rd SK10 . . 87 F2
Greystone Pk CW1 . . 190 D6
Greystone Rd WA5 . . . 14 F4
Greystones CH66 . . . . 69 D4
Greystones Rd CH3 . . 119 C1
Grice La CW1 . . . . 16 C1
Griffin Cl
Blacon CH1 . . . . 117 F6
New Mills SK22 . . . . . 39 D6
Norton in Hales TF9 . . 236 C2
Griffin La SK9 . . . . 34 D7
Griffith Ave WA3 . . . . . 3 B3
Griffith Mews WA8 . . . . 9 E5
Griffiths Dr CW9 . . . . 104 D6
Griffiths Rd
Lostock Gralam CW9 . . 79 F1
Northwich CW9 . . . . . 104 E8
Griffiths St WA4 . . . . . 16 F4
Grig Pl ST7 . . . . 193 C5
Grimsditch La WA4 . . . 52 B5
Grimshaw Ave SK10 . . 88 A7
Grimshaw La SK10 . . . 88 A7
Grindley Bank CH2 . . 119 F8
GRINDLEY BROOK . . 225 C3
Grindley Gdns CH65 . . 70 C2
Grindley Gn SY13 . . . 228 B3
Grisedale Ave WA2 . . . 8 B3
Grisedale Cl WA7 . . . . 49 E5
Grisedale Rd CH66 . . . 69 D3
Grisedale Way SK11 . . 112 A5
Gritstone Dr SK10 . . . 112 A8
Grizedale WA8 . . . . . . 12 B2
Grizedale Cl CW7 . . . . 149 C7
Grizedale Cl CH62 . . . 189 D2
Groarke Dr WA5 . . . . . 15 B7
Groby Rd CW1 . . . . . 190 E8
Groombridge Row [2]
CW5 . . . . 204 E5
Grosvenor Ave
Alsager ST7 . . . . 193 D5
[3] Golborne WA3 . . . . 3 D8
Hartford CW8 . . . . . . 103 A4
Warrington WA4 . . . . . 16 F7
Grosvenor Cl
Warrington WA5 . . . . . 15 C5
Wilmslow SK9 . . . . . . 60 A4
Grosvenor Cotts CH4 . 141 D7
Grosvenor Ct
Chester CH1 . . . . 237 C2
[12] Crewe CW1 . . . . 190 B5
Winsford CW7 . . . . . . 149 C7
Grosvenor Ctr SK11 . . 112 D8
Grosvenor Dr SK12 . . . 36 D3
Grosvenor Gdns WA12 . 2 C2
Grosvenor Grange WA1 . 9 B1
Grosvenor Mus*
CH1 . . . . 237 A1
Grosvenor Nuffield Hospl
CH4 . . . . 141 C6
Grosvenor Pk Rd CH1 . 237 C2
Grosvenor Pk Terr CH1,
CH3 . . . . 237 C2
Grosvenor Pl CH1 . . . 237 A2
Grosvenor Rd
Chester CH4 . . . . 141 C7
Congleton CW12 . . . . 156 A3
Haydock WA11 . . . . . . 1 B7
Tarvin CH3 . . . . 121 A2
Widnes WA8 . . . . 13 B5
Grosvenor Sh Ctr The
CH1 . . . . 237 B2
Grosvenor St
Chester CH1 . . . . 237 A2
Crewe CW1 . . . . 190 B5
[3] Macclesfield SK10 . 112 C8
Runcorn WA7 . . . . 23 B3
Winsford CW7 . . . . . . 149 C7
Grotsworth La SY14 . . 214 E8
Grotto La WA16 . . . . . 108 B7
Grounds St WA2 . . . . . 16 B7
Grove Arc SK9 . . . . . . 60 A2
Grove Ave
Chester CH3 . . . . 119 B3

Grove Ave continued
Kidsgrove ST7 . . . . . . 194 E1
Lawton-gate ST7 . . . . 194 A4
Lostock Gralam CW9 . . 80 A3
Lymm WA13 . . . . 18 C3
Wilmslow SK9 . . . . . . 60 B7
Grove Cl CW3 . . . . . . 149 B8
Grove Cres CW3 . . . . 232 C1
Grove Ct
Alsager ST7 . . . . 193 E4
Lymm WA13 . . . . 18 C3
Grove Gdns CH3 . . . . 119 E7
Grove Ho SK8 . . . . 35 B6
Grove La SK8 . . . . 35 A6
Grovemount CW9 . . . . 103 F2
Grove Park Ave ST7 . . 194 A4
Grove Pk WA16 . . . . . . 57 A1
Grove Rd CH1 . . . . 94 E4
Grove Rise WA13 . . . . 18 E3
Grove St
New Mills SK22 . . . . . 39 B7
Runcorn WA7 . . . . 22 F3
Warrington WA4 . . . . . 16 C4
Wilmslow SK9 . . . . . . 60 B7
Groves The
Chester CH1 . . . . 237 B2
Ellesmere Port CH66 . . 95 A8
Grove Terr WA16 . . . . 73 C4
Grove The
Cheadle SK8 . . . . 35 A6
Knutsford WA16 . . . . . 57 C4
Lawton-gate ST7 . . . . 194 A4
Lymm WA13 . . . . 18 E3
Tarporley CW6 . . . . . 146 C2
Warrington WA5 . . . . . 14 F4
Whitchurch SY13 . . . 225 F1
Grove Way SK9 . . . . . 60 B7
Grovewood Mews
SK11. . . . . 112 C6
Grub La CW6 . . . . 122 C5
Grundy Cl WA3 . . . . . . 12 F3
Grundy St WA3 . . . . . . 3 A7
Guardian St WA5 . . . . 15 F5
Guardian Street Ind Est
WA5 . . . . 15 F6
Guernsey Cl
Congleton CW12 . . . . 157 A2
Middlewich CW10 . . . 128 D2
Warrington WA4 . . . . . 26 D8
Guernsey Dr CH65 . . . 70 C1
Guernsey Ho CH2 . . . 119 B5
Guernsey Rd WA8 . . . 13 E3
Guests Slack WA6 . . . 100 B8
Guilden Gn CH3 . . . . 119 E4
Guilden St CH3 . . . . . 119 E4
GUILDEN SUTTON . . 119 F5
Guilden Sutton CE Prim
Sch CH3 . . . . 119 F5
Guilden Sutton La
CH3 . . . . 119 D5
Guildford Ave SK8 . . . 35 A6
Guildford Cl
[1] Chester CH4 . . . . 140 F6
Warrington WA2 . . . . . . 9 A1
Guillemot Cl CW1 . . . 190 F5
Gullane Cl SK10 . . . . . 87 B4
Gull Cl SK12 . . . . 36 B3
Gullet The CW5 . . . . . 204 E5
Gulivers World Theme
Pk* WA5 . . . . 7 E1
Gulls Way CH60 . . . . . 40 E7
Gunco La
Macclesfield SK11 . . . 112 E6
Prestbury SK10 . . . . . 87 C8
Gunn Gr CH64 . . . . . . 66 F8
Gutticar Rd WA8 . . . . 12 B1
Gutterscroft CW1 . . . 191 D5
Gutticar Rd WA8 . . . . 12 B1
Guy La CH3 . . . . 143 D5
Gypsy La CH1 . . . . 94 F2

H

Hacked Way La SK11 . 113 F6
HACK GREEN 218 D5
Hack Green Secret
Nuclear Bunker*
. . . . 218 D4
Haddon Cl
Alderley Edge SK9 . . . 59 F2
High Lane SK6 . . . . . . 37 E6
Holmes Chapel CW4 . 130 B3
Macclesfield SK11 . . . 112 B5
Wistaston CW2 . . . . . 206 B7
Haddon Dr WA8 . . . . . 12 C3
Haddon La CH64 . . . . 66 E4
Haddon La CH64 . . . . 67 C4
Haddon Rd
Burton CH64 . . . . 67 D2
Gatley SK8 . . . . 34 C7
Hadfield Cl WA8 . . . . . 13 E2
Hadfield St CW9 . . . . . 79 B1
Hadleigh Cl WA5 . . . . 14 E5
Hadley Ave CH62 . . . . 43 C8
Hadley Cl WA7 . . . . . 207 E4
Hadlow La CH64 . . . . 67 F7
Hadlow Rd CH64 . . . . 67 F6
Hadlow Terr CH64 . . . 67 F6
Hadrian Dr CH1 . . . . . 117 C6
Hadrian Way
Cuddington CW8 . . . . 102 B2
Middlewich CW10 . . . 128 C2
Hadyn Jones Dr CW5 . 204 F4

Hafod Cl
Blacon CH1 117 D3
Connah's Quay CH5 91 C1
Hag Bank La SK12 38 D7
HAGUE BAR 38 F8
Hague Bar Prim Sch
SK22 38 E8
Hague Bar Rd SK22 39 A7
Hague Fold Rd SK22 38 F8
Haig Ave
Irlam M44 11 C4
Warrington WA5 15 A5
Haig Ct WA16 57 C4
Haighton Ct 11 CW5 204 E6
Haig Rd
Knutsford WA16 57 C4
Widnes WA8 13 A1
Hailwood Ho SK10 88 B8
HALE
Altrincham 32 B8
Liverpool 21 D1
Hale Ave SK12 36 D2
HALE BANK 22 A4
Hale Bank CE Prim Sch
WA8 22 A5
Halebank Rd WA8 21 F5
Hale Bank Terr WA8 22 A4
HALE BARNS 32 D8
Hale CE Prim Sch L24 21 E1
Hale Ct WA8 22 A4
Hale Gate Rd
Hale WA8 21 F3
Widnes WA8 22 A3
Hale Gr WA5 15 A6
HALE HEATH 21 A1
Hale Rd
Hale L24 21 B2
Widnes WA8 22 C7
Hale Road Ind Est WA8 22 B4
Hale St WA2 16 B7
Hale View WA7 48 E8
Hale View Rd WA6 73 C4
HALEWOOD 21 B7
Halewood Lane Ends
L26 21 A8
HALEWOOD VILLAGE 21 A8
Haley Rd N WA5 6 E6
Haley Rd S WA5 6 E5
Halfacre La WA4 17 F2
Half St SK11 112 D6
Halghton La LL13 222 B2
Halifax Cl WA2 8 D2
Halkett Cl CH4 140 E5
Halkyn Rd CH2 237 C4
Hall Acres La SK8 34 E8
Hallams Dr CW5 205 B4
Hallastone Rd WA6 73 C4
Hall Ave WA8 12 A1
Halla-Way WA4 16 E3
Hall Bank WA16 58 C4
Hall Bank N WA16 58 C4
Hall Bank S WA16 58 C4
Hall Cl SK10 87 D4
Hallcroft M31 11 F4
Hallcroft Pl WA4 17 A2
Hall Dr
Alsager ST7 193 C3
Marston CW9 79 B6
Warrington WA4 26 D6
Willaston CW5 205 C6
Hallefield Cres 5
SK11 112 E7
Hallefield Dr 4 SK11 112 E7
Hallefield Rd SK10,
SK11 112 E7
Hall Farm CH62 44 A4
Hall Farm Cl SK23 65 D8
Hallfield Dr CH2 72 B3
Hallfield Pk CH66 69 D4
Hallfields Rd
Tarvin CH3 121 C2
Warrington WA2 8 D1
Hall Gr SK10 87 D3
HALL GREEN
Scholar Green 194 E5
Whitchurch 224 E1
Hallgreen La CW12 155 D8
Hall Hill SK10 87 E7
Halliday Cl WA3 9 F3
Halliwel Jones Stad
(Warrington Wolves
RLFC) The WA2 16 A6
Halliwell's Brow WA16 29 B3
Hall La
Appleton Thorn WA4 27 B8
Audlem CW3 230 C7
Brown Knowl CH3 199 C7
Cronton L35 12 C7
Daresbury WA4 25 D2
Haughton CW6 186 D5
Kelsall CW6 122 D6
Little Leigh CW9 77 F8
Lostock Gralam CW9 79 F3
Mobberley WA16 58 D4
Newton-le-W WA5 7 B8
Ollerton WA16 83 B5
Partington M31 11 F4
Pickmere WA16 55 B1
Sandbach CW11 174 B5
Shotwick CH1 93 B5
St Helens WA9 6 A4
Stretton WA4 52 D8
Sutton Lane Ends SK11 112 F3
Utkinton CW6 146 C6
Winsford CW7 149 B3
Hall La The CW6 147 D2
Hall Moss La SK7 35 C4
Hall Nook WA5 14 F3
Hall O'shaw St CW1 190 E4
Hallows Ave WA2 16 D8
Hallows Cl CW6 122 C4
Hallows Dr CW6 122 C4
HALLOWSGATE 122 C4
Hallowsgate Ct CW6 122 C4
Hall Rd
Handforth SK9 34 E3
Haydock WA11 1 E7
Warrington WA1 17 C7
Wilmslow SK9 60 A7
Hallsgreen La CH2 96 F7
Hallshaw Ave CW1 190 E5
Hallside Pk WA16 57 C1
Halls Rd
Biddulph ST8 179 C1
Mow Cop ST7 195 C7
Hall St
Audley ST7 209 D2
Macclesfield SK10 112 C8
New Mills SK22 39 B8
Warrington WA1 16 C5
Hall Terr WA5 14 E7
Hall View CH3 166 B1
Hall View Cl CW8 102 A7
Hall Wood Ave WA11 1 E8
Hallwood Cl WA7 49 B6
Hallwood Ct CH64 66 E7
Hallwood Dr CH66 68 D4
Hallwood Link Rd WA7 49 F6
HALLWOOD PARK 49 F6
Hallwood Park Ave
WA7 49 E6
Hallwood Park Prim Sch
WA7 49 E6
Hallwood Rd SK9 34 D2
Halsall Ave WA2 16 D8
Halsall Cl WA7 50 C5
Halsall's Cotts WA8 21 E5
Halstone Ave SK9 59 E4
HALTON BROOK 23 D1
Halton Brook Ave WA7 23 D1
Halton Brow WA7 23 E1
Halton Castle* WA7 23 F1
Halton Cres CH66 69 F2
Halton Ct WA7 23 D2
Halton Dr CW2 189 D5
Halton General Hospl
WA7 49 F7
Halton High Sch WA7 50 C6
Halton Lea S Ctr WA7 49 E8
Halton Link Rd WA7 49 E8
HALTON LODGE 49 D7
Halton Lodge Ave
WA7 49 D7
Halton Lodge Prim Sch
WA7 49 D8
Halton Rd
Chester CH2 118 F6
Ellesmere Port CH66 69 E2
Runcorn WA7 23 D2
Warrington WA5 14 F6
Halton St WA11 1 E6
Halton Station Rd WA7 49 F3
HALTON VIEW 13 C1
Halton View Rd WA8 13 C1
HALTON VILLAGE 49 F8
Halton Way CH66 69 E1
Hambledon Cl CH66 69 A6
Hamble Dr WA5 14 F3
Hambleton Cl WA8 12 C3
Hambleton Rd SK8 34 C8
Hambleton Way CW7 149 A7
Hambletts Hollow
WA6 100 F6
Hamble Way SK10 86 E1
Hamilton Ave
Irlam M44 11 D4
Sandycroft CH5 116 A3
Hamilton Cl
Haslington CW1 191 C4
Macclesfield SK10 113 A8
Neston CH64 41 B2
Hamilton Ct CH64 66 F8
Hamilton Pl CH1 237 A2
Hamilton Rd CH5 91 D1
Hamilton St CH2 118 F3
Hamlin Cl WA7 49 A6
Hammersmith Way
WA8 13 D4
Hammond Sch CH2 119 B7
Hammond St CW2 190 C3
Hamnett Ct WA3 9 E3
Hampshire Cl CW12 156 D4
Hampshire Gdns ST7 194 F2
Hampshire Rd M31 11 D2
Hampshire Wlk SK10 86 F2
Hampson Ave WA3 4 F3
Hampson Cres SK9 34 C4
Hampstead Ct 7
CW7 149 A8
Hampstead Dr CW2 221 C8
Hampton Cl
Neston CH64 66 E6
Widnes WA8 13 E3
Hampton Court Way
WA8 13 D4
Hampton Cres
Neston CH64 66 E6
No Man's Heath SY14 214 A5
Hampton Ct
Gatley SK9 34 D5
Runcorn WA7 24 C4
Hampton Dr
Cronton WA8 12 C5
Hampton Dr *continued*
Warrington WA5 15 C4
Hampton Gdns CH65 70 A5
HAMPTON GREEN 214 B7
HAMPTON HEATH 213 E7
Hampton Heath Ind Est
SY14 213 D7
Hampton Rd
Chester CH4 140 F6
Irlam M44 11 D4
Hamson Dr SK10 63 B1
Hamsterley Cl WA3 10 B6
Hanbury Cl CW2 206 B7
Hancock Ct WA4 16 C4
Hancock Rd CW12 156 F4
Handa Dr CH65 95 B8
HANDBRIDGE 141 E7
Handbridge CH4 237 B1
Handford Ave CH62 43 F5
Handford Rd CH2 118 F6
HANDFORTH 34 C4
Handforth Cl WA4 17 C3
Handforth La WA7 49 D6
Handforth Rd
Crewe CW2 189 E3
Handforth SK9 34 E1
Handforth Sta SK9 34 D3
HAND GREEN 168 B6
HANDLEY 182 D8
Handley Dr WA2 8 E1
Handley Hill CW7 149 C8
Handley Hill Prim Sch
CW7 149 C8
Handley St WA7 22 F3
Hand St SK11 112 B8
Hangman's La
Lostock Green CW9 105 C7
Smallwood CW11 177 B5
HANKELOW 230 C7
Hankelow Cl
Chester CH2 237 B4
Middlewich CW10 151 C6
Hankey St 2 WA7 22 F2
Hankins Heys La CW3 231 A1
Hankinson Cl M31 11 E2
Hanley Cl
Disley SK12 38 D5
Widnes WA8 12 C1
Hanley Rd WA8 12 C1
Hannah's Wlk 2
CW10 151 C8
Hanns Hall Farm CH64 67 D8
Hanns Hall Rd CH64 67 D8
Hanover Ct WA7 50 A6
Hanover Dr 2 CW7 149 D6
Hanover Ho 6 CW8 103 C5
Hanover St WA1 16 A4
Hapsdale View WA6 72 E1
HAPSFORD 72 F1
Hapsford Cl WA3 9 C4
Hapsford La
Dunham-on-t-H WA6 97 E8
Elton CH2 72 D4
Hapsford Mews WA6 72 E2
Harbord St WA1 16 C4
Harbour Cl
Chester CH2 118 E7
Runcorn WA7 50 D6
Harbour La SK11 111 C1
Harburn Wlk M22 33 E8
Harcourt Cl WA3 9 E3
HARDEN PARK 60 A3
Harden Pk SK9 60 A3
Harding Ave
Tattenhall CH3 166 C2
Warrington WA2 8 E1
Harding Rd
Chester CH2 118 B8
Nantwich CW5 204 C4
Hardings Mdw ST7 194 F2
Hardings Row ST7 195 D7
Hardings Wood ST7 194 E2
HARDING'S WOOD 194 E2
Hardingswood Rd
ST7 194 E2
Hardknott Rd CH62 43 E8
Hardwick Cl SK6 37 F6
Hardwick Dr SK11 112 B5
Hardwicke Ct CW1 190 E4
Hardwicke Rd SK12 36 F4
Hardwick Grange WA1 17 E8
Hardwick Rd WA7 23 D3
Hardy Cl
Ellesmere Port CH66 69 F3
Wistaston CW2 205 F8
Hardy Dr SK7 35 D7
Hardy Rd WA13 18 C2
Hardy St WA2 16 B6
Harebell Cl
Huntington CH3 142 A6
Widnes WA8 12 E4
Harebell Gr ST7 195 F1
Harecastle Ave ST7 194 E1
Harecastle Ct ST7 210 E6
Harecastle Villas ST7 194 E2
Harefield Dr SK9 60 B5
Harefield Rd SK9 34 E4
Hare Hill Gdn* SK10 86 B6
Hare La CH3 119 D3
Hare's La WA6 73 F7
Harewood Ave CH66 69 C4
Harewood Cl
Northwich CW9 103 F4
Winsford CW7 126 A1
Harewood Way SK11 112 B5
Harfield Gdns CH66 69 C5
Harford Cl WA5 14 F4
HARGRAVE 144 A1
Hargrave Ave CW2 189 F3
Hargrave Dr CH66 69 E5
Hargrave La
Bebington CH64 43 A4
Thornton Hough CH63,
CH64 42 F5
Hargreave Ho 7 CH64 66 E8
Hargreaves Ct WA8 13 D1
Hargreaves Ho 5
WA8 13 D1
Hargreaves Rd CW9 104 C8
Harington Cl CH2 118 C8
Harland Gn L24 21 A3
Harlech Cl WA5 7 E2
Harlech Ct CH65 70 D3
Harlech Gr 3 WA7 23 F1
Harlech Way CH65 70 D3
Harlow Cl WA4 17 C3
Harlyn Ave SK7 35 F7
Harlyn Gdns WA5 14 D3
Harn The CH66 69 C3
Haroldgate SY13 225 F1
Harold Rd WA11 1 F7
Harper Cl CH66 69 D4
Harper Gr CW12 156 E4
Harpers Rd WA2 9 B2
Harpur Cl SK11 112 D6
Harpur Cres ST7 193 B5
Harrier Rd WA2 8 F2
Harriet St M44 11 E5
Harrington Dr SK11 111 D1
Harris Cl CW1 173 B1
HARRISEAHEAD 195 E4
Harriseahead La ST7 195 D4
Harrison Cl WA1 16 C6
Harrison Dr
Crewe CW1 190 B4
Goostrey CW4 107 B1
Haydock WA11 1 A6
Harrison Gr CH5 116 A3
Harrisons Pl 4 CW8 103 E8
Harrison Sq WA5 7 F1
Harrison St WA8 22 B6
Harrisons Terr CH66 69 C6
Harrison Way WA12 2 C4
Harris Rd CW9 80 A2
Harris St WA8 13 C1
Harrogate Cl
Bebington CH62 43 D4
Warrington WA5 7 A1
Harrogate Rd CH62 43 D4
Harrop La SK10 62 E5
Harrop Rd
Bollington SK10 88 C8
Runcorn WA7 23 B1
Harrow Cl
Crewe CW2 190 A1
Warrington WA4 26 E6
Wilmslow SK9 60 D8
Harrow Dr WA7 23 E2
Harrow Gr CH62 43 E8
Harrow Rd CH65 70 D4
Harrow Way CW9 103 E3
HARTFORD 103 C4
Hartford Ave SK9 59 F5
HARTFORDBEACH 103 A6
Hartford Bsns Ctr
CW8 102 F4
Hartford Cl CW11 175 C7
Hartford Dr CH65 69 F4
Hartford High Sch
CW8 103 C5
Hartford Manor Com Prim
Sch CW8 103 C5
Hartford Mews 3
CH3 119 B1
Hartford Prim Sch
CW8 103 B4
Hartford Rd CW9 103 E3
Hartford Sta CW8 103 A4
Hartford Way CH1 118 A2
HARTHILL 183 E3
Harthill Cl CW9 103 E5
Harthill La CH3 183 E4
Harthill Prim Sch
CH3 183 E3
Harthill Rd
Blacon CH1 117 E6
Burwardsley CH3 184 A6
Hartington Dr SK7 36 E8
Hartington Rd
Bramhall SK7 35 E6
Gatley SK8 34 D8
High Lane SK12, SK6 37 F7
Hartington St CH4 141 E7
Hartland Cl
Poynton SK12 36 D5
Widnes WA8 13 A5
Hartley Cl WA13 18 F3
Hartley Gdns CW12 179 B8
Hartley Gn SK10 87 F8
Harton Cl WA8 12 E3
Hartswood Cl WA4 26 E3
Hartwell Gr CW7 126 F4
Harty Rd WA11 1 A5
Harvard Cl WA7 24 D2
Harvard Ct WA2 8 A3
Harvest Cl CW9 126 F8
Harvest Rd SK10 87 C3
Harvey Ave
Nantwich CW5 205 A6
Newton-le-W WA12 1 F3
Harvey Ct WA2 8 B3
Harvey La WA3 3 A8
Harvey Rd CW12 157 A5
Harwood Gdns WA4 17 A2
Haryngton Ave WA5 15 F7
Haseley Cl SK12 36 E5
Haslemere Ave WA15 32 C6
Haslemere Dr WA5 14 D4
Haslemere Way CW1 190 D6
Haslin Cres CH3 142 D7
HASLINGTON 191 D4
Haslington Cl ST5 210 D1
Haslington Gr L26 21 A6
Haslington Prim Sch
CW1 191 D4
HASSAL 192 C7
HASSALL GREEN 176 A2
Hassall Rd
Alsager ST7 193 B5
Haslington CW11 192 B7
Sandbach CW11 175 C4
Winterley CW11 191 F8
Hassall Way 7 SK9 34 E5
Hassals La CH2 96 F3
Hastings Ave WA2 8 B4
Hastings Rd CW5 204 F5
Hasty La
Altrincham WA15 32 E8
Hale WA15 32 E8
Wythenshawe WA15 32 F8
Hatchery Cl WA4 27 B4
Hatchings The WA13 18 E2
HATCHMERE 100 D4
Hatch Mere* WA6 100 C4
Hatchmere Cl
Sandbach CW11 174 F7
Warrington WA5 15 E5
Hatchmere Dr CH3 142 B8
Hatchmere Pk WA6 100 C5
Hatfield Ct CW4 130 B3
Hatfield Gdns WA4 26 E4
Hathaway Cl SK8 34 B7
Hathaway Dr SK11 112 C5
HATHERTON 219 E3
Hatherton Cl
Newcastle-u-Lyme
ST5 210 D2
5 Northwich CW9 103 F4
Hatherton Gr L26 21 A6
Hatherton Way CH2 237 B4
Hatley La WA6 73 F7
Hatter St CW12 156 E3
HATTON 26 A2
Hatton Ave CH62 43 E3
Hatton Bldgs CH2 237 C4
Hatton Brow Terr
SK11 112 F4
HATTON HEATH 143 B1
Hatton La
Hartford CW8 103 D6
Stretton WA4 26 B1
Hatton Rd CH1 117 E6
Hatton St SK11 112 C7
HAUGHTON 186 C6
Haughton Cl SK10 86 F1
HAVANNAH 157 A6
Havannah Bsns Ctr 6
CW12 156 F4
Havannah La
Congleton CW12 156 F6
St Helens WA9 1 B3
Havannah Prim Sch
CW12 157 A5
Havannah St CW12 156 F4
Haven The
Crewe CW1 190 D7
Sandbach CW11 174 E7
Havergal St 4 WA7 22 F1
Haverhill Cl CW2 207 C3
Haverty Prec WA12 2 B1
Havisham Cl WA3 9 D5
Hawarde Cl WA12 2 A4
Hawarden Airport CH4,
CH5 139 D7
Hawarden Gdns CH65 70 D2
Hawarden Ind Pk
CH5 139 B6
Haweswater Ave
Crewe CW1 173 B1
Haydock WA11 1 A6
Haweswater Cl WA7 50 A5
Haweswater Dr CW7 126 D2
Hawick Cl CH66 69 A5
Hawker Cl CH4 139 C4
Hawkins La SK10 88 D4
Hawkins Rd CH64 41 F1
Hawkins View CH3 120 E6
Hawk Rd SK22 39 E8
Hawks Ct WA7 49 E6
Hawksey Dr CW5 204 F4
Hawkshaw Cl WA3 9 C4
Hawkshead Cl WA7 50 A4
Hawkshead Rd WA5 6 E6
Hawkshead Way CW7 126 D2
Hawk St CW11 175 B6
Hawkstone Gr WA6 73 C4
Hawks Way CH60 40 E8
Hawley Dr WA15 32 B8
Hawley La WA15 32 B8
Hawley's Cl WA5 7 F1
Hawley's La WA2, WA5 8 A1
Hawley's Lane Trad Pk
WA2 8 A1
Haworth Ave CW12 157 A5
Haworth Cl SK11 112 B5
Hawthorn Ave
3 Nantwich CW5 204 F5
Newton-le-W WA12 2 D3
Runcorn WA7 23 A1
1 Widnes WA8 13 B2
Wilmslow SK9 60 A7
Hawthorn Bank SK22 39 B6
Hawthorn Cl
Holmes Chapel CW4 130 D3

Hawthorn Cl continued
Winsford CW7 . . . . 126 C3
Hawthorn Cotts CH60 . . . . 40 F8
Hawthorn Dr M44 . . . . .11 D5
Hawthorne Ave
Audley ST7 . . . . .209 F1
Fowley Common WA3 . . . . . . 5 C4
Warrington WA5 . . . . 15 A6
Warrington, Woolston
WA1 . . . . .17 B7
Hawthorne Bsns Pk
WA5 . . . . .16 A8
Hawthorne Cl
Congleton CW12 . . . . 156 A4
Haydock WA11 . . . . 1 A5
Hawthorne Ct ST7 . . . . . .193 E4
Hawthorne Dr
Sandbach CW11 . . . . 175 D6
Willaston CH64 . . . . 43 B1
Hawthorne Gr
Barnton CW8 . . . . .77 F4
Poynton SK12 . . . . .37 C4
Warrington, Bruche WA1 . . .16 F7
Warrington WA4 . . . . .16 D3
Winsford CW7 . . . . .127 A1
Hawthorne Rd
Frodsham WA6 . . . . .49 B1
Warrington WA4 . . . . .26 C8
Hawthorne St WA5 . . . . . .16 A8
Hawthorn Gdns ST7 . . 210 D8
Hawthorn Gn SK9 . . . . . .60 A7
Hawthorn Gr
Bramhall SK7 . . . . .35 C6
Crewe CW1 . . . . .190 D7
Warrington WA4 . . . . .16 D1
Wilmslow SK9 . . . . .60 B7
Hawthorn La
Bebington CH62 . . . . .43 D8
Congleton CW12 . . . . 155 C6
Crewe CW2 . . . . .189 F2
Wilmslow SK9 . . . . .60 A7
Hawthorn Pk SK9 . . . . . . .60 A7
Hawthorn Rd
Bollington SK10 . . . . .87 F8
Chester CH4 . . . . .141 A6
Christleton CH3 . . . . .142 E7
Ellesmere Port CH66 . . . . .69 D6
Lymm WA13 . . . . .18 D3
Neston CH64 . . . . .41 C1
Newcastle-u-Lyme ST5 . . 210 E1
Plumley WA16 . . . . .80 F3
Weaverham CW8 . . . . 102 C8
Hawthorn Rise SK10 . . . .86 E6
Hawthorn St SK9 . . . . . . .60 A6
Hawthorns The
Bunbury CW6 . . . . .185 E8
Ellesmere Port CH66 . . . . .69 F7
Haslington CW1 . . . . 191 D5
Northwich CW8 . . . . .103 C7
Tarporley CW6 . . . . 146 D1
Hawthorn Terr SK9 . . . . .60 A6
Hawthorn View
Connah's Quay CH5 . . . . . 116 A7
Lindow End WA16 . . . . .59 B2
Wilmslow SK9 . . . . .60 A7
Hawthorn Villas CW4 . 130 C3
Hawthorn Way SK10 . . . .87 E2
Hawthorn Wlk
3 Partington M31 . . . . . . .11 E3
Wilmslow SK9 . . . . .60 A7
Wincham CW9 . . . . .79 C3
Haycroft SK8 . . . . .34 E8
Haycroft CH66 . . . . .69 D2
Haydan Ct CH2 . . . . .118 D4
Haydan Mews WA6 . . . . . .73 E6
Haydn Jones Dr CW5 . . 204 F3
HAYDOCK 1 D6
Haydock Cl
Chester CH1 . . . . .118 B2
Macclesfield SK10 . . . . . . .87 C3
Haydock English Martyrs'
RC Prim Sch WA11 . . . . . . 1 E7
Haydock La Ind Est
WA11 . . . . 1 E8
Haydock Park Racecourse
WA3 . . . . .2 E8
Haydock Sports Coll
WA11 . . . . 1 C6
Haydock St
Newton-le-W WA12 . . . . 2 A3
Warrington WA2 . . . . .16 B6
Hayes Cl CW5 . . . . .204 E7
Hayes Cres WA6 . . . . .49 C1
Hayes Dr CW8 . . . . .78 C3
Hayes Pk CH1 . . . . .237 A4
Haye's Rd M44 . . . . .11 E5
Hayfield Cl SK10 . . . . .87 B3
Hayfield Rd
New Mills SK22 . . . . .39 D8
Warrington WA1 . . . . .17 C7
Hayfields WA16 . . . . .57 C3
Hayfields Gr CW3 . . . . . .229 F3
Haygarth Hts **5** CH1 . . 237 C3
Hayhead Cl ST7 . . . . 195 B2
Hayhurst Ave CW10 . . . . 151 C8
Hayhurst Cl CW9 . . . . . . 103 F8
Hayle Cl SK10 . . . . .86 D1
Hayling Cl CW1 . . . . .190 B8
Haymakers Cl CH4 . . . . .140 F4
Haymakers Way CH1 . . . 117 A8
HAYMOOR GREEN 205 E2
Haymoor Green Rd
CW5 . . . . .205 E3
Hayscastle Cl WA5 . . . . . . 7 E1
Hayside Wlk SY14 . . . . .213 A2
Hayton St WA16 . . . . .56 F1
Haywood Cres WA7 . . . . .24 D2

Hazel Ave
Macclesfield SK11 . . . . . . 112 A5
Runcorn WA7 . . . . .48 E8
Hazelbadge Cl SK12 . . . .36 C4
Hazelbadge Rd SK12 . . . .36 C4
Hazelbank CH65 . . . . .69 F3
Hazelborough Cl WA3 . . .10 B5
Hazel Cl
1 Ellesmere Port
CH66 . . . . .69 F1
Kidsgrove ST7 . . . . .195 B3
Hazelcroft SK9 . . . . .85 A8
Hazelcroft Gdns SK9 . . . .85 A8
Hazelean Ct **17** SK9 . . . .34 E1
Hazel Dr
Gatley M22 . . . . .34 A8
Lymm WA13 . . . . .18 F2
Poynton SK12 . . . . .36 F3
Weaverham CW8 . . . . 102 D7
Winsford CW7 . . . . .149 C8
Hazel Gr
Alsager ST7 . . . . .194 A3
Crewe CW1 . . . . .190 C7
Golborne WA3 . . . . .3 B8
Warrington WA1 . . . . .17 A8
Hazel Grove High Sch
SK7 .36 C8
Hazelhurst Dr SK10 . . . . .88 A8
Hazelmere Cl CW8 . . . . . 103 C5
Hazel Rd CH4 . . . . .140 F6
Hazel St WA1 . . . . .16 D7
Hazel Wlk M31 . . . . .11 E3
Hazelwood Cl WA8 . . . . . .22 A8
Hazelwood Mews WA4 . . .17 C1
Hazelwood Rd
Barnton CW8 . . . . .78 B4
Wilmslow SK9 . . . . .60 D8
Wythenshawe M22 . . . . . . .33 D8
Hazlehurst Rd WA6 . . . . .74 D6
Hazlemere Ave SK11 . . . 112 A6
Headland Cl WA3 . . . . 3 E6
Headlands The CH1,
CH3 . . . . 237 C2
Headworth Cl CW9 . . . . .103 F4
HEALD GREEN 34 B8
Heald Green Sta M22 . . .34 A8
Heald St WA12 . . . . 1 F3
Healey Cl CW1 . . . . .190 A8
Heapy St SK11 . . . . 112 C8
Hearn's La CW5 . . . . .202 E5
HEATH 49 A6
Heath Ave
Ellesmere Port CH65 . . . . .70 A1
Rode Heath ST7 . . . . .193 F7
Sandbach CW11 . . . . 175 C6
Heath Bank CH3 . . . . 119 D5
Heathbank Rd SK8 . . . . . .34 F8
Heathbrook Cotts
CW9 . . . . .104 E7
Heath Cl
Chester CH3 . . . . .142 B8
Sandbach CW11 . . . . 175 D6
Tarvin CH3 . . . . .121 B1
Heathcote Cl CW4 . . . . . 118 C4
Heathcote Gdns CW9 . . 104 D7
Heathcote St ST7 . . . . . .195 A2
Heath Ct
Alsager ST7 . . . . .193 F6
Ellesmere Port CH66 . . . . .69 B6
Heath Dr
Knutsford WA16 . . . . .56 F2
Runcorn WA7 . . . . .49 A7
Tarvin CH3 . . . . .121 B1
Heath End Rd ST7 . . . . .193 B5
Heather Ave M44 . . . . .11 D6
Heather Brae WA12 . . . . . . 2 A4
Heather Brae Mews
CW12 . . . . .156 A3
Heather Cl
Ellesmere Port CH66 . . . . .69 E3
Macclesfield SK11 . . . . . . 112 C3
Runcorn WA7 . . . . .49 E4
Warrington WA3 . . . . .9 D5
Heather Ct CH3 . . . . .142 A8
Heather Falls SK22 . . . . .39 B8
Heatherfield Ct SK9 . . . . .60 E8
Heathergate Pl CW2 . . . 206 B8
Heatherside ST7 . . . . 195 C6
Heatherways CW6 . . . . . .146 C3
Heather Wlk M31 . . . . .11 E3
Heathfield SK9 . . . . .60 A3
Heathfield Ave CW1 . . . .190 C4
Heathfield Cl
Congleton CW12 . . . . 155 F3
Nantwich CW5 . . . . .204 F6
Heathfield Ct
Ellesmere Port, Whitby
CH65 . . . . .70 B5
Ellesmere Port, Whitbyheath
CH66 . . . . .95 A8
Heathfield Dr ST5 . . . . . 210 D1
Heathfield Pk
Warrington WA4 . . . . .17 A2
Widnes WA8 . . . . .12 D3
Heathfield Rd
Audlem CW3 . . . . .230 A5
Ellesmere Port CH65 . . . . .70 B5
Heathfields Cl CH2 . . . . 237 B4
Heathfield Sq WA16 . . . . .56 F2
Heathgate Ave L24 . . . . . .21 A2
Heath Gn CW6 . . . . .146 C4
Heath Gr CH66 . . . . .69 B7
Heath La
Chester CH3 . . . . .142 A8
Culcheth WA3 . . . . .4 A1

Heath La continued
Ellesmere Port, Little Sutton
CH66 . . . . .69 B7
Ellesmere Port, Little Sutton
CH66 . . . . .69 B7
Golborne, Kenyon WA3 . . . . 3 F2
Golborne WA3 . . . . .3 D6
Great Barrow CH3 . . . . . . 120 E6
Great Budworth CW9 . . . . .54 A1
High Legh WA16 . . . . .28 D5
Little Leigh WA4, CW8 . . . .77 B7
Marbury SY13 . . . . .226 E6
Stoak CH2 . . . . .95 E7
Stoak CH2 . . . . .95 F7
Swan Green WA16 . . . . . . 106 F6
Willaston CH64, CH66 . . . .68 D7
Wincham CW9 . . . . .79 C3
Heathlands Ho WA16 . . . .56 F2
Heathlands Rd CH66 . . . .69 B7
Heathland Trail* . . . .
CW6 . . . . .147 E2
Heathmoor Ave WA3 . . . . . 3 D5
Heath Park Gr WA7 . . . . .48 F8
Heath Rd
Bollington SK10 . . . . .87 E6
Chester CH2 . . . . .118 E7
Congleton CW12 . . . . 156 A2
Runcorn WA7 . . . . .23 B2
Sandbach CW11 . . . . 175 D6
Warrington WA5 . . . . .14 F5
Weaverham CW8 . . . . .77 E1
Widnes WA8 . . . . .12 D2
Heath Rd S WA7 . . . . .48 F6
Heath Road Cres WA7 . . .49 B8
Heath Sch The WA7 . . . . .49 B7
Heathside CW6 . . . . .204 F6
Heaths La CW6 . . . . 123 D2
Heath St
Crewe CW1 . . . . .190 D4
Golborne WA3 . . . . .3 D4
Warrington WA4 . . . . .26 C8
Heath Terr
Chester CH2 . . . . .118 E8
Smallwood CW11 . . . . . . 154 B1
Heathview CW1 . . . . 191 D3
Heath View
Alsager ST7 . . . . .193 E5
Weston CW2 . . . . .207 B5
Heathview Cl WA8 . . . . . .22 A5
Heathview Rd WA8 . . . . . .22 A5
Heathway CH60 . . . . .41 B7
Heath Way CW6 . . . . 168 D8
Heathwood Dr ST7 . . . . .193 F7
Heathwood Gr WA1 . . . . .17 B7
HEATLEY 19 C5
Heatley Cl WA13 . . . . .19 A4
Heatley La CW5 . . . . .217 F3
Heatley Way **5** SK9 . . . .34 D4
HEATON 159 E2
Heaton Cl CW10 . . . . 151 B6
Heaton Ct WA3 . . . . 9 F6
Heaton Sq CW7 . . . . .149 C8
Heaton Way CW2 . . . . . . 207 E4
Heaward Cl CW2 . . . . . . .206 B4
Hebden Ave WA3 . . . . 5 B5
HEBDEN GREEN 148 F7
Hebden Green Com Sch
CW7 . . . . .149 A7
Heber's Cl SY14 . . . . .213 C5
Heber Wlk CW9 . . . . .104 A8
Hedge Hey WA7 . . . . .24 A1
Hedge Row SK10 . . . . . . .63 E1
Hedgerow Dr CW9 . . . . . .79 C3
Hedgerows The WA11 . . . . 1 F7
Hedingham Cl **7**
SK10 . . . . .111 F8
Hefferston Grange Dr
CW8 . . . . .102 A7
Heights The WA6 . . . . .73 C4
Helena Cl WA16 . . . . .57 C2
Hellath Wen CW5 . . . . . .204 E2
Hellyar-Brook Rd
ST7 . . . . .193 B4
Helmdon Cl CW7 . . . . . . .127 A3
Helmsdale Cl CW1 . . . . .190 B6
Helmsdale La WA5 . . . . . .15 C6
Helmsley Cl WA5 . . . . . . .15 E7
HELSBY 73 C3
Helsby Ave CH62 . . . . .43 F3
Helsby High Sch WA6 . . .73 D5
Helsby Hillside Prim Sch
WA6 . . . . .73 C4
HELSBY MARSH 73 B5
Helsby Pk WA6 . . . . .73 C4
Helsby Rd WA6 . . . . .73 C1
Helsby St WA1 . . . . .16 D6
Helsby Sta WA6 . . . . .73 B4
Helsby Way **5** SK9 . . . .34 D4
Helston Cl
Bramhall SK7 . . . . .35 F7
Runcorn WA7 . . . . .50 B5
Warrington WA5 . . . . .14 E5
Helston Gr SK8 . . . . .34 C8
Helton Cl CW4 . . . . .130 A3
Hemingford Cl CH66 . . . .69 D2
Hemlegh Vale WA6 . . . . . .73 B2
Hemmingshaw La
CW11 . . . . .176 B8
Hemming St CW2 . . . . . .190 B2
Hemsworll Cl CW7 . . . . .149 E8
Hemsworth Ave CH66 . . .69 C5
HENBURY 111 B8
Henbury Cl CW10 . . . . . .151 C7
Henbury Gdns WA11 . . . .26 E3
Henbury High Sch
SK10 . . . . .111 E8
Henbury La SK8 . . . . .34 F6
HENBURY MOSS 110 D5

Henbury Pl WA7 . . . . .49 B6
Henbury Rd SK9 . . . . .34 D4
Henbury Rise SK11 . . . . 111 C8
Henderson Cl WA5 . . . . . .14 D6
Henderson Rd
Widnes, Lower House
WA8 . . . . .22 F8
2 Widnes WA8 . . . . .13 A1
Henderson St SK11 . . . . 112 C7
Hendon Cl CW1 . . . . .190 F5
Henley Ave M44 . . . . .11 E6
Henley Cl
Macclesfield SK10 . . . . . . .87 B4
Neston CH64 . . . . .66 E6
Warrington WA4 . . . . .26 E6
Henley Ct WA2 . . . . .23 D2
Henley Dr CW7 . . . . .126 F1
Henley Rd
Chester CH4 . . . . .140 F6
Chorlton CW2 . . . . .207 B1
Neston CH64 . . . . .66 E6
Henrietta St CW12 . . . . . 156 C3
Henry Pl CH1 . . . . .237 B3
Henry St
Crewe CW1 . . . . .190 D5
Haslington CW1 . . . . 191 D4
2 Lymm WA13 . . . . .18 E3
Tarporley CW6 . . . . .146 C2
Warrington WA1 . . . . .16 A5
4 Widnes WA8 . . . . .13 C1
Henry Wood Ct CH4 . . . .140 E6
Henshall Ave WA4 . . . . . . .16 F4
Henshall Dr CW11 . . . . . 175 D8
Henshall Hall Dr
CW12 . . . . .157 B1
Henshall La WA14 . . . . . . .20 C6
Henshall Rd SK10 . . . . . . .87 F7
Henshall St CH1 . . . . . . .237 A4
Henshaw La SK11 . . . . . .110 E2
Hepherd St WA5 . . . . .15 D4
Hepley Rd SK12 . . . . .37 A3
Herald Dr CW1 . . . . .190 E3
Herald Pk CW1 . . . . .190 E3
Heralds Cl WA8 . . . . .22 C8
Heralds Gn WA5 . . . . 7 A2
Herberts La CH60 . . . . . . .40 F8
Herbert St
Burtonwood WA5 . . . . 6 E6
Congleton CW12 . . . . 156 F3
Crewe CW1 . . . . .191 A5
Lostock Gralam CW9 . . . . .80 A2
Herbert Swindells Cl
CW2 . . . . .190 D1
Herdman St CW2 . . . . . . .190 D2
Hereford Ave
Ellesmere Port CH66 . . . . .94 E8
Golborne WA3 . . . . .3 C7
Hereford Cl
Macclesfield SK10 . . . . . . .86 F1
Warrington WA1 . . . . .17 A8
Hereford Dr SK9 . . . . .34 E3
Hereford Pl CH1 . . . . 118 A5
Hereford Way CW10 . . . .128 E2
Hereward Rd CH3 . . . . . . 119 B1
Heritage Ct CH1 . . . . 237 B2
Hermitage Ct
Holmes Chapel CW4 . . . .130 D3
Saughall CH1 . . . . .117 A8
Hermitage Dr CW4 . . . . .130 D3
Hermitage Green La WA2,
WA12 . . . . .3 A8
Hermitage La CW4 . . . . .130 C2
Hermitage Prim Sch
CW4 . . . . .130 D4
Hermitage Rd CH1 . . . . .117 B7
Hermitage The CH60 . . . .40 F7
Heron Bsns Pk WA8 . . . .23 D8
Heron Cl
Broughton CH4 . . . . .139 C4
Farndon CH3 . . . . .180 F1
Knutsford WA16 . . . . .57 B3
Runcorn WA7 . . . . .50 D8
Winsford CW7 . . . . .149 D5
Heron Cres CW1 . . . . .190 F5
Heron Ct
Neston CH64 . . . . .66 C7
Northwich CW9 . . . . .79 C2
Heron Dr SK12 . . . . .36 A3
Heron Pl CH2 . . . . .237 B4
Herons Reach WA3 . . . . . . 5 C6
Herons Way
Chester CH4 . . . . .141 B2
Runcorn WA7 . . . . .24 F4
Herrick Cl CW2 . . . . .206 A8
Hertford Apartments
WA2 . . . . 9 A3
Hertford Cl
Congleton CW12 . . . . 156 E4
Warrington WA1 . . . . .17 A8
Hertford Dr M44 . . . . .11 C6
Hesketh Cl WA5 . . . . .14 F4
Hesketh Croft CW1 . . . . .190 A8
Hesketh Dr CW9 . . . . .80 A3
Hesketh Grange Cotts
CH63 . . . . .42 A7
Hesketh Meadow La
WA3 . . . . 3 F8
Hesketh Rd L24 . . . . .21 E2
Hesketh St N WA5 . . . . . .15 D4
Hesketh St S WA5 . . . . . .15 C8
Hessall Cl WA3 . . . . 3 E8
Hessle Dr CH60 . . . . .40 F7
HESWALL 40 D7
Heswall Ave WA3 . . . . 4 E4
Heswall Point **7** CH60 . .41 A8
Heswall Rd CH66 . . . . . . .94 E8
Heswall St Peter's CE Prim
Sch CH60 . . . . .40 F8

Heswall Sta CH60 . . . . . . .41 D8
HETHERSON GREEN . . 214 D8
Hetherson Green La
SY14 . . . . .214 D8
Hewetson Cres SK11 . . . 111 E7
Hewitt Dr CW7 . . . . .150 B8
Hewitt Gr CW9 . . . . .79 F5
Hewitt St
Chester CH2 . . . . .118 F3
Crewe CW2 . . . . .190 D2
Northwich CW9 . . . . .79 D2
Warrington WA4 . . . . .16 C3
Hexham Ct CH1 . . . . .118 B2
Hexham Way **4** SK10 . .87 C4
Heybridge La SK10 . . . . . .87 B6
Heydon Cl
Congleton CW12 . . . . 156 C3
Halewood L26 . . . . .21 A7
Heyes Ave WA11 . . . . 1 D5
Heyes Dr WA13 . . . . .18 C2
Heyes Farm Rd SK11 . . .111 E8
Heyes Rd WA11 . . . . 1 D8
Heyes La
Alderley Edge SK9 . . . . . . .60 B3
Warrington WA4 . . . . .26 E8
Heyes Pk CW8 . . . . .102 F4
Heyes Rd WA8 . . . . .22 C8
Heyeswood La CW8 . . . .103 A4
Heyfield Park Rd CH66 . .69 B7
Heygarth Prim Sch
CH62 . . . . .43 E5
Heygarth Rd CH62 . . . . . .43 E5
Hey Lock Cl WA12 . . . . 7 C8
Heys Ave CH62 . . . . .43 D8
Heysbank Rd SK12 . . . . . .38 D5
Heysham Cl WA7 . . . . .50 D6
Hey Shoot La WA3 . . . . 5 C5
Heysoms Ave CW8 . . . . .103 D7
Heysoms Cl CW8 . . . . . . 103 D7
Heys The
Bebington CH62 . . . . .43 F5
Runcorn WA7 . . . . .23 E1
Heythrop Dr CH60 . . . . . . .41 D8
Heywood Cl SK9 . . . . .60 B2
Hey Wood Cl WA12 . . . . . . 7 C8
Heywood Gn CW2 . . . . . 206 C8
Heywood Ho CW3,
SY13 . . . . .234 C7
Heywood Rd
Alderley Edge SK9 . . . . . . .60 B2
Ellesmere Port CH66 . . . . .69 D5
Heywoods Ridge
CW3 . . . . .229 E3
Heywood St CW12 . . . . . 156 C2
Heywoods The CH2 . . . . 118 C4
Hibbert St
New Mills SK22 . . . . .39 B6
6 Widnes WA8 . . . . .23 B8
Hibel Rd SK10 . . . . .87 D1
Hickhurst La CW6 . . . . . .147 D3
Hickmore Heys CH3 . . . .119 F5
Hickory Cl WA1 . . . . .17 E7
Hickson St CW8 . . . . .78 B3
Hidcote Cl CW2 . . . . .206 B8
HIDEBANK 39 C8
Hield Brow CW9 . . . . .79 C7
Hield Gr CW9 . . . . .79 C7
Hield La CW9 . . . . .79 C8
Higginbotham Gn
SK11 . . . . .112 E6
Higginson Cl CW12 . . . . 179 C8
Higham Ave WA5 . . . . 7 F1
Highbank Cl CW8 . . . . . . .78 B3
High Bank Cl M44 . . . . . . .11 D6
Highbank Dr
Kingsley WA6 . . . . .75 C2
Northwich CW8 . . . . .103 D7
High Bent Ave SK8 . . . . . .35 A6
HIGH CARR 210 F3
High Carr Bsns Pk
ST5 . . . . .210 F2
High Carr Network Ctr
ST5 . . . . .210 F2
Highcliffe Ave CH1 . . . . .118 B4
Highcroft Ave CW12 . . . .156 F2
High Cross La CH3 . . . . .182 D1
High Ct SK10 . . . . .88 B8
High Elm Dr WA15 . . . . . .32 C8
High Elm Rd WA15 . . . . . .32 D7
High Elms SK8 . . . . .35 B5
Higher Ash Rd ST7 . . . . 210 D8
Higher Ashton WA8 . . . . .12 F3
HIGHER BUNBURY 168 F1
HIGHER BURWARDSLEY
. . . . .184 C5
HIGHER CARDEN 198 D7
Higher Carden La
SY14 . . . . .198 D6
HIGHER DISLEY 38 E4
Higher Downs WA16 . . . . .57 C2
HIGHERFENCE 113 A8
Higher Fence Rd SK10 . . .87 F1
HIGHER FERRY 140 C8
Higher Heyes Dr WA6 . . .75 C1
HIGHER HURDSFIELD . . .88 A2
HIGHER KINNERTON
. . . . .161 B8
Higher Knutsford Rd
WA4 . . . . .16 F2
Higher La
Bollington SK10 . . . . .88 B6
Disley SK12 . . . . .38 E1
Dutton WA4 . . . . .51 D4
Kettleshulme SK23 . . . . . . .64 C6
Lymm WA13 . . . . .19 B1

Highland Ct **6** ST7 . . . . . 195 A2
HIGHER MARSTON 79 C6
HIGHER POYNTON 35 D8
Higher Rd L26, WA8 . . . . . . 21 C5
HIGHER RUNCORN 23 A1
HIGHER SHURLACH 104 E6
HIGHER WALTON 80 A8
HIGHER WHITLEY 52 D5
HIGHER WINCHAM 79 F4
Higher Works Cotts
SK11 . . . . 158 C6
HIGHER WYCH 224 D4
Highfield
Elton CH2 . . . . 72 A4
Prestbury SK10 . . . . 87 A5
High Field WA14 . . . . 20 B2
Highfield Ave
Audlem CW3 . . . . 230 A4
Golborne WA3 . . . . 2 F8
Kidsgrove ST7 . . . . 195 D2
Lostock Gralam CW9 . . . . . . 80 A3
Warrington, Dudlow's Green
WA4 . . . . 26 D4
Warrington WA5 . . . . 15 A5
Highfield Cl CH64 . . . . 66 E8
Highfield Com Prim Sch
CH1 . . . . 117 F4
Highfield Cres
Handforth SK9 . . . . 34 C1
Widnes WA8 . . . . 13 A2
Highfield Dr
Lymm WA13 . . . . 18 C2
Macclesfield SK10 . . . . 87 A1
Nantwich CW5 . . . . 205 A6
Highfield Est SK9 . . . . 34 C1
Highfield La
Coddington CH3 . . . . 181 E4
Golborne WA3 . . . . 3 C5
Winwick WA2 . . . . 8 C7
Highfield Parkway
SK7 . . . . 35 D4
Highfield Pl **1** CW8 . . . . 103 E8
Highfield Rd
Blacon CH1 . . . . 117 D5
Bollington SK10 . . . . 88 A8
Cheadle SK8 . . . . 34 F8
Congleton CW12 . . . . 156 C2
Ellesmere Port CH65 . . . . . . 70 C2
Ellesmere Port, Little Sutton
CH66 . . . . 69 B6
Lymm WA13 . . . . 18 C2
Macclesfield SK11 . . . . 112 C7
Neston CH64 . . . . 66 F8
Northwich CW8 . . . . 103 F7
Poynton SK12 . . . . 36 A4
Widnes WA8 . . . . 13 A2
Highfield Rd N **1**
CH65 . . . . 70 C6
Highfields SY13 . . . . 224 A2
Highfield Sch L26 . . . . 21 A7
Highfields Com Prim Sch
CW5 . . . . 204 F6
Highfield Terr SK22 . . . . . 39 D8
Highgate Cl
Crewe CW1 . . . . 190 A8
Runcorn WA7 . . . . 24 D1
High Gates Cl WA5 . . . . . . 15 E7
High Gates Lo WA5 . . . . . . 15 E7
Highgrove Mews **2**
SK9 . . . . 60 A6
High Hill Rd SK22 . . . . . . 39 D8
Highlands Rd WA7 . . . . . . 48 F8
Highlands The CW6 . . . . . 185 E8
Highland Way WA16 . . . . . 82 A7
HIGHLANE 134 C6
HIGH LANE 37 E8
High Lane Prim Sch
SK6 . . . . 37 F8
High Lea Rd SK22 . . . . 39 A8
HIGH LEGH 29 B5
High Legh Prim Sch
WA16 . . . . 29 C5
High Legh Rd WA13 . . . . . 29 C8
High Lowe Ave CW2 . . . . . 157 A4
Highmarsh Cres WA12 . . . 2 B4
High Mdw **2** SK8 . . . . . 34 E8
High Mount CH60 . . . . 40 F8
High St
Audley ST7 . . . . 210 A1
Bollington SK10 . . . . 88 B8
Clutton CW6 . . . . 145 D4
Congleton CW12 . . . . 156 D2
Crewe CW2 . . . . 190 D3
Farndon CH3 . . . . 180 E2
Frodsham WA6 . . . . 49 B1
Golborne WA3 . . . . 3 A8
Great Budworth CW9 . . . . . 79 A7
Hale L24 . . . . 21 D1
Harriseahead ST7 . . . . 195 E5
Kidsgrove, The Rookery
ST7 . . . . 195 C4
Macclesfield SK11 . . . . 112 D6
Malpas SY14 . . . . 213 B3
Mow Cop ST7 . . . . 195 D7
Nantwich CW5 . . . . 204 E5
Neston CH64 . . . . 66 E7
New Mills SK22 . . . . 39 C8
Newton-le-W WA12 . . . . 2 D4
Norley WA6 . . . . 100 F5
Northwich CW9 . . . . 103 F8
Runcorn WA7 . . . . 23 A2
Saltney CH4 . . . . 140 E7
Sandbach CW11 . . . . 175 B6
Talke ST7 . . . . 210 D6

High St continued
Tarporley CW6 . . . . 146 C2
Tarvin CH3 . . . . 121 B2
Tattenhall CH3 . . . . 166 B1
Warrington WA1 . . . . 16 C5
Weaverham CW8 . . . . 77 C1
Winsford CW7 . . . . 126 D1
Hightown
Crewe CW1 . . . . 190 C4
Middlewich CW10 . . . . 128 C1
Sandbach CW11 . . . . 175 B6
Hightown Appts **6**
CW1 . . . . 190 C4
Hightree Dr SK11 . . . . 111 C8
High View
Helsby WA6 . . . . 73 C4
Mount Pleasant ST7 . . . . . 195 B5
HIGH WARREN 26 C6
High Warren Cl WA4 . . . . . 26 C5
Highwood Rd WA4 . . . . . . 26 C7
Hignett Ave WA9 . . . . 1 B2
Hilary Ave SK8 . . . . 34 D8
Hilary Cl
Chester CH3 . . . . 119 B1
Warrington WA5 . . . . 14 D6
Widnes WA8 . . . . 13 E3
Hilbre Ave CH60 . . . . 40 E6
Hilbre Bank CW6 . . . . 169 D4
Hilbre Dr CH65 . . . . 70 C1
Hilden Pl WA2 . . . . 16 D8
Hilden Rd WA2 . . . . 8 E1
Hilary Ave CW12 . . . . 157 A2
Hilary Dr CW3 . . . . 230 A4
Hilary Rd
Bebington CH62 . . . . 43 E5
Kidsgrove ST7 . . . . 195 B3
Hillberry Cres WA4 . . . . . . 16 B3
Hillbre Way **1** SK9 . . . . 34 D4
Hillbrook Rd SK7 . . . . 35 D6
Hill Cl
Bunbury CW6 . . . . 185 E7
Neston CH64 . . . . 67 B5
HILLCLIFFE 26 C8
Hill Cliffe Rd WA4 . . . . 26 B8
Hill Cotts CH3 . . . . 164 A4
Hillcourt Rd SK6 . . . . 37 F7
Hillcrest WA7 . . . . 23 D1
Hillcrest Ave WA4 . . . . 130 B3
Hillcrest Dr CH66 . . . . 69 A6
Hillcrest Rd
Bollington SK10 . . . . 87 F7
Ellesmere Port CH66 . . . . . . 69 B6
Kelsall CW6 . . . . 122 E6
Warren SK11 . . . . 112 A4
Hill Ct CH64 . . . . 67 B5
Hill Dr
Handforth SK9 . . . . 34 E3
Whaley Bridge SK23 . . . . . . 65 D8
Hillesden Rise CW12 . . . . 156 F2
Hillfield
Frodsham WA6 . . . . 74 B7
Runcorn WA7 . . . . 50 D8
Hillfield Gdns CW5 . . . . . 204 E4
Hillfield Pl CW5 . . . . 204 E4
Hillfield Rd CH66 . . . . 69 D7
Hill Fields CW12 . . . . 156 D4
Hill Fields Cl CW12 . . . . . 156 D4
Hillfield View CW5 . . . . . . 204 E4
Hillfoot Cres WA4 . . . . 26 B7
Hillfoot La WA4 . . . . 74 E3
Hilliards Ct CH4 . . . . 141 B3
Hillingden Ave L26 . . . . . . 21 A7
Hill La
Brown Knowl CH3 . . . . 199 C8
Peckforton CW6 . . . . 184 E6
Hillock La WA1 . . . . 17 C8
Hill Rd CH4 . . . . 141 E2
Hill Rd N WA6 . . . . 73 D3
Hill Rd S WA6 . . . . 73 C3
Hillsboro Ave WA6 . . . . . . 74 C7
Hillsdown Way CH66 . . . . . 69 C2
Hillside
Broomedge WA13 . . . . 19 E1
Northwich CW8 . . . . 103 C7
Hillside Ave
Newton-le-W WA12 . . . . 1 F2
Runcorn WA7 . . . . 48 E8
Hillside Cl
Bramhall SK7 . . . . 36 A7
Chorlton CW2 . . . . 207 E3
Helsby WA6 . . . . 73 D4
Tarvin CH3 . . . . 121 B2
Hillside Ct
Macclesfield SK10 . . . . 88 A1
Warrington WA4 . . . . 26 D3
Hillside Dr
Crewe CW1 . . . . 190 E5
Ellesmere Port CH66 . . . . . . 69 E7
Macclesfield SK10 . . . . 88 A1
Hillside Gr WA5 . . . . 14 F4
Hillside Ho **3** CW8 . . . . 103 C5
Hillside La CW9 . . . . 126 E7
Hillside Rd
Blacon CH1 . . . . 117 E4
Frodsham WA6 . . . . 74 C7
Heswall CH60 . . . . 41 A7
Kelsall CW6 . . . . 122 D4
Knutsford WA16 . . . . 57 A2
Warrington WA4 . . . . 26 D3
Hillside View SK22 . . . . . . 39 A8
Hill St
Crewe CW1 . . . . 190 D4
Macclesfield SK11 . . . . 112 D4
Runcorn WA7 . . . . 23 A3
Sandbach CW11 . . . . 174 D7
Warrington WA1 . . . . 16 B5

Hill St continued
Winsford CW7 . . . . 126 F1
Hill Terr ST7 . . . . 209 D2
Hill The
Knutsford WA16 . . . . 82 B8
Sandbach CW11 . . . . 175 D5
HILLTOP 60 B8
Hilltop WA7 . . . . 50 C7
Hill Top
Altrincham WA15 . . . . 32 A8
Barnton CW8 . . . . 78 B2
Hill Top Ave
Cheadle SK8 . . . . 35 B8
Wilmslow SK9 . . . . 60 B8
Winsford CW7 . . . . 126 C1
Hilltop Com Prim Sch
ST7 . . . . 210 D7
Hill Top La
Heswall CH60 . . . . 41 B8
Neston CH64 . . . . 67 B5
Hilltop Pk WA16 . . . . 79 F7
Hilltop Rd
Guilden Sutton CH3 . . . . . . 119 F5
Lymm WA13 . . . . 18 C2
Hill Top Rd
Acton Bridge CW8 . . . . 76 F2
Dutton WA4 . . . . 51 C1
Runcorn WA7 . . . . 50 F6
Warrington, Stockton Heath
WA4 . . . . 16 F2
Warrington, Woolston
WA4 . . . . 17 C7
Hill Top Rise SK23 . . . . . . 65 D8
Hill View
Bollington SK10 . . . . 87 F7
Whaley Bridge SK23 . . . . . . 65 C8
Widnes WA8 . . . . 12 F5
Hill View Ave WA6 . . . . 73 A1
Hillview Cl WA6 . . . . 74 C7
Hill View Prim Sch
WA7 . . . . 49 E4
Hillview Rise CW8 . . . . 78 E1
Hilton Ave WA5 . . . . 15 B5
Hilton Cl
9 Macclesfield SK11 . . . 111 F7
Middlewich CW10 . . . . 151 B8
Hilton Dr M44 . . . . 11 C5
Hilton Gr SK12 . . . . 36 D4
Hilton Rd
Disley SK12 . . . . 38 B7
Poynton SK12 . . . . 37 C5
Himalayan Birch Cl
CH66 . . . . 69 C6
Hinchley Cl CW8 . . . . 103 A5
Hinckley Ct CW12 . . . . . . 156 A3
Hinderton Dr CH60 . . . . . . 40 F6
Hinderton Gn CH64 . . . . . 66 F8
Hinderton Rd CH64 . . . . . . 66 F8
Hinderton Sch CH65 . . . . . 69 F3
Hinde St WA5 . . . . 204 D4
Hind Heath La CW11 . . . . 174 F4
Hind Heath Rd CW11 . . . . 174 E4
Hindle Ave WA5 . . . . 7 F1
Hindley Cres CW8 . . . . 78 A3
Hinton Cres WA4 . . . . 26 E8
Hinton Rd
Crewe CW2 . . . . 206 D8
Runcorn WA7 . . . . 23 A1
Hirsch Cl SK11 . . . . 205 A4
Hitchen's Cl WA7 . . . . 50 D7
Hitchens La SY14 . . . . . . 184 D1
Hitch Lowes SK11 . . . . 84 A3
Hobart Cl SK7 . . . . 35 F4
Hobart Way CW1 . . . . 12 F4
Hobb La WA4 . . . . 25 C5
Hobbs Cl CW1 . . . . 191 D4
Hobbs Hill La WA16 . . . . . . 28 E1
Hobby Ct WA7 . . . . 49 E6
Hobcroft La WA16 . . . . 58 A7
Hob Hey La WA3 . . . . 4 D3
Hob La
Chorlton CW2 . . . . 180 F5
Dunham-on-t-H WA6 . . . . . 97 C6
Hobson St SK11 . . . . 112 D6
Hockenhull Ave CH3 . . . . 121 B2
Hockenhull Cres CH3 . . . 121 B2
Hockenhull La
Tarvin, Broom Bank
CH3 . . . . 121 B1
Tarvin CH3 . . . . 121 B2
Hocker La
Adder's Moss SK10 . . . . 85 F4
Nether Alderley SK10 . . . . . 85 C4
Hockerley Ave SK23 . . . . . . 65 D8
Hockerley Cl SK23 . . . . 65 D8
Hockerley La SK23 . . . . 65 D8
Hockerley New Rd
SK23 . . . . 65 D8
HOCKLEY 37 A2
Hockley Cl SK12 . . . . 37 A3
Hockley Paddock SK12 . . . 36 F3
Hockley Rd SK12 . . . . 37 A3
HODGEHILL 132 E8
Hodgehill La SK11 . . . . . . 132 E5
Hodge La
Hartford CW8 . . . . 103 A6
Weaverham CW8 . . . . 102 D5
Hodgkinson Ave WA5 . . . . 7 F7
Hoghton Rd L24 . . . . 21 E2
Hogshead La CW8 . . . . . . 124 C7
Holbeck WA7 . . . . 50 C7
Holbein Cl CH4 . . . . 141 E6
Holborn Rd CW8 . . . . 12 F1
Holbrook Cl WA5 . . . . 14 C3
Holbury Ct CW1 . . . . 190 B8
Holcombe Ave WA3 . . . . 3 C8

Holcombe Dr SK10 . . . . . . 87 B3
Holcot Ct CW7 . . . . 127 A4
Holcroft La WA3 . . . . 5 D2
Holdings La CW3 . . . . 232 F4
Hole House La
Langley SK11 . . . . 113 C4
Scholar Green ST7 . . . . 194 D8
Whiteley Green SK10 . . . . . 62 D2
Hole House La CW8 . . . . . 77 E4
Hole La WA16 . . . . 106 E4
Holes La WA1 . . . . 17 B7
Holford Ave
Lostock Gralam CW9 . . . . . 80 A3
Warrington WA5 . . . . 15 F8
Holford Cres WA16 . . . . . . 57 B1
Holford Moss WA7 . . . . . . 24 D3
Holford St CW12 . . . . 156 D3
Holford Way WA12 . . . . 2 F3
Holgrave Cl WA16 . . . . 29 C4
Holkam Cl CW9 . . . . 103 F5
Holker Cl SK12 . . . . 36 F4
Holland Ave WA8 . . . . 12 F1
Holkham The CH3 . . . . . . 119 B1
Holland Cl CW11 . . . . 175 C5
Holland Ct SK12 . . . . 36 E3
Holland Rd SK7 . . . . 35 E7
Hollands La CW6 . . . . 122 C5
Hollands Pl SK11 . . . . 112 F7
Hollands Rd CW9 . . . . 103 F7
Holland St
Crewe CW1 . . . . 190 B6
5 Macclesfield SK11 . . . 112 C7
Holland Wlk CW5 . . . . 204 D6
Hollies La SK9 . . . . 60 F7
Hollies The
Moulton CW9 . . . . 126 E8
1 Northwich CW9 . . . . 104 A8
Runcorn WA7 . . . . 49 D8
Shavington CW2 . . . . 206 B4
HOLLINFARE 11 A3
Hollingford Pl WA16 . . . . . 82 A8
HOLLIN GREEN 202 E8
Hollingreen La CW5 . . . . 229 B7
Hollin Green La CW5 . . . . 202 E6
Hollinhey Prim Sch
SK11 . . . . 112 F3
Hollin La
Langley SK11 . . . . 113 A1
Newhall CW5 . . . . 228 D8
Styal SK9 . . . . 33 F5
Sutton Lane Ends SK11 . . . 136 C6
Hollin Rd SK10 . . . . 88 A7
HOLLINS 210 E8
Hollins Cres ST7 . . . . 194 E1
Hollins Dr WA2 . . . . 8 A6
Hollins Grange ST7 . . . . . 210 D8
HOLLINSGREEN 10 F2
HOLLINS GREEN 11 B2
Hollins Green St Helens
CE Prim Sch WA3 . . . . 11 B2
Hollinshead Cl ST7 . . . . . 194 F7
Hollins Hill CW6 . . . . 146 F8
Hollins La
Antrobus CW9 . . . . 53 F4
Marbury SY13 . . . . 226 E7
Warrington WA2 . . . . 7 F6
HOLLINS-LANE 226 E6
Hollins Park Hospl WA2 . . 7 F6
Hollins Rd SK11 . . . . 112 F6
Hollins Terr SK11 . . . . 112 F6
Hollins Way WA8 . . . . 22 B5
Hollinwood Cl ST7 . . . . . . 210 E8
Hollinwood Rd
Disley SK12 . . . . 38 D6
Talke ST7 . . . . 210 E8
Holloway WA7 . . . . 22 F1
Hollow Dr WA4 . . . . 16 E1
Hollow La
Kingsley WA6 . . . . 75 B3
Knutsford WA16 . . . . 57 B1
Hollowmoor Heath
CH3 . . . . 121 A6
Hollow Oak La CW8 . . . . . 101 D4
Hollowood Rd SY14 . . . . . 213 B5
Hollow The ST7 . . . . 195 B5
Holly Ave WA3 . . . . 2 D3
Hollybank
Audlem CW3 . . . . 229 E3
Moore WA4 . . . . 25 E5
Holly Bank
Chester CH1 . . . . 237 A4
Frodsham WA6 . . . . 74 C8
Helsby WA6 . . . . 73 D2
Lymm WA13 . . . . 18 D2
Hollybank Cl CW8 . . . . 78 D1
Hollybank Ct WA8 . . . . 12 F1
Holly Bank Cvn Pk
WA3 . . . . 11 A1
Hollybank Rd WA7 . . . . . . 49 F8
Holly Bank Rd SK9 . . . . . . 34 B1
Hollybush Cres CW5 . . . . 205 D5
Holly Bush La WA3 . . . . . . 10 C2
Holly Cl
Connah's Quay CH5 . . . . . . 91 C1
Hale L24 . . . . 21 D2
Mickle Trafford CH2 . . . . . 119 F8
Holly Cotts CW12 . . . . . . 132 C1
Holly Croft CW12 . . . . . . 154 F6
Holly Ct
Helsby WA6 . . . . 73 C5
Middlewich CW10 . . . . 128 B2
Holly Dr CW7 . . . . 149 D8
Holly Farm Ct WA8 . . . . . . 12 E4
Hollyfield Rd CH65 . . . . . . 70 B5
Hollyfields CW3 . . . . 191 F8
Holly Gr
Over Tabley WA16 . . . . 56 A3
Warrington WA1 . . . . 17 A7

Holly Heath Cl CW11 . . . . 175 C5
Holly Hedge La WA4 . . . . . 25 D6
Holly House Est
CW10 . . . . 129 C6
HOLLYHURST 227 A5
Hollyhurst Rd SY13 . . . . . 227 B7
Holly La
Alsager ST7 . . . . 193 E3
Harriseahead ST7 . . . . 195 F5
Wythenshawe SK9 . . . . 33 E5
Holly Mount CW2 . . . . 206 E5
Holly Rd
Bramhall SK7 . . . . 35 E5
Chester CH4 . . . . 140 F5
Ellesmere Port CH65 . . . . . . 70 C5
Golborne WA3 . . . . 3 C8
Haydock WA11 . . . . 1 B6
High Lane SK6 . . . . 37 F7
Lymm WA13 . . . . 19 B5
Macclesfield SK11 . . . . 112 B7
Newcastle-u-Lyme ST5 . . . 210 D1
Poynton SK12 . . . . 36 E3
Warrington WA5 . . . . 14 E5
Weaverham CW8 . . . . 102 C8
Holly Rd N SK9 . . . . 60 B6
Holly Rd S SK9 . . . . 60 B5
Holly Terr
Tilston SY14 . . . . 198 C3
Warrington WA5 . . . . 14 F5
Hollythorn Ave SK8 . . . . . 35 C7
Holly Tree Dr
Biddulph ST8 . . . . 179 C2
Swan Green WA16 . . . . . . 106 D7
Hollytree Rd WA16 . . . . . . 80 F3
Holly Wlk
Northwich CW8 . . . . 103 C7
Partington M31 . . . . 11 D3
Holm Dr CH2 . . . . 72 C3
HOLMES CHAPEL 130 C4
Holmes Chapel Bsns Pk
CW4 . . . . 130 D3
Holmes Chapel Comp Sch
CW4 . . . . 130 A2
Holmes Chapel Prim Sch
CW4 . . . . 130 B3
Holmes Chapel Rd
Allostock WA16 . . . . 106 B3
Brereton Green CW4,
CW12 . . . . 154 D8
Congleton CW12 . . . . 155 C4
Knutsford WA16 . . . . 82 C3
Lach Dennis CW9 . . . . 105 E4
Middlewich CW10 . . . . 128 E2
Sandbach CW11 . . . . 153 E1
Sproston Green CW4,
CW10 . . . . 129 B2
Holmes Chapel Sta
CW4 . . . . 130 D2
Holmes Ct WA3 . . . . 9 C4
Holme St CH3 . . . . 120 F2
Holmesville Ave
CW12 . . . . 156 B3
Holmeswood Cl SK9 . . . . . 60 C8
Holmfield Ave WA7 . . . . . . 85 A8
Holmfield Ave WA7 . . . . . . 23 C2
Holmfield Dr
Cheadle SK8 . . . . 35 B8
Ellesmere Port CH66 . . . . . . 69 D3
Holmlea Dr CW9 . . . . 190 F3
Holmlee Way SK10 . . . . . . 86 D6
Holm Oak Way CH66 . . . . 94 F8
Holmsfield Rd WA1 . . . . . . 16 D5
Holmshaw La CW1 . . . . . . 192 B3
Holmwood Dr CH65 . . . . . 70 B2
HOLT 196 E8
Holt Gdns WA16 . . . . 58 E6
Holt Hey CH64 . . . . 67 A5
Holtis La SK9 . . . . 33 F3
Holt La WA7 . . . . 49 F8
HOLTRIDGE 215 E6
Holtridge La SY13 . . . . . . 215 E6
Holt's Com Prim Sch
LL13 . . . . 196 D8
Holt St WA1 . . . . 190 B4
Holyhead Cl WA5 . . . . 7 D3
Holyrood Ave WA8 . . . . . . 13 A4
Holyrood Dr CW2 . . . . 205 E8
Holyrood Way CH3 . . . . . 119 B2
Holy Spirit RC Prim Sch
WA9 . . . . 1 A3
Holy Spirit RC Prim Sch
The WA7 . . . . 49 D8
Holywell Cl CH64 . . . . 41 B1
Holywell Dr WA1 . . . . 16 C5
Holywell La CH3 . . . . 182 D2
Homecrofts CH64 . . . . 66 E5
Homedee Ho CH1 . . . . . . 237 A3
Home Farm WA16 . . . . 56 B8
Home Farm Pk CW5 . . . . . 172 A8
Home Pk CH1 . . . . 94 F1
Homeshire Ho ST7 . . . . . 193 D3
Homestead Ave WA11 . . . . . 1 B6
Homestead La CW9 . . . . . 104 D7
Homestead Rd SK12 . . . . . 38 D6
Homesteads The
CW5 . . . . 172 A6
Homeway WA3 . . . . 3 C3
Homewood Cres CW8 . . . 103 B5
Honey Fields CW6 . . . . . . 146 C1
Honeysuckle Cl
Broughton CH4 . . . . 139 C3
Widnes WA8 . . . . 13 B4

Honey Suckle Cl 3 CH66 94 F8
Hong Kong Ave M90 33 A8
Honister Ave WA2 8 C2
Honister Gr WA7 49 E5
Honiton Way
Middlewich CW10 128 D2
Warrington WA5 14 E4
HONKLEY 161 C3
Hood La WA5 15 C4
Hood La N WA5 15 C6
HOOD MANOR 15 D5
Hood Rd WA8 12 F1
HOOFIELD 145 A2
Hoofield La CH3 145 A1
HOO GREEN 29 F2
Hoo Green La WA16 29 E1
Hooker St CW8 103 E7
Hook La CW6 145 A6
Hookstone Dr CH66 69 C6
HOOLE 119 A3
HOOLE BANK 119 C7
Hoole CE Prim Sch CH2 119 A3
Hoole Gdns CH2 119 B3
Hoole Ho CH2 119 B4
Hoole La CH2 119 A3
HOOLE PARK 118 F3
Hoole Pk CH2 118 F2
Hoole Rd CH2 118 F3
Hoole Way CH1 237 B3
Hooleyhey La SK10, SK11 89 D4
Hoolpool La WA6 72 F5
Hooten Hey CH66 69 D5
HOOTON 44 A1
Hooton Gn CH66 44 B2
Hooton La CH66 44 B1
Hooton Rd CH64, CH66 43 D1
Hooton Sta CH66 43 D1
Hooton Way
14 Handforth SK9 34 D5
Hooton CH66 44 A2
Hooton Works CH66 43 E1
Hope Ave SK9 34 C3
Hope Croft CH66 69 F2
Hope Farm Prec CH66 69 F2
Hope Farm Rd CH66 69 E2
Hopefield Rd WA13 19 B4
Hope Green Way SK10 36 D2
Hope La
Midway SK10 36 D1
Wardsend SK10 36 E1
Hope Rd CH4 139 B3
Hope St W SK10 112 C8
Hope St
Audley ST7 209 F3
Chester CH4 140 F7
Crewe CW2 190 D2
Macclesfield SK10 112 E8
Newton-le-W WA12 2 B3
Northwich CW8 103 E7
Sandbach CW11 175 B6
Hopkins Cl CW12 156 B3
Hopkinson Ct CH1 118 B1
Hopwood Cl 5 WA3 3 F8
Hopwood St WA1 16 C6
Horace Black Gdns CH65 70 C6
Horace Lawton Ct 2 CW12 156 D3
Horbury Gdns CH66 69 C5
Hornbeam Ave CH66 69 F1
Hornbeam Cl
Chester CH2 119 B3
Runcorn WA7 24 C1
Hornbeam Dr CW8 102 E4
Hornbeam Rd L26 21 A7
Hornby Dr
Congleton CW12 156 A3
Nantwich CW5 205 A5
Hornby La WA2 8 A6
Horncastle Cl 4 WA3 3 F8
Horn's Mill Prim Sch WA6 73 A1
Hornsmill Way WA6 73 A3
Horridge Ave WA12 2 C5
Horrocks La WA1 16 B5
Horrocks Rd CH2 118 E5
Horsemarket St WA1 16 B5
Horseshoe Cl WA6 75 B2
Horseshoe Cres WA2 8 E3
Horseshoe Dr SK11 112 B7
Horseshoe La SK9 60 A2
Horsley La CW6 167 E1
Horstone Cres CH66 69 F2
Horstone Gdns CH66 70 A2
Horstone Rd CH66 69 F2
HORTON GREEN 212 A8
Horton Way CW5 205 A4
HORWICH END 65 D5
Hoscar Ct WA8 22 D7
Hospital La CW5 203 E2
Hospital of St John Almhouses CH1 237 A3
Hospital St
Crewe CW1 190 D6
Nantwich CW5 204 E5
Hospital Way WA7 49 F7
Hotel Rd M90 33 C7
Hotel St WA12 2 B3
Hothershall Cl CW1 173 B1
HOUGH
Alderley Edge 60 D1
Crewe 206 F3
Hough Cl SK10 88 D5
HOUGH COMMON 206 F2
Hough Cotts CW2 206 E3
Hougher Wall Rd ST7 209 D1
Hough Gn
Ashley WA15 31 E5
Chester CH4 141 B7
HOUGH GREEN 12 B2
Hough Green Rd WA8 12 B3
Hough Green Sta WA8 12 B2
Hough La
Alderley Edge SK9 60 D3
Barnton CW8, CW9 78 B4
Comberbach CW9 78 A7
Norley WA6 100 F5
Houghley Cl SK10 87 C2
Hough's La WA4 26 A6
Houghton Cl
Chester CH2 118 F3
Newton-le-W WA12 2 B3
9 Northwich CW9 103 F4
Widnes WA8 13 D2
Houghton Croft WA8 12 C5
HOUGHTON GREEN 8 E4
Houghton St
Newton-le-W WA12 2 B3
Warrington WA2 16 B6
Widnes WA8 13 D2
Houndings La CW11 175 B4
Hourd Way CH66 94 E8
Housesteads Dr CH2 118 F3
Housman Cl CH1 118 A5
Houston Gdns WA5 15 A8
Hove Cl CW1 190 B8
Hove The WA7 50 D6
Hovis Mill SK11 112 E7
Howard Ave
Bebington CH62 43 D8
Lymm WA13 19 B4
Howard Ct
Neston CH64 41 F1
Runcorn WA7 24 C4
Howard Rd
Culcheth WA3 5 A2
Saltney CH4 140 D6
Howard St CW1 191 A5
Howards Way CH64 67 A6
Howarth Ct 4 WA7 23 B2
HOWBECK BANK 219 E8
Howbeck Cres CW5 220 A8
Howbeck Wlk CW2 206 D8
Howells Ave CH66 69 D3
Howe Rd CH4 141 B7
Howe St SK10 87 F1
Howey Hill CW12 156 D1
Howey La
Congleton CW12 156 D2
Frodsham WA6 74 B7
Howey Rise WA6 74 B7
Howgill Cl CH66 68 F6
HOWLEY 16 D5
Howley La WA1 16 E5
Howley Quay Ind Est WA1 16 D5
Howson Rd WA2 8 C3
Howty Cl SK9 34 D1
Hoylake Cl WA7 50 C6
Hoyle St WA5 15 F7
Hubert Dr CW10 151 C8
Hubert Worthington Ho 9 SK9 60 A1
Hudson Cl WA5 15 D8
Hudson Gr 9 WA3 3 E8
Hudson Rd WA2 8 E2
Hughes Ave WA2 8 D2
Hughes Dr CW2 189 F4
Hughes Pl WA2 8 D2
Hughes St WA4 16 C3
Hugh St CH4 141 D7
Hulley Pl SK10 87 F1
Hulley Rd SK10 87 F2
Hullock's Pool Rd ST7 209 E5
HULME 8 B3
Hulme Hall Ave SK8 35 B8
Hulme Hall Cres SK8 35 A8
Hulme Hall Gram Sch SK8 35 A8
Hulme Hall La WA16 106 B4
Hulme Hall Rd SK8 35 A8
Hulme La WA16 106 C7
Hulme Sq SK11 112 D5
Hulme St CW1 189 F5
HULME WALFIELD 156 B7
HULSEHEATH 30 A4
Hulseheath La WA16 30 A3
Hulse La CW9 105 D6
Hulton Cl CW12 157 B1
Humber Cl WA8 13 F3
Humber Dr ST8 179 E1
Humber Rd
Ellesmere Port CH66 69 F2
Warrington WA2 8 E2
Humble Bee Bank Cotts CW5 187 C8
Hume St WA1 16 D6
Humphrey's Cl WA7 50 D7
Hungerford Ave CW1 190 E4
Hungerford Pl
Barthomley CW2 208 D5
Sandbach CW11 175 A5
Hungerford Prim Sch CW1 190 E4
Hungerford Rd CW1 190 F4
Hungerford Terr CW1 190 F4
Hungerford Villas CW1 190 F4
HUNSTERSON 220 B1
Hunsterson Rd
Bridgemere CW5 231 D8
Hatherton CW5 220 B3
Hunt Cl WA5 15 B8
Hunter Ave
Shavington CW2 206 D7
Warrington WA2 8 B3
Hunters Cl SK9 34 F1
Hunter's Cres CH3 121 C1
Hunters Ct
Helsby WA6 73 D4
Runcorn WA7 49 E6
Hunter's Dr CH3 121 C1
Huntersfield CW2 206 B3
Hunters Field CW8 103 D7
Hunters Hill
Kingsley WA6 75 C1
Weaverham CW8 77 C1
Hunters Lo SK9 34 F1
Hunters Mews SK9 60 C7
Hunters Pointe CW12 155 C6
Hunters Pool La SK10 86 C8
Hunters Rise CW7 126 C1
Hunter St CH1 237 A3
Hunter's View SK9 34 C3
Hunters Way
Neston CH64 66 C8
Talke ST7 210 D8
Hunters Wlk CH1 237 A2
Hunting Lodge Mews CW8 102 A4
HUNTINGTON 142 A5
Huntington Com Prim Sch CH3 142 A5
Huntley St WA5 15 C4
Huntly Chase SK9 60 C7
Hunt Rd WA11 1 E6
Huntsbank Bsns Pk CW2 205 E7
Huntsbank Dr ST5 210 D1
Hunts Cl CH3 119 B1
Hunts Field Cl WA13 18 D2
Hunts La WA4 16 F2
Huntsman Dr M44 11 F7
HURDSFIELD 87 E2
Hurdsfield Cl CW10 151 C7
Hurdsfield Com Prim Sch SK10 87 F2
Hurdsfield Gn SK10 87 E2
Hurdsfield Ind Est SK10 87 E3
Hurdsfield Rd SK10 87 E1
Hurford Ave CH65 69 F3
Hurlbote Cl SK9 34 D5
Hurleston Bldgs CW5 204 E6
Hurlestone Cl CH2 96 F1
Hurley Cl WA5 15 C5
Hurn Cl CW1 190 B8
HURST 179 F3
Hurst Ave SK8 35 C6
Hurst Cl
Bunbury CW6 185 E8
Talke ST7 210 D6
Hurst Ct CW6 185 F8
Hursthead Inf Sch SK8 35 C6
Hursthead Jun Sch SK8 35 C7
Hursthead Rd SK8 35 B7
Hurst La
Bollington SK10 88 A8
Glazebury WA3 5 C7
Hurst Lea Ct SK9 60 A2
Hurst Lea Rd SK22 39 C7
Hurst Mews WA6 75 C2
Hurst Mill La WA3 5 C8
Hurst Rd ST8 179 F4
Hurst St WA8 23 A4
Hurst The WA6 75 C2
Hurstwood CH3 143 A4
Hush Ho CH1 237 A2
Huskisson Way WA12 2 B4
Hutchins' Cl CW10 151 E6
Hutchinson St WA8 22 F6
Huttfield Rd L24 21 A4
Hutton Cl WA3 4 E5
Hutton Dr CW12 157 A2
HUXLEY 167 A8
Huxley CE Prim Sch CH3 167 A7
Huxley Cl
Bramhall SK7 35 E7
Macclesfield SK10 87 B2
Huxley Ct CH66 69 F8
Huxley Dr SK7 35 E7
Huxley La CW6 168 B6
Huxley St CW8 103 E7
Hyacinth Cl WA11 1 F6
Hyde Bank Ct SK22 39 C7
Hyde Bank Mill SK22 39 C8
Hyde Bank Rd SK22 39 C8
Hyde Cl
Ellesmere Port CH65 69 F4
Runcorn WA7 49 D6
Hydrangea Way WA9 6 A7
Hylton Ct CH65 70 E2
Hylton Dr SK8 35 C8
Hythe Ave CW1 190 B8

I

Ian Rd ST7 195 D3
Iberis Gdns WA9 6 A7
Ibis Ct WA1 16 A3
Ikey La CW5 202 F6
Ikins Dr ST7 209 F2
Ilex Ave WA2 8 B7
Ilford Way WA16 58 A4
ILLIDGE GREEN 154 C4
Imperial Ave CH1 117 C4
Imperial Mews
Crewe CW2 190 D3
Ellesmere Port CH65 70 B6
INCE 71 F6
Ince Ave CH62 43 E3
Ince Dr CH3 180 F1
Ince & Elton Sta CH2 72 B4
Ince La
Elton CH2 72 B3
Wimbolds Trafford CH2 96 F5
Ince Orchards CH2 72 B4
Indigo Rd CH65 70 F6
Ingersley Ct SK10 88 B8
Ingersley Rd SK10 88 C8
Ingersley Vale SK10 88 B8
Ingham Ave WA12 2 C1
Ingham Cl CH3 119 A1
Ingham Rd WA8 12 F4
Inglegreen CH60 41 B8
Inglenook Rd WA5 14 F4
Ingleton Cl
Holmes Chapel CW4 130 A3
Newton-le-W WA12 2 B4
Ingleton Gr WA7 49 D5
Inglewood Ave CW10 151 D5
Inglewood Cl
Partington M31 11 F4
Warrington WA3 10 B6
Inglewood Cvn Pk M31 11 F4
Inman Ave WA9 1 B2
Inner Gosling Cl WA4 25 F1
Innisfree Cl 4 CH66 69 C5
Innovation Ho CW7 149 A7
Insall Rd WA2 8 F2
Intack La WA16 28 B3
Intake Cl CH64 68 A8
International App M90 33 C7
Int Peace Ctr WA5 15 D5
Inveresk Rd SY14 198 C3
Inward Way CH65 70 B7
Ion Path CW7 127 C1
Irby Cl CH66 69 E4
Ireland Blackburne Ho WA1 16 E7
Ireland Rd
Hale L24 21 E1
Haydock WA11 1 C6
Ireland St
Warrington WA2 16 B8
Widnes WA8 13 D2
Iris Cl WA8 12 C2
Iris Wlk 7 M31 11 E2
Irlam & Cadishead Com High Sch M44 11 E7
Irlam Ind Est M44 11 E7
Irlam Sta M44 11 E7
Ironbridge Dr CW4 130 C2
Irons La CH3 120 F7
Irvin Dr M22, SK8 34 A8
Irving's Cres CH4 140 E6
Irwell La WA7 23 B3
Irwell Rd WA4 16 B2
Irwell Rise SK10 87 F7
Irwell St WA8 23 A4
Irwin Dr SK9 34 C5
Isabella Ct CH4 140 E6
Isherwood Cl WA2 8 F3
Isis Cl CW12 156 F1
Islay Cl CH65 70 C1
Islington Gn WA8 13 D4
ISYCOED 196 C1
Iveagh Cl WA7 50 A7
Iver Cl
Chester CH2 118 E7
Cronton WA8 12 C6
Iver Rd CH2 118 E7
Ivy Ave WA12 2 C2
Ivy Bank Prim Sch SK11 112 A5
Ivychurch Mews WA7 23 D2
Ivy Cotts SY13 225 A8
Ivy Ct CH4 162 D2
Ivy Dr CW8 102 A2
Ivy Farm Ct L24 21 D1
Ivy Farm Dr CH64 66 F6
Ivy Farm Gdns WA3 4 D4
Ivy Farm La CH3 183 C1
Ivy Gdns CW12 156 C2
Ivy Ho
Macclesfield SK11 112 A7
Nether Alderley SK9 84 C7
Ivy House Rd ST8 179 C2
Ivy La
Alsager ST7 193 E2
Macclesfield SK11 112 A6
Ivy Meade Cl 10 SK11 111 F7
Ivy Meade Rd SK11 111 F6
Ivy Mews CH2 119 A5
Ivy Rd
Golborne WA3 3 B8
Macclesfield SK11 112 A7
Poynton SK12 36 E3
Warrington WA1 17 E7
Ivy St WA7 23 A1
Ivy Wlk M31 11 D3

J

Jackie Stewart Bsns Ctr CW6 147 D6
Jack La
Moulton CW9, CW10 127 A7
Weston CW2 207 D6
Jackson Ave
Culcheth WA3 4 E3
Nantwich CW5 204 F5
Warrington WA1 16 F6
Jackson Ct CH5 139 B7
Jackson La SK10 88 B7
Jackson Rd CW12 156 E5
Jacksons Cl SK10 88 B7
Jacksons Edge Rd SK12 38 B6
Jackson's La SK7 36 C8
Jackson St
Burtonwood WA5 6 E6
Haydock WA11 1 A7
Macclesfield SK11 112 D6
Jacobs Way WA16 79 F7
Jamage Ind Est ST7 210 C5
Jamage Rd ST7 210 D5
James Atkinson Way CW1 189 F7
James Ave CH66 69 C3
James Cl WA8 23 A4
James Hall St CW5 204 E6
James Pl CH2 118 F2
James Rd WA11 1 F7
James St
Chester CH1 237 B3
Macclesfield SK11 112 D6
Northwich CW9 104 C8
5 Warrington WA1 16 B5
Jamieson Cl
Alsager ST7 193 E4
Chester CH3 119 A2
Jane Maddock Homes ST7 193 B3
Jan Palach Ave CW5 204 F4
Japonica Gdns WA9 6 A7
Jarman SK11 112 F4
Jasmine Cres ST7 195 D2
Jasmine Gdns WA9 6 A7
Jasmine Gr WA8 22 D8
Jasmine Wlk M31 11 F2
Jasmin Way ST7 195 F2
Jay Cl WA3 10 A4
Jays Cl WA7 50 E7
Jedburgh Ave CH66 69 A6
Jefferson Dr WA5 15 B7
Jefferson Gdns WA8 12 F3
Jellicoe Ave M44 11 E6
Jennet's La WA3 5 C8
Jenny La SK7 35 E4
Jensen Ct WA7 23 C3
Jersey Ave CH65 70 C1
Jersey Cl CW12 157 A2
Jersey Way CW10 128 D2
Jervis Cl WA2 9 A3
Jesmond Cres CW2 190 B2
Jesmond Gr SK8 35 B8
Jesmond Rd CH1 118 B2
Jessop Ho WA7 22 E3
Jessop Way CW1 191 C4
JH Godwin Prim Sch CH1 117 D4
Jockey St WA2 16 B7
JODRELL BANK 108 D2
Jodrell Bank Obsy* CW4 108 C3
Jodrell Bank Visitor Ctr* SK11 108 D3
Jodrell Cl
Holmes Chapel CW4 130 A3
Macclesfield SK11 112 E7
Jodrell Dr WA4 27 A7
Jodrell Mdw SK23 65 E8
Jodrell Rd SK23 65 D8
Jodrell St
Macclesfield SK11 112 E7
New Mills SK22 39 B7
John Brunner Cres CW9 103 E6
John Ford Way CW11 154 B1
John Fryer Ave CW9 80 A5
John Gresty Dr CW5 205 D6
John Lloyd Ct M44 11 F8
John May Ct SK10 87 B2
John Middleton Cl L24 21 E2
John Nicholas Cres CH65 70 C6
John Rd WA13 18 C3
Johns Ave
Haydock WA11 1 E7
Runcorn WA7 48 F8
Johns Cl SK10 88 D5
Johnson Ave WA12 2 B5
Johnson Cl CW12 157 B1
Johnsons Cl CH4 141 B5
Johnson's La WA8 13 E1
Johnson St SK23 65 E8
John St
Bollington SK10 88 B8
Congleton CW12 156 C2
Crewe CW1 190 C5
Ellesmere Port CH65 70 B6
Golborne WA3 3 A8
Irlam M44 11 E5
Macclesfield SK11 112 D6
1 Northwich CW9 104 A8
Utkinton CW6 146 B7
Warrington WA2 16 B6
Winsford CW7 126 C1
John Street Com Prim Sch CH65 70 B6
Jonathan's Way CH1 117 E5
Jones's La CW10 152 D6
Jonson Rd CH64 66 E8
Jordangate SK10 112 D8
Joseph Cres ST7 193 F2
Joseph Groome Twrs 10 CH65 70 C6

Joseph St WA8 . . . .**13** C2
Joyce Ave CW7 . . . .**126** C2
Joy La WA5 . . . .**6** E4
Jubilee Almshouses
  CW5 . . . .**204** E6
Jubilee Ave
  Crewe CW2 . . . .**190** B3
  Warrington, Padgate
  WA1 . . . .**16** F8
  Warrington WA5 . . . .**14** E4
Jubilee Cres WA11 . . . .**1** F7
Jubilee Ct
  2 Handforth SK9 . . . .**34** E5
  Holmes Chapel CW4 . . . .**130** A3
Jubilee Gdns
  Nantwich CW5 . . . .**204** E4
  New Mills SK22 . . . .**39** C7
Jubilee Gn CH65 . . . .**70** C4
Jubilee Gr WA13 . . . .**18** C4
Jubilee Rd CW12 . . . .**156** E2
Jubilee St SK22 . . . .**39** C7
Jubilee Terr CW5 . . . .**204** E4
Jubilee Villas CW11 . . . . . .**175** C2
Jubilee Way
  Widnes WA8 . . . .**12** E1
  5 Winsford CW7 . . . . . .**126** D1
Jubits La WA8 . . . .**13** A8
Juddfield St WA11 . . . .**1** A7
Judy La SK11 . . . .**113** A3
Julian Way WA8 . . . .**12** F4
July Bglws CH4 . . . .**141** E2
Jumper La SK10 . . . .**88** F7
Junction Eight Bsns Ctr
  CH65 . . . .**70** A7
Junction Ho CW1 . . . .**190** A5
Junction La WA12 . . . .**2** B3
June Ave CH62 . . . .**43** E8
Juniper CI ST5 . . . .**210** E1
Juniper Ct CW2 . . . .**119** B4
Juniper Dr CH66 . . . .**69** E1
Juniper Gr CH66 . . . .**69** F1
Juniper La WA3 . . . .**18** A7
Juniper Rise SK10 . . . .**86** E1
Jupiter Dr CH1 . . . .**117** C2
Jurby Ct WA2 . . . .**8** F1
Justice St SK10 . . . .**87** D1

K

Kansas Pl WA5 . . . .**15** B7
Karen CI WA5 . . . .**7** A6
Karen Way CH66 . . . .**69** D3
Kaye Ave WA3 . . . .**4** F3
Kay La WA13 . . . .**29** B8
Keats CI
  Ellesmere Port CH66 . . . . .**94** E8
  Widnes WA8 . . . .**22** F8
Keats Dr
  Macclesfield SK10 . . . .**86** F1
  Rode Heath ST7 . . . .**193** E8
  Wistaston CW2 . . . .**206** A8
Keats Gr WA2 . . . .**8** C2
Keats La CW9 . . . .**80** A5
Keats Terr CH1 . . . .**118** A5
Keble St WA8 . . . .**23** B7
KECKWICK **25** A3
Keckwick La WA4 . . . .**25** A3
Keele Cres SK11 . . . .**112** B6
Keel Hey CH64 . . . .**43** B1
Keepers CI WA16 . . . .**57** D3
Keepers La CW9 . . . .**53** D4
Keeper's La CW8 . . . .**102** E8
Keeper's Rd WA4 . . . .**27** A7
Keepers Wlk WA7 . . . .**23** F2
Keith Ave WA5 . . . .**14** E6
Keith Dr CH63 . . . .**43** D5
Kelburn Ct WA3 . . . .**9** F6
Kelmscott CI CH66 . . . .**69** D2
KELSALL **122** C4
Kelsall Ave CH62 . . . .**43** F3
Kelsall CI
  Bebington CH62 . . . .**43** E3
  Warrington WA3 . . . .**9** C3
  Widnes WA8 . . . .**12** D1
Kelsall Com Prim Sch
  CW6 . . . .**122** C4
Kelsall Rd CH3 . . . .**121** C4
Kelsall St CW12 . . . .**156** E3
Kelsall Way
  Audley ST7 . . . .**209** D1
  8 Handforth SK9 . . . .**34** D5
Kelsborrow CI CW9 . . . . . .**103** E3
Kelsborrow Way
  CW6 . . . .**122** D4
Kelso Way SK10 . . . .**87** C4
Kelstern CI **2** CW9 . . . . . .**104** B8
KELSTERTON **91** B2
Kelsterton Ct CH5 . . . .**91** C1
Kelsterton La CH5 . . . .**91** B1
Kelsterton Rd
  Connah's Quay CH5,
  CH6 . . . .**91** C2
  Kelsterton CH6 . . . .**91** A3
Kelvin CI WA3 . . . .**9** D6
Kelvin Gr CH2 . . . .**118** E4
Kelvin St WA3 . . . .**9** F5
Kemberton Dr WA8 . . . .**13** A5
Kemble CI CW2 . . . .**206** B8
Kemmel Ave WA4 . . . .**16** C3
Kempsell Way L26 . . . .**21** A7
Kempsell Wlk L26 . . . .**21** A7
Kempton Ave CW1 . . . .**190** C7
Kempton CI
  Chester CH1 . . . .**118** B2

Kempton CI continued
  Newton-le-W WA12 . . . .**2** D5
  Runcorn WA7 . . . .**49** C6
Kempton Way SK10 . . . .**87** C4
Kendal Ave WA2 . . . .**8** C2
Kendal CI
  Chester CH2 . . . .**119** A6
  Ellesmere Port CH66 . . . . .**69** D2
  Macclesfield SK11 . . . . . .**111** E6
Kendal Ct CW12 . . . .**156** A2
Kendal Dr
  Bramhall SK7 . . . .**35** C5
  Ellesmere Port CH66 . . . . .**69** E2
Kendal Rd
  Macclesfield SK11 . . . . . .**111** F6
  Widnes WA8 . . . .**12** C1
Kendal Rise WA7 . . . .**49** D5
Kendal Way CW2 . . . .**207** C1
Kendrick CI SW8 . . . .**77** D1
Kendrick St WA1 . . . .**16** A5
Kenilworth Ave
  Handforth SK9 . . . .**34** D3
  Knutsford WA16 . . . .**57** C2
  Runcorn WA7 . . . .**49** B8
Kenilworth CI
  Macclesfield SK11 . . . . . .**111** F6
  Wistaston CW2 . . . .**206** A7
Kenilworth Ct CH65 . . . .**70** E2
Kenilworth Dr
  Hazel Grove SK7 . . . .**36** D8
  Warrington WA4 . . . .**16** F8
Kenilworth Gdns WA12 . . . .**2** C1
Kenilworth Gn SK11 . . . . . .**111** F6
Kenilworth Ho **6**
  CH1 . . . .**237** C3
Kenilworth Rd
  Golborne WA3 . . . .**3** E7
  Macclesfield SK11 . . . . . .**111** F6
  Neston CH64 . . . .**66** E5
Kenley Ave WA8 . . . .**12** D5
Kenmare Bank CW9 . . . . . .**104** A5
Kenmore Gr M44 . . . .**11** D6
Kennedy Ave SK10 . . . .**86** F2
Kennedy CI CH2 . . . .**119** A5
Kennedy Ct **4** WA5 . . . .**15** B7
Kennel La
  Cuddington CW8 . . . .**102** A1
  Little Budworth CW8 . . . . .**124** E7
Kennelwood Rd CW9 . . . . . .**78** C7
Kennerley's CI SK9 . . . .**60** A7
Kennerley's La SK9 . . . .**60** A7
Kennet CI SK9 . . . .**34** D2
Kennet Dr CW12 . . . .**156** F1
Kenneth Rd WA8 . . . .**22** C8
Kennet Rd WA11 . . . .**1** A6
Kennet Way **10** SK11 . . . . . .**111** F8
Kennington Pk WA8 . . . .**12** E4
Kenrick CI CW3 . . . .**232** C1
Kensington Ave WA4 . . . . . .**17** C2
Kensington CI
  Chester CH4 . . . .**141** A6
  Widnes WA8 . . . .**13** D4
Kensington Ct
  Alsager ST7 . . . .**192** F3
  9 Nantwich CW5 . . . . . .**204** E6
  Wilmslow SK9 . . . .**60** A6
  Winsford CW7 . . . .**149** C7
Kensington Dr
  Congleton CW12 . . . .**156** F4
  Wistaston CW5 . . . .**205** D4
Kensington Gn CH4 . . . . . .**140** F6
Kensington Rd
  Chester CH4 . . . .**141** A6
  Ellesmere Port CH65 . . . . .**70** A5
Kensington Sq **11**
  SK10 . . . .**111** F8
Kensington Way CW9 . . . . .**103** E3
Kent Ave SK10 . . . .**87** E6
Kent CI CH63 . . . .**43** B8
Kent Gdns CW12 . . . .**118** F5
Kent Gr WA7 . . . .**23** B1
Kent Ho ST7 . . . .**210** D6
Kent Wlk SK10 . . . .**88** F1
Kenview CI WA8 . . . .**22** A4
Kenwick CI CH66 . . . .**69** C3
Kenwood Ave SK7 . . . .**35** D5
KENYON **3** F3
Kenyon Ave WA5 . . . .**14** E5
Kenyon Ct WA8 . . . .**23** A6
Kenyon La
  Culcheth WA3 . . . .**4** A4
  Golborne, Kenyon WA3 . . . .**3** F3
  Golborne WA3 . . . .**3** F5
Kenyons La N WA11 . . . .**1** F8
Kenyon's La S WA11 . . . .**1** F7
Kerfoot Bsns Pk WA2 . . . . .**16** A8
Kerfoot St WA2 . . . .**16** A7
Keristal Ave CH3 . . . .**142** A7
KERRIDGE **88** A4
Kerridge CI CW10 . . . .**151** B8

KERRIDGE-END **88** D3
Kerridge Rd SK10 . . . .**88** B3
Kerry Croft CH66 . . . .**69** E1
Kershaw Gr SK11 . . . .**112** B8
Kershaw St WA8 . . . .**12** D1
Kershaw Way WA12 . . . .**2** C5
Kestrel Ave WA16 . . . .**57** B3
Kestrel CI
  Congleton CW12 . . . .**156** E1
  Middlewich CW10 . . . .**151** D6
  Winsford CW7 . . . .**149** D5
Kestrel Dr CW1 . . . .**190** B8
Kestrel La WA3 . . . .**9** E4
Kestrel Rd
  Heswall CH60 . . . .**41** C7
  Northwich CW8 . . . .**103** C7
Kestrels Way WA7 . . . .**49** F6
Keswick Ave
  Bebington CH63 . . . .**43** C4
  Macclesfield SK11 . . . . . .**111** F5
  Warrington WA2 . . . .**8** C2
Keswick CI
  Chester CH2 . . . .**119** A5
  Crewe CW2 . . . .**189** E3
  Irlam M44 . . . .**11** D4
  Macclesfield SK11 . . . . . .**111** F6
  Widnes WA8 . . . .**12** C1
  Winsford CW7 . . . .**126** D2
Keswick Cres WA2 . . . .**8** C2
Keswick Ct SK12 . . . .**156** A2
Keswick Dr
  Bramhall SK7 . . . .**35** C5
  Frodsham WA6 . . . .**74** D8
Keswick Gdns CH63 . . . . . .**43** C5
Keswick Rd SK6 . . . .**37** E8
Ketlan Ct CH4 . . . .**140** E7
Kettell Ave CW1 . . . .**190** A6
Kettle La CW3 . . . .**230** C2
KETTLESHULME **64** F4
Kettleshulme St James CE
  Prim Sch SK22 . . . .**64** F4
Kettleshulme Way
  SK12 . . . .**37** A3
Kew Gardens CI WA8 . . . . . .**13** D4
Keyes CI WA3 . . . .**9** F4
Keyes Gdn WA3 . . . .**9** F4
KEY GREEN **157** E4
Keysbrook CH3 . . . .**166** C2
Keysbrook Ave CH3 . . . . . .**166** C2
Kidderton CI CW5 . . . .**202** E7
Kidderton La CW5 . . . .**202** F7
KIDNAL **212** E8
KIDSGROVE **195** B1
Kidsgrove Sta ST7 . . . .**194** F1
Kidston Dr CW1 . . . .**189** F7
Kilbuck La WA11 . . . .**2** A8
Kilburn Ave CH62 . . . .**43** E6
Kilburn CI SK8 . . . .**34** B7
Kildare CI L24 . . . .**21** D2
Kildonan Rd WA4 . . . .**17** A2
Kilford CI WA5 . . . .**7** E2
Killingworth La WA3 . . . .**11** B5
Kilmorey Park Rd
  CH2 . . . .**118** F3
Kilmorey Pk CH2 . . . .**118** F4
Kilmorey Pk Ave CH2 . . . . .**237** C4
Kilncroft WA7 . . . .**50** B5
Kiln Croft La SK9 . . . .**34** E4
Kiln La CW5 . . . .**220** B8
Kilsby Dr WA8 . . . .**13** E2
Kilshaw Rd WA5 . . . .**6** F6
Kilsyth CI WA7 . . . .**49** F4
Kimberley Dr WA4 . . . .**16** C1
Kimberley St WA5 . . . .**15** E5
Kimberley Terr CH2 . . . . . .**118** F2
Kinder Dr CW2 . . . .**189** D3
Kinderton CI WA16 . . . .**29** C4
Kinderton Mobile Home
  Pk CW10 . . . .**152** A7
Kinderton St CW10 . . . .**128** D1
Kinder View ST7 . . . .**39** C7
King Arthur's Wlk WA7 . . . . .**24** A1
King Charles Ct CH1 . . . . . .**237** A3
King Edward Bldgs **4**
  CH3 . . . .**119** A1
King Edward Ct CW9 . . . . .**103** F5
King Edward Rd
  Knutsford WA16 . . . .**57** A2
  3 Macclesfield SK10 . . . .**112** D8
King Edward St
  Macclesfield SK10 . . . . . .**112** D8
  Middlewich CW10 . . . .**128** C1
  Warrington WA1 . . . .**16** E7
Kingfisher CI
  Congleton CW12 . . . .**156** E1
  Farndon CH3 . . . .**180** F1
  Nantwich CW5 . . . .**204** E8
  Runcorn WA7 . . . .**49** F5
  Warrington WA3 . . . .**9** F4
Kingfisher Ct
  Chester CH2 . . . .**237** A4
  Northwich CW9 . . . .**79** C2
Kingfisher Dr **5** CW7 . . . . .**149** D6
Kingfisher Gr CW9 . . . .**79** F5
King George Ave
  CW9 . . . .**104** B8
King George Cres WA1 . . . .**16** F7
King George Rd WA11 . . . . . .**2** A7
King George St **1**
  ST7 . . . .**195** C1
Kingham CI **3** WA8 . . . . . .**13** D1
King Ho ST7 . . . .**210** D5
King James Ct WA7 . . . .**49** E6
King PI CW5 . . . .**204** E6
King's Ave WA3 . . . .**3** F7
King's Bldgs CH1 . . . .**237** A3

Kingsbury CI WA4 . . . .**26** D3
Kingsbury Dr **14** SK9 . . . . . .**34** D1
Kingsbury Rd WA8 . . . .**13** D4
Kings CI
  Chester CH4 . . . .**140** F5
  Wilmslow SK9 . . . .**60** A6
King's Cres CW10 . . . .**128** C2
King's Cres E CH3 . . . .**119** A1
King's Cres W CH3 . . . .**119** A1
Kings Croft CH5 . . . .**91** D1
Kings Ct
  Nantwich CW5 . . . .**204** D5
  Runcorn WA7 . . . .**24** D4
King's Ct
  Chester CH1 . . . .**237** A3
  Middlewich CW10 . . . .**128** D2
Kingsdale Rd WA5 . . . .**14** F7
Kingsdown CI CW2 . . . .**207** C1
Kings Dr
  Helsby WA6 . . . .**73** B3
  Wistaston CW2 . . . .**205** E8
Kingsfield Ct CH4 . . . .**141** C3
King's Gate CW8 . . . .**102** A2
Kings Grove Sch
  CW2 . . . .**190** A3
Kingshead CI WA7 . . . .**24** D2
Kings La CW6 . . . .**147** D4
King's La
  Allostock CW10,
  WA16 . . . .**106** C1
  Nantwich CW5 . . . .**204** D5
Kingslawn CI **4** CW9 . . . . .**103** F5
Kings Lea Ho CH3 . . . .**142** A8
KINGSLEY **75** C2
Kingsley Ave
  Bebington CH62 . . . .**43** E3
  Handforth SK9 . . . .**34** C2
Kingsley CI
  Northwich CW8 . . . .**103** C5
  Talke ST7 . . . .**210** D6
Kingsley Cres WA7 . . . .**23** A1
Kingsley Ct CW11 . . . .**174** D8
Kingsley Dr
  Northwich CW9 . . . .**104** A6
  Warrington WA4 . . . .**26** C7
Kingsley Gdns CH3 . . . . . .**142** B8
Kingsley Gn WA6 . . . .**74** F5
Kingsley Rd
  Chester CH4 . . . .**142** B8
  Congleton CW12 . . . .**157** A3
  Crowton WA6 . . . .**76** B1
  Ellesmere Port CH65 . . . . .**70** C5
  Frodsham WA6 . . . .**74** E4
  Haslington CW1 . . . .**191** C4
  Runcorn WA7 . . . .**23** A1
  Talke ST7 . . . .**210** D6
Kingsley St John's CE
  Prim Sch WA6 . . . .**75** C2
Kingsley Wlk CW7 . . . .**126** B2
Kings Mdw
  Hough CW2 . . . .**206** E2
  Runcorn WA7 . . . .**50** C8
KINGSMEAD **103** E5
Kingsmead
  Chester CH2 . . . .**118** C8
  Northwich CW9 . . . .**103** F5
Kingsmead Crossroads **10**
  CW9 . . . .**103** F4
Kingsmead Ct WA3 . . . .**9** A8
Kingsmead Prim Sch
  CW9 . . . .**103** E5
Kingsmead Sq CW9 . . . . . .**103** E4
Kings Mews CH66 . . . .**69** C7
Kings Rd
  Connah's Quay CH5 . . . . . .**91** D1
  Ellesmere Port CH66 . . . . .**69** C7
  Golborne WA3 . . . .**3** A1
  Irlam M44 . . . .**11** E6
  Warrington WA2 . . . .**9** A2
King's Rd SK9 . . . .**59** E8
King's Sch The
  Chester CH4 . . . .**141** B4
  Macclesfield SK10 . . . .**87** C1
  Macclesfield SK10 . . . . . .**112** B8
King St
  Audley ST7 . . . .**209** D1
  Chester CH1 . . . .**237** A3
  Congleton CW12 . . . .**156** F4
  Ellesmere Port CH65 . . . . .**70** C6
  Hartford CW8 . . . .**103** B5
  Kidsgrove ST7 . . . .**195** A2
  Knutsford WA16 . . . .**57** A2
  Macclesfield SK10 . . . . . .**112** D8
  Middlewich CW10 . . . .**128** B5
  Newton-le-W WA12 . . . .**2** B3
  Northwich CW9 . . . .**104** F6
  Runcorn WA7 . . . .**23** A3
  Sandbach CW11 . . . .**174** E8
  Talke ST7 . . . .**210** D5
Kingston Ave
  Macclesfield SK11 . . . . . .**112** F7
  Warrington WA5 . . . .**14** E6
Kingston CI WA7 . . . .**23** E2
Kingston Ct
  14 Handforth SK9 . . . . . .**34** E1
  Saughall CH1 . . . .**94** B2
Kingston PI ST8 . . . .**179** E2
Kingston Rd SK9 . . . .**34** D5
Kingstreet SK7 . . . .**35** B1
King Street Trad Est
  CW10 . . . .**128** C2
KINGSWAY **23** A8
Kingsway
  Bollington SK10 . . . .**87** E7
  Chester CH2 . . . .**118** F5

Kingsway continued
  Crewe CW2 . . . .**190** A5
  Frodsham WA6 . . . .**74** B8
  Heswall CH60 . . . .**41** C6
  Newton-le-W WA12 . . . .**2** C2
  Northwich CW9 . . . .**104** B8
  Widnes WA8 . . . .**13** A1
  Winsford CW7 . . . .**126** F1
Kingsway Ho WA4 . . . .**16** F4
Kingsway N WA1 . . . .**16** F6
Kingsway S WA1, WA4 . . . .**16** F4
Kingsway W CH2 . . . .**118** E4
KINGSWOOD **74** C1
KINGSWOOD **7** B2
Kingswood Ave **7** B2
Kingswood Ave
  Chorlton CW2 . . . .**207** B3
  Saughall CH1 . . . .**94** C1
Kingswood Cres
  CW10 . . . .**151** E5
Kingswood La CH1 . . . .**94** C1
Kingswood Rd WA5 . . . .**7** A2
Kings Wood Wlk
  CW6 . . . .**122** D5
Kinloch CI
  Crewe CW1 . . . .**190** B6
  Halewood L26 . . . .**21** A7
Kinnerley Rd CH65 . . . .**70** A3
Kinnersley Ave ST7 . . . . . .**210** F8
Kinnersley St **1** ST7 . . . . .**195** A2
Kinnerton CI CH4 . . . .**161** A7
Kinnerton Hts CH4 . . . .**161** A7
Kinnerton La CH4 . . . .**161** A8
Kinnerton Rd CH4 . . . .**162** A7
Kinnington Way CH1 . . . . . .**94** F7
Kinnock Pk WA5 . . . .**6** E6
Kinross CI WA2 . . . .**8** F4
Kinsale Dr WA3 . . . .**9** C4
KINSEY HEATH **230** B1
Kinsey Rd CH65 . . . .**70** D1
Kinsey's La CH2 . . . .**71** F6
Kinsey St CW12 . . . .**156** E2
Kintore CI
  Bebington CH63 . . . .**43** C4
  Winsford CW7 . . . .**127** A3
Kintore Dr WA5 . . . .**14** D6
Kintyre CI CH65 . . . .**70** C1
Kipling Ave WA2 . . . .**8** C1
Kipling Cres WA8 . . . .**22** F8
Kipling Rd CH1 . . . .**117** F5
Kipling Way CW1 . . . .**190** F4
Kirby CI CW2 . . . .**118** D5
Kirkacre Ave WA12 . . . .**7** C8
Kirkby Rd WA3 . . . .**4** F3
Kirkcaldy Ave WA5 . . . .**14** D6
Kirkfell Dr SK6 . . . .**37** E8
Kirkham Ave WA3 . . . .**3** E6
Kirkham Ct WA5 . . . .**15** B4
Kirkham Rd
  Gatley SK8 . . . .**34** C8
  Widnes WA8 . . . .**13** C2
Kirkstall CI
  Macclesfield SK10 . . . .**87** B2
  Poynton SK12 . . . .**36** C6
Kirkstead Rd SK8 . . . .**35** C6
Kirkstead Way WA3 . . . .**3** A8
Kirkstone Ave WA2 . . . .**8** C2
Kirkstone Cres WA7 . . . . . .**50** A4
Kirkstone Ct CW12 . . . .**156** A1
Kirkwall Dr WA5 . . . .**15** A3
Kirkwood CI CH3 . . . .**119** A2
Kishfield La SK23 . . . .**65** A6
Kitchener Ave M44 . . . .**11** C4
Kitchen St CH1 . . . .**118** B1
Kite Gr ST7 . . . .**195** D3
Kitfield Ave CW10 . . . .**151** D7
Kitt's Moss La SK7 . . . .**35** D6
Knap The CH60 . . . .**41** A6
Knebworth Ct CW12 . . . . . .**179** B8
Knight Rd WA5 . . . .**6** F6
Knightsbridge Ave
  1 Handforth SK9 . . . . . .**103** E3
  Warrington WA4 . . . .**17** C2
Knightsbridge Ct
  13 Handforth SK9 . . . . . .**34** D1
  Widnes WA8 . . . .**13** D4
Knightsbridge Ct
  Chester CH4 . . . .**237** C2
  Warrington WA1 . . . .**16** A5
Knight's Ct SK11 . . . .**112** E7
Knight's Grange (Sports
  Complex) CW7 . . . .**126** B3
Knights La CW6 . . . .**123** E1
Knights Mdw CW7 . . . .**126** C3
Knight St SK11 . . . .**112** E7
Knightwake Rd SK22 . . . . . .**39** A8
Knole Ave SK12 . . . .**36** F4
KNOLLS GREEN **58** C3
Knoll St SK22 . . . .**39** B8
Knoll The WA7 . . . .**49** F7
KNOTBURY **138** F5
Knottingley Dr CH66 . . . . . .**69** C5
Knott's Hos WN7 . . . .**4** B8
Knotty La CW12 . . . .**179** F8
Knowe The CH64 . . . .**68** A8
Knowl CI CW8 . . . .**78** C3
Knowle Gn SK9 . . . .**34** C3
Knowle Pk SK9 . . . .**34** C3
Knowles Ind Est SK23 . . . . .**39** D3
Knowles St **2** WA8 . . . . . .**13** C2
Knowl Hey Rd L26 . . . .**21** A6
Knowl La CH3 . . . .**180** E5
Knowl The CH3 . . . .**180** F5
Knowsley Ave WA3 . . . .**3** F8

Knowsley Ct CH2 ...... 118 F4
Knowsley Expressway L35,
  WA8 .... 21 F8
Knowsley La ST7 .... 194 F4
Knowsley Rd
  Chester CH2 .... 118 F4
  Hazel Grove SK7 ..... 36 F8
  Macclesfield SK11 ... 112 C5
KNUTSFORD 57 A3
Knutsford & Dist Hospl
  WA16 .... 56 F1
Knutsford High Sch
  (Lower Sch) WA16 .... 56 E1
Knutsford High Sch
  (Upper Sch) WA16 .... 56 F1
Knutsford Rd
  Alsager ST7 .... 193 F6
  Antrobus CW9 .... 53 D4
  Chelford SK7 .... 84 A2
  Grappenhall WA4 ..... 17 C1
  Great Budworth CW9 ... 54 A2
  Holmes Chapel CW4 ... 130 B5
  Mobberley WA16 ...... 57 E4
  Row-of-Trees SK9,
  WA16 .... 59 D3
  Warrington WA4 ...... 16 D3
Knutsford Road Wlk [12]
  SK11 .... 112 E7
Knutsford Sta WA16 .... 57 A1
Knutsford View WA15 ... 32 C8
Knutsford Way CH1 .... 117 F2
Kohima Cres CH3 .... 142 B5
Kronsbec Ave CH66 .... 69 D6
KUS Ind Est CH5 ..... 139 A6
Kynaston Dr CH4 .... 140 C7

L

Laburnum Ave
  [2] Nantwich CW5 ..... 189 F2
  [2] Nantwich CW5 .... 204 F5
  Warrington WA1 ...... 17 C7
Laburnum Cl
  Congleton CW12 .... 156 A4
  Talke ST7 .... 210 E8
Laburnum Cres CW8 ... 78 B3
Laburnum Ct
  Lymm WA13 .... 19 B4
  Wistaston CW2 ...... 205 F7
Laburnum Farm Cl
  CH64 .... 67 A5
Laburnum Gr
  Crewe CW1 .... 190 D6
  Ellesmere Port CH66 ... 95 A8
  Runcorn WA7 .... 49 C7
  Saltney CH4 .... 140 E6
  Weaverham CW8 .... 102 D8
Laburnum La
  Altrincham WA15 ..... 31 E8
  Warrington WA5 ...... 14 C5
Laburnum Pl ST5 .... 210 D1
Laburnum Rd
  Davenham CW9 ..... 103 F3
  Golborne WA3 .... 3 F7
  Irlam M44 .... 11 D5
  Macclesfield SK11 ... 112 E5
  Northwich CW9 ..... 104 C6
Laburnum Way LL13 ... 180 D1
Lacey Ct
  Handforth SK9 .... 34 B1
  Widnes WA8 .... 23 B7
Lacey Gn SK9 .... 34 B1
Lacey Gr SK9 .... 34 C1
LACEY GREEN 34 B1
Lacey Green Prim Sch
  SK9 .... 34 B1
Lacey St WA8 .... 23 A7
LACH DENNIS 105 D5
Lache CH4 .... 140 F5
Lache Hall Cres CH4 .. 140 F4
Lache La
  Chester, Westminster Park
  CH4 .... 141 B5
  Roughhill CH4 ...... 140 E3
Lache Park Ave CH4 ... 141 A6
Lache Prim Sch CH4 .... 141 A5
Lacy Ct CW12 .... 156 F2
Ladies Mile WA16 .... 56 F2
Ladies Wlk CH64 ..... 66 E8
Lady Acre Cl WA13 .... 18 D2
Ladybarn Ave WA3 .... 2 F7
Ladybarn Cres SK7 .... 35 E8
Ladybarn Manor SK7 ... 35 E8
Ladybrook Gr [8] SK9 ... 34 D2
Ladybrook Prim Sch
  SK7 .... 35 F7
Ladycroft Cl WA1 ..... 60 B7
Ladyfield St SK9 ...... 60 C7
Ladyfield Terr SK9 ..... 60 C7
Lady Helen Wlk CW5 .. 204 E6
Lady Heyes Craft &
  Antique Restoration
  Ctr* WA6 .... 74 F4
Lady La
  Croft WA3 .... 9 C8
  Culcheth WA3 .... 4 C1
  Mobberley WA16 ..... 58 C6
Lady Mary's Sq WA16 .. 30 E3
Ladypit Rd ST7 ...... 210 A8
Ladypool L24 .... 21 C2
Lady Richeld Cl WA7 ... 24 D3
Ladys Cl SK12 .... 14 A8
Ladythorn Cres SK7 ... 35 F6
Ladythorn Gr SK7 ..... 35 F6
Ladythorn Rd SK7 ..... 35 E6

Ladywood Rd WA5 ...... 7 D1
Lagos Gr CW2 .... 126 E2
Laidon Ave CW2 .... 206 A7
Laira Ct WA2 .... 16 C7
Laira St WA2 .... 16 C7
Lake House Cl CW8 .... 77 D1
Lake La WA4 .... 52 F5
Lakelands Cl SK10 ... 112 F7
Lakemore Ctry Pk*
  CW1 .... 174 C1
Lakeside
  Bosley SK11 .... 158 D8
  Chester CH4 .... 141 B2
Lakeside Cl
  Chester CH2 .... 118 F7
  Widnes WA8 .... 22 A8
Lakeside Cvn Pk CW7 .. 149 F7
Lakeside Dr
  Poynton SK12 .... 36 E5
  Warrington WA1 ..... 16 A3
Lakeside Rd WA13 .... 18 D2
Lakeside View
  Moulton CW7 .... 126 F7
  Nantwich CW5 ..... 204 E3
Lake View
  Alsager ST7 .... 193 C2
  Congleton CW12 .... 156 B2
  Furness Vale SK23 ... 39 D8
Lakewood CH4 ...... 141 B2
Laleston Cl WA8 .... 22 E8
Lamb Cottage Cvn Pk
  CW8 .... 125 C7
Lambert Cres CW5 ... 204 C6
Lambert's La CW12 ... 156 E1
Lambert Way CW8 ... 103 A4
Lamb La WA14 .... 31 D4
Lambourn Ave WA8 ... 12 C5
Lambourn Cl SK12 ..... 36 D4
Lambourn Dr CW1 ... 173 B1
Lambourne Cl
  [4] Ellesmere Port
  CH66 .... 94 F8
  Wythenshawe M22 ... 33 D8
Lambourne Gr
  [1] Middlewich CW10 .. 128 C1
  St Helens WA9 .... 1 A4
Lambs House Sch
  CW12 .... 156 F4
Lambsickle Cl WA7 .... 48 A6
Lambsickle La WA7 .... 49 A6
Lambs La
  Warrington, Padgate
  WA1 .... 17 A8
  Warrington WA1 ..... 17 A7
Lamb St ST7 .... 195 A2
Lamerton Cl WA5 ...... 14 D4
Lamerton Way CW9 ... 34 E2
Lampeter Cl WA5 ...... 7 F2
Lampits La CH3 ...... 120 E6
Lamport Cl WA8 ...... 13 E3
Lanark Gdns WA8 ..... 12 E3
Lanark Rd CW4 .... 88 F2
Lancashire Rd M31 .... 11 E2
Lancaster Ave
  Golborne WA3 .... 3 C8
  Irlam M44 .... 11 D5
  Widnes WA8 .... 13 B3
Lancaster Cl
  Hazel Grove SK7 ..... 36 D8
  Newton-le-W WA12 ... 2 F4
  Warrington WA2 ...... 8 F2
  Winsford CW7 ...... 149 D6
Lancaster Ct [3] WA4 ... 16 E1
Lancaster Dr CH3 ..... 119 B2
Lancaster Fields WA5 .. 191 A2
Lancaster Gdns CH65 .. 70 C2
Lancaster Pk CH4 .... 139 A3
Lancaster Rd
  Handforth SK9 .... 34 E1
  Irlam M44 .... 11 D5
  Widnes WA8 .... 13 B3
Lancaster St WA5 ..... 15 E5
Lanceley Ct SY14 .... 213 B3
Lancelyn Dr SK9 ...... 60 D8
Lancer Ct WA7 .... 23 E3
Lancers Croft CH66 ... 69 E1
Lancing Ave WA2 ...... 8 A4
Lancing Rd CH65 ..... 70 D4
Land Cut La WA3 ...... 9 D3
Lander Cl WA5 .... 15 D7
Landican Cl SK9 .... 60 C6
Landor Cl WA3 .... 31 A5
Landscape Dene WA6 ... 73 D4
Landseer Ave
  Neston CH64 .... 66 F7
  Warrington WA4 ..... 16 D3
Landseer Dr SK10 .... 111 E8
Landswood Pk CW8 ... 103 B4
LANE ENDS 173 D3
Lane Ends WA8 .... 21 D5
LANE HEAD 3 E6
Lane Head Ave WA3 .... 3 E6
Lanehead Rd SK23 .... 65 C5
Lanehouse Rd SK22 ... 39 E7
Lane The SY13, SY14 .. 223 C3
Langcliffe SY14 .... 4 E3
Langdale Ave WA13 ... 18 F4
Langdale Cl
  Bramhall SK7 .... 35 C5
  Crewe CW2 .... 189 D2
  Partington M31 ...... 11 E3

Langdale Rd continued
  Runcorn WA7 .... 23 B1
Langdale Way WA6 .... 49 C1
Langden Cl WA3 .... 4 D4
Langdon Ho CH4 .... 141 B7
Langfield WA3 .... 3 E7
Langfield Gr CH62 ..... 43 D5
Langford L24 .... 21 C2
Langford Ct CH3 ..... 121 C2
Langford Rd CW9 ..... 80 A3
Langford St [1] SK11 .. 112 C8
Langford Way WA4 ... 27 D4
Langland Cl WA3 ...... 7 E2
LANGLEY 113 C3
Langley Ave WA2 ...... 2 C1
Langley Cl
  Newcastle-u-Lyme
  ST5 .... 210 D2
  Sandbach CW11 .... 175 C8
Langley Ct CH65 ...... 70 E3
Langley Dr
  Crewe CW2 .... 190 A2
  Handforth SK9 .... 34 E3
  Macclesfield SK11 ... 112 B4
Langley Hall Cl SK11 .. 113 B4
Langley Hall Cotts
  SK11 .... 113 B4
Langley Rd
  Langley SK11 .... 113 A3
  Northwich CW9 ..... 104 A6
Langport Dr CH3 ..... 119 C2
Langton Cl
  Newton-le-W WA12 ... 2 A4
  Widnes WA8 .... 12 B3
Langton Gr WA7 ..... 17 D7
Langwell Cl WA3 ..... 10 A5
Lanreath Cl SK10 ..... 86 D1
Lansbrook Cl WA7 .... 23 C2
Lansdown Cl SK8 ..... 35 C7
Lansdowne
  Culcheth WA3 .... 4 E2
  Frodsham WA6 .... 74 D6
Lansdowne Gr CH4 ... 141 A7
Lansdowne Rd
  Connah's Quay CH5 ... 91 D1
  Crewe CW1 .... 190 F5
  Great Barrow CH3 ... 120 D3
Lansdowne St SK10 ... 87 E1
Lansdown Rd CH4 .... 139 B4
Lanyard Way CW11 ... 175 C3
Lapwing Cl
  Golborne WA3 .... 3 D8
  Newton-le-W WA12 ... 2 C3
  Packmoor ST7 ..... 195 E1
  Winsford CW7 ...... 149 C5
Lapwing Gr
  Moore WA4 .... 25 A8
  Whisterfield SK11 ... 109 C4
  Whisterfield SK11 ... 109 C6
Lapwing Rd ST7 ..... 195 D3
Lapwing Rise CH60 ... 40 F6
Larch Ave
  Haydock WA11 ...... 1 E7
  Macclesfield SK11 ... 112 A5
  Newton-le-W WA12 ... 2 C5
  Warrington WA5 ..... 14 E5
  Widnes WA8 .... 13 B2
Larch Cl
  Golborne WA3 .... 3 F6
  Poynton SK12 .... 36 F3
  Runcorn WA7 .... 49 C7
  Weaverham CW8 .... 102 D7
Larchdale Cl CH66 .... 94 F8
Larches The WA16 .... 58 E2
Larchfields CH1 ...... 117 A8
Larch Rd
  Crewe CW2 .... 189 E2
  Haydock WA11 ...... 1 E7
  Partington M31 ...... 11 E3
  Runcorn WA7 .... 49 C7
Larch Rise SK10 ...... 86 D6
Larchtree Cl CW8 ..... 78 B4
Larchway
  Bramhall SK7 .... 35 C7
  High Lane SK6 .... 37 F7
Lark Way CW4 ...... 140 E6
Larchways WA4 ...... 26 D5
Larchwood Dr SK9 ... 60 D8
LARDEN GREEN 202 D4
Lark Ave ST7 .... 195 D3
Larkfield ST7 .... 195 B1
Larkfield Ave WA1 .... 17 A7
Lark Hall Cl SK10 .... 113 A7
Lark Hall Rd SK10 ... 113 A7
Lark Hill Cotts SK22 ... 39 A8
Larkspur Cl
  Chester CH4 .... 140 F4
  Nantwich CW5 ..... 204 E8
  Runcorn WA7 .... 49 F4
Larkspur Gr WA5 .... 15 E3
Larkstoke Cl WA4 .... 26 E6
Larksway CH60 ...... 41 B8
Larkwood Way SK10 .. 87 E5
Larne Ct WA8 .... 12 E2
Larne Dr CH4 .... 139 D4
Laskey La WA4 .... 17 F4
LATCHFORD 16 B4
Latchford CE Prim Sch
  WA4 .... 16 B4
Latchford Rd CH60 ... 41 B6
Latchford St WA4 .... 17 A3
Latham Ave
  Helsby WA6 .... 73 B1
  Newton-le-W WA12 ... 2 C4
  Runcorn WA7 .... 23 C1
Latham Ho WA12 ..... 2 B4

Latham Rd CW11 .... 175 A5
Latham St CW7 ..... 126 C1
Lathom Ave WA2 ..... 16 B8
Lathom Rd M44 ...... 11 F8
Lathom Way SK10 .... 87 F2
Latimer Dr CW2 .... 190 A4
Launceston Cl
  Runcorn WA7 .... 50 C6
  Winsford CW7 ...... 149 B7
Launceston Dr
  Bramhall SK7 .... 35 F7
  Warrington WA5 ..... 14 E3
Laura St CW2 ...... 190 D1
Laurel Ave
  Newton-le-W WA12 ... 2 D3
  Warrington WA4 ..... 17 D7
Laurel Bank
  Warrington WA1 ..... 17 C1
  Widnes WA8 .... 13 A3
  Winsford CW7 ...... 149 D8
Laurel Cl
  Barnton CW8 .... 78 A4
  Middlewich CW10 ... 128 B2
  Nantwich CW5 ..... 175 C5
Laurel Dr
  Crewe CW2 .... 189 F2
  Ellesmere Port CH65 ... 70 B2
  Harrisead ST7 ..... 195 E4
  Willaston CH64 ...... 43 B1
Laurel Gr
  Chester CH2 .... 119 A3
  Golborne WA3 .... 3 D8
Laurel Pk CW6 ...... 145 A6
Laurels Farm Ct CH2 .. 72 B3
Laurels The
  High Lane SK6 .... 37 E8
  Milton Green CH3 ... 165 C2
Laurel Way SK8 ...... 35 C8
Laurel Wlk M31 ..... 11 E2
Laurelwood Dr [4]
  CH66 .... 69 E1
Laureston Ave CW1 ... 190 F4
Lavender Cl WA7 ..... 23 C1
Lavender Dr CW9 .... 104 E7
Lavender Gdns WA9 ... 6 A7
Lavender Wlk M31 ... 11 E2
Lavenham Cl
  Hazel Grove SK7 ..... 36 E8
  Macclesfield SK10 ... 87 C2
LAVISTER 162 C1
Lavister Cl [6] CW9 ... 103 F4
Lavister Wlks LL12 ... 162 C1
Lawford Cl CW1 ..... 189 F8
Lawford Dr CH60 ..... 41 C8
Lawn Ave WA1 .... 16 F8
Lawn Dr CW2 .... 118 D2
Lawns Ave CH63 ..... 43 B6
Lawnsdale CH3 ...... 101 D5
Lawns The SK9 ...... 59 E4
Lawnswood Gr CW2 .. 72 B3
Lawrence Ave
  [3] Middlewich CW10 .. 128 C1
  Moulton CW9 .... 126 E8
Lawrence Ave E [2]
  CW10 .... 128 C1
Lawrence Pl SK12 .... 36 D2
Lawrence St
  Crewe CW1 .... 190 C4
  Sandycroft CH5 ..... 116 A3
Lawson Cl CH3 ...... 142 A8
Lawson Cl WA1 ...... 17 E7
Law St CH2 .... 118 D3
Lawton Ave
  Bramhall SK7 .... 35 E8
  Lawton-gate ST7 ... 194 D3
Lawton Cl WA3 .... 4 E3
Lawton Coppice ST7 .. 194 E4
Lawtongate Est ST7 .. 194 A5
Lawton Hall ST7 .... 194 C4
Lawton Hall Dr ST7 ... 194 C4
LAWTON HEATH 193 E6
LAWTON HEATH END
  .... 193 C6
Lawton Heath Rd ST7 .. 193 F5
Lawton Rd ST7 ..... 193 E4
Lawton St
  Congleton CW12 .... 156 E2
  Crewe CW2 .... 190 C3
  Kidsgrove ST7 ..... 195 C3
Lawton Way CW11 ... 174 E2
Laxey Ave WA1 ...... 17 D6
Laxton Cl CH66 ...... 94 F8
Laxton Way CW10 .... 128 C2
Layland Ave WA3 ..... 3 A8
Layton Cl WA3 .... 9 E3
Lea Ave
  Crewe CW1 .... 190 F4
  Goostrey CW4 .... 107 C3
Lea Bank Cl SK11 ... 112 A8
Lea Cl CW11 .... 175 C5
Leacroft Rd WA3 .... 10 A7
Lea Cross Gr WA8 ... 12 C3
Leadbeaters Cl WA11 .. 112 F7
Leadbeaters Rd SK11 . 112 F7
Leadgate La CH3 .... 144 F2
Lea Dr
  Nantwich CW5 ..... 204 C4
  Wimboldsley SK10 ... 151 A4
Leadsmithy St CW10 .. 128 C1
Leadworks La CH1 ... 237 C3
Leaf Gr CW7 .... 126 A1
Leafield Dr SK8 ...... 34 F6
Leafield Rd SK12 .... 38 C6
Leaf La CW7 .... 127 A2

Leaf Lane Inf Sch
  CW7 .... 127 A2
Leafy Way CW8 ..... 102 D7
LEA GREEN 172 A8
Lea Hall Barns CW5 .. 220 E6
Lea Hall Pk CH1 ..... 95 A3
Lea Homes CW5 ..... 217 B7
Leahurst Cl CH2 ..... 118 F4
Lea La CH3 .... 164 C3
Leamington Ave WA12 .. 2 C1
Leamington Cl
  Neston CH64 .... 66 E6
  Warrington WA5 ..... 15 F8
Leamington Rd
  Congleton CW12 .... 155 F3
  Macclesfield SK10 ... 86 F1
Lear Dr CW2 .... 205 F8
Leas Cl [3] CH66 ..... 69 C5
Leaside CW2 .... 23 D1
Leaside Rd CH1 ..... 117 E6
Leaside Way WA16 ... 60 C6
Lea's Pas CW10 ..... 128 B1
Lea St SK22 .... 39 A8
Leatham Cl WA3 ...... 9 E3
Leathers La L26 ..... 21 A7
Lea Way WA7 .... 193 D3
Leawood Cl CW8 .... 103 A6
Ledbury Cl CW8 ..... 206 A7
Ledbury Dr CW2 ..... 18 C3
Ledger Rd WA11 ...... 1 A5
Ledley St CW7 .... 87 F7
LEDSHAM 68 F2
Ledsham Cl WA3 ...... 9 C3
Ledsham Ct CH66 ..... 69 B6
Ledsham Hall La CH66 . 68 E4
Ledsham La CH66 .... 68 F3
Ledsham Park Dr
  CH66 .... 69 A6
Ledsham Rd CH66 .... 69 B6
Ledsham Village CH66 . 68 F4
Ledston Cl WA7 ...... 24 D1
Ledward St CW7 .... 127 A1
Ledyard Cl WA5 ...... 15 D7
Leech Rd SY14 ..... 213 B3
Lee Cl WA16 .... 56 F1
Lee Ct
  Runcorn WA7 .... 23 D2
  Warrington WA2 ...... 8 C7
Lee Dr CW8 .... 103 E7
Lee Green Cres WA5 .. 150 A1
Leek Old Rd SK11 ... 112 C2
Leek Rd CW12 ...... 179 A8
Leen La CH1 .... 237 B2
Lees La
  Ellesmere Port CH65 ... 70 E4
  Mottram St Andrew
  SK10 .... 61 B7
Lees Mill [4] SK22 .... 39 C7
Lees Rd SK7 .... 35 D5
Lees The WA8 .... 15 A8
LEFTWICH 104 B5
Leftwich Com Prim Sch
  CW9 .... 104 A4
Leftwich Warehouse
  CW9 .... 103 F7
Legh Cl SK12 .... 36 E4
Legh Ct
  Golborne WA3 .... 3 A8
  Knutsford WA16 ..... 57 D4
Legh Gdns WA16 .... 57 B1
Legh Ho [2] WA16 .... 57 B1
Legh Rd
  Adlington SK10 ...... 62 C5
  Haydock WA11 ...... 1 A6
  High Lane SK12 ..... 38 A6
  Knutsford WA16 ..... 82 B8
  Prestbury SK10 ...... 87 A8
Legh St
  Golborne WA3 .... 3 A8
  [3] Lymm WA13 ..... 18 E3
  Newton-le-W WA12 ... 2 A3
  Warrington WA1 ..... 16 A5
Legh Vale Prim Sch
  WA11 .... 1 D5
Leicester Ave ST7 ... 193 D5
Leicester St
  Northwich CW9 ...... 79 A1
  Warrington WA5 ..... 15 F5
Leigh Ave
  Knutsford WA16 ..... 57 C3
  Widnes WA8 .... 13 A1
Leigh Green Cl [4]
  WA8 .... 22 C8
Leigh La CW8 .... 77 C5
Leigh Rd
  Congleton CW12 .... 157 B5
  Wilmslow SK9 .... 59 D5
Leigh's Brow CW8 .... 77 F3
Leigh St [1] SK11 ... 112 F7
Leighstone Ct CW2 ... 237 A4
Leighton Chase CH64 . 41 D1
Leighton Cotts CH64 .. 41 D5
Leighton Ct CH64 .... 66 D8
Leighton Dr WN7 ..... 4 B8
Leighton Hospl CW1 .. 172 E1
Leighton Prim Sch
  CW1 .... 189 F8
Leighton Rd CH64 ... 41 D2
Leighton St [1] CW1 .. 190 B5
Leightons The CW4 .. 130 A4
Leighton View CW1 .. 190 A8
Leigh Way CW8 .... 77 C1

Leinster Gdns WA7 . . . . . . .22 F3
Leinster St WA7 . . . . .22 F3
Leiria Way WA7 . . . . .23 B2
Lenham Wlk M22 . . . . .33 D8
Lenthall Ave CW12 . . . . . . .178 F8
Leonard St
  Chester CH1 . . . . .118 B3
  Runcorn WA7 . . . . .48 D7
  Warrington, Stockton Heath
  WA4 .16 C1
  Warrington WA2 . . . . .16 C7
Leon Cl WA5 . . . . .14 D7
Leslie Rd CW7 . . . . .149 A7
Lessingham Rd WA8 . . . . . . .12 F3
Lester Cl ST7 . . . . .193 D6
Leven Ave CW7 . . . . .126 F2
Levens Cl WA5 . . . . .15 F6
Levens Way 1 WA8 . . . . .22 C8
Leven Wlk CH66 . . . . .70 A7
Leveret Rd L24 . . . . .21 A3
Levisham Gdns WA5 . . . . . . .15 E7
Lewin St CW10 . . . . .128 C1
Lewis Ave WA5 . . . . .7 F2
Lewis Cl
  Ellesmere Port CH65 . . . . . . .95 C8
  Nantwich CW5 . . . . .205 A5
Lewis Cres WA8 . . . . .23 A7
Lewis Gr WA8 . . . . .12 D1
Lewis St CW1 . . . . .190 C3
Lexden St WA5 . . . . .15 E6
Lexington Wlk 2 WA5 . . . . .15 C7
Leycester Cl WA16 . . . . .82 C8
Leycester Dr WA16 . . . . .57 F7
Leycester Rd WA16 . . . . .82 B8
Leyfield Ct CH4 . . . . .140 F5
Leyland Dr CH4 . . . . .140 C6
Leyland Gr
  Haslington CW1 . . . . .191 C4
  Haydock WA11 . . . . .1 B6
Leyland Wlk CW7 . . . . .149 C6
Leyton Cl WA7 . . . . .49 B6
Libris Ho 1 WA16 . . . . .57 A1
Libris Pk 2 WA16 . . . . .57 A1
Libris Pl 3 WA16 . . . . .57 A1
Libson Cl WA2 . . . . .9 A3
Lichfield Ave
  Golborne WA3 . . . . .3 D8
  Grappenhall Heys WA4 . . . . . .27 A7
Lichfield Cl WA16 . . . . .57 D2
Lichfield Ct CW7 . . . . .149 D7
Lichfield Dr CH66 . . . . .94 E8
Lichfield Rd
  Blacon CH1 . . . . .117 F5
  Talke ST7 . . . . .210 D7
Lichfield St CW10 . . . . .128 D2
Lidgetts La SK10 . . . . .88 C3
Lift La CW9 . . . . .78 D3
Light Alders La SK12 . . . . . . .38 A6
Lightburn St 6 WA7 . . . . . . .22 F1
Lightfoot Cl CH60 . . . . .41 B7
Lightfoot La
  Eaton CW6 . . . . .147 A4
  Heswall CH60 . . . . .41 B7
Lightfoot St CH2 . . . . .118 F2
Lighthouse Rd L24 . . . . .47 E7
Lightley Cl CW11 . . . . .175 A4
Lightley Ct CW11 . . . . .175 A4
Light Oaks Rd WA3 . . . . .5 C6
LIGHTWOOD GREEN 229 B3
Lightwood Green Ave
  CW3 . . . . .229 A2
Lightwood Rd ST5 . . . . .210 D1
Lilac Ave
  Knutsford WA16 . . . . .56 E1
  Warrington WA5 . . . . .15 A5
  Widnes WA8 . . . . .13 B2
Lilac Cl
  Kelsall CW6 . . . . .122 E2
  Newcastle-u-Lyme ST5 . . . . .210 D1
Lilac Cres WA7 . . . . .49 C8
Lilac Ct CW12 . . . . .156 E2
Lilac Dr CW8 . . . . .103 D6
Lilac Gr
  Ellesmere Port CH66 . . . . . . .95 A8
  Warrington WA4 . . . . .16 E1
Lilac Wlk M31 . . . . .11 E3
Lilford Ave WA5 . . . . .15 F8
Lilford Dr WA5 . . . . .14 F6
Lilford Sq SK11 . . . . .112 D5
Lilford St WA5 . . . . .15 F7
Lillyfield CH60 . . . . .40 F6
Lily Ave WA12 . . . . .2 D2
Lilybrook Dr WA16 . . . . .57 B1
Lily La CW10 . . . . .129 B6
Limbrick Rd ST7 . . . . .209 A1
Lime Ave
  Frodsham WA6 . . . . .74 C8
  Northwich CW9 . . . . .103 F5
  Weaverham CW8 . . . . .102 D8
  5 Widnes WA8 . . . . .13 B2
Lime Cl
  Hollinfare WA3 . . . . .11 A2
  Middlewich CW10 . . . . .128 B2
  Sandbach CW11 . . . . .175 A7
  Tarporley CW6 . . . . .146 D2
Lime Ct
  Leftwich CW9 . . . . .104 A5
  Northwich CW9 . . . . .103 F5
Limefield Ave WA13 . . . . .18 F2
Lime Gr
  Alsager ST7 . . . . .193 E2
  Chester CH2 . . . . .119 A3
  Elton CH2 . . . . .72 A3
  Golborne WA3 . . . . .3 E6
  Macclesfield SK10 . . . . .112 E8

Lime Gr continued
  Runcorn WA7 . . . . .49 C8
  Saltney CH4 . . . . .140 D6
  Shavington CW2 . . . . .206 C4
  Winsford CW7 . . . . .127 A1
Limehurst Gr CH62 . . . . .43 D6
Limekiln La WA5 . . . . .6 E3
Lime Kiln La ST7 . . . . .194 E2
Limekiln Row WA7 . . . . .50 A8
Limerick Cl WA8 . . . . .12 E3
Limes Cl CW1 . . . . .191 C4
Limes La WA4 . . . . .52 D6
Lime St
  Congleton CW12 . . . . .156 D2
  Crewe CW1 . . . . .190 C6
  Ellesmere Port CH65 . . . . . . .70 C7
Limes The
  Culcheth WA3 . . . . .4 D4
  Golborne WA3 . . . . .3 D6
  Middlewich CW10 . . . . .128 B1
Limetree Ave
  Warrington, Stockton Heath
  WA4 .16 E1
  Warrington WA1 . . . . .17 A8
Lime Tree Ave
  Congleton CW12 . . . . .156 B3
  Crewe CW1 . . . . .190 E6
Lime Tree Cl
  Ellesmere Port CH66 . . . . . . .95 A8
  Winsford CW7 . . . . .149 C8
Lime Tree Dr CH3 . . . . .180 F1
Lime Tree Gr CH66 . . . . .69 E1
Lime Trees La WA16 . . . . . . .29 D6
Limeways WA4 . . . . .26 E5
Lime Wlk
  6 Handforth SK9 . . . . .34 D1
  Partington M31 . . . . .11 D3
Lime Wood CH2 . . . . .118 F4
Limewood Cres WA8 . . . . . . .78 B4
Limewood Gr CW8 . . . . .78 B4
Linacre La WA8 . . . . .12 E5
Lincoln Ave
  Gatley SK8 . . . . .34 B7
  Irlam M44 . . . . .11 C4
Lincoln Cl
  Golborne WN7 . . . . .4 C8
  Macclesfield SK10 . . . . .86 F2
  Rainow SK10 . . . . .88 E5
  Runcorn WA7 . . . . .49 C6
  Warrington WA1 . . . . .17 E6
Lincoln Ct
  Helsby WA6 . . . . .73 B3
  5 Warrington WA5 . . . . .15 B7
Lincoln Dr CH2 . . . . .119 A5
Lincoln Ho 13 CH1 . . . . . . .237 C3
Lincoln Pl WA7 . . . . .86 F2
Lincoln Rd
  Blacon CH1 . . . . .117 F5
  Ellesmere Port CH66 . . . . . . .69 D3
  Handforth SK9 . . . . .34 E1
  Kidsgrove ST7 . . . . .194 F2
Lincoln Sq WA8 . . . . .13 B2
Lincoln St 3 CW1 . . . . .190 B5
Lincoln Wlk CH65 . . . . .86 F2
Lincombe Hey SK10 . . . . . . .87 C8
Lincombe Rd M22 . . . . .33 D8
Lindale Cl CW12 . . . . .157 A5
Linden Cl
  Congleton CW12 . . . . .179 A8
  Ellesmere Port CH66 . . . . . . .94 F8
  Lymm WA13 . . . . .19 A4
  Warrington WA1 . . . . .17 D7
Linden Ct
  Macclesfield SK10 . . . . .87 B2
  Sandbach CW11 . . . . .174 F3
  Widnes WA8 . . . . .12 F4
Linden Dr
  Biddulph ST8 . . . . .179 C1
  Crewe CW1 . . . . .190 F4
  Helsby WA6 . . . . .73 B1
  Mickle Trafford CH2 . . . . .96 F1
Linden Gr
  Biddulph ST8 . . . . .179 C1
  Bramhall SK7 . . . . .35 D4
  Chester CH2 . . . . .119 A4
  Saltney CH4 . . . . .140 D6
Linden Way
  High Lane SK6 . . . . .38 A7
  Widnes WA8 . . . . .12 F4
Lindfield Cl WA4 . . . . .25 A5
Lindfield Est N SK9 . . . . . . .60 A6
Lindfield Est S SK9 . . . . . . .59 F6
Lindfields CH4 . . . . .140 F6
Lindi Ave WA4 . . . . .17 C2
Lindisfarne Ave
  Ellesmere Port CH65 . . . . . . .70 C2
  Golborne WA3 . . . . .4 C8
Lindisfarne Cl CW10 . . . . . .128 B1
Lindisfarne Ct WA8 . . . . .12 F6
Lindisfarne Dr SK12 . . . . . . .36 D4
Lindley Ave WA4 . . . . .16 F4
Lindop Ct WA16 . . . . .57 C1
Lindow Com Prim Sch
  SK9 .59 D3
Lindow Court Pk WA16 . . . . .59 B5
Lindow Ct SK9 . . . . .59 E8
LINDOW END 59 B2
Lindow Fold Dr SK9 . . . . . . .59 C5
Lindow La SK9 . . . . .59 E6
Lindow Par SK9 . . . . .59 F6
Lindrick Cl SK10 . . . . .87 C4
Lindrum Ave SK11 . . . . .112 D2
Lindsay Way WA11 . . . . .193 A4
Lindsay Wlk WA8 . . . . .102 A4
Lindsworth Cl WA5 . . . . .15 C6
Linear View WA12 . . . . .2 C1
Linen Hall Pl CH1 . . . . .237 A2
Lines Rd M44 . . . . .11 F8

Lingdale Wlk SK11 . . . . .112 D5
Lingfield Cl SK10 . . . . .87 C4
Lingfield Dr CW1 . . . . .190 C7
Lingfield Ho WA7 . . . . .48 E8
Lingfield Rd WA7 . . . . .22 E1
LINGLEY GREEN 14 C7
Lingley Green Ave
  WA5 .14 D8
Lingley Mere Bsns Pk
  WA5 .14 C8
Lingley Rd WA5 . . . . .14 D8
Linglongs Ave WA3 . . . . .65 C5
Linglongs Rd SK23 . . . . .65 C5
Lingmell Gdns CW4 . . . . . . .129 F3
Lingwell Ave WA8 . . . . .12 D2
Lingwell Pk WA8 . . . . .12 E2
Lingwood Rd WA5 . . . . .14 F6
Links Ave CH66 . . . . .69 C7
Links Cl CH63 . . . . .43 B6
Linkside Ave WA3 . . . . .8 B6
Linkside Way CH66 . . . . .94 F8
Links Rd SK9 . . . . .59 E4
Links View CH66 . . . . .69 C7
Linksway
  Chester CH2 . . . . .118 C7
  Congleton CW12 . . . . .178 E8
Linksway Cl CW12 . . . . .178 F8
Link The SK9 . . . . .34 D3
Linkway WA3 . . . . .9 C8
Link Wlk M31 . . . . .11 D2
Linley Gr ST7 . . . . .193 F3
Linley La ST7 . . . . .194 A2
Linley Rd
  Alsager ST7 . . . . .193 F2
  Cheadle SK8 . . . . .35 B8
  Talke ST7 . . . . .210 C8
Linley Trad Est ST7 . . . . . . .194 C1
Linnards La CW9, WA16 . . . . .80 B5
Linnet Cl
  Newton-le-W WA12 . . . . .2 C3
  Warrington WA3 . . . . .8 D3
  Winsford CW7 . . . . .150 B8
Linnet Gr
  Macclesfield SK10 . . . . .87 A1
  Warrington WA3 . . . . .9 E4
Linnets Pk WA7 . . . . .23 C3
Linnets Way CH60 . . . . .40 E8
Linnett Cl CW1 . . . . .190 A7
Linnett Gr ST7 . . . . .195 E1
Linton Ct CW7 . . . . .127 A3
Linum Gdns WA9 . . . . .6 B7
Linwood CW7 . . . . .150 B8
Linwood Cl WA7 . . . . .50 C5
Lion Salt Works Mus*
  CW9 .79 C3
Lion St CW12 . . . . .156 D2
Liskeard Cl WA7 . . . . .50 B6
Liskeard Dr SK7 . . . . .35 F7
Lismore Wlk M22 . . . . .33 E8
Lister Cl CW10 . . . . .151 D6
Lister Rd WA7 . . . . .23 C3
Little Abbey Gateway
  CH1 .237 A3
Little Aston Cl WA10 . . . . . . .87 C4
LITTLE BOLLINGTON 20 B2
Little Bollington CE Prim
  Sch WA14 . . . . .20 B2
Littlebourne WA7 . . . . .50 E7
LITTLE BUDWORTH 147 F8
Little Budworth Ctry Pk*
  CW6 . . . . .147 C8
Littlecote Gdns WA4 . . . . . . .26 E5
Littledale Rd WA5 . . . . .14 F7
Littledales La CW8 . . . . .102 E4
Little Delph WA11 . . . . .1 C7
Littlegate WA7 . . . . .49 E8
Little Gn CH66 . . . . .69 D3
LITTLE HEATH 230 A5
Little Heath CW3 . . . . .230 A5
Little Heath La WA14 . . . . . . .20 D5
Little Heath Rd
  Chester CH3 . . . . .119 E1
  Christleton CH3 . . . . .142 E8
Little La CH64 . . . . .41 C1
Little Lakes CW7 . . . . .207 D2
Little Mdw CW8 . . . . .102 A4
Little Moss Cl ST7 . . . . .194 E6
Little Moss La ST7 . . . . .194 E5
LITTLE NESTON 66 D6
LITTLER 126 A2
Little Rake La CH2 . . . . .95 D5
Littler Grange Ct
  CW7 . . . . .126 A1
Littler La CW7 . . . . .125 F1
Little Roodee CH5 . . . . .139 B7
Little Row 5 ST7 . . . . .195 B2
Little St
  Congleton CW12 . . . . .156 D2
LITTLE STANNEY 70 E1
Little Stanney La CH2 . . . . . .95 F8
Littlestone Cl WA8 . . . . .13 A4
LITTLE SUTTON 69 B5
Little Sutton CE Prim Sch
  CH66 . . . . .69 A6
Little Sutton Sta CH66 . . . . .69 C6
LITTLETON 119 E1
Littleton Cl
  1 Northwich CW9 . . . . . . .103 F4

Littleton Cl continued
  Warrington WA5 . . . . .15 D4
Littleton La CH3 . . . . .119 E2
LITTLE TOWN 4 C1
Little Wissage CH66 . . . . . . .69 F2
Littondale Cl CW12 . . . . . . .157 A5
Liverpool Pl WA8 . . . . .12 C1
Liverpool Rd
  Backford CH1, CH2 . . . . .95 B4
  Chester CH2 . . . . .118 C6
  Haydock, Stanley Bank
  WA11 .1 A7
  Haydock WA11 . . . . .1 A1
  Irlam, Cadishead M44 . . . . . .11 D4
  Kidsgrove ST7 . . . . .195 A1
  Neston CH64 . . . . .41 F1
  Newcastle-u-Lyme ST5 . . . . .210 D2
  Warrington, Great Sankey
  WA5 .14 C6
  Warrington, Penketh
  WA5 .15 A4
  Warrington WA5, WA1 . . . . . . .15 F5
  Widnes WA8 . . . . .12 C1
Liverpool Rd E ST7 . . . . . . .194 E2
Liverpool Rd W ST7 . . . . . . .194 B4
Liverpool Row WA12 . . . . .7 D8
Liverpool St CW7 . . . . .104 C8
Livingstone Cl
  Macclesfield SK10 . . . . .111 F8
  Warrington WA5 . . . . .15 D7
Livingstone Rd CH65 . . . . . . .70 C7
Livingstone Way
  CW10 . . . . .151 D6
Liz Kaye Ho SK11 . . . . .112 E7
Llandaff Cl CH66 . . . . .69 E1
Llandovery Cl CW7 . . . . .149 B7
Lloyd Cl CH3 . . . . .180 E2
Lloyd Cres WA12 . . . . .1 F3
Lloyd Dr CH65 . . . . .70 D1
Lloyd Pl CH1 . . . . .117 E4
Llyndir La LL12 . . . . .162 B1
Llys Bernsdale/Bernsdale
  Ct CH5 . . . . .116 A3
Llys Cadnant/Cadnant Ct
  CH4 .139 A3
Llys Caer CH4 . . . . .139 A3
Llys Catrin/Catherine Ct
  CH5 .139 B6
Llys Derwen CH4 . . . . .140 F6
Llys Maes Y Ffynnon /
  Springfield Ct CH4 . . . . .161 A8
Llys Perenna/Perenna Ct
  CH66 . . . . .91 B2
Llys Rhuddlan/Rhuddlan
  Ct **5** CH4 . . . . .140 F6
Llys Sant Iago/St James
  Ct CH5 . . . . .91 D1
Llys Y Faenol CH5 . . . . .139 B7
Loachbrook Ave
  CW12 . . . . .156 A2
Lobelia Gr WA7 . . . . .49 F4
Lobelia Wlk 6 M31 . . . . .11 E2
Lochinvar Ave CH66 . . . . .68 F6
Lochleven Rd CW2 . . . . .206 A7
Lochmaben Cl CH4 . . . . .130 B2
Loch St
  4 Runcorn WA7 . . . . .23 A2
  Runcorn WA7 . . . . .23 A3
Locke Ho CW1 . . . . .190 B4
Locker Ave WA2 . . . . .8 B2
Lockerbie Cl
  Holmes Chapel CW4 . . . . . . .130 C2
  Warrington WA2 . . . . .8 E3
Lockett Rd WA8 . . . . .13 B1
Lockett St WA4 . . . . .16 F3
Lockgate E WA7 . . . . .24 C2
Lockgate W WA7 . . . . .24 C2
LOCKING STUMPS 9 C5
Locking Stumps Com Prim
  Sch WA3 . . . . .9 D4
Locking Stumps La WA3 . . . . .9 B4
Lockitt St CW2 . . . . .190 D3
Lock La M31 . . . . .11 E3
Lock Rd
  Bebington CH62 . . . . .44 A8
  Warrington WA1 . . . . .16 F6
Locks The
  Grappenhall WA4 . . . . .17 B3
  Middlewich CW10 . . . . .151 D8
Lockton La WA5 . . . . .15 E7
Lockwood View WA7 . . . . . . .50 F5
Lodge Brow SK10 . . . . .63 A1
Lodgebury Ct SY14 . . . . .211 C2
Lodge Cl WA13 . . . . .19 B4
Lodge Dr
  Culcheth WA3 . . . . .4 F3
  Moulton CW9 . . . . .126 E8
  Winsford CW7 . . . . .127 A1
Lodgefields Com Prim Sch
  CW2 . . . . .189 E4
Lodgefields Dr CW2 . . . . . . .189 E4
Lodge Gdns CH65 . . . . .118 D6
Lodge Hollow WA6 . . . . .73 B2
Lodge La
  Antrobus CW9 . . . . .54 A6
  Dutton WA4 . . . . .76 C8
  Hartford CW8 . . . . .103 B4
  Hatherton CW5 . . . . .220 A4
  Haydock WA11, WA12,
  WN4 . . . . .2 C4
  Lostock Gralam CW9 . . . . . . .80 A2
  Runcorn WA7 . . . . .49 D8
  Saughall CH1 . . . . .94 A2
  Warrington WA5 . . . . .15 F7
  Widnes WA8 . . . . .12 B4
Lodge Rd
  Alsager ST7 . . . . .193 C4
  Knutsford WA16 . . . . .57 C3

Lodge Rd continued
  Sandbach CW11 . . . . .174 E5
  Talke ST7 . . . . .210 D6
  Widnes WA8 . . . . .22 A8
Lodmore La SY13 . . . . .233 C6
Lofthouse Gate WA8 . . . . . . .12 F4
Lomas Sq SK11 . . . . .112 D5
Lomax Rd CW5 . . . . .205 D6
Lomond Gr CH66 . . . . .69 F3
London Rd
  Adlington SK10 . . . . .62 C5
  Alderley Edge SK9 . . . . .60 A1
  Allostock WA16 . . . . .106 F3
  Bridgemere CW5, CW3 . . . . .232 A5
  Davenham CW9 . . . . .104 A1
  Frodsham WA6 . . . . .74 B8
  Hatherton CW5 . . . . .220 C1
  Holmes Chapel CW4 . . . . . . .130 C2
  Macclesfield SK11 . . . . .112 D3
  Nantwich CW5 . . . . .204 F5
  Northwich, Leftwich
  CW9 . . . . .104 A5
  Sandbach CW11 . . . . .174 D8
  Stapeley CW5 . . . . .205 B3
  Warrington WA4 . . . . .26 D5
  Woore CW3 . . . . .232 C1
London Rd N SK12 . . . . .36 E5
London Rd S SK12 . . . . .36 D3
London Road Terr
  SK11 . . . . .112 D5
London Row WA12 . . . . .7 D8
Loney St SK11 . . . . .112 C7
Long Acre
  Cuddington CW8 . . . . .101 D4
  Warrington CW8 . . . . .77 C1
Longacres Rd WA15 . . . . .32 D7
Long Acres Rd CH64 . . . . . . .41 E2
Longacre St SK10 . . . . .112 C8
LONGBARN 9 B1
Longbarn Bvd WA2 . . . . .9 C2
Longbarn Com Prim Sch
  WA2 . . . . .9 B1
Long Barn La
  Warrington WA2 . . . . .9 B2
  Warrington, Woolston
  WA1 .17 D8
Longbenton Way WA7 . . . . . .24 B4
Longburgh Cl CH2 . . . . .118 F3
Longbutt La WA13 . . . . .19 A2
Longbutts La SK11 . . . . .111 E2
Longclough Rd ST5 . . . . .210 D2
Long Croft La SK8 . . . . .34 E8
Longcross Ct CW10 . . . . . . .128 C1
Longdale Dr CH1 . . . . .117 C5
Longden Ct SK7 . . . . .35 E5
Longden La SK11 . . . . .113 A6
Longden St WA4 . . . . .16 F3
Longdin St WA4 . . . . .16 F3
Longdown Rd CW12 . . . . . . .155 F4
Longfield Ave
  Chester CH2 . . . . .118 E7
  Gatley SK8 . . . . .34 C7
Longfield Rd WA2 . . . . .8 C1
LONGFORD 8 B1
Longford Dr WA8 . . . . .12 E2
Longford Rd
  4 Crewe CW2 . . . . .190 D2
  Warrington WA2 . . . . .16 B7
Long Gn CH3 . . . . .97 E1
LONG GREEN 97 F1
LONGHILL 230 E5
Long Hill SK23 . . . . .65 F2
Longhill La CW3 . . . . .230 E5
Longhorn Cl CW10 . . . . .128 D2
Long La
  Alpraham CW6 . . . . .169 E4
  Bickerton SY14 . . . . .199 F4
  Biddulph SK10 . . . . .63 B2
  Burland CW5 . . . . .203 A8
  Chester CH2 . . . . .118 F7
  Hargrave CH3 . . . . .143 D2
  Harriseahead ST7 . . . . .195 E4
  Haughton CW6 . . . . .186 A6
  Horwich End SK23 . . . . .65 F3
  Huxley CH3 . . . . .166 D4
  Middlewich CW10 . . . . .151 C7
  Over Tabley WA16 . . . . .94 B2
  Swan Green WA16 . . . . .107 D7
  Swettenham CW12 . . . . .131 F5
  Tilston SY14 . . . . .198 B3
  Warrington WA2 . . . . .8 C1
  Wettenhall CW7, CW6 . . . . .170 C6
Longlands Dr SK22 . . . . .39 B8
Longlands Rd SK22 . . . . .39 B8
Long La CW10 . . . . .151 D7
Longley Ave CH6 . . . . .122 D6
Longley La CW6 . . . . .99 D1
Long Looms CH3 . . . . .121 A6
Longlooms Rd CH65 . . . . . . .70 D1
Long Marl Dr SK9 . . . . .34 F4
Long Mdw CH60 . . . . .40 F6
Longmeade Gdns SK9 . . . . . .60 C6
Longmeadow
  Chester CH3 . . . . .35 C7
  Weaverham CW8 . . . . .102 C8
LONGMOSS 86 C1
Longmoss Cl CW10 . . . . .151 B8
Longmynd Rise WA7 . . . . . . .149 B8
Longnor Rd
  Gatley SK8 . . . . .34 D8
  Hazel Grove SK7 . . . . .37 D3
Longridge WA16 . . . . .57 D3
Longridge Trad Est
  WA16 . . . . .57 D3
Long Row WA5 . . . . .195 A1
Longsdon Cl ST5 . . . . .210 C1

Longshaw St
Warrington, Bewsey
WA5 . . . . .15 F8
Warrington, Dallam WA5. . . .7 F1
Long Shoot CW4 . . . . .130 D8
Long Shoot Rd SK11 . . . . .108 E1
Longsides Rd WA15. . . . . . .32 C7
Longsight La SK8. . . . . .34 F6
Long Spinney WA7 . . . . . . .50 C8
Longster CI WA6 . . . . .73 B2
Longstone La CW6. . . . . . .124 E3
Longton Ave WA3. . . . . .3 C7
Long Valley Rd ST8 . . . . . .179 C2
Longview Ave ST7 . . . . . . .193 E4
Long Wlk WA11 . . . . .11 D3
Longwood CI CW10 . . . . . .151 C7
Longwood Rd WA4 . . . . . . .26 E5
Lonsdale CI
Warrington WA5 . . . . .14 F8
☑ Widnes WA8. . . . . .22 C8
Lonsdale Ct CW4 . . . . . . .140 F4
Lon Y Cryddion / Cobblers
La LL12 . . . . .161 B1
Lon yr Orsaf / Station App
CH1 . . . . .116 F7
Lon yr Yuen / Yree Tree
Ave CH1 . . . . .116 F7
Looe CI WA4 . . . . .12 E2
Looms The CH64. . . . . .41 B2
Loont The CW7 . . . . .149 C7
Lord Nelson St WA1 . . . . . .16 C5
Lordship La WA6 . . . . .73 B7
Lordshire PI ST7. . . . . .195 F2
Lords La WA3 . . . . .9 C4
Lords Mill Rd CW2. . . . . . .206 B4
Lord's St M44 . . . . .11 C5
Lord St
Bollington SK10. . . . . .88 B8
Chester CH3 . . . . .118 F2
Crewe CW2 . . . . .190 D3
Croft WA3 . . . . .9 A8
Macclesfield SK11 . . . . . .112 D6
Macclesfield SK11. . . . . . .112 D7
Newton-le-W WA12. . . . . . .2 A3
Runcorn WA7 . . . . .23 B2
Warrington WA4 . . . . .16 B4
Lorne St CH1 . . . . .237 A3
Lorraine St ST7. . . . . .195 F1
Lostock Ave
Poynton SK12 . . . . .36 B4
Warrington WA5 . . . . .15 E8
Lostock CI ☑ CW9. . . . . . .103 E5
Lostock Gn CW9. . . . . .80 A1
LOSTOCK GRALAM 80 A3
Lostock Gralam CE Prim
Sch CW9. . . . . .80 A2
Lostock Gralam Sta
CW9. . . . . .80 A2
LOSTOCK GREEN 105 B8
Lostock Hall Prim Sch
SK12. . . . . .36 B3
Lostock Hall Rd SK12. . . . . .36 B3
Lostock Hollow CW9. . . . . .80 A2
Lostock Rd SK12. . . . . .36 D2
Lostock Way SK9 . . . . .34 D4
Lotus Gdns WA9. . . . . .6 A7
Louise St CH1 . . . . .237 A3
Loushers La WA4 . . . . .16 D2
Lovage CI WA2 . . . . .9 C1
Lovatt Dr WA16 . . . . .52 B7
Lovatt Ct WA13 . . . . .19 B4
Lovatts The ST7 . . . . .195 A1
Love La
Hassall Green CW11 . . . . .176 C3
Malpas SY14 . . . . .213 A4
Nantwich CW5. . . . . .204 E5
Lovell Ct CW4 . . . . .130 C3
Love Terr WA8 . . . . .22 B5
Lovely La WA5. . . . . .15 E6
Love St CH1 . . . . .237 B2
Lowcross La SY14 . . . . . . .198 D3
Lowe Ave
Congleton CW12 . . . . . . .156 E2
Warrington WA4 . . . . .16 F4
Lowe Cres CW9. . . . . .53 C4
Lowe Dr WA16. . . . . .57 B2
Lower Appleton Rd
WA8 . . . . .13 B1
Lower Ash Rd ST7 . . . . . . .194 E1
Lower Bank St ☑
SK11. . . . . .112 E7
Lower Beech Cotts
SK10. . . . . .87 D2
Lower Bridge St CH1 . . . . .237 B1
Lower Brook St CW5. . . . . .91 D1
LOWER BUNBURY 185 F8
LOWER CARDEN 198 C6
Lower Church St WA3 . . . . .23 A5
Lower Cl L26 . . . . .21 A8
Lower Darwin St
CW9. . . . . .103 E6
Lower Exchange St ☑
SK11. . . . . .112 E7
Lower Farm Mews
CW6. . . . . .147 B3
Lowerfield Rd SK10. . . . . . .87 E1
Lower Field Rd CH4 . . . . . .141 A5
Lower Fold Cott SK6. . . . . .37 D7
Lower Greenhall La
SK12. . . . . .38 F6
Lower Hague SK22 . . . . . . .38 E8
Lower High St ☑
CW7. . . . . .149 C8
Lower Hall La L24 . . . . . . .182 D2
Lower Hall Mews
CH3 . . . . .182 C2
Lower Hall Rd SY13. . . . . .215 D4
LOWER HEATH 156 E5

Lower Heath CW12 . . . . . .156 E4
Lower Heath Ave
CW12. . . . . .156 E4
Lower Heath Terr
CW12. . . . . .156 E4
Lower High St ST7. . . . . . .195 D2
LOWERHOUSE 87 E8
Lowerhouse SK10. . . . . . . .87 E8
LOWER HOUSE 22 E8
Lower House La WA8 . . . . .22 F8
LOWER KINNERTON 139 D1
Lower La
Aldford CH3 . . . . .164 A2
Churton CH3 . . . . .181 A7
Eaton CW6. . . . . .147 A3
Lowerlea SK12 . . . . .38 C6
Lower Macclesfield Rd
SK23. . . . . .65 E6
Lower Meadow Dr
WA14. . . . . .156 C3
Lower Meadow Rd
SK9. . . . . .34 E4
Lower Mersey St CH65. . . .70 C7
Lower Park Cres SK12 . . . .36 C6
Lower Park Prim Sch
SK12. . . . . .36 C4
Lower Park Rd
Chester CH4 . . . . .237 C2
Poynton SK12 . . . . .36 B5
Lower Park St CW12 . . . . .156 E3
LOWER PEOVER 81 E1
Lower Peover CE Prim
Sch WA16. . . . . .81 E1
Lower Rake La WA6 . . . . . .73 B4
Lower Rd L26, WA8. . . . . . .21 C7
Lower Robin Hood La
WA6. . . . . .73 B3
Lower Rock St ☑ SK22 . . .39 C7
Lower Sandy La CH3 . . . . .199 C7
LOWER STRETTON 52 F8
LOWER THREAPWOOD
. . . . .222 E6
Lower Walton CH 26 A8
Lower Wash La WA4 . . . . . .16 E3
LOWER WHITLEY 52 D3
LOWER WITHINGTON
. . . . .132 A8
LOWER WYCH 224 B6
Lowes La SK11 . . . . .111 F2
Lowe St
Golborne WA3 . . . . .3 A8
Macclesfield SK11 . . . . . .112 D7
Loweswater CI WA11 . . . . . .8 B3
Loweswater Cres WA11 . . . .1 A6
Lowfield Gdns WA5 . . . . . . .5 C7
Lowfields Ave CH62. . . . . . .43 E3
Lowfields CI CH62 . . . . .43 E3
Low Hill WA6. . . . . .97 D5
Lowlands Rd ☑ WA7 . . . . .22 F2
Lowland Way WA16. . . . . . .82 A8
LOW LEIGHTON 39 D8
Low Leighton Rd SK22 . . . .39 D8
Low Mdw SK23. . . . . .65 D8
Lowndes Rd M22 . . . . .33 E8
Lowry CI WA5. . . . . .15 D6
Low St ST7. . . . . .193 E8
Lowther Ave WA3 . . . . .4 F4
Lowther St SK10. . . . . .88 C8
LOWTON 4 A7
Lowton Bsns Pk WA3 . . . . . .4 A7
LOWTON COMMON 4 A7
Lowton Com Sports Coll
WA3. . . . . .4 B8
Lowton Gdns WA3 . . . . .3 B5
LOWTON HEATH 4 A7
Lowton Jun & Inf Sch
WA3. . . . . .4 A7
Lowton Rd WA3 . . . . .3 D8
LOWTON ST MARY'S 3 F8
Lowton St Mary's CE Prim
Sch WA3. . . . . .4 A8
Lowton West Prim Sch
WA3. . . . . .3 D8
Loxdale Dr CH65. . . . . .69 F4
Loxley CI
Macclesfield SK11 . . . . . .112 B7
Warrington, Paddington
WA1. . . . . .17 B8
Winsford CW7. . . . . .149 B7
Loyola Hey L35. . . . . .12 E8
Lucerne CI CH3 . . . . .142 B6
Ludford St CW1. . . . . .190 C5
Ludlow CI
Macclesfield SK10. . . . . . .87 C2
Warrington, Paddington
WA1. . . . . .17 B8
Ludlow Cres WA7. . . . . . . .49 B8
Ludlow Rd CH65. . . . . .70 E3
Ludlow Rd CH1. . . . . .118 A5
Ludwell CI CH4. . . . . .141 B6
LUGSDALE 23 C7
Lugsdale Rd WA8 . . . . .23 B7
Lulworth CI CW7 . . . . .149 B7
Lumb Brook Mews ☑
WA4. . . . . .16 E1
Lumb Brook Rd
Appleton Thorn WA4. . . . . .27 A5
Warrington WA4 . . . . .26 F8
Lumb CI SK7. . . . . .35 E6
Lumber La WA5 . . . . .6 F8
Lumb La SK15. . . . . .35 E6
Lumley PI CH1 . . . . .237 B2
Lumley Rd
Chester CH2 . . . . .118 C4
Macclesfield SK11. . . . . . .111 F7
Lumley Wlk L24 . . . . .21 E1
Lumpy St CW12 . . . . .156 C3

Lundy Dr CH65 . . . . .95 C8
Lune CI ☑ CW12. . . . . . . .157 A1
Lunehurst ☑ WA3 . . . . .3 E8
Lune Way WA8 . . . . .12 C1
Lunt Ave CW2 . . . . .190 C2
LUNTS HEATH 13 A5
Lunts Heath Prim Sch
WA8. . . . . .13 B5
Lunt's Heath Rd WA8 . . . . .13 B5
Lunts Moss ST7 . . . . .194 C6
Luntswood Gr WA12 . . . . . .2 A1
Lupin Dr
Haydock WA11. . . . . .1 F6
Huntington CH3 . . . . .142 B6
Lupus Way CH66 . . . . .69 F3
Luscombe CI L26 . . . . .21 A8
Luther Gr WA9 . . . . .1 B2
Luton Rd CH65 . . . . .70 A5
Luton St WA8 . . . . .23 A7
Lutyens CI SK10. . . . . .111 F8
Lyceum CI CW1. . . . . .190 A8
Lyceum Way WA1 . . . . . . .190 A8
Lychgate WA4. . . . . .25 F7
Lycroft CI WA7 . . . . .49 B6
Lydbury Ct WA3 . . . . .9 F4
Lydden Rd CH65 . . . . .70 B7
Lydgate CI CW12 . . . . .205 F8
Lydiate CI
Runcorn WA7 . . . . .48 D7
Willaston CH64 . . . . .42 E1
Lydiate The
Heswall CH60 . . . . .40 F7
Willaston CH64 . . . . .42 D1
Lydiat La SK9. . . . . .60 A1
Lydney Ave SK8 . . . . .34 C7
Lydstep Ct WA5 . . . . .7 E2
Lydyett La CW8 . . . . .78 B3
Lymcote Dr WA9 . . . . .103 A4
Lyme Ave
Handforth SK9 . . . . .34 B1
Macclesfield SK11 . . . . . .112 D5
Lyme Com Prim Sch
SK11. . . . . .1 F4
Lyme Gr WA13. . . . . .18 C2
LYME GREEN 112 D2
Lyme Green Bsns Pk
SK11. . . . . .112 C3
Lyme Green Settlement
SK11. . . . . .112 D2
Lyme Lea CI SK8 . . . . .35 B8
Lyme Pk* SK12. . . . . .38 B1
Lyme Rd
High Lane SK6 . . . . .38 A6
Poynton SK12 . . . . .37 C3
Lyme St
Haydock WA11. . . . . .1 E6
Newton-le-W WA12. . . . . . .1 F4
☑ Warrington WA1 . . . . . .16 B5
Lyme View SK11 . . . . .112 D2
Lymewood Dr
Disley SK12. . . . . .38 C6
Wilmslow SK9 . . . . .60 E8
LYMM 18 E4
Lymm Brook ☑ WA13. . . . .18 E3
Lymm Hall WA13 . . . . .18 E3
Lymmhay La WA13 . . . . . . .18 E4
Lymm High Sch WA13 . . . .19 B3
Lymmington Ave
WA13. . . . . .18 C3
Lymm Rd
Little Bollington WA14. . . . .20 B1
Warrington WA4 . . . . .17 F3
Lynalls CI CW12 . . . . .155 F3
Lynbrook Rd CW1 . . . . . . .190 F4
Lyncastle Way WA4. . . . . . .27 D4
Lyncastle Way WA4. . . . . . .27 D4
Lyncombe CI SK8. . . . . .35 B6
Lyncroft CI CW1 . . . . .190 B8
Lyndale ☑ WA7 . . . . .49 C8
Lyndale Ave
Bebington CH62 . . . . .43 E4
Warrington, Fearnhead
WA2. . . . . .16 D8
Lyndale CI CW7 . . . . .127 A3
Lyndale Sch The CH62 . . . .43 F5
Lyndhurst CI SK9 . . . . .59 D5
Lyndon Gr WA7 . . . . .49 B8
Lyneal Ave CH66. . . . . .69 C3
Lyngard CI SK9. . . . . .34 E1
Lynham Ave WA5 . . . . .15 B5
Lynn Ave ST7 . . . . .210 C8
Lynn CI WA7 . . . . .49 C7
Lynndene CI CH66 . . . . . . .69 D7
Lynn Gr SK11. . . . . .112 C6
Lynnside Wlk M22 . . . . . . .33 E8
Lynthorpe Ave M44 . . . . . .11 E6
Lynton Ave WA14 . . . . .11 E6
Lynton CI
Chester CH4 . . . . .140 F6
Heswall CH60 . . . . .41 B6
Knutsford WA16 . . . . .57 C1
Warrington WA5 . . . . .14 E4
Lynton Cres WA8 . . . . .12 E2
Lynton Dr SK6. . . . . .37 E8
Lynton Gdns WA4 . . . . .26 E8
Lynton Gr CW2 . . . . .191 D5
Lynton La SK9 . . . . .60 A1
Lynton Mews SK9. . . . . . . .60 A2
Lynton Park Rd SK8 . . . . . .34 F8
Lynton PI
Alsager ST7 . . . . .193 D4
Broughton CH4 . . . . .139 B4
Lynton Way CW2 . . . . .206 A8
Lynwood
Altrincham WA15. . . . . . . .32 A8

Lynwood continued
Wilmslow SK9 . . . . .60 A6
Lynwood Ave
Golborne WA3 . . . . .3 E6
Warrington WA4 . . . . .26 C7
Lynwood Rd CH1 . . . . .117 F5
Lyon CI WA4 . . . . .16 F3
Lyon's La WA4. . . . . .26 E6
Lyons Rd WA5 . . . . .15 A4
Lyon St
Chester CH1 . . . . .237 B3
Crewe CW1 . . . . .190 D4
Macclesfield SK11 . . . . . .112 C7
Warrington WA4 . . . . .16 F3
Lysander Dr WA2 . . . . .8 E2
Lyster CI WA3 . . . . .9 F3
Lytham CI WA5 . . . . .15 B3
Lytham Dr
Bramhall SK7. . . . . .36 A7
Winsford CW7 . . . . .126 C2
Lytham Rd WA8 . . . . .13 C2
Lytherton Ave M44. . . . . . .11 D4
Lythgoes La WA2 . . . . .16 B6

M

Mableden CI SK8. . . . . .34 D8
Mablins La CW1 . . . . .190 B8
Mablins Lane Com Prim
Sch CW1. . . . . .190 B8
Macbeth Ho ST7. . . . . .12 E8
McCarthy CI WA3. . . . . . . .10 A3
Mc Clellan PI WA3 . . . . . . .13 B1
MACCLESFIELD 112 B4
Macclesfield Coll
SK11. . . . . .112 B6
Macclesfield District
General Hospl SK10. . . . .112 B8
MACCLESFIELD FOREST
. . . . .114 D5
Macclesfield Forest
Walks* SK11. . . . . .114 A3
Macclesfield Rd
Alderley Edge SK9. . . . . . .85 D7
Congleton CW12 . . . . . . .156 F6
Eaton CW12. . . . . .134 B2
Hazel Grove SK7 . . . . .36 F8
Holmes Chapel CW4 . . . . .130 E4
Kettleshulme SK23,
SK10. . . . . .64 D3
Prestbury SK10. . . . . .87 B7
Rainow SK10 . . . . .89 B7
Wilmslow SK9 . . . . .60 D6
Macclesfield Sta
SK11. . . . . .112 D8
Macdermott Rd WA8. . . . . .22 F5
Macdonald Rd M44 . . . . . . .11 E8
McEllin CI ST7 . . . . .209 E2
McGarva Way CH65. . . . . . .70 C4
McGowan Ho ST7 . . . . . . .210 D8
McKeagney Gdns WA8 . . . .22 C7
McKee Ave WA8 . . . . .8 B2
McKinley St WA5 . . . . .15 A3
McKinley Way WA8 . . . . . . .12 F3
McLaren St CW1 . . . . .190 C7
McMinnis Ave WA9 . . . . . . .1 B2
McNeill Ave CW1 . . . . .190 A5
Macon Ct CW1 . . . . .190 E3
Macon Ind Pk CW1 . . . . . .190 E3
Macon Way CW1 . . . . .190 E3
Maddocks Hill WA6 . . . . . .100 F5
Maddock St ST7 . . . . .209 D1
Madeley CI
Broughton CH4 . . . . .139 C4
Warrington WA4. . . . . .31 E8
Madeley St CW2 . . . . .190 D1
Madeline McKenna Ct
WA8. . . . . .12 C3
Madron Ave SK10. . . . . . . .86 D1
Maelor CI CH63. . . . . .43 C6
Maes-y-Coed CH4. . . . . . .140 E6
Magdala PI CW9 . . . . .104 C8
Magdalen Ct CW2 . . . . . . .190 A1
Magecroft CW1. . . . . .173 B1
Magenta Ave M44 . . . . . . .11 E6
Maggoty La SK11 . . . . .111 D1
Mag La WA13, WA16. . . . . .28 F6
Magnolia CI
☑ Ellesmere Port
CH66. . . . . .69 F1
☑ Partington M31 . . . . . .11 E2
Warrington WA1 . . . . .17 E7
Magnolia Dr WA7 . . . . .49 F4
Magnolia Rise SK10. . . . . . .86 E6
Magpie Cres ☑ ST7 . . . . .195 B2
Maiden Gr CW4. . . . . .228 C8
Maiden Gdns CH65 . . . . . . .70 D3
Maidenhills CW10 . . . . . . .128 D1
Maidstone CI SK10. . . . . . .87 B2
Maidwell CI CW7 . . . . .127 A4
Main CI WA11 . . . . .11 A6
Main Dr WA14 . . . . .20 E3
Main La WA3 . . . . .3 F3
Main Rd
Betley CW2, CW3. . . . . . .221 F8
Broughton CH4 . . . . .139 B4
Goostrey CW4 . . . . .107 C1
Higher Kinnerton CH4 . . . .161 A8
Langley SK11 . . . . .113 E2
Moulton CW9. . . . . .126 F8
Norton in Hales TF9. . . . .236 C1
Shavington CW2. . . . . . . .206 B4
Weston CW2 . . . . .207 C6
Worleston CW5 . . . . .188 F5
Wybunbury CW5 . . . . . . .220 B8
Main St
Frodsham WA6 . . . . .74 B8

Main St continued
Great Barrow CH3. . . . . . .120 E5
Runcorn WA7 . . . . .49 F8
Maintree Cres L24 . . . . .21 A4
Mainwaring CI CW5 . . . . . .205 A4
Mainwaring Dr
Saltney CH4. . . . . .140 C7
Wilmslow SK9 . . . . .60 D8
Mainwaring Rd
Bebington CH62. . . . . .43 D8
Over Peover WA16 . . . . . .108 A8
Mairescia Ave WA4. . . . . . .17 B2
Maisterson Ct ☑
CW5. . . . . .204 E5
Maitland Way CH1. . . . . . .117 D4
Maitland-Wood CI
CW9. . . . . .104 D7
Major Cross St ☑ WA8 . . . .23 A7
Makepeace CI CH3 . . . . . .119 C3
Makerfield Dr WA12 . . . . . . .2 A5
Malaga Ave M90. . . . . .33 B7
Malahide Ct WA8 . . . . .12 E2
Malam Dr CW9 . . . . .104 D6
Malbank CI WA5 . . . . .204 E6
Malbank Rd CW2 . . . . .189 E4
Malbank Sch & Sixth Form
Coll CW5 . . . . .204 C6
Malcolm Ave WA2 . . . . .8 D1
Malcolm Cres CH63. . . . . . .43 C6
Malcolm St WA7 . . . . .23 B2
Malet's La WA5 . . . . .14 E8
Malhamdale Rd
CW12. . . . . .157 A5
Malin CI L24 . . . . .21 D2
Maliston Rd WA5 . . . . .15 B5
MALKINS BANK 175 C3
Mallaig CI CW4 . . . . .130 C2
Mallard CI
Knutsford WA16 . . . . .57 B3
Warrington WA2 . . . . .9 F3
Mallard Cres SK12 . . . . . . .36 A4
Mallard Ct
Chester CH2 . . . . .118 F7
Crewe CW1 . . . . .191 A2
Gatley SK8. . . . . .34 B8
Mallard La WA3 . . . . .9 F3
Mallard Way
Crewe CW1 . . . . .191 A2
Winsford CW7 . . . . .149 D6
Mallory CI WA16. . . . . .58 A4
Mallory Ct
Congleton CW12 . . . . . . .155 F3
Mobberley WA16. . . . . . . .58 A4
Mallory Rd CH65. . . . . .70 A4
Mallowdale CI CH62. . . . . . .43 F5
Mallow Wlk M31. . . . . .11 F2
Mall The WA1 . . . . .16 A5
Malmesbury CI
Middlewich CW10 . . . . . .128 B1
Poynton SK12 . . . . .36 D4
Malmesbury Pk WA7 . . . . . .24 C2
Malmesbury Rd SK8 . . . . . .35 B6
Malory CI CW1 . . . . .190 F5
MALPAS 213 B2
Malpas Alport Prim Sch
SY14. . . . . .213 B4
Malpas CI
Handforth SK9 . . . . .34 E1
Northwich CW9 . . . . .104 B7
Malpas Dr WA5. . . . . .15 C4
Malpas Rd
Ellesmere Port CH65. . . . . .69 F4
Northwich CW9 . . . . .104 C7
Runcorn WA7 . . . . .49 C7
Malpas Way WA5 . . . . .15 C4
Malta Rd CH2 . . . . .95 B1
Malt Kiln Rd WA16 . . . . . . .80 F4
Malt Kiln Way CW11. . . . . .175 B2
Maltmans Rd WA13 . . . . . .18 D3
Malton Ave WA3 . . . . .12 C5
Malton CI WA8 . . . . .12 C5
Malton Dr SK7. . . . . .36 D7
Malt St WA5 . . . . .52 A2
Malvern Ave CH65 . . . . . . .70 D3
Malvern CI
Congleton CW12 . . . . . . .155 F3
Shavington CW2 . . . . .206 B4
Warrington WA5 . . . . .15 A8
Malvern Dr SK10 . . . . .87 E4
Malvern Rd
Blacon CH1. . . . . .118 A5
Haydock WA9. . . . . .1 A4
Knutsford WA16 . . . . .81 F8
Malvern Way CW7 . . . . . . .149 B7
Manchester Airport Sta
M90. . . . . .33 B7
Manchester Bridge
CW1 . . . . .190 E4
Manchester Bsns Pk
M22. . . . . .33 D8
Manchester International
Airport M90. . . . . .33 A7
Manchester Met Univ
(Alsager Campus)
ST7. . . . . .193 A5
Manchester New Rd
M31. . . . . .11 F4
Manchester Rd
Congleton CW12 . . . . . . .156 E5
Handforth SK9 . . . . .34 C2
Hollinfare WA3 . . . . .11 A2
Hollins Green WA3 . . . . . .11 B3
Knutsford WA16 . . . . .56 E4

Manchester Rd *continued*
Macclesfield SK10 87 D4
Warrington, Bruche WA1 16 E6
Warrington WA3 18 D7
Warrington, Woolston WA1 17 C7
Wincham CW9 79 D1
Manchester Row WA12 7 D8
Mancroft Cl WA1 17 E7
Mandarin Ct WA1 16 A3
Manhattan Gdns 1 WA5 15 B7
Manifold Cl CW11 174 E8
Manifold Dr SK6 37 F6
MANLEY 99 A4
Manley Cl
Antrobus CW9 53 C4
Holmes Chapel CW4 130 A3
Northwich CW9 104 A5
MANLEY COMMON 99 C5
Manley Gdns WA5 15 F5
Manley Gr SK7 35 E6
Manley La
Dunham-on-t-H WA6 97 F5
Manley WA6 98 C4
Manley Mere* WA6 98 B5
Manley Rd
Frodsham WA6 74 B3
Manley WA6 98 E7
Warren SK11 112 A5
Manley View CH2 72 C3
Manley Village Sch WA6 99 A5
Manna Dr CH2 72 C3
Manners La CH60 40 E6
Mannings La CH2 119 B6
Mannings La S CH2 119 A5
Manning St CW2 190 D1
Manora Rd CW9 104 A8
Manor Ave
Crewe CW2 190 A1
Golborne WA3 3 C8
Goostrey CW4 107 F1
Marston CW9 79 B6
Newton-le-W WA12 1 F4
Manor Bsns Pk CW4 130 D3
Manor Cl
Broughton CH5 139 C7
Cheadle SK8 35 C8
Congleton CW12 157 A1
Great Barrow CH3 120 E6
Lymm WA13 18 E2
Neston CH64 66 C7
Warrington WA1 17 D7
Wilmslow SK9 59 F8
Manor Cres
Broughton CH4 139 C8
Knutsford WA16 57 B2
Macclesfield SK10 87 D3
Middlewich CW10 151 C7
Manor Ct
Acton CW5 204 B4
Crewe CW2 190 B1
Golborne WA3 3 C8
Knutsford WA16 57 B1
2 Nantwich CW5 204 E6
Manor Dr
Barnton CW8 78 B2
Chester CH3 119 C1
Northwich, Rudheath CW9 104 C7
Manor Farm Cl CH2 119 F8
Manor Farm Cres CH1 94 B8
Manor Farm Ct
Broughton CH5 139 B7
5 Frodsham WA6 49 C1
Manor Farm Mews WA7 24 D4
Manor Farm Rd WA7 24 D4
Manor Fell WA7 50 B7
Manorfield Cl CH1 69 A1
Manor Fields CW10 151 C7
Manor Gdns
Nantwich CW5 204 E6
Wilmslow SK9 60 D7
Manor Gr CW8 103 C6
Manor Ho
Bebington CH62 43 D8
Ellesmere Port CH66 69 D2
Row-of-Trees SK9 59 D3
Manorial Rd CH64 66 C8
Manorial Rd S CH64 66 C7
Manor Ind Est WA4 16 E4
Manor La
Broughton CH5 139 B7
Davenham CW9 104 D2
Ellesmere Port CH66 69 D3
Holmes Chapel CW4 130 D3
3 Middlewich CW10 151 C8
Ollerton WA16 82 E6
MANOR PARK
Middlewich 151 B7
Runcorn 24 B3
Manor Park Ave WA7 24 C4
Manor Park Dr CH66 69 D2
Manor Park N WA16 57 C2
Manor Park Prim Sch WA16 57 C2
Manor Park Rd CW12 134 D2
Manor Park S WA16 57 C1
Manor Pk CH5 139 B7
Manor Pk CH3 120 E6
Manor Pl
Hatherton CW5 220 B1
Widnes WA8 12 B1
Manor Rd
Bebington CH62 43 E6
Chester CH4 141 B5
Cuddington CW8 101 F2
Frodsham WA6 49 C1
Haydock WA11 1 F7
Horwich End SK23 65 E5
Lymm WA13 18 E2
Mow Cop ST7 195 D7
Nantwich CW5 204 E6
Runcorn WA7 23 D2
Sandbach CW11 175 D6
Sealand CH5 116 A6
Thornton Hough CH63 42 A7
Widnes WA8 12 B1
Wilmslow SK9 59 E8
Manor Rd N CW5 204 E7
Manor Sq CW7 149 A8
Manor St CW8 103 D6
Manor Terr SK11 113 B3
Manor The WA1 17 F7
Manor Way
Crewe CW2 190 C1
Sandbach CW11 175 E6
Manse Field Rd WA6 75 B1
Manse Gdns WA12 2 D4
Mansell Cl WA8 13 C5
Mansfield Apartments WA2 9 A3
Mansfield Cl WA3 10 A4
Mansfield Prim Sch CH65 69 F3
Mansfield Rd CH65 70 A2
Mansion Ct 5 CW5 204 F5
Mansion Dr WA16 57 B2
Manston Rd WA5 14 F3
Manuel Perez Rd WA5 15 B6
Manx Rd WA4 16 B3
Maori Dr WA6 74 A8
Maple Ave
Alsager ST7 193 E2
Aston WA7 50 A4
Disley SK12 39 A6
Ellesmere Port CH66 69 D6
Golborne WA3 3 F7
Haydock WA11 1 B7
Macclesfield SK11 112 D5
Newcastle-u-Lyme ST5 210 E1
Newton-le-W WA12 2 D2
Poynton SK12 36 F3
Runcorn WA7 49 C8
Talke ST7 210 D8
5 Widnes WA8 13 B2
Maple Cl
Brereton Green CW11 153 F5
Congleton CW12 155 F4
Holmes Chapel CW4 130 D4
Sandbach CW11 175 C6
Maple Cres WA5 14 F3
Maple Ct CW7 127 A3
Maple Gr
Barnton CW8 78 B4
Bebington CH62 43 C8
Chester CH2 119 B4
Crewe CW1 190 E6
Ellesmere Port CH66 95 A8
Northwich, Greenbank CW8 103 C7
Saltney CH4 140 D5
Warrington WA4 16 D3
Winsford CW7 127 A1
Maple La CW8 101 F2
Maple Pl ST7 193 F7
Maple Rd
Alderley Edge SK9 60 B3
Bramhall SK7 35 E6
Partington M31 11 E3
Warrington WA1 17 E7
Winwick WA2 8 B6
Maples SK9 59 F6
Maples The
Mobberley WA16 58 E1
Winsford CW7 127 A3
Mapleton Dr WA7 49 F3
Maplewood SK11 112 D5
Maplewood Cl WA8 22 A7
Maplewood Gr CH1 117 B8
Maplewood Rd SK9 60 E8
Mapplewell Cres WA5 15 A6
Marble Arch 5 WA16 57 A2
MARBURY 226 D8
Marbury Gdns CH65 69 F6
Marbury House Farm WA4 52 E5
Marbury La CW9 78 E5
Marbury Park Ctry Pk* CW9 78 E5
Marbury Rd
Chester CH3 119 C2
Comberbach CW9 78 D6
Handforth SK9 34 B1
Norbury SY13 215 B3
Marbury St WA4 16 C3
March St CW1 190 E4
Marchwiel Rd CH65 70 D4
Marcien Way WA8 12 F3
Marcliff Gr WA16 57 A1
Marcross Cl WA5 7 E1
Mardale Ave WA2 8 C3
Mardale Cl CW12 157 B5
Mardale Cres WA13 18 F3
Mardale Ct CW4 130 A2
Mardon Cl WA16 57 D3
Marfield Ave WA13 19 A2
Marford Cl CW9 103 E5
Marfords Ave CH63 43 C7
Margaret Ave WA1 17 B7
Margaret Ct WA8 23 B7
Margaret's La CH66 69 A7
Margery Ave ST7 194 E7
Marian Ave WA12 1 F3
Marian Dr CH3 142 B8
Marian Rd WA11 1 E7
Marie Cl CW5 216 F4
Marie Dr WA4 17 D2
Marigold Cl SK11 111 F8
Marigold Pl WA5 15 D3
Marigold Way WA9 6 A7
Marina Ave WA5 15 C4
Marina Cl SK9 34 D5
Marina Dr
Chester CH2 118 E7
Ellesmere Port CH65 70 B5
Warrington WA2 8 C1
Marina Flats CH3 142 E7
Marina Gr WA7 23 B1
Marina La WA7 50 E7
Marina Village WA7 50 E7
Marina Wlk CH65 70 B5
Marine App 10 CW9 103 F8
Marine Ave M31 11 D3
Marine Dr CH60 40 D6
Mariner Cl WA7 50 D6
Marion Dr
Mobberley WA16 58 A4
Runcorn WA7 48 F6
Maritime Cl WA12 2 C5
Mark Ave CH66 69 C4
Mark Cl CH2 118 F2
Market Cl CW1 190 D5
Market Ct CW6 146 C2
Market Ctr The CW1 190 D4
Market Gate WA1 16 B5
Market Pl
Bollington SK10 88 B8
Hampton Heath SY14 213 D7
Macclesfield SK10, SK11 112 D8
Winsford CW7 126 F1
Market Sq
Chester CH1 237 A2
Congleton CW12 156 D2
Crewe CW1 190 D4
4 Sandbach CW11 175 B6
Market St
Congleton CW12 156 D3
Crewe CW1 190 D4
Crewe CW1 190 D5
Disley SK12 38 D6
Kidsgrove ST7 195 A1
Nantwich CW5 204 E5
New Mills SK22 39 B7
Newton-le-W WA12 2 A3
9 Northwich CW9 103 F8
Whaley Bridge SK23 65 E7
Widnes WA8 23 A7
Market Way 7 CW9 103 F8
Marlborough Ave
Alderley Edge SK9 60 B2
Winsford CW7 126 C3
Marlborough Cl
Knutsford WA16 57 C4
Macclesfield SK10 87 D4
Wistaston CW2 205 E8
Marlborough Cres
Warrington WA4 16 F2
Widnes WA8 13 A5
Marlborough Ct
1 Chester CH3 119 B2
3 Macclesfield SK11 112 D7
Marlborough Dr
Helsby WA6 73 B2
Macclesfield SK10 87 D4
Sandbach CW11 175 B8
Marlborough Ho 8 SK11 111 F8
Marlborough Prim Sch The SK10 87 D4
Marlborough Rd CH65 70 D3
Marlborough Way WA11 1 E8
Marlborough Wlk CH65 70 C3
Marl Cl CW8 102 A4
Marl Croft CH3 142 B7
Marl Edge SK10 87 A5
Marley Ave CW1 190 B7
Marley Gn SY13 227 C8
MARLEY GREEN 227 C8
Marley Rd SK12 36 E2
Marley Way CH4 140 E7
Marlfield Rd
Altrincham WA15 32 D7
Warrington WA4 17 A2
Marlfields Prim Sch CW12 156 C2
Marl Heys CH2 118 E7
Marline Ave CH63 43 C6
Marling Cl WA6 74 D6
Marling Pk WA8 12 B1
Marlow Ave CH2 118 F7
Marlow Cl
Sandbach CW11 174 D5
Warrington WA3 9 C5
Marlow Dr
Altrincham WA14 20 F2
Handforth SK9 34 C5
Marlowe Cl
Blacon CH1 118 A5
Widnes WA8 12 F1
Wistaston CW2 206 A8
Marlowe Ct SK11 112 C5
Marlowe Dr CW5 204 F3
Marlowe Rd
1 Neston CH64 66 E8
Northwich CW9 104 C6
Marlston Ave CH4 141 A6
Marlston Ct CH4 140 E1
Marlston Pl WA7 49 B6
Marlwood Pl CH4 139 A3
Maroon Rd M22 33 F7
Marple Cres CW2 189 E2
Marple Rd CW9 104 C8
Marquis Dr SK8 34 D7
Marriott Rd CW11 174 F3
Marron Ave WA2 8 B2
Marryat Cl WA2 8 A6
Marsden Ave WA4 17 A4
Marsden Ct WA8 12 E4
Marsden Terr 3 SK11 112 C7
Marshall Ave WA5 7 F2
Marshall Gr CW12 179 B8
Marshall La CW8 103 D6
Marshall Rd WA1 17 D7
Marshalls Ct 2 CW8 103 C5
Marsh Ave ST7 195 E2
Marsh Brook Cl WA3 11 A2
Marsh Cl ST7 193 A3
Marshfield Ave CW2 189 D4
MARSHFIELD BANK 189 C4
Marshfield Bank CW2 189 D4
Marshfield La ST8 179 C2
Marshgate WA8 22 B6
Marshgate Pl WA6 49 D2
Marsh Gr ST8 179 C3
MARSH GREEN
Biddulph 179 D3
Frodsham 74 A8
Marsh Green Cl ST8 179 D2
Marshgreen Rd ST8 179 D3
Marsh Green Rd CW11 174 E8
Marsh Hall Pad WA8 13 B4
Marsh House La WA1, WA2 16 C7
Marsh La
Alsager ST7 193 A3
Barton CH3, SY14 181 E3
Churton CH3 181 B5
Dutton WA4 51 E3
Elton CH2 72 B4
Frodsham WA6 74 A8
Holmes Chapel CW4 130 E2
Ince CH2 72 D6
Mere WA16 30 F3
Nantwich CW5 204 C5
New Mills SK22, SK23 39 D6
Norley CW8, WA6 101 B7
Ravensmoor CW5 203 F2
Runcorn WA7 23 F3
Warrington, Penketh WA5 14 C2
Marshlands Rd CH64 66 E5
Marsh Lane Trad Est SK22 39 D7
Marsh Rd WA4 27 B4
Marsh St
Warrington WA1 16 D7
Widnes WA8 23 A6
Marshway Dr WA12 2 B5
Marson St WA2 16 A6
MARSTON 79 B4
Marston Cl CH62 43 E3
Marston Gdns CH65 69 F6
Marston La CW9 79 C6
Marten Ave CH63 43 C7
Martens Rd M44 11 E5
MARTHALL 83 E4
Marthall La WA16 83 B7
Marthall Way 8 SK9 34 E5
Martham Cl WA4 17 A3
Martin Ave
Newton-le-W WA12 2 C5
Warrington WA2 8 E1
Martin Cl
Chester CH2 118 C8
Runcorn WA7 50 A7
Martindale Gr WA7 49 D5
Martin Rd
Chester CH2 118 C8
Frodsham WA6 74 B8
MARTIN'S ASH 227 B2
MARTINSCROFT 17 F7
Martinscroft Gn WA1 17 F7
Martinsfields CW8 77 A5
Martin's La CH3 143 F3
Martins Mill CW12 179 C8
MARTIN'S MOSS 176 E6
Martland Ave WA3 3 E7
Martlet Ave SK12 38 C6
MARTON 133 B5
Marton Cl
Congleton CW12 156 E5
Culcheth WA3 4 E4
Hough CW2 206 E3
Macclesfield SK10 86 F1
Marton & District CE Prim Sch SK11 133 C5
MARTON GREEN 125 C4
Marton Hall La SK11 133 B3
Marton La
Marton SK11 133 D7
Warren SK11 111 B1
Marton Rd CH4 139 C3
MARTONSANDS 125 F4
Marton Way 5 SK9 34 E5
Martree Ct CW11 174 D8
Maryfield Cl WA3 3 A7
Maryhill Cl ST7 195 A3
Maryhill High Sch ST7 195 A3
Maryhill Prim Sch ST7 195 A3
Maryhill Rd WA7 49 A8
Maryland Cl WA5 15 C7
Marys Gate CW2 205 E8
Mary St
Crewe CW1 190 E5
Widnes WA8 23 D7
Maryville Cl 3 CH65 70 C6
Masefield Ave WA8 22 F8
Masefield Dr
Blacon CH1 117 E6
Crewe CW1 190 F4
Winwick WA2 8 A5
Masefield Way CW11 174 D5
Maskery Pl CW12 156 E4
Mason Ave
Warrington WA1 16 E8
Widnes WA8 13 B4
Mason Cl CH66 69 D2
Masons La SK10 87 F1
Mason's Row CW6 169 E2
Mason St
Chester CH2 237 A3
Runcorn WA7 23 C3
Warrington WA1 16 C5
Massey Ave
Hartford CW8 103 A4
Lymm WA13 18 B2
Warrington WA5 7 F2
Winsford CW7 126 F1
Massey Brook La WA13 18 B2
Massey Cl CW5 205 A4
Masseyfield Rd WA7 50 B5
Massey Hall Sch WA4 17 F2
Massey St 6 SK9 60 A1
Masters Ct WA16 56 F1
Mastiff La SY14 213 B1
Mates La SY14 213 B6
Mather Ave
Golborne WA3 3 E6
Runcorn WA7 48 D7
Mather Cl CW10 151 C8
Mather Dr
Comberbach CW9 78 C8
Northwich CW9 104 D7
Mathers Cl WA2 9 A4
Mathieson Rd WA8 22 E5
Matlock Cl WA5 15 A8
Matlock Dr SK7 36 E8
Matlock Rd SK8 34 C7
Matterdale Cl WA6 74 D7
Matthew Cl CH2 118 F2
Matthews Pl CW12 157 A2
Matthews St WA1 16 D7
Matty's La WA6 74 A7
Mavor Ct CW1 190 B4
Mawdsley Ave WA1 17 E7
Mawdsley Cl ST7 193 A3
MAW GREEN 190 E7
Maw Green Cl CW1 190 E7
Maw Green Rd CW1 190 F7
Maw La CW1 191 C7
Mawson Cl WA5 15 D8
Maxfield Cl SK11 111 F8
Maxwell Cl CH65 70 A2
Maxwell Rd CW12 179 A8
Maxwell St
Crewe CW2 190 C3
Warrington WA3 9 E6
May Ave SK8 35 B6
Mayberry Gr WA2 9 A1
Maybrook Pl WA4 16 F3
Maydor Ave CH4 140 C7
Mayfair Cl
Poynton SK12 36 E4
Warrington WA5 14 D7
Mayfair Ct CH4 162 E5
Mayfair Dr
Crewe CW1 190 F6
Northwich CW9 103 F3
Mayfair Gr WA8 12 D1
Mayfield Ave
Macclesfield SK11 112 C5
Widnes WA8 12 B1
Mayfield Cl CW4 130 D3
Mayfield Ct WA8 13 A2
Mayfield Dr
Bebington CH62 44 B6
Cuddington CW8 102 A4
Golborne WN7 4 C8
Winsford CW7 127 A3
Mayfield Gdns CH64 41 E1
Mayfield Gr
Cuddington CW8 102 A4
Wilmslow SK9 59 E5
Mayfield Mews CW1 189 F6
Mayfield Rd
Blacon CH1 117 D5
Bramhall SK7 35 E4
Mobberley WA16 57 F4
Northwich CW9 104 C8
Warrington WA4 17 A2
Mayfield Terr SK11 112 C5
Mayfield View WA13 18 F2
Mayflower Rd CW5 204 E3
May Rd
Cheadle SK8 35 B6
Heswall CH60 41 A8
Maythorn Ave WA3 9 A7
Maytree Ave CH3 119 B2
May Wlk 2 M31 11 E3
Mead Ave ST7 194 E7
Mead Cl WA16 56 F1
Meade The SK9 60 C8
Meadow Ave
Congleton CW12 156 C1

Meadow Ave continued
Goostrey CW4 . . . . 107 C1
Warrington WA4 . . . . .16 B2
Weston CW2 . . . . .207 B5
MEADOWBANK 126 D5
Meadow Bank
Adderley TF9 . . . . 235 A4
Kelsall CW6 . . . . 122 C4
Meadow Bank Cvn Pk
WA4 . . . . .25 C6
Meadowbank Dr CH66 . .69 A6
Meadowbank Gdns
WA3 .5 C7
Meadow Brow SK9 . . . . . .60 A2
Meadow Cl
Cuddington CW8 . . . . 102 A4
Farndon CH3 . . . . 180 F1
Goostrey CW4 . . . . 107 C1
Helsby WA6 . . . . 73 B3
High Lane SK6 . . . . .37 F8
Neston CH64 . . . . .66 E6
Newton-le-W WA12 . . . . . . .1 F3
Shavington CW2 . . . . 206 D5
Tarvin CH3 . . . . 121 B2
Whaley Bridge SK23 . . . . . .65 C8
Widnes WA8 . . . . 12 D3
Willaston CH64 . . . . .67 F8
Wilmslow SK9 . . . . .59 E4
Winsford CW7 . . . . 126 C3
Meadow Com Prim Sch
CH66 . . . . .69 E2
Meadow Cotts [5]
CW12 . . . . 156 D3
Meadowcroft
Higher Kinnerton CH4 . . . 161 A7
Saughall CH1 . . . . .94 B1
Meadow Croft
Alsager ST7 . . . . .193 E2
Willaston CH64 . . . . .67 E7
Meadowcroft Ct WA7 . .50 A8
Meadow Ct
Frodsham WA6 . . . . .49 C1
Mollington CH1 . . . . .94 F1
Newchapel ST7 . . . . 195 E2
No Man's Heath SY14 . . . 214 A5
Meadow Dr
Barnton CW8 . . . . .78 A3
Knutsford WA16 . . . . .81 F8
Prestbury SK10 . . . . .87 B7
Weston CW2 . . . . .205 F7
Meadowfield
Tarporley CW6 . . . . 146 C1
Whaley Bridge SK23 . . . . . .65 D8
Meadow Field Rd
CH4 . . . . 141 A5
Meadow Gate CW9 . . . . . .79 F5
Meadowgate Cl
CW11 . . . . 174 D5
Meadowgate Farm
WA7 . . . . .49 F2
Meadow Gr
Northwich CW9 . . . . 104 B5
Winsford CW7 . . . . 126 E5
Meadow Home Pk
CW7 . . . . 126 D6
Meadow House Pk
CW6 . . . . 185 D5
Meadow La
Comberbach CW9 . . . . 78 C7
Disley SK12 . . . . .38 D6
Ellesmere Port CH65 . . . . . .70 D6
Huntington CH3 . . . . 142 A5
Moulton CW9 . . . . 126 F8
Warrington WA2 . . . . .9 A2
Willaston CH64 . . . . .67 F8
Meadow Lane Ind Pk
CH65 . . . . .70 D5
Meadow Mill Ct
CW12 . . . . 156 E3
Meadow Rd
Broughton CH4 . . . . 139 B4
Weaverham CW8 . . . . 102 E7
Meadow Rise
Clutton CH3 . . . . 182 D2
Winsford CW7 . . . . 126 A1
Meadow Row WA7 . . . . . .24 A1
Meadowside
Disley SK12 . . . . .39 A6
Fourlane-ends SK10 . . . . . .63 B8
Frodsham WA6 . . . . .74 A8
Northwich CW8 . . . . 103 D7
Whaley Bridge SK23 . . . . . .65 D8
Meadowside Ave ST7 . . . 209 D2
Meadowside Com Prim
Sch WA2 . . . . .9 C4
Meadowside La ST7 . . .195 B7
Meadowside Mews
CH1 . . . . 118 B2
Meadowside Rd CH62 . .43 D8
Meadows La
Chester CH4 . . . . 237 C1
Saughall CH1 . . . . 117 A8
Tilston SY14 . . . . .212 B6
Meadows Pl CH4 . . . . . . 141 E7
Meadows Rd
Cheadle SK8 . . . . 34 F8
Kidsgrove ST7 . . . . 194 F1
Meadow St
[N] Nantwich CW5 . . . . . . .39 C8
Northwich CW9 . . . . 104 A8
Meadows The
Ashton Hayes CH3 . . . . . . 121 E8
Bebington CH62 . . . . .43 D7
Irlam M44 . . . . .11 E6
Neston CH64 . . . . .66 F6
Meadowsway CH2 . . . . . 118 D8

Meadowsweet Rd
WA16 . . . . .57 F3
Meadow The CW4 . . . . . 130 D8
Meadowvale Cl CW5 . . .204 E7
Meadow View
Chester CH4 . . . . 118 F1
Ellesmere Port CH2 . . . . . . .70 C1
Elton CW2 . . . . .72 A3
Lymm WA13 . . . . .18 D4
Middlewich CW10 . . . . 128 B2
Sealand CH5 . . . . 116 A6
Meadow View Dr WA6 . .74 A7
Meadow Way
Lawton-gate ST7 . . . . 194 A5
Macclesfield SK10 . . . . .87 E2
Sandbach CW11 . . . . .59 E4
Meadow Wlk
Partington M31 . . . . .11 E3
[M] Runcorn WA7 . . . . .49 F7
Mead Rd WA1 . . . . .17 A8
Meadscroft Dr SK9 . . . . .59 F1
Meads Rd ST7 . . . . 193 D4
Meadway
Bramhall SK7 . . . . .35 E5
Ellesmere Port CH66 . . . . . .69 B7
Golborne WA3 . . . . .3 D8
Heswall CH60 . . . . .40 F6
High Lane SK6 . . . . .37 F8
Poynton SK12 . . . . .36 B4
Prestbury SK10 . . . . .87 A5
Widnes WA8 . . . . 12 A1
Meakin Cl CW12 . . . . . . .157 B1
Mealors New Cotts
CH64 . . . . .67 A4
Mealors Weint CH64 . . .41 B1
Meal St SK22 . . . . .39 C8
Meddings Cl SK9 . . . . . . .85 A8
Medina Ave CW7 . . . . . . 126 F2
Medina Way ST7 . . . . . . 195 B2
Medlar Cl CH4 . . . . 140 F5
Medway Cl
Golborne WN7 . . . . .4 C8
Handforth SK9 . . . . .34 D2
Warrington WA3 . . . . .8 E2
Medway Dr ST8 . . . . 179 D1
Medway Rd WA3 . . . . .5 A2
Meeanee Dr CW5 . . . . . . 204 D4
Mee St SK11 . . . . 112 E5
Meeting House La
WA6 . . . . .74 E2
Meeting La WA5 . . . . .14 E5
MEGACRE 210 A1
Megacre ST7 . . . . 210 A1
Meg La
Langley SK11 . . . . 113 D1
Macclesfield SK10 . . . . 111 E8
Megs La CW9 . . . . .53 B4
Melbourne Ave M90 . . . .33 A8
Melbourne Gr CW1 . . . .191 C5
Melbourne Rd
Blacon CH1 . . . . 117 D4
Bramhall SK7 . . . . .35 F5
Melbury Ct WA3 . . . . .9 F6
Melbury Rd SK8 . . . . .35 B6
Melchett Cres CW9 . . . . 104 D7
Melford Cl CW2 . . . . 206 C8
Melford Ct WA1 . . . . .17 D8
Melford Dr
Macclesfield SK10 . . . . .87 C2
Runcorn WA7 . . . . .23 C1
Meliden Gr WA6 . . . . .73 B1
Melkridge Cl CH2 . . . . . . 119 A3
Melksham Cl SK11 . . . . . 112 A7
Mellard St ST7 . . . . 209 D1
Mellock Cl CH64 . . . . .66 F6
Mellock La CH64 . . . . .66 F5
Mellor Cl WA7 . . . . .24 D1
Mellor Cres WA16 . . . . . . .56 E1
Mellors Bank ST7 . . . . . 195 D6
Mellor St
Crewe CW1 . . . . 190 D5
Packmoor ST7 . . . . 195 F2
Mellor View SK12 . . . . . . .38 E6
Melrose Ave
Burtonwood WA5 . . . . .6 F7
Chester CH3 . . . . 119 B2
Warrington WA4 . . . . .26 D8
Melrose Cres SK12 . . . . . .37 D5
Melrose Ct [16] SK9 . . . . . .34 E1
Melrose Dr
Crewe CW1 . . . . 190 B8
Ellesmere Port CH66 . . . . . .94 F8
Melton Ave WA4 . . . . .26 B8
Melton Cl CW12 . . . . 155 F3
Melton Dr CW12 . . . . 155 F3
Melton Rd WA7 . . . . .49 C7
Melverly Dr CH1 . . . . 117 C4
Melville Cl
Warrington WA2 . . . . .16 B7
[M] Widnes WA8 . . . . .13 D1
Melville Rd M44 . . . . 11 C5
Mendell Cl CH62 . . . . .43 E8
Mendell Prim Sch
CH62 . . . . .43 E8
Mendip Ave WA2 . . . . .8 B3
Mendip Cl
Ellesmere Port CH66 . . . . . .69 E3
Gatley SK8 . . . . .34 B7
Winsford CW7 . . . . 149 B8
Menin Ave WA4 . . . . .16 C3
Menlow Cl WA4 . . . . .17 C1
Mentmore Gdns WA4 . . .26 F5
Meols Cl
Ellesmere Port CH66 . . . . . .69 E4
Hale LA24 . . . . .21 E2
Mercer Cl SY14 . . . . .213 B3
Mercer Rd WA11 . . . . .1 D6

Mercer St
Burtonwood WA5 . . . . .6 E6
Newton-le-W WA5 . . . . .2 D4
Mercer Way
Chester CH4 . . . . 140 F6
Nantwich CW5 . . . . 204 E7
Mercer Wlk CH65 . . . . . . .70 C4
Merchants Ct CW1 . . . . 190 C7
Mercian Cl CW2 . . . . 206 B4
Mercury Ct CH1 . . . . 117 E2
MERE 56 B8
Mere Ave CH63 . . . . .43 B6
Mere Bank CW9 . . . . 127 A8
Merebank Rd CW2 . . . . . 190 B1
Merebrook Cl SK11 . . . . 112 A8
Merebrook Rd SK11 . . . . 111 F8
Mere Brook Wlk CW2 . . 190 C1
Mere Cl
Ellesmere Port CH66 . . . . . .69 D2
Haslington CW1 . . . . 191 D4
Pickmere WA16 . . . . .80 A7
Mere Cres CW8 . . . . 123 F6
Merecroft [1] CH3 . . . . . . 119 A1
Mere Ct
Alsager ST7 . . . . 193 D4
Chelford SK11 . . . . .83 F3
[6] Knutsford WA16 . . . . . . .57 A2
Weston CW2 . . . . .207 B5
Meredith Ave WA4 . . . . . .17 B2
Meredith St CW1 . . . . . . 190 C5
Mere Hall WA16 . . . . .56 A8
Merehaven Cl WA16 . . . . .80 A7
MERE HEATH 127 A8
Merehaath La WA16 . . . . .56 F3
Merehaath Pk WA16 . . . . .56 F3
Mere Ho ST7 . . . . 193 C3
Mere La
Cuddington CW8 . . . . 102 A2
Pickmere WA16 . . . . .79 F7
Merelake Rd ST7 . . . . 210 B8
Meremore Dr ST5 . . . . . . 210 D2
Mere Rd
Marston CW9 . . . . .79 B6
Newton-le-W WA12 . . . . . . .2 F4
Warrington WA7 . . . . .9 A2
Weston CW2 . . . . .207 B5
Mereside Ave CW12 . . . . 156 B3
Mereside Cl SK10 . . . . . . .87 A1
Mereside Gdns SK23 . . . .65 D6
Mereside Rd WA16 . . . . . .30 C2
Mere St CW1 . . . . 191 D4
Merevale Cl WA7 . . . . .49 E6
Mere View WA6 . . . . .73 A2
Mere View Gdns WA4 . . .26 E5
Merewood Cl WA2 . . . . . . .8 D3
Mereworth Dr CW9 . . . . 103 F5
Meridian Ho CW7 . . . . . . 127 B3
Merino Rd SK9 . . . . .34 D4
Merlin Ave WA16 . . . . .57 B3
Merlin Cl
Runcorn WA7 . . . . .24 A1
Winsford CW7 . . . . 150 A4
Merlin Way
Crewe CW1 . . . . 190 A8
Kidsgrove ST7 . . . . 195 D3
Merrick Cl WA7 . . . . .8 E3
Merridale The WA15 . . . .32 A8
Merriden Rd SK10 . . . . . . .87 B2
Merrill's Ave CW2 . . . . . 189 E5
Merriman Ave WA16 . . . . .57 C3
Merrivale Rd CW2 . . . . . 206 B8
Merrydale Cl WA16 . . . . . .86 F1
Merryman's La SK9 . . . . .84 B7
Mersey Pl CW7 . . . . 127 B1
Mersey Rd
Runcorn WA7 . . . . .23 A3
Widnes WA8 . . . . 23 A4
Mersey St
St Helens WA9 . . . . .1 A3
Warrington WA1 . . . . .16 B5
Merseyton Rd CH65 . . . . .70 B8
Merseyton Road
Workshops CH65 . . . . .70 C7
Mersey View WA7 . . . . . . .48 D7
Mersey View Rd WA8 . . .22 B4
Mersey Wlk WA4 . . . . .16 F5
Mersham Ct WA8 . . . . 12 F4
Merton Ave SK7 . . . . .36 F8
Merton Cl CH64 . . . . .66 E5
Merton Dr CH4 . . . . 141 A4
Merton House Sch
CH2 . . . . 118 C4
Merton Rd
Bebington CH65 . . . . .44 B3
Ellesmere Port CH66 . . . . . .69 F3
Poynton SK12 . . . . .37 B4
Mertoun Rd WA4 . . . . . . .16 B1
Mervyn Rd CH64 . . . . .77 E1
Merwood Ave SK8 . . . . . . .34 D8
Messuage La CW12 . . . . .132 E4
Meteor Cres WA2 . . . . .8 D2
Mevagissey Rd WA7 . . . . .50 C5
Mevril Rd SK10 . . . . .65 E5
Mevril Springs Way
SK23 . . . . .65 E5
Mews The
Barnton CW8 . . . . .78 B2
Burtonwood WA5 . . . . .6 E6
Holmes Chapel CW4 . . . . . 130 C3
New Mills SK22 . . . . .39 D8
Tarporley CW6 . . . . 146 C2
Willaston CH64 . . . . .68 A8
Wilmslow SK9 . . . . .33 D4
Meynell Cl CW2 . . . . 190 A1
Meynell Pl CH1 . . . . 118 A5
Meyrick Cl WA12 . . . . .2 E2
Miami Cl [9] WA5 . . . . .15 B7
Micawber Rd SK12 . . . . . .36 E2

Micklegate
Mickle Trafford CH2 . . . . . 119 E8
Runcorn WA7 . . . . .50 D7
MICKLE TRAFFORD 119 E8
Mickle Trafford Village
Sch CH2 . . . . 119 E8
Micklewright Ave
CW1 . . . . 190 D5
Mickley Mall La CW5 . . . 218 A4
Mid-Cheshire Coll
(Hartford Campus)
CW8 . . . . 103 C6
Mid Cheshire Coll (London
Road Studios) CW1 . . . . 190 D5
Mid Cheshire Coll (Verdin
Ctr) CW7 . . . . 126 D1
Middlecroft CH3 . . . . 119 E5
Middlehills SK11 . . . . 113 A6
Middlehurst Ave CW8 . . 102 E8
Middlehurst Rd WA4 . . . .17 A2
Middle La
Aldford CH3 . . . . 163 F3
Congleton CW12 . . . . 157 D4
Kingsley WA6 . . . . .74 F2
MIDDLEWICH 128 D3
Middlewich High Sch
CW10 . . . . 151 C8
Middlewich Prim Sch
CW10 . . . . 151 B8
Middlewich Rd
Allostock WA16 . . . . 106 D5
Church Minshull CW1,
CW10 . . . . 172 E5
Cranage CW4, CW10 . . . . 129 E6
Crewe CW1 . . . . 189 D6
Delamere CW6, CW8 . . . . 123 D5
Holmes Chapel CW4 . . . . 130 B3
Knutsford WA16 . . . . .82 A3
Lower Peover WA16 . . . . . .81 F2
Nantwich CW5 . . . . 189 B1
Nantwich CW5 . . . . 204 F7
Northwich CW9 . . . . 104 D7
Sandbach CW11 . . . . 174 E7
Winsford CW7, CW10 . . . 127 E1
Middlewich Road Ind Est
CW10 . . . . 129 A6
Middlewich St CW1 . . . . 190 D6
Middle Wlk
Frodsham WA6 . . . . .74 B7
Knutsford WA16 . . . . .57 B2
MIDDLEWOOD 37 C5
Middlewood WA3 . . . . .3 E8
Middlewood Rd
Hazel Grove SK7, SK12 . . .37 C7
High Lane SK6 . . . . .37 B4
Poynton SK12 . . . . .37 B4
Middlewood View SK6 . . .37 D7
Midfield Cl ST8 . . . . 179 C2
Midhurst Cl SK8 . . . . .34 F8
Midland St WA8 . . . . .13 B1
Midland Terr SK22 . . . . . .39 C7
Midland Way WA1,
WA5 . . . . .16 B5
Midlothian Ho [4]
CH1 . . . . 237 C3
Midpoint 18 Motorway Ind
Est CW10 . . . . 128 E1
MIDWAY 36 D2
Midway St SK8 . . . . .35 B5
Midway Dr SK12 . . . . .36 D2
Milborne Cl CH2 . . . . 118 E5
Mildenhall Cl WA5 . . . . . .15 B6
Mile Bank Rd SY13 . . . . 226 D3
Miles Cl WA3 . . . . .9 F3
Milford Gdns WA4 . . . . . .26 D4
Milford St CW12 . . . . 156 D3
Miltar Cres WA8 . . . . .23 A7
Mill Ave WA5 . . . . .14 E7
Millbank WA13 . . . . 18 B5
Mill Bank CH64 . . . . .67 A5
Millbank Cl SK11 . . . . .84 A3
Millbank Cotts CH3 . . . . 166 C2
Millbank Ct WA6 . . . . .74 A8
Millbank Dr SK10 . . . . . . .86 F1
Millbeck Cl CW2 . . . . 207 B5
Mill Bridge Cl CW1 . . . . 190 F3
Millbridge Gdns WA12 . . .2 E3
Millbrook Cl
Fowley Common WA3 . . . . . .5 C5
Winsford CW7 . . . . 148 F8
Millbrook Ct
Middlewich CW10 . . . . 128 D1
Warrington WA2 . . . . .8 B2
Millbrook End CH3 . . . . 166 A2
Millbrook Fold SK7 . . . . .35 D8
Millbrook Gr [1] SK9 . . . . .34 D1
Mill Brow WA8 . . . . 13 C1
Millbuck Pk CW11 . . . . . 174 C5
Millbuck Way CW11 . . . . 174 C6
Mill Cl
Chester CH2 . . . . 118 D6
Knutsford WA16 . . . . .57 D7
Warrington WA7 . . . . .8 A1
Mill Cotts
Bollington SK10 . . . . .88 B8
Christleton CH3 . . . . 142 D8
Willaston CH64 . . . . .42 F1
Millcroft
Neston CH64 . . . . .41 D1
Sandbach, Wheelock
CW11 . . . . 191 F8
Mill Cross CH3 . . . . 143 A5
Mill Ct CH65 . . . . .70 B4
Milldale Rd WN7 . . . . .4 B8
MILLEND 209 C5
Millend La ST7 . . . . 209 C5
Millenium Way [8] WA5 . .15 B7

Millennium Ct CH64 . . . . .41 E2
Millennium Way ST5 . . . 210 F2
Millers Cl CH3 . . . . 143 A4
Millers Croft [8] SK10 . . . 112 C8
Millers Cl [7] SK10 . . . . . 112 C8
Millersdale Cl CH62 . . . . .43 F5
Millersdale Gr WA7 . . . . .49 D6
Millers La WA13 . . . . .19 B5
Millers Mdw SK10 . . . . . . .88 E5
Miller St WA4 . . . . .16 C4
Millers View ST7 . . . . 195 A1
Millers Wharf ST7 . . . . . 193 E7
Milley La WA16 . . . . .80 C7
Mill Farm Cl WA2 . . . . .8 B3
Mill Farm Cotts CW7 . . . 149 B3
Mill Farm Est CW5 . . . . . 217 A3
Millfield
Holt LL13 . . . . 196 D7
Neston CH64 . . . . .41 E1
Millfield Bsns Ctr WA11 . . .1 B8
Mill Field Cl CH3 . . . . 180 F2
Millfield La
Haydock WA11 . . . . .1 E8
Saighton CH3 . . . . 142 F1
Tarporley CW6 . . . . 146 C2
Millfield Rd WA8 . . . . .13 C2
Millfields CW5 . . . . 204 D4
Millfields Prim Sch
Bebington CH62 . . . . .43 E4
Nantwich CW5 . . . . 204 C5
Millfield Terr CH66 . . . . . .69 C7
Millgate CW5 . . . . 101 F4
Mill Gn
Congleton CW12 . . . . 156 D3
Willaston CH64 . . . . .67 F8
Mill Gr
Bulkeley SY14 . . . . 184 C5
Kidsgrove ST7 . . . . 194 D1
Mill Green La WA8 . . . . . .13 E5
Mill Green Sch WA12 . . . .2 E3
Mill Hill Ave SK12 . . . . . . .36 D7
Mill Hill Dr CW11 . . . . . . 175 A5
Mill Hollow SK12 . . . . . . .36 D7
Mill Hill La CW11 . . . . . . 175 A4
Mill Ho CW5 . . . . 204 D5
Millhouse Ave WA4 . . . . .16 D1
Millhouse La WA3 . . . . .9 A6
Milling Field The
CW4 . . . . 130 C2
Millingford Ind Est WA3 . . .3 A8
Millington Cl
Runcorn WA7 . . . . .49 F3
Widnes WA8 . . . . .22 F8
Millington Hall La
WA14 . . . . .30 B5
Millington La
Rostherne WA14 . . . . .30 B6
Weaverham CW8 . . . . 102 B6
Mill La
Adlington SK10 . . . . .62 B6
Aldford CH3 . . . . 163 F3
Alsager CW11 . . . . 192 E8
Altrincham WA15 . . . . .32 E4
Audlem, Little Heath
CW3 . . . . 230 A4
Audlem, Swanbach
CW3 . . . . 229 E2
Barthomley CW2 . . . . 208 C7
Blakenhall CW5 . . . . 221 B4
Bold Heath WA8 . . . . 13 D6
Bollington SK10 . . . . .88 C8
Brereton Green CW4 . . . . . 153 E8
Bulkeley SY14 . . . . 184 E2
Burton CH64 . . . . .67 C1
Chester CH2 . . . . 118 D6
Christleton CH3 . . . . 120 D2
Congleton CW12 . . . . 179 C8
Cronton WA8 . . . . .12 D6
Cuddington CW8 . . . . 101 F4
Duddon CW6 . . . . 145 A7
Eaton CW6 . . . . 147 B2
Ellesmere Port CH66 . . . . . .69 E5
Frodsham WA6 . . . . .69 C5
Goostrey CW4 . . . . 107 E2
Great Barrow CH3 . . . . 120 E5
Hazel Grove SK7 . . . . .36 F8
Heswall CH60 . . . . .41 B8
Higher Walton WA4 . . . . . . .25 E7
Holmes Chapel CW4 . . . . 154 A8
Huxley CH3 . . . . 166 C4
Kingsley WA6 . . . . .75 E3
Lindow End SK9 . . . . .84 A7
Little Budworth CW6 . . . . 148 A8
Lymm WA13 . . . . 19 C4
Macclesfield SK11 . . . . 112 D7
Marton CW12 . . . . 132 F2
Middlewich CW10 . . . . 128 D1
Middlewich, Newtonia
CW10 . . . . 128 B1
Middlewich, Stud Green
CW11 . . . . 152 C1
Mobberley WA16 . . . . .58 B4
Mottram St Andrew
SK10 . . . . .61 C5
Neston CH64 . . . . .67 C5
Newton-le-W WA12 . . . . . . .2 E3
Over Peover WA16,
SK11 . . . . 108 D8
Prestbury SK10 . . . . .61 F6
Sandbach CW11 . . . . 174 C8
Sandbach, Wheelock
CW11 . . . . 175 B2
Siddington SK11 . . . . 109 F6
Smallwood CW11 . . . . 176 D7

Mill La continued
Tarvin St CW1 . . . . 121 C4
The Bank ST7 . . . . 195 A7
Warrington, Houghton Grn
WA2 . . . . 8 E4
Warrington, Stockton Heath
WA4 . . . . 16 E1
Warrington WA2 . . . . 7 F4
Weston CW2 . . . . 207 B6
Whitegate CW7, CW8 . . . . 126 B6
Willaston CH64 . . . . 42 F1
Mill Lane Cotts CH3 . . . . 120 E5
Mill Lane End CW5 . . . . 221 C4
Mill Mdw WA12 . . . . 2 E3
Millmead ST7 . . . . 193 F7
Mill Park Dr CH62 . . . . 43 E3
Mill Pool La CW5 . . . . 187 C6
Millport Cl CW2 . . . . 9 A2
Millrace Dr CW2 . . . . 206 B8
Mill Rd
Macclesfield SK11 . . . . 112 D6
Wilmslow SK9 . . . . 60 B7
Mill Rise
Helsby WA6 . . . . 73 C4
Kidsgrove ST7 . . . . 195 A1
Mill Row CW11 . . . . 175 C6
Mill St
Chester CH4 . . . . 237 B1
Congleton, Buglawton
CW12 . . . . 156 F4
Congleton CW12 . . . . 156 D3
Crewe CW2 . . . . 190 D3
Golborne WA3 . . . . 3 A8
Macclesfield SK11 . . . . 112 D7
Nantwich CW5 . . . . 204 E5
Neston CH64 . . . . 66 D8
Wilmslow SK9 . . . . 60 B7
Millstone Ave ST7 . . . . . 194 E1
Millstone Cl WA12 . . . . 36 F5
Millstone La CW5 . . . . . . 204 F5
Millstone Pas SK11 . . . . 112 E6
Mill Stream Cl CW4 . . . . 107 E1
Mills Way CW1 . . . . 173 B1
Mill The ST7 . . . . 195 C5
Mill View Cl SY14 . . . . . . 184 E2
Mill View Prim Sch
CH2 . . . . 118 E6
Millway
Altrincham WA15 . . . . 32 C7
Waverton CH3 . . . . 143 B5
Mill Way CW5 . . . . 204 F2
Millway Rd L24 . . . . 21 A4
Mill Wharf CH3 . . . . 143 B5
Millwood WA7 . . . . 24 C1
Millwood Cl SK8 . . . . 34 E8
Millwood Ct L24 . . . . 21 A4
Millyard The CH4 . . . . . . 162 C1
Milne Cl CW2 . . . . 189 F1
Milner Cop CH60 . . . . 41 A8
Milner Rd
Heswall CH60 . . . . 41 A8
Northwich CW8 . . . . 103 C6
MILNERS GREEN 143 C2
Milner St WA5 . . . . 15 F5
Milnthorpe Rd WA5 . . . . 6 E6
Milton Ave
Irlam M44 . . . . 11 E6
Newton-le-W WA12 . . . . 2 B3
Widnes WA8 . . . . 22 F8
Milton Cl
Ellesmere Port CH65 . . . . . . 70 D4
Higher Wincham CW9 . . . . . 80 A5
Middlewich CW10 . . . . 151 D5
Milton Cres ST7 . . . . 210 C8
Milton Ct SK7 . . . . 35 F6
Milton Dr
Poynton SK12 . . . . 36 D4
Wistaston CW2 . . . . 206 A8
Milton Gr
Helsby WA6 . . . . 73 A1
Warrington WA4 . . . . 16 D3
MILTON GREEN 165 C2
Milton Rd
Blacon CH1 . . . . 117 F6
Bramhall SK7 . . . . 35 E7
Ellesmere Port CH65 . . . . . . 70 D4
Golborne WA3 . . . . 3 D7
Widnes WA8 . . . . 23 A8
Milton Rough CW8 . . . . . . 76 E2
Milton St
Chester CH1 . . . . 237 B3
Widnes WA8 . . . . 174 C6
Milton Way CW11 . . . . . . 174 D6
Milvain Dr WA2 . . . . 8 C1
Milverton Dr SK7 . . . . 35 B5
Mimosa Cl CH2 . . . . 72 C4
Miners Way
Speke L24 . . . . 21 A3
Widnes WA8 . . . . 23 A7
Minerva Ave CH1 . . . . . . 117 E2
Minerva Cl WA4 . . . . 16 D2
Minerva Ct CH1 . . . . 117 E2
Mine Way WA11 . . . . 1 F7
Minn-End-La SK11 . . . . . 159 B6
Minor Ave SK11 . . . . 112 D3
Minshull La CW5,
CW7 . . . . 171 D4
Minshull New Rd
CW1 . . . . 189 F7
Minshull St WA16 . . . . 57 A2
MINSHULL VERNON . . 172 E5
Minster Cl CW7 . . . . 149 D5
Minster Ct
Runcorn WA7 . . . . 48 E8
Wistaston CW2 . . . . 205 E8

Minster Dr WA14 . . . . 31 A8
Minton Cl CW12 . . . . 157 B1
Minton Way WA8 . . . . 13 B5
Mirfield Cl WA3 . . . . 3 D7
Mirion St CW1 . . . . 190 D4
Mission Mews CH2 . . . . 118 F2
Misty Cl WA8 . . . . 12 C2
Mitchell Ave
Burtonwood WA5 . . . . 6 E5
Kidsgrove ST7 . . . . 194 D1
Mitchell Dr ST7 . . . . 194 D1
Mitchell Fold
Fourlane-ends SK10 . . . . 63 D8
High Lane SK6 . . . . 37 D1
Mitchell St
Golborne WA3 . . . . 3 A8
Warrington WA4 . . . . 26 C8
Mithril Cl WA8 . . . . 13 E3
Mitton Cl WA3 . . . . 4 E5
MMU Cheshire (Crewe
Campus) CW1 . . . . 190 F3
Moat Ho [17] CW8 . . . . . . 103 F8
Moat La
Audley ST7 . . . . 209 B3
Hollins Green WA3 . . . . 10 E2
MOBBERLEY 58 A4
Mobberley CE Prim Sch
WA16 . . . . 58 C5
Mobberley Rd
Ashley WA14, WA15,
WA16 . . . . 31 E3
Knutsford WA16 . . . . 57 B3
Wilmslow SK9 . . . . 33 D1
Mobberley Sta WA16 . . . . . 57 F7
MOBLAKE 230 D4
Modyn CH2 . . . . 118 C4
Moelfre Dr SK8 . . . . 35 C7
Moggie La SK10 . . . . 36 F1
Mold Rd CH4 . . . . 139 A3
MOLLINGTON 94 E2
Mollington Ct CH1 . . . . . . 94 F2
Mollington Grange Bsns
Pk CH1 . . . . 117 F8
Mollington Rd M22 . . . . . . 33 E8
Molly Potts Cl WA16 . . . . 82 B8
Molyneux Ave WA5 . . . . . 15 F8
Monarch Cl
Crewe CW2 . . . . 189 F4
Irlam M44 . . . . 11 E6
Monarch Dr CW9 . . . . 103 E5
Monck Dr CW5 . . . . 204 D6
Mond Rd WA8 . . . . 23 A8
Mond St CW8 . . . . 78 B3
Monica Dr WA8 . . . . 13 A5
Monks Coppenhall Prim
Sch CW1 . . . . 190 C7
Monks Gr CH65 . . . . 70 B6
MONKS HEATH 85 A1
Monk's Heath Crossroads
SK10 . . . . 85 A1
Monks Heath Hall
Wrkshps SK10 . . . . 85 B1
Monks La
Acton CW5 . . . . 203 F7
Crewe CW1 . . . . 189 F5
Nantwich CW5 . . . . 204 E5
Monk's La CW3 . . . . 230 C5
Monks Orch CW5 . . . . . . 204 F5
Monks Pl WA2 . . . . 16 C7
Monks St WA5 . . . . 15 C6
Monk St CW1 . . . . 190 A5
Monks Way CW8 . . . . . . 103 B4
Monkswood Cl WA5 . . . . . . 7 E2
Monmouth Cl WA1 . . . . . . 17 E7
Monroe Cl WA1 . . . . 17 B8
Monsall Cl SK11 . . . . 112 F7
Monsall Dr SK11 . . . . 112 F7
Montague Rd WA8 . . . . . . 22 A6
Montana Cl WA5 . . . . 15 C7
Montclare Cres WA4 . . . . 16 F2
Montcliffe Cl WA3 . . . . 9 C5
Montgomery Cl
Knutsford WA16 . . . . 57 C4
Warrington WA5 . . . . 15 A8
Montgomery Rd WA8 . . . 22 D8
Montgomery Way
CW7 . . . . 149 B7
Montmorency Rd
WA16 . . . . 57 D3
Montpelier Ave WA7 . . . . 48 F6
Montrose Cl
Macclesfield SK10 . . . . 87 A1
Shavington CW2 . . . . 206 B3
Warrington WA2 . . . . 8 F4
Montrose Ct
Chester CH4 . . . . 140 F7
Holmes Chapel CW4 . . . . . 130 B2
Monument Rd ST7 . . . . . 210 D6
Monument View ST7 . . . 209 F2
Moody St CW12 . . . . 156 D2
Moor Cl ST8 . . . . 179 E1
Moor Cres CW4 . . . . 139 D1
Moorcroft WA16 . . . . 80 C5
Moorcroft Ave CH3 . . . . . 119 B1
Moorcroft Cres CH3 . . . . 119 C4
Moorcroft Ct CH3 . . . . . . 119 B1
Moorcroft Mews CH4 . . . 140 D6
Moordale Rd WA16 . . . . . . 57 B2
Moorditch La
Frodsham WA6 . . . . 48 D1
Frodsham WA6 . . . . 48 F1
MOORE 25 B6
Moore
St Helens WA9 . . . . 1 B3
Warrington WA3 . . . . 17 D3
Moore Cl WA8 . . . . 13 D2
Moore Dr WA11 . . . . 1 F6

Moore Gr WA13 . . . . 19 B5
Moore La WA4 . . . . 25 C7
Moore Prim Sch WA4 . . . . . 25 A5
Moorfield Cres WA3 . . . . . 4 A7
Moorfield Gr
Neston CH64 . . . . 41 C1
Wilmslow SK9 . . . . 59 E5
Moorfield Prim Sch
Blacon CH1 . . . . 117 E4
Moorfield Rd WA8 . . . . . . 13 D3
Moorfields CW5 . . . . 205 E6
Moorhead La CW8 . . . . . . 101 A6
Moorhill Rd SK11 . . . . 112 C4
Moor Ho WA6 . . . . 74 B8
Moorhouse Ave ST7 . . . . 193 E4
Moorhouse Cl CH2 . . . . . 118 D5
Mooring Cl WA7 . . . . 50 D6
Moorings CW12 . . . . 156 E1
Moorings Cl CH64 . . . . . . 41 B1
Moorings The
Christleton CH3 . . . . 142 E7
Disley SK12 . . . . 38 E6
Heswall CH60 . . . . 40 C8
Middlewich CW10 . . . . 128 C1
Moor La
Bramhall SK7 . . . . 35 E3
Elton WA6 . . . . 72 E1
Frodsham WA6 . . . . 74 B8
Heswall CH60 . . . . 40 F8
Higher Kinnerton CH4 . . . . 161 D8
Lower Kinnerton CH4 . . . . 161 C6
Sandycroft CH5 . . . . 116 A2
Waverton CH3 . . . . 143 A5
Widnes WA8 . . . . 22 F7
Widnes WA8 . . . . 23 A7
Wilmslow SK9 . . . . 59 E5
Moorland Cl CH60 . . . . . . 41 A7
Moorland Dr
Cheadle SK8 . . . . 34 F8
Runcorn WA7 . . . . 50 E7
Moorland Pk CH60 . . . . . . 41 A7
Moorland Rd
Biddulph ST8 . . . . 179 D1
Ellesmere Port CH66 . . . . . 69 E8
Goostrey CW4 . . . . 107 E1
Moorlands Ave CW8 . . . . 102 A4
Moorlands Cl SK10 . . . . . . 87 C3
Moorlands Dr CW8 . . . . . . 78 B3
Moorlands Pk CW8 . . . . . 102 A4
Moor Lane Bsns Ctr
WA8 . . . . 23 A7
Moor La S WA8 . . . . 22 F7
Moor-Park Way CW9 . . . . . 103 E4
Moorsbrook Gr SK9 . . . . . 34 E1
Moorsfield Ave CW3 . . . 229 F3
MOORSIDE 66 C7
Moorside
Knutsford WA16 . . . . 57 A2
Warrington WA4 . . . . 16 E4
Moorside Ave CH64 . . . . . 66 C8
Moorside Ct WA8 . . . . 22 F7
Moorside La
Neston CH64 . . . . 66 D8
Pott Shrigley SK10 . . . . 63 E4
Moors La CW7 . . . . 149 D5
Moorson Ave ST7 . . . . . . 194 F8
Moor St CW12 . . . . 156 E2
Moorview Gdns ST7 . . . . 195 E6
Moorway CH60 . . . . 41 B8
Moran Cl SK9 . . . . 34 E2
Moran Cres SK11 . . . . . . 112 B7
Moran Dr WA5 . . . . 15 A6
Moran Rd SK11 . . . . 112 B7
Morcott La L24 . . . . 21 D2
Moresby Cl WA7 . . . . 50 E7
Moreton Ave SK7 . . . . 35 E5
Moreton Cl CW11 . . . . . . 175 C7
Moreton Dr
Alsager ST7 . . . . 193 C3
Handforth SK9 . . . . 34 E3
Holmes Chapel CW4 . . . . . 130 B3
Poynton SK12 . . . . 36 F4
Moreton Pl ST7 . . . . 194 E6
Moreton Rd CW9 . . . . 189 F3
Moreton St CW8 . . . . 78 D1
Moreton Terr WA6 . . . . . . 74 A8
Moreville Cl CW9 . . . . 103 E3
Morgan Ave WA2 . . . . 8 C2
Morgan Cl
Blacon CH1 . . . . 117 F6
Crewe CW2 . . . . 190 A4
Morgans Way WA3 . . . . . . 4 A8
Morgan Wlk CW5 . . . . . . 204 D6
Morland Ave
Bebington CH62 . . . . 43 D6
Neston CH64 . . . . 41 F1
MORLEY 33 C2
Morley Cl CH2 . . . . 119 F8
MORLEY COMMON 15 F1
Morley Dr CW12 . . . . 157 A1
MORLEY GREEN 33 C1
Morley Green Rd SK9 . . . . . 33 C1
Morley Rd
Runcorn WA7 . . . . 23 A1
Warrington WA4 . . . . 16 A1
Morley St WA1 . . . . 16 D6
Mornant Ave CW8 . . . . . . 103 A3
Mornington Ave CH65 . . . 70 C5
Mornington Cl CW11 . . . 174 D7
Morphany La WA4 . . . . 51 E4
Morreys La CW6 . . . . 122 F6
Morris Ave WA4 . . . . 16 F4
Morris Cl WA11 . . . . 1 A5
Morris Dr CW8 . . . . 77 D1
Morrison Cl WA3 . . . . 15 A5
Morris Pk CW8 . . . . 103 B4
Mort Ave WA4 . . . . 17 A5
Mortimer Ave WA2 . . . . . 16 B8

Mortimer Dr CW11 . . . . . 175 C5
Mortlake Cl WA8 . . . . 12 C3
Mortlake Cres CH3 . . . . . 119 A1
Morton Ave WA6 . . . . 73 B1
Morton Cl WA5 . . . . 15 C8
Morton Dr SK11 . . . . 112 F3
Morton Gdns CH1 . . . . . . 117 F4
Morton Rd
Blacon CH1 . . . . 117 E4
Runcorn WA7 . . . . 50 D8
Morval Cres WA7 . . . . 23 D1
Morven Cl WA2 . . . . 8 E3
Mosedale Gr WA7 . . . . . . 49 E5
Moseley Ave WA4 . . . . . . 17 A3
Moses Ct CH1 . . . . 237 C3
MOSS BANK 23 D8
Moss Bank
Bramhall SK7 . . . . 35 C5
Chester CH2 . . . . 118 C4
Winsford CW7 . . . . 126 C1
Moss Bower Rd SK11 . . . 112 C4
MOSSBROW 19 F7
Moss Brow CW8 . . . . 87 E7
Moss Brow La WA16 . . . . 28 D4
Moss Cl
Warrington WA4 . . . . 16 E2
Willaston CH64 . . . . 68 A8
Moss Croft CW1 . . . . 190 A8
Mossdale Cl
Crewe CW2 . . . . 189 E4
Warrington WA5 . . . . 15 A7
Moss Dr
Manley WA6 . . . . 98 F4
Middlewich CW10 . . . . 151 D6
MOSSEND 154 E1
MOSS END 54 C2
Moss End La CW11 . . . . . 176 E8
Moss Farm Barns
CW8 . . . . 102 D4
Moss Farm Recn Ctr
CW8 . . . . 103 D8
Mossfield Cres [4]
ST7 . . . . 195 B2
Moss Fields
Alsager ST7 . . . . 193 A3
Crewe CW1 . . . . 173 A1
Mossford Ave CW1 . . . . . 190 B7
Moss Gate WA3 . . . . 10 A5
Moss Gr
Lymm WA13 . . . . 19 B4
Newcastle-u-Lyme ST5 . . . 210 D3
Saltney CH4 . . . . 140 D6
Moss Green Way WA9 . . . . 1 A1
Moss Hall La CW6 . . . . . 147 C4
Moss Hey Prim Sch
SK7 . . . . 35 C5
MOSS HOUSES 111 F2
Moss La
Alderley Edge SK9 . . . . 60 B1
Bollington SK10 . . . . 87 E8
Bramhall SK7 . . . . 35 D5
Brereton Green CW12 . . . . 154 F5
Byley CW10 . . . . 129 B7
Congleton CW12 . . . . 156 E6
Crewe CW1 . . . . 173 A2
Cuddington CW8 . . . . 102 A3
Dunham Woodhouses
WA13 . . . . 20 B8
Fowley Common WA3 . . . . . . 5 D5
Golborne WA3 . . . . 3 B5
Higher Wincham CW9 . . . . . 79 E6
High Legh, Sink Moss
WA16 . . . . 28 D4
High Legh WA16 . . . . 29 E6
Hollins Green WA3 . . . . 10 E5
Irlam M44 . . . . 11 D5
Lawton-gate ST7 . . . . 194 F4
Lostock Green CW9 . . . . . 105 D8
Macclesfield SK11 . . . . 112 C4
Manley WA6 . . . . 99 A4
Mere WA16 . . . . 56 C5
Mobberley WA16 . . . . 58 F4
Moore WA4 . . . . 25 A6
Mottram St Andrew
SK10 . . . . 61 A2
Norbury SY13 . . . . 215 C5
Norley WA6 . . . . 101 B5
Northwich CW8 . . . . 103 D7
Over Peover WA16 . . . . 83 C3
Partington M31 . . . . 11 F3
Partington, Mossbrow
WA13 . . . . 11 F1
Saddlebach CW11 . . . . 174 C7
St Helens, Moss Nook
WA9 . . . . 1 A1
Tarporley CW6 . . . . 146 B2
Warrington WA1 . . . . 173 C3
Warrington WA3 . . . . 9 E1
Wybunbury CW5 . . . . 206 A1
Wythenshawe SK9 . . . . 33 E6
Moss Lane Bsns Ctr
CW11 . . . . 174 D6
Moss Lane Ind Est
CW11 . . . . 174 D6
MOSSLEY 179 A8
Mossley Ave CH62 . . . . . . 43 D8
Mossley CE Prim Sch
CW12 . . . . 179 B8
Mossley Garth [4]
CW12 . . . . 179 B8
Moss Mere CW11 . . . . . . 176 F7
MOSS NOOK 33 F7
Moss Pl ST7 . . . . 195 B3

Moss Rd
Alderley Edge SK9 . . . . 60 C2
Congleton CW12 . . . . 178 F7
Irlam M44 . . . . 11 C7
Northwich CW8 . . . . 103 D8
Warrington WA4 . . . . 17 A3
Moss Rose SK9 . . . . 60 B2
Moss Rose Football Gnd
SK11 . . . . 112 D4
Moss Side La
Antrobus CW9 . . . . 53 D7
Hollins Green WA3 . . . . 10 F3
Moore WA4 . . . . 24 F7
Moss Side Rd M44 . . . . . . 11 E6
Moss Sq
Crewe CW1 . . . . 190 D4
Macclesfield SK11 . . . . 112 D4
Moss St
Weaverham CW8 . . . . 77 D1
Widnes WA8 . . . . 23 D7
Moss Terr
Warren SK11 . . . . 112 A5
Wilmslow SK9 . . . . 60 F8
Winnington CW8 . . . . 78 D1
Moss The CW9 . . . . 78 D7
Mossvale CH66 . . . . 69 D8
Moss View Rd SK11 . . . . 112 A4
Moss Way ST7 . . . . 193 A3
Mossways Pk SK9 . . . . . . 59 C7
Mosswood Rd SK9 . . . . . . 34 E3
MOSTON 95 C1
Moston Ct [5] CW2 . . . . . 156 F3
Moston Gr WA13 . . . . 18 D3
MOSTON GREEN 174 B8
Moston Rd
Chester CH2 . . . . 118 D8
Sandbach CW11 . . . . 174 D6
Moston Way CH66 . . . . . . 69 F3
Mostyn Ave CH60 . . . . . . 40 C8
Mostyn Gdns CH64 . . . . . 41 B1
Mostyn House Sch
CH64 . . . . 66 C8
Mostyn Pl CH1 . . . . 117 E6
Mostyn Sq CH64 . . . . 41 B1
Mote Hill Ct WA1 . . . . 16 D6
Motherwell Cl WA8 . . . . . 12 E3
Mottershall Cl [1]
WA8 . . . . 23 A8
Mottershead Rd WA8 . . . 23 A8
Mottram Cl
Middlewich CW10 . . . . 151 B7
Warrington WA4 . . . . 17 B3
Mottram Dr CW5 . . . . 205 A4
Mottram Rd SK9 . . . . 60 D1
MOTTRAM ST ANDREW
. . . . 61 B2
Mottram St Andrew Prim
Sch SK10 . . . . 61 B1
Mottram Way SK10 . . . . . . 87 E2
Moughland La WA7 . . . . . 49 A8
Moulders La WA1 . . . . 16 B4
MOULDSWORTH 98 F2
Mouldsworth Cl [2]
CW9 . . . . 103 E4
Mouldsworth Motor Mus*
CH3 . . . . 98 E1
Mouldsworth Sta CH3 . . . 99 A2
MOULTON 126 E7
Moulton Cl
Knutsford WA16 . . . . 57 C1
Northwich CW9 . . . . 103 E4
Runcorn WA7 . . . . 49 F4
Moulton Sch CW9 . . . . . . 126 F8
Mountain View
Helsby WA6 . . . . 73 B3
Saltney CH4 . . . . 140 E6
Mount Ave CH60 . . . . 40 F8
Mount Barns CH2 . . . . 95 C6
Mountbatten Cl CW7 . . . 149 A7
Mountbatten Way
CW12 . . . . 156 E3
Mount Cl CW5 . . . . 204 F8
Mount Ct [3] CH60 . . . . . . 40 F8
Mount Dr CW5 . . . . 204 F8
Mount Farm Way CH66 . . 69 C2
Mountfield Rd SK7 . . . . . . 35 E5
Mount Haven CH60 . . . . . . 40 F8
Mount Pl CH2 . . . . 118 F2
Mount Pleasant
Audlem CW3 . . . . 230 A4
Chester CH4 . . . . 140 F7
Congleton CW12 . . . . 156 E2
Crewe CW1 . . . . 190 B6
Elton CH2 . . . . 72 A4
Haslington CW1 . . . . 191 D4
Kidsgrove ST7 . . . . 195 A1
Macclesfield SK10 . . . . 87 B1
MOUNT PLEASANT 195 B6
Mount Pleasant
Rainow SK10 . . . . 88 D3
Widnes WA8 . . . . 13 B2
Wilmslow SK9 . . . . 60 B8
MOUNT PLEASANT 149 A7
Mount Pleasant Ave
WA9 . . . . 1 B3
Mount Pleasant Dr
CW7 . . . . 149 A7
Mount Pleasant Rd
Davenham CW9 . . . . 103 F2
The Bank ST7 . . . . 195 B7
Mount Pleasant
Residential Pk CW4 . . . . 130 D8
Mount Rd
Kidsgrove ST7 . . . . 195 B2
Runcorn WA7 . . . . 49 F8
Mount St WA8 . . . . 13 A1
Mount Terr SK11 . . . . 112 F7

Mount The
Chester CH3 . . . . .118 F1
Congleton CW12 . . . . . . .156 A2
Great Budworth CW9 . . . . .79 A7
Hale WA15 . . . . .32 C8
Heswall CH60 . . . . .40 F8
Kidsgrove ST7 . . . . .195 A1
Scholar Green ST7 . . . . . .194 E7
Mount Way CH3 . . . . .143 A4
Mourne Cl CH66 . . . . .69 A6
MOW COP 195 C7
Mow Cop Rd ST7 . . . . . . .195 D6
Mowcroft La WA5 . . . . . . .14 B3
Mow La
Mount Pleasant ST7 . . . .195 A5
Mow Cop ST7 . . . . .179 B2
Mowpen Brow WA16 . . . . . .29 B6
Moxon Ave WA4 . . . . .16 F5
Moyles Cl WA8 . . . . .12 C2
Mudhouse La CH64 . . . . . .67 F2
Mudhurst La SK12 . . . . . . .38 E3
Muirfield Cl
Northwich CW9 . . . . . . .104 A5
Warrington WA2 . . . . .9 A3
Wilmslow SK9 . . . . .60 D8
Muirfield Dr
Macclesfield SK10 . . . . . .87 D4
Winsford CW7 . . . . .126 C2
Muirfield Mews CW7 . . . .126 C2
Muir Rd CH1 . . . . .117 E3
Mulberry Ave WA3 . . . . . . .3 F7
Mulberry Cl
Elton CH2 . . . . .72 C3
Gatley SK8 . . . . .34 C7
Warrington WA1 . . . . .17 C4
Mulberry Ct
Macclesfield SK11 . . . . . .112 C4
Warrington WA4 . . . . . . .16 D1
Mulberry Dr SK10 . . . . . . .87 E1
Mulberry Gdns CW11 . . . .174 D7
Mulberry Rd CW2 . . . . . .189 E2
Mulberry Rise CW8 . . . . .103 C7
Mulcaster Ct CW7 . . . . . .191 D5
Mull Cl CH65 . . . . .70 C1
Mullein Cl WA3 . . . . .3 D8
Mullins Cl WA5 . . . . .7 F1
Mullins Ave WA12 . . . . . . .2 C5
Mullion Cl WA7 . . . . .50 B6
Mullion Gr WA2 . . . . .9 A1
Mulsford Cl LL13 . . . . . . .222 A8
Mulsford La LL13,
SY14 . . . . .222 B8
MURDISHAW 50 D7
Murdishaw Ave WA7 . . . . .50 D6
Murdishaw West Com
Prim Sch WA7 . . . . .50 D6
Muriel Cl WA5 . . . . .14 D6
Murray Cl SK10 . . . . .87 A1
Murrayfield SK10 . . . . . . .87 A5
Murrayfield Dr CW5 . . . . .205 D5
Museum St WA1 . . . . .16 A4
Music Hall Pass CH1 . . . .237 B2
Muslin Row WA5 . . . . . . .172 A5
Mustard La WA3 . . . . .4 B1
Myddleton La WA2 . . . . . . .8 C6
Myrica Gr CH2 . . . . .119 B3
Myrtle Ave
Haydock WA11 . . . . .1 B7
Higher Kinnerton CH4 . . .161 A7
Newton-le-W WA12 . . . . . .2 C2
Myrtle Cl
Warrington WA4 . . . . .16 D3
Widnes WA8 . . . . .22 D8
Myrtle Rd M31 . . . . .11 D3
Myrtle St
Crewe CW2 . . . . .190 C3
Ellesmere Port CH65 . . . . .70 C7
Mytholme Ave M44 . . . . . .11 C2
Mytton Dr CW5 . . . . .204 D6

N

Nabbs Cl ST7 . . . . .195 B2
Nabbswood Rd ST7 . . . . . .195 B2
Nab Cl SK10 . . . . .63 C1
Nab La SK10 . . . . .63 C1
Nairn Ave CW4 . . . . .130 B2
Nairn Cl
Bebington CH62 . . . . .43 D4
Warrington WA2 . . . . .9 B3
Nancy View SK10 . . . . . . .88 B8
Nansen Cl WA5 . . . . .15 D7
Nansmoss La SK9 . . . . . . .33 D1
Nant Peris CH1 . . . . .117 D3
NANTWICH 204 D6
Nantwich Mus* CW5 . . . .204 E5
Nantwich Rd
Audley ST7 . . . . .209 B1
Barbridge CW5 . . . . .187 B8
Betley ST7 . . . . .208 E1
Broxton CH3 . . . . .183 C1
Chorley Bank CW5 . . . . .201 E2
Crewe CW2 . . . . .190 C2
Ellesmere Port CH66 . . . .69 F3
Middlewich CW10 . . . . . .151 A7
Sound CW5 . . . . .217 B5
Tarporley CW6 . . . . .168 D7
Wimboldsley CW10 . . . . .150 F5
Wistaston CW2, CW5 . . . .189 C2
Woore CW3 . . . . .232 B1
Nantwich Sta CW5 . . . . . .204 E4
Nantwich Trade Yd
CW5 . . . . .204 F4
Nantwich Way 6 SK9 . . . . .34 E5
Naomi Cl CH1 . . . . .117 D5
Napier Gdns 3 ST7 . . . . . .195 A2
Napier Rd CH2 . . . . .118 C8

Napier St WA1 . . . . .16 C5
Napley Dr TF9 . . . . .236 C2
NAPLEY HEATH 236 F1
Napley Rd TF9 . . . . .236 D1
Nares Cl WA3 . . . . .7 C1
Narrow La
Crewe, Crewe Green
CW1 . . . . .191 C3
Wardsend SK10 . . . . .37 A1
Naseby Rd CW12 . . . . . . .156 A3
Nathan Dr WA11 . . . . .1 E6
Nathans Mdw CW12 . . . . .179 A2
Nat La CW7 . . . . .126 F2
Nat Lane Ret Pk CW7 . . . .126 F2
Naughton Lea WA8 . . . . . .12 D3
Naughton Rd 3 WA8 . . . . .23 A8
Navan Ct CW1 . . . . .190 B5
Navigation Cl WA7 . . . . . . .50 D6
Navigation Ho 10
CW9 . . . . .103 F8
Navigation Rd CW8 . . . . .103 F7
Navigation St WA1 . . . . . .16 D5
Naylor Ave WA3 . . . . .3 B8
Naylor Cl CH66 . . . . .69 F8
Naylor Cres
Ellesmere Port CH66 . . . . .69 E6
Nantwich CW5 . . . . .205 A4
Naylor Ct
Ellesmere Port CH66 . . . . .69 E6
2 Northwich CW9 . . . . . .103 F8
Naylor Gn CH66 . . . . .69 F8
Naylor Pl CH66 . . . . .69 F8
Naylor Rd
Overpool CH66 . . . . .69 F7
Widnes WA8 . . . . .13 D1
Naylor Wlk CH1 . . . . .16 B5
Nazareth House La
WA8 . . . . .22 C7
Neal Ave SK8 . . . . .34 A8
Neath Cl SK12 . . . . .36 D5
Needham Cl WA7 . . . . .23 D2
Needham Dr
Cranage CW4 . . . . .130 A5
Hartford CW8 . . . . .103 A4
Needhams Bank
CW11 . . . . .174 C6
Needhams Wharf Cl
SK10 . . . . .88 A1
Neills Rd WA5 . . . . .6 B6
Neil St WA8 . . . . .13 C2
Nelson Ave SK12 . . . . .37 A3
Nelson Bldgs ST7 . . . . . .195 A1
Nelson Cl CW12 . . . . .156 A3
Nelson Dr M44 . . . . .11 E6
Nelson Gr WA3 . . . . .3 E7
Nelson Ind Est ST7 . . . . .194 C1
Nelson Rd CH66 . . . . .70 C7
Nelson St
Chester CH1 . . . . .237 C3
Congleton CW12 . . . . . . .156 D2
Crewe CW2 . . . . .190 C2
Macclesfield SK11 . . . . . .112 D7
Newton-le-W WA12 . . . . . .2 A3
5 Runcorn WA7 . . . . .23 A6
Widnes WA8 . . . . .23 A6
Nemos Cl WA4 . . . . .73 C2
Neptune Cl WA7 . . . . .50 D7
Nesfield Cl CW11 . . . . . . .191 F7
Nesfield Dr CW11 . . . . . . .191 F7
NESS 67 B4
Ness Acre La CH64 . . . . . .67 E8
Ness Botanic Gdns*
CH64 . . . . .67 A3
Nesse Ho CH64 . . . . .66 D8
NESS HOLT 66 F5
Nessina Gr CW2 . . . . .205 F8
NESTON 66 D7
Neston Dr CH2 . . . . .118 E5
Neston Gn CH66 . . . . .69 D4
Neston High Sch CH64 . . . .41 F1
Neston Prim Sch CH64 . . . .66 E7
Neston Rd
Heswall CH63, CH64 . . . . .41 F5
Neston CH64 . . . . .67 B3
Willaston CH64 . . . . .67 F8
Neston Road Cotts
CH63 . . . . .42 A6
Neston Sta CH64 . . . . .66 E8
Neston Way SK9 . . . . .34 D3
NETHER ALDERLEY 85 A6
Nether Alderley Mill*
SK10 . . . . .85 A5
Nether Alderley Prim Sch
SK10 . . . . .85 A6
Netherfield WA8 . . . . .22 E8
Netherfields SK9 . . . . .85 A8
Nether Fold SK10 . . . . . . .87 A8
Nether Lea CW4 . . . . .130 C8
Netherley Rd WA8 . . . . . . .12 A2
Netherpool Rd CH66 . . . . .69 F8
NETHER TABLEY 80 F8
NETHERTON 74 A6
Netherton Dr WA6 . . . . . . .74 A7
Netherton Farm Cotts
WA6 . . . . .74 A7
Neumann St CW9 . . . . . . .104 B8
Nevada Cl WA5 . . . . .15 C8
Neville Ave
St Helens WA9 . . . . .1 B2
Warrington WA4 . . . . .8 D1
Neville Cres WA5 . . . . .15 A3
Neville Dr CH3 . . . . .119 B1
Neville Rd
Bebington CH62 . . . . .43 E8
Chester CH3 . . . . .119 B1
Neville St
Crewe CW2 . . . . .190 D1

Neville St continued
Newton-le-W WA12 . . . . . .2 A3
Nevin Cl SK7 . . . . .36 A7
Nevin Rd CH1 . . . . .117 D3
Nevis Dr CW2 . . . . .189 D3
New Albert Terr WA7 . . . . .23 B3
Newall Ave CW11 . . . . . . .175 A5
Newall Cl CH3 . . . . .166 B1
Newall Cres CW7 . . . . . . .127 A1
Newarth Dr WA13 . . . . . . .19 A2
New Bank Pl WA8 . . . . . . .12 B1
New Bank Rd WA8 . . . . . . .12 B1
New Barnet WA8 . . . . .12 F4
Newbiggin Way 10
SK10 . . . . .112 C8
Newbold Ct 9 CW12 . . . . .156 F3
New Bold Ct WA9 . . . . .6 A7
Newbold Way CW5 . . . . . .204 E3
Newborough Cl WA5 . . . . . .7 E2
NEW BOSTON 1 E7
Newbridge Cl
Warrington WA7 . . . . .50 C6
Warrington WA5 . . . . .7 D2
New Bridge Rd CH65,
CH2 . . . . .70 F3
Newburgh Cl WA7 . . . . . . .24 D1
Newbury Ave
Crewe CW1 . . . . .190 C7
5 Winsford CW7 . . . . . . .149 A8
Newbury Cl
Cheadle SK8 . . . . .35 A6
Widnes WA8 . . . . .13 A3
Newbury Ct SK9 . . . . .60 A6
Newbury Rd
Chester CH4 . . . . .140 F6
Gatley SK8 . . . . .34 C7
Newby Ct CW12 . . . . .156 A1
Newcastle Rd
Astbury CW12 . . . . .178 A7
Brereton Green CW11 . . . .153 F4
Congleton CW12 . . . . . . .156 A2
Hassall Green CW11 . . . . .176 A3
Nantwich CW5 . . . . .205 B4
Shavington CW2, CW5 . . . .206 C3
Smallwood CW11 . . . . . .176 D6
Talke ST7 . . . . .210 E7
Willaston CW5 . . . . .205 E4
Woore CW3 . . . . .232 E1
Newcastle Rd N
CW11 . . . . .153 E5
Newcastle Rd S CW11 . . . .153 F5
Newcastle Road Cvn Pk
CW11 . . . . .175 C5
Newcastle St WA5 . . . . . .190 A5
NEWCASTLE-UNDER-
LYME 210 D3
NEWCHAPEL 195 E2
Newchapel Obsy*
ST7 . . . . .195 E2
Newchapel Rd ST7 . . . . . .195 C3
New Chester Rd CH62 . . . .43 E7
Newchurch Com Prim Sch
WA3 . . . . .4 E2
Newchurch La WA3 . . . . . . .4 F2
Newcombe Ave WA2 . . . . .16 E8
New Cotts
Hampton Heath SY14 . . . .213 E7
Manley WA6 . . . . .99 C7
New Crane Bank CH1 . . . . .118 B1
New Crane St CH1 . . . . . . .118 B1
Newcroft CH1 . . . . .94 B2
New Cut Ind Est WA1 . . . . .17 C7
New Cut La WA1 . . . . .17 B7
Newdigate St
Crewe CW1 . . . . .190 C4
Crewe CW1 . . . . .190 C5
New Farm Cotts WA3 . . . . .11 A7
New Farm Ct
Great Barrow CH3 . . . . . .120 E5
Malpas SY14 . . . . .213 A5
NEWFIELD 195 D7
Newfield Cl WA13 . . . . . . .19 A5
Newfield Dr CW11 . . . . . . .190 E5
Newfield Rd WA13 . . . . . . .18 D3
Newfield St CW11 . . . . . . .175 B7
Newfield Terr WA6 . . . . . . .73 B2
Newgate
1 Macclesfield SK11 . . . .112 D7
Wilmslow SK9 . . . . .59 E7
Newgate Rd SK9 . . . . .59 D7
Newgate St CH1 . . . . .237 B2
Newgate Wlk CH1 . . . . . . .237 B2
New Grosvenor Rd
CH65 . . . . .70 B7
NEWHALL 228 C8
New Hall Ave SK8 . . . . . . .34 B7
Newhall Ct CH2 . . . . .118 E6
New Hall La
Culcheth WA3 . . . . .5 A2
Culcheth, Wigshaw WA3 . . .4 E1
New Hall Manor CH64 . . . . .41 E6
Newhall Rd CH2 . . . . .118 F6
New Hall St SK10 . . . . .87 D1
Newham Cl SK11 . . . . .112 F3
New Hampshire Cl 7
WA8 . . . . .15 B7
Newhaven Ct CW5 . . . . . .204 F5
Newhaven Rd WA2 . . . . . . .8 B4
New Heyes CH64 . . . . .41 E1
New Hey La CH64 . . . . . . .68 A6
New Home Farm Cotts
CH64 . . . . .93 A7
NEW HORWICH 65 C6
New Horwich Rd SK23 . . . .65 E7
New Hos CW5 . . . . .187 D6
New Houses CH3 . . . . . . .143 B7
New Inn Cotts WA16 . . . .108 C8

New Inn La CW11 . . . . . . .176 A2
New King St
Audley ST7 . . . . .209 C1
Middlewich CW10 . . . . . .128 C2
New La
Appleton Thorn WA4 . . . . .27 B5
Churton CH3 . . . . .180 F6
Croft WA3 . . . . .9 B7
Harthill CH3 . . . . .183 F3
Winsford CW7 . . . . .149 F4
Newland Cl WA8 . . . . .12 C3
Newland Mews WA3 . . . . . .4 E5
Newlands Ave
Bramhall SK7 . . . . .35 F8
Cheadle SK8 . . . . .35 A7
Newlands Cl
Cheadle SK8 . . . . .35 A7
Frodsham WA6 . . . . .74 C8
Newlands Dr
Golborne WA3 . . . . .3 D8
Wilmslow SK9 . . . . .59 E5
Newlands Rd
Macclesfield SK10 . . . . . .111 E7
Warrington WA4 . . . . .16 F2
Newland Way CW5 . . . . . .205 B4
NEW LANE END 4 A2
New Lane End WA3 . . . . . . .4 A2
Newlyn Ave
Congleton CW12 . . . . . . .178 F8
Macclesfield SK10 . . . . . .86 D1
Newlyn Cl WA7 . . . . .50 B6
Newlyn Gdns WA5 . . . . . . .14 D3
New Manchester Rd
WA1 . . . . .17 A7
Newman Cl CW12 . . . . . . .156 B3
New Manor Rd WA4 . . . . . .51 B6
Newman's La CW5 . . . . . .219 D8
Newman St WA4 . . . . .16 F3
Newmarket Cl 1 SK10 . . . .87 C4
New Market Wlk 10
WA1 . . . . .16 B5
New Meadowside
Residential Cvn Pk
CW5 . . . . .217 E5
NEW MILLS 39 D7
New Mills Central Sta
SK22 . . . . .39 B7
New Mills Heritage Ctr*
SK22 . . . . .39 B7
New Mills Newtown Sta
SK22 . . . . .39 B6
New Mills Prim Sch
SK22 . . . . .39 B8
New Mills Sch & Sixth
Form Ctr SK22 . . . . .39 C8
Newmoore La WA7 . . . . . . .24 F4
New Moss Rd M44 . . . . . . .11 D6
Newnham Dr CH65 . . . . . .70 C4
New Pale Rd WA6 . . . . . . .99 C6
New Park Ct SK22 . . . . . . .39 D7
New Platt La CW4 . . . . . . .107 B1
Newport Gr ST5 . . . . .210 E2
Newquay Cl WA7 . . . . .50 B6
Newquay Ct CW12 . . . . . .178 E8
Newquay Dr
Bramhall SK7 . . . . .35 F7
Macclesfield SK10 . . . . . .111 D8
New Rd
Anderton CW9 . . . . .78 D4
Antrobus CW9 . . . . .27 D1
Astbury CW12 . . . . .178 B4
Audley ST7 . . . . .209 E3
Duddon CW6 . . . . .145 B6
Ellesmere Port CH66 . . . . .69 A8
Horwich End SK23 . . . . . .65 E6
Lymm WA13 . . . . .18 E3
Marton CW12 . . . . .132 D1
Mossend CW11 . . . . .154 F2
Prestbury SK10 . . . . .87 A7
Rostherne WA16 . . . . . . .30 C3
Warrington WA4 . . . . .16 C4
Whaley Bridge, Bridgemont
SK23 . . . . .39 F1
Winsford CW7 . . . . .126 C2
Wrenbury CW5 . . . . .216 D3
New Road Bsns Ctr
CW7 . . . . .126 C2
New Russia Hall Craft
Ctr* CH3 . . . . .165 E5
Newry Ct CH2 . . . . .118 D4
Newry Pk CH2 . . . . .118 D4
Newry Pk E CH2 . . . . .118 D4
NEWSBANK 132 F1
New School La CH66 . . . . . .44 B1
Newsham Cl WA8 . . . . . . .12 B4
Newsholme Cl WA3 . . . . . . .4 F3
Newspaper Ho WA5 . . . . . .14 D3
New St
Congleton CW12 . . . . . . .156 E2
Haslington CW1 . . . . .191 C5
Neston CH64 . . . . .66 E5
New Mills SK22 . . . . .39 D7
9 Runcorn WA7 . . . . .23 A2
Sandbach CW11 . . . . . . .174 D7
Widnes WA8 . . . . .23 A6
Wilmslow SK9 . . . . .59 E5
Newstead Cl SK12 . . . . . . .36 D5
Newstead Rd WA8 . . . . . . .21 F6
New Street Cotts
CW12 . . . . .157 A6
Newtech Sq CH5 . . . . .92 F2
NEWTON
Chester 118 F5
Frodsham 74 D3
Tattenhall 166 E4
Newton Ave WA3 . . . . .9 E5
Newton Bank
Middlewich CW10 . . . . . .128 B1

Newton Bank continued
Preston on t H WA4 . . . . .51 B8
Newton Bank Sch WA12 . . . .2 E4
Newton Com Hospl
WA12 . . . . .2 B2
Newton Cotts CH3 . . . . . .166 C4
Newton Gdns WA3 . . . . . . .4 A8
Newton Gr WA2 . . . . .8 F3
Newton Hall Ct CH2 . . . . .118 F5
Newton Hall Ct CH2 . . . . .118 F5
Newton Hall Dr CH2 . . . . .118 F5
Newton Hall La WA16 . . . . .58 E5
Newton Hall Mews 1
CW10 . . . . .151 C8
Newton Heath CW12 . . . . .128 B3
Newton Ho CH2 . . . . .118 F5
Newton Hollow WA6 . . . . . .74 D1
NEWTONIA 128 B1
Newton La
Chester CH2 . . . . .118 F4
Daresbury WA4 . . . . .51 C8
Daresbury WA4 . . . . .51 E7
Golborne WA12 . . . . .2 E6
Tattenhall CH3 . . . . .166 D4
NEWTON-LE-WILLOWS 2 B2
Newton-le-Willows Com
High Sch WA12 . . . . .2 D5
Newton-le-Willows Prim
Sch WA12 . . . . .2 C3
Newton-le-Willows Sta
WA12 . . . . .2 E3
Newton Park Dr WA12 . . . . .2 F3
Newton Park View
CH2 . . . . .118 D4
Newton Pl CW12 . . . . .156 F2
Newton Prim Sch
CH2 . . . . .118 E4
Newton Rd
Ellesmere Port CH65 . . . . .70 C5
Golborne, Lowton Common
WA3, WN7 . . . . .4 A8
Golborne, Town of Lowton
WA12, WA3 . . . . .3 D5
Handforth SK9 . . . . .34 A1
St Helens WA3 . . . . .1 A3
Winwick WA2 . . . . .8 A5
Newtons Cres CW11 . . . . .191 F7
Newtons Gr CW11 . . . . . . .191 E7
Newtons La CW11 . . . . . . .191 E7
Newton St
Crewe CW1 . . . . .190 D5
Macclesfield SK11 . . . . . .112 C7
NEWTOWN
Burwardsley 183 E8
Frodsham 49 D1
Newtown
Neston CH64 . . . . .66 F7
Newchapel ST7 . . . . .195 F2
NEWTOWN
New Mills 39 B6
Poynton 37 A3
Sound 217 E4
Widnes 23 A6
Newtown Cl CH1 . . . . .237 B3
Newtown Prim Sch
SK22 . . . . .39 B6
New Warrington Rd
CW9 . . . . .79 C2
New William Cl M31 . . . . . .11 F4
NEW WOODHOUSES 227 E1
New York Cotts WA16 . . . . .29 F2
New York Cvn Pk CW9 . . . .104 C6
Nicholas Ave CH3 . . . . . . .237 A2
Nicholas Rd
Weaverham CW8 . . . . .77 D1
Widnes WA8 . . . . .22 C8
Nicholas St Mews
CH1 . . . . .237 A2
Nicholas St CH1 . . . . .237 A2
Nicholls St WA4 . . . . .17 B2
Nicholson Ave SK10 . . . . . .87 E1
Nicholson Cl SK10 . . . . . . .87 E1
Nicholson St WA1 . . . . .15 F5
NICK I' TH' HILL 179 B4
Nickleby Rd SK12 . . . . .36 E3
Nickleford Hall Dr
WA8 . . . . .12 F6
Nickolson Cl CH2 . . . . . . .119 F8
Nicol Ave WA1 . . . . .17 F8
Nidderdale Cl CW12 . . . . .157 A5
Niddries Ct CW9 . . . . .126 F7
Niddries La CW9 . . . . .126 F7
Nield Ct CH2 . . . . .118 D7
Nigel Gresley Cl CW1 . . . .191 A4
Nigel Rd CH60 . . . . .41 C8
Nightingale Cl
Farndon CH3 . . . . .180 F1
Handforth SK9 . . . . .34 B1
Middlewich CW10 . . . . . .151 D6
Runcorn WA7 . . . . .49 F5
Warrington WA3 . . . . .9 F4
Nightingale Ct 4
CW7 . . . . .149 D6
Nightingale Way ST7 . . . . .193 B3
Nile St CW2 . . . . .190 D2
Nine Hos The CH3 . . . . . .166 B1
Nixon Dr CW7 . . . . .126 B2
Nixon Rd CW8 . . . . .101 F3
Nixon's Row CW5 . . . . . . .204 C5
Nixon St
Crewe CW1 . . . . .189 F5
Macclesfield SK11 . . . . . .112 B8
No 1 Road N CW2 . . . . . .192 F1
No 1 Road S CW2 . . . . . . .192 F1

No 2 Road N CW2 ....192 F1
No 2 Road S CW2 ....192 F1
No 156 CH1 ....237 C2
Noahs Ark La WA16......58 F1
Noble Cl WA3 ....9 E3
NO MAN'S HEATH 214 B4
Nook La
 Antrobus CW9 ....53 E6
 Golborne WA3 ....3 B8
 Warrington, Fearnhead
  WA2 ....9 B2
 Warrington WA4 ....17 A3
Nook The
 Backford CH1 ....95 B4
 Bramhall SK7 ....35 D5
 Chester CH2 ....118 E4
 Guilden Sutton CH3 ....119 C4
 Hankelow CW3 ....230 C8
 Saltney CH4 ....140 E6
Noon Ct WA12 ....2 B1
Noonsun Farm WA16 ....58 E1
Nora St WA1 ....16 C5
Norbreck Ave CW2 ......190 B2
Norbreck Cl WA5 ....15 A4
NORBURY 215 D4
Norbury Ave WA2........16 D8
Norbury Cl
 Hough CW2 ....206 E3
 Knutsford WA16 ....57 C3
 Widnes WA8 ....13 E1
NORBURY COMMON
 ....215 C6
Norbury Dr
 Congleton CW12 ....156 E4
 Middlewich CW10 ......151 B8
Norbury Hollow Rd
 SK7..........................37 B8
Norbury St
 Macclesfield SK11 ......112 C7
 Northwich CW9 ....104 B8
Norbury Town La
 SY13........................215 C3
Norbury Way 9 SK9....34 D5
Norcott Ave WA4 ....16 D2
NORCOTT BROOK 52 C6
Norcott Dr WA5 ....9 C6
Norden Cl WA3 ....9 D5
Norfolk Cl WA4 ....11 C5
Norfolk Dr WA5 ....14 E6
Norfolk Gr ST8 ....179 C1
Norfolk Ho ST7 ....210 D6
Norfolk House Prep Sch
 CW11.......................175 B7
Norfolk Pl WA8...........22 C8
Norfolk Rd
 Chester CH2 ....118 F4
 Congleton CW12 ....156 E4
 Ellesmere Port CH65...70 C5
 Kidsgrove ST7 ....194 F2
Norfolk St WA7 ....23 B3
Norfolk Wlk SK10........86 F2
Norgrove Cl WA7 ....50 E8
Norland's La L35, WA8....12 F7
Norlands Pk WA8........12 F6
Norland St WA8 ....13 D1
Norleane Cres WA7......49 B8
NORLEY 100 F6
Norley Ave
 Bebington CH62..........43 E3
 Ellesmere Port CH65...69 F6
Norley CE Prim Sch
 WA6 ....100 F5
Norley Cl WA5..............15 E6
Norley Dr CH3 ....119 C1
Norley La CW8 ....101 A8
Norley Pl CW7 ....103 E5
Norley Rd
 Cuddington CW8,
  WA6 ....101 E4
 Kingsley WA6..............75 A1
 Norley WA6 ....100 D7
 Sandiway CW8............102 A3
Norman Ave
 Haydock WA11.............2 A7
 Newton-le-W WA12 ......2 E3
Normanby Cl WA5 ....15 E7
Norman Cl CH66..........94 F8
Norman Dr CW7 ....149 C6
Normandy Ave 2
 CW7..........................149 D8
Normandy Rd CH2......95 C1
Norman Ho 3 CW8......103 C5
Norman Rd WA7.........23 A1
Normans Cotts 1
 CH64 ....66 F7
Norman's Hall Farm
 ....63 B5
Norman's La WA4 ......52 F4
Norman St WA2 ....16 B6
Norman Way CH1.......117 E5
Norreys Ave WA5.........15 F8
Norris Rd CH1.............117 E5
Norris St WA2 ....16 D8
North Ave WA2............16 B8
Northbank Ind Pk WA4...11 F6
Northbank Wlk CW2...206 C8
North Brook Rd CW6...146 B7
Northbury Rd CH66......69 E1
North Cheshire Coll
 (Museum St Ctr)
 WA1.........................16 A4
North Cheshire Hospl
 WA4..........................26 D1
Northcote Rd SK7........35 F7
North Crofts CW5........204 E5

Northdale Rd WA1........17 A8
North Downs WA16......57 D2
North Dr
 Heswall CH60 ....41 A7
 High Legh WA16.........29 C4
 Northwich CW9 ....104 E7
Northern La WA8..........12 A3
Northern Pathway
 CH4 ....237 C1
Northern Rise CH66......69 E4
Northfield Dr
 Biddulph ST8 ....179 E2
 Wilmslow SK9 ....60 D8
Northfield Pl CW2 ......206 C5
Northfields WA16........57 C3
NORTH FLORIDA 1 D8
North Florida Rd WA11...1 D8
Northgate CW6...........146 B7
Northgate Ave
 Chester CH2 ....237 B4
 Macclesfield SK10......87 C1
Northgate Row CH1....237 B2
Northgate St CH1.......237 A3
North Gn CH5 ....116 A6
Northlands CW3 ....232 C1
Northmead SK10........87 A5
Northolt Ct WA2..........8 E1
North Par CH64..........41 B2
North Park Brook Rd
 WA5...........................7 E1
North Rd
 Altrincham WA15........32 A8
 Bebington CH65..........44 E3
 Connah's Quay CH5....91 F2
 Ellesmere Port CH65...70 B8
 Halewood L26 ....21 A5
NORTH RODE 134 E2
North St
 Chester CH3 ....119 A1
 Congleton CW12 ....156 D3
 Crewe CW1 ....190 C7
 Haydock WA11............1 E6
 Mount Pleasant ST7...195 B6
 Newton-le-W WA12 ......1 F4
 Saltney CH4 ....140 B7
 Sandycroft CH5 ....116 A3
North Stafford St
 CW1.........................190 D4
Northumberland Rd
 M31............................11 E2
North View
 Crewe CW1 ....190 A6
 Ellesmere Port CH66...69 C7
 Middlewich CW10 ......128 B2
 Warrington WA5 ....14 E7
Northward Rd SK9......59 F6
Northway
 Chester CH4 ....141 A7
 Lymm WA13...............18 D4
 Runcorn WA7..............49 F8
 Warrington WA2 ....8 B2
 Widnes WA8 ....12 D1
 Winnington CW8.........78 D1
North Way
 Holmes Chapel CW4 ..130 C3
 Shavington CW2 ....206 D5
NORTHWICH 103 D8
Northwich Rd
 Allostock CW4, WA16..106 E1
 Antrobus CW9 ....53 B2
 Dutton WA4...............51 B3
 Great Budworth CW9..78 F8
 Knutsford WA16 ....56 D1
 Runcorn, Brookvale WA7..50 C5
 Weaverham CW8........102 E7
 Northwich Ret Pk CW9 ...79 C1
 Northwich Sta CW9 ...104 B8
Northwood Ave
 Middlewich CW10 ......151 C5
 Newton-le-W WA12....2 F3
Northwood La WA16....28 F1
Northwood Rd WA7....23 C2
NORTON 24 C1
Norton Ave
 Saltney CH4 ....140 D6
 Warrington WA5 ....14 E5
Norton Cotts WA7 ......50 E7
Norton Gate WA7........50 C8
Norton Hill WA7..........24 C2
NORTON IN HALES 236 C1
Norton in Hales CE Prim
 Sch TF9 ....236 C2
Norton La
 Runcorn, Norton WA7....24 D1
 Runcorn, Town Park
  WA7 ....50 A8
 Runcorn WA7.............50 B8
Norton Priory Mus*
 WA7..........................24 B3
Norton Priory Walled
 Gdn* WA7 ....24 B3
Norton Rd CH3 ....119 C2
Nortons La CW6 ....122 F7
Norton's La CH3.........98 B2
Norton St SK10 ....112 E8
Norton Station Rd
 WA7..........................50 A8
Norton View WA7........50 A8
Norton Village WA7....24 D1
Norton Way CW11.....174 D7
Nortonwood La WA7...24 C1
Norville CH66 ....69 D7
Norwich Ave WA3.........3 D8
Norwich Dr CH66........94 E8
Norwood Ave
 Bramhall SK7..............35 D5
 Golborne WA3 ....3 F7
 High Lane SK6............37 D7

Norwood Dr CH4 ....141 B6
Nottingham Cl WA1.....17 E6
Nova Ct 14 CW1 ....190 B5
NOVA SCOTIA 125 C6
Nun House Cl CW7......127 B2
Nun House Dr CW7.....127 B2
Nunsmere Cl CW7......127 B1
Nuns Rd CH1.............237 A1
Nursery Ave WA15......31 E8
Nursery Cl
 Crewe CW2 ....190 A2
 Kidsgrove ST7 ....194 D1
 Shavington CW2 ....206 C3
 Widnes WA8 ....13 D3
Nursery Dr
 Biddulph ST8 ....179 C2
 Poynton SK12............36 D4
Nursery Gr M31...........11 F4
Nursery La
 Congleton CW12 ....156 E2
 Nether Alderley SK10...84 D5
 Siddington SK11 ....110 A3
 Wilmslow SK9 ....59 F5
Nursery Pk WA6.........100 B7
Nursery Rd
 Barnton CW8 ....78 B3
 Bollington SK10..........87 E7
 Oakhanger CW1, ST7 ...192 D3
 Scholar Green ST7.....194 E5
Nursery The CW8 ......103 C6
Nutfield Ave CW1.......190 B7
Nuthurst Gdns 4
 CW5..........................204 F5
Nuttall Ct WA3 ....9 C4
Nuttall St M44.............11 E6

O

Oak Ave
 Alsager ST7 ....193 E2
 Disley SK12 ....39 A6
 Golborne WA3 ....3 B8
 Haydock WA11.............1 E7
 Irlam M44 ....11 D5
 Macclesfield SK11 ......112 A5
 Newton-le-W WA12......2 D3
 Wilmslow SK9 ....59 F5
 Winsford CW7............149 D7
Oak Bank
 Alderley Edge SK9.......60 A2
 Disley SK12 ....39 A6
Oak Bank Cl CW5......205 E4
Oak Bank Dr SK10......63 B1
Oak Bank La CH2 ......119 C6
Oak Brow Cotts SK9....33 E4
Oak Cl SK9 ....59 F6
Oak Cotts
 Styal SK9 ....33 E4
 Wrenbury CW5 ....216 F4
Oakdale Ave
 Frodsham WA6 ....74 D6
 Warrington WA4 ....16 D1
Oakdale Cl
 Broughton CH4 ....139 B3
 Chorlton CW2 ....207 B3
Oakdene Ave
 Ellesmere Port CH66...69 C5
 Gatley SK8................34 C7
 Warrington WA1 ....17 C7
Oakdene Cl CH2.........43 D5
Oakdene Ct SK9..........34 B1
Oakdene Way CW6 .....168 D8
Oak Dr
 Cheadle SK7 ....35 C7
 Higher Kinnerton CH4..161 A7
 Middlewich CW10 ......151 D7
 Runcorn WA7.............49 C7
 Scholar Green ST7.....194 E6
Oakenbank La SK10....88 D7
Oakenclough Cl SK9...34 D2
Oakes Cnr CW5..........219 E3
Oak Farm CW6 ....186 C5
Oakfield Ave
 Chester CH2 ....118 E8
 Knutsford WA16 ....57 C3
 Wrenbury CW5 ....216 F3
Oakfield Cl
 Alderley Edge SK9.......60 B3
 Bramhall SK7..............35 E4
 Wrenbury CW5 ....216 F3
Oakfield Com Prim Sch
 WA8..........................22 B8
Oakfield Dr
 Chester CH2 ....118 E8
 Widnes WA8 ....22 A8
Oakfield Rd
 Alderley Edge SK9.......60 B2
 Bebington CH62..........43 C8
 Blacon CH1 ....117 D4
 Ellesmere Port CH66...68 E8
 Plumley WA16 ....80 F3
 Poynton SK12............36 F4
Oakfield Rise CW4......130 B3
Oakfield Terr CH66......68 E8
Oakfold SK10 ....88 A6
Oak Gr
 Ellesmere Port CH65...70 A3
 Nantwich CW5...........204 E3
 Poynton SK12............36 D4
Oak Gr/Gelli Dderw
 CH4 ....140 D5
OAKGROVE 135 D7
Oak Grove Sch SK8....34 C7
OAKHANGER 192 C2
Oakhill Cl SK10...........87 B4
Oak Ho
 Chester CH2 ....118 C5

Oak Ho continued
 7 Sandbach CW11......175 B6
Oak House La CW7 ....149 B8
Oakhurst Chase SK9....60 A2
Oakhurst Dr CW2.......206 B7
Oak La
 Astbury CW12 ....178 B4
 Cuddington CW8 ....101 F2
 Kerridge SK10............88 A6
 Marton SK11 ....133 C5
 Wilmslow SK9 ....59 F6
Oakland Ave CW1.......191 C4
Oakland Ct SK12.........36 D4
Oakland Gdns WA1.....16 E7
Oaklands
 Bebington CH62..........43 D6
 Guilden Sutton CH3....119 F4
Oaklands Ave CH3 .....166 B2
Oaklands Cl SK9..........34 E1
Oaklands Cres CH3 ....166 B2
Oaklands Dr WA13......18 D2
Oaklands Inf Sch SK9...34 E1
Oaklands Rd
 Golborne WA3 ....3 F7
 Ollerton WA16............82 F6
Oaklands Sch CW7.....149 B7
Oakland St
 Warrington WA1 ....16 E7
 Widnes WA8 ....23 A4
Oaklea Ave CH2.........118 F4
Oak Lea Ave SK9.........60 A5
Oakleaf Lo SK11.........112 D5
Oakleigh WA16............82 C7
Oakleigh Cl CW12 ......155 F3
Oakleigh Ho SK10......88 B8
Oakleigh Rd SK8........34 E8
Oakleigh Rise CW8 .....78 E1
Oakley Cl CW11 ....175 A8
Oakley Ct CH65..........70 C4
Oakley St WA1 ....190 C5
Oak Lo SK7................35 F7
Oakmere CW8 ....102 E7
OAKMERE 124 A7
Oakmere Barns CW8...124 A7
Oakmere Cl CW11......174 F7
Oakmere Dr
 Chester CH3 ....142 B8
 Ellesmere Port CH66...69 F1
 Warrington WA5 ....14 F3
Oakmere Hall CW8....101 E1
Oakmere Pl 8 CW1....190 B5
Oakmere Rd
 Handforth SK9............34 D5
 Winsford CW7............149 B8
Oak Mews SK9............34 C1
Oakmoore WA7...........24 F4
Oak Rd
 Chelford SK11.............84 A3
 Chester CH4 ....140 F6
 Hooton CH66 ....43 E1
 Lymm WA13...............18 C3
 Mottram St Andrew
  SK10.......................86 B7
 Paddockhill WA16 ......59 B5
 Partington M31 ....11 D2
 Warrington WA5 ....14 F3
Oaks Com Prim Sch The
 CH65 ....70 D3
Oaks Dr The CH2 ......118 D7
Oaks Gdns WA5..........14 E4
Oaks Pl WA8 ....23 A7
Oak St
 Crewe CW2 ....190 D3
 Croft WA3 ....9 A7
 Ellesmere Port CH65...70 C7
 Northwich CW9 ....79 A1
 Rode Heath ST7........193 E8
 Sandbach CW11 ....174 D8
Oaks The
 Bebington CH62..........43 C8
 Goostrey CW4 ....130 D8
 Mobberley WA16.........58 E1
 8 Northwich CW9 .....103 E6
Oaksway CH60.............41 C6
Oakthorn Gr WA11......11 C6
Oaktree Cl
 Barnton CW8 ....78 B4
 Tarporley CW6...........146 D2
Oak Tree Cl CW1........190 F5
Oaktree Ct CH2 ....119 A3
Oak Tree Ct CW6........146 D1
Oak Tree Dr CW1.......190 F5
Oak Tree Gate CW3...229 F3
Oaktree La ST7 ....210 D5
Oak Tree La CW10 .....129 E7
Oak View
 Knutsford WA16 ....57 C1
 Marton SK11 ....133 C5
 Speke L24 ....21 A3
Oak Villas CW5............26 D4
Oakways WA4..............26 D5
OAKWOOD 9 F4
Oakwood Ave
 Warrington WA1 ....16 E7
 Wilmslow SK9 ....59 E6
Oakwood Avenue Com
 Prim Sch WA1............16 D7
Oakwood Cl CH66......69 D1
Oakwood Cres
 Crewe CW2 ....189 E4
 Sandbach CW11 ....175 E6
Oakwood Ct WA14......31 B8
Oakwood Dr SK10 ......87 C6
Oakwood Gate WA3....9 D4

Oakwood Ho
 Alderley Edge SK9......85 B8
 Barnton CW8 ....78 A2
Oakwood La
 Altrincham WA14.......31 B8
 Barnton CW8 ....78 A2
 Sandbach CW11 ....174 B8
Oakwood Pk CH62......43 D5
Oakwood Rd
 Disley SK12 ....38 D6
 Rode Heath ST7........193 F8
Oak Wood Rd WA16....29 F2
Oakworth Cl CW12....156 C3
Oathills SY14.............213 B5
Oathills Cl CW6..........146 D1
Oathills Dr CW6 ....146 D1
Oathills Lea CW6.......146 D1
Oatlands SK9..............85 B8
Oat Market 3 CW5....204 E5
Oban Dr CH60.............41 A8
Oban Gr WA3...............9 A3
Obelisk Way CW12....156 C3
OCCLESTONE GREEN
 ....151 B2
O'Connell Cl WA11......1 C6
Oddfellows Pas CW10..128 B1
Odeon Bldg CH1........237 A3
Offal Pit La WA6..........74 F2
Offley Ave CW11........175 B7
Offley Prim Sch
 CW11.......................175 B7
Offley Rd CW11..........175 B7
Off Spring Bank SK22...39 C8
Ogden Rd SK7.............35 D5
Oglet La L24 ....45 C6
Oil Sites Rd CH65.......71 C5
Okell St WA7 ....23 A2
Old Albert Terr WA7....23 B3
Old Alder La WA2, WA5...7 D5
Old Applecroft CW11...174 C5
OLD BOSTON 2 A8
Old Boston WA11..........2 A7
Old Boston Trad Est
 WA11..........................2 B8
Old Brickworks Ind Est
 SK10..........................63 E4
Old Butt La ST7 ....194 D2
OLDCASTLE HEATH 223 E8
Oldcastle La SY14......222 E8
Old Cherry La WA13....28 A7
Old Chester Ct CW5...187 D6
Old Chester Rd
 Barbridge CW5 ....187 D6
 Ellesmere Port CH66...69 D4
 Helsby WA6 ....73 C4
 Higher Walton WA4.....25 F7
Old Church Cl CH65....70 C7
Old Coach Rd
 Brown Knowl SY14,
  CH3..........................199 B6
 Kelsall CW6 ....122 D5
 Runcorn WA7.............24 F4
Old Constabulary The 1
 CW5..........................204 D5
Old Court Ho The 9
 WA16..........................57 A2
Olde George The CH1...237 B3
Old Farm Cl
 Macclesfield SK10......87 A2
 Willaston CH64 ....68 A8
Old Farm Cotts CH1...116 E3
Old Farm Mews SK8...35 C7
Oldfield Cres CH4 .....140 F5
Oldfield Dr
 Chester CH3 ....119 C2
 Mobberley WA16.........58 A4
Oldfield La WA4 ....20 F4
Oldfield Prim Sch
 CH3 ....119 C3
Oldfield Rd
 Ellesmere Port CH65...70 B5
 Lymm WA13...............18 C4
 Sandbach CW11 ....174 F3
Oldgate WA8 ....22 C7
Old Gate Cl CW10......151 B7
Old Gorse Cl CW2......189 C3
OLD HALL 15 C8
Old Hall Cl WA4 ....26 A8
Oldhall Cres SK9........34 E3
Old Hall Ct
 Ashton Hayes CH3......121 F7
 Malpas SY14 ....213 B3
Old Hall Dr
 Ellesmere Port CH65...70 B4
 Horwich End SK23 .....65 E4
Old Hall Gdns CH2....237 C4
Old Hall La
 Elton CH2 ....72 B3
 Hargrave CH3 ....144 A1
 Over Tabley WA16 ......55 E4
 Woodford SK7 ....35 D1
Old Hall Pl CH1 ....119 F5
Old Hall Pl CH1 ....237 A2
Old Hall Rd
 Northwich CW9 ....104 A5
 Warrington WA5 ....15 D7
Oldhall St SY14.........213 B3
Old Hall St SK10........87 D1
Oldhams Hill
 Kingsmead CW8 ....103 F8
 Winsford CW8............78 F1
Oldham's Rise SK10...87 D3
Oldham St
 Bollington SK10..........88 B8
 Warrington WA4 ....16 D3
Old Hey Wlk WA12......2 C1
Old Higher Rd WA8....21 D5
Oldhill Cl ST7 ....210 E5

Old Hutte La L26 ....21 A6
Old Knutsford Rd
ST7 ....194 A6
Old La
Acton Bridge CW8 ......76 F3
Antrobus CW9 ....53 C3
Davenham CW9 ....104 D2
Heswall CH60 ....41 D8
Mouldsworth CH3 ......99 C2
Pulford CH4 ....162 E4
Old Library The CW7 ..126 E1
Old Liverpool Rd WA5 ..15 E4
Old Man of Mow'*
ST7 ....195 D8
Old Market PI
8 Knutsford WA16 .....57 A2
12 Warrington WA1 .....16 B5
Old Marsh Farm Ho
CH5 ....116 A8
Old Mill CI
Heswall CH60 ....41 B7
Lymm WA13 ....18 D1
Old Mill Ct CW2 ......118 D6
Old Mill La
Hazel Grove SK7 ....37 A8
Higher Whitley WA4 ....52 F3
Macclesfield SK11 .....112 E6
Old Mill PI CH3 ....166 B1
Old Mill Rd CW11 ......175 C6
Old Mill The
Crowton CW8 ....76 B2
Ellesmere Port CH66 ....69 C7
OLD MOSS 144 D7
Old Moss La
Fowley Common WA3 ....5 E6
Tarvin CH3 ....144 D7
Old Newcastle Rd
CW5 ....205 D4
Old Orchard The
Antrobus CW9 ....53 C4
Cuddington CW8 ....101 F4
Old Paddock The
CW4 ....130 F8
Old Pale Cotts CH8 ...123 C7
Old Pale Hts CW8 .....123 C7
Old Park Rd CW1 ......207 D8
Old Pearl La CH3 .....119 B1
Old Penny La WA11 ....2 B8
Old Pewterspear La
WA4 ....26 E4
Old Port Sq CH1 .....118 B2
Old Pump Ho The
CH66 ....68 E8
Old Quay CI CH4 ....66 C7
Old Quay La CW8 ......66 D7
Old Quay St WA7 ......23 B3
Old Quays The WA4 ....16 E3
Old Rd
Anderton CW9 ....78 D3
Audley ST7 ....209 A3
Furness Vale SK23 .....39 D4
Handforth SK9 ....34 D3
Hornick End, New Horwich
SK23 ....65 E6
Horwich End SK23 ......65 E5
Warrington WA4 ....16 B4
Wilmslow SK9 ....60 B8
Old Ribbon Mill The
SK11 ....112 D6
Old School CI
Barnton CW8 ....78 B2
Farndon CH3 ....180 E2
Kidsgrove ST7 ....195 A1
Neston CH64 ....66 F5
Old School House La
WA2 ....8 A7
Old School La SK8 .....35 A8
Old Seals Way CH1 ....118 A3
Old Smithy La WA13 ...18 C2
Old Smithy Row SK22 ...39 C7
Old Stack Yd CH3 .....120 C6
Old Tannery CW5 .....204 F6
Old Upton La WA8 .....12 E4
Old Vicarage Gdn
CW3 ....230 A3
Old Vicarage La CW8 ..103 C5
Old Vicarage Rd CH64 ..68 A8
Old Wargrave Rd WA12 ..2 C3
Old Warrington Rd
CW9 ....79 A2
Old Wesleyan
Schoolhouse The
SK22 ....39 B6
Old Whint Rd WA11 .....1 A6
Old Woman's La CH3 ...142 D7
OLD WOODHOUSES 227 C2
Old Wrexham Rd CH4 ..141 C7
O'leary St WA2 ....16 C7
Olive Dr CH6 ....66 F8
Olive Gr ST5 ....210 D1
Oliver CI SK10 ....87 F7
Olive Rd CH64 ....66 E8
Oliver Ho CH66 ....69 D4
Oliver La CH66 ....69 D4
Oliver St WA2 ....16 B6
Ollersett Ave SK22 ....39 D8
Ollersett Dr SK22 .....39 D8
Ollersett Ho SK22 .....39 D8
Ollershaw La CW9 ......79 C4
Ollerton CI WA4 ....17 B3
Ollerton Pk WA5 ....6 E7
Ollerton Rd SK9 ....34 E5
Ollier St 1 WA8 ....13 A7
Olympia PI WA5 ....15 A7
Omega Bvd WA5 ....6 D1
One Oak La SK9 ....60 F7

ONNELEY 232 F3
Onslow Rd CH1 ....117 D4
ONSTON 76 E1
Onston La CW8 ....101 E8
On The Air', The
Broadcasting Mus &
Vintage Sound Shop*
CH1 ....237 B2
Openshaw La M44 ....11 E6
Orange Gr WA2 ....8 E2
Orchard Ave
Acton Bridge CW8 ......76 E4
Lymm WA13 ....18 F3
Partington M31 ....11 F4
Whaley Bridge SK23 ....65 D7
Orchard Brow WA3 ......11 A2
Orchard CI
Barnton CW8 ....78 B3
Bunbury CW6 ....185 F8
Cheadle SK8 ....35 C7
Chester CH4 ....118 D5
Ellesmere Port CH66 ....69 F1
Frodsham WA6 ....74 A6
Goostrey CW4 ....107 E1
Higher Wincham CW9 ....80 A6
Macclesfield SK11 .....112 B6
Middlewich CW10 ......151 D7
Poynton SK12 ....36 E3
Weaverham CW8 ....77 B1
Wilmslow SK9 ....59 F5
Winsford CW7 ....149 D7
Orchard Cotts CW6 ....146 D1
Orchard Cres
Kidsgrove ST7 ....194 D1
Nantwich CW5 ....204 E3
Nether Alderley SK10 ...84 F6
Orchard Croft CH3 ....119 E5
Orchard Ct
Alsager ST7 ....193 E4
3 Chester CH3 ....119 A1
Croft WA3 ....9 A8
Frodsham WA6 ....74 A8
Haslington CW7 ....191 D4
Orchard Dene CW8 ....101 D5
Orchard Dr
Handforth SK9 ....34 E2
Little Leigh CW8 ......77 D5
Neston CH64 ....66 E5
Orchard Gdns
Congleton CW12 ......156 A3
Tarporley CW6 ....168 D8
Weaverham CW8 ....77 B1
Orchard Gn SK9 ....60 B1
Orchard Gr CH3 ......180 F1
Orchard Haven CH66 ...69 C1
Orchard Ho SK10 ....86 E1
Orchard La CH66 ....69 A8
Orchard Park La CH2 ...72 B4
Orchard Pk CH2 ....72 B4
Orchard PI
Helsby WA6 ....73 C4
Poynton SK12 ....36 D4
Orchard Rd
Ellesmere Port CH65 ...70 B2
Lymm WA13 ....19 B5
Whaley Bridge SK23 ....65 D7
Orchard Rise CW9 ....126 E8
Orchard St
Chester CH1 ....237 A3
Crewe CW1 ....190 C5
Northwich CW9 ....104 B8
Warrington, Fearnhead
WA2 ....9 A2
Warrington, Stockton Heath
WA4 ....26 C8
Warrington WA1 ....16 C5
Willaston CW5 ....205 D6
Orchards The
Holt LL13 ....196 D8
Pickmere WA16 ....79 F7
Saltney CH4 ....140 D6
Shavington CW2 ....206 C4
Orchard The
Alderley Edge SK9 .....85 B8
Chester CH3 ....142 A8
Disley SK12 ....38 D6
Helsby WA6 ....73 B2
Orchard Way
Congleton CW12 ......156 A3
Kelsall CW6 ....122 D5
Widnes WA8 ....13 D5
Orchard Wlk
Neston CH64 ....66 E8
3 Runcorn WA7 ....49 F7
Orchid CI
Huntington CH3 ......142 A6
Irlam M44 ....11 E8
Orchid Way WA9 ....6 B7
Orchil CI CH66 ....69 A6
Ordnance Ave
Warrington, Birchwood
WA3 ....10 A5
Warrington WA3 ....9 F4
Ordsall CI CW11 ......174 F3
ORFORD 8 D2
Orford Ave
Disley SK12 ....38 D6
Warrington WA1, WA2 ...16 C7
Orford CI
Golborne WA3 ....3 A7
Hale L24 ....21 E2
High Lane SK6 ....37 E7
Orford Gn WA2 ....8 D1
Orford La WA2 ....16 B8
Orford Rd WA2 ....16 B8
Orford St WA1 ....16 A5
Organsdale Cotts
CW6 ....123 B5

Oriel Ho CH2 ....118 C4
Orion Bvd WA5 ....6 E1
Orkney CI
3 Ellesmere Port
CH65 ....70 C1
Widnes WA8 ....13 E3
Orlando Dr WA5 ....15 C7
Orme CI
Macclesfield SK10 .....87 D3
Prestbury SK10 ....87 A8
Orme Cres SK10 ....87 D3
Ormerod CI CW11 .....175 C5
Ormesby Gr CH63 ......43 B6
Orme St SK9 ....60 A1
Ormond CI WA8 ....12 C2
Ormonde Rd CH2 ......118 C4
Ormonde St CH1 ......237 C3
Orrell CI WA5 ....15 A6
Orton CI CW7 ....127 A4
Orwell CI SK9 ....34 D2
Osborne Ave WA2 ....8 D1
Osborne CI CW11 .....174 D5
Osborne Gr CW2 ......206 C5
Osborne Rd
Golborne WA3 ....3 E7
Warrington WA4 ....16 B1
Osbourne CI
Bebington CH62 ....43 E7
Wilmslow SK9 ....60 D6
OSCROFT 121 E2
Osier CI CH7 ....72 C3
Osmere CI SY13 ......226 B1
Osnath Wks WA2 ....16 B6
Osprey Ave CW7 ......149 D5
Osprey CI
Middlewich CW10 ......151 D5
Runcorn WA7 ....49 F5
Warrington WA2 ....8 E3
Osprey Ct CH2 ....237 A4
Osprey Dr SK9 ....60 C8
Osprey View ST7 ......195 D3
Ossett CI WA7 ....50 D8
Ossmere CI CW11 ......174 F8
Ostler's La WA16 ......58 E7
Oteley Ave CH62 ....43 D8
Otters Bank 2 CW7 ...126 A1
Ottersbank Mews
CW8 ....123 F3
OUGHTRINGTON 19 C4
Oughtrington Com Prim
Sch WA13 ....19 B4
Oughtrington Cres
WA13 ....19 B4
Oughtrington La WA13 ..19 A2
Oughtrington View
WA13 ....19 B4
Oulton Ave CH2 ....118 E7
Oulton Ct WA4 ....17 B2
Oulton Dr CW12 ......155 F3
Oulton Mill La CW6 ...147 B7
Oulton PI CH1 ....237 B3
Our Lady Mother of the
Saviour RC Prim Sch
WA7 ....50 A6
Our Lady of Lourdes RC
Prim Sch M31 ....11 C3
Our Lady of Perpetual
Succour RC Prim Sch
WA8 ....22 A8
Our Lady's RC Inf & Jun
Sch CH65 ....70 A3
Our Lady's RC Prim Sch
WA4 ....16 E3
Ousel Nest CW8 ....101 D4
Out La CH3 ....184 C6
Outwood Dr SK8 ....34 A8
Outwood La M90 ....33 C7
Outwood La W M90 ....33 B8
Outwood Prim Sch
SK8 ....34 D7
Outwood Rd SK8 ....34 B7
Oval The
Ellesmere Port CH65 ...70 C3
Gatley SK8 ....34 B8
Ovenhouse La SK10 ....87 E7
Oven La SK11 ....114 D5
OVER 149 B8
Overdale La CW8 ......101 D1
Overdale Rd
New Mills SK12 ....38 F6
Willaston CH64 ....43 A1
Overdene Rd CW7 .....149 D8
Overfields WA16 ....57 D3
Over Hall Com Prim Sch
CW7 ....149 B7
Over Hall Dr CW7 ....149 C7
Overhill Dr SK9 ....60 E7
Overhill Gr SK9 ....60 E7
Overhill La SK9 ....60 D7
Overhill Rd SK9 ....60 D7
OVER KNUTSFORD 57 C1
OVER LEIGH 65 F6
Overleigh Ct CH4 ....141 D7
Overleigh Rd CH4 ....141 D7
Overleigh St Mary's CE
Prim Sch CH4 ....141 D6
Overleigh Terr CH4 ...141 C7
OVER PEOVER 83 A1
Over PI WA16 ....82 C8
OVERPOOL 69 F7
Overpool Gdns CH66 ...69 F3
Overpool Rd
Ellesmere Port CH65 ...70 A2
Ellesmere Port, Great Sutton
CH65, CH66 ....69 F5
Overpool Sta CH66 ....69 E6
Over Rd
Church Minshull CW5 ...172 A7
Winsford CW7 ....149 F1

Over St John's CE Prim
Sch CW7 ....126 B1
OVER TABLEY 56 A5
OVERTON 74 C7
Overton CI
Congleton CW12 ......156 C3
Middlewich CW10 ......151 B8
Overton Dr WA6 ....74 C6
Overton Heath La
SY14 ....212 F5
Overton Rd ST8 ....179 F6
Overton Way 2 SK9 ...34 C5
Overway CW7 ....126 E1
Overwood Ave CH1 .....94 E1
Overwood La
Blacon CH1 ....117 C4
Mollington CH1 ....94 E1
Ovington CI WA7 ....49 F3
Owen CI CH1 ....117 E6
Owens Cnr WA4 ....26 D3
Owen St
Crewe CW2 ....190 C2
Northwich CW9 ....104 B8
Warrington WA2 ....16 A7
Owlers The SK23 ....65 E6
Owley Wood Rd CW8 ....77 C1
Owlhurst The SK10 .....88 B8
Owl Ind Est The CH5 ..116 B6
Owlsfield WA12 ....2 E3
Oxborough CI CW8 .....12 F4
Oxenham Rd WA2 ....8 E3
Oxford CI CH66 ....94 E8
Oxford Ct WA1 ....16 D6
Oxford Dr
Halewood L26 ....21 A8
Heswall CH63 ....41 F6
Oxford Gr WA44 ....11 C6
Oxford Rd
Chester CH4 ....140 F6
Macclesfield SK11 ....112 B7
Runcorn WA7 ....49 A8
Oxford St
Crewe CW1 ....190 B5
Newton-le-W WA12 ......2 B3
Warrington WA4 ....16 C4
Widnes WA8 ....23 B7
Ox-Hey Cres ST8 ......179 D1
Ox-Hey Dr ST8 ....179 D1
Oxhey Fst Sch ST8 ....179 E1
Oxheys WA7 ....50 C8
Oxheys La CW6 ....169 C8
Oxmead CI WA2 ....9 B1
Oxmoor CI WA7 ....50 A5
Oxney CI SK11 ....111 F8
Oxton CI WA8 ....12 C4
Oxton Gn CH66 ....69 D4

Padstow CI
Crewe CW1 ....190 C8
Macclesfield SK10 ....111 E8
Warrington WA5 ....14 E3
Padstow Dr SK7 ....35 F7
Padstow Sq WA7 ....50 B5
Padworth PI CW1 ......173 B1
Page Gr CW2 ....206 B3
Page La WA8 ....13 C1
Paignton CI WA5 ....14 E4
Painswick Rd CH66 ....69 E2
Paisley Ave CH62 ......43 E4
PALACE FIELDS 50 A6
Palace Fields Ave WA7 ..50 A6
Palace Fields Local Ctr
WA7 ....50 A6
Palace Fields Prim Sch
WA7 ....50 A6
Palace Hey CH64 ....67 A5
Palatine CI CH1 ......117 C6
Palatine Ind Est WA4 ..16 C3
Palgrave CI CH1 ......118 A5
Palin Dr WA5 ....14 F6
Palliser CI WA3 ....10 A3
Pall Mall CW5 ....204 E5
Palma Ave M90 ....33 B8
Palmer CI 3 CW9 .....103 F5
Palmer Cres WA5 ......15 D8
Palmer Rd CW11 ......175 C5
Palmerston CI CW1 ....191 C5
Palmerston CI CH1 ....118 B4
Palmerston Rd SK11 ...112 A7
Palmerston St SK10 ....88 B8
Palmerston Way ST8 ...179 D1
Palm Gr CH66 ....70 A1
Palmyra Sq N WA1 .....16 A5
Palmyra Sq S WA1 .....16 A5
PANDY 222 A3
Pangbourne CI WA4 .....26 E6
Panton PI CH2 ....118 F3
Panton Rd CH2 ....118 F3
Parade Rd M90 ....33 C7
Parade The
8 Alderley Edge SK9 ...60 A1
Blacon CH1 ....117 C5
Culcheth WA3 ....4 E3
Neston CH64 ....41 B1
Paradise CH4 ....237 B1
Paradise La CW5 ......171 E7
PARADISE GREEN 171 E6
Paradise Mill Mus*
SK11 ....112 D7
Paradise St SK11 .....112 C7
Paragon CI WA8 ....13 B5
Parbold Ct WA8 ....22 D8
Parc Ddiwydiannol
Glannau Dyfrdwy/
Deeside Ind Pk CH5 ...92 E2
Parc Ddiwydiannol Y Ffin/
Borders Ind Pk CH4
LL4 ....140 C7
Parchments The WA12 ...2 D4
Parish CI ST7 ....193 B4
Park Ave
Bramhall SK7 ....35 D5
Furness Vale SK23 .....39 D3
Haydock WA11 ....1 A6
Poynton SK12 ....36 E4
Saltney CH4 ....140 E6
Saughall CH1 ....94 A2
Talke ST7 ....210 E8
Tattenhall CH3 ....166 B2
Warrington WA4 ....16 D3
Weaverham WA4 ....77 D1
Widnes WA8 ....13 B1
Wilmslow SK9 ....60 C8
Park Ave N WA12 ....2 C2
Park Ave S WA12 ....2 C2
Park Bank CW2 ....156 F2
Park Brook Rd SK11 ...112 A8
Park Bvd CH3 ....16 B4
Park CI CH3 ....121 B2
Park Cres
Cuddington CW8 ......101 F4
Furness Vale SK23 .....39 D3
Handforth SK9 ....34 B1
Warrington WA4 ....26 D6
Park Ct
Chester CH1 ....237 C2
Frodsham WA6 ....74 A8
Runcorn WA7 ....49 A8
1 Warrington WA1 .....16 A5
Parkdale Ind Est WA1 ..16 C4
Parkdale Rd WA1 ....17 A7
Park Dr
Chester CH2 ....119 A4
Ellesmere Port CH65 ...70 B3
Handforth SK9 ....34 B1
Wistaston CW2 ....205 F8
Park Drive Gdns CW2 ..205 F8
Park Dr S CW2 ....205 F8
PARK END 209 A4
Park End Rd CH66 .....103 A6
Parker Dr CH3 ....180 E1
Parker's Bldgs CH1 ...237 C3
Parkers Ct WA7 ....49 E6
Parker's Row CH3 .....180 F6
Parker St
Macclesfield SK11 ....112 E7
Runcorn WA7 ....23 D3
Warrington WA1 ....16 A5
Parker Way CW12 ......156 A3

Park Est CW2 . . . . 206 D5
Parkett Heyes Rd
  SK11. . . . . .111 E7
Parkfield CW1. . . . . .173 A1
Parkfield Ave WA4 . . . . . .17 A4
Parkfield Dr
  Ellesmere Port CH65. . . . .70 A3
  Helsby WA6. . . . . .73 B3
  Nantwich CW5. . . . . .204 E4
Parkfield Rd
  Broughton CH4 . . . . .139 C3
  Knutsford WA16 . . . . .82 B8
  Northwich CW9 . . . . .104 C8
Parkfields La WA2 . . . . 8 F2
Parkgate WA16 . . . . .57 C3
PARKGATE
  Neston 41 C1
  Over Peover. 108 B8
Parkgate Ave WA16. . . . .108 B8
Parkgate Ct
  Chester CH4 . . . . .118 B4
  Warrington WA4 . . . . .16 C2
Parkgate Ho
  Neston CH64 . . . . .41 B1
  Neston CH64 . . . . .41 B1
Parkgate La
  Heswall CH64 . . . . .41 F5
  Knutsford WA16 . . . . .57 C3
Parkgate Prim Sch
  CH64 . . . . .41 C1
Parkgate Rd
  Blacon CH1 . . . . .118 A6
  Macclesfield SK11. . . . . .112 C4
  Neston CH64 . . . . .66 D8
  Puddington CH66. . . . . . . .68 C2
  Saughall CH1. . . . . .94 C3
  Warrington WA4 . . . . .16 D1
  Woodbank CH1 . . . . .93 E7
Parkgate Trad Est
  WA16. . . . . .57 C4
Parkgate Way
  7 Handforth SK9 . . . . . .34 D4
  Runcorn WA7. . . . . .50 D7
Park Gn SK11 . . . . .112 D7
Park Gr SK11 . . . . .112 C6
Parkhill Ct WA16 . . . . . . .57 B1
Park House Dr
  Prestbury SK10 . . . . .87 A8
  Sandbach CW11 . . . . . . .175 C8
Parkhouse Ind Est
  ST5. . . . . .210 F1
Park House La SK10 . . . . .87 A8
Park House Mews
  CW11. . . . . .175 D8
Parkhouse Rd E ST5. . . . .210 F1
Parkhouse Rd W ST5 . . . .210 F1
Park La
  Audley ST7. . . . . .209 B4
  Congleton CW12 . . . . . . .156 F2
  Frodsham WA6 . . . . .74 B8
  Hargrave CH3 . . . . .144 E3
  Hartford CW8 . . . . .103 B4
  Hatherton CW5 . . . . .219 E4
  Higher Walton WA4 . . . . . .25 F5
  Little Bollington WA14. . . .20 B2
  Littleton CH3 . . . . .119 F3
  Macclesfield SK11. . . . . .112 C6
  Macclesfield SK11. . . . . .112 D7
  Moulton CW9. . . . . .126 F7
  Pickmere CW9, WA16 . . . .79 E8
  Poynton SK12 . . . . .36 F3
  Pulford CH4. . . . . .162 E5
  Sandbach CW11 . . . . . . .174 F6
Parkland Cl WA4 . . . . .27 B4
Parkland Dr CH2 . . . . .72 B3
Parklands
  Ellesmere Port CH66. . . . .69 D6
  Kidsgrove ST7. . . . . .195 B1
  Widnes WA8 . . . . .12 C3
Parklands Com Prim Sch
  CH66 . . . . .69 D5
Parklands Dr
  Chorlton CH2 . . . . .207 E3
  Heswall CH60 . . . . .41 C6
Parklands Gdns CH66. . . .69 D6
Parklands The
  Congleton CW12 . . . . . . .157 A2
  Middlewich CW10 . . . . . .151 B7
Parklands View CH66 . . . .69 D5
Parklands Way SK12 . . . . .36 F4
Parkland View CW5 . . . . .204 D4
  Park Lane Schl SK11 . . . .112 B6
Parklea CH66 . . . . .69 D6
Parkleigh CW12 . . . . .156 E2
Park Mills Cl CW5 . . . . . .205 D5
Park Mount Cl SK11 . . . .112 A6
Park Mount Dr SK11 . . . .112 A6
Park Prim Sch The
  WA7. . . . . .24 A1
Park Rd
  Bebington, Eastham
    CH62. . . . . .43 F6
  Congleton CW12 . . . . . . .156 E3
  Ellesmere Port CH65. . . . .70 C4
  Golborne WA3 . . . . 3 A7
  Haslington CW1. . . . . . . .191 D5
  Heswall CH60 . . . . .41 B8
  High Lane SK12 . . . . .38 A6
  Horwich End SK23. . . . . . .65 D6
  Little Budworth CW6. . . . .124 F1
  Lymm WA13. . . . . .29 D8
  Middlewich CW10 . . . . . .128 C1
  Nantwich CW5. . . . . .204 E3
  New Mills SK22. . . . . .39 C7
  North Rode CW12. . . . . . .134 F2

Park Rd continued
  Partington, Warburton
    WA13. . . . . .19 C8
  Runcorn WA7. . . . . .49 A8
  Tarporley CW6. . . . . .146 D2
  Thornton-le-M CH2 . . . . . .71 E1
  Warrington, Orford WA2 . . . 8 D1
  Warrington, Orford WA4. . .16 E6
  Widnes WA8 . . . . .13 B1
  Willaston CH64 . . . . .68 B8
  Willaston(nr Nantwich)
    CW5. . . . . .205 C5
  Wilmslow SK9 . . . . .59 F7
  Winnington WW8 . . . . . . .78 D1
Park Rd N WA12. . . . . 2 E4
Park Rd S WA12. . . . . 2 E4
Park Rd W CH4. . . . . .141 A7
Park Road Com Prim Sch
  WA5. . . . . .14 E6
Parkroyal Com Sch
  SK11. . . . . .112 C7
Parkside Bsns Pk WA5 . . . . 3 A8
Parkside Cl
  High Lane SK6. . . . . .37 D8
  Neston CH64 . . . . .66 D8
Parkside Ct WA8 . . . . .13 A2
Parkside Rd WA12, WA2 . . . 3 B2
Park St
  Bollington SK10 . . . . .88 B8
  Chester CH1 . . . . .237 B2
  Congleton CW12 . . . . . . .156 D2
  Haydock WA11. . . . . 1 A6
  Macclesfield SK11. . . . . .112 D7
  Neston CH64 . . . . .66 E8
  Northwich CW8 . . . . .103 E7
Park Vale Rd SK11 . . . . . .112 C6
Park View
  Audlem CW3 . . . . .230 C8
  Bebington CH62. . . . . .43 C8
  Congleton CW12 . . . . . . .156 E3
  Hazel Grove SK7 . . . . .37 B8
  Little Bollington WA14. . . .20 B2
  Nantwich CW5. . . . . .204 F6
  Newton-le-W WA12. . . . . . 2 E3
  Warrington WA2 . . . . 8 E3
Parkview Ct CH60 . . . . . . .40 F8
Park View Ct SK11 . . . . . . .36 E4
Parkview Pk WA13. . . . . . .29 D8
Park View Rd ST7. . . . . . .195 B3
Park W CH60 . . . . .40 E7
Parkway
  Connah's Quay CH5. . . . . .92 E1
  Holmes Chapel CW4 . . . .130 C3
  Widnes WA8 . . . . .60 B6
Park Way CH1. . . . . .94 A2
Parkway Bsns Ctr CH5. . . .92 E1
Park Wlk CH2 . . . . .118 E4
Parkwood Cl
  Bebington CH62. . . . . .43 E8
  Lymm WA13. . . . . .18 D2
Parliament St **4**
  CW8. . . . . .103 E7
Parliament Way **9**
  CH66 . . . . .94 F8
Parlington Cl WA8. . . . . . .22 C7
Parnell Sq CW12 . . . . . . .157 A2
PARRAH GREEN 231 E7
Parr Gr WA11 . . . . 1 A6
Parr St
  Macclesfield SK11. . . . . .112 C8
  Warrington WA1 . . . . .16 C4
  1 Widnes WA8. . . . . . . .13 C1
Parrs Wood View WA4 . . .17 B1
Parry Dr WA4 . . . . .17 E3
Parsonage Gn
  Hale L24 . . . . .21 E1
  Wilmslow SK9 . . . . .60 B7
Parsonage Rd WA8 . . . . . .23 A4
Parsonage St SK11 . . . . .112 D7
Parsonage Way WA5 . . . .15 A5
Parsons La CH2 . . . . .118 A7
Parson St CW12 . . . . . . .156 C2
PARTINGTON 11 F4
Partington Prim Sch
  M31. . . . . .11 F3
Partington Sh Ctr M31. . . .11 F3
Partridge Cl
  Congleton CW12 . . . . . . .156 E1
  Warrington WA3 . . . . 9 F3
  Winsford CW7 . . . . .149 D5
Partridge Way CW9 . . . . . .79 F5
Parvey La SK11 . . . . .112 E2
Pasture Cl
  Kelsall CW6. . . . . .122 C4
  Macclesfield SK10. . . . . . .87 C3
Pasture Dr WA3 . . . . 9 B7
Pasture La WA2 . . . . 9 B1
Pastures Dr CW2 . . . . . . .207 D3
Pastures The WA9 . . . . 6 A7
Patch La SK7. . . . . .35 D5
Patmos La WA16 . . . . . . .105 F8
Patrivale Cl WA1. . . . . . . .16 F6
Patten La WA1 . . . . .16 B5
Patterdale Ave WA2 . . . . . . 8 C2
Patterdale Cl CW2 . . . . . .189 D3
Patterdale Rd M31. . . . . . .11 E3
Patterson Cl WA3 . . . . 9 E3
Patterson St WA12. . . . . . . 2 B3
Patton Dr WA5 . . . . .15 E6
Paul Cl WA5. . . . . .14 D6
Paulden Rd CW9 . . . . .80 A2
Paul St WA3 . . . . .18 A6
Pavement La WA16 . . . . . .57 F3

Pavilion Ct WA12 . . . . 2 A3
Pavilions The
  Chester CH4 . . . . .141 B3
  Davenham CW9 . . . . .103 E2
Pavilion Way
  Congleton CW12 . . . . . . .156 C3
  Macclesfield SK10. . . . . . .86 F1
Paxford Pl SK9 . . . . .60 A5
Payne Cl WA5. . . . . .15 D6
Paythorne Cl WA3 . . . . 4 F3
Peace Dr WA5. . . . . .15 D5
Peach Field CH3. . . . . . . .142 B7
Peach Gr WA11. . . . . 1 E7
Peach La CW5. . . . . .189 A1
Pear Tree Cl L24 . . . . .21 E2
Peacock Ave
  Warrington WA1 . . . . .16 E6
  Winsford CW7 . . . . .149 C5
Peacock Dr SK8 . . . . .34 B6
Peacock Hay Rd ST7. . . . .210 F4
Peacock La CW6 . . . . .29 E6
Peacock Way **5** SK9. . . . .34 D5
Peak Rd SK22. . . . . .39 D8
Pearle St SK10 . . . . .87 D1
Pearlings The CH3. . . . . . .119 F1
Pearl La
  Chester CH3 . . . . .119 C1
  Littleton CH3 . . . . .119 D1
Pearl St SK10. . . . . .87 A7
Pearson Ave WA4. . . . . . . .16 D2
Pearson St **9** SK11 . . . . .112 E7
Pear Tree Ave
  Crewe CW1. . . . . .190 B7
  Runcorn WA7 . . . . .49 C7
Pear Tree Bank CW12 . . .156 E2
Peartree Cl CW11. . . . . . .175 E6
Pear Tree Cl
  Frodsham WA6 . . . . .49 D1
  Hale L24 . . . . .21 E1
  Weaverham CW8. . . . . . . .77 C1
  Winsford CW7 . . . . .149 D7
Pear Tree Dr CW9. . . . . . . .80 A6
Pear Tree Farm Cotts
  CW9. . . . . .104 F4
Pear Tree Field CW5 . . . . .205 A4
Peartree La SY14 . . . . . . .222 D1
Pear Tree La
  Acton Bridge CW8 . . . . . . .76 E4
  Whitchurch SY13. . . . . . .225 D1
Pear Tree Rd ST7 . . . . . . .209 F1
Pear Tree Sch CW5 . . . . . .205 A4
Pear Tree Way
  Chester CH2 . . . . .118 F6
  5 Ellesmere Port CH66. . .69 E1
Pearwood Cl CW6 . . . . . .146 D1
Peasley Cl WA2. . . . . 9 B1
Pebble Brook Prim Sch
  CW2. . . . . .190 C1
Peckfield Cl WA7. . . . . .50 A5
PECKFORTON 184 F5
Peckforton Castle*
  CW6. . . . . .167 E1
Peckforton Cl CW11 . . . . .174 E7
Peckforton Dr
  Ellesmere Port CH66. . . . .69 E3
  Runcorn WA7. . . . . .49 F4
Peckforton Hall Farm
  CW6. . . . . .185 A6
Peckforton Hall La
  CW6. . . . . .185 B6
Peckforton Rd CW6. . . . . .168 A2
Peckforton Way
  Chester CH2 . . . . .118 F6
  2 Northwich CW8 . . . . .103 E7
Peckforton Wlk 11 SK9 . . .34 E1
Peckmill Cl SK9 . . . . .34 E2
Peck Mill La WA6. . . . . .98 A7
Peckmill Rdbt CW9 . . . . .127 B8
Pedley Hill
  Booth Green SK10. . . . . . .62 F7
  Rainow SK10 . . . . .88 E4
Pedley House La WA16. . . .58 E1
Pedley La
  Chelford WA16. . . . . .83 D8
  Congleton CW12 . . . . . . .157 F4
Pedley St CW2 . . . . .190 D2
Peebles Cl
  Ellesmere Port CH66. . . . .68 F6
  Holmes Chapel CW4 . . . .130 B2
Peel Cl WA1. . . . . .17 D6
Peel Cres CH3. . . . . .119 A1
Peel Ct ST7 . . . . .195 A2
Peel Dr CW12 . . . . .178 B7
Peel Hall La CH3 . . . . .121 E7
Peel Hall Pk CH3 . . . . . . .121 D8
Peel Hollow ST7. . . . . . . .209 A2
Peel House La WA8. . . . . . .13 B2
Peel La CW12 . . . . .178 D7
Peel Sq **1** CW1 . . . . .190 B5
Peel St
  Crewe CW1. . . . . .190 B5
  Macclesfield SK11. . . . . .112 D6
  Newton-le-W WA12. . . . . . 2 A3
  Runcorn WA7. . . . . .22 F3
Peel Terr CH1 . . . . .237 C3
Peerswood Ct CH64. . . . . .66 E5
Peewit Cl CW7 . . . . .149 D5
Peggie's La SK10 . . . . .62 D2
Pelham Cl WA5. . . . . .191 C5
Pelham Rd WA4 . . . . .17 C3
Pelican Cl CW1. . . . . .191 A5
Pemberton Cl CH64. . . . . .68 A8
Pemberton Rd CH1 . . . . .237 A3
Pembridge Cl CH65. . . . . .70 E3
Pembridge Gdns CH65. . . .70 E3
Pembroke Apartments
  WA2. . . . . 9 A3

Pembroke Cl CH4. . . . . . .141 E6
Pembroke Ct WA7. . . . . . .24 D5
Pembroke Dr CH65 . . . . . .70 A3
Pembroke Gdns WA4 . . . . .26 D4
Pembroke Gr M44 . . . . . . .11 C6
Pembroke Rd SK11 . . . . . .111 F7
Pembroke Way CW7 . . . . .149 B7
Penare WA7. . . . . .50 C6
Penbrook Cl CW2. . . . . . .189 D3
Penda Way CW11. . . . . . .175 B6
Pendine Cl WA5. . . . . 7 C2
Pendlebury Gdns
  SK11. . . . . .112 D2
Pendlebury St WA4 . . . . . .17 A3
Pendle Cl
  Crewe CW1. . . . . .191 A5
  Ellesmere Port CH66. . . . .68 F6
Pendle Gdns WA3 . . . . 4 E8
Penfold Cl CH1. . . . . .94 B8
Penfold Hey CH2 . . . . .118 D7
Penfolds WA7 . . . . .23 D1
Penfold Way CH4. . . . . . . .162 A7
Peninsula Ho WA7. . . . . . .16 C7
Penistone Dr CH66 . . . . . .69 B5
PENKETH 14 D4
Penketh Ave WA5. . . . . . . .15 F8
Penketh Bsns Pk WA5 . . . .15 B4
Penketh Com Prim Sch
  WA5. . . . . .15 B4
Penketh Ct
  Runcorn WA7. . . . . .23 B2
  Warrington WA5 . . . . .14 D4
Penketh High Sch
  WA5. . . . . .15 A5
Penketh Rd WA5 . . . . .15 A4
Penketh's La 16 WA7 . . . . .23 A3
Penketh South Com Prim
  Sch WA5. . . . . .14 E3
Penkford La WA5. . . . . 1 D2
Penkford Sch WA12 . . . . . . 1 E2
Penkford St WA12 . . . . 1 E2
Penkmans La WA6. . . . . . .74 C6
Penlington Ct CW5 . . . . . .204 E6
Penmann Cres L26 . . . . . . .21 A7
Penmark Cl WA5. . . . . .7 D1
Penmon Cl CH1 . . . . .117 D3
Pennant Cl WA3 . . . . .10 A3
Penn Bridge SK11 . . . . . .158 E6
Penn Gdns CH65. . . . . . . .70 B5
Penn House Cl SK7 . . . . . .35 E8
Pennine Cl SK10. . . . . .87 E2
Pennine Rd WA2 . . . . 8 E2
Pennine Way
  Biddulph ST8 . . . . .179 E1
  Winsford CW7 . . . . .149 B8
Pennine Wlk CH66. . . . . . .69 B6
Pennington Cl WA6. . . . . . .49 D2
Pennington Dr WA12 . . . . . 2 E3
Pennington Gn CH66. . . . .69 C3
Pennington La WA5,
  WA9. . . . . 1 D2
Penningtons La SK11 . . . .111 F5
Penn La WA7. . . . . .49 F4
Penny Bank Cl WA4 . . . . .139 A3
Pennyfields Rd ST7. . . . . .195 D2
Penny La
  Collins Green WA5. . . . . . . 1 D1
  Cronton L35, WA8 . . . . . . .12 B6
  Haydock WA11. . . . . 1 B7
  Rainow SK10 . . . . .88 D3
Pennymoor Dr CW10. . . . .128 D2
Pennypleck La CW9 . . . . . .28 A2
Penny's La
  Northwich CW9 . . . . .104 F7
  Rudheath CW9. . . . . .105 B5
Penrhyn Cres
  Hazel Grove SK7 . . . . .36 C8
  Runcorn WA7. . . . . .49 B7
Penrhyn Rd CW8 . . . . .103 E8
Penrith Ave
  Macclesfield SK11. . . . . .111 F5
  Warrington WA2 . . . . 8 C2
Penrith Cl
  Frodsham WA6 . . . . .49 D1
  Partington M31. . . . . .11 E4
Penrith Ct CW12. . . . . . . .156 A2
Penrose Gdns WA5 . . . . . .14 D3
Penry Ave M44 . . . . .11 E6
Penryn Cl WA5. . . . . .14 E3
Pensarn Gdns WA5 . . . . . .15 A5
Pensby Ave CH2 . . . . .118 D5
Pensby Dr CH66 . . . . .69 D4
Pensby Rd CH60 . . . . .40 F8
Penshaw Ct WA7 . . . . .49 E7
Pentland Ave WA5. . . . . 8 B3
Pentland Cl
  Chester CH3 . . . . .119 A2
  Winsford CW7 . . . . .149 B8
Pentland Pl WA2 . . . . 8 B3
Pentre Cl CH3. . . . . .121 F7
Pentre La CH3. . . . . .121 F7
Penzance Cl SK10 . . . . . . .111 E8
Peony Gdns WA9 . . . . 6 B7
Peover Hall & Gdns*
  WA16. . . . . .107 E8
PEOVER HEATH 108 C8
Peover La
  Chelford SK11 . . . . .108 F8
  Congleton CW12 . . . . . . .157 F6
Peover Prim Sch
  WA16. . . . . .108 B8
Peover Rd SK9 . . . . .34 E5
Pepper Cl SK9. . . . . .60 A6
Pepper St
  Appleton Thorn WA4 . . . . .27 A3
  Ashley WA16 . . . . .31 F1
  Chelford SK11 . . . . .83 E2

Pepper St continued
  Chester CH1 . . . . .237 B2
  Christleton CH3 . . . . .142 D8
  Hale L24 . . . . .21 D1
  Henbury SK11. . . . . .111 B8
  Lymm WA13. . . . . .18 F3
  Middlewich CW10 . . . . . .128 C1
  Nantwich CW5. . . . . .204 E5
Peppers The WA13. . . . . . .18 F3
Percival Cl CH2. . . . . .118 C8
Percival La WA7 . . . . .22 E2
Percival Rd
  Chester CH2 . . . . .118 C8
  Ellesmere Port CH66. . . . .70 B6
Percivals La WA16 . . . . . . .83 B3
Percival St WA1 . . . . .16 C5
Percy James Cl ST7 . . . . .193 E4
Percy Rd CH4 . . . . .141 D7
Percy St
  Northwich CW9 . . . . .104 A8
  Warrington WA5 . . . . .15 E5
Percyvale St SK10 . . . . . .112 E8
Peregrine Cl CW7 . . . . . . .149 D5
Perenna Ct/Llys Perenna
  CH6 . . . . .91 B2
Perimeter Rd CH2 . . . . . . .72 D5
Perrin Ave WA7 . . . . .48 E8
Perrins Rd WA5 . . . . 6 F6
Perry Fields CW1. . . . . . . .173 B1
Perry St WA7. . . . . .23 B2
Perth Cl
  Bramhall SK7. . . . . .35 F5
  Holmes Chapel CW4 . . . .130 B2
  Warrington WA3 . . . . 8 F3
Peterborough Cl
  Ellesmere Port CH66. . . . .94 F7
  Macclesfield SK10. . . . . . .87 A2
Peter Destapleigh Way
  CW5. . . . . .205 A3
Peter Ellson Cl CW2 . . . . .190 D1
Peter House Rd SK11 . . . .112 F3
Peter Pl **7** CW1 . . . . .190 B5
Peter St W 11 SK11 . . . . . .112 C7
Peters Cl WA11 . . . . 1 A7
Petersfield Gdns WA3 . . . . 4 E4
Petersfield Way CW7 . . . .207 D3
Petersgate WA7 . . . . .50 D7
Petersham Dr WA4 . . . . . . .26 E5
Peter St
  Golborne WA3 . . . . 3 A8
  Macclesfield SK11. . . . . .112 C7
  Northwich CW9 . . . . .79 B1
Peterstone Cl WA5 . . . . 7 D2
Petham Ct WA8 . . . . .12 E4
Petrel Ave SK12 . . . . .36 B4
Petrel Cl CW7 . . . . .149 D5
Petunia Cl
  Macclesfield SK11. . . . . .112 B5
  St Helens WA9. . . . . 6 A7
Petworth Ave WA2. . . . . . . 8 B3
Petworth Cl CW2 . . . . . . .206 B8
Pevensey Dr WA16. . . . . . .82 A8
Peveril Cl WA4 . . . . .26 D8
Peveril Dr SK7 . . . . .36 F8
Peveril Gdns WA4 . . . . . . .26 D8
Peveril Mews SK12 . . . . . .39 A6
Peveril Wlk 3 SK11 . . . . .111 F7
Pewithall Prim Sch
  WA7. . . . . .49 B7
Pewit La CW5 . . . . .231 C7
PEWTERSPEAR 26 A4
Pewterspear Green Rd
  WA4. . . . . .26 A3
Pewterspear La WA4 . . . . .26 C4
Pexall Rd SK11 . . . . .134 C3
Pex Hill Ct WA8 . . . . .12 E5
Pexhill Dr SK10. . . . . .111 E7
Pexhill Rd SK11 . . . . .111 C5
Pex Hill Visitor Ctr*
  WA8. . . . . .12 E5
Pheasant Cl WA3. . . . . 9 F5
Pheasant Dr CW9 . . . . .79 F5
Pheasant Field L24 . . . . . .21 C2
Pheasant Way CW7 . . . . .149 D5
Pheasant Wlk WA16 . . . . . .29 C4
Philip Rd WA8. . . . . .22 B8
Philips Dr WA5. . . . . .14 E7
Philips La CH66. . . . . .69 C4
Philip St CH5. . . . . .116 A2
Phillips Rd CH1. . . . . .117 D3
Phillip St CW2 . . . . .118 F3
Phillips Way CH60 . . . . . . .40 F8
Phipps' La WA5. . . . . 6 F7
Phoenix Ave WA5. . . . . 7 F2
Phoenix Cl ST7. . . . . .195 C2
Phoenix Ctr The CW7 . . . .127 C1
Phoenix St CH5. . . . . .116 A3
Phythian Cres WA5 . . . . . .14 F4
Pichael Nook WA4 . . . . . . .17 D3
Pickenham Cl SK11 . . . . . .111 F6
Pickering Cres WA4 . . . . . .17 D3
Pickerings Cl WA7. . . . . . . .49 C6
Pickerings Lock Cvn PK
  CW8. . . . . .76 A5
Pickerings O the Boat
  CW8. . . . . .76 B5
Pickering's Pasture
  (Nature Reserve)***
  WA8. . . . . .22 B3
Pickerings Rd WA8 . . . . . .22 C3
Pickering St CH2 . . . . . . .237 C4
Pickering Way CW5. . . . . .204 F4
Pickford St SK11 . . . . .112 D7
PICKMERE 80 A7
Pickmere Cl CW11. . . . . . .174 F7
Pickmere Ct
  Crewe CW1. . . . . .190 C5
  10 Handforth SK9 . . . . . .34 D5

Pickmere Dr
Bebington CH62 . . . . .43 F3
Bebington CH62 . . . . .43 F4
Chester CH3 . . . . .142 B8
Runcorn WA7 . . . . .50 C5
Pickmere La
Higher Wincham CW9 . . . . .79 F6
Pickmere WA16 . . . . .55 D2
Pickmere Rd SK9 . . . . .34 D5
Pickmere St WA15 . . . . . . .15 E5
Pickwick CI CW11 . . . . . .175 C8
Pickwick PI ST7 . . . . .194 D2
Pickwick Rd SK12 . . . . . . .36 D3
Picow Farm Rd WA7 . . . . . .22 E1
Picow St 2 WA7 . . . . .22 E1
PICTON
Picton Ave
Ellesmere Port CH65 . . . . . .70 C5
Runcorn WA7 . . . . .23 B2
Picton CI
Bebington CH62 . . . . .43 E3
2 Northwich CW9 . . . . . .103 F4
Warrington WA3 . . . . .9 E7
Picton Dr
Handforth SK9 . . . . .34 E2
Winsford CW7 . . . . .126 A1
Picton Gorse La CH2 . . . .119 B7
Picton La CH2 . . . . .96 C4
Picton Sq CW4 . . . . .130 C3
Piele Rd WA11 . . . . .1 E8
Pierce St SK11 . . . . .112 C8
Pierpoint La CH1 . . . . . . .237 B2
Pierpoint St WA1 . . . . .15 F7
Pigginshaw SK9 . . . . .59 E8
Pigot PI WA4 . . . . .16 F5
Pike La WA6 . . . . .75 A3
Pikemere Prim Sch
ST7 . . . . .193 B5
Pikemere Rd ST7 . . . . . . .193 B5
Pikenall La CW8 . . . . .76 D3
Pike Rd SK10 . . . . .89 B6
Pike St WA4 . . . . .16 D1
Pike The CW5 . . . . .204 E3
Pilgrim CI WA7 . . . . .24 D2
Pilgrims Way WA7 . . . . . . .24 D2
Pillar Box La CW11 . . . . . .153 B3
Pillmoss La WA4 . . . . .52 B8
Pillory St CW5 . . . . .204 E5
Pimblett Rd WA11 . . . . .1 E7
Pimblett St 3 . . . . .3 A7
Pimlico Rd WA7 . . . . .22 E2
Pinders Farm Dr WA1 . . . .16 C5
Pineapple Pk CW7 . . . . . .127 B2
Pine Ave
Newton-le-W WA12 . . . . . . .2 D2
4 Widnes WA8 . . . . .13 B2
Pine CI
Haydock WA11 . . . . .1 C6
Macclesfield SK10 . . . . .87 F1
Talke ST7 . . . . .210 D7
Pine Ct ST7 . . . . .193 E4
Pinedale CI CH66 . . . . .95 A8
Pine Gdns CH2 . . . . .118 C6
Pine Gr
Chester CH2 . . . . .119 B4
Ellesmere Port CH66 . . . . . .70 A1
Golborne WA3 . . . . .3 C8
Sandbach CW11 . . . . .175 C6
Warrington WA1 . . . . .17 A7
Winsford CW7 . . . . .127 A1
Pinehey CH64 . . . . .41 D1
Pine Ho CH2 . . . . .118 C5
Pinehurst SK10 . . . . .86 E6
Pinellas WA7 . . . . .23 B3
Pine Lo SK7 . . . . .35 F7
Pine Rd
Bramhall SK7 . . . . .35 F8
Heswall CH60 . . . . .41 C8
Macclesfield SK10 . . . . .87 F1
Poynton SK12 . . . . .36 F3
Runcorn WA7 . . . . .49 C8
Pines The
Mobberley WA16 . . . . .58 E1
3 Northwich CW9 . . . . . .103 E6
Widnes WA8 . . . . .13 D4
Pinetree CI
Barnton CW8 . . . . .78 B4
Winsford CW7 . . . . .127 A1
Pine Tree CI CH4 . . . . . . .139 C3
Pine Trees WA16 . . . . .57 F8
Pineways WA4 . . . . .26 D5
Pine Wlk
Nantwich CW5 . . . . .204 F4
1 Partington M31 . . . . .11 E3
Pinewood Ave WA11 . . . . . .16 E7
Pinewood CI CH2 . . . . .72 C3
Pinewood Ct CW2 . . . . . .206 B7
Pinewood Dr CH60 . . . . . . .41 B8
Pinewood Gr ST5 . . . . . . .210 E1
Pinewood Rd
Burtonwood WA5 . . . . .6 F7
Wilmslow SK9 . . . . .60 E8
Winsford CW7 . . . . .126 B1
Pinfold CI WA15 . . . . .32 D7
Pinfold Craft Ctr*
CW5 . . . . .188 B3
Pinfold Ct CH4 . . . . .141 E6
Pinfold La
Chelford WA16 . . . . .83 D6
Chester CH4 . . . . .141 D6
Chester CH4 . . . . .141 E7
Little Budworth CW6 . . . . .147 E7
Middlewich CW10 . . . . . . .128 B1
Plumley WA16 . . . . .81 B4
Wythenshawe M90,
WA15 . . . . .32 F6
Pinfold St 10 SK11 . . . . . .112 C8

Pinfold The LL13 . . . . . . .196 D8
Pinfold Way CW8 . . . . .77 D1
Pingard's La CW8 . . . . . . .101 C6
Pingate Dr SK8 . . . . .35 A6
Pingate La SK8 . . . . .35 A6
Pingate La S SK8 . . . . .35 A6
Pingot Croft CH3 . . . . . . .142 B7
Pingot La WA6 . . . . .99 A5
Pingot Rd SK22 . . . . .39 D8
Pinmill Brow WA6 . . . . .74 B7
Pinmill CI WA6 . . . . .74 C7
Pinners Brow WA1 . . . . . . .16 B6
Pinners Brow Ret Pk
WA2 . . . . .16 B6
Pinners Fold WA7 . . . . . . .24 B1
PINSLEY GREEN 216 D2
Pinsley Green Rd
CW5 . . . . .216 E2
Pinsley View CW5 . . . . . .216 E4
Pintail PI CW7 . . . . .149 D6
Pinwood Ct 13 SK9 . . . . . .34 E1
Pipers Ash CW7 . . . . .126 A1
PIPER'S ASH 119 D4
Piper's CI CH60 . . . . .40 D8
Pipers Ct CH2 . . . . .119 B4
Piper's End CH60 . . . . .40 D8
Pipers La
Chester CH2 . . . . .119 B4
Puddington CH64 . . . . .93 A8
Piper's La CH60 . . . . .40 D8
Pipers The
Golborne WA3 . . . . .3 F8
Heswall CH60 . . . . .40 D8
Pipit Ave WA12 . . . . .2 C3
Pipit La WA3 . . . . .9 E3
Pippin CI CW10 . . . . .151 C7
Pippits Row WA7 . . . . .49 E4
Pirie CI CW12 . . . . .157 A4
Pirie Rd CW12 . . . . .157 A4
Pitcher La CW11 . . . . .177 A8
Pit La
Hough CW2 . . . . .206 E2
Talke ST7 . . . . .210 C6
Widnes WA8 . . . . .13 A4
Pitt La SK11 . . . . .132 B8
Pitts CI CH3 . . . . .121 C2
Pitts Heath La WA7 . . . . . .24 E3
Pitt St
Macclesfield SK11 . . . . . . .112 D6
Warrington WA4 . . . . .15 F7
Widnes WA8 . . . . .23 A5
Pitville Terr WA8 . . . . .22 C7
Plaistow Ct WA7 . . . . .49 E7
Plane Gr ST5 . . . . .210 E1
Plane Tree Dr CW1 . . . . .190 E6
Plane Tree Gr WA11 . . . . . .2 A7
Plane Tree Rd M31 . . . . . .11 D3
Plantagenet CI 3
CW7 . . . . .149 D6
Plantation CI WA7 . . . . . . .24 A1
Plantation Dr CH66 . . . . . .69 E7
Plant La CW11 . . . . .174 B7
Plant St CW11 . . . . .175 A7
Plas Dinas CH1 . . . . .117 D3
Plas Newton La CH2 . . . .118 F5
Plas Newydd CH4 . . . . . .161 B6
Plat Ave CW11 . . . . .175 A7
Platts La
Christleton CH3 . . . . .143 D8
Duddon CH3, CW6 . . . . . .144 E7
Tarvin, Broom Bank
CH3 . . . . .144 B8
Tarvin CH3 . . . . .121 B2
Tattenhall CH3 . . . . .183 F7
Platt's La CH3 . . . . .164 E5
Platts St WA11 . . . . .1 A6
Pleasance Way WA12 . . . . .2 A7
Pleasant St
Macclesfield SK10 . . . . .87 F1
Northwich CW8 . . . . .103 E7
Pleasant View SK10 . . . .111 C8
Pleasant Way SK8 . . . . . . .35 C6
Pleck Rd CH65 . . . . .70 A2
PLEMSTALL 97 B1
Plemstall CI CH2 . . . . . . .119 F8
Plemstall La CH2 . . . . .97 A1
Plemstall Way CH2 . . . . . .96 F1
Plemston Ct CH66 . . . . . . .69 F8
Plex The ST7 . . . . .193 D4
Plinston Ave WA4 . . . . .16 F4
Plough Croft ST7 . . . . . . .193 A3
Plough Inn Pk The
CW8 . . . . .125 E5
Plough La CH3 . . . . .143 B7
Ploughmans CI CH66 . . . . .94 E8
Ploughmans Way
Ellesmere Port CH66 . . . . . .94 E8
Macclesfield SK10 . . . . .87 B3
Plover Ave CW7 . . . . .149 D5
Plover CI
Farndon CH3 . . . . .180 F1
Macclesfield SK10 . . . . .87 B4
Newton-le-W WA12 . . . . . . .2 C3
Plover Dr WA7 . . . . .50 D8
Plovers La WA6 . . . . .73 C5
Plover Way WA3 . . . . .3 E8
Plumbs Fold CW8 . . . . . . .78 A2
Plumley CI CW7 . . . . .80 F3
PLUMLEY
Plumley CI
Chester CH3 . . . . .119 C1
10 Macclesfield SK11 . . . .112 E7
Plumley Gdns WA8 . . . . . .12 A1
PLUMLEY MOOR 81 C2
Plumley Moor Rd
WA16 . . . . .81 C2
Plumley Rd SK9 . . . . .34 D5
Plumley Sta WA16 . . . . . . .81 A3
Plumpstons La WA6 . . . . . .49 B1

Plumpton Cross 6
WA8 . . . . .13 B2
Plum Terr CH1 . . . . .237 A3
Plumtre Ave WA5 . . . . .15 F8
Plymouth CI WA7 . . . . .50 E6
Plymouth Dr SK7 . . . . .35 F7
Plymyard Ave CH62 . . . . . .43 D5
Plymyard CI CH62 . . . . . . .43 D5
Plymyard Ct CH62 . . . . . . .43 C6
Poachers' La WA4 . . . . . . .16 F3
Pochard Ave CW7 . . . . . .149 D6
Pochard Dr SK12 . . . . .36 A4
Pochard Rise WA7 . . . . . . .50 D8
Pochin Way CW10 . . . . . .128 E1
Pocket Nook La WA3 . . . . . .4 B7
Pocklington Ct WA2 . . . . . .8 F1
Points Ho CW1 . . . . .190 A5
Polden CI CH66 . . . . .69 A6
Poleacre Dr WA8 . . . . .12 D2
Pole La CW9 . . . . .53 E2
Pole Lane Ends CW9 . . . . .53 C4
Pollard Ave WA6 . . . . .74 D7
Pollard Dr CW5 . . . . .205 B4
Polperro CI
Macclesfield SK10 . . . . .86 D1
Warrington WA5 . . . . .14 E3
Pond Cotts CH2 . . . . .72 A3
Pond St WA3 . . . . .4 A8
Pond View CI CH60 . . . . . .41 C8
Pond Wlk WA9 . . . . .1 A1
Pool Bank Cotts CH3 . . .121 C3
Poole Ave WA2 . . . . .8 B2
Poole Cres WA2 . . . . .8 B2
Poole Hall La CH66 . . . . . .69 E8
Poole Hall Rd CH66 . . . . . .69 F8
POOLEHILL 188 A2
Poole Hill Rd CW5 . . . . . .188 A2
Poole La CH2 . . . . .71 E2
Pool End CI SK10 . . . . .87 D4
Pool End Rd SK10 . . . . . . .87 D4
Poole Old Hall La
CW5 . . . . .188 D4
Pooles La CW11 . . . . .177 A6
POOLFOLD 179 F4
Poolford La CW4 . . . . .129 E2
Pool Hall Ind Est CH65,
CH66 . . . . .70 A8
Pool House Rd SK12 . . . . .37 D5
Pool La
Cuddington CW8 . . . . .102 B2
Haslington CW11 . . . . .192 A7
Ince CH2 . . . . .71 F4
Lymm WA13 . . . . .18 D3
Malpas SY14 . . . . .212 D1
Runcorn WA7 . . . . .23 B2
Tarvin CH3 . . . . .121 C4
Warrington WA4 . . . . .16 A1
Pool Meadows Rd
CW1 . . . . .191 B4
Pool Rd WA3 . . . . .11 A3
Pool Side ST7 . . . . .194 A8
Poolside CI ST7 . . . . .193 E4
Poolside Rd WA7 . . . . .23 B1
Pools Platt La CW9 . . . . . .53 E6
Pool St
Macclesfield SK11 . . . . . . .112 E6
Widnes WA8 . . . . .23 B7
Pooltown Rd CH65 . . . . . . .69 F5
Pool View CW11 . . . . .191 F7
Poplar Ave
Culcheth WA3 . . . . .4 F3
Moulton CW9 . . . . .126 F8
Newton-le-W WA12 . . . . . . .2 D3
Runcorn WA7 . . . . .49 C7
Warrington WA5 . . . . .14 E3
Wilmslow SK9 . . . . .59 F5
Poplar CI
Congleton CW12 . . . . .156 A4
Cuddington CW8 . . . . .102 A3
Ellesmere Port CH65 . . . . . .70 B4
Runcorn WA7 . . . . .49 C7
Winsford CW7 . . . . .149 B8
Poplar Dr
Alsager ST7 . . . . .193 E2
Kidsgrove ST7 . . . . .195 A1
Middlewich CW10 . . . . . . .151 D7
Poplar Gr
Bollington SK10 . . . . .88 A8
Crewe CW1 . . . . .190 E5
Elton CW2 . . . . .7 A4
Haydock WA11 . . . . .1 C6
Irlam M44 . . . . .11 C6
Poplar Hall La CH2 . . . . . .95 C6
Poplar La TF9 . . . . .236 F5
Poplar Rd
Chester CH4 . . . . .140 F5
Haydock WA11 . . . . .1 C6
Macclesfield SK11 . . . . . . .112 D6
Weaverham CW8 . . . . .102 D8
Poplars Ave
Warrington, Hulme WA2 . . . .8 C3
Warrington, Winwick Quay
WA2 . . . . .8 A4
Poplars PI WA2 . . . . .8 C3
Poplars The
Golborne, Wash End
WN7 . . . . .4 D8
Lymm WA13 . . . . .18 D4
Wistaston CW2 . . . . .205 F8
Poplar View WA4 . . . . .25 A7
Poplar Way SK10 . . . . .87 B4
Poplar Weint 2 CH64 . . . .66 E8
Poplar Wlk M31 . . . . .11 D3
Poppy CI CW7 . . . . .207 C5
Poppyfields ST7 . . . . .193 B3

Porlock CI
Heswall CH60 . . . . .41 B6
Warrington WA5 . . . . .14 E4
Port Arcades The
CH65 . . . . .70 C5
Porter Ave WA12 . . . . .2 C5
Porter CI CW9 . . . . .104 C6
Porters Croft CH3 . . . . . .119 F5
Porter St WA7 . . . . .23 C2
Porter Way CW9 . . . . . . .104 C6
Portford CI SK10 . . . . .86 F1
Porthcawl CI WA8 . . . . .12 C3
Porthleven Rd WA7 . . . . . .50 B5
Portland Dr
Biddulph ST8 . . . . .179 D2
Scholar green ST7 . . . . . .194 E6
Winsford CW7 . . . . .149 B8
Portland Gr CW1 . . . . . . .191 D5
Portland PI WA6 . . . . .73 C4
Portland Rd WA5 . . . . .15 A8
Portland St
Newton-le-W WA12 . . . . . . .1 F4
Runcorn WA7 . . . . .22 F3
Portland Trad Pk WA2 . . . .16 A6
Portloe Rd SK9 . . . . .34 B7
Portman PI 3 CW7 . . . . .149 A8
Portmarnock CI SK10 . . . . .87 B2
Portola CI WA4 . . . . .17 C2
Portree Ave CH66 . . . . . . .43 D5
Portree Dr CW4 . . . . .130 B2
Portrush CI
Macclesfield SK10 . . . . .87 C4
Warrington WA8 . . . . .12 E3
Portside WA7 . . . . .50 E7
Portside Bsns Pk CH65 . . .70 B8
Portsmouth PI WA7 . . . . . .50 E6
Portway M22 . . . . .33 E8
Postles PI CW9 . . . . .103 F6
Post Office La
Betley CW2 . . . . .207 F1
Hampton Heath SY14 . . . .213 D7
Macclesfield SK10 . . . . . . .100 C5
Runcorn WA7 . . . . .48 D7
Post Office PI 1 CW9 . . . .79 A1
Potter CI CW5 . . . . .205 D4
Potters Barn The*
CW11 . . . . .176 A1
Potters End ST8 . . . . .179 C1
Potters La WA8 . . . . .21 F5
Pott Hall SK10 . . . . .63 D3
POTT SHRIGLEY
SK10 . . . . .63 C3
Pott Shrigley Church Sch
SK10 . . . . .63 C3
POULTON 163 B2
Poulton Cres WA1 . . . . . . .17 D8
Poulton Dr WA8 . . . . .12 A1
Poulton Hall Rd CH63 . . . . .43 A7
Poulton Rd CH63 . . . . .43 A8
Pound Rd CH66 . . . . .69 C7
Povey Rd WA2 . . . . .8 D1
Powell's Orch CH4 . . . . . .141 C7
Powell St WA4 . . . . .16 F3
Powey La CH1 . . . . .94 B5
Pownall Ave SK7 . . . . .35 F7
Pownall Ct SK9 . . . . .59 E8
POWNALL GREEN 35 E6
Pownall Green Prim Sch
SK7 . . . . .35 E6
Pownall Hall Sch SK9 . . . .59 E8
POWNALL PARK 59 E7
Pownall Rd SK9 . . . . .59 F8
Pownall Sq SK11 . . . . . . .112 C8
Pownall St SK10 . . . . .87 D1
Powy Dr ST7 . . . . .195 B2
Powys Ct CH1 . . . . .237 A3
Powys St WA5 . . . . .15 F5
POYNTON 36 E4
Poynton Ct WA4 . . . . .17 B3
Poynton High Sch
SK12 . . . . .36 D1
Poynton St 18 SK10 . . . .112 C8
Poynton Sta SK12 . . . . . . .36 C4
Pratchitts Row CW5 . . . . .204 E5
Precinct The CW2 . . . . . . .189 F2
Preece CI WA11 . . . . .12 C4
Preece Ct CW1 . . . . .190 B5
Preesall Ave SK8 . . . . .34 B8
Premier Pk CW7 . . . . .127 B3
Prenton PI CH4 . . . . .141 E7
Prescot Dr WA8 . . . . .12 D2
Prescot St CH2 . . . . .118 F3
Prescott Rd SK9 . . . . .34 B1
Prescott St WA4 . . . . .16 E3
PRESTBURY 87 B7
Prestbury CE Prim Sch
SK10 . . . . .86 F7
Prestbury CI
6 Northwich CW9 . . . . . .103 F4
Widnes WA8 . . . . .22 E8
Prestbury Ct SK10 . . . . . . .86 F6
Prestbury La SK10 . . . . . . .87 D4
Prestbury Pk SK10 . . . . . . .86 E6
Prestbury Rd
Adder's Moss SK10 . . . . . . .85 E6
Macclesfield SK10 . . . . .87 B1
Nether Alderley SK10 . . . . . .86 A5
Wilmslow SK9 . . . . .60 E5
Prestbury Sta SK10 . . . . . .87 A7
Preston Ave M44 . . . . .11 F7
PRESTON BROOK 50 F5
PRESTON ON THE HILL
. . . . .51 A6
Preston St W SK11 . . . . . .112 B6
Prestwich Ave WA3 . . . . . . .4 E3

Pic–Pri 273

Prestwick CI
Macclesfield SK10 . . . . .87 C5
Widnes WA8 . . . . .12 F3
Winsford CW7 . . . . .126 C2
Prestwood Ct WA3 . . . . . . .10 A7
Pretoria St CH4 . . . . .141 D7
Price Ave CW11 . . . . .175 A5
Price Dr CW11 . . . . .175 A5
Pride Gr WA9 . . . . .1 A2
Pride CI WA12 . . . . .2 E2
Priestfield Rd CH65 . . . . . .70 C5
Priest La SK10 . . . . .61 B1
Priestley Bsns Ctr WA5 . . .15 F5
Priestley Coll WA4 . . . . . . .16 C3
Priestley St WA4 . . . . .16 B3
Priestley St WA5 . . . . .15 F5
Priesty Ct 13 CW5 . . . . . .204 E5
Priestner Dr WA6 . . . . .73 B4
Priestway La CH64 . . . . . . .67 E1
Priesty Ct CW12 . . . . .156 D2
Priesty Fields CW12 . . . . .156 D2
Primary CI M44 . . . . .11 D5
Primitive St ST7 . . . . .195 C7
Primrose Ave
Haslington CW1 . . . . .191 C5
Macclesfield SK11 . . . . . . .112 B5
Primrose Chase CW4 . . . .130 D8
Primrose CI
Huntington CH3 . . . . .142 A6
Runcorn WA7 . . . . .50 A8
Warrington WA3 . . . . .8 D2
Widnes WA8 . . . . .12 E1
Primrose Gr WA11 . . . . .1 E7
PRIMROSE HILL 28 C6
Primrose Hill
Crewe CW2 . . . . .189 E5
Cuddington SK10 . . . . . . .101 F4
Kelsall CW6 . . . . .122 C6
Primrose La WA4 . . . . .73 B1
Primula CI WA9 . . . . .6 A7
Primula Dr WA3 . . . . .3 D8
Prince Albert St WA1 . . . .190 D4
Prince Edward St
CW5 . . . . .204 E6
Prince Henry Sq 3
WA1 . . . . .16 B5
PRINCE HILL 231 F6
Prince Rd SK12 . . . . .37 C5
Princes Ave
Bebington CH62 . . . . .43 E6
Chester CH1 . . . . .237 C3
Northwich CW9 . . . . .104 B8
Princes CI WA7 . . . . .23 F1
Princes Ct CW5 . . . . .204 E7
Princes Pk CW8 . . . . .78 A2
Princes Rd WA8 . . . . .12 E1
Princes St CH65 . . . . .70 B6
Princess Ave
Audley ST7 . . . . .209 D1
Haydock WA11 . . . . .2 A1
Warrington, Bruche WA1 . . .16 F6
Warrington, Great Sankey
WA5 . . . . .14 E2
Warrington, Padgate
WA1 . . . . .17 A8
Princess CI CW2 . . . . . . .205 F8
Princess Cres
Middlewich CW10 . . . . . . .151 D6
Warrington WA1 . . . . .16 F6
Princess Ct ST7 . . . . .210 D5
Princess Dr
Bollington SK10 . . . . .87 E7
Nantwich CW5 . . . . .205 A6
Sandbach CW11 . . . . .175 A7
Wistaston CW2 . . . . .205 F8
Princess Gr CW2 . . . . . . .205 F8
Princess Rd
Allostock WA16 . . . . .106 E3
Lymm WA13 . . . . .18 C3
Wilmslow SK9 . . . . .59 F5
Princess St
Bollington SK10 . . . . .87 F7
Chester CH1 . . . . .237 A2
Congleton CW12 . . . . .156 D3
Crewe CW1 . . . . .190 C6
Knutsford WA16 . . . . .57 A2
Northwich CW9 . . . . .79 E2
Talke ST7 . . . . .210 D5
Warrington WA5 . . . . .15 D4
Winsford CW7 . . . . .127 A2
Princes St S WA12 . . . . . . .2 B3
Prince's St WA8 . . . . .23 A8
Princes Wlk SK7 . . . . .36 A7
Princes Way SK11 . . . . . .111 E7
Princeway WA6 . . . . .74 B8
Prince William Ave
CH5 . . . . .116 B3
Priory Ave CW9 . . . . .103 F4
Priory CI
Chester CH2 . . . . .118 C4
Congleton CW12 . . . . .179 B7
Crewe CW1 . . . . .190 A8
Runcorn WA7 . . . . .24 A1
Winsford CW7 . . . . .126 C3
Priory Ct SK10 . . . . .86 F1
Priory Dr ST10 . . . . .86 E2
Priory La SK10 . . . . .86 E2
Priory PI
Chester CH2 . . . . .237 B2
Kidsgrove ST7 . . . . .195 B3
Priory Rd
Altrincham WA14 . . . . .31 B8
Runcorn WA7 . . . . .24 C2

Priory Rd continued
Wilmslow SK9 ....59 E8
Priory St
Northwich CW9 ....104 A8
Warrington WA4 ....16 B3
Priory The
Neston CH64 ....41 E1
Winwick WA2 ....8 A7
Priory Way CW8 ....103 B4
Pritchard Dr CW9 ....103 E2
Private Wlk CH3 ....142 A8
Probert Cl CW2 ....190 A4
Proctors Cl WA8 ....13 D2
Proctors La CW11 ....174 E5
Proffits La WA6 ....73 B4
Promenade Cvn Pk
WA4 ....25 B7
Promised Land La
CH3 ....142 E5
Prospect Ave M44 ....11 E6
Prospect Dr
Altrincham WA15 ....32 D8
Davenham CW9 ....103 E2
Prospect La WA3 ....10 D3
Prospect Rd M44 ....11 E6
Prospect Row WA7 ....48 F7
Prospect St CW12 ....156 C2
Prosperity Ct CW10 ....128 D1
Prosperity Way CW10 ....128 D1
Prosser Rd CH2 ....95 C1
Protector Way M44 ....11 F8
Provan Way CH1 ....117 D5
Provident St WA1 ....1 A3
Prunus Rd CW1 ....190 E6
Pryors The CH3 ....121 C3
Ptarmigan Pl CW7 ....149 D5
Public Hall St 18 WA7 ....23 A3
Pudding La CW6 ....168 A7
PUDDINGLAKE 129 A8
PUDDINGTON 92 F8
Puddington La CH64 ....92 E8
Puddle Bank La CW12 ....178 F5
Puffin Ave SK12 ....36 B4
Puffin Cl CH65 ....95 C8
PULFORD 162 D3
Pulford App
Aldford CH3 ....163 D3
Pulford CH4 ....162 E2
Pulford Cl
Northwich CW9 ....103 E4
Runcorn WA7 ....49 E6
Pulford Ct CH4 ....162 D2
Pulford La CH4 ....162 A6
Pulford Rd
Blacon CH1 ....117 E5
Ellesmere Port CH65 ....69 F4
Winsford CW7 ....126 C1
Pullman Cl CH60 ....104 C8
Pullman Dr CW9 ....104 C8
Pump Ct ST7 ....209 E2
Pumping Station Hos
CW6 ....184 E3
Pump La
Churton CH3 ....181 A5
Runcorn WA7 ....49 F8
Tattenhall CH3 ....182 C6
Pumptree Mews
SK11 ....111 E7
Purdy Cl WA5 ....7 D1
Puritan Bldgs WA7 ....23 C2
Purley Dr M44 ....11 C5
Purser La SY14 ....211 E4
Puss Bank Sch SK10 ....112 F8
Putney Ct WA7 ....49 F7
Pye Cl WA11 ....2 B8
Pyecroft Cl WA5 ....14 D6
Pyecroft Rd WA5 ....14 D6
Pyecroft St CH4 ....141 E7
Pye Rd CH60 ....41 A8
Pym's La CW1 ....189 E6
Pyrus Ave CW1 ....190 E6
Pyrus Gr WA6 ....73 C4
Pytcheley Hollow
WA6 ....100 F6

Q

Quadrant Cl WA7 ....50 D6
Quadrant The CH1 ....117 E2
Quadrant The WA3 ....9 F5
Quad The CH1 ....117 E2
Quail Cl WA2 ....8 D3
Quaintways CW8 ....103 C4
Quakers Coppice
CW1 ....191 A2
Quakers Way LL13 ....180 E1
Quamlock Cl
Ellesmere Port CH66 ....69 A6
Winsford CW7 ....149 A7
Quarry Ave CH3 ....180 F1
QUARRYBANK 146 C8
Quarrybank CW6 ....184 F6
Quarry Bank Cotts
CW6 ....184 F6
Quarry Bank Mill*
SK9 ....33 F2
Quarry Bank Rd SK9 ....33 F3
Quarry Bank Rise
CW7 ....149 B8
Quarry Cl
Chester CH4 ....141 C7
Runcorn WA7 ....23 D1

Quarry Ct
Chester CH3 ....180 F1
Widnes WA8 ....12 C1
Quarry Hill CH3 ....180 F1
Quarry La
Christleton CH3 ....142 E7
Kelsall CW6 ....122 D5
Warrington WA4 ....26 C6
Quarry Rd
Neston CH64 ....42 C1
New Mills SK22 ....39 D7
Quarry Terr ST7 ....195 A1
Quarter The CH1 ....237 B3
Quay Fold WA5 ....15 F4
Quayle Cl WA11 ....1 C6
Quay Pl WA7 ....50 E7
Quayside
Congleton CW12 ....156 E1
Neston CH64 ....66 E5
Quay Side WA6 ....49 D1
Quayside Mews WA13 ....18 F3
Quayside Way SK11 ....112 E7
Quay The WA6 ....49 D2
Queastybirch La
Hatton WA4 ....25 F1
Hatton WA4 ....26 A1
Quebec Rd WA2 ....16 D7
Queen Anne Ct SK9 ....60 C6
Queen Annes Ct 8
SK11 ....112 B6
Queen Elizabeth Ho
CW9 ....79 A1
Queens Ave
Ellesmere Port CH65 ....70 A3
Warrington WA1 ....16 E7
Queen's Ave CH1 ....237 C3
Queen's Ave CW5 ....91 D1
Queen's Ave
Glazebury WA3 ....5 C7
Macclesfield SK10 ....87 E2
Sandycroft CH5 ....116 A3
Widnes WA8 ....22 B8
Queensbury Cl
15 Handforth SK9 ....34 D1
Wilmslow SK9 ....60 D8
Queensbury Way WA8 ....12 E3
Queens Cl SK10 ....87 E6
Queen's Cl
Macclesfield SK10 ....87 E2
Runcorn WA7 ....22 F1
Queens Cres
Chester CH2 ....118 E7
Warrington WA1 ....17 A8
Queen's Cres CW1 ....172 E2
Queens Ct
Chester CH4 ....237 C1
Winsford CW7 ....126 D1
Queen's Ct CW10 ....128 D1
Queens Dr
Golborne WA3 ....3 C8
Helsby WA6 ....73 B3
Heswall CH60 ....40 E8
Newton-le-W WA12 ....2 C5
Warrington WA4 ....17 A2
Queen's Dr
Chester CH4 ....237 C1
Middlewich CW10 ....151 D7
Nantwich CW5 ....204 D4
Sandbach CW11 ....175 A8
Queensford LL13 ....222 A8
Queensgate
Bramhall SK7 ....35 E5
Northwich CW8 ....103 E8
Queensgate Prim Sch
SK7 ....35 E4
Queens Gdns
Ellesmere Port CH65 ....70 B5
Talke ST7 ....210 D5
Queen's Par 1 CW7 ....126 D1
QUEEN'S PARK 141 F8
Queen's Park Dr CW1 ....189 F3
Queen's Park Gdns
CW2 ....189 E4
Queens Park High Sch
CH4 ....237 B1
Queen's Park Ho CH4 ....237 B1
Queen's Park Rd CH4 ....237 B1
Queen's Park View
CH4 ....237 B1
Queens Pk CH60 ....40 D8
Queens Pl CH1 ....237 B3
Queens Rd
Chester CH3 ....119 B3
Ellesmere Port CH66 ....69 C7
Haydock WA11 ....2 A7
Queen's Rd
Chester CH1 ....237 C3
Runcorn WA7 ....22 F1
Wilmslow SK9 ....60 A6
Queen's Sch (Lower) The
CH2 ....118 C4
Queen's Sch The CH1 ....237 A2
Queen St
Audley ST7 ....209 C1
Bollington SK10 ....88 B8
Bunbury CW6 ....185 E8
Chester CH1 ....237 B2
Congleton, Buglawton
CW12 ....156 F4
Congleton CW12 ....156 C2
Crewe CW1 ....190 E5
Ellesmere Port CH65 ....70 C7
Golborne WA3 ....3 B8
Kidsgrove ST7 ....195 A2
Knutsford WA16 ....56 F2
Macclesfield SK10 ....112 D8
Middlewich CW10 ....128 C1
Nantwich CW5 ....204 E5

Queen St continued
Newton-le-W WA12 ....2 B3
Northwich CW9 ....103 F7
8 Runcorn WA7 ....23 A3
Shavington CW2 ....206 C4
Queens Terr SK9 ....34 D3
Queensway
Alsager ST7 ....193 B5
Chester CH2 ....118 F5
Crewe CW1 ....190 C4
Frodsham WA6 ....74 B8
Gatley SK8 ....34 C8
Heswall CH60 ....41 C6
Knutsford WA16 ....56 E3
Partington M31 ....11 F4
Poynton SK12 ....36 D3
Runcorn WA7 ....22 F3
Widnes WA8 ....22 F6
Winsford CW7 ....149 D8
Queen's Way CH4 ....139 B4
Queensway Trad Est
WA8 ....23 A5
Queen Victoria St 14
SK11 ....112 D8
Quill Ct M44 ....11 E6
Quillet The CH64 ....66 F7
Quinn St WA8 ....23 B7
Quinta Prim Sch The
CW12 ....156 A2
Quinta Rd CW12 ....156 A3
QUOISLEY 226 B8

R

RABY 42 C4
Raby Ave CH63 ....43 B6
Raby Cl
Bebington CH63 ....43 A7
Heswall CH60 ....40 F7
Widnes WA8 ....13 E2
Raby Ct CH65 ....70 D3
Raby Dr CH63 ....43 A6
Raby Gdns CH64 ....66 E8
Raby Hall Rd CH63 ....43 A6
RABY MERE 43 B7
Raby Mere Rd CH63 ....42 D5
Raby Park Cl CH64 ....66 E8
Raby Park Rd CH64 ....41 F1
Raby Rd
Neston CH64 ....66 E8
Thornton Hough CH63 ....42 B5
Racecourse La CW6 ....124 A1
Racecourse Pk SK9 ....59 F6
Racecourse Rd SK9 ....59 E6
Racefield CW13 ....18 F3
Racefield Rd WA16 ....56 F2
Race The SK9 ....34 D2
Rackdale Cl CW11 ....175 D8
Radcliffe Ave WA3 ....4 E3
Radcliffe Cl CH3 ....121 C3
Radcliffe Rd
Sandbach CW11 ....174 F3
Sutton Lane Ends SK11 ....135 D7
Winsford CW7 ....149 B6
Raddel La WA4 ....52 C5
Raddle Wharf CH65 ....70 C7
Raddon Pl WA4 ....16 B8
Radford Cl WA8 ....22 C7
Radlett Cl WA5 ....14 E3
Radley Dr CH63 ....41 F6
Radley La WA2 ....8 E4
RADMORE GREEN 186 E3
RADNOR 155 E6
Radnor Cl
Congleton CW12 ....156 B3
Sandbach CW11 ....174 E7
Radnor Dr
Chester CH4 ....141 A4
Widnes WA8 ....12 D2
Radnor Park Ind Ctr
CW12 ....156 A4
Radnor Park Trad Est
CW12 ....156 A4
Radnor St WA5 ....15 E6
Radway Gn CH66 ....69 C5
RADWAY GREEN 192 F1
Radway Green Bsns &
Tech Ctr CW2 ....192 F1
Radway Green Rd
Alsager CW2 ....208 E8
Barthomley CW2 ....208 D6
Raeburn Ave
Bebington CH62 ....43 E6
Neston CH64 ....66 F7
Raeburn Prim Sch
CH62 ....43 D6
Raglan Ct WA3 ....9 F6
Raglan Rd SK10 ....87 F2
Ragley Cl SK12 ....36 F4
Railbrook Ct CW2 ....190 D2
Railton Ave CW1 ....190 C8
Railway Age Mus The*
CW1 ....190 D3
Railway Cotts
Congleton CW12 ....157 A1
Hollinfare WA3 ....11 B5
Hooton CH66 ....43 E1
Wimboldsley CW10 ....150 F1
Railway St
Crewe CW2 ....190 D2
Newton-le-W WA12 ....2 B3
Railway Terr
Disley SK12 ....38 D6
Sandycroft CH5 ....116 B3
Railway View WA5 ....1 D1
Rainbow St CW1 ....190 D4

Rainford Cl ST7 ....195 F1
RAINOW 88 D5
Rainow Cl CW10 ....151 B7
Rainow Dr SK12 ....37 A2
Rainow Prim Sch SK10 ....88 D4
Rainow Rd SK10 ....88 B8
Rainow View SK10 ....63 C1
Rainow Way 13 SK9 ....34 E1
Rajar Cotts WA16 ....57 F4
Rajar Wlk WA16 ....58 A4
Rake House Mews
WA6 ....73 B4
Rake La
Backford CH2 ....95 D6
Broughton CH5 ....139 A8
Christleton CH3 ....143 A7
Dunham-on-t-H WA6 ....97 B7
Dunham-on-t-H WA6 ....97 E7
Eccleston CH4 ....141 C1
Helsby, Helsby Marsh
WA6 ....73 A5
Helsby WA6 ....73 C4
Rake The
Bebington CH62 ....43 C8
Burton CH64 ....67 D1
Rake Way CH1 ....94 A1
Raleigh Cl WA5 ....7 D1
Raleigh Rd CH64 ....41 F1
Rampit Cl WA11 ....1 F7
Ramp Rd E M90 ....33 C7
Ramp Rd S M90 ....33 C7
Ramp Rd W M90 ....33 B7
Ramsay Cl WA3 ....9 E3
Ramsbottom St 2
CW1 ....190 B5
Ramsbrook La L24,
WA8 ....21 C3
Ramsdale Rd SK7 ....35 E8
Ramsden Ct CH4 ....140 F4
Ramsey Cl WA8 ....13 E3
Ramsey Rd CH65 ....70 C1
Ramsfield Rd L24 ....21 A4
Randal Cres SK23 ....65 E5
Randall Cl WA12 ....2 B4
Randle Bennett Cl
CW11 ....174 E7
Randle Mdw CH66 ....69 F1
Randle Meadow Ct
CH66 ....69 F2
Randle's View CW12 ....179 C8
Range Ct SK10 ....87 E1
Rangemoor Cl WA3 ....10 A6
Rannoch Cl CW6 ....69 F3
Ranulph Cl WA6 ....74 C7
Ranwonath Ct CH2 ....237 B4
Ranworth Dr WA3 ....3 E7
Ranworth Rd WA5 ....14 E6
Rappax Rd WA15 ....32 A8
Raquets Ct The CW10 ....127 D5
Rathbone Pl CW6 ....146 D2
Rathlin Cl WA8 ....13 E3
Rathmell Cl WA3 ....4 E3
Rathvale Dr M22 ....33 C8
Ravenbank Com Prim Sch
WA13 ....18 F3
Raven Cl CW11 ....174 F3
Ravendale Cl CW7 ....149 E8
Ravenfield Dr WA8 ....12 C3
Ravenho La SK10 ....88 D4
Ravenhurst Ct WA3 ....9 F5
Ravenoak Park Rd SK8 ....35 B8
Ravenoak Rd SK8 ....35 B8
Ravenscar Cres M22 ....33 D8
Ravens Cl ST7 ....209 E3
Ravenscliffe Rd ST7 ....195 A1
RAVENSCLOUGH 101 E3
Ravens Cnr CW5 ....203 E2
Ravenscroft CW4 ....130 A3
Ravenscroft Cl CW11 ....175 C7
Ravenscroft Rd CW2 ....189 E3
Ravensdale Cl WA2 ....8 D3
Ravensfield CW8 ....101 D4
Ravensholme Cl CH3 ....166 A2
Ravensholme La CH3 ....166 A2
Ravens La CW5 ....203 E5
Raven's La CW7 ....209 F3
Ravensmead Com Prim
Sch ST7 ....209 E3
RAVENSMOOR 203 E2
Ravenswood CW8 ....103 B4
Ravenswood Dr SK8 ....35 B8
Ravenswood Rd SK9 ....59 E4
Ravenwood Dr WA15 ....32 D7
Rawcliffe Cl WA8 ....12 F4
Rawdon Cl WA7 ....50 A7
Rawlings Cl WA3 ....9 F3
Rawlinson Cres L26 ....21 B8
Rawson Rd CH1 ....117 E3
Ray Ave CW5 ....204 F7
Raycliffe Cl WA7 ....49 D5
Rayleigh Ave CW9 ....127 A8
Rayleigh Way SK10 ....86 E1
Raymond Ave WA4 ....16 D2
Raymond St CH1 ....237 A3
Raymond Way CH4 ....67 A7
Rays Brow CW8 ....78 B2
Readesdale Ave CW2 ....189 F2
Reade's La CW12 ....179 B8
Reading Room La SY14,
CH3 ....199 D8
Rean Mdw CH3 ....166 B2
Reaper Cl WA3 ....15 D6
REASE HEATH 188 C2
Reaseheath Coll CW5 ....188 D1
Reay St WA8 ....13 C2
Rectory Ave WA3 ....3 C8

Rectory Cl
Farndon CH3 ....180 E1
Heswall CH60 ....40 F7
8 Nantwich CW5 ....204 E5
Winwick WA2 ....8 A6
Wistaston CW2 ....205 E8
Rectory Gdns
Lymm WA13 ....18 E3
Talke ST7 ....210 D6
Rectory La
Adderley TF9 ....235 B5
Capenhurst CH1 ....94 A8
Heswall CH60 ....40 E7
Lymm WA13 ....18 E3
Winwick WA2 ....8 A6
Rectory View ST7 ....210 D6
Redacre SK12 ....36 F6
Redacre Cl WA4 ....51 A3
Red Bank Ave WA12 ....2 F1
Redbourne Dr
Chorlton CW2 ....207 D1
Widnes WA8 ....12 B4
Redbrook Cl CH62 ....43 D6
Redbrook Gr 2 SK9 ....34 D1
Redbrook Rd M31 ....11 E2
Redbrook Way SK10 ....62 C5
Red Brow La WA7, WA4 ....50 F8
RED BULL 194 E3
Redcar Dr CH62 ....43 D5
Red Cow Yd 11 WA16 ....57 A2
Reddish Ave SK23 ....65 D6
Reddish Cres WA13 ....18 F4
Reddish La
Horwich End SK23 ....65 D6
Lymm WA13 ....19 A5
Reddish Rd SK23 ....65 D6
Reddy La WA14 ....30 B8
Redesdale Cl WA2 ....8 E2
Redesmere Cl
Macclesfield SK10 ....87 A1
Northwich CW9 ....104 A5
Sandbach CW11 ....174 F7
Redesmere Dr SK9 ....60 A1
Redesmere La SK11 ....110 B3
Redesmere Rd SK9 ....34 D5
Redfern Ave CW12 ....156 F4
Red Gables WA4 ....27 B3
Redgate CW8 ....103 D7
Redhill Mews CH65 ....70 B6
Redhill Rd
Chester CH4 ....140 F6
Kelsall CW6 ....122 C5
Red Ho SK10 ....87 E1
Redhouse La SK12 ....38 E7
Red House La WA14 ....20 C8
Redhouses SK11 ....113 D3
Red La
Disley SK12 ....38 C5
Frodsham WA6 ....74 C7
Huxley CH3 ....166 D6
Lower Whitley WA4 ....52 C1
Sandbach CW11 ....174 C6
Warrington WA4 ....26 C7
Redland Cl CH4 ....141 A7
Redland Ho CH4 ....141 B7
Red Lion Cl ST7 ....210 D7
Red Lion La
Ellesmere Port CH66 ....69 C7
Nantwich CW5 ....204 D5
Red Lo SK12 ....38 A6
Redmain Gr WA3 ....3 E8
Redmayne Cl WA12 ....2 B4
Redmere Dr CH60 ....41 D8
Redmoor La
Disley SK12 ....39 A4
New Mills SK22 ....39 B6
Red Pike CH66 ....69 D8
Redpoll La WA3 ....9 F3
Redrock Cres ST7 ....195 C1
Red Row SK7 ....37 B8
Redruth Ave SK10 ....86 E1
Redruth Cl WA7 ....50 C6
Redshank Ave CW7 ....149 C5
Redshank Cl WA12 ....2 C4
Redshank Dr SK10 ....87 C5
Redshank La WA3 ....9 F3
Redshaw Cl CW10 ....151 C6
Redstart Cl 7 WA3 ....3 E8
Redstone Dr 3 CW7 ....126 A1
Red Stone Hill WA6 ....73 C4
RED STREET 210 E3
Redtail Cl WA7 ....22 F3
Redvales Ct WA3 ....9 C4
Redvers Ave CH66 ....44 A2
Redway La SK10 ....88 B7
Redwing Cl ST7 ....195 F1
Redwood Cl
Barnton CW8 ....78 B4
Holt LL13 ....196 D8
Lostock Gralam CW9 ....140 E6
Warrington WA1 ....17 E7
Redwood Cl SK10 ....87 C5
Redwood Dr
Crewe CW1 ....189 F7
Ellesmere Port CH66 ....69 F1
Elton CH2 ....72 C4
Reece Cl CW2 ....119 E8
Reedgate La CW9 ....77 F1
Reed La CW9 ....53 C6
Reedsmere Cl WA4 ....16 E2
Reedsmere Wlk CW9 ....78 D8
Reeman Ct SK9 ....34 D2
Rees Cres CW4 ....130 C3
Reeves Rd CH3 ....142 B8
Reeve St WA3 ....4 B8
Regal Cl
Ellesmere Port CH66 ....69 E3
Northwich CW9 ....103 E4

Regal Cres WA8 . . . . .22 B8
Regency Cl ST7 . . . . .210 D5
Regency Ct
  Chester CH2 . . . . .119 E8
  Winsford CW7 . . . . .149 C7
Regency Gdns SK8 . . . . .34 E8
Regency Hospl SK11 . . . . . .112 B8
Regency Pk SK9 . . . . .59 F5
Regency Sq WA5 . . . . .15 F6
Regency Way CW9 . . . . . . .103 E4
Regent Ave
  Haydock WA11 . . . . .1 B7
  Macclesfield SK11 . . . . . . .112 B6
  Warrington WA1 . . . . .17 A8
Regent Bank SK9 . . . . .59 F5
Regent Cl
  Bramhall SK7 . . . . .35 D4
  Shavington CW2 . . . . .206 B3
  Wilmslow SK9 . . . . .59 F5
Regent Ct WA15 . . . . .6 C6
Regent Rd WA8 . . . . .13 B1
Regents Cl CH3 . . . . .119 B2
Regents Gate CW5 . . . . . . .205 A5
Regent St
  Ellesmere Port CH65 . . . . . .70 A5
  Moulton CW9 . . . . .126 F8
  Newton-le-W WA12 . . . . .2 A3
  ⚹ Runcorn WA7 . . . . .23 A3
  Warrington WA1 . . . . .16 A5
Regents The SK9 . . . . .60 C8
Regents Theological Coll
  CW5 . . . . .205 A5
Regents Way ⁴ CW7 . . . . . .149 A8
Reginald Mitchell Prim
  Sch The ST7 . . . . .194 D1
Registry Ct CW7 . . . . .103 E4
Reid Ave WA5 . . . . .15 F8
Reid Ct CH66 . . . . .69 C7
Reid St CW1 . . . . .190 C6
Reins Croft CH64 . . . . .41 E1
Rembury Pl WA4 . . . . .51 A3
Remer St CW1 . . . . .190 D7
Renaissance Way
  CW1 . . . . .191 A3
Rendel Cl WA12 . . . . .2 D2
Rendlesham Cl WA3 . . . . . . .10 B6
Renfrew Ave CH62 . . . . .43 E5
Renfrew Cl SK10 . . . . .86 F2
Renown Cl WA3 . . . . .9 D4
Renshaw St CW9 . . . . .79 D2
Rensherds Pl WA16 . . . . . . .29 C5
Renton Ave WA7 . . . . .23 D2
Repton Cl WA16 . . . . .29 C4
Repton Dr CW1 . . . . .191 D5
Repton Rd CH65 . . . . .70 D4
Reservoir Rd SK23 . . . . .65 D7
Reservoir Terr CH2 . . . . . . .118 F2
Retreat The CW1 . . . . .190 C6
Revesby Cl WA8 . . . . .12 D2
Rex Bldgs SK9 . . . . .60 B6
Reynolds Ave
  St Helens WA9 . . . . .1 B2
  Warrington WA3 . . . . .9 E5
Reynolds La CW11 . . . . . . .175 F6
Reynolds Mews SK9 . . . . . . .60 E8
Reynolds St WA4 . . . . .16 F3
Rhoden St CW1 . . . . .191 A6
Rhodes Cl CW1 . . . . .191 D4
Rhodes St WA2 . . . . .16 C7
Rhodesway CH60 . . . . .41 B7
Rhona Cl CH63 . . . . .43 C4
Rhona Dr WA5 . . . . .14 E6
Rhone Ct CH3 . . . . .142 A8
RHUDDALL HEATH 146 E1
Rhuddlan Ct CW7 . . . .
Rhuddlan ⁵ CH4 . . . . .140 F6
Rhuddlan Rd CH1 . . . . .117 D3
Rhum Cl CH65 . . . . .70 C1
Rhyl St WA8 . . . . .22 F7
Ribble Ave CW7 . . . . .127 B1
Ribble Cl
  Culcheth WA3 . . . . .4 E2
  Widnes WA8 . . . . .13 F3
Ribble Dr ST8 . . . . .179 E1
Ribble Pl CW7 . . . . .127 B1
Ribblesdale Ave
  CW12 . . . . .157 A5
Ribblesdale Cl CH62 . . . . . . .43 F5
Ribchester Gdns WA3 . . . . . .5 A3
Richard Cl WA7 . . . . .24 A2
Richard Moon St
  CW1 . . . . .190 B4
Richard Reynolds Ct
  CW1 . . . . .11 E6
Richards Croft CH3 . . . . . . .142 A7
Richards Gr CW12 . . . . .156 A3
Richardson Cl
  ⁴ Sandbach CW11 . . . . . .174 D6
  Shavington CW2 . . . . .206 D5
Richardson St WA2 . . . . . . .16 C8
Richard St
  Crewe CW1 . . . . .190 B5
  Northwich CW9 . . . . .104 C7
Richbell Cl WA4 . . . . .11 F7
Richmond Ave
  Grappenhall WA4 . . . . .17 C3
  Handforth SK9 . . . . .34 D4
  Haydock WA11 . . . . .1 B7
  Warrington WA7 . . . . .23 E2
  Warrington WA4 . . . . .17 A4
Richmond Cl
  Chorlton CW2 . . . . .207 D1
  Culcheth WA3 . . . . .4 D1

Richmond Cl continued
  Lymm WA13 . . . . .19 B4
  Sandbach CW11 . . . . .174 E7
Richmond Cres CH3 . . . . . .119 C2
Richmond Ct
  Chester CH3 . . . . .118 F2
  Ellesmere Port CH65 . . . . . .70 D3
  Warrington WA4 . . . . .17 A3
  Widnes WA8 . . . . .13 D4
Richmond Dr
  Lymm WA13 . . . . .19 B4
  Northwich CW9 . . . . .104 A8
Richmond Gdns WA12 . . . . . .2 C2
Richmond Gr SK7 . . . . .35 F6
Richmond Hill
  ❶ Knutsford WA16 . . . . . . .57 B1
  Macclesfield SK11 . . . . . . .112 E6
Richmond Mews CH2 . . . . .118 F2
Richmond Pl SK11 . . . . .112 E6
Richmond Rd CW1 . . . . .190 E5
Richmond St
  Warrington WA4 . . . . .17 A3
  Widnes WA8 . . . . .13 C1
Richmond Village
  CW5 . . . . .205 A5
Rickaby Cl CH4 . . . . .43 C8
Ridding La WA7 . . . . .50 B5
Riddings Ct CW8 . . . . .103 B4
Riddings La
  Hartford CW8 . . . . .103 B4
  Wybunbury CW5 . . . . .220 A8
Riddings The CH65 . . . . .70 B4
Rides The WA11 . . . . .1 D6
Ridge Ave WA15 . . . . .32 D6
Ridgeborne Cl WA5 . . . . .7 D2
Ridge Hill
  Langley SK11 . . . . .113 B2
  Utkinton CW6 . . . . .146 B5
Ridge Pk SK7 . . . . .35 D6
Ridge The CW8 . . . . .123 D7
Ridge View SK11 . . . . .112 C5
Ridgeway
  Golborne WA3 . . . . .3 E7
  Wilmslow SK9 . . . . .60 F7
Ridgeway Cl CH66 . . . . .69 C2
Ridgeway Ho CH3 . . . . .121 C3
Ridgeway The
  Alvanley WA6 . . . . .74 A1
  Cronton WA8 . . . . .12 C6
  Disley SK12 . . . . .38 C6
  Heswall CH60 . . . . .41 B7
  Runcorn WA7 . . . . .50 D6
  Tarvin CH3 . . . . .121 C3
Ridgewell Ave ⁴ WA3 . . . . . .3 E8
Ridgmont Rd SK7 . . . . .35 E5
RIDGWARDINE 235 E1
Ridgway Gdns WA13 . . . . . .18 D3
Ridgway St
  Crewe CW1 . . . . .190 D5
  Warrington WA2 . . . . .16 D8
Ridings Com Inf Sch The
  CH1 . . . . .94 A1
Ridings The
  Saughall CH1 . . . . .117 B8
  Wilmslow SK9 . . . . .59 D4
Ridley Cl CW2 . . . . .206 C8
Ridley Dr WA5 . . . . .15 C4
Ridley Gn CW6 . . . . .185 D1
Ridley Hill Farm CW6 . . . . .185 C3
Ridley Rd SK10 . . . . .87 E8
RIDLEYWOOD 196 C3
Ridley Wood Rd LL13 . . . . .196 A3
Ridsdale ❷ WA8 . . . . .22 C8
Rigby Ave CW1 . . . . .190 A7
Rigby Dr WA7 . . . . .49 F7
Rigby's Row CW5 . . . . .204 E5
Rigby St WA3 . . . . .3 A8
Rigg St ⁵ CW1 . . . . .190 B5
Riley Bank Mews WA6 . . . . .74 B1
Riley Cl CW11 . . . . .174 E5
Riley Dr WA7 . . . . .49 A8
Rileys Way ST7 . . . . .209 F2
Rilshaw La CW7 . . . . .150 B8
Rilston Ave WA3 . . . . .4 E3
Rimington Cl WA3 . . . . .4 E3
Rimsdale Cl CW2 . . . . .206 A7
Ring-o-Bells La SK12 . . . . . .38 D6
Ring Rd
  Chester CH2, CH3 . . . . . . .119 C3
  Connah's Quay CH5 . . . . . . .91 E2
Ringfield Rd L24 . . . . .21 A2
Ringstead Cl SK9 . . . . .34 D1
Ringstead Dr SK9 . . . . .34 D1
Ringstone Way SK23 . . . . . . .65 D8
Ringway
  Ellesmere Port CH66 . . . . . .69 E4
  Neston CH64 . . . . .41 E1
  Waverton CH3 . . . . .143 B5
Ringway Cl SK10 . . . . .87 B4
Ringway Prim Sch
  M22 . . . . .33 D8
Ringway Rd
  Runcorn WA7 . . . . .50 D6
  Wythenshawe M22, M90 . . .33 D7
Ringway Rd W M22,
  M90 . . . . .33 D8
Ringway Trad Est M22 . . . . .33 E8
Ringwood Cl WA3 . . . . .10 B5
Ripley Ave SK8 . . . . .35 B5
Ripley St WA5 . . . . .15 E6
Ripon Ave
  Ellesmere Port CH66 . . . . . .69 C5
  Golborne WA3 . . . . .3 D8
Ripon Cl
  Macclesfield SK10 . . . . .87 C3
  Newton-le-W WA12 . . . . .2 C5
Ripon Dr CW2 . . . . .206 A7

Ripon Row WA7 . . . . .49 D6
Riseley St SK10 . . . . .112 C8
Rise The SK23 . . . . .65 C6
Rising Sun Cl SK11 . . . . . . .112 A5
Rising Sun Rd SK11 . . . . . .112 A4
RISLEY 9 E6
Risley Moss Local Nature
  Reserve Visitor Ctr *
  WA3 . . . . .10 B5
Risley Rd WA3 . . . . .9 F6
Rivacre Brow CH66 . . . . .69 E8
Rivacre Bsns Ctr CH66 . . . . .69 E5
Rivacre Rd CH62, CH65,
  CH66 . . . . .44 C2
Rivacre Valley Ctry Pk*
  CH66 . . . . .69 D8
Rivacre Valley Prim Sch
  CH66 . . . . .69 E7
Riverbank Cl
  Bollington SK10 . . . . .87 F8
  Heswall CH60 . . . . .40 F6
  Nantwich CW5 . . . . .204 E8
Riverbank Rd CH60 . . . . .40 E6
Riverdane Rd CW12 . . . . . .156 F4
River La
  Chester CH4 . . . . .141 C7
  Farndon CH3 . . . . .180 E2
  Partington M31 . . . . .11 F4
  Saltney WA4 . . . . .140 E7
Rivermead Ave WA15 . . . . . .32 C7
River Rd
  Connah's Quay CH5 . . . . . . .91 F1
  Warrington, Latchford
    WA4 . . . . .16 B3
  Warrington, Wilderspool
    WA4 . . . . .16 C2
Riversdale
  Frodsham WA6 . . . . .49 C1
  Warrington WA1 . . . . .17 F7
Riversdale Rd WA7 . . . . .49 E8
Rivershill Gdns WA15 . . . . . .32 D6
Riverside
  Nantwich CW5 . . . . .204 D5
  Northwich CW9 . . . . .104 B5
Riverside Bsns Pk SK9 . . . . .60 B7
Riverside Cl WA1 . . . . .16 D4
Riverside Coll Halton
  (Kingsway Campus)
  WA8 . . . . .23 A8
Riverside Coll Halton
  Runcorn Campus
  WA7 . . . . .22 E3
Riverside Cres CW4 . . . . . .130 C4
Riverside Ct
  Huntington CH3 . . . . .141 F7
  Langley SK11 . . . . .113 C4
Riverside Dr SK10 . . . . .87 A5
Riverside Gr WA7 . . . . .189 D3
Riverside Pk CW9 . . . . .103 E6
Riverside Ret Pk WA1 . . . . . .16 C4
Riverside Trad Est
  Northwich WA8 . . . . .103 F7
  Warrington WA5 . . . . .14 D1
Riverside Trad Pk
  CH4 . . . . .140 E7
Riverton Wlk CH64 . . . . .66 D5
Riversmead CH3 . . . . .142 A6
River St
  Congleton CW12 . . . . .156 D3
  Macclesfield SK11 . . . . . . .112 E6
  Wilmslow SK9 . . . . .60 B8
River View CH2 . . . . .126 E1
Riverview Rd CH64 . . . . .66 F5
River Wlk WA7 . . . . .49 F7
Rivington Ct WA1 . . . . .16 E3
Rivington Gr WA14 . . . . .11 D6
Rivington Rd
  Ellesmere Port CH65 . . . . . .70 C5
  Runcorn WA7 . . . . .50 F3
Rixton Ave WA5 . . . . .14 D3
Rixton Park Homes
  WA3 . . . . .10 F2
Roaches The SK11 . . . . . . .112 B5
Road Beta CW10 . . . . .151 D8
Road Five CW7 . . . . .127 C2
Road Four CW7 . . . . .127 B2
Road One
  Weston CW1 . . . . .207 D8
  Winsford CW7 . . . . .127 B3
Roadside Ct WA3 . . . . .3 C8
Road Three CW7 . . . . .127 B2
Road Two
  Anderton CW9 . . . . .78 C3
  Weston CW1 . . . . .207 C8
  Winsford CW7 . . . . .127 B2
Roan Ct SK11 . . . . .112 F7
Roan House Way
  SK11 . . . . .112 F7
Roan Mews SK11 . . . . .112 F7
Roan Way SK11 . . . . .88 B8
Robert Moffat WA16 . . . . . . .29 C5
Roberts Ave WA11 . . . . .1 A5
Roberts Ct WA7 . . . . .49 F6
Roberts Dr CW9 . . . . .104 D6
Roberts Fold WA3 . . . . .9 D5
Roberts Rd CW9 . . . . .80 A2
Robert St
  Northwich CW9 . . . . .103 E6
  Runcorn WA7 . . . . .23 C2
  Warrington WA5 . . . . .15 F6
  Widnes WA8 . . . . .13 B1
Robert's Terr CH1 . . . . .118 B1
Robin Cl
  Chelford SK11 . . . . .84 A2
  Rainow SK10 . . . . .88 E5
  Runcorn WA7 . . . . .49 F6
  Sandbach CW11 . . . . .175 A8
Robin Cres SK11 . . . . .112 D2

Robin Hood Ave
  SK11 . . . . .112 D5
Robin Hood La WA6 . . . . . . .73 B2
Robin La
  Chelford SK11 . . . . .84 A3
  Sutton Lane Ends SK11 . . .112 D2
Robinsbay Rd M22 . . . . .33 E8
Robins Cl SK7 . . . . .35 E7
Robins Croft CH66 . . . . .69 F2
Robins La WA3 . . . . .4 D2
Robin's La SK7 . . . . .35 E7
Robinsons Croft CH3 . . . . . .142 B7
Robins Way WA3 . . . . .88 A7
Rob La WA12 . . . . .2 E5
Robson Cl WA11 . . . . .1 B7
Robson Way ❸ WA3 . . . . .3 F8
Roby Gr WA5 . . . . .15 A6
Roche Gdns SK8 . . . . .35 B6
Rochester Cl
  Golborne WA3 . . . . .3 A8
  Warrington WA5 . . . . .15 C7
Rochester Cres CW1 . . . . . .190 F6
Rochester Dr CH65 . . . . .70 D3
Rochester Ho SK10 . . . . .86 F1
Rochester Rd WA8 . . . . .22 D8
Rock Bank SK23 . . . . .65 E6
Rock Bank Rise SK10 . . . . . .63 A1
Rock Cotts CH5 . . . . .91 D1
Rock Dr WA6 . . . . .49 C1
Rock Farm Cl CH64 . . . . .67 A6
Rock Farm Dr CH64 . . . . .67 A6
Rock Farm Gr CH64 . . . . .67 A6
Rockfield Dr WA8 . . . . .12 D2
Rockfield Dr WA6 . . . . .73 C2
Rockfield Mews WA4 . . . . . .16 F2
Rockford Gdns WA5 . . . . . . .15 A8
Rockford Lo WA16 . . . . .57 C1
Rockhouse La ST7 . . . . .210 C7
Rockingham Cl WA3 . . . . . . .10 C6
Rock La
  Burwardsley CH3 . . . . .184 C6
  Chester CH2 . . . . .237 A4
  Widnes WA8 . . . . .12 F4
Rocklands La CH63 . . . . .42 C8
Rocklee Gdns CH64 . . . . . . .67 A6
Rockliffe La CH6 . . . . .91 A3
Rock Mill La SK22 . . . . .39 B7
Rock Rd
  Connah's Quay CH5 . . . . . . .91 E1
  Warrington WA4 . . . . .16 E4
ROCKSAVAGE 49 B4
Rock Savage Rdbt
  WA7 . . . . .49 E4
Rockside ST7 . . . . .195 C6
Rock St SK22 . . . . .39 C7
Rock The WA6 . . . . .73 C2
Rock Villas LL13 . . . . .180 E1
Rockwood Ave CW2 . . . . . .190 A3
Rockwood Cl WA7 . . . . .190 A3
Rocky La
  Heswall CH60 . . . . .40 F8
  Tattenhall CH3 . . . . .182 F7
Rocky La S CH60 . . . . .41 A8
Roddy La WA7 . . . . .75 E2
Rode Ct ⁷ CW12 . . . . .156 F3
Rode Hall * ST7 . . . . .194 B7
RODEHEATH 134 B3
RODE HEATH 193 E7
Rodeheath Cl SK9 . . . . .60 D7
Rode Heath Prim Sch
  ST7 . . . . .193 F7
Rodehouse Cl ST7 . . . . .193 F7
Rodepool Cl SK9 . . . . .34 D2
Rode St CW6 . . . . .146 A3
Rode The ST7 . . . . .193 D4
Rodgers Cl WA6 . . . . .49 B1
Rodney St WA1 . . . . .16 C5
Roebourne Rise CH1 . . . . . .117 D4
Roebuck St CW1 . . . . .190 C5
Roeburn Way WA5 . . . . .14 D3
Roedean Wlk CW1 . . . . . . .190 F5
Roehampton Dr WA7 . . . . . .49 E7
Rehurst La CW7 . . . . .126 D2
Roemarsh Ct WA7 . . . . .49 E6
Roe Pk CW12 . . . . .178 E1
Roe St
  Congleton CW12 . . . . .156 E2
  Macclesfield SK11 . . . . . . .112 D7
Roewood La
  Higher Hurdsfield
    SK10 . . . . .88 A1
  Macclesfield SK10 . . . . . . .113 A8
Roften Ind Est CH6 . . . . .43 D1
Rokeby Ct WA7 . . . . .24 D5
Rokeden WA12 . . . . .2 C4
Roklis Grange ❿ CH64 . . . . .66 E8
Roland Ave WA7 . . . . .22 F1
Rolands Wlk CW7 . . . . .23 F2
Rolleston St WA2 . . . . .16 E6
Rolls Ave WA5 . . . . .190 A6
Rolt Cres CW10 . . . . .151 C7
Roman Cl
  Newton-le-W WA12 . . . . .2 C2
  Runcorn WA7 . . . . .50 A5
Roman Ct CH64 . . . . .66 F7
Roman Dr CH1 . . . . .117 D6
Romanes St CW8 . . . . .103 E7
Roman Rd WA4 . . . . .26 C3
Roman Way CW11 . . . . .174 E7
Romiley Rd CH66 . . . . .69 D2
Romney Cl
  Neston CH64 . . . . .66 E7
  Widnes WA8 . . . . .22 C8
Romney Croft CH64 . . . . . . .66 F7
Romney Way CH64 . . . . .66 E7
Romsey Dr SK8 . . . . .35 C6
Rona Ave CH65 . . . . .70 C1
Ronald Dr WA2 . . . . .9 B2
Ronaldshay WA8 . . . . .13 E2

Ronaldsway
  Halewood L26 . . . . .21 A8
  Heswall CH60 . . . . .40 F6
Ronan Rd WA8 . . . . .22 E5
ROODEE 237 A1
Rood Hill CW12 . . . . .156 D3
Rood La CW12 . . . . .156 E4
Rookery Cl
  ❶ Nantwich CW5 . . . . . . .204 F5
  Sandbach CW11 . . . . .174 C5
Rookery Ct CW11 . . . . .174 C5
Rookery Dr
  Nantwich CW5 . . . . .204 E4
  Tattenhall CH3 . . . . .166 B2
Rookery Farm Rd
  CW6 . . . . .169 A6
Rookery Gdns CW9 . . . . . . .103 E3
Rookerypool Cl SK9 . . . . . . .34 D2
Rookery Rd
  Newton-le-W WA12 . . . . . .195 C3
  Tilston SY14 . . . . .198 B3
Rookery Rise CW7 . . . . .150 A8
Rookery The
  Broughton CH4 . . . . .139 B3
  Newton-le-W WA12 . . . . .2 D4
Rook St CW2 . . . . .190 C2
Rooks Way CH60 . . . . .40 E8
Roome St WA2 . . . . .16 C7
Rope Bank Ave CW2 . . . . . .206 A7
Rope La
  Shavington CW2 . . . . .206 A5
  Shavington CW2 . . . . .205 F7
Ropewalk The 66 C8
Rope Wlk CW12 . . . . .156 D3
Ropeworks The CH1 . . . . . .118 B2
Rosam Ct WA7 . . . . .49 E6
Roscoe Ave
  Newton-le-W WA12 . . . . .2 E3
  Warrington WA2 . . . . .16 D8
Roscoe Cres WA7 . . . . .48 E1
Roscoe Rd M44 . . . . .11 F8
Roscoe Yd ⁴ WA16 . . . . .57 A2
Roscommon Way WA8 . . . . .12 E1
Roscote Cl CH60 . . . . .40 F7
Roscote The CH60 . . . . .40 F7
Rose Ave WA11 . . . . .1 E6
Rose Bank
  Bollington SK10 . . . . .87 F7
  Lymm WA13 . . . . .18 E3
Rosebank Cl CW7 . . . . .149 F8
Rosebank Mews
  CW10 . . . . .129 C5
Rosebank Rd M44 . . . . .11 C5
Rosebank Sch CW8 . . . . . . .78 A3
Rosebank Wlk CW8 . . . . . . .78 A4
Rosebery Way CW1 . . . . . . .191 C4
Rose Cl
  Blacon CH1 . . . . .117 D4
  Halewood L26 . . . . .21 A7
  Runcorn WA7 . . . . .50 D5
Rose Cotts CW12 . . . . .154 F6
Rose Cres WA8 . . . . .22 E7
Rosecroft CW12 . . . . .43 C6
Rosedale Ave
  Golborne WA3 . . . . .3 C7
  Warrington WA1 . . . . .17 C7
Rosedene Cl CW2 . . . . .118 E8
Rose Farm Cl CW9 . . . . .79 E4
Rose Farm Mews WA6 . . . . .73 B4
Rose Gdns CH66 . . . . .66 F6
Rosehaven Dr L26 . . . . .21 A6
Rosehill Ave WA9 . . . . .6 B5
Rosehill Rd CW2 . . . . .190 B1
Roselands Ct LL12 . . . . .162 C1
Rose Lea Cl WA8 . . . . .13 A4
Rosemary Ave
  Runcorn WA7 . . . . .49 F4
  Warrington WA4 . . . . .16 E2
Rosemary Cl
  Broughton CH4 . . . . .139 C3
  Warrington WA5 . . . . .15 C6
Rosemary Dr WA12 . . . . .2 F3
Rosemary La CW12 . . . . . . .161 D1
Rosemary Row CH3 . . . . . .166 A1
Rosemary Wlk M31 . . . . .11 F2
Rosemere Dr CH1 . . . . .94 F7
Rosemere Gdns WA6 . . . . . .26 F5
Rosemount CW10 . . . . .128 C1
Rosemount Cotts WA2 . . . . . .8 B8
Rose Terr
  Blacon CH1 . . . . .117 D4
  Crewe CW1 . . . . .190 C5
Rosetree Mdw CW5 . . . . . . .80 A2
Rosevale Rd ST5 . . . . .210 D1
Rose View Ave WA8 . . . . . . .13 A2
Roseville Dr CW2 . . . . .179 B8
Roseway SK11 . . . . .112 D5
Rose Wharf SK11 . . . . .112 E7
Rose Wlk M31 . . . . .11 E3
Rosewood Ave
  Chester CH2 . . . . .118 D5
  Frodsham WA6 . . . . .74 D7
Rosewood Cl CW1 . . . . .190 E6
Rosewood Dr CW7 . . . . .126 A1
Rosewood Farm Ct
  WA8 . . . . .12 E4
Rosewood Gr
  Saughall CH1 . . . . .117 B8
  Widnes WA8 . . . . .22 B8
Rossall Ave WA2 . . . . .8 D2
Rossall Cl L24 . . . . .21 E2
Rossall Rd SK7 . . . . .35 E6

276 Ros–St J

Rossall Dr SK7 35 E6
Rossall Gr CH66 69 D6
Rossall Rd
Warrington WA5 15 B4
Widnes WA8 13 D2
Rossbank Rd CH65 70 A7
Ross Cl WA5 15 D7
Rosscliffe Rd CH65 70 A6
Ross Dr CH66 69 C5
Rossenclough Rd SK9 34 D1
Rossendale Dr WA3 10 A6
Rossendale Rd SK8 34 C8
Rossett Ave 1 M22 33 D8
Rossett Bsns Village LL12 162 B1
Rossett Cl
Northwich CW9 103 E4
Warrington WA5 7 E2
Rossett Pk LL12 162 C1
Rossett Rd LL13 180 A1
Rossfield Rd CH65 70 A6
Rossfield Rd N CH65 70 B7
Rosslyn Cl CH5 116 A2
Rosslyn La CW8 102 A3
Rosslyn Rd CH3 119 B3
Rossmill La WA15 32 B7
Rossmore Bsns Pk CH65 70 B7
Rossmore Ct CH66 69 E6
Rossmore Gdns CH66 69 D6
Rossmore Ind Est CH65 70 A6
Rossmore Rd E CH65 69 F7
Rossmore Rd W CH66 69 D7
Rossmore Sch CH66 69 C7
Rossmore Terraced Factories CH65 70 A6
Rossmount Rd CH65 70 A6
Ross Rd CH65 70 A6
Ross St WA8 13 B1
Rosswood Rd CH65 70 A6
ROSTHERNE 30 E4
Rostherne Ave
Ellesmere Port CH66 69 E4
Golborne WA3 3 D8
High Lane SK6 37 E8
Rostherne Cl 1 WA5 15 D4
Rostherne Cres WA8 12 D2
Rostherne La WA16 30 E4
Rostherne Rd SK9 59 F4
Rostherne Way CW11 174 F7
Rosyth Cl WA2 8 F3
Rothay Dr WA5 14 D3
Rothbury Cl WA7 49 D6
Rother Dr CH65 70 A7
Rother Dr Bsns Ctr CH65 70 A7
Rotherhead Dr SK11 112 B5
Rotherwood Rd SK9 59 D6
Rothesay Cl WA7 23 F2
Rothesay Dr CH62 43 E4
Rothesay Rd CH4 141 A7
Rough Bank CW12 179 E8
Rough Heys La SK11 111 A8
ROUGHHILL 140 E1
Roughlea Ave WA3 4 D4
Roughley Ave WA5 15 D4
Roughlyn Cres CH4 140 E1
Roughwood La
Alsager CW11, ST7 193 B7
Hassall Green CW11 176 A1
Roundabout The WA8 12 D6
Round Gdns SK10 88 A8
Roundhey SK8 34 C8
Round Hill Mdw CH3 142 B7
Round Mdw SK10 88 E5
Round Thorn WA3 9 A8
Roundway SK7 35 D6
Round Way SK22 39 D8
Roundy La SK10 62 F6
Routledge St WA8 13 B1
Rowan Ave WA3 3 F7
Rowan Cl
Alsager ST7 193 D3
Delamere CW8 123 D7
Lawton Heath ST7 193 D6
Middlewich CW10 151 E6
Runcorn WA7 49 C7
Sandbach CW11 174 F7
Warrington WA5 14 F6
Winsford CW7 126 D3
Rowan Ct SK9 60 B7
Rowan Dr SK8 35 C8
Rowan Gr CH5 91 C1
Rowan Ho CH2 237 C4
Rowan Lo SK7 35 F7
Rowan Pk CH3 142 E7
Rowan Pl CH2 119 B4
Rowan Rd CW8 102 D8
Rowan Rise CW8 78 A3
Rowans Cl CW1 189 F7
Rowanside SK10 86 E6
Rowanside Dr SK9 60 E8
Rowans The
Broughton CH4 139 B3
4 Northwich CW9 103 E6
Widnes WA8 13 D4
Rowan Tree Rd WA16 59 B5
Rowan Way SK10 87 E1
Rowan Wlk M31 11 E2
Rowcliffe Ave CH4 141 A4
Rowena Ct CH2 118 F3
Rowland Cl WA2 9 A3
Rowlands Hts 1 CH1 237 C3
Rowlands View CW6 146 B7
Rowley Bank La WA16 29 B1
ROWLEYHILL 181 B1
Rowley Rd SK7 36 E8
Rowley Way WA16 82 B7
ROWLINSON'S GREEN 28 C5
ROW-OF-TREES 59 D3
Rowson Dr M44 11 D6
Rowswood Ctyd WA4 25 E5
Rowswood Farm WA4 25 E5
Row The
3 Winsford CW7 126 D1
Wrenbury CW5 217 B5
Rowthorn Cl WA8 22 E8
ROWTON 142 E5
Rowton Bridge Rd CH3 142 E7
Rowton Cl 7 CW9 103 F4
Rowton La CH3 142 F6
Rowton Rd CW2 189 D4
Roxborough Cl WA5 7 A6
Roxburgh Cl SK10 87 A1
Roxburgh Rd CH66 68 F6
Roxby Way WA16 82 A7
Roxholme Wlk M22 33 C8
Royal Arc 5 CW1 190 C4
Royal Ave WA8 12 A1
Royal Ct 3 WA16 57 A2
Royal Gdns
Altrincham WA14 20 F2
Northwich CW9 103 E3
Royal La CW6 147 A3
Royal Mdws SK10 87 A1
Royal Mews CW9 104 D5
Royal Pl WA8 22 B8
Royal Rd SK12 38 D5
Royal Schools for The Deaf & Communication Disorders SK8 34 D6
ROYAL'S GREEN 228 E1
Royal Sh Arc The 9 CH64 66 E8
Royce Cl CW1 190 A7
Royce Ct WA16 56 F2
Royden Ave
Irlam M44 11 F8
Runcorn WA7 49 A8
Royds Cl CW8 103 B4
Royds Ct CW11 174 D5
Roylance Dr CW10 151 C8
Royleen Dr WA6 74 D6
Royle Pk CW12 156 D3
Royle's Pl CW8 103 D6
Royles Sq 2 SK9 60 A1
Royle St
Congleton CW12 156 D3
Northwich CW9 104 B8
Winsford CW7 126 E1
Royston Ave WA1 17 A7
Royston Cl
Ellesmere Port CH66 69 F3
2 Golborne WA3 3 E8
Rozel Cres WA5 15 B5
Rubin Dr CW1 189 F7
Rudd Ave WA9 1 B2
RUDHEATH 104 D6
Rudheath Cl CW2 189 D5
Rudheath Com High Sch CW9 104 D7
Rudheath Com Prim Sch CW9 104 D6
Rudheath La WA7 24 D3
Rudheath Way CW9 104 E5
Rudloe Ct WA2 8 F1
Rudstone Cl CH66 69 B5
Rudyard Cl SK11 112 B6
Rue De Bohars CW6 168 D8
Rufford Cl
Widnes WA8 12 C2
Wistaston CW2 206 B8
Rufford Ct WA1 17 E8
Rufus Ct CH1 237 A3
Rugby Cl SK10 87 E4
Rugby Dr SK10 87 E4
Rugby Ho SK10 87 D3
Rugby Rd CH65 70 D3
Rugby Wlk CH65 70 D3
Ruislip Ct WA2 8 F1
RULOE 101 D7
RUNCORN 23 C1
Runcorn All Saints CE Prim Sch WA7 23 A3
Runcorn Docks Rd WA7 22 E2
Runcorn East Sta WA7 50 D7
Runcorn Mkt WA7 23 A3
Runcorn Rd
Barnton CW8 78 B2
Higher Walton WA4 25 D6
Little Leigh CW8 77 D5
Runcorn Spur Rd WA7 23 B1
Runcorn Sta WA7 22 F2
Runger La M90, WA15 32 F8
Runnell The CH64 41 D4
Runnymede WA1 17 D7
Runnymede Ct 2 WA8 13 C1
Runnymede Dr WA11 1 A6
Runnymede Gdns 5 WA8 13 C1
Runnymede Wlk 3 WA8 13 C2
Rupert Row WA7 50 A8
Ruscoe Ave CW11 174 E6
Ruscolm Cl WA5 14 D7
Rushes Mdw WA13 19 B5
Rushey Cl WA15 32 D7
Rushfield Cres WA7 50 B5
Rushfield Rd
Cheadle SK8 35 A6
Chester CH4 141 B5
Rush Gdns WA13 19 A4
RUSHGREEN 19 A4
Rushgreen Rd WA13 19 A4
Rushmere Cl SK10 62 F2
Rushmere La CH3 163 F3
Rushmore Gr WA1 17 A7
Rusholme Cl L26 21 A6
Rushside Rd SK8 35 A6
RUSHTON 147 C5
Rushton Ave WA12 2 B4
Rushton CE Prim Sch SK11 159 B2
Rushton Cl
Burtonwood WA5 6 F7
Northwich CW9 104 C7
Widnes WA8 12 F3
Rushton Dr
Chester CH2 118 E7
Hough CW2 206 E2
Middlewich CW10 151 C7
Rushton Fold SK10 61 A2
Rushton La CW6 147 D6
Rushton Rd SK8 35 A6
RUSHTON SPENCER 159 B2
Rushy View WA12 2 A4
Ruskin Ave
Newton-le-W WA12 2 C4
Warrington WA2 8 C2
Ruskin Ct WA16 57 A2
Ruskin Dr CH65 70 D3
Ruskin Rd
Congleton CW12 156 C2
Crewe CW2 190 C2
Ruskin Sports Coll & Com High Sch CW2 190 C2
Ruskin Way WA16 57 A3
Russel Ct WA8 13 B4
Russell Ave
Alsager ST7 193 D5
High Lane SK6 37 E7
Russell Cl CW12 179 A8
Russell Dr CW1 191 C5
Russell Rd
Runcorn WA7 48 E8
Winsford CW7 149 C8
Russell St CH1, CH3 237 C3
Russet Cl CW10 128 B2
Russet Rd CW8 102 D8
Russett Sch & Cheshire MSI Unit The CW8 102 E8
Russet Way SK9 59 E3
Rutherford Dr WA16 82 C7
Ruthin Cl WA5 7 E3
Ruthin Ct CH65 70 D3
Ruthin Wlk WA6 73 A1
Rutland Ave
Golborne WA3 3 D7
Halewood L26 21 A8
Warrington WA4 26 B8
Rutland Cl
Congleton CW12 156 E4
Sandbach CW11 174 C5
Rutland Dr
Middlewich CW10 151 C7
Weaverham CW8 77 C1
Rutland Pl CH2 119 A5
Rutland Rd
Hazel Grove SK7 36 E8
Irlam M44 11 D5
Kidsgrove ST7 195 A2
Macclesfield SK11 112 D4
Partington M31 11 E2
Rutland St 1 WA7 22 F2
Rutter Ave WA5 7 F2
Ryburn Cl CW2 207 B3
Ryburn Rd SK11 112 A5
Rydal Ave
High Lane SK6 37 E8
Warrington WA4 16 A2
Rydal Cl
Ellesmere Port CH65 70 C2
Holmes Chapel CW4 130 B2
Neston CH64 66 F6
Winsford CW7 126 D3
Rydal Ct CW12 156 A2
Rydal Dr WA15 32 D8
Rydal Gr
Chester CH4 141 A6
Helsby WA6 73 B1
Runcorn WA7 49 B8
Rydal Mount CW1 173 B1
Rydal Pl SK11 112 A6
Rydal St WA12 2 C3
Rydal Way
Alsager ST7 193 C5
Widnes WA8 12 C1
Ryde Cl CW1 190 B8
Ryder Rd
Warrington WA1 17 C7
Widnes WA8 13 B4
Ryders St CW8 103 E8
Ryebank Ave CW1 190 B7
Ryebank Way SK10 87 C3
Rye Cl ST7 193 B3
Ryecroft CH2 72 B3
Ryecroft Cl CW10 151 B7
Ryecroft La
Duddon CH3, CW6 144 C6
Mobberley WA16 57 E4
Ryecroft Rd CH60 41 C7
Ryedale Way CW12 179 C8
Ryehills ST7 209 E1
RYE HILLS 209 E1
Rylands Cl SY14 213 B4
Rylands Dr WA2 16 C7
Rylands St
Warrington WA1 16 B5
5 Widnes WA8 23 B8
Ryles Cl SK11 112 C5
Ryles Cres SK11 112 C5
Ryles Ho SK11 112 C5
Ryle's Park Rd SK11 112 C6
Ryle St SK11 112 D6
Ryleys Farm SK9 59 F1
Ryleys La SK9 59 F1
Ryleys Sch The SK9 59 F1

S

Sabre Cl WA7 50 D7
Sack La CW9 54 F6
Sacred Heart RC Prim Sch WA5 15 E5
Saddleback Dr SK10 86 F7
Saddlers Rise WA7 50 C8
Saddlery Way CH1 118 B1
Sade Ct 4 CW1 190 B5
Sadler Cl CW7 126 D1
Sadler Rd CW7 126 D1
Sadler's Cl CW4 130 B3
Sadlers La CW6 124 A1
Sadler St WA8 13 C1
Sadlers Wells CW6 185 E8
Saffron Cl
Golborne WA3 3 E8
Warrington WA2 9 B1
Saffron Wlk M31 11 F2
Sagars Rd
Handforth SK9 34 C3
Styal SK9 34 B4
Sage Cl WA2 9 C2
SAIGHTON 142 E1
Saighton CE Prim Sch CH3 142 E1
Saighton La CH3 142 F2
St Aelred's RC Tech Coll WA12 2 D4
St Aidans Dr WA8 12 F6
St Alban Rd WA5 14 E5
St Albans Cl WA11 2 A7
St Albans Dr CW5 204 F3
St Alban's RC Prim Sch
Macclesfield SK10 86 F1
Warrington WA5 15 F6
St Albans St SK22 39 C8
St Ambrose Coll WA15 32 B8
St Ambrose Ct WA4 16 B2
St Ambrose RC Prim Sch L24 21 A2
St Ambrose Rd WA8 13 C1
St Andrew's Ave CW2 190 C1
St Andrew's CE Prim Sch WA2 8 C3
St Andrews Cl
Northwich CW9 104 E7
Warrington WA2 9 A4
St Andrews Ct
Crewe CW2 190 C1
Ellesmere Port CH65 70 E2
Macclesfield SK11 112 B7
St Andrews Dr
Holmes Chapel CW4 130 B2
Kidsgrove ST7 195 C3
St Andrew's Gdns ST7 193 E2
St Andrew's Rd
Ellesmere Port CH65 70 E3
Macclesfield SK11 112 B7
St Andrews Wlk
Mickle Trafford CH2 96 F1
New Mills SK22 39 D8
St Annes CH1 237 B3
St Annes Ave WA4 17 B2
St Anne's Ave CW10 151 D8
St Annes Ave E WA4 17 B2
St Anne's Fulshaw CE Prim Sch SK9 59 F6
St Anne's La CW5 204 D5
St Anne's RC Prim Sch CW5 204 E3
St Anne's Rd WA8 13 B2
St Anne St CH1 237 B3
St Ann's Rd CW10 151 C8
St Ann's Rd S SK8 34 C8
St Ann's Sq SK8 34 C8
St Anthony Pl WA2 8 B6
St Anthony's RC Prim Sch CH4 140 E6
St Asaph Dr WA5 7 E3
St Asaph Rd CH66 94 E8
St Augustine's Ave WA4 16 F4
St Augustines Dr CW2 207 E3
St Augustine's RC Prim Sch
Runcorn WA7 24 A2
Warrington WA4 16 F4
St Austell Cl WA5 14 E3
St Austell Ave SK10 86 E1
St Austell Cl
Macclesfield SK10 86 E1
Runcorn WA7 50 B6
St Austell Dr SK8 34 B8
St Austins La WA1 16 B4
St Barnabas CE Prim Sch
Macclesfield SK11 112 D6
Warrington WA5 15 F5
St Barnabas Ct SK11 112 D6
St Barnabas Pl WA5 15 E6
St Bartholomews Ct CH5 116 E6
St Basil's RC Prim Sch WA8 12 A2
St Bede's Ave CW8 77 D1
St Bede's RC Inf Sch WA8 13 A1
St Bede's RC Jun Sch WA8 13 A1
St Bede's RC Prim Sch CW8 102 F7
St Benedicts Cl WA2 16 B7
St Benedict's RC Prim Sch
Handforth SK9 34 E3
Warrington WA2 16 D7
St Bernard's RC Prim Sch CH65 70 D3
St Berteline's CE Prim Sch WA7 50 C8
St Brannocks Rd SK8 35 B7
St Brides Cl WA5 14 E3
St Bridgets Cl
Warrington WA2 8 F3
Widnes WA8 23 A5
St Bridgets Ct CH4 141 B6
St Bridget's RC Prim Sch WA2 8 E3
St Catherine Dr CW8 103 A4
St Catherine's RC Prim Sch WA3 3 E7
St Chad's CE Prim Sch
Newcastle-u-Lyme ST5 210 D2
Winsford CW7 149 E8
St Chads Cl CW5 220 A8
St Chad's Fields CW7 149 C5
St Chad's RC High Sch WA7 49 D7
St Chad's Rd CH1 117 F4
St Chad's Terr ST5 210 D2
St Chads Way TF9 236 C2
St Christophers Cl CH2 118 D8
St Clair St CW2 190 D1
St Clare's RC Prim Sch CH4 141 A5
St Clements Ct CW2 207 B1
St Clement's RC Prim Sch WA7 49 A8
St David Rd CH62 44 A6
St Davids Dr
12 Ellesmere Port CH66 94 F8
Warrington WA5 7 E2
St David's High Sch CH4 140 C6
St Davids' Ret Pk CH4 140 D7
St David's Terr CH4 140 C6
St Edwards Cl SK11 112 D6
St Edward's RC Prim Sch
Macclesfield SK11 112 C5
Runcorn WA7 23 B3
St Elmo Pk SK12 37 C4
St Elphins Cl WA1 16 C5
St Elphin's (Fairfield) CE Prim Sch WA1 16 D6
SS Peter & Paul RC High Sch WA8 12 F2
St Gabriels Ct ST7 193 C3
St Gabriel's RC Prim Sch ST7 193 C3
St George's CH1 237 B3
St Georges Ave 13 CH66 94 F8
St George's CE Prim Sch SK22 39 C8
St Georges Cl WA4 26 E3
St George's Cl WA16 82 C8
St George's Cres
Chester CH4 237 C1
Waverton CH3 143 A5
St George's Ct WA8 22 D8
St George's Pl 11 SK11 112 D7
St Georges Rd SK22 39 C8
St George's Rd CW7 149 C8
St George's St SK11 112 D6
St George's Way
Northwich CW9 103 F5
Thornton Hough CH63 42 A7
St Gerard's RC Prim Sch WA8 23 B7
St Gregory's RC High Sch WA5 15 D5
St Gregory's RC Prim Sch SK10 87 F8
ST HELENS 1 A1
St Helens Cl WA3 11 B3
St Helens Coll Newton Campus WA12 2 B4
St Helens Rd
Golborne WN7 4 B8
5 Northwich CW9 104 A8
St Hilarys Pk SK9 85 A8
St Hilda's Dr WA6 49 C1
St Ives Cl SK10 86 E1
St Ives Pk CH5 116 A3
St Ives Way CH5 116 A3
St James Ave
Chester CH2 118 F7
Congleton CW12 156 C2
Warren SK11 111 E2
St James' CE Prim Sch WA11 1 E6
St James Cl
Audlem CW3 230 A4
1 Frodsham WA6 49 C1
St James Ct
Audley ST7 209 D2

St James Ct *continued*
Cheadle SK8 34 F6
Chester CH2 118 F3
St James' Ct
Biddulph ST8 179 E3
Warrington WA4 16 B3
St James Ct/Llys Sant Iago CH5 91 D1
St James' Dr SK9 60 A6
St James' RC High Sch SK8 34 F6
St James' Sq SK22 39 C8
St James St CH1 237 B3
St James Terr 9 CW7 149 A8
St James' Way SK8 34 F6
St James Wlk 1 CW8 103 E7
St John Ave WA4 16 B2
St John Fisher RC Prim Sch WA8 13 D1
St John's Ave
Knutsford WA16 56 F1
Lostock Gralam CW9 79 F3
St John's Brow WA7 23 B3
St John's CE Prim Sch
Bollington SK10 88 A7
Sandbach CW11 175 E6
St John's Cl CW9 104 E8
St Johns Ct
Chester CH1 237 B2
Winsford CW7 126 B1
St John's Ct
Knutsford WA16 57 C2
Warrington WA1 16 F7
St Johns Dr CW7 149 A8
St John's Rd
Bebington CH62 44 A5
Chester CH4 237 C1
Congleton CW12 157 A5
Knutsford WA16 57 A1
7 Macclesfield SK11 112 C7
Wilmslow SK9 59 E3
St John's Rear Rd CH4 237 C1
St John's St WA7 23 B3
St John St
Chester CH1 237 B2
Newton-le-W WA12 2 A3
St John's Way
Cuddington CW8 102 B2
Sandbach CW11 175 E6
St John's Wood ST7 194 F1
St John's Wood Com Sch WA16 57 D2
St John The Evangelist CE Prim Sch SK11 112 A7
St John The Evangelist RC Prim Sch ST7 194 F1
St Joseph's Cl WA5 14 E5
St Joseph's RC Prim Sch
Warrington WA5 14 E5
Winsford CW7 149 B8
St Josephs Way CW5 205 A5
St Katherines Way WA1 16 D5
St Kilda Cl CH65 70 C1
St Lawrence Ct CW5 204 F6
St Lawrence Rd WA6 74 B8
St Leonard's Way CW3 232 C1
St Lewis RC Prim Sch WA3 4 B1
St Luke's Ave WA3 3 D8
St Luke's CE Prim Sch WA3 3 E7
St Lukes Cl CW4 130 D3
St Luke's Cres WA8 13 B4
St Luke's Ho 3 SK10 111 F8
St Luke's RC Prim Sch WA6 74 C8
St Luke's Way WA6 49 B1
St Margaret's Ave WA2 8 D1
St Margaret's CE Prim Sch WA2 8 C1
St Mark's CE Prim Sch CW9 53 C4
St Marks Cres CH66 94 F8
St Mark's RC Prim Sch L26 21 A8
St Marks Rd CH4 140 F6
St Mark's St WA11 1 A6
St Martins Dr CH66 69 D2
St Martins La WA7 50 D7
St Martins RC Prim Sch WA7 50 D7
St Martin's Rd ST7 210 E6
St Martin's Way CH1 237 A3
St Mary of the Angels RC Prim Sch CH66 69 D6
St Mary's Ave CW8 77 D1
St Mary's CE Prim Sch
Bebington CH62 44 A5
Bosley SK11 158 D8
Irlam M44 11 C5
Runcorn WA7 50 A8
St Mary's Cl
Alsager ST7 193 C5
Hale L24 21 E2
Warrington WA4 26 C6
St Marys Ct CW5 204 A7
St Mary's Ct CW12 156 A2
St Mary's Ct
Golborne WA3 4 B8
Partington M31 11 F4
St Mary's Dr CW8 126 A8
St Mary's Hill CH1 237 B1
St Mary's Hospl The Phineas Gage Ctr WA2 8 B1
St Mary's RC Inf Sch WA12 2 C4
St Mary's RC Jun Sch WA12 2 B3
St Mary's RC Prim Sch
Congleton CW12 156 D3
Crewe CW2 190 A1
Middlewich CW10 151 C8
New Mills SK22 39 B8
St Mary's Rd
Disley SK12 38 D5
Dodleston CH4 162 A7
Nantwich CW5 204 E7
New Mills SK22 39 B8
Runcorn WA8 23 F1
Warrington WA5 14 F5
Widnes WA8 23 A4
St Mary's St
Crewe CW1 190 C4
Warrington WA4 16 D3
St Mary's Way CH4 139 C5
St Matthews CE Prim Sch WA4 26 E2
St Matthews Cl
Haslington CW1 191 D4
Warrington WA4 26 D7
St Mawes Cl WA8 12 E2
St Mawes Ct SK10 86 E1
St Mawgan Ct WA2 8 F2
St Michael's Ave SK7 35 E8
St Michael's Cl
Little Leigh CW8 77 D5
Widnes WA8 22 C7
St Michael's Cotts CW12 156 B7
St Michael's Ind Est WA8 22 C7
St Michael's RC Prim Sch WA8 22 C7
St Michael's Rd WA8 22 C7
St Michael's Row CH1 237 B2
St Michael's Sq CH1 237 B2
St Michaels Terr 10 SK11 112 D8
St Michael's View CW1 190 B5
St Michael's Way CW10 128 C1
St Monicas Cl WA4 26 D7
St Monica's RC Prim Sch WA4 26 D7
St Nicholas Ct CW5 204 F5
St Nicholas RC High Sch CW8 103 D6
St Nicholas Rd WA3 4 A8
St Olave St CH1 237 B1
St Oswalds CH1 237 B3
St Oswald's CE Prim Sch CH1 94 F2
St Oswalds Cl
Malpas SY14 213 B3
Winwick WA2 8 B6
St Oswald's Cres CW11 153 F5
St Oswald's RC Prim Sch WA1 16 F8
St Oswalds Way CH1, CH2 237 B3
St Oswald's Worleston CE Prim Sch CW5 188 E6
St Patricks Cl WA8 23 A5
St Paul of the Cross RC Prim Sch WA5 6 E6
St Paul's Cl CW1 190 C4
St Paul's Ct
2 Macclesfield SK11 112 E7
Warrington WA2 16 A6
St Pauls Gdns CH66 69 B7
St Paul's Pl 2 CW9 79 A1
St Paul's RC Prim Sch SK12 36 E2
St Paul's Rd
3 Macclesfield SK11 112 E7
Widnes WA8 23 A7
St Paul's St CW1 190 C4
St Peter's Ave WA16 56 F1
St Peter's CE Prim Sch WA12 2 E4
St Peter's Cl
Heswall CH60 40 F7
Lymm WA13 19 A4
St Peter's Ct WA2 16 C6
St Peter's Dr CW6 147 F7
St Peter's Ho SK11 112 E6
St Peter's RC Prim Sch WA1 17 C7
St Peters Rd CW12 156 E1
St Peter's Rise CW11 174 E7
St Peters Way CH2 119 F8
St Peter's Way WA2 16 B6
St Philip (Westbrook) CE Prim Sch WA5 7 B1
St Saviour's CE Prim Sch ST7 194 D1
St Saviour's RC Inf Sch CH66 69 E3
St Saviour's RC Jun Sch CH66 69 E3
St Saviour's St ST7 194 D1
St Stephen Rd WA5 14 F5
St Stephen's Ave WA2 8 B3
St Stephens Cl CH60 41 C6
St Stephens Ct
11 Congleton CW12 156 F3
Sandbach CW11 174 D7
St Stephen's RC Prim Sch WA2 8 B2
St Teresa's RC Prim Sch M44 11 E8
St Theresa's RC Prim Sch CH1 117 F5
St Thomas CE Prim Sch ST7 195 A1
St Thomas Ct WA8 12 E1
St Thomas More RC High Sch CW2 190 A2
St Thomas of Canterbury Blue Coat CE Jun Sch CH1 237 A4
St Thomas's CE Prim Sch WA4 16 D1
St Thomas's Pathway CH1 237 B2
St Thomas St ST7 195 E7
St Thomas Terr WA8 12 E1
St Thomas' View CH65 70 B4
St Vincent Dr CW8 102 F3
St Vincent Rd WA5 14 F5
St Vincent's RC Prim Sch
Knutsford WA16 57 C1
Warrington WA5 14 F3
St Wenefredes Gn SY13 214 F6
St Werburgh's & St Columba's RC Prim Sch CH2 118 F2
St Werburgh St CH1 237 B2
St Wilfrids Cl CW9 104 A3
St Wilfrid's Dr WA4 17 C1
St Wilfrid's RC Prim Sch CW8 103 D5
St Winefride's RC Prim Sch CH64 66 F7
Salander Cres CW2 206 A7
Salerno Rd CH2 95 B1
Salesbrook La CW5 228 C7
Salford CW3 230 A4
Salford Pl CW12 156 E3
Salisbury Ave
Crewe CW2 190 C1
Saltney CH4 140 E6
Salisbury Cl
Crewe CW2 190 C1
10 Ellesmere Port CH66 94 F8
Salisbury Pl SK10 87 E4
Salisbury Rd WA11 1 E8
Salisbury St
Chester CH1 118 B3
Golborne WA3 3 A8
Runcorn WA7 23 A1
Warrington WA1 16 D6
4 Widnes WA8 23 B8
Salkeld St 8 CW9 104 B8
Salmon Leap CH4 237 B1
Salop Pl ST7 195 A3
Salop Wlk SK10 86 F2
Saltash Cl WA7 50 B6
Saltersbrook Gr 12 SK9 34 E1
Salters Ford CW8 77 F3
Saltersford Cnr CW4 130 E3
Saltersgate CH66 69 F2
Salters La
Lower Withington SK11 132 B8
Windyharbour SK11 109 D1
Salter's La
Bickerton SY14 199 F8
Broxton CH3, SY14 183 E1
Hoole Bank CH2 119 C8
SALTERSWALL 125 F3
Salt Line Way CW11 174 D6
Salt Mdws CW5 204 C5
Salt Mus The* CW9 103 F7
SALTNEY 140 D6
Saltney Bsns Ctr CH4 140 F7
Saltney Ferry Prim Sch CH4 140 B6
Saltney Ferry Rd CH4 140 B7
Saltney Terr CH4 140 B7
Salton Gdns WA5 15 E7
Saltwood Dr WA7 50 C5
Saltworks Cl WA6 49 D2
Samian Cl CW10 128 C2
Samphire Gdns WA9 6 B7
Samuel St
Chester CH1 237 C3
Crewe CW1 190 B5
Macclesfield SK11 112 D7
Packmoor ST7 195 F1
Warrington WA5 15 E4
Sanbec Gdns WA8 12 D5
Sandalwood WA7 24 C1
Sandalwood Cl WA2 8 D2
SANDBACH 175 B5
Sandbach Com Prim Sch CW11 175 A6
Sandbach Crosses* CW11 175 B6
Sandbach Dr CW9 103 E6
SANDBACH HEATH 175 D6
Sandbach High Sch & Sixth Form Coll CW11 175 A7
Sandbach Rd
Congleton CW12 156 A3
Rode Heath ST7 193 E7
Sandbach Rd N ST7 193 C4
Sandbach Rd S ST7 193 D3
Sandbach Sch CW11 175 A6
Sandbach Sta CW11 174 D8
Sanderling Rd WA12 2 C4
Sanders Hey Cl WA7 50 B5
Sanderson Cl
Crewe CW2 206 C8
Sanderson Cl *continued*
Warrington WA5 14 D6
Sanderson Way CW10 128 E1
Sanders Sq SK11 112 D5
Sandfield Ave CW5 216 F3
Sandfield Cl 3 WA3 3 E8
Sandfield Cres WA3 5 C7
Sandfield Ct
3 Frodsham WA6 74 B8
Wrenbury CW5 216 F4
Sandfield Hall WA3 3 A4
Sandfield La
Acton Bridge CW8 76 E1
Hartford CW8 103 C4
Sandfield Pk CH60 40 D8
Sandfields WA6 74 B8
Sandfield Terr CW8 76 F1
Sandford Cres CW2 207 D2
Sandford Rd CW5 204 F7
Sandgate Rd SK10 87 F2
Sandham Gr CH60 41 D7
Sandham Rd L24 21 A4
Sandheys CH64 41 C1
Sandhill Terr WA4 16 E3
Sandhole Cotts 2 CW7 149 B8
Sandhole La
Chelford WA16 83 D4
Crowton CW8 101 B7
Sandhurst Ave CW2 190 A1
Sandhurst Dr 2 SK9 60 C8
Sandhurst Rd L26 21 A6
Sandhurst St WA4 16 F3
Sandicroft Cl WA3 9 C5
Sandiford Rd CW4 130 C3
Sandiford Sq CW9 104 A8
Sandileigh Ave WA16 56 F2
Sandington Dr CW8 101 F2
SANDIWAY 102 B3
Sandiway
Bebington CH63 43 C6
Knutsford WA16 57 B2
Sandiway Ave WA8 12 A1
Sandiway Cl CW8 102 A2
Sandiway La CW9 53 A2
Sandiway Pk CW8 102 E4
Sandiway Prim Sch CW8 102 B3
Sandiway Rd
Crewe CW1 190 A7
Handforth SK9 34 D5
Sand La SK10 84 F5
Sandlebridge Farm SK9 83 F6
Sandle Bridge La WA16, SK9 83 E5
Sandle Bridge Rise WA16 83 F6
SANDLOW GREEN 131 B1
Sandmoor Pl WA13 19 A2
Sandon Cres CH64 66 E5
Sandon Park Gdns CW2 189 D4
Sandon Pl WA8 13 D1
Sandon Rd CH2 118 E4
Sandon St CW1 190 D4
Sandown Cl
Culcheth WA3 4 F4
Middlewich CW10 151 C8
Runcorn WA7 49 C6
Wilmslow SK9 60 D8
Sandown Cres CW8 102 A3
Sandown Dr WA15 32 D6
Sandown Pl SK11 111 F7
Sandown Rd CW1 190 C7
Sandown Reach CW5 229 D7
Sandown Terr CH3 118 F1
Sandpiper Cl
Macclesfield SK10 87 B4
Newton-le-W WA12 2 C4
Sandpiper Ct
Chester CH4 141 B2
Kidsgrove ST7 195 C2
Sandpiper Way CH4 141 B3
Sandra Dr WA12 2 E3
Sandringham Ave
Chester CH3 119 A2
Helsby WA6 73 B4
Sandringham Cl
Altrincham WA14 20 F1
Northwich CW9 103 E4
Winsford CW7 126 C3
Sandringham Ct
Golborne WA3 3 E7
5 Wilmslow SK9 60 A6
Sandringham Dr
Poynton SK12 36 D3
Warrington WA5 15 C4
Wistaston CW2 205 E8
Sandringham Gdns 2 CH65 70 D2
Sandringham Rd
Congleton CW12 156 F4
Macclesfield SK10 87 F1
Widnes WA8 13 A4
Sandringham Way 4 SK9 60 A6
Sandrock Rd CH3 142 E7
Sandsdown Cl ST8 179 C1
Sandside Rd ST7 193 B3
Sands Rd ST7 195 E6
Sandstone Mews WA8 12 E4
Sandstone Wlk CH60 41 A7
Sandwich Dr SK10 87 C4
Sandwood Ave CH4 139 B3
Sandybank CW8 78 D1
Sandy Brow La WA3 3 E2
Sandy Cl SK10 87 F7
SANDYCROFT 116 B2
Sandyfield Ct ST8 179 C1
Sandyhill Pl 1 CW7 149 D6
Sandyhill Rd CW7 149 D6
Sandy La
Allostock CW4 106 E1
Astbury CW12 177 E6
Aston CW5 217 C2
Bold Heath WA8 14 B6
Brown Knowl CH3 199 C7
Bulkeley SY14 184 C1
Chester CH3 119 A1
Congleton, Astbury Marsh CW12 156 B2
Congleton CW12 155 D3
Croft WA3 9 A8
Cronton WA8 12 D5
Golborne, Lowton Common WA3 4 A8
Golborne WA3 2 F8
Goostrey CW4 107 D1
Haslington CW11 192 B7
Hatherton CW5 219 F5
Helsby WA6 73 B2
Higher Kinnerton CH4 161 A6
Huntington CH3 141 F8
Knutsford WA16 82 D3
Lymm WA13 19 B4
Macclesfield SK10 86 C2
Neston CH64 67 A7
Runcorn, Preston Brook WA7 50 F6
Runcorn WA7 48 E7
Saighton CH3 142 C3
Saltney CH4 140 D6
Sandbach CW11 174 D5
Swan Green WA16 106 E6
Swettenham CW12 131 F3
Tarvin CH3 121 C4
Threapwood SY14 222 E8
Warrington, Longford WA2 8 C2
Warrington, Penketh WA5 15 A4
Warrington, Stockton Heath WA4 26 D8
Weaverham CW8 77 C2
Whitegate CW8 125 D6
Wilmslow SK9 59 E8
Sandylands Cres ST7 193 F5
Sandylands Pk CW2 205 D7
Sandylane Mews CW12 156 C5
Sandy La W WA2 8 B3
Sandymere Ct CW7 126 B1
Sandymoor La WA7 24 D3
Sandy Moor La WA7 24 D3
Sandy Rd ST8 179 C2
Sandy Way CW7 149 B8
SANKEY BRIDGES 15 C4
Sankey Bridges Ind Est WA5 15 C4
Sankey for Penketh Sta WA5 14 F6
Sankey La WA4 25 F1
Sankey St
Golborne WA3 3 A8
Newton-le-W WA12 2 A3
Warrington WA1 16 A5
Widnes WA8 23 A6
Sankey Valley Ind Est WA12 2 A2
Sankey Valley Pk*
Newton-le-W WA5 1 D3
Warrington WA5 15 D5
Sankey Valley St James CE Prim Sch WA5 15 C6
Sankey Way WA5 15 D5
Santon Dr WA3 3 E8
Sapling La CW6 146 F3
Sark Ave CH65 95 B8
Sark Ho CH2 119 B4
Sarl Williams Ct CH1 237 A3
Sarn Bank Rd SY14 222 E6
Sarn Rd SY14 222 D8
Sarra La CH3 184 B5
Sarsfield Ave 1 WA3 3 D8
Sarus Ct WA7 24 B4
SAUGHALL 117 B8
Saughall Cl CW9 103 E4
Saughall Hey CH1 94 A1
Saughall Rd
Blacon, Abbot's Meads CH1 118 A4
Blacon CH1 117 E5
Saundersfoot Cl WA5 7 E2
Saunders St CW1 190 B4
Saunderton Cl WA11 1 C7
Saunton Cl CW7 126 A2
Savannah Pl 5 WA5 15 C7
Saville Ave WA5 15 F7
Saville St SK11 112 E7
Savoy Rd CW1 207 A8
Sawley Cl
Culcheth WA3 5 A2
Runcorn WA7 50 E7
Sawley Dr SK8 35 C6
Sawpit St WA13, WA14 20 A6
Sawyer Dr ST8 179 C1
Saxon Cl WA4 26 B5
Saxon Crossway CW7 126 B1
Saxon Rd WA7 23 C2
Saxons La CW8 103 D7
Saxon Terr 4 WA8 13 B1

Saxon Way
Blacon CH1 . . . . .117 E6
6 Ellesmere Port CH66 . . . . 94 F8
Sandbach CW11 . . . . 175 C6
Sayce St WA8 . . . . .13 B1
Scafell Ave WA2 . . . . 8 C3
Scafell Cl
Bebington CH62 . . . . .43 D3
High Lane SK6 . . . . .37 E8
Scaife Rd CW5 . . . . 204 F5
Scaliot Cl SK22 . . . . .39 B8
Scar La SY14 . . . . 198 F1
Sceptre Cl WA12 . . . . 2 A3
SCHOLAR GREEN 194 E8
Scholar Green Prim Sch
ST7 . . . . 194 E6
Scholar Rise CW7 . . . . 127 A2
Scholars Cl
Macclesfield SK10 . . . . 111 D8
Saltney CH4 . . . . 140 E6
Scholar's Ct 8 CH64 . . . . . . 66 E8
Scholars Green La
WA13 . . . . .18 F2
School Ave CH64 . . . . .66 F6
School Bank
Norley WA6 . . . . 101 A6
Wybunbury CW5 . . . . 220 B8
School Brow WA1 . . . . .16 C6
School Cl
Audley ST7 . . . . 210 A1
Knutsford WA16 . . . . .56 E1
Marbury SY13 . . . . 226 E8
Poynton SK12 . . . . .36 F3
School Cotts
Bradwall Green
CW11 . . . . 153 B4
Wimboldsley CW10 . . . . 150 F4
School Cres CW1 . . . . 190 E4
School Dr
Barnton CW8 . . . . .78 A3
Lymm WA13 . . . . .19 C5
School Field Cl CW3 . . . . 230 F4
Schoolfold La SK10 . . . . .63 A7
School Gn CH3 . . . . 182 C1
SCHOOL GREEN 149 C5
School Hill CH60 . . . . .40 F7
School Hos SK11 . . . . 109 A1
School House Cotts
CH66 . . . . .69 B6
School La
Aldford CH3 . . . . 163 F2
Antrobus CW9 . . . . .53 C3
Astbury CW12 . . . . 178 B8
Audlem CW3 . . . . 230 A4
Bold Heath WA8 . . . . .13 E7
Brereton Green CW11 . . . . . . 153 F5
Bunbury CW6 . . . . 168 E1
Burwardsley CH3 . . . . 184 B6
Cuddington CW8 . . . . 102 A2
Eaton (nr Congleton)
CW12 . . . . 156 E8
Ellesmere Port CH66 . . . . . . .69 A8
Elton CH2 . . . . .72 B3
Frodsham WA6 . . . . .74 C7
Great Budworth CW9 . . . . . . .79 B8
Guilden Sutton CH3 . . . . 119 E5
Hartford CW8 . . . . 103 C4
Henbury SK11 . . . . 111 B6
Higher Whitley WA4 . . . . .52 E6
Hollinfare WA3 . . . . .11 A2
Hooton CH66 . . . . .43 F1
Irlam, Cadishead M44 . . . . . . .11 D5
Lostock Gralam CW9 . . . . .80 A2
Manley WA6 . . . . .99 A5
Marton SK11 . . . . 133 C5
Mickle Trafford CH2 . . . . 119 E8
Moulton CW9 . . . . 126 F8
4 Nantwich CW5 . . . . 204 E6
Neston CH64 . . . . .42 B2
Neston, Little Neston
CH64 . . . . .66 F6
Neston, Parkgate CH64 . . . . . .41 B1
Nether Alderley SK10 . . . . . . .86 A6
Norbury SY13 . . . . 215 E2
Norley WA6 . . . . 100 D5
Ollerton WA16 . . . . .83 B4
Onneley CW3 . . . . 232 F3
Partington WA14 . . . . .20 D5
Poynton SK12 . . . . .36 F4
Runcorn WA7 . . . . .49 F8
Sandbach CW11 . . . . 174 D7
Sandbach Heath CW11 . . . . . 175 E6
Smallwood CW11 . . . . 176 F5
Warmingham CW11 . . . . 173 E7
Warrington WA3 . . . . .10 D5
School Mews SK7 . . . . .35 E7
School Rd
Ellesmere Port CH65 . . . . . . .70 B5
Handforth SK9 . . . . .34 D4
Higher Shurlach CW9 . . . . . . 104 D5
Warrington WA2 . . . . 8 C1
Winsford, Meadowbank
CW7 . . . . 126 E5
Winsford, Wharton
CW7 . . . . 127 A2
School Rd N CW9 . . . . 104 E6
School Rd S CW9 . . . . 104 E6
School St
Chester CH2 . . . . 118 F3
Golborne WA3 . . . . 3 A8
Haslington CW1 . . . . 191 D5
Newton-le-W WA12 . . . . 2 B3
Warrington WA4 . . . . .16 B4
School Terr WA3 . . . . 3 A8

School Way
Northwich CW9 . . . . 104 A8
Widnes WA8 . . . . .13 D3
Schooner Cl WA7 . . . . .50 D6
Scilly Cl CH65 . . . . .70 C1
Scope Ho CW1 . . . . 190 E1
Scotch Hall La CW9 . . . . .53 A3
Scotia Wlk 11 WA3 . . . . 3 F8
Scotland Rd WA1 . . . . .16 B5
Scott Ave
Crewe CW1 . . . . 190 F4
Widnes WA8 . . . . .22 F8
Scott Cl
Macclesfield SK10 . . . . 113 A7
Rode Heath ST7 . . . . 193 E8
2 Sandbach CW11 . . . . 174 D6
Scott Ct WA2 . . . . .16 B6
Scotthope Cl SK11 . . . . 111 F6
Scotton Ave CH66 . . . . .69 B5
Scott Rd SK10 . . . . .87 A7
Scotts Ind Est WA5 . . . . .16 A7
Scott St WA2 . . . . .16 C6
Scott Wlk WA12 . . . . 2 C1
Scroggins La M31 . . . . .11 F4
Sea Bank CW3 . . . . 128 D1
Seabank Rd CH60 . . . . .40 E6
Seabury St WA4 . . . . .17 A3
Seacombe Dr CH66 . . . . .69 E3
Seafield Ave CH60 . . . . .40 E6
Seaford Cl WA7 . . . . .24 D1
Seaford Pl WA2 . . . . 8 A4
Seagrave Cl CW9 . . . . 103 F5
Seagull Cl CW1 . . . . 190 F5
Seahill Rd CH1 . . . . 116 F8
Sea La WA7 . . . . .23 D2
SEALAND 116 E6
Sealand Cl WA3 . . . . 8 E1
Sealand Ind Est CH1 . . . . 117 F2
Sealand Rd
Blacon CH1 . . . . 117 C3
Chester CH1 . . . . 118 A2
Sealand CH1, CH5 . . . . 116 D6
Sealand Trad Pk CH1 . . . . 117 F2
Sealand Way 2 SK9 . . . . .34 D4
Seal Rd SK7 . . . . .36 A7
Seathwaite Cl WA7 . . . . .49 E5
Seaton Cl CW1 . . . . 190 B8
Seaton Pk WA7 . . . . .24 E3
Seaton St CH3 . . . . 237 D1
Seattle Cl 3 WA5 . . . . .15 B7
Sea View CH64 . . . . .66 E4
Seaview Ave CH62 . . . . .44 B6
Seaville St CH3 . . . . 237 C3
Secker Ave WA4 . . . . .16 D2
Secker Cl WA4 . . . . .16 D2
Second Ave
Connah's Quay CH5 . . . . .92 F3
Crewe CW1 . . . . 190 F2
Kidsgrove ST7 . . . . 194 E1
Poynton SK12 . . . . .36 D1
Runcorn WA7 . . . . .49 F8
Sandbach CW11 . . . . 175 A5
Second Dig La CW5 . . . . 219 C8
Second Wood St
CW5 . . . . 204 D5
Sedbergh Cl CW4 . . . . 130 A3
Sedbergh Gr WA7 . . . . .49 E5
Seddon St CW10 . . . . 128 C2
Sedgefield Cl 3 SK10 . . . . . .87 C4
Sedgefield Rd CH1 . . . . 118 B2
Sedgeford Cl SK9 . . . . .34 D1
Sedgemere Ave CW1 . . . . 190 A8
Sedum Cl CH3 . . . . 142 A6
Sefton Ave
Congleton CW12 . . . . 157 A1
Widnes WA8 . . . . .13 A3
Sefton Dr SK9 . . . . .34 C2
Sefton Rd CH2 . . . . 119 A4
Sefton St WA12 . . . . 1 F3
Selby Cl
Poynton SK12 . . . . .36 D5
Runcorn WA7 . . . . .24 F4
Selby Gdns SK8 . . . . .35 C6
Selby Gn CH66 . . . . .69 B5
Selby St WA5 . . . . .15 E5
Selkirk Ave
Bebington CH62 . . . . .43 E4
Warrington WA4 . . . . .17 A3
Selkirk Cl
Ellesmere Port CH66 . . . . . . .68 F5
Macclesfield SK10 . . . . .86 F2
Selkirk Rd CH4 . . . . 141 A7
Seller St CH1 . . . . 237 C3
Selsdon Ct CW4 . . . . 141 C7
Selsey Cl CW1 . . . . 190 B8
Selworthy Dr
Crewe CW1 . . . . 190 B7
Warrington WA4 . . . . .17 D3
Selwyn Cl
Newton-le-W WA12 . . . . 2 B5
Widnes WA8 . . . . .13 E3
Selwyn Dr
Cheadle SK8 . . . . .35 C7
Sutton Lane Ends SK11 . . . . . 112 F3
Semper Cl CW12 . . . . 157 A4
Seneschal Ct WA7 . . . . .49 E6
Senna La CW9 . . . . .78 C8
Sennen Cl WA7 . . . . .50 C5
Sens Cl CH1 . . . . 237 A2
Sephton Ave WA3 . . . . 4 E3
Serin Cl WA12 . . . . 2 C3
Serpentine The CH4 . . . . 141 B7
Servite Cl CH65 . . . . .69 F6
Servite Pl CH64 . . . . .66 E7

Sett Cl SK22 . . . . .39 B8
Sevenoaks Cl SK10 . . . . .87 B2
Seven Row CH64 . . . . .66 E5
Seven Sisters La SK11 . . . . . . .82 E5
Severn Cl
Biddulph ST8 . . . . 179 E1
Congleton CW12 . . . . 156 F1
Macclesfield SK10 . . . . .86 F2
Warrington WA2 . . . . 8 E2
Widnes WA8 . . . . .13 F3
Severn Dr SK7 . . . . .35 C6
Severn Rd WA3 . . . . 4 F2
Severnvale CH65 . . . . .70 B3
Severn Wlk CW7 . . . . 127 A2
Sewell St 7 WA7 . . . . .23 B2
Sextant Cl WA7 . . . . .50 D7
Sexton Ave WA9 . . . . 1 B2
Seymour Chase WA16 . . . . . . .82 A8
Seymour Cl WA7 . . . . .24 C4
Seymour Dr
Ellesmere Port CH66 . . . . . . .69 E6
Warrington WA1 . . . . .17 A8
Seymour Ho 8 SK9 . . . . .34 D1
Seymour St WA8 . . . . .35 A8
Sgt York Loop WA5 . . . . .15 B6
Shackleton Cl WA5 . . . . .15 D8
Shade Terr SK6 . . . . .37 F7
Shadewood Cres WA4 . . . . . . .17 B2
Shadewood Rd SK11 . . . . 112 A6
Shadowmoss Rd M22 . . . . . . .33 E8
Shady Brook La CW8 . . . . .77 C1
Shady Gr ST7 . . . . 193 D4
Shaftesbury Ave
Chester CH3 . . . . 119 C2
Warrington WA5 . . . . .14 E2
Shaftesbury Way WA5 . . . . 6 F7
Shaftway Cl WA11 . . . . 1 F7
Shakerley Ave CW12 . . . . 156 F3
Shakespeare Cl CW9 . . . . 104 C7
Shakespeare Dr CW1 . . . . . . 191 A4
Shakespeare Rd WA2 . . . . 8 C2
Shakespeare Rd
Neston CH64 . . . . .41 E1
Widnes WA8 . . . . .13 A1
Shalcombe Cl L26 . . . . .21 A7
Shallacres CH65 . . . . .69 F7
Shallcross Ave SK23 . . . . .65 F4
Shallcross Cres SK23 . . . . . . .65 E4
Shallcross Hall Barns
SK23 . . . . .65 E4
Shallcross Mill Rd
SK23 . . . . .65 E5
Shallcross Rd SK23 . . . . .65 E4
Shambles The WA16 . . . . .57 B1
Shanklin Cl WA5 . . . . .14 C6
Shannon Cl
Chester CH4 . . . . 140 E5
Willaston CW5 . . . . 205 D6
Shannon Gr WA8 . . . . .12 E2
Shargate Cl SK9 . . . . .34 C1
Sharnbrook Dr CW2 . . . . 189 D4
Sharon Park Cl WA4 . . . . .17 C1
Sharpley St 11 SK10 . . . . 112 C8
Sharp St
Warrington WA2 . . . . .16 C6
Warrington WA5 . . . . .15 F6
Sharston Cres WA16 . . . . .57 B1
SHAVINGTON 206 C5
Shavington Ave CW2 . . . . 118 F4
Shavington High Sch
CW2 . . . . 206 A5
Shavington Prim Sch
CW2 . . . . 206 C4
Shavington Way CW9 . . . . 103 F4
Shawbury Gr WA1 . . . . .17 A8
Shaw Cl CH66 . . . . .69 E4
Shaw Dr WA16 . . . . .57 C3
Shawell Ct WA8 . . . . .13 E2
Shaw Entry L35, WA8 . . . . . . .12 A7
SHAW HEATH 57 D3
Shaw Heath View
WA16 . . . . .57 C3
Shaw's Ave WA2 . . . . .16 C8
Shaws Fold SK9 . . . . .33 F3
Shawn La
Winsford CW7 . . . . 126 F4
Winsford, Wharton
CW7 . . . . 127 A3
Shaw St
Culcheth WA3 . . . . 5 A3
Haydock WA11 . . . . 1 E6
Macclesfield SK11 . . . . 112 C8
Runcorn WA7 . . . . .22 F2
Shay La
Ashton Hayes CH3 . . . . 121 F7
Hampton Heath SY14 . . . . . . 200 A1
Tarvin CH3 . . . . 121 E3
Shay's La CW6 . . . . 124 E4
Sheaf Cl CH3 . . . . 121 C2
Shearbrook La CW8 . . . . 107 E1
Sheardhall Ave SK12 . . . . .38 E5
Sheath St CW9 . . . . 104 A8
Shed La CH3 . . . . 119 B2
Sheepfield Cl CH66 . . . . .69 C7
Sheerwater Cl WA8 . . . . .14 F7
Sheffield Cl WA5 . . . . .15 C5
Sheffield Row WA12 . . . . 2 B4
Sheilings The WA3 . . . . 3 F8
Shelagh Ave WA8 . . . . .13 B1
Shelbourne Mews 2
SK10 . . . . 111 F8
Shelburne Dr CW1 . . . . 191 C5
Sheldon Ave
Chester CH3 . . . . 119 B2
Congleton CW12 . . . . 157 A1
Sheldon Cl M31 . . . . .11 E3
Sheldon Rd SK10 . . . . 111 B4
Sheldon St SK10 . . . . .88 B8

Sheldon Rd
Hazel Grove SK7 . . . . .36 E8
Poynton SK12 . . . . .37 C2
Sheldrake Gr CH64 . . . . .66 E5
Shellbrook Gr 3 SK9 . . . . . . .34 D1
Shelley Ave CW9 . . . . .80 A5
Shelley Cl
Crewe CW1 . . . . 190 F4
Middlewich CW10 . . . . 151 E5
Rode Heath ST7 . . . . 193 E8
Shelley Ct 5 CW11 . . . . 174 D6
Shelley Dr WA2 . . . . 189 F1
Shelley Gr WA4 . . . . .16 F4
Shelley Rd
Blacon CH1 . . . . 117 F6
Widnes WA8 . . . . .13 A1
SHELL GREEN 13 E1
Shell Green Est WA8 . . . . .23 E8
Shellow La CW12,
SK11 . . . . 134 C5
Shellway Rd CH2 . . . . .71 A3
Shelton Cl WA8 . . . . .13 F3
Shenhurst Cl SK9 . . . . .59 E4
Shepcroft La WA4 . . . . .26 C3
Shepherds Fold Dr
CW7 . . . . 126 C3
Shepherd's La CH2 . . . . 118 D5
Shepherds Row WA7 . . . . .23 F2
Shepherds View WA7 . . . . .78 B2
Shepley Cl SK7 . . . . .36 D8
Sheppard Cl CW1 . . . . 190 D5
Sheppenhall Gr CW5 . . . . 217 C1
Sheppenhall La CW5,
SY13 . . . . 228 D5
Shepperton Cl WA4 . . . . .26 E6
Shepsides Cl CH66 . . . . .69 C3
Shepton Rd CH66 . . . . .69 E2
Sheraton Rd CH3 . . . . 143 B5
Sherborne Cl WA7 . . . . .24 F3
Sherborne Rd CW1 . . . . 190 D6
Sherbourne Ave CH4 . . . . 141 B5
Sherbourne Cl SK8 . . . . .35 B6
Sherbourne Rd
Ellesmere Port CH65 . . . . . . .70 D3
Macclesfield SK11 . . . . 111 F7
Sherbourne Way WA5 . . . . 6 F6
Sherbrooke Rd SK12 . . . . .38 D6
Sherbrook Rise SK9 . . . . .60 C6
Sheridan Ave WA3 . . . . 3 D7
Sheridan Cl CW1 . . . . 173 B1
Sheridan Pl WA2 . . . . 8 A5
Sheridan Way WA7 . . . . .24 D2
Sheri Dr WA12 . . . . 2 E2
Sheringham Cl CH4 . . . . 140 E5
Sheringham Dr CW1 . . . . 190 B8
Sheringham Rd WA5 . . . . .14 E6
Sherlock Ave WA11 . . . . 1 E7
Sherratt Cl
Congleton CW12 . . . . 156 E2
Nantwich CW5 . . . . 204 F4
Sherrington's La CH3 . . . . . . 199 D8
Sherwin St CW2 . . . . 190 C1
Sherwood Cl WA8 . . . . .12 C1
Sherwood Cres WA5 . . . . 6 E6
Sherwood Gr WA6 . . . . .73 A3
Sherwood Rd
Blacon CH1 . . . . 117 E5
Macclesfield SK11 . . . . 112 D5
Shetland Cl
Warrington WA2 . . . . 8 E4
Widnes WA8 . . . . .13 E3
Shetland Dr
Bebington CH62 . . . . .43 E8
Ellesmere Port CH65 . . . . . . .70 C1
Shevington Cl WA8 . . . . .13 E3
Shevington Wlk WA8 . . . . .13 E3
Shiggins Cl WA5 . . . . .15 D6
Shillingford Cl WA4 . . . . .26 E5
Shilton Cl CW10 . . . . 151 E5
Shipbrook Rd
Chester CH2 . . . . 118 F6
Davenham CW9 . . . . 104 C3
Northwich CW9 . . . . 104 C6
Shipgate St CH1 . . . . 237 B1
Shipgate The CH1 . . . . 237 B1
Shipley Gdns ST7 . . . . 210 D6
Ship St WA6 . . . . .49 C1
Shipton Cl
Warrington WA5 . . . . .15 B8
Widnes WA8 . . . . .12 D3
Shirley Ave SK8 . . . . .34 C6
Shirley Dr WA4 . . . . .17 A2
Shirleys Cl SK10 . . . . .87 A6
Shirleys Dr SK10 . . . . .87 A6
SHOCKLACH 211 D7
SHOCKLACH GREEN 211 C7
Shocklach Oviatt CE Prim
Sch SY14 . . . . 211 C7
Shocklach Rd CH2 . . . . 118 F6
Shones Croft CH64 . . . . .67 A5
Shop La
Congleton CW12 . . . . 156 E2
Little Budworth CW6 . . . . . . 124 F2
Shopping Precinct The
CH2 .72 B3
Shoreham Dr WA5 . . . . .15 A3
Shores Green Dr CW9 . . . . . . .79 F5
Shores La CW5 . . . . 203 D7
Short Cl WA12 . . . . 1 E3
Shorthorn Cl CW10 . . . . 128 D2
Short St
Haydock WA11 . . . . 1 E6
11 Macclesfield SK11 . . . . . . 112 D8
Newton-le-W WA12 . . . . 1 E3
Widnes WA8 . . . . .23 A5
Shorwell Cl WA5 . . . . .14 C7
Shot Tower Cl CH1 . . . . 237 C3
SHOTWICK 93 B4

Shotwick La CH1 . . . . .93 D6
Shotwick Rd CH5 . . . . .92 F3
SHRALEYBROOK 209 A1
Shrewsbury Cres
CW5 . . . . 204 E4
Shrewbridge Rd CW5 . . . . . . 204 D4
Shrewsbury Dr ST5 . . . . 210 E2
Shrewsbury Gdns SK8 . . . . . . .35 C6
Shrewsbury Rd 4
CH65 . . . . .70 C5
Shrewsbury St WA4 . . . . .16 B3
Shrewsbury Way CH4 . . . . . . 140 F6
Shrigley Cl SK9 . . . . .34 D1
Shrigley Ct SK10 . . . . .88 B8
Shrigley Rd SK10 . . . . .63 B5
Shrigley Rd N SK12 . . . . .37 C3
Shrigley Rd S SK10,
SK12 . . . . .37 C2
Shrigley Rise SK10 . . . . .63 C1
Shropshire Cl
Middlewich CW10 . . . . 151 C8
Warrington WA1 . . . . .17 E6
Shropshire Rd CH2 . . . . 227 E2
Shropshire Rd CH2 . . . . .70 F3
Shropshire St CW3 . . . . 229 F4
Shuldham Cl WA16 . . . . .29 C4
Shurlach Rd CW9 . . . . 104 D6
Shutley La CW8 . . . . .77 D6
Shutlingsloe Way
SK10 . . . . 112 A8
Sibberhalld La CH3 . . . . 180 F4
Sibell St CH1 . . . . 237 C3
Siddall St 7 CW9 . . . . 104 B8
Siddals Ct CW5 . . . . 204 C5
Siddeley Cl CH4 . . . . 139 C4
Siddeley Dr WA12 . . . . 1 F4
SIDDINGTON 110 A3
Siddington Ave CW9 . . . . 104 A4
SIDDINGTON HEATH . . . .
. . . . 109 E1
Siddington Rd
Handforth SK9 . . . . .34 D5
Poynton SK12 . . . . .36 F2
Siddorn St CW7 . . . . 126 E1
Side End La SK23 . . . . .64 F3
Side La CW6 . . . . 144 E6
Sidings Cl WA1 . . . . .16 C6
Sidings The SK23 . . . . .65 E8
Sidlaw Cl CH66 . . . . .69 A6
Sidmouth Cl WA5 . . . . .14 C4
Sidmouth Gr SK8 . . . . .34 F7
Sidney Cl CH64 . . . . .41 F1
Sidney Rd CH64 . . . . .41 F1
Siemens Rd M44 . . . . .11 E5
Sienna Cl M44 . . . . .11 E6
Signal Ct CW2 . . . . 118 F2
Silk Hill SK23 . . . . .65 E8
Silk Mill Cl
Macclesfield SK11 . . . . 112 D6
Poynton SK12 . . . . .36 C4
Silk Mill St WA16 . . . . .57 A2
Silk Mus Heritage Ctr*
SK11 . . . . 112 D7
Silk Rd The
Bollington SK10 . . . . .87 E4
Macclesfield SK10 . . . . 112 E7
Silk St CW12 . . . . 156 C2
Silkstone Cres WA7 . . . . .50 B7
Silsden Ave WA3 . . . . 4 B8
Silvan Ct SK10 . . . . .87 B1
Silver Ave WA11 . . . . 1 A5
Silverbirch Croft CH4 . . . . . . 139 B3
Silverbirch Way CH66 . . . . . . .94 F8
Silverdale CW8 . . . . 103 D7
Silverdale Cl
Chorlton CW2 . . . . 207 C2
Frodsham WA6 . . . . .74 C7
High Lane SK6 . . . . .37 E8
Silverdale Dr SK9 . . . . .60 A4
Silverdale Rd
Newton-le-W WA12 . . . . 2 B4
Warrington WA4 . . . . .16 B2
Silvergate Ct CW12 . . . . 178 E8
Silver La
Croft WA3 . . . . 9 F7
Warrington WA3 . . . . .10 C6
Silvermine Cl 8 ST7 . . . . 195 B2
Silvermuir CH1 . . . . 117 E3
Silverne Dr CH65 . . . . .70 A2
Silver St
Bollington SK10 . . . . .88 B8
Congleton CW12 . . . . 156 E2
Warrington WA2 . . . . .16 B6
Silver Terr CW11 . . . . 175 D6
Silverwood ST7 . . . . 195 B1
Simkin Ave WA4 . . . . .17 C2
Simmonds Cl CW9 . . . . 103 E3
SIMM'S CROSS 23 A8
Simms Cross Prim Sch
WA8 .23 A8
Simonside WA8 . . . . .12 C2
Simons La WA6 . . . . .74 B5
Simonstone Rd CH4 . . . . 139 B3
Simonswood Cl CW10 . . . . . . 151 B8
Simpson Cl CH2 . . . . .95 C1
Simpson Ct CW1 . . . . 173 B1
Simpson La CH2 . . . . .95 C1
Simpson Rd CH2 . . . . .95 C1
Simpson's Ct 17 SK11 . . . . . . 112 C8
Simpson St CW9 . . . . .79 F6
Simpsons Way CH4 . . . . 139 B3
Sinclair Ave
Alsager ST7 . . . . 193 B3
Warrington WA2 . . . . 8 B2
Widnes WA8 . . . . .23 A8
Sinderland La
Partington WA13 . . . . .20 B8
Partington WA13 . . . . .20 E8

Singapore Ave M90 . . . . .33 A8
Singleton Cl WA7 . . . . .190 C6
Singleton Rd CH65 . . . . .69 F4
SINK MOSS 28 D3
Sir John Deane's Coll
CW9 . . . . .103 F6
Sir Thomas Boteler CE
High Sch WA4 . . . . .16 E3
Siskin Cl WA12 . . . . .2 C3
Six Acre Gdns WA4 . . . . . . .25 A5
Six Acre La WA4 . . . . .25 A5
Sixth Ave CH5 . . . . .92 E1
Skeath Cl CW1 . . . . .175 E6
Skellern St ST7 . . . . .194 D2
SKELLORN GREEN 62 E8
Skellorn Green La
SK10 . . . . .62 F8
Skiddaw Cl WA7 . . . . .50 A4
Skip's La CH3 . . . . .142 F7
Skipton Cl
Hazel Grove SK7 . . . . .36 C8
2 Runcorn WA7 . . . . .23 F1
Skipton Dr CH66 . . . . .69 C5
Skye Cl
Ellesmere Port CH65 . . . . .70 C1
Widnes WA8 . . . . .13 E3
Skylark Cl CW1 . . . . .189 F7
Sky Lark Rise WA9 . . . . .1 A3
Slacken La ST7 . . . . .194 D2
Slack St SK11 . . . . .112 E6
Slade La
Mobberley WA16 . . . . .58 A7
Nether Alderley SK10 . . . . .85 E5
Slade St **5** CW9 . . . . . . .104 B8
Slag La
Golborne WA3 . . . . .3 D8
Haydock WA11 . . . . .1 E7
Slater St
Macclesfield SK11 . . . . . .112 C6
Warrington WA4 . . . . .16 D3
Slicks Bsns Ctr CW8 . . . . . .78 C2
Slindon Cl ST5 . . . . .210 D1
Slutchers La WA1 . . . . .16 A3
Small Ave WA3 . . . . .8 C2
Smallbrook Wlk CW2 . . . .206 C8
Small Cres WA2 . . . . .8 C2
Small La WA16 . . . . .58 A8
Smallman Rd CW2 . . . . . . .190 C1
SMALLWOOD 176 F5
Smallwood CE Prim Sch
CW11 . . . . .176 F5
Smallwood Cl
4 Middlewich CW10 . . . .151 C8
Newcastle-u-Lyme ST5 . .210 D1
Smallwood Ct **1**
CW12 . . . . .156 F3
Smallwood Forge
CW11 . . . . .176 D5
Smeaton Wood CW5 . . . . . .216 E2
SMETHWICK GREEN 154 F4
Smethwick La CW11,
CW12 . . . . .154 E4
Smith Cl ST7 . . . . .193 B4
Smith Cres WA2 . . . . .16 D8
Smith Dr WA2 . . . . .16 D8
Smithers Cl CW5 . . . . .204 F4
Smithfield Dr/Ffordd
Smithfield LL13 . . . . .196 D8
Smithfield Gn LL13 . . . . . .196 D8
Smithfield La CW11 . . . . . .175 C6
Smithfields CH3 . . . . .166 C2
Smithfield St LL13 . . . . . . .196 D8
Smith Gr CW1 . . . . .190 A6
Smithills Cl WA3 . . . . .9 D5
Smith La
Mobberley WA16 . . . . .57 F6
Rainow SK10 . . . . .89 A5
Smith Rd WA8 . . . . .22 F7
Smiths Cotts CH64 . . . . .66 E5
SMITHS GREEN 109 A2
SMITH'S GREEN 208 B7
Smith's La CW8 . . . . .77 C1
Smiths Lawn SK9 . . . . .60 A5
Smith St
Macclesfield SK11 . . . . . .112 D6
Warrington WA1 . . . . .16 B5
Smith's Terr SK11 . . . . .112 E6
Smithy Bank
Acton CW5 . . . . .204 A6
Winsford CW7 . . . . .149 A3
Smithy Brow
Bollington SK10 . . . . .88 C8
Winwick WA3 . . . . .8 F7
Smithy Cl
Cronton WA8 . . . . .12 C5
Neston CH64 . . . . .67 A4
Saughall CH1 . . . . .94 A1
Shocklach SY14 . . . . .211 E7
Smithy Cotts SY14 . . . . . .213 A2
Smithy Ct
Christleton CH3 . . . . .142 E7
Duddon CW6 . . . . .145 C5
5 Ellesmere Port CH66 . . .69 C6
Smithy Dr WA14 . . . . .20 D3
Smithy Gn
Cheadle SK8 . . . . .35 A8
Gatesheath SK8 . . . . .165 E5
Smithy Gr CW11 . . . . .176 A2
SMITHY GREEN
Cheadle Hulme 35 B7
Lower Peover 81 E2
Smithy Hill CH63 . . . . .42 A6
Smithy La
Alsager CW7 . . . . .208 D7
Altrincham WA14 . . . . .20 D3
Barthomley CW2 . . . . .208 C6
Biddulph ST8 . . . . .179 D2
Bosley SK11 . . . . .158 E6

Smithy La continued
Broxton CH3 . . . . .183 D1
Congleton CW12 . . . . .156 C7
Crewe CW1 . . . . .189 E8
Croft WA3 . . . . .9 A7
Cronton WA8 . . . . .12 C5
Cuddington CW8 . . . . .102 A5
Ellesmere Port CH66 . . . . .69 C6
Great Budworth CW9 . . . . .79 A8
Helsby WA6 . . . . .73 C5
Kingsley WA6 . . . . .75 B2
Little Leigh CW8 . . . . .77 B6
Lostock Gralam CW9 . . . . .80 A2
Malpas SY14 . . . . .213 A2
Mottram St Andrew
SK10 . . . . .61 C2
Mouldsworth CH3 . . . . .98 F2
Partington M31 . . . . .11 F3
Rainow SK10 . . . . .88 E5
Utkinton CW6 . . . . .146 C6
Weston CW2 . . . . .207 C5
Willaston CH64 . . . . .68 A7
Smithy Pathway CH4 . . . . .140 F4
Smithy The CW2 . . . . .118 E8
Smithy Wlk CW11 . . . . .174 F3
Smokehall La CW7,
CW9 . . . . .126 F6
Smokehall Lane Ind Est
CW7 . . . . .127 A5
Smokey La SY13 . . . . .224 A1
Smokies Way ST8 . . . . .179 C1
Smyth Rd WA8 . . . . .13 D2
Snab La
Neston CH64 . . . . .66 F4
Norbury SY13 . . . . .215 B5
Snabwood Cl CH64 . . . . .66 F5
Snaefell Rise WA4 . . . . .26 C7
Snapebrook Gr **6** SK9 . . .34 E1
Snape Hollow CW2 . . . . . . .207 F4
Snape La CW2 . . . . .207 F4
Snape Rd
Crewe CW2 . . . . .206 D8
Macclesfield SK10 . . . . .87 E2
Snelson La
Chelford, Marthall WA16,
SK9 . . . . .83 D3
Chelford SK11 . . . . .108 E7
Snipe Cl SK12 . . . . .36 A4
Snowberry Cl WA8 . . . . .13 E4
Snowberry Cres WA5 . . . . . .15 E3
Snowberry Way **5**
CH66 . . . . .94 F8
Snowberry Wlk M31 . . . . . . .11 E3
Snowdon Cl
Ellesmere Port CH66 . . . . .69 A6
Warrington WA5 . . . . .14 E6
Snowdon Cres CH4 . . . . . . .141 A5
Snowdon Dr CW2 . . . . .189 D3
Snowdonia Way CW7 . . . . .149 B7
Snowdon St CW9 . . . . .77 F3
Snowdrop Cl WA7 . . . . .49 F4
SNOW HILL 204 D6
Snow Hill SK11 . . . . .112 E6
Solly Cres CW12 . . . . .156 A2
Solvay Rd CW8 . . . . .78 D1
Solway Cl WA3 . . . . .8 F4
Solway Ct CW1 . . . . .191 A2
Solway Gr WA7 . . . . .49 D5
SOMERFORD 154 F7
Somerford Ave CW2 . . . . . .190 A3
Somerford Cl CW11 . . . . . .175 C8
Somerford Ct **2**
CW12 . . . . .156 F3
Somerford Ho SK10 . . . . . . .36 E4
Somerford Rd CH4 . . . . . . .139 C4
Somerford Way **3** SK9 . .34 E5
Somerford Wlk WA8 . . . . . . .13 E3
Somerley Cl CW1 . . . . .190 B8
Somerset Ave ST7 . . . . .194 F2
Somerset Cl
Congleton CW12 . . . . .156 D4
Irlam M44 . . . . .11 D6
Somerset Rd CH2 . . . . .118 F5
Somerset St **1** 237 B4
Somerset Way WA11 . . . . . .17 B8
Somerton Cl **5** SK11 . . . .111 F7
Somerton Rd SK11 . . . . . . .111 F7
Somerville Cl
Bebington CH63 . . . . .43 B6
High Legh WA16 . . . . .29 C4
Neston CH64 . . . . .66 E5
Somerville Cres CH65 . . . . . .70 C4
Somerville Rd WA8 . . . . .22 C8
Somerville St CW2 . . . . . . .190 B2
Soot Hill CW8, CW9 . . . . . . .78 C3
Sorbus Cl CH2 . . . . .72 C3
Sorbus Dr CW1 . . . . .190 E6
Sorby Rd M44 . . . . .11 F7
Sorrel Cl
Huntington CH3 . . . . .142 A6
Warrington WA2 . . . . .9 C2
Soss Moss Hospl (Mary
Dendy Unit) SK10 . . . . . . .84 C6
Sossmoss La SK10 . . . . .84 D6
SOUND 217 F6
Sound & District Prim Sch
CW5 . . . . .217 E5
SOUND HEATH 217 E5
Sound La
Ravensmoor CW5 . . . . . . .203 E1
Sound CW5 . . . . .217 D7
Souter's La CH1 . . . . .237 B2
South Acre Dr
Handforth SK9 . . . . .34 D3
Macclesfield SK11 . . . . . . .113 A7
Southampton Way
WA7 . . . . .50 E6

South Ave
Chester CH2 . . . . .237 C4
Warrington WA4 . . . . .191 D1
Warrington, Stockton Heath
WA4 . . . . .16 C1
Warrington WA2 . . . . .16 B8
Southbank CW9 . . . . .79 A7
South Bank CH2 . . . . .118 C4
Southbank Ave CW2 . . . . . .206 C5
South Bank Cl SK9 . . . . .60 B2
South Bank Gr CW12 . . . . .156 F2
South Bank Terr WA7 . . . . . .22 F2
South Cheshire Coll
CW2 . . . . .190 B2
South Cheshire Private
Hospl The CW1 . . . . .172 E1
South Cl
Tarporley CW6 . . . . .146 C2
Wilmslow SK9 . . . . .59 F6
South Crescent Rd
CH4 . . . . .237 C1
South Croft CW6 . . . . .185 D6
South Crofts CW5 . . . . .204 F5
South Dale WA5 . . . . .14 F5
Southdale Rd WA1 . . . . .17 A7
Southdown Cl SK10 . . . . .87 A4
Southdown Cres SK8 . . . . . .34 F8
South Downs WA1 . . . . .16 F7
South Downs Dr WA14 . . . . .31 D8
South Downs Rd WA14 . . . .31 D8
South Dr
Heswall CH60 . . . . .41 A7
Northwich CW9 . . . . .104 D6
Plumley WA16 . . . . .80 F3
Wilmslow SK9 . . . . .60 B6
Southern St WA4 . . . . .16 C1
Southey Cl
1 Sandbach CW11 . . . . .174 D6
Widnes WA8 . . . . .22 F8
Southfield CH65 . . . . .87 A4
Southfield Cl SK9 . . . . .34 C3
Southfield Rd CH66 . . . . . . .69 C7
Southfields WA16 . . . . .57 C3
Southfields Ave WA5 . . . . . .14 F6
Southfields Cl CW5 . . . . . . .220 A8
South Gn CH5 . . . . .116 A6
South Gr SK9 **10** 60 A1
South La
Warrington WA5, WA8 . . . .14 E5
Widnes WA8 . . . . .13 F4
Southlands Ave CW4 . . . . . .14 F3
Southlands Ct
2 Runcorn WA7 . . . . . . .22 F1
Widnes WA8 . . . . .48 F8
Southlands Mews **8**
WA7 . . . . .22 F1
Southlands Rd CW12 . . . . .157 A1
Southlands View
CW4 . . . . .107 E1
Spinney Cl
Handforth SK9 . . . . .34 C3
Winsford CW7 . . . . .150 A8
South Lane Entry WA8 . . . . .13 F5
Southlawn WA5 . . . . .60 A5
South Lo CW5 . . . . .168 D8
South Mead SK12 . . . . .36 B5
South Meadway SK6 . . . . . . .37 F7
South Oak La SK9 . . . . .59 F5
South Par WA7 . . . . .48 D7
South Park Dr SK12 . . . . . . .36 E5
South Park Rd SK11 . . . . . .112 C7
South Pier Rd CH65 . . . . . . .70 D7
Southport St WA9 . . . . .1 A3
South Rd
Altrincham, Ashley Heath
WA14 . . . . .31 E8
Ellesmere Port CH65 . . . . .70 C3
Halewood L24 . . . . .21 A4
Runcorn WA7 . . . . .48 D7
Stanlow CH65 . . . . .70 F4
South St
Alderley Edge SK9 . . . . . . .60 A1
Chester CH3 . . . . .119 A1
Congleton CW12 . . . . .156 D3
Crewe CW2 . . . . .190 D2
Mount Pleasant ST7 . . . . .195 B6
3 Widnes WA8 . . . . . . .23 B8
South Terr **14** SK9 . . . . . . .60 A1
South View
Chester CH4 . . . . .141 D7
Christleton CH3 . . . . .142 F7
Lower Whitington SK11 . .132 A8
New Mills SK22 . . . . .39 B8
South View Ave WA11 . . . . .111 D2
South View Cotts ST7 . . . . .193 F4
South View La CW7 . . . . . . .170 F2
South View Rd CH2 . . . . . . .118 B2
Southward Rd WA11 . . . . . . .2 A7
Southwark Pl CW7 . . . . .149 A8
Southway
Middlewich CW10 . . . . . .128 C1
Runcorn WA7 . . . . .49 F7
Widnes WA8 . . . . .22 D8
South Way CH1 . . . . .117 F4
Southway Ave WA4 . . . . .26 D7
Southwell Cl WA3 . . . . .3 C8
South West Ave SK10 . . . . . .87 F6
South Wirral High Sch
CH62 . . . . .43 D4
Southwold Cres WA5 . . . . . .14 E5
Southwood Ave WA4 . . . . . .24 C2
Southworth Ave WA5 . . . . . .15 F8
Southworth La WA2,
WA3 . . . . .8 F4
Southworth Rd WA12 . . . . . .2 F4
Sovereign Cl
Golborne WA3 . . . . .3 F8
Northwich CW9 . . . . .104 F6
Runcorn WA7 . . . . .50 D7
Sovereign Ct WA3 . . . . .9 C4

Sovereign Way CH1 . . . . . .117 E2
Sowcar Way SK10 . . . . .88 C8
Spark Hall Cl WA4 . . . . .26 E1
Spark La
Runcorn WA7 . . . . .23 F1
Smallwood CW11 . . . . . . .154 C2
Sparks Cl CH3 . . . . .142 B7
Sparrowbutts Gr ST7 . . . . .195 C2
Sparrowhawk Cl WA7 . . . . . .50 A7
Sparrow La WA16 . . . . .57 B1
Spath La SK8 . . . . .34 F5
Spath La E SK8 . . . . .35 B5
Spath Wlk SK8 . . . . .35 B5
Spawell Cl WA3 . . . . .3 E8
Speakman Ave WA12 . . . . . . .2 C5
Speakman St WA7 . . . . .22 F3
Speed's Way CH3 . . . . .180 E2
Speedwell Cl
11 Golborne WA3 . . . . . . .3 E8
Heswall CH60 . . . . .41 C8
Speedwell Dr CH60 . . . . . . .41 C8
Speedwell Rd CH65 . . . . . .210 F1
Speedwell Wlk ST7 . . . . .21 A3
SPEKE 21 A3
Speke Bvd L24, L26,
WA8 . . . . .21 B5
Speke Ho L24 . . . . .21 A2
Speke Rd WA8 . . . . .22 C6
Spencer Brook SK10 . . . . . . .86 F6
Spencer Cl
Alsager ST7 . . . . .192 F4
Wistaston CW2 . . . . .206 A8
Spencer Mews SK10 . . . . . . .86 F6
Spencer St
Barnton CW8 . . . . .78 B3
Northwich CW9 . . . . .103 E7
SPEN GREEN 177 B6
Spenlow Cl SK12 . . . . .36 E1
Spennymoor Ct WA7 . . . . . . .49 E7
Spenser Cl WA8 . . . . .12 F1
Spenser Rd CH4 . . . . .141 E1
Spey Cl
Middlewich CW10 . . . . . .128 D3
Winsford CW7 . . . . .126 F2
Spey Dr ST7 . . . . .195 C2
Spike Island (Nature
Reserve) * WA8 . . . . .23 A5
Spike Island Visitor Ctr *
WA8 . . . . .23 A6
Spindle St CW12 . . . . .156 E2
Spink La WA8 . . . . .80 A6
Spinnaker Cl WA7 . . . . .50 D5
Spinner Cres CW9 . . . . .78 D7
Spinners La SK12 . . . . .36 C4
Spinners Pl WA1 . . . . .16 C6
Spinners Way SK10 . . . . .87 F7
Spinney Ave
Goostrey CW4 . . . . .107 F1
Widnes WA8 . . . . .12 A1
Spinney Dr
Ellesmere Port CH66 . . . . .69 D2
Weston CW2 . . . . .207 B5
Spinney End CH3 . . . . .166 A1
Spinney La WA16 . . . . .56 E3
Spinney Mead SK10 . . . . . . .87 E2
Spinney The
Cuddington CW8 . . . . .101 D5
Heswall CH60 . . . . .41 C5
Lawton-gate ST7 . . . . .194 E4
Neston CH64 . . . . .41 D1
Norley WA6 . . . . .100 E5
Sandbach CW11 . . . . .175 C6
Willaston CW5 . . . . .205 D6
Spinney Wlk WA7 . . . . .24 A1
Spires Gdns WA2 . . . . .8 A7
Spital Wlk CH2 . . . . .118 F2
Spodegreen La WA14 . . . . . .30 C8
Spout La WA16 . . . . .58 B4
Spragg St CW12 . . . . .156 E3
Spring Ave **2** CH66 . . . . . .69 C6
Springbank SK10 . . . . .87 F7
Springbank Dr WA6 . . . . . . .49 W6
Springbank Cl WA7 . . . . . . .49 W6
Springbank Cres
CW7 . . . . .149 C8
Springbank Gdns
Lymm WA13 . . . . .19 B5
New Mills SK22 . . . . .39 B8
Spring Bank Rd SK22 . . . . . .39 C8
Springbourne WA6 . . . . .74 D6
Springburn Gdns WA1 . . . . .17 F7
Spring Cl ST7 . . . . .193 E8
Springcroft CH64 . . . . .41 C1
Spring Ct **8** WA7 . . . . .23 B2
Springe La CW5 . . . . .203 B5
Springfield Ave
Golborne WA3 . . . . .2 F8
Grappenhall WA4 . . . . .17 B3
Helsby WA6 . . . . .73 B3
Lymm WA13 . . . . .19 B5
Malpas SY14 . . . . .213 C3
Warrington, Padgate
WA1 . . . . .17 A8
Springfield Cl CH4 . . . . . . .161 A7
Springfield Cres CW8 . . . . . .77 F3
Springfield Ct / Llys Maes
Y Ffynnon CH4 . . . . .161 A8
Springfield Dr
Talke ST7 . . . . .210 E8
Wilmslow SK9 . . . . .59 D5
Wistaston CW2 . . . . .205 F7
Springfield Pk WA11 . . . . .1 C7
Springfield Rd
Macclesfield SK11 . . . . . .111 F8

Springfield Rd continued
Malpas SY14 . . . . .213 B3
Mobberley WA16 . . . . .57 F4
Widnes WA8 . . . . .22 A8
Springfields
Cuddington CW8 . . . . .101 D4
Helsby WA6 . . . . .73 B3
Knutsford WA16 . . . . .57 C3
Mickle Trafford CH2 . . . . .119 E8
Prestbury SK10 . . . . .87 A7
Springfield Sch CW1 . . . . . .191 A3
Springfields Dr CW12 . . . . .156 D3
Springfield St WA1 . . . . .16 A5
Spring Gdns
Crewe CW1 . . . . .190 E5
Ellesmere Port CH66 . . . . .69 C6
Macclesfield SK10 . . . . .87 D1
Mobberley WA16 . . . . .58 D5
Nantwich CW5 . . . . .204 F5
Springhead Cl ST7 . . . . . . .210 D6
Springhead Prim Sch
ST7 . . . . .210 D6
Springhill SK10 . . . . .88 A1
Spring Hill WA6 . . . . .168 C8
Springhill Ave CH62 . . . . . . .43 D6
Springholm Dr WA4 . . . . . . .26 D3
Spring La
Coddington CH3 . . . . .181 E6
Croft WA3 . . . . .9 B6
Lymm WA13 . . . . .19 E3
Spring Mdw CW8 . . . . .78 E1
Springmount WA3 . . . . .3 E7
Spring Mount SK22 . . . . .39 C8
Spring Rd SK12 . . . . .36 F2
Spring St
Congleton CW12 . . . . .156 E2
Widnes WA8 . . . . .23 A6
Wilmslow SK9 . . . . .60 A7
Springvale Bsns Ctr
CW11 . . . . .174 D6
Springvale Cl CW11 . . . . . .174 D5
Springvale Ind Pk
CW11 . . . . .174 C6
Springwater Cl CW2 . . . . . .207 C1
Springwater Dr CW2 . . . . . .206 C8
Springwood Ave WA16 . . . . .57 C3
Springwood Cl
Blacon CH1 . . . . .117 C4
Macclesfield SK10 . . . . .87 D5
Springwood Way SK10 . . . . .87 D5
Sprink La CW12 . . . . .157 D5
SPROSTON GREEN 129 C2
Sproston Way WA7 . . . . . . .103 E4
Spruce Ave CW8 . . . . .102 B3
Spruce Cl
Golborne WA3 . . . . .3 F7
Warrington WA1 . . . . .17 E7
Spruce Gr ST7 . . . . .193 F7
Spuley La SK10 . . . . .63 D2
Spunhill Ave CH66 . . . . .69 D2
Spurling Rd WA5 . . . . .6 F6
Spurston Cl WA10 . . . . .2 D7
SPURSTOW 185 D6
Spurstow Mews SK9 . . . . . . .35 C8
Square St SK11 . . . . .112 E6
Square The
Altrincham WA15 . . . . .32 C8
Audlem CW3 . . . . .229 F4
Chester CH1 . . . . .237 C3
Christleton CH3 . . . . .142 E8
Holmes Chapel CW4 . . . . .130 C3
Ince CH2 . . . . .71 F5
6 Lymm WA13 . . . . .18 E3
Woore CW3 . . . . .232 C1
Squires Ave WA8 . . . . .23 A8
Squires Cl WA11 . . . . .1 B6
Squirrel Cl CW8 . . . . .103 C7
Squirrels Chase SK10 . . . . . .86 F5
Squirrel's Jump SK9 . . . . . . .60 C1
Stable La
Mouldsworth CH3 . . . . .99 A3
Utkinton CW6 . . . . .123 F1
Stables The
Bostock Green CW10 . . . .127 D5
Brereton Heath CW12 . . . .155 A7
Guilden Sutton CH3 . . . . .119 F5
Lawton-gate ST7 . . . . .194 C4
Stadium Cl WA4 . . . . .16 A3
Stadium Way WA1 . . . . .118 B3
Stadmorslow La ST7 . . . . . .195 F4
Staffin Ave CH65 . . . . .95 B8
Stafford Cl SK10 . . . . .86 F2
Stafford Gdns CH65 . . . . . . .70 B5
Stafford Rd WA4 . . . . .16 C2
Stafford St
Audlem CW3 . . . . .230 A4
Crewe CW1 . . . . .190 C5
Stafford Wlk SK10 . . . . .86 F2
Stage La WA13 . . . . .19 C4
Stainer Cl WA12 . . . . .2 A4
Staines Cl WA4 . . . . .26 E5
Stainforth Cl WA3 . . . . .4 D4
Stainmore Cl WA3 . . . . .10 B6
Staithes Rd M22 . . . . .33 D8
Stalbridge Rd CW2 . . . . . . .190 C3
Stallard Way CW10 . . . . . . .151 C8
Stalmine Ave SK8 . . . . .34 B8
Stamford Ave CW2 . . . . . . .190 C3
STAMFORD BRIDGE 120 D4
Stamford Cl SK11 . . . . .112 C4
Stamford Ct
Chester CH3 . . . . .119 C2
Lymm WA13 . . . . .18 F3
Macclesfield SK11 . . . . . .112 C5
Stamford La CH3 . . . . .120 A1

Stamford Rd
Alderley Edge SK9 . . . . .60 B1
Blacon CH1 . . . . .117 E6
Handforth SK9 . . . . .34 A1
Little Bollington WA14 . . . . .20 B2
Macclesfield SK11 . . . . .112 C4
Stamford St CH65 . . . . .70 A5
Stamp Ave CW1 . . . . .190 D6
Stamp Cl CW11 . . . . .190 D6
Standford Dr CW9 . . . . . . .104 A5
Standish Ct WA8 . . . . .22 D8
Standon Ave ST5 . . . . .210 C2
Stanford Cl 2 CW9 . . . . . .103 F5
Stanhope Ave CW1 . . . . . .190 E3
Stanhope Cl SK9 . . . . .60 D8
Stanier Cl
Crewe CW1 . . . . .191 A4
Sutton Lane Ends SK11 . . .112 D2
Stanlaw Rd CH65 . . . . .70 C4
Stanley Ave
Warrington, Stockton Heath
WA4 . . . . .16 F2
Warrington WA5 . . . . .14 D7
STANLEY BANK 1 A7
Stanley Bank Rd WA11 . . . .1 A7
Stanley Bank Way WA11 . .1 A7
Stanley & Brocklehurst Ct
3 SK10 . . . . .112 C8
Stanley Cl
Hartford CW8 . . . . .103 A4
Widnes WA8 . . . . .13 C2
Stanley Ct ST7 . . . . .193 C4
Stanley Dr
Gatley SK8, SK9 . . . . .34 D6
Newcastle-u-Lyme ST5 . . .210 C1
Stanley Gr CW9 . . . . .79 E2
STANLEY GREEN 34 E6
Stanley Green Ind Est
SK8 . . . . .34 E5
Stanley Green Ret Pk
SK8 . . . . .34 F6
Stanley Hall La SK12 . . . . .38 C6
Stanley La CH62 . . . . .43 F4
Stanley Park Ct CH4 . . . . .140 E5
Stanley Park Dr CH4 . . . . .140 E5
Stanley Pl
Chester CH1 . . . . .237 A2
Warrington WA4 . . . . .16 F2
Stanley Place Mews
CH1 . . . . .237 A2
Stanley Rd
Biddulph ST8 . . . . .179 C2
Ellesmere Port CH65 . . . . . .70 C7
Handforth SK8, SK9 . . . . . . .34 E6
Knutsford WA16 . . . . .56 F2
Stanley Rd Ind Est
WA16 . . . . .57 A1
Stanley St
Chester CH1 . . . . .237 A2
2 Crewe CW1 . . . . .190 C4
7 Macclesfield SK11 . . . .112 D8
Newton-le-W WA12 . . . . .2 A3
Northwich CW9 . . . . .104 C8
Runcorn WA7 . . . . .23 B3
Warrington WA1 . . . . .16 B4
Stanley Villas 7 WA7 . . . .22 F1
STANLOW 71 B5
Stanlow Abbey Bsns Ctr
CH65 . . . . .70 D2
Stanlow & Thornton Sta
CH2 . . . . .71 D5
Stanmore Rd WA7 . . . . .23 D2
Stannage La CH3 . . . . .180 F5
Stanner Cl WA5 . . . . .7 D2
Stannerhouse La
CW11 . . . . .175 E4
Stanneybrook Cl
WA6 . . . . .101 A6
Stanney Cl
Bebington CH62 . . . . .43 E3
Neston CH64 . . . . .66 E7
Stanney Grange Sports
Complex The CH65 . . . . . .70 E3
Stanney La
Ellesmere Port CH65 . . . . . .70 C3
Stoak CH2 . . . . .70 E1
Stanneylands Cl SK9 . . . . .34 C2
Stanneylands Dr SK9 . . . . .34 B2
Stanneylands Rd SK9 . . . . .34 B2
Stanney Mill Ind Est
CH2 . . . . .70 F3
Stanney Mill La CH2 . . . . .70 F2
Stanney Mill Rd CH2 . . . . .70 F2
Stanney Ten Ind Est
CH2 . . . . .70 F1
Stanney Woods Ave
CH65 . . . . .70 C1
Stanney Woods Ctry Pk*
CH65 . . . . .70 B1
Stansfield Ave WA16 . . . . .16 F6
Stansfield Dr WA4 . . . . .27 A7
Stanstead Ave WA5 . . . . . . .14 F3
Stanthorne Ave CW2 . . . . .190 A3
Stanthorne Park Mews
CW10 . . . . .150 E6
Stanton Cl WA11 . . . . .1 C6
Stanton Ct CH64 . . . . .66 E8
Stanton Dr CH2 . . . . .118 D5
Stanton Rd WA4 . . . . .17 D3
Stanyer Ct CW5 . . . . .205 A4
STAPELEY 219 D8
Stapeley Broad Lane CE
Prim Sch CW5 . . . . .205 A1
Stapeley Cl CW9 . . . . .103 E4
Stapeley Ct CW1 . . . . .190 B5

Stapeley Gdns L26 . . . . . . .21 A6
Stapeley Terr CW5 . . . . . . .205 A4
Stapeley Water Gdns*
CW5 . . . . .205 A3
Stapleford Ct CH66 . . . . . . .69 F8
Stapleton Ave WA2 . . . . . . .16 D8
Stapleton Ct WA6 . . . . .74 C8
Stapleton Rd SK10 . . . . . . .87 B2
Stapleton Way WA8 . . . . . . .22 B5
Stapley Cl WA7 . . . . .22 F1
Starbeck Dr CH66 . . . . .69 B5
Starkey Gr WA4 . . . . .16 F4
Star La
Lymm WA13 . . . . .18 C4
Macclesfield SK11 . . . . . . .112 D4
Starling Cl
Farndon CH3 . . . . .180 F1
Kidsgrove ST7 . . . . .195 D3
Runcorn WA7 . . . . .50 D7
Start La SK23 . . . . .65 B7
STATHAM 18 C4
Statham Ave
Lymm WA13 . . . . .18 D3
Warrington WA2 . . . . .8 C2
Statham Cl WA13 . . . . .18 D3
Statham Com Prim Sch
WA13 . . . . .18 C4
Statham Dr WA13 . . . . .18 D3
Statham La WA13 . . . . .18 B5
Statham St SK11 . . . . .112 D7
Station App / Lon yr Orsaf
CH1 . . . . .116 F7
Station Ave
Ellesmere Port CH66 . . . . . .69 C7
Helsby WA6 . . . . .73 B4
Station Cl CH64 . . . . .66 F7
Station Cotts
Mouldsworth CH3 . . . . .99 A2
Saughall CH1 . . . . .116 F7
Station Gn CH66 . . . . .69 C7
Station Hill CW8 . . . . .76 F2
Station La
Dunham-on-t-H CH3 . . . . . . .97 D3
Guilden Sutton CH2,
CH3 . . . . .119 F7
Rushton Spencer SK11 . . .159 B2
Station Rd
Adderley TF9 . . . . .235 A5
Alsager ST7 . . . . .193 D3
Astbury ST7, CW12 . . . . . .178 B1
Aston WA7 . . . . .50 B4
Backford CH1 . . . . .95 A3
Biddulph ST8 . . . . .179 C1
Bosley CW12 . . . . .135 A2
Burton CH64 . . . . .67 B1
Calveley CW6 . . . . .169 E2
Chelford SK11 . . . . .84 A2
Chester CH1 . . . . .237 C4
Crowton CW8 . . . . .76 D2
Delamere CW8 . . . . .123 D8
Ellesmere Port CH65 . . . . . .70 C6
Ellesmere Port, Little Sutton
CH66 . . . . .69 C6
Elton CH2 . . . . .72 A5
Furness Vale SK23 . . . . .39 D4
Goostrey CW4 . . . . .131 A8
Handforth SK9 . . . . .34 D3
Haydock WA11 . . . . .1 C6
Heswall CH60 . . . . .40 F6
Holmes Chapel CW4 . . . . .130 D2
Irlam M44 . . . . .11 E7
Kidsgrove ST7 . . . . .194 F1
Lostock Gralam CW9 . . . . . .80 A2
Mobberley WA16 . . . . .57 F7
Mouldsworth CH3 . . . . .99 A2
Mow Cop ST7 . . . . .195 C8
Nantwich CW5 . . . . .204 E5
Neston CH64 . . . . .66 F7
Neston, Parkgate CH64 . . . .66 C8
Newchapel ST7 . . . . .195 E2
New Mills SK22 . . . . .39 B7
Northwich CW9 . . . . .79 B1
Partington WA14 . . . . .20 B5
Runcorn WA7 . . . . .22 F2
Sandbach CW11 . . . . .174 D7
Sandycroft CH5 . . . . .116 A2
Scholar Green ST7 . . . . . . .194 F7
Styal SK9 . . . . .34 A4
Warrington, Fearnhead
WA2 . . . . .9 A2
Warrington, Great Sankey
WA5 . . . . .14 F6
Warrington, Penketh
WA5 . . . . .14 B3
Warrington WA4 . . . . .16 E2
Weaverham CW8 . . . . .77 A1
Wilmslow SK9 . . . . .60 B7
Winsford CW7 . . . . .127 A1
Worleston CW5 . . . . .188 E6
Wrenbury CW5 . . . . .216 F3
Station Rd N WA2 . . . . .9 A1
Station Rd S WA2 . . . . .9 A1
Station St SK10 . . . . .87 D1
Station Terr WA7 . . . . .50 B4
Station View
Chester CH3 . . . . .118 F2
Hampton Heath SY14 . . . .213 D7
Nantwich CW5 . . . . .204 E4
Sandbach CW11 . . . . .174 D7
Station Yard Trad Est
CW4 . . . . .130 D3
Staveley Dr CW7 . . . . .126 D2
Steadings Rise WA16 . . . . .56 D6
Steadings The CH3 . . . . . . .120 A4
Steam Mill St CH1,
CH3 . . . . .237 C3
Stearns Cl CH1 . . . . .118 A5
Stearns Ho CH1 . . . . .118 A5

Steele Rd CW10 . . . . .151 D5
Steele St CH1 . . . . .237 B2
Steel St WA1 . . . . .16 D7
Steeple Ct CH64 . . . . .66 E7
Steeple St SK10 . . . . .87 E1
Stein Ave WA3 . . . . .3 E8
Stendall Rd CH1 . . . . .118 A3
Stenhills Cres WA7 . . . . . . .23 C2
Stephens Gdns CH66 . . . . .69 B6
Stephen's Gr WA6 . . . . .73 B2
Stephenson Dr CW1 . . . . .191 A4
Stephenson Rd WA12 . . . . . .2 D2
Stephenson Wlk CW7 . . . .149 A8
Stephen St WA1 . . . . .16 D6
Stephens Terr CH66 . . . . . .69 B6
Stephens Way ST7 . . . . . . .209 F2
Sterling Cl 1 CW9 . . . . . .103 F5
Sterne Ct CW1 . . . . .174 D6
Stetchworth Rd WA4 . . . . . .16 B1
Stevenage Cl SK11 . . . . . .112 B7
Stevenage Dr SK11 . . . . . .112 B7
Steven Ct CH3 . . . . .237 C3
Stevens Rd CH60 . . . . .41 C7
Stevens St WA9 . . . . .60 A1
Steventon WA7 . . . . .24 E4
Steward's Ave WA8 . . . . . . .22 F8
Stewart St CW2 . . . . .190 A3
Stile End CH2 . . . . .119 F8
Stiles The CW8 . . . . .101 D5
Stiperstones CT CH66 . . . . .69 A6
Stirling Cl
Chester CH3 . . . . .119 A2
Congleton CW12 . . . . .156 C3
Macclesfield SK10 . . . . .86 F2
Warrington WA1 . . . . .17 E7
Winsford CW7 . . . . .127 A3
Stirling Dr
Ellesmere Port CH65 . . . . . .70 D3
Holmes Chapel CW4 . . . . .130 B2
Stirrup Cl WA2 . . . . .9 A3
Stirrup La CH64 . . . . .43 B1
Stoak Cl CH65 . . . . .70 C4
Stoak Lo CH65 . . . . .70 C4
Stockdale Dr WA5 . . . . .14 E7
Stockham Cl WA7 . . . . .50 A8
Stockham La WA7 . . . . .50 B7
Stock La CW7, CW5 . . . . . .206 B2
Stockley La WA4 . . . . .52 F7
Stockport Rd WA4 . . . . .17 E3
Stocks Ave 3 CH3 . . . . . . .119 A1
Stocks Ct The WA3 . . . . .3 D8
Stocks Hill CW7 . . . . .149 F7
Stocks La
Chester CH3 . . . . .119 A1
Ollerton SK10 . . . . .82 E1
Rainow SK10 . . . . .88 E5
Warrington WA4 . . . . .16 D8
Stockswell Rd WA8 . . . . . . .12 A3
STOCKTON HEATH 16 D1
Stockton Heath Prim Sch
WA4 . . . . .16 C1
Stockton La WA4 . . . . .16 F1
Stockton Rd SK9 . . . . .59 F4
Stockton View WA4 . . . . . . .16 B2
Stockwell Farm Ct
WA8 . . . . .12 E4
Stoke Abbott Cl SK7 . . . . . .35 E7
Stoke Cl CH62 . . . . .43 E3
Stoke Gdns CH65 . . . . .70 C4
Stokehall La CW5 . . . . .187 E6
Stokesay Ct CH65 . . . . .70 E3
Stokes St WA3 . . . . .9 E5
Stoke Wlk CH65 . . . . .70 C4
Stoneacre Gdns WA7 . . . . .24 C1
Stonebank Dr CH64 . . . . . . .67 A6
Stone Bank Rd ST7 . . . . . .195 B1
Stone Barn La WA7 . . . . . . .49 F6
Stonebridge Rd CW5 . . . . .204 E3
Stone Chair La ST7 . . . . . .194 E7
Stonechat Cl
10 Golborne WA3 . . . . .3 E8
Runcorn WA7 . . . . .49 E5
Stone Cotts CW12 . . . . . . .157 E2
Stone Croft
Chester CH3 . . . . .142 B7
Kingsmead CW9 . . . . .103 F5
Stonecrop Cl
Runcorn WA7 . . . . .49 F4
Warrington WA3 . . . . .9 C4
Stone Cross Dr WA8 . . . . . .12 E5
Stone Cross La N WA3 . . . . .3 C6
Stone Cross La S WA3 . . . . .3 C6
Stone Cross Pk WA3 . . . . . . .3 B7
Stonehaven Dr WA2 . . . . . . .9 A3
Stoneheads SK23 . . . . .65 C8
Stoneheads Rise SK23 . . . .65 D8
Stone Heyes La CW8,
CW9 . . . . .77 F5
Stonehill Cl WA4 . . . . .26 D4
Stonehills Cl WA7 . . . . .23 C2
Stonehills La WA7 . . . . .23 C2
Stonehouse Gn 6
CW12 . . . . .156 D3
Stone House La CW6 . . . . .184 E4
Stonelea WA7 . . . . .24 B2
Stoneleigh Cl SK10 . . . . . . .87 C2
Stoneleigh Ct WA4 . . . . . . .17 D1
Stoneleigh Gdns WA4 . . . .17 D1
Stoneley Ave CW1 . . . . . . .190 D7
STONELEY GREEN 203 D4
Stoneley Rd CW1 . . . . .190 D8
Stone Mead Ave WA15 . . . .32 C7
Stone Pit La WA3 . . . . .3 F2
Stonepail Cl CH2 . . . . .118 F3
Stones Manor La
CW8 . . . . .103 C5
Stoneway Ct 1 CH60 . . . . .40 F8
Stoneyfold La SK11 . . . . . .113 A6

Stoneyford La CW8 . . . . . .101 C2
Stoney Holt WA7 . . . . .50 C8
Stoney La
Delamere CW6 . . . . .123 C6
Wilmslow SK9 . . . . .59 F5
Stoneyland Dr SK22 . . . . . . .39 B8
Stonyhurst Cres WA3 . . . . . .4 D5
Stony La CW12 . . . . .156 C1
Stopsley Cl CW12 . . . . .155 F4
Stores Rd M90 . . . . .33 A6
Store St SK10 . . . . .88 B8
Stour Ct CH65 . . . . .70 B7
STOWFORD 207 C8
Straight Dr 4 WA3 . . . . .4 A7
Straight Length WA6 . . . . . .73 E7
Straight Mile CH4 . . . . .162 F5
Straker Ave CH65 . . . . .69 F6
Stratford Gdns CH1 . . . . . .117 E4
Stratford Rd
Blacon CH1 . . . . .117 E4
Neston CH64 . . . . .66 C6
Stratford Sq SK8 . . . . .34 C7
Stratford Way SK11 . . . . . .112 C5
Strathaven Ave CW2 . . . . .205 E8
Strathearn Rd CH60 . . . . . .40 F7
Strathmore Cl CW4 . . . . . .130 B2
Stratton Cl WA7 . . . . .50 B6
Stratton Pk WA8 . . . . .12 F5
Stratton Rd WA5 . . . . .15 B5
Strawberry Cl WA3 . . . . .9 C4
Strawberry Dr CH66 . . . . . .95 A8
Strawberry Fields
CH3 . . . . .142 B7
Strawberry Gn CH66 . . . . . .95 A8
Strawberry La
Acton Bridge CW8 . . . . .76 F3
Mollington CH1 . . . . .94 D4
Wilmslow SK9 . . . . .59 E6
Street Forest Walks The*
SK17 . . . . .90 E4
Street Hey La CH64 . . . . . . .43 B1
Street La
Lower Whitley WA4 . . . . . . .52 C3
Rode Heath ST7 . . . . .176 F2
Skellorn Green SK10 . . . . . .62 D8
Street The
Mickle Trafford CH2 . . . . . .119 D8
Whaley Bridge SK10,
SK17 . . . . .90 C5
STRETTON
Farndon 197 F6
Warrington 26 E2
Stretton Ave WA3 . . . . .3 E7
Stretton Cl CH62 . . . . .43 E3
Stretton Hall Mews
WA4 . . . . .52 E8
Stretton Mill* SY14 . . . . .198 A7
Stretton Rd WA4 . . . . .26 E2
Stretton Way 3 SK9 . . . . . .34 D5
Stretton Wlk CW9 . . . . .103 F4
Strickland Cl WA4 . . . . .27 A7
Strines Rd SK6 . . . . .38 D8
Stringer Ave CW11 . . . . . . .175 C5
Stringer Cres WA4 . . . . .16 E4
Stringer's La LL12,
CH4 . . . . .161 B4
Stroma Ave CH65 . . . . .95 B8
Stromness Cl WA2 . . . . .9 B3
Stuart Cl
Chester CH3 . . . . .119 C3
Winsford CW7 . . . . .149 C5
Stuart Cr SK10 . . . . .87 B2
Stuart Dr WA4 . . . . .16 F2
Stuart Pl CH1 . . . . .237 B3
Stuart Rd WA7 . . . . .24 C4
Stubbs La
Lostock Gralam CW9 . . . . . .80 A2
Mobberley WA16 . . . . .58 E4
Stubbs Pl CH1 . . . . .117 E3
Stubbs Terr 17 SK11 . . . . .112 E7
Stubby La SK10 . . . . .84 E2
STUD GREEN 152 C1
Stud Green Ind Pk
CW11 . . . . .152 C1
Sturgess St WA12 . . . . .1 F3
STYAL 33 F4
Styal Cl 4 CW9 . . . . .103 F4
Styal Cl SK9 . . . . .33 E4
Styal Ctry Pk* SK9 . . . . . . .33 E3
Styal Gn SK9 . . . . .33 F3
STYAL GREEN 34 A3
Styal Prim Sch SK9 . . . . . . .33 E4
Styal Rd
Wilmslow SK9 . . . . .60 B8
Wythenshawe M22 . . . . . . .33 F7
Styal St WA5 . . . . .34 A4
Styal View SK9 . . . . .34 B2
Styperson Way SK12 . . . . . .36 E3
Sudbrook Cl WA3 . . . . .3 E8
Sudbury Dr SK8 . . . . .34 C8
Sudbury Rd SK7 . . . . .36 E8
Sudlow La
Knutsford WA16 . . . . .56 D1
Plumley WA16 . . . . .81 C7
Suez St
Newton-le-W WA12 . . . . .2 B3
Warrington WA1 . . . . .16 B5
Suffolk Ave CH65 . . . . .69 F5
Suffolk Cl
Congleton CW12 . . . . .156 D4
Macclesfield SK10 . . . . .86 F1
Warrington WA1 . . . . .17 E6
Suffolk Dr SK9 . . . . .34 C1
Suffolk Ho 3 CH1 . . . . . . .237 C3
Suffolk Pl WA8 . . . . .22 C7
Suffolk St WA7 . . . . .23 A3
Sugar La
Bollington SK10 . . . . .63 A3

Sugar La continued
Manley WA6 . . . . .98 E5
Rainow SK10 . . . . .88 D5
Sugar Pit La WA16 . . . . .56 E3
Sugar St SK11 . . . . .159 C2
Sulby Ave WA4 . . . . .16 B3
Sulgrave Ave SK12 . . . . . . .36 F4
Summer Cl 7 WA7 . . . . .23 F1
Summercroft CW3 . . . . .3 F8
Summer Dr CW11 . . . . .175 C6
Summerfield ST7 . . . . .195 B1
Summerfield Ave WA5 . . . . .7 F2
Summerfield Cl CH4 . . . . . .139 A3
Summerfield Dr CH9 . . . . .126 F8
Summerfield Ho CH3 . . . . .119 F5
Summerfield Pl SK9 . . . . . . .60 A5
Summerfield Rd
Guilden Sutton CH3 . . . . . .119 F5
Mobberley WA16 . . . . .57 F4
Summerfields WA16 . . . . . .57 C3
Summerfields Ctr 10
SK9 . . . . .34 D2
Summerhill Dr ST5 . . . . . . .210 D1
Summerhill Rd SK10 . . . . . .86 F4
Summer La
Daresbury WA4 . . . . .51 D7
Hatton WA4 . . . . .25 F1
Runcorn WA7 . . . . .23 F1
Summerlea SK8 . . . . .35 B8
Summerlea Cl SK10 . . . . . . .87 D1
Summers Cl WA16 . . . . .82 A7
Summers Way WA16 . . . . . .82 A7
Summertrees Rd CH66 . . . .69 E3
Summerville Gdns
WA4 . . . . .16 F1
Summerville Wlk 1
WA5 . . . . .15 C7
Summit Cl WA4 . . . . .26 E1
Sumner Rd CH1 . . . . .117 E4
Sumner St WA11 . . . . .1 A7
Sumpter Pathway
CH2 . . . . .118 F3
Sunart Cl CW2 . . . . .206 B6
Sunbank La WA15 . . . . .32 E6
Sunbeam Cl WA7 . . . . .22 F3
Sunbeam St WA12 . . . . .2 C3
Sunbury Cl SK9 . . . . .34 E2
Sunbury Cres 3 CH4 . . . . .140 F6
Sunbury Gdns WA4 . . . . . . .26 E7
Suncroft Cl WA1 . . . . .17 E7
Suncroft Rd CH60 . . . . .41 C7
Sundale Dr CW2 . . . . .189 D4
Sunderland St SK11 . . . . . .112 D7
Sundial Ho WA3 . . . . .4 F3
Sundown Cl SK22 . . . . .39 A8
Sunfield Cl CH66 . . . . .69 D3
Sunflower Cl WA9 . . . . .6 A7
Sunflower Dr WA5 . . . . .15 D3
Sunningdale Ave WA8 . . . .12 B1
Sunningdale Cl
Burtonwood WA5 . . . . .6 F6
Northwich CW9 . . . . .104 E7
Winsford CW7 . . . . .126 A2
Sunningdale Dr
Bebington CH63 . . . . .43 B6
Bramhall SK7 . . . . .36 A7
Sunningdale Rd
Cheadle SK8 . . . . .35 A7
Macclesfield SK11 . . . . . . .112 A6
Sunningdale Way
CH64 . . . . .66 E4
Sunninghey Ct SK9 . . . . . . .59 F2
Sunnybank SK9 . . . . .60 B6
Sunny Bank SK11 . . . . .112 D5
Sunnybank Cl WA12 . . . . . . .2 C4
Sunny Bank Cl SK11 . . . . .112 C5
Sunny Bank Cotts
Ashton Hayes CH3 . . . . . . .121 E7
Warrington WA8 . . . . .14 A4
Sunnybank Dr SK9 . . . . .59 D4
Sunnybank Rd CW1,
CW2 . . . . .189 E5
Sunny Bank Rd WA14 . . . . .31 C8
Sunny Lea Mews SK9 . . . . .60 A6
Sunnymill Dr CW11 . . . . . .175 A6
Sunnyside
Alsager ST7 . . . . .193 A4
4 Ellesmere Port CH65 . . .70 C6
Malpas SY14 . . . . .212 F2
Warrington WA5 . . . . .14 E6
Sunnyside La WA7 . . . . .24 E4
Sunnyside Wlk CW11 . . . . .154 B1
Sunset Cotts CH64 . . . . .67 A4
Surrey Dr CW12 . . . . .156 E5
Surrey Rd
Chester CH2 . . . . .119 A5
Kidsgrove ST7 . . . . .195 A2
Warren SK11 . . . . .112 A4
Surrey St
Crewe CW1 . . . . .190 E4
4 Runcorn WA7 . . . . .23 A3
Warrington WA4 . . . . .16 D3
Surridge WA16 . . . . .29 C5
Susan Dr WA5 . . . . .14 D5
Susan St WA8 . . . . .13 C2
Sussex Ave SK11 . . . . .112 A5
Sussex Dr ST7 . . . . .194 F2
Sussex Pl CW12 . . . . .156 E5
Sussex Rd
Chester CH2 . . . . .118 F4
Irlam M44 . . . . .11 C6
Partington M31 . . . . .11 F3
Sussex St WA8 . . . . .13 D1
Sussex Way CH2 . . . . .118 F4
Sutch La WA13 . . . . .19 A3
Sutherland Cr 5 WA7 . . . . .23 B2
Sutherland Dr
Bebington CH62 . . . . .43 D4

Sutherland Dr *continued*
Macclesfield SK10 . . . . .87 A1
Sutherland Way CH3 . . . .119 B3
Sutton Ave
Culcheth WA3 . . . . .4 F4
Neston CH64 . . . . .66 E6
Sutton Cl
Bebington CH62 . . . . .43 E3
Higher Wincham CW9 . . . . . . .79 F6
Macclesfield SK11 . . . . .112 D5
Mickle Trafford CH2 . . . . . . .119 F8
Nantwich CW5 . . . . .204 C5
Sutton Cswy WA6, WA7 . . .49 E2
Sutton Dr CH2 . . . . .118 E5
Sutton Field CW8 . . . . .126 A7
SUTTON GREEN 69 C3
Sutton Green Prim Sch
CH66 .69 C5
Sutton Hall Dr CH66 . . . . . . .69 A6
Sutton Hall Gdns CH66 . . . .69 A6
Sutton High Sch CH66 . . . . .69 E6
Sutton La CW10 . . . . .151 C7
SUTTON LANE ENDS
. . . . .112 E2
Sutton Quays Bsns Pk
WA7 . . . . .49 E3
Sutton Rd
Alderley Edge SK9 . . . . .59 F2
Poynton SK12 . . . . .37 A2
Sutton's La 4 WA8 . . . . . . .23 B7
Sutton St
Runcorn WA7 . . . . .23 B2
Warrington WA1 . . . . .16 C4
Sutton Way
Ellesmere Port CH66 . . . . .69 E4
1 Handforth SK9 . . . . .34 E5
SUTTON WEAVER 50 B3
Swale Cl SK9 . . . . .34 E2
Swaledale Ave CW12 . . . . . .157 A5
Swaledale Cl
Bebington CH62 . . . . .43 E5
Warrington WA5 . . . . .14 F7
Swale Rd CH65 . . . . .70 A7
Swallow Cl
1 Kidsgrove ST7 . . . . .195 B2
Macclesfield SK10 . . . . .113 A7
Warrington WA3 . . . . .9 F4
Swallow Ct
Handforth SK9 . . . . .34 B1
Winsford CW7 . . . . .149 D5
Swallow Dr
Alsager ST7 . . . . .193 B3
Kelsall CW6 . . . . .122 D5
Sandbach CW11 . . . . .175 A8
Swallowfield Cl CW2 . . . . . .206 A8
Swallowfield Gdns
WA4 . . . . .26 F5
Swallowfields CH3 . . . . . . .180 E2
Swallowmere View
ST7 .195 F1
Swallow Rd ST7 . . . . .195 F1
Swanage Cl WA4 . . . . .16 E2
Swanage Ct 6 CW7 . . . . . .149 D6
Swan Ave WA9 . . . . .1 A2
SWANBACH 229 E1
Swan Bank
Congleton CW12 . . . . .156 D2
Talke ST7 . . . . .210 D7
Swan Cl
Ellesmere Port, Great Sutton
CH66 .69 D2
Poynton SK12 . . . . .36 B4
Talke ST7 . . . . .210 D8
Swan Ct
Bunbury CW6 . . . . .185 E8
Crowton CW8 . . . . .101 E2
Swan Farm La CW3 . . . . . . .232 B1
Swan Gr WA16 . . . . .106 D8
SWAN GREEN 106 D8
Swan Ho ST7 . . . . .210 D7
Swan La
Bunbury CW6 . . . . .185 E8
Cheadle SK8 . . . . .35 B8
SWANLEY 203 C5
Swanley La CW5 . . . . .203 D4
Swanlow Ave CW7 . . . . .149 D5
Swanlow Dr CW7 . . . . .149 D6
Swanlow La CW7 . . . . .149 E5
Swan Rd WA12 . . . . .1 E4
Swanscoe Ave SK10 . . . . . . .88 A7
Swanscoe Cl CW10 . . . . . . .151 B8
Swanscoe La SK10 . . . . .88 B3
Swan St
Congleton CW12 . . . . .156 D2
Wilmslow SK9 . . . . .60 B7
Swanwick Cl CW4 . . . . .107 C1
Swanwick Gn SY13 . . . . . . .215 C5
SWANWICK GREEN 215 C5
Swanwick Ho SK10 . . . . .86 F6
Sweet Briar Cres
CW2 .189 F3
Sweet Brier Cl CW8 . . . . . . .78 B4
Sweetfield Gdns CH66 . . . . .69 D7
Sweetfield Rd CH66 . . . . . . .69 D7
Sweettooth La CW11 . . . . . .175 A7
SWETTENHAM 131 E3
Swettenham Cl
Alsager ST7 . . . . .193 C3
Sandbach CW11 . . . . .175 D7
SWETTENHAM HEATH
. . . . .132 B3
Swettenham La CW12 . . . . .131 E3
Swettenham Rd
Handforth SK9 . . . . .34 D5
Swettenham CW12 . . . . .132 B2
Swettenham St SK11 . . . . . .112 E7
Swift Cl
Kidsgrove ST7 . . . . .195 B2

Swift Cl *continued*
Warrington WA2 . . . . .8 E3
Wistaston CW2 . . . . .205 F8
Swinburne Dr CW1 . . . . . . .190 F4
Swindale Ave WA8 . . . . .8 B3
Swinden Cl WA7 . . . . .24 D2
Swine Market 2
CW5 . . . . .204 E5
Swineyard La WA16 . . . . . . .28 C4
Swinford Ave WA8 . . . . .13 E2
Swinhoe Pl WA3 . . . . .4 D3
Swinley Chase SK9 . . . . .34 E1
Swinleys Hey CH3 . . . . .142 A7
Swinnerton St CW2 . . . . . . .190 C2
Swinton Sq 18 WA16 . . . . . .57 A2
Swireford Rd WA6 . . . . .73 B2
Swiss Cott
Alderley Edge SK9 . . . . .60 C1
Macclesfield SK10 . . . . .87 B2
Swiss Hill SK9 . . . . .60 B1
Swithin Rd M22 . . . . .33 E8
SWORTON HEATH 28 E5
Swynnerton Way WA8 . . . . .13 B5
Sycamore Ave
Alsager ST7 . . . . .193 E2
Congleton CW12 . . . . .155 F4
Crewe CW1 . . . . .190 D6
Haydock WA11 . . . . .1 A5
Newton-le-W WA12 . . . . .2 C3
Rode Heath ST7 . . . . .193 F7
Widnes WA8 . . . . .13 B2
Winsford CW7 . . . . .149 D8
Sycamore Cl
Audlem CW3 . . . . .230 A4
Biddulph ST8 . . . . .179 E2
Handforth SK9 . . . . .34 B2
Holmes Chapel CW4 . . . . . . .130 D3
Nantwich CW5 . . . . .204 F7
Talke ST7 . . . . .210 E8
Sycamore Cres
Barnton CW8 . . . . .78 B4
Hollinfare WA3 . . . . .11 B2
Macclesfield SK11 . . . . .112 A7
Sycamore Ct WA7 . . . . .24 D5
Sycamore Dr
Aston WA7 . . . . .50 B4
Chester CH4 . . . . .140 F5
Ellesmere Port CH66 . . . . . . .70 A1
Lymm WA13 . . . . .18 D4
Middlewich CW10 . . . . .151 E5
Sycamore Gr
Broughton CH4 . . . . .139 B3
Sandbach CW11 . . . . .175 A8
Sycamore La WA5 . . . . .15 B6
Sycamore Lane Com Prim
Sch WA5 . . . . .15 B5
Sycamore Lo SK7 . . . . .35 F7
Sycamore Rd
Paddockhill WA16 . . . . .59 B5
Partington M31 . . . . .11 E3
Runcorn WA7 . . . . .49 D8
Sycamore Rise WA11 . . . . . . .1 A6
Sycamores The WA16 . . . . .58 E2
Syddal Cl SK7 . . . . .35 D5
Syddal Cres SK7 . . . . .35 D4
Syddal Gn SK7 . . . . .35 D5
Syddal Rd SK7 . . . . .35 D5
SYDNEY 191 A5
Sydney Ave M90 . . . . .33 A8
Sydney Rd
Bramhall SK7 . . . . .35 F5
Chester CH1 . . . . .118 B3
Crewe CW1 . . . . .190 F6
Sydney St
Northwich CW8 . . . . .103 C7
Runcorn WA7 . . . . .48 D7
Syers Ct WA1 . . . . .16 E8
Sylvan Ave SK9 . . . . .59 F5
Sylvan Cl CW8 . . . . .103 C7
Sylvan Mews CH1 . . . . .117 E6
Sylvia Cres WA2 . . . . .8 D1
Symondley Rd SK11 . . . . . . .112 F2
Synge St WA2 . . . . .16 C7
Sytch Croft CH64 . . . . .66 E8

T

Tabley Ave WA8 . . . . .12 D2
Tabley Cl
Knutsford WA16 . . . . .56 E3
Macclesfield SK10 . . . . .112 A8
Sandbach CW11 . . . . .174 E7
Tabley Ct WA16 . . . . .56 B4
Tabley Gr WA16 . . . . .56 E1
Tabley Hill La WA16 . . . . . . .56 B2
Tabley Ho* WA16 . . . . .81 B8
Tabley Rd
Crewe CW2 . . . . .189 E3
Handforth SK9 . . . . .34 D5
Knutsford WA16 . . . . .56 E3
Tabley St SK9 . . . . .79 A1
Tabley Stables WA16 . . . . . .81 A8
Tabor St SK11 . . . . .112 E6
Tadgers La WA6 . . . . .73 D8
Tailors View CW5 . . . . .204 E6
Talbot Cl
Neston CH64 . . . . .66 F6
Shavington CW2 . . . . .206 B4
Warrington WA3 . . . . .9 E3
Talbot Gdns CH64 . . . . .66 F6
Talbot Rd
Alderley Edge SK9 . . . . .60 B1
Dunham-on-t-H WA6 . . . . .97 E7
Ellesmere Port CH66 . . . . .69 D3

Talbot St
Chester CH1 . . . . .237 B4
Golborne WA3 . . . . .3 A8
Talbot Way CW5 . . . . .205 A3
Talfryn Cl CH5 . . . . .91 D1
Talisman Cl WA7 . . . . .50 D7
TALKE 210 C7
Talke Rd
Alsager ST7 . . . . .193 E3
High Carr ST5 . . . . .210 F2
Newcastle-u-Lyme ST7,
ST5 .210 D4
TALLARN GREEN/
TALLWRN GREEN 222 E5
Tall Ash Ave CW12 . . . . .157 A4
Tall Chys CW11 . . . . .175 D4
Tall Trees Cl CW8 . . . . .103 C6
Tally Ho La CW5 . . . . .203 E3
Tamar Cl
Congleton CW12 . . . . .156 F1
Macclesfield SK10 . . . . .86 E1
Tamar Rd
Haydock WA11 . . . . .1 C6
Kidsgrove ST7 . . . . .195 B2
Tamar Wlk CW7 . . . . .127 A2
Tame Cl
Biddulph ST8 . . . . .179 D1
Sandbach CW11 . . . . .174 E8
Tame Wlk 8 SK9 . . . . .34 D2
Tamworth Cl SK7 . . . . .36 D8
Tamworth St WA12 . . . . .2 A3
Tanhouse WA7 . . . . .23 E1
Tanhouse Ind Est WA8 . . . . .23 C7
Tan House La
Burtonwood WA5 . . . . .7 A5
Widnes WA8 . . . . .22 D8
Tankersley Gr WA5 . . . . .15 B6
Tanners La WA2 . . . . .16 A6
Tanner's La WA3 . . . . .3 B8
Tanner St CW12 . . . . .156 E2
Tanners Way CW5 . . . . .204 E4
Tannery La
Neston CH64 . . . . .66 E8
Warrington WA5 . . . . .14 D3
Tanning Ct 8 WA1 . . . . .16 C5
Tanyard Dr WA15 . . . . .32 C6
Tanyard La WA15 . . . . .32 A5
Tapley Ave SK12 . . . . .36 E2
Taplow Cl WA4 . . . . .26 E6
Taporley War Meml Hospl
. . . . .146 D2
Target Cl ST7 . . . . .210 E6
Target Rd CH60 . . . . .40 C8
Tarnbeck WA7 . . . . .50 D8
Tarn Cl CW7 . . . . .126 C3
Tarn Ct WA1 . . . . .17 F7
Tarn Mount SK11 . . . . .112 A5
Tarnway WA3 . . . . .3 F7
TARPORLEY 146 C1
Tarporley Bsns Ctr
CW6 .168 C8
Tarporley CE Prim Sch
CW6 .146 D2
Tarporley Com High Sch
CW6 .146 D1
Tarporley Rd
Duddon CH3 . . . . .144 E7
Ellesmere Port CH66 . . . . .69 E4
Little Budworth CW6,
CW8 . . . . .124 C5
Lower Whitley WA4 . . . . .52 C4
Tarvin CH3 . . . . .121 C1
Utkinton CH6 . . . . .146 E6
Whitchurch SY13 . . . . .225 F3
Tarporley Wlk SK9 . . . . .34 E2
Tarrant Ct CH1 . . . . .94 F1
TARVIN 121 C3
Tarvin Ave CW2 . . . . .189 D4
Tarvin Bridge CH3 . . . . .119 A2
Tarvin Cl
Ellesmere Port CH65 . . . . .70 C4
Golborne WA3 . . . . .3 E7
Macclesfield SK11 . . . . .112 E5
Middlewich CW10 . . . . .151 D5
Northwich CW9 . . . . .103 F5
Runcorn WA7 . . . . .49 C6
Tarvin Prim Sch CH3 . . . . . .121 B1
Tarvin Rd
Alvanley WA6 . . . . .73 F4
Bebington CH62 . . . . .43 F3
Chester, Boughton CH3 . . . . .119 A2
Chester, Vicarscross
CH3 . . . . .119 E2
Christleton CH3 . . . . .120 C3
Manley WA6 . . . . .99 A4
Tarvin Rdbt CH3 . . . . .121 A2
TARVIN SANDS 121 D4
Tarvin Sands Industries
CH3 .121 B4
Tarvin Way
1 Handforth SK9 . . . . .34 D5
Winsford CW7 . . . . .126 C2
Tasman Cl WA5 . . . . .15 C8
Tate Cl WA8 . . . . .12 D2
Tate Dr CW1 . . . . .191 C4
TATTENHALL 166 B1
Tattenhall La
Beeston CW6 . . . . .167 F2
Tattenhall CH3 . . . . .167 B3
Tattenhall Park Prim Sch
CH3 .166 B2
Tattenhall Rd CH3 . . . . .166 F2
Tatton Cl
Alsager ST7 . . . . .193 C3
Chester CH4 . . . . .140 E5
Northwich CW9 . . . . .103 F4
Winsford CW7 . . . . .126 C1

Tatton Ct
4 Handforth SK9 . . . . .34 E5
2 Knutsford WA16 . . . . .57 A2
Warrington WA1 . . . . .9 D1
TATTON DALE 30 E1
Tatton Dr CW11 . . . . .175 C7
Tatton Lo 17 WA16 . . . . .57 A2
Tatton Pk* WA16 . . . . .57 B7
Tatton Rd
Crewe CW2 . . . . .189 F2
Handforth SK9 . . . . .34 E5
Tatton St WA16 . . . . .57 A2
Tatton Stile WA16 . . . . .58 A4
Taurus Pk WA5 . . . . .7 D3
Tavener Cl CH63 . . . . .43 C5
Tavistock Cl WA5 . . . . .14 E4
Tavlin Ave WA5 . . . . .5 F1
Tawney Cl ST7 . . . . .195 B2
Tawny Ct WA7 . . . . .49 E7
TAXAL 65 D4
Taxal & Fernilee CE Prim
Sch SK23 . . . . .65 D6
Taxal Moor Rd SK23 . . . . . . .65 C3
Taxi Rd M90 . . . . .33 B7
Taxmere Cl CW11 . . . . .174 F7
Tay Cl ST8 . . . . .179 E1
Taylor Bsns Pk WA3 . . . . . . .4 F1
Taylor Dr CW5 . . . . .204 C5
Taylor Rd
Altrincham WA14 . . . . .20 F5
Haydock WA11 . . . . .1 F7
Taylor's La
Oakhanger CW1 . . . . .192 C3
Warrington WA5 . . . . .14 A2
Taylors Row WA7 . . . . .23 C2
Taylor St
Warrington WA4 . . . . .16 A1
Widnes WA8 . . . . .13 C1
Teal Ave
Knutsford WA16 . . . . .56 F7
Poynton SK12 . . . . .36 A4
Tealby Cl CW9 . . . . .104 B8
Teal Cl
Warrington WA4 . . . . .8 E3
Winsford CW7 . . . . .149 D5
Teal Gr WA3 . . . . .9 F3
Teals Way CH60 . . . . .40 E8
Tebay Rd CH62 . . . . .43 E8
Technology Ctr The
CH65 .70 B7
Tedder Dr M22 . . . . .33 F7
Tedder Sq WA14 . . . . .22 D8
Teddington Cl WA4 . . . . .26 E5
Tees Cl CH65 . . . . .70 A7
Teesdale Cl WA5 . . . . .14 F7
Teesdale Rd WA11 . . . . .1 C7
Tegg's Nose Ctry Pk*
SK11 .113 D6
Teggsnose La SK11 . . . . .113 D6
Tegid Way CH4 . . . . .140 D5
Tegsnose Mount
SK11 . . . . .113 C4
Telegraph Rd CH60 . . . . .41 A7
Telfer Ct CW10 . . . . .151 C6
Telford Cl
Congleton CW12 . . . . .157 B2
Macclesfield SK10 . . . . .88 A1
Talke ST7 . . . . .210 E8
Widnes WA8 . . . . .12 D4
Telford Ct CH1 . . . . .94 D6
Telford Gdns CW11 . . . . . . .174 F3
Telford Ho ST7 . . . . .195 B3
Telford Pl CW5 . . . . .204 C5
Telford Rd CH65 . . . . .70 E4
Telford's Quay CH65 . . . . . . .70 D7
Telford Way
Audlem CW3 . . . . .230 A3
Chester CH4 . . . . .140 F6
Middlewich CW10 . . . . .128 E1
Tempest Rd SK9 . . . . .60 C1
Templar Ct SK10 . . . . .87 A1
Temple Chambers
CH1 .237 B3
Temple Ct WA3 . . . . .9 E6
Templeton Dr WA2 . . . . .9 A8
Tenbury Cl WA5 . . . . .15 A8
Tenby Cl WA5 . . . . .7 D3
Tenby Dr WA7 . . . . .23 D2
Tenby Rd SK11 . . . . .111 F6
Tenchersfield CW5 . . . . .205 A4
Tennyson Ave CW1 . . . . .190 F4
Tennyson Cl
Crewe CW2 . . . . .190 A1
Macclesfield SK11 . . . . .111 E6
Northwich CW9 . . . . .104 C6
Rode Heath ST7 . . . . .193 E8
Tennyson Dr WA2 . . . . .8 C2
Tennyson Rd
Ellesmere Port CH65 . . . . .70 A4
Widnes WA8 . . . . .13 A1
Tennyson Wlk CH1 . . . . .118 A5
Tensing Cl WA5 . . . . .15 B8
Tenth Ave CH5 . . . . .92 D3
Terence Ave WA1 . . . . .16 F6
Terminal Rd N M90 . . . . .33 B7
Terminal Rd S M90 . . . . .33 B7
Tern Ave ST7 . . . . .195 C2
Tern Cl WA8 . . . . .12 B3
Tern Dr SK12 . . . . .36 B4
Terrace Rd WA8 . . . . .22 B5
Terra Nova Sch CW4 . . . . . .108 D1
Terrick Mews SY13 . . . . . . .226 B2
Terrick Rd SY13 . . . . .226 A2
Tetchill Cl
Ellesmere Port CH66 . . . . .69 D2
Runcorn WA7 . . . . .50 D8
Tetton Cl 8 CW12 . . . . .156 F3
Tetton La CW10 . . . . .151 E3

Tewkesbury Cl
Cheadle SK8 . . . . .35 B6
Chester CH2 . . . . .118 F7
Ellesmere Port CH66 . . . . .94 E8
Middlewich CW10 . . . . .128 B1
Poynton SK12 . . . . .36 D4
Tewkesbury Dr SK10 . . . . . . .87 E4
Tewkesbury Rd WA3 . . . . . . .3 B8
Thackeray Dr CH3 . . . . .119 C3
Thackeray Twrs 2
CH1 .237 C3
Thackery Ct 6 CW11 . . . . .174 D6
Thames Cl
Congleton CW12 . . . . .156 F1
Warrington WA2 . . . . .8 D2
Thamesdale CH65 . . . . .70 B4
Thames Dr
Biddulph ST8 . . . . .179 D1
Biddulph ST8 . . . . .179 E1
Thames Gdns CH65 . . . . .70 B3
Thames Pl CW7 . . . . .127 B1
Thames Side CH65 . . . . .70 B3
Thames Trad Ctr M44 . . . . . .11 F7
Thatchers Mount WA5 . . . . . .1 D1
Thaxted Wlk SK22 . . . . .33 C8
Theatre Ct CW9 . . . . .103 F8
THE BANK 195 B7
THE BARONY 204 F6
THELWALL 17 E3
Thelwall Com Inf Sch
WA4 . . . . .17 C3
Thelwall Com Jun Sch
WA4 . . . . .17 D3
Thelwall La
Warrington WA4 . . . . .16 F3
Warrington WA4 . . . . .17 B3
Thelwall New Rd WA4 . . . . . .17 C3
Thelwall New Rd Ind Est
WA4 . . . . .17 C3
Thelwall Rd CH66 . . . . .69 B1
THE QUARRY 209 E1
THE ROOKERY 195 C3
Thetford Cl SK10 . . . . .87 C3
Thetford Rd WA5 . . . . .14 E6
THE VALLEY 190 A4
The Verdin High Sch
CW7 .126 C1
Thewlis St WA5 . . . . .15 E5
Third Ave
Connah's Quay CH5 . . . . .92 F1
Crewe CW1 . . . . .190 F1
Kidsgrove ST7 . . . . .194 F1
Poynton SK12 . . . . .36 D1
Runcorn WA7 . . . . .49 F8
Sandbach CW11 . . . . .175 A5
Thirlmere
Macclesfield SK11 . . . . .111 F5
Macclesfield SK11 . . . . .112 A5
Thirlmere Ave WA2 . . . . .8 C3
Thirlmere Cl
Alderley Edge SK9 . . . . .59 F1
Frodsham WA6 . . . . .49 D1
Holmes Chapel CW4 . . . . . . .130 A3
Winsford CW7 . . . . .126 F3
Thirlmere Ct CW12 . . . . .156 A2
Thirlmere Dr WA13 . . . . .18 F3
Thirlmere Lo 5 WA13 . . . . .18 F3
Thirlmere Rd
Chester CH2 . . . . .119 A5
Crewe CW2 . . . . .190 A2
Ellesmere Port CH65 . . . . .70 C2
Neston CH64 . . . . .66 F7
Partington M31 . . . . .11 E4
Thirlmere Way WA8 . . . . .22 C8
Thirsk Cl WA7 . . . . .49 C6
Thistle Cl WA16 . . . . .79 F7
Thistle Sq M31 . . . . .11 E2
Thistleton Cl SK11 . . . . .112 D6
Thistle Wlk 4 M31 . . . . .11 E2
Thistlewood Dr SK9 . . . . .60 D8
Thomas Ave CW5 . . . . .205 A3
Thomas Brassey Cl
CH2 .237 C4
Thomas Cl
Alsager ST7 . . . . .193 E4
Blacon CH1 . . . . .117 F6
Ellesmere Port CH65 . . . . .70 B2
Mickle Trafford CH2 . . . . . . .119 F8
Thomas Ct WA7 . . . . .49 F7
Thomas Ho CH1 . . . . .118 A5
Thomas Hodges Ct
CW4 .130 D3
Thomasons Bridge La
WA4 . . . . .25 E6
Thomas Row 8 CW5 . . . . . .204 E6
Thomas St
Biddulph ST8 . . . . .179 D1
Congleton CW12 . . . . .156 E3
Crewe CW1 . . . . .190 D4
Golborne WA3 . . . . .3 A8
Packmoor ST7 . . . . .195 F1
Runcorn WA7 . . . . .23 B3
Talke ST7 . . . . .210 D8
2 Widnes WA8 . . . . .23 A7
Thomas Wedge CE Jun
Sch The CH1 . . . . .94 A1
Thompson Ave WA3 . . . . .4 E3
Thompson Cl CW12 . . . . .2 C1
Thompson Gdns CW12 . . . .156 A3
Thomson St WA3 . . . . .9 E5
Thoresway Rd SK9 . . . . .59 F5
Thorlby Rd WA3 . . . . .4 F3
Thorley Gr CW2 . . . . .190 A1

Thorley La
Wythenshawe M90 ....**33** A8
Wythenshawe M90 ....**33** B8
Thorley Mews SK7 ....**35** F7
Thornberry CI CH1......**117** B8
Thornbrook Way
CW1.......................**174** D5
Thornbury Ave WA3 .....**3** E7
Thorn CI
Runcorn WA7............**49** C7
Warrington WA5 ....**14** F3
Thorn Dr M22 ....**34** A8
Thorne CI SK10...........**87** A5
Thorne Dr CH66 ....**69** B4
Thorneycroft Dr WA1....**16** C6
Thorney Dr SK8 ....**35** C6
Thorneyholme Dr
WA16.....................**57** B2
Thornfield SK9 ....**60** A4
Thornfield CI WA3.........**3** C8
Thornfield Hey SK9 .....**60** E8
Thornfields CW7........**173** B1
Thorn Gr SK8.............**35** A7
Thorngrove Dr SK9 ......**60** C6
Thorngrove Hill SK9 ....**60** C6
Thorn Grove Prim Sch
SK8.......................**35** A7
Thorngrove Rd SK9 .....**60** C6
Thornhills WA8...........**12** A3
Thornhill CI CH2.........**118** F6
Thorn La CW8...........**103** C5
Thornleigh Ave CH2 .....**43** F3
Thornleigh Dr CH66 .....**69** E6
Thornley CI **1** WA3......**3** C3
Thornley Rd WA13........**18** C3
Thorn Rd
Bramhall SK7.............**35** E5
Runcorn WA7............**49** C7
Warrington WA1 ....**17** A8
THORNS GREEN **32** C5
Thornsgreen Rd M22 ....**33** B8
Thornton WA8............**22** E8
Thornton Ave SK11......**112** A5
Thornton Bank CW6 ...**169** D4
Thornton CI CW7 ....**127** A3
Thornton Common Rd
CH63.....................**42** D7
Thornton Cres CH60 ....**41** B6
Thorntondale Dr WA5....**14** F7
Thornton Dr
Chester CH2 ....**118** D5
Handforth SK9...........**34** D3
Wistaston CW2 ....**206** A7
Thornton Green La
CH2.......................**71** E1
Thornton Ho
Audlem CW3 ....**230** A5
Thornton Hough **42** B6
THORNTON HOUGH **42** A7
Thornton Hough Prim Sch
CH63.....................**42** A6
THORNTON-LE-MOORS
.............................**71** F1
Thornton Mews CH66 ...**69** B8
Thornton Rd
Ellesmere Port CH65....**70** E3
Gatley SK8................**34** C8
Warrington WA5 ....**15** B4
Thornton Sq SK11 ......**112** A5
Thorntree Bglws
SK11......................**132** A8
Thorn Tree CI L24.......**21** E2
Thorn Tree Dr CW1.....**173** A1
Thorntree Gn WA4.......**27** B5
Thornway
Bollington SK10...........**88** A7
Bramhall SK8.............**35** C7
High Lane SK6............**37** F7
Thorn Wlk WA11.........**1** E6
Thornwythe Gr CH66....**69** E4
Thornycroft CW7 ....**126** A1
Thornycroft CI SK11 ...**111** E1
Thornycroft **7**
SK11......................**112** E7
Thorpe CI CW1.........**189** F8
Thorp St SK10 ....**112** D8
Thowler La WA14........**30** A5
Threaphurst La SK12....**37** C8
THREAPWOOD **222** E7
Three Acre La SK8......**34** E7
Three Fields CI CW12 ..**156** B3
Threeways CW8 ....**101** D4
Thrush Way CW7 ......**126** F4
Thurlow WA3.............**3** E7
THURLWOOD **193** E7
Thursfield Ave ST7 ....**195** C3
Thursfield Ct CH1......**118** B1
Thursfield Prim Sch
ST7.......................**195** A3
Thurstaston Rd CH60 ...**40** F8
Thurston CI WA5 ....**15** D6
Thurston Gn SK9 ....**60** A1
Thurston Rd CH4.......**140** C6
Thynne St WA1..........**16** A4
Tibbs Cross La WA8 ....**13** D8
Tibb St ST7..............**210** F8
Tidal La WA13 ....**16** F8
Tideswell CI SK8 ....**34** D8
Tideswell Rd SK7........**36** E8
Tidnock Ave CW12.....**156** E5
Tiffield CI CW7 ....**127** A4
Tilbey Dr WA6 ....**74** A8
Tilbury Pl WA7 ....**50** E6
Tidsley Cres WA7 ....**48** F6
Tilewright CI ST7......**195** B2

Tilley St WA1............**16** C6
Tilman CI WA5 ....**15** B8
TILSTON **198** B3
Tilston Ave WA4 ....**17** A4
Tilston CE Prim Sch
.............................**198** B3
TILSTONE BANK **168** F4
Tilstone CI
Hough CW2 ....**206** E2
Northwich CW9 ....**104** A5
TILSTONE FEARNALL
.............................**168** F6
Tilston Rd SY14 ....**213** A5
Tilston Wlk **5** SK9......**34** E1
Timberfields Rd CH1...**117** A8
Timber La **2** CW9 ....**103** F8
TIMBERSBROOK **157** E2
Timbersbrook Gr **5**
SK9.......................**34** D2
Timberscombe Gdns
WA1.......................**17** E6
Timber St SK10...........**87** F1
Timberell Ave CW1 ...**190** A6
Timmis CI WA2 ....**9** A3
Timmis Cres WA8 ....**13** A1
Timperley Ave WA4 .....**17** A4
Tinkersfield CW5 ......**205** A4
Tinkwood La SY14 .....**211** F1
Tinsley St WA4 ....**16** F3
Tintagel CI
Macclesfield SK10......**111** E8
Warrington WA7.........**50** B6
Tintern Ave CH2........**118** F6
Tintern CI
Poynton SK12 ....**36** D5
Warrington WA5 ....**7** E2
Tintern Rd SK8 ....**35** B6
Tipping Brow WA16.....**58** C4
Tirley La CW6 ....**123** A2
Tithebarn CI CH64......**40** F7
Tithebarn Dr CH64.....**41** B2
Tithebarn Rd WA15....**32** C8
Tithings The WA7........**23** E1
TIVERTON **168** C6
Tiverton CI
Chester CH2 ....**118** F5
Sandbach CW11........**175** C7
Widnes WA8 ....**12** C3
Tiverton Ct **6** CW9...**103** E5
Tiverton Dr SK9 ....**34** D1
Tiverton Sq WA5 ....**14** E4
Tiveton Ct CW9........**103** F5
Tobermory CI WA11.......**1** A5
Todbrook CI SK23.......**65** D6
Todds Bldgs WA8 ....**23** A6
Toft CI
Chester CH4 ....**140** E5
Widnes WA8 ....**12** F1
Toft Rd WA16............**82** B7
Toft Way SK9 ....**34** E4
Tolland La WA16.........**31** F8
Tollard CI SK8 ....**35** B6
Toll Bar Ave SK11......**112** F7
Toll Bar Pl WA2 ....**8** A4
Toll Bar Rd
Chester CH3 ....**142** C8
Macclesfield SK11......**111** F8
Warrington WA3 ....**8** A3
Tollemache Cotts
CW5......................**203** C8
Tollemache Dr CW1 ...**190** A8
Tollemache Terr CH2..**118** F2
Tollgate CI SY3.........**229** E4
Tollitt St CW1 ....**190** C4
Tom Brads Croft SK23 ..**65** E8
Tom Fields ST7 ....**209** F1
Tomkinson CI CW1....**189** F7
Tomkinson St CH2.....**237** C4
Tom La WA14.............**30** E6
Tomlinson Ave WA2.....**16** D8
Tomlins Terr CH1 ......**117** E5
Tommy's La
Congleton CW12......**156** F4
Crewe CW1 ....**190** E2
Tonbridge CI SK10......**87** B2
Toogood CI CW2 ......**119** F8
Top Farm La CW7.....**170** F2
Topgate CI CH60........**41** B8
Topping Ct WA3 ....**9** B4
Top Rd
Frodsham WA6 ....**74** D5
Kingsley WA6.............**75** B1
Top Station Rd ST7 ...**195** C7
Torbrook Gr **1** SK9....**34** D2
Torkington Rd SK9 .....**60** D6
Toronto Ave M90 ....**33** B7
Torr Dr CH62.............**44** A7
Torridon Gr CH66 ....**69** F3
Torr Rd SK11 ....**112** C4
Torr Rise WA6..........**146** D1
Torrs Valley SK22 ....**39** C7
TORR TOP **39** C8
Torr Top St SK22........**39** C7
Torrvale Rd SK22 ....**39** C7
Totland CI WA5 ....**14** C7
Totland Gr CH2.........**118** E4
Tourney Gn WA5..........**7** A2
Towcester CI CW7 ....**118** B1
TOWER HILL **88** D4
Tower Hill Rd SK10 .....**88** D4
Tower Hill Rd ST7 .....**195** F7
Tower Ho The **20**
SK11......................**112** C8
Tower La
Lymm WA13 ....**18** E2
Runcorn WA7............**50** D7
Weaverham CW8.........**77** B1

Tower Rd CH1 ....**118** B2
Towers CI
Poynton SK12 ....**36** F5
Wistaston CW2 ....**206** A7
Towers Ct
Towers CI WA5 ....**15** C7
Towers La WA6...........**98** C7
Towers Rd SK12 ....**36** F5
Towers The **6** SK10...**111** F8
Towers Yard Barns
SK12......................**36** F5
Tower Way CW1 ....**190** C4
Townbridge Ct **14**
CW8......................**103** F8
Towneley Ct WA8 ....**13** A1
TOWN END
CW8......................**12** C6
Town Farm La WA6....**100** E7
Townfield Ave CH3.....**180** E2
Townfield CI ST7 ......**194** D2
Townfield Ct CW8 ....**78** A3
Townfield La
Barnton CW8 ....**78** A3
Blacon CH1 ....**117** F8
Farndon CH3 ....**180** D2
Frodsham WA6...........**74** D7
Lymm WA13 ....**19** B7
Mollington CH1 ....**94** D2
Swan Green WA16....**106** E5
Tarvin CH3 ....**121** B2
Tiverton CW6...........**168** C6
Townfield Rd
Mobberley WA16.........**58** A4
Runcorn WA7............**24** C2
Townfields WA16........**57** C5
TOWN FIELDS **149** D7
Town Fields Cotts **6**
CW7......................**149** C5
Townfields Cres CW7 ..**149** D7
Townfields Dr CW7 ....**149** D7
Townfields Gdns
CW7......................**149** D7
Townfields Rd CW7 ...**149** D7
Townfield View WA7 ....**24** C2
Townfield Villas CH2 ....**72** B3
Towngate Bsns Ctr
WA8.......................**22** B7
Town Gn The WA4......**52** D5
Town Hill WA1...........**16** B5
Town La
Hale L24, WA8...........**21** E2
Mobberley WA16........**58** B4
Neston CH64............**66** F6
Townley Mill **6** SK11 ..**112** D7
Townley Pl **5** SK11....**112** D7
Townley St **4** SK11...**112** D7
TOWN OF LOWTON
.............................**50** B8
Townsend Farm ST7 ..**193** D2
Townsend La ST7 .....**194** A8
Townsend Rd CW12...**156** E2
Townsfield Dr CW6 ....**147** F7
Townshend La WA2 ......**4** B3
Townshend Rd CW9 ....**80** A3
Township CI CH3 .....**182** C1
Town Sq
6 Northwich CW9 ...**103** F8
6 Runcorn WA7 ....**49** F7
Town Well WA6..........**75** C2
Townwell Ct CW5.....**204** D5
Town Wlk **9** WA7......**49** F7
Trackside Bsns Pk
CW11......................**174** C6
Tracy Dr WA12...........**2** E3
Trafalgar Ave SK12 .....**37** A3
Trafalgar Ct
Northwich CW9 ....**103** E3
Poynton SK12 ....**37** A3
Trafalgar Ct
3 Macclesfield SK11 ..**112** D7
Widnes WA8 ....**23** A6
Trafford Ave WA5.......**15** F7
Trafford Cres WA7......**49** C6
Trafford Pl WA5 ....**60** D6
Trafford Rd
Alderley Edge SK9......**60** B1
Handforth SK9...........**34** B1
Trafford St CH1........**237** B3
Tragan Dr WA5 ....**14** D3
Tramway Rd M44 ....**11** F7
Tramway St CH1 ......**237** C3
Trammere Dr SK9 ......**34** E2
Trap Rd CW12 ....**132** C3
Trap St SK11 ....**132** B6
TRAP STREET **132** C3
Travellers Rest Cvn Pk
CW7......................**150** C8
Travers' Entry WA9 .....**6** A7
Travis St **10** WA8 ......**23** B8
Tredorth Rd CH1......**117** D3
Tree Bank CI WA7 ......**49** A8
Treen CI SK10 ....**86** D1
Tree Tops CH64..........**66** E4
Treetops CI WA1 ....**16** F7
Tree Way WA16..........**82** A7
Trefoil CI
Huntington CH3 ....**142** B6
Warrington WA3 ....**9** C5
Tregele CI CH1.........**117** D3
Trenance CI WA7 ....**50** C5
Trenchard Dr M22 ......**33** F7
Trent Ave CW7.........**127** B1
Trent CI
Bramhall SK7............**35** C6
Culcheth WA3 ....**5** A2
Widnes WA8 ....**13** B4
Winsford CW7............**127** B1
Trentdale CH65...........**70** B3
Trentham CI WA8 ....**13** B4

Trentham St WA7........**22** F3
Trent Way CH60 ....**41** C6
Tresham Dr WA4 ....**27** A8
Trevithick CI CW7 .....**191** A4
Trevone CI WA16 ....**57** A1
Trickett La CW8 ....**102** A3
Tricketts La CW5 ......**205** E5
Tricketts Mews CW5 ..**205** E5
Trident Ind Est WA3 .....**9** E6
Trident Ret Pk WA7.....**49** E7
Trident Way SK11......**112** A5
Trinity CI CW2 ....**190** A1
Trinity Ct
Congleton CW12......**157** B1
1 Knutsford WA16.....**57** A2
Warrington WA3 ....**9** F5
Trinity Gdns **4** WA6...**49** C1
Trinity Ho **3** WA6 .....**49** C1
Trinity Sq SK8 ....**87** F1
Trinity St
Chester CH1 ....**237** A2
Runcorn WA7............**23** B3
Trinity Terr **2** CW8 ..**103** E8
Troon CI
Bebington CH63.........**43** C5
Bramhall SK7............**36** A7
Haydock WA11............**1** A5
Holmes Chapel CW4 ..**130** C2
Trossach CI WA2 ....**8** E2
Troutbeck Ave
Congleton CW12 ......**156** A2
Newton-le-W WA12 ......**1** E4
Warrington WA5 ....**15** F8
Troutbeck CI WA7 ......**50** D6
Troutbeck Gr CW7 ....**126** D2
Trouthall La WA16 ......**81** A2
Trubshaw Ct ST7 .....**195** C3
Trubshaw Pl ST7 .....**195** B3
Truman CI WA8 ....**12** F3
Truman Ct **5** WA5....**15** B7
Trumans La CH66 ....**69** C7
Truro CI
Bramhall SK7............**35** F7
Congleton CW12......**178** E8
Ellesmere Port CH66...**94** F8
Macclesfield SK10......**86** E1
Runcorn WA7............**50** C6
Warrington WA1 ....**17** B8
Tudor CI
Ellesmere Port CH66...**94** F8
Middlewich CW10 ......**128** D1
Northwich CW9 ....**104** E6
Warrington WA4 ....**17** A2
Winsford CW7..........**149** D6
Tudor Ct
Congleton CW12 ......**156** D2
4 Warrington WA4 ....**16** E1
Tudor Dr SK10............**86** D7
Tudor Gn
Blacon CH1 ....**117** E6
Handforth SK9...........**34** E1
Tudor Rd
Handforth SK9...........**34** E1
Runcorn WA7............**24** C3
Tudorway CH60 ....**41** B8
Tudor Way
Chester CH3 ....**142** A7
Congleton CW12 ......**156** D1
Nantwich CW5.........**204** E3
Tue La WA8 ....**12** B6
Tulip Gr WA5 ....**15** E3
Tulip Rd
Haydock WA11............**1** F6
Partington M31 ....**11** E2
Tully Ave WA12 ....**1** F3
Tulworth Rd SK12.......**36** D4
Tunbridge CI
Warrington WA3 ....**15** A8
Wistaston CW2 ....**206** A8
Tunnel Rd CW8 ....**78** B2
Tunnicliffe Rd WA13...**112** F3
Tunnicliffe St **1**
SK10......................**112** D8
Tunstall Rd
Biddulph ST7, SK11 ...**158** C7
Congleton CW12 ......**157** F2
Turf La SK11 ....**112** C3
Turnall Rd WA8..........**22** B7
Turnberry CI
Lymm WA13 ....**18** F3
Macclesfield SK10......**87** C4
Northwich CW9 ....**104** E7
Winsford CW7..........**126** C2
Turnberry Dr SK9 ....**60** D8
Turner Ave ST7 ....**210** A1
Turner CI
Crewe CW1 ....**190** A8
Widnes WA8 ....**12** D3
Turner Rise SK10 ....**88** C8
Turner St
Bollington SK10..........**88** B8
Nantwich CW5.........**204** F5
Turner's View CW4.....**41** D2
Turnhurst Rd ST7 .....**195** F1
Turnock St SK11 ......**112** E7
Turnstone Ave WA12 ....**2** C4
Turret Hall Dr **1** WA3 ..**3** E8
Turriff Dr CH63..........**43** C4
Turrocks CI CH64 ....**66** E5
Turrocks Croft CH64 ..**66** E5
Turton CI
Hale L24 ....**21** E1
Warrington WA3 ....**9** C5
Turton St WA3...........**3** A8

Turville Ho SK9 ....**34** D2
Tuscan CI WA8 ....**13** B5
Tushingham CI CH3....**142** B7
Tushingham-with-
Grindley CE Prim Sch
SY13.....................**214** C1
Tuson Dr WA8 ....**12** F4
Tutor Bank Dr WA12 ....**2** D3
Tweedsmuir CH3 ......**119** A2
Tweedsmuir CI WA2 .....**9** A4
Twemlow Ave CW11 ..**175** B7
TWEMLOW GREEN ...**131** A5
Twemlow La CW4 .....**130** D6
Twenty Acre Rd WA5 ..**15** C8
Twinnies Rd SK9.........**34** B1
TWISS GREEN **4** E4
Twiss Green Com Prim
Sch WA3...................**4** E4
Twiss Green Dr WA3 .....**4** E4
Twiss Green La WA3 .....**4** E4
Twist Ave WA3............**3** C8
Two Acre Gr CH66 .....**69** F1
TWO MILLS **93** E8
Twyford CI WA8 ....**13** B5
Twyford La WA8 ....**13** D6
Tyldesley Way CW5 ...**204** D6
Tyler St WA9..............**60** A1
Tyne CI WA2 ....**8** C2
Tynedale Ave CW2 ....**190** C2
Tynedale CI SK11 .....**112** C8
Tynemouth Rd WA7....**50** C6
Tynesdale CH65..........**70** B3
Tynwald Cres WA8 .....**12** F5
Tynwald Dr WA4........**26** C7
Tyrer Rd WA12 ....**2** C1
Tyrer Wlk **2** WA3 ....**3** F8
TYTHERINGTON **87** C3
Tytherington Bsns Pk
SK10.......................**87** D5
Tytherington CI
CW10......................**151** C6
Tytherington Ct SK10 ..**87** D3
Tytherington Dr SK10...**87** E4
Tytherington Gn SK10...**87** C4
Tytherington High Sch
SK10.......................**87** D2
Tytherington La SK10 ..**87** D5
Tytherington Park Rd
SK10.......................**87** D3
Tytherington Sh Ctr **1**
SK10.......................**87** D3

U

Ullapool CI CH66 ....**68** F6
Ullswater SK11 ....**111** F5
Ullswater Ave
Crewe CW1 ....**189** E3
Warrington WA2 ....**8** D3
Winsford CW7 ....**126** C2
Ullswater Cres CH2 ...**119** A6
Ullswater Gr WA7 ....**49** D5
Ullswater Mans SK11 .**111** F6
Ullswater Rd
Congleton CW12 ......**156** A2
Ellesmere Port CH65...**70** C2
Handforth SK9...........**34** C4
Ulverston Ave WA2 ......**8** B4
Ulverston CI WA11.......**1** A6
Ulviet Gate WA16.......**29** C4
Underbridge La WA4 ...**25** E6
Undercliffe Ho WA4 ....**26** D8
Under Rainow Rd
CW12......................**157** C1
Underway The WA7.....**49** F8
Underwood Bsns Pk
CW1......................**190** A6
Underwood CI SK10.....**86** F1
Underwood Ct CW1...**190** B6
Underwood Dr CH65...**70** C2
Underwood La CW1...**190** B6
Underwood Rd SK9....**60** C1
Underwood West Prim
Sch CW1.................**190** A5
Unicorn Gateway 3
SK10......................**112** D8
Union CI
Crewe CW12 ....**156** D3
Union Ind Est SK11 ...**112** E7
Union Pl CH1...........**237** A2
Union Rd
Macclesfield SK11......**112** E7
New Mills SK22 ....**39** C7
Union St
Chester CH1 ....**237** C2
Congleton CW12 ......**156** D3
Crewe CW2 ....**190** D3
Macclesfield SK11......**112** D7
Runcorn WA7............**23** B2
Sandbach CW11 ......**175** B6
Warrington WA1 ....**16** B5
Union Terr CH1 ....**237** B3
Union Wlk CH1 ....**237** B2
Unity Way ST7 ....**210** D8
University Way CW1 ...**191** B2
Univ of Chester CH1..**237** A4
Univ of Chester
(Chichester House)
CH1.......................**237** A3
Univ of Chester
Warrington Campus
WA2........................**9** B3
Univ of Liverpool, Faculty
of Veterinary Science
(Leahurst) CH64.......**67** D8

Univ of Manchester
School of Physics &
Astronomy The
SK11 . . . . .108 D2
Unsworth Ct WA2 . . . . .8 F1
Upcast La SK9 . . . . .59 E3
Uplands CW8 . . . . .101 D4
Uplands Rd CW9 . . . . .78 E4
Uplands The
 Biddulph ST8 . . . . .179 E2
 Macclesfield SK11 . . . . . . .112 A8
 Runcorn WA7 . . . . .50 A7
Upper Cambrian Rd
 CH1 . . . . .118 B2
Upper Haigh St CW7 . . . . . .149 C8
Upper Mersey Rd WA8 . . . . .23 A5
Upper Mersey St CH65 . . . . .70 C7
Upper Northgate St
 CH1 . . . . .237 A3
Upper Raby Rd CH64 . . . . . .42 A2
UPPER THREAPWOOD
 . . . . .222 E7

UPTON
 Chester 118 D6
 Widnes 12 C4
Upton Ave SK8 . . . . .35 A8
Upton Bridle Path
 WA8 . . . . .12 F4
Upton-by-Chester High
 Sch CH2 . . . . .118 F6
Upton Cl
 Golborne WA3 . . . . .3 D8
 Winsford CW7 . . . . .126 F4
Upton Dr
 Chester CH2 . . . . .118 C6
 Warrington WA5 . . . . .14 F5
Upton Grange WA8 . . . . . . .12 D4
UPTON HEATH 118 F8
Upton Health CE Prim Sch
 CH2 . . . . .118 E8
Upton La
 Chester CH2 . . . . .118 D7
 Widnes WA8 . . . . .12 F4
Upton Mount SK10 . . . . . . .87 A1
Upton Pk CH2 . . . . .118 D6
Upton Priory Inf Sch
 SK10 . . . . .86 F2
Upton Priory Jun Sch
 SK10 . . . . .86 F2
Upton Rd CH66 . . . . .69 D4
UPTON ROCKS 12 E4
Upton Rocks Ave WA8 . . . .12 E4
Upton Rocks Mews
 WA8 . . . . .12 E4
Upton Way 12 SK9 . . . . . . .34 D5
Upton Westlea Prim Sch
 CH2 . . . . .118 D7
Upwood Rd WA3 . . . . .3 D7
Ure Ct CH65 . . . . .70 A7
Urmston Ave WA12 . . . . . . .2 B5
Ursuline Way CW9 . . . . . . .190 B1
UTKINTON 146 B7
Utkinton La CW6 . . . . .146 E7
Utkinton Rd CW6 . . . . .146 C5
Utkinton St Paul's CE Prim
 Sch CW6 . . . . .146 B8

V
Vahler Terr WA7 . . . . .23 C2
Vale Ave WA2 . . . . .16 B8
Vale Bank CW5 . . . . .220 A8
Vale Bsns Ctr CW12 . . . . . .156 D2
Vale Cl CW4 . . . . .139 C3
Vale Ct WA4 . . . . .51 A3
Vale Gdns
 Alsager ST7 . . . . .193 E4
 Ellesmere Port CH65 . . . . .70 B4
 Helsby WA6 . . . . .73 B4
Vale Head SK9 . . . . .34 D2
Valentine Rd
 Kidsgrove ST7 . . . . .195 A1
 Newton-le-W WA12 . . . . . . .1 F3
Vale Owen Rd WA2 . . . . . . .8 D1
Vale Rd
 Alpraham CW6 . . . . .169 A4
 Ellesmere Port CH65 . . . . .70 B4
 Hartford CW8 . . . . .103 C4
 Marston CW9 . . . . .79 B6
 Wilmslow SK9 . . . . .59 E8
Vale Royal Clyd CW8 . . . . .126 B8
Vale Royal Dr CW8 . . . . . .126 A8
Vale Royal River Park Cvn
 Site CW9 . . . . .126 E6
Vale View CW9 . . . . .79 D1
Vale Wlk CW12 . . . . .156 D2
Valiant Cl WA2 . . . . .8 F2
Valley Brook Bsns Ctr
 CW2 . . . . .190 D3
Valley Cl
 Alsager ST7 . . . . .192 F3
 Knutsford WA16 . . . . .82 A7
Valley Ct
 Crewe CW2 . . . . .190 B3
 Middlewich CW10 . . . . . . .128 E1
 Warrington WA2 . . . . .8 F1
Valley Dr
 Chester CH2 . . . . .118 C5
 Ellesmere Port CH66 . . . . .69 D5
 Handforth SK9 . . . . .34 C3
Valley La
 Cuddington CW8 . . . . . . .101 F3
 Sandiway CW8 . . . . .102 A3
Valley Rd
 Bebington CH62 . . . . .43 D8
 Bramhall SK7 . . . . .35 F8
 Crewe CW2 . . . . .189 F1

Valley Rd continued
 Macclesfield SK11 . . . . . . .112 A6
 Weaverham CW8 . . . . .77 C1
Valley Sch SK7 . . . . .35 C5
Valley View
 Congleton CW12 . . . . . . .156 C3
 Ellesmere Port CH66 . . . . .69 D5
 Newton-le-W WA12 . . . . . . .2 B1
 Northwich CW9 . . . . .104 C7
Valley Way WA16 . . . . .82 A7
Vanguard Ct WA3 . . . . .9 D4
Varden Rd SK12 . . . . .36 E3
Varden Town Cotts
 SK10 . . . . .86 A4
Vardon Dr SK9 . . . . .60 D6
Varey Rd CW12 . . . . .156 F4
Vaudrey Cres CW12 . . . . . .156 F3
Vaudrey Dr WA1 . . . . .17 D7
Vaughan Rd SK23 . . . . .65 E5
Vaughans La CH3 . . . . .142 A8
Vauxhall Cl WA5 . . . . .14 F4
Vauxhall Rd CW5 . . . . .204 E7
Vauxhall Way CW7 . . . . . . .149 C6
Vearows Pl CW8 . . . . .103 F7
Venables Rd CW9 . . . . .79 A1
Venable's Rd CH1 . . . . . . .117 F4
Venables Way
 High Legh WA16 . . . . .29 C4
 Middlewich CW10 . . . . . . .151 E6
Venetian Marina Village
 CW5 . . . . .188 B8
Venns Rd WA2 . . . . .16 D7
Ventnor Cl
 Middlewich CW10 . . . . . . .151 C8
 Warrington WA5 . . . . .14 D7
Venture Ho SK11 . . . . .112 D6
Venture Way WA12 . . . . . . .36 F3
Verbena Cl
 Partington M31 . . . . .11 F3
 Runcorn WA7 . . . . .49 F4
Verdin Ave WA7 . . . . .78 F1
Verdin Cl
 Moulton CW9 . . . . .126 F7
 Winsford CW7 . . . . .126 C2
Verdin Ct CW1 . . . . .190 A8
Verdin St CW9 . . . . .104 C8
Vere St CW1 . . . . .190 C5
Verity Cl CW1 . . . . .190 D5
Verity Ct CW10 . . . . .128 E2
Vermont Cl WA5 . . . . .15 C7
Vermont Gdns SK7 . . . . . . .35 B5
Vernay Gn CH4 . . . . .141 B5
Vernon Ave
 Audley ST7 . . . . .209 D2
 Congleton CW12 . . . . . . .178 F8
 Hooton CH66 . . . . .44 A2
Vernon Cl
 Audley ST7 . . . . .209 D2
 Poynton SK12 . . . . .36 D2
 Saughall CH1 . . . . .117 A8
Vernon Dr CW3 . . . . .230 F4
Vernon Inf Sch SK12 . . . . . .36 E3
Vernon Jun Sch SK12 . . . . .36 E3
Vernon Rd
 Chester CH1 . . . . .118 B2
 Poynton SK12 . . . . .36 E2
Vernon St
 Crewe CW1 . . . . .190 B5
 Macclesfield SK10 . . . . . . .112 F8
 Warrington WA1 . . . . .16 B4
Vernon Way CW1 . . . . .190 D4
Veronica Mews WA8 . . . . . .12 D1
Veronica Way CH66 . . . . . . .69 D7
Vetch Cl WA3 . . . . .11 B5
Vetches The CH3 . . . . .119 F5
Viaduct St WA12 . . . . .2 A3
Vicarage Ave SK8 . . . . .35 B7
Vicarage Cl
 Guilden Sutton CH3 . . . . .119 F5
 Hale L24 . . . . .21 E1
Vicarage Ct LL13 . . . . .196 E8
Vicarage Dr WA11 . . . . .1 B7
Vicarage Gdns WA5 . . . . . .174 E8
Vicarage Gr CW7 . . . . .149 D5
Vicarage Hill WA6 . . . . .73 C4
Vicarage La
 Audlem CW3 . . . . .230 A4
 Bunbury CW6 . . . . .168 F1
 Burton CH64 . . . . .67 D2
 Frodsham WA6 . . . . .74 C7
 Helsby WA6 . . . . .73 C4
 Little Budworth CW6 . . . . .147 F7
 Poynton SK12 . . . . .36 E5
 Sandbach CW11 . . . . .174 E8
Vicarage Rd
 Chester CH2 . . . . .118 F3
 Haslington CW1 . . . . .191 D6
 Haydock WA11 . . . . .1 A7
 Northwich CW9 . . . . .104 B8
 Widnes WA8 . . . . .23 A7
Vicarage Row CH62 . . . . . . .44 A5
Vicarage Way 1
 SK11 . . . . .111 F7
Vicarage Wlk
 Northwich CW9 . . . . .104 B8
 Warrington WA4 . . . . .26 C8
Vicar's Cl CH3 . . . . .121 F7
VICARSCROSS 119 E2
Vicars Cross Ct 2
 CH3 . . . . .119 B2
Vicars Cross Rd CH3 . . . . .119 C2
Vicar's La CH1 . . . . .237 B2
Vickers Rd WA8 . . . . .22 F4
Vickers Way CW9 . . . . .104 A7
Victoria Ave
 Crewe CW2 . . . . .190 A4
 Grappenhall WA4 . . . . .17 A2
 Haslington CW1 . . . . .191 C4

Victoria Ave continued
 Heswall CH60 . . . . .41 A6
 Holmes Chapel CW4 . . . . .130 C2
 Kidsgrove ST7 . . . . .194 F2
 Warrington WA5 . . . . .7 E8
 Widnes WA8 . . . . .13 A3
Victoria Cl SK7 . . . . .35 D6
Victoria Com Tech Sch
 CW1 . . . . .190 C5
Victoria Cres
 Chester CH2 . . . . .237 A4
 Chester, Queen's Park
 CH4 . . . . .237 C1
Victoria Ct
 Chester CH2 . . . . .237 A4
 3 Crewe CW1 . . . . .190 C4
 Haslington CW1 . . . . .191 C4
 8 Kidsgrove ST7 . . . . . . .195 A2
 Knutsford WA16 . . . . .56 F1
 2 Widnes WA8 . . . . .23 A8
Victoria Gr WA8 . . . . .13 A3
Victoria Infmy CW8 . . . . . .103 E8
Victoria Inf Sch CH1 . . . . .237 A4
Victoria Mews CH65 . . . . . .70 B5
Victoria Mill Dr CW5 . . . . .205 D6
Victoria Pathway
 CH4 . . . . .237 C1
Victoria Pk CW8 . . . . .78 F1
Victoria Pl
 Chester CH1 . . . . .237 B3
 2 Warrington WA4 . . . . . . .16 C1
Victoria Rd
 Chester CH1, CH2 . . . . . .237 B3
 Chester CH2 . . . . .237 A4
 Ellesmere Port CH65 . . . . .70 C5
 Macclesfield SK10 . . . . . . .87 A1
 Neston CH64 . . . . .67 A6
 Newton-le-W WA12 . . . . . . .2 C3
 Northwich CW9 . . . . .104 B8
 Runcorn WA7 . . . . .23 A2
 Saltney CH4 . . . . .140 D5
 Warrington, Great Sankey
 WA5 . . . . .15 B4
 Warrington, Penketh
 WA5 . . . . .14 D4
 Warrington, Stockton Heath
 WA4 . . . . .16 D1
 Warrington WA4 . . . . .16 F2
 Widnes WA8 . . . . .23 A6
 Wilmslow SK9 . . . . .60 A6
Victoria Road Prim Sch
 Northwich CW9 . . . . .104 B8
 Runcorn WA7 . . . . .23 A2
Victoria Sq
 Warrington WA4 . . . . .16 C1
 4 Widnes WA8 . . . . .23 A7
 Winsford CW7 . . . . .149 A8
Victoria St
 Congleton CW12 . . . . . . .156 D2
 Crewe CW1 . . . . .190 C4
 Knutsford WA16 . . . . .56 F2
 New Mills SK22 . . . . .39 B6
 Northwich CW9 . . . . .78 F1
 Sandbach CW11 . . . . .175 B7
 Warrington WA1 . . . . .16 C5
 Widnes WA8 . . . . .23 B7
Victoria Stadium
 (Northwich Victoria FC)
 CW9 . . . . .79 D3
Victoria Trad Ctr WA8 . . . . .23 A6
Victoria Way SK7 . . . . .35 D6
Victoria Wlk SK10 . . . . . . .112 E8
Victory Rd WA1 . . . . .11 C4
Viewlands Dr SK9 . . . . .34 D2
Viking Way CW11 . . . . .156 C4
Villa Farm CW11 . . . . .176 B8
Village Cl
 Lostock Green CW9 . . . . . .105 A8
 Runcorn WA7 . . . . .50 A8
Village Ct SK9 . . . . .34 D1
Village Farm CW5 . . . . . . .172 A5
Village La WA4 . . . . .52 D4
Village Mews SK10 . . . . . . .87 A6
Village Rd
 Christleton CH3 . . . . .142 E8
 Great Barrow CH3 . . . . . .120 E6
 Heswall CH60 . . . . .40 F7
 Waverton CH3 . . . . .143 C4
Village St WA7 . . . . .24 E2
Village Terr The 6
 WA4 . . . . .16 C1
Village The
 Astbury CW12 . . . . .178 B8
 Burton CH64 . . . . .67 D1
 Prestbury SK10 . . . . .86 F6
 4 Weaverham CW8 . . . . . .77 D1
Villa Rd CH5 . . . . .116 B7
Villars St WA1 . . . . .16 C5
Villas The CW4 . . . . .131 A8
Villiers Russell Cl
 CW1 . . . . .190 D5
Vincent Cl WA5 . . . . .15 C8
Vincent Dr CH1 . . . . .141 C6
Vincent St
 Crewe CW1 . . . . .190 E4
 Macclesfield SK11 . . . . . . .112 D7
Vine Bank Rd ST7 . . . . . . .195 A1
Vine Cl SK11 . . . . .112 A6
Vine Cres WA5 . . . . .14 F6
Vine Rd CH66 . . . . .69 F1
Vine St
 Bollington SK10 . . . . .88 B8
 11 Runcorn WA7 . . . . .23 A3
 Widnes WA8 . . . . .23 A7
Vine Terr WA8 . . . . .12 A2

Vine Tree Ave
 Crewe CW2 . . . . .190 B1
 Shavington CW2 . . . . .206 B5
Vine Tree Prim Sch
 CW2 . . . . .190 A1
Vineyard The CW2 . . . . . . .206 B4
Violet Cl WA3 . . . . .9 C5
Violet St WA8 . . . . .23 A7
Virginia Chase SK8 . . . . . . .34 F8
Virginia Dr CH1 . . . . .117 C4
Virginia Gdns WA5 . . . . . . .15 B8
Virginia Terr CH66 . . . . .69 B8
Virtual Bsns Ctr CH1 . . . . .117 E2
Viscount Dr
 Gatley SK8 . . . . .34 D7
 Wythenshawe M90 . . . . . . .32 F7
Viscount Rd WA2 . . . . .8 E2
Vista Ave WA12 . . . . .2 A4
Vista Rd
 Newton-le-W WA11,
 WA2 . . . . .2 A6
 Runcorn WA7 . . . . .49 A8
Vista The M44 . . . . .11 C4
Vista Way WA12 . . . . .2 A4
Vixen Gr WA8 . . . . .12 F4
Volunteer Ave 7
 CW5 . . . . .204 E6
Volunteer Fields CW5 . . . .204 E6
Volunteer St
 Chester CH1 . . . . .237 B2
 Frodsham WA6 . . . . .49 D1
Vose Cl WA5 . . . . .15 D6
Vulcan Cl
 Newton-le-W WA12 . . . . . . .2 C1
 Warrington WA2 . . . . .8 F2
Vulcan Ind Est WA12 . . . . . .2 D1
VULCAN VILLAGE 7 C8
Vyrnwy Rd CW4 . . . . .140 D6

W
Waddington Cl
 Golborne WA3 . . . . .3 F8
 Warrington WA2 . . . . .8 F1
Wade Ct WA3 . . . . .4 SK9. . . .34 D1
Wadebrook Trad Est
 CW9 . . . . .104 C8
Wade Cres CW8 . . . . .78 A3
Wade Ct ST7 . . . . .195 A1
Wade Deacon High Sch
 WA8 . . . . .13 A2
WADES GREEN 171 F5
Wades La CW7 . . . . .126 D3
Wadeson Way CW1 . . . . .9 B7
Wadeson St CW5 . . . . .79 B1
Wadsworth Cl SK9 . . . . .34 E3
Waggon Cotts ST7 . . . . . . .208 E1
Waggs Rd CW12 . . . . .156 C1
Wagg St CW12 . . . . .156 D2
Wagon La WA11 . . . . .1 B6
Waine St CW1 . . . . .190 D5
Wain Ho CH1 . . . . .94 A1
Wain St CW1 . . . . .195 F4
Wakefield Cl CW1 . . . . . . .189 F7
Wakefield Ct CW9 . . . . . . .104 A5
Wakefield Ho WA5 . . . . .15 E6
Wakefield Rd CH66 . . . . . . .69 E1
Wakefield St WA3 . . . . .3 A7
Wakeham Chase 8
 SK11 . . . . .111 F7
Wakes Mdw CW6 . . . . .185 E8
Walden Cl WA4 . . . . .17 D3
Walden Dr CH1 . . . . .93 D8
Waldon Rd SK11 . . . . .112 A5
Waldron Gdns CW2 . . . . . .189 F1
Waldron Rd CW1 . . . . .191 D3
Waldron's La CW1 . . . . . . .173 D1
Walfield Ave CW12 . . . . . . .156 D5
Walford Ave CW2 . . . . .190 B3
WALGHERTON 220 B6
Walgrave Cl CW2 . . . . .156 A3
Walker Cl CW1 . . . . .191 D4
Walker Dr CW10 . . . . .151 C8
Walker La SK11 . . . . .112 E2
Walkers Green CW1 . . . . . . .152 D7
Walkersgreen Rd
 ST5 . . . . .210 D2
Walkers La
 Ellesmere Port CH66 . . . . .69 C6
 Farndon CH3 . . . . .180 F2
 Scholar Green ST7 . . . . . .177 B2
 Tarporley CW6 . . . . .146 D1
 Warrington WA5 . . . . .14 D7
Walker St
 Chester CH2 . . . . .237 C4
 Crewe CW1 . . . . .190 B5
 2 Macclesfield SK10 . . . .112 C8
 Warrington WA5 . . . . .16 A6
Wallace Ct CW7 . . . . .127 D1
Wallace St
 Northwich CW8 . . . . .103 E7
 Widnes WA8 . . . . .23 A8
Wallcroft CH64 . . . . .68 A7
Wallcroft Gdns CW10 . . . .128 C1
Walled Gdn The
 CH1 . . . . .127 D5
Wallerscote Cl CW8 . . . . . .102 E8
Wallerscote Com Sch
 CW8 . . . . .102 E8
Wallerscote Rd CW8 . . . . .102 E8
Waller St WA11 . . . . .1 A7
WALLEY'S GREEN 172 E7
Walleys La CW5 . . . . .203 C7
Wallfields Cl CW5 . . . . . . .204 E7
Wall Fields Rd CW5 . . . . . .204 E7
Wallhill La CW11 . . . . .177 D7
Wall Hill Way CW8 . . . . . . .76 F3

Uni–War 283
Wallingford Rd SK9 . . . . . .34 C5
Wallis St
 Crewe CW1 . . . . .190 D4
 Warrington WA4 . . . . .16 B3
Wall La CW5 . . . . .204 E6
Wallrake CH60 . . . . .40 F7
Walls Ave CH1 . . . . .118 B1
Wallsend Ct WA8 . . . . .12 F3
Wallworth's Bank
 CW12 . . . . .156 E2
Wallworth Terr SK9 . . . . . . .59 E8
Walmer Pl CH7 . . . . .149 C6
Walmoor Pk CH3 . . . . .119 A1
Walmsley St
 Newton-le-W WA12 . . . . . . .2 D4
 Widnes WA8 . . . . .23 C8
Walnut Ave CW8 . . . . .102 D7
Walnut Cl
 Chester CH2 . . . . .118 D7
 Warrington WA1 . . . . .17 E7
 Wilmslow SK9 . . . . .60 E8
Walnut Cotts LL13 . . . . . . .196 D8
Walnut Croft CH3 . . . . .180 F6
Walnut Dr CW7 . . . . .127 A1
Walnut Gr CH66 . . . . .70 A1
Walnut La CW8 . . . . .103 A5
Walnut Rd M31 . . . . .11 D3
Walnut Rise CW12 . . . . . . .156 B2
Walnut Tree La
 Bradwall Green
 CW11 . . . . .153 A4
 Warrington WA4 . . . . .26 F4
Walpole Cl CW1 . . . . .191 C5
Walpole Gr WA2 . . . . .8 C2
Walpole Rd WA7 . . . . .49 C6
Walpole St CH1 . . . . .237 A4
Walsh Cl WA12 . . . . .2 C1
Walsingham Dr WA7 . . . . . .24 D2
Walsingham Rd WA5 . . . . . .14 F5
Walter St
 Chester CH1 . . . . .237 B4
 Crewe CW1 . . . . .16 E7
 Widnes WA8 . . . . .13 D1
Walters Wood SK23 . . . . . .65 F5
Walthall St CW2 . . . . .190 C2
Waltham Ave WA3 . . . . .3 A8
Waltham Cl WA7 . . . . .24 E4
Waltham Dr SK8 . . . . .35 B6
Waltham Pl CH4 . . . . .141 A6
Walton Ave CW5 . . . . .14 E5
Walton Gr ST7 . . . . .210 C8
Walton Hall* WA4 . . . . .25 F7
Walton Hall Gdns*
 WA4 . . . . .25 F6
Walton Heath Dr SK10 . . . .87 B4
Walton Heath Rd WA4 . . . . .16 B1
Walton La WA3 . . . . .9 E5
Walton Lea Rd WA4 . . . . . . .26 A7
Walton New Rd WA4 . . . . . .26 B8
Walton Pl CH1 . . . . .117 C4
Walton Rd
 Culcheth WA3 . . . . .4 F3
 Warrington WA4 . . . . .26 C8
Waltons The CH4 . . . . .141 E6
Walton Way ST7 . . . . .210 C8
Wandsworth Way WA8 . . . .22 F5
Wansfel Pl WA2 . . . . .8 A3
WARBURTON 19 C8
Warburton Bridge Rd
 WA13, WA3 . . . . .11 A1
Warburton Cl
 Altrincham WA15 . . . . .32 D6
 Barnton CW8 . . . . .77 F4
 Lymm WA13 . . . . .19 A4
Warburton Dr WA15 . . . . . .32 D6
WARBURTON GREEN 32 D6
Warburton La
 Partington M31 . . . . .11 F4
 Partington M31, WA13 . . .11 F2
Warburton Rd SK9 . . . . . . .34 D4
Warburton St WA4 . . . . .16 D1
Warburton View WA3 . . . . .11 A2
Ward Ave SK10 . . . . .88 A8
Ward Cl WA3 . . . . .7 B1
Ward La SK12 . . . . .38 F4
Wardle Ave CW5 . . . . .187 C7
Wardle Cotts CW5 . . . . . . .187 C7
Wardle Cres CW5 . . . . .111 E1
Wardle Ind Est CW5 . . . . . .187 A7
Wardle Mews CW10 . . . . . .151 D8
Wardle St 7 SK11 . . . . . . .112 D7
Wardley Rd WA4 . . . . .16 B1
Wardour Cl 6 SK11 . . . . . .111 F7
Wardour St WA5 . . . . .15 E6
WARDSEND 37 A1
Wards La CW12 . . . . .179 C8
Ward's La CW11 . . . . .153 C5
Ward's Terr CH2 . . . . .118 F3
Wareham Cl
 Haydock WA11 . . . . .1 C7
 Warrington WA1 . . . . .17 E7
Wareham Dr CW1 . . . . . . .190 B8
Wareham St SK9 . . . . .60 B7
Warford Ave SK12 . . . . .37 A2
Warford Cres SK9 . . . . .84 B7
Warford Hall Dr SK9 . . . . . .84 B6
Warford La WA16 . . . . .59 B1
WARFORD PARK 58 E1
Warford Terr WA16 . . . . . . .59 B2
WARGRAVE 2 D3
Wargrave CE Prim Sch
 WA12 . . . . .2 C1
Wargrave House Sch
 WA12 . . . . .2 C1

Wargrave Mews WA12 . . . . **2** C1
Wargrave Rd WA12 . . . . . . **2** C2
Waring Ave
St Helens WA9 . . . . **1** B2
Warrington WA4 . . . . **16** F5
Warkworth Cl WA8 . . . . . **12** C3
Warkworth Ct CH65 . . . . . **70** E3
WARMINGHAM **173** D7
Warmingham CE Prim Sch
CW11 . . . . **173** E8
Warmingham Ct
CW10 . . . . **151** D7
Warmingham La
Middlewich CW10 . . . . . . **151** D5
Sandbach CW11 . . . . **174** B8
Warmingham Rd
CW1 . . . . **173** D4
Warnley Cl WA8 . . . . **12** D3
WARREN **111** D1
Warren Ave
Knutsford WA16 . . . . **56** E2
Lostock Gralam CW9 . . . . . **80** A3
Warren Cl
Knutsford WA16 . . . . **56** F2
Middlewich CW10 . . . . . . **151** B7
Poynton SK12 . . . . **36** B4
Warren Croft WA7 . . . . . . **50** D7
Warren Ct
Ellesmere Port CH66 . . . . . **69** D3
Frodsham WA6 . . . . **74** D6
Warren Dr
Altrincham WA15 . . . . **32** D7
Broughton CH4 . . . . **139** A3
Ellesmere Port CH66 . . . . . **69** E7
Newton-le-W WA12 . . . . **2** F4
Warren Gr SK11 . . . . **111** D1
Warren Hey SK9 . . . . **60** E8
Warren La
Hartford CW8 . . . . **103** A4
Warrington WA1 . . . . **17** D8
Warren Lea SK12 . . . . . . **36** E5
Warren Rd
Warrington, Orford WA2 . . . **8** B1
Warrington WA4 . . . . **26** C7
Warren The
Cuddington CW8 . . . . . . **101** D5
Newton-le-W WA12 . . . . . . **2** A3
Warren Way CW6 . . . . . **168** D8
Warrilow Heath Rd
ST5 . . . . **210** C1
WARRINGTON **16** E6
Warrington Ave
Crewe CW1 . . . . **190** C6
Ellesmere Port CH65 . . . . . **70** B2
Warrington Bank Quay Sta
WA1 . . . . **15** F4
Warrington Bsns Pk
WA2 . . . . **8** C1
Warrington Bsns Pk
[10] Warrington WA1 . . . . . **16** B5
Warrington WA2 . . . . **16** A6
Warrington Central Sta
WA2 . . . . **8** C1
Warrington Central Trad
Est WA2 . . . . **16** A6
Warrington Collegiate
WA2 . . . . **8** B1
Warrington Hospl WA5 . . **15** F6
Warrington La WA13 . . . . **19** E2
Warrington Mus & Art
Gallery* WA1 . . . . **16** A4
Warrington Rd
Bold Heath L35, WA8 . . . . **13** D7
Comberbach CW9 . . . . **78** D7
Cronton L35 . . . . **12** E8
Cronton L35 . . . . **12** F8
Cuddington CW8 . . . . **102** A5
Fowley Common WA3,
WN7 . . . . **5** C5
Golborne WA3, WA12 . . . . . **3** A6
Hatton WA4 . . . . **25** F4
Little Leigh CW8 . . . . **77** B7
Lymm WA13 . . . . **18** B4
Mere WA16 . . . . **56** B7
Mickle Trafford CH2 . . . . . **119** E7
Runcorn, Castlefields
WA7 . . . . **23** E2
Runcorn, Manor Park
WA7 . . . . **24** B4
Warrington, Risley WA3 . . . **9** E7
Warrington WA5 . . . . **14** F4
Widnes WA8 . . . . **13** D1
Warrington St Ann's CE
Prim Sch WA2 . . . . **16** C8
Warton Cl
Bramhall SK7 . . . . **36** A7
Warrington WA5 . . . . **15** A3
Warwick Ave
Kidsgrove ST7 . . . . **195** A3
Macclesfield SK11 . . . . **57** C1
Macclesfield SK11 . . . . . . **111** F6
Neston CH64 . . . . **66** E5
Warwick Ct
Ellesmere Port CH65 . . . . . **70** E2
Warrington WA1 . . . . **16** D6
Warwick Dr SK7 . . . . **36** D8
Warwick Gate CW5 . . . . . **217** C2

Warwick Gr [1] WA7 . . . . . **23** F1
Warwick Mews SK11 . . . . **111** F6
Warwick Pl CW7 . . . . **149** C6
Warwick Rd
Blacon CH1 . . . . **117** F5
Irlam M44 . . . . **11** D5
Macclesfield SK11 . . . . . . **111** E6
Warrington Wlk SK11 . . . . **111** F6
Wasdale Gr WA7 . . . . **173** B1
WASH END **4** C8
Washington Cl
Biddulph ST8 . . . . **179** C2
Cheadle SK8 . . . . **34** F8
Widnes WA8 . . . . **12** F3
Wash La
Allostock WA16 . . . . **106** E3
Warrington WA4 . . . . **16** E3
Wasley Cl WA2 . . . . **8** F3
Waste La
Cuddington CW8 . . . . **101** E3
Delamere CW8 . . . . **123** F6
Kelsall CW6 . . . . **122** F4
Watch La CW11 . . . . **174** A6
Waterbank Row CW9 . . . **103** F7
Waterbridge Ct
[2] Lymm WA13 . . . . **18** C3
Warrington WA4 . . . . **26** D8
Waterbridge Mews
WA7 . . . . **24** A2
Waterfoot La SK23 . . . . . . **65** D6
Waterford Dr CH64 . . . . . **67** A7
Waterford Pl SK8 . . . . **34** B8
Waterford Way WA7 . . . . **50** C6
Waterfront WA4 . . . . **50** F6
Watergate Row S
CH1 . . . . **237** A2
Watergate Row S
CH1 . . . . **237** A2
Watergate Sq CH1 . . . . . **237** A2
Watergate St CH1 . . . . . **237** A2
Waterhouse Ave SK10 . . . **87** F8
Water La SK9 . . . . **60** A2
Water-Lode CW5 . . . . . . **204** E5
Waterloo Cl [1] CH65 . . . . **70** C5
Waterloo Cotts WA6 . . . . **99** F8
Waterloo Gr ST7 . . . . . . **195** A2
Waterloo Ho [15] CW8 . . . **103** F8
Waterloo La WA6 . . . . **74** F1
Waterloo Rd
Bramhall SK7 . . . . **35** F8
Chester CH2 . . . . **118** C4
Haslington CW1 . . . . **191** D4
Northwich CW8 . . . . **103** E7
Poynton SK12 . . . . **37** A2
[3] Runcorn WA7 . . . . **22** F2
Runcorn WA7 . . . . **22** F3
Widnes WA8 . . . . **23** A5
Waterloo St W SK11 . . . . **112** F8
Watermead Dr WA7 . . . . . **50** F5
Watermill Dr SK11 . . . . . **112** F7
Watersedge WA8 . . . . **49** D2
Waters Edge
Anderton CW9 . . . . **78** D3
Chester CH1 . . . . **118** B2
Waters Edge Mews
CW10 . . . . **151** C8
Watersfield Cl SK8 . . . . . . **34** F8
Waters Gn SK11 . . . . **112** D8
Waterside
Disley SK12 . . . . **38** E7
Furness Vale SK23 . . . . **39** E3
Macclesfield SK11 . . . . . . **112** E7
Warrington WA4 . . . . **26** D8
Waterside Cotts CW5 . . . **216** E5
Waterside Ct WA7 . . . . . . **22** E3
Waterside Dr WA6 . . . . . . **49** D2
Waterside La WA8 . . . . . . **22** C5
Waterside Mews
CW11 . . . . **174** F3
Waterside Rd SK12,
SK22 . . . . **38** E7
Waterside View
Chester CH1 . . . . **237** B3
Northwich CW9 . . . . **104** E6
Waterside Way CW10 . . . **128** B2
Waters Reach SK12 . . . . . **36** F5
Water's Reach SK6 . . . . . . **37** E7
Waters Reams CH3 . . . . . **142** B8
Water St
Bollington SK10 . . . . **88** B8
Macclesfield SK11 . . . . . . **112** C8
Newcastle-u-Lyme ST5 . . . **210** D2
Newton-le-W WA12 . . . . . . **2** C4
Northwich CW9 . . . . **104** A7
Runcorn WA7 . . . . **23** A3
Widnes WA8 . . . . **23** A6
Watertower View
CH2 . . . . **118** F2
Waterway CH3 . . . . **143** B5
Waterways WA5 . . . . **15** D6
Waterworks Dr WA12 . . . . **2** F4
Watery La
Astbury CW12 . . . . **178** C5
Frodsham WA6 . . . . **74** E6
Winwick WA2 . . . . **8** D4
Watkins Ave WA12 . . . . . . **1** F3
Watkins Rd WA12 . . . . . . **13** C5
Watkin St
Sandycroft CH5 . . . . **116** A3
Warrington WA2 . . . . **16** B7
Watlands Rd ST7 . . . . . . **209** E2
Watling Cres CH4 . . . . . . **141** E7
Watling Ct
Chester CH3 . . . . **119** C2

Watling Ct *continued*
Cuddington CW8 . . . . **102** B2
Watling Dr CW6 . . . . **123** C6
Watling St CW9 . . . . **103** F8
Watson's Cl CH4 . . . . **139** C3
Watton Cl WA4 . . . . **17** C3
Wavell Ave WA8 . . . . **22** D8
Wavells Way CH3 . . . . . . **142** B5
Waveney Dr SK9 . . . . **34** D2
Waverley Ave WA4 . . . . . **26** D8
Waverley Cl SK10 . . . . . . **113** A8
Waverley Ct [1] CW7 . . . . **190** D2
Waverley Dr SK8 . . . . **35** B7
Waverley Terr CH2 . . . . . **118** E4
WAVERTON **143** B4
Waverton App CH3 . . . . **164** E6
Waverton Bsns Pk
CH3 . . . . **142** F4
Waverton Cl
Hough WA2 . . . . **206** E2
Northwich CW9 . . . . **143** B5
Waverton Com Prim Sch
CH3 . . . . **143** A5
Waverton Mill Quays
CH3 . . . . **143** B5
Waverton Pk CH3 . . . . . . **143** B5
Waverton Rd CH66 . . . . . **69** E5
Wavertree Ave
Scholar Green ST7 . . . . . . **194** E7
Widnes WA8 . . . . **23** A8
Wavertree Ct CH66 . . . . . **69** F7
Wavertree Dr CW10 . . . . **151** B7
Wavertree Rd CH1 . . . . . **117** C5
Wayburlt La CW2 . . . . . **221** D8
Wayfarers Ct CW9 . . . . . . **79** F7
Wayfarers Dr WA12 . . . . . **2** E2
Wayford Cl WA6 . . . . **49** B1
Wayford Mews WA7 . . . . **49** B1
Way's Gn CW7 . . . . **149** E8
WAY'S GREEN **149** E8
Wayside Cl WA3 . . . . **18** D2
Wayside Ct CH2 . . . . **119** F8
Wayside Dr SK12 . . . . . . **36** C4
Wayside Linley ST7 . . . . . **193** F2
Wayside Rd SK10 . . . . . . **112** F8
Waystead Cl CW9 . . . . . **103** F4
Waywell Cl WA7 . . . . **8** F3
Weald Dr CH66 . . . . **69** A6
Wealstone Ct CH2 . . . . . **118** E5
Weal Stone La CH2 . . . . **118** E6
Wearhead Cl WA3 . . . . **2** F7
Weaste La WA4 . . . . **17** E2
Weates Cl WA8 . . . . **13** F3
Weathercock La
CW12 . . . . **157** E3
Weatherstones Cotts
CH64 . . . . **67** D8
Weatherstones Mews
CH64 . . . . **67** C8
Weaver Bank CW5 . . . . . **204** D5
Weaver Cl
Alsager ST7 . . . . **193** A3
Biddulph ST8 . . . . **179** D1
Sandbach CW11 . . . . **174** E7
Weaver Cres WA6 . . . . . . **49** D1
Weaver Ct
Macclesfield SK11 . . . . . . **112** C7
Northwich CW9 . . . . **103** F8
Weaver Gr
Mickle Trafford CH2 . . . . **119** F8
St Helens WA9 . . . . **1** A3
Weaver Grange CW9 . . . **126** E8
Weaverhall La CW7 . . . . **150** B5
WEAVERHAM **77** C2
Weaverham Forest Prim
Sch CW8 . . . . **77** C1
Weaverham High Sch
CW8 . . . . **102** C8
Weaverham Rd CH66 . . . **102** B4
Weaverham Way SK9 . . . . **34** E4
Weaver Ho [18] CW8 . . . . **103** F8
Weaver La WA6 . . . . **49** B2
Weaver Park Ind Est
WA6 . . . . **49** D2
Weaver Prim Sch
CW5 . . . . **204** E3
Weaver Rd
Culcheth WA3 . . . . **5** A2
Ellesmere Port CH65 . . . . . **70** C2
Frodsham WA6 . . . . **49** D1
Moulton CW9 . . . . **126** E7
Nantwich CW5 . . . . **204** E6
Northwich CW9 . . . . **103** E7
Runcorn, Heath WA7 . . . . . **49** A6
Weavers Cotts [3]
CW12 . . . . **156** D3
Weaverside CW5 . . . . . . **204** E2
Weaverside Ave WA7 . . . . **49** F4
Weavers La SK7 . . . . **35** D6
Weaver St
Chester CH1 . . . . **237** A2
Winsford CW7 . . . . **126** E1
Weavervale Pk CH8 . . . . . **77** A6
Weaver Valley Rd
CW7 . . . . **126** F3
Weaver View
Audlem CW3 . . . . **229** E3
Church Minshull CW5 . . . **172** A6
Northwich CW8 . . . . **103** F7
Weaverham CW8 . . . . **77** D1
Weaver Way CW9 . . . . **78** F1
Webb Dr WA5 . . . . **6** F1
Webb's Ct CW9 . . . . **103** F7
Webb's La CW10 . . . . . . **128** C2
Webbs Orch SK23 . . . . . . **65** D8
Webster Cl CH4 . . . . **139** C3
Websters La CH66 . . . . . . **69** F2
Weddell Cl WA5 . . . . **15** D7

Wedge Ave WA11 . . . . **1** A5
Wedgwood Ave ST7 . . . . **210** A1
Wedgwood Dr WA8 . . . . . **13** B4
Wedgwood La ST8 . . . . . **179** C2
Wedgwood Rd ST7 . . . . . **210** D7
Wednesbury Dr WA5 . . . . **14** F6
Weedon Ave WA12 . . . . . . **2** B5
WEETWOOD COMMON . . .
. . . . **122** C2
Weighbridge Rd
Connah's Quay CH5 . . . . . **92** B4
Connah's Quay CH5 . . . . . **92** C5
Weint The WA3 . . . . **11** B3
Weir Gr ST7 . . . . **195** B2
Weir La WA1 . . . . **17** E6
Weir St
Northwich CW9 . . . . **103** F7
Warrington WA4 . . . . **16** A1
Welbeck Ave WA12 . . . . . . **2** D2
Welbeck Cl CW10 . . . . . **128** B1
Welbeck Rd WA3 . . . . **3** C7
Welford Cl SK9 . . . . **60** E8
Welland Cl CW11 . . . . . . **174** C5
Welland Rd SK9 . . . . **34** E2
Well Ave SY14 . . . . **213** B3
Well Bank CW11 . . . . . . **175** B6
Well Bank Cotts
WA16 . . . . **108** C8
Wellbank Ct CW12 . . . . . **156** E2
Well Bank La WA16,
SK11 . . . . **108** C7
Wellbrook Cl WA7 . . . . . . **50** C5
Well Cl CH64 . . . . **67** A4
Wellcroft Cl CW2 . . . . . . **206** B7
Wellcroft Gdns WA13 . . . **19** A2
Weller Ave SK12 . . . . **36** D2
Weller Cl SK12 . . . . **36** D2
Wellesbourne Cl
Macclesfield SK10 . . . . **86** F1
Neston CH64 . . . . **66** D6
Wellesley Ave
Ellesmere Port CH65 . . . . . **70** C5
Haslington CW1 . . . . **191** C4
Wellesley Cl WA12 . . . . . . **2** D2
Wellesley Wlk [6] CH65 . . . **70** C5
Welles St CW11 . . . . **175** B6
Well Farm Cl
Malpas SY14 . . . . **213** B3
Warrington WA1 . . . . **17** D8
Wellfield
Runcorn WA7 . . . . **50** E5
Widnes WA8 . . . . **13** A3
Winsford CW7 . . . . **127** A2
Wellfield Cl WA16 . . . . **80** A7
Wellfield Rd WA3 . . . . **4** F4
Wellfield St
Warrington, Bank Quay
WA5 . . . . **15** E5
Warrington, Whitecross
WA5 . . . . **15** E5
Wellfield Way SY13 . . . . **225** F1
Wellington Cir SK10 . . . . **112** E8
Wellington Cl
Congleton CW12 . . . . . . **156** D4
[3] Ellesmere Port CH65 . . . **70** C5
Knutsford WA16 . . . . **57** C4
Newton-le-W WA12 . . . . . . **2** A3
Warrington WA2 . . . . **8** F2
Wellington Gate L24 . . . . **21** E2
Wellington Gdns WA12 . . . **2** A3
Wellington Pl CH1 . . . . . **237** B3
Wellington Rd
Bollington SK10 . . . . **87** F8
Broughton CH4 . . . . **139** C3
Ellesmere Port CH65 . . . . . **70** B4
Hazel Grove SK7 . . . . **37** B8
Kidsgrove ST7 . . . . **195** A2
Nantwich CW5 . . . . **204** D6
Wellington Rd N CH65 . . . **70** C5
Wellington St Wrkshps [4]
WA1 . . . . **16** C5
Wellington St
[18] Macclesfield SK11 . . . **112** D8
Newton-le-W WA12 . . . . . . **2** A3
Northwich CW8 . . . . **103** E7
[3] Runcorn WA7 . . . . **23** A3
Warrington WA1 . . . . **16** C5
Widnes WA8 . . . . **23** A6
Wellington Street Ind Est
WA8 . . . . **23** A6
Well La
Alsager ST7 . . . . **193** C3
Antrobus CW9 . . . . **53** A4
Biddulph ST8 . . . . **179** D3
Chester CH2 . . . . **118** E5
Heswall CH60 . . . . **41** B6
Kingsley WA6 . . . . **75** C2
Little Budworth CW6 . . . . **147** F7
Macclesfield SK10 . . . . **88** B2
Manley WA6 . . . . **99** F3
Mollington CH1 . . . . **94** F2
Neston CH64 . . . . **66** F5
Prestbury SK10 . . . . **87** A6
Stretton WA4 . . . . **52** E8
Warrington WA5 . . . . **14** D3
Weaverham CW8 . . . . **77** C1
Wells Ave CW1 . . . . **191** D5
Wells Cl
Ellesmere Port CH66 . . . . . **94** E8
Gatley SK8 . . . . **34** C7
Mickle Trafford CH2 . . . . **119** F8
Wells Green **205** F8
Well St
Malpas SY14 . . . . **213** B3
Mow Cop ST7 . . . . **195** D7
New Mills SK22 . . . . **39** B8
Winsford CW7 . . . . **126** C1

Wellswood Dr CW2 . . . . **205** F7
Wellswood Rd CH66 . . . . **69** E7
Welsby Cl WA2 . . . . **8** F3
Welshampton Cl CH66 . . . **69** D2
Welsh La CW7 . . . . **149** D6
Welshmen's La CW5 . . . . **204** C7
Welshpool Cl WA5 . . . . . . **7** D3
Welsh Rd
Connah's Quay CH5 . . . . . **116** A7
Ellesmere Port CH66 . . . . . **68** E4
Woodbank CH1 . . . . **93** C6
Welsh Road Cotts CH1 . . . **93** D8
Welton Cl SK9 . . . . **59** F4
Welton Dr SK9 . . . . **59** E4
Welton Gr SK9 . . . . **59** E4
Welwyn Cl WA4 . . . . **17** C3
Wem Gr ST5 . . . . **210** E2
Wemyss Rd CH1 . . . . **117** D4
Wendover Cl WA11 . . . . . . **1** D7
Wenger Rd WA8 . . . . **13** B5
Wenlock Cl
Macclesfield SK10 . . . . **87** B2
Newcastle-u-Lyme ST5 . . . **210** E2
Warrington WA1 . . . . **17** A8
Wenlock Gdns CH66 . . . . **69** F2
Wenlock La CH66 . . . . . . **69** F2
Wenlock Rd WA7 . . . . **50** A4
Wenlock Way CH4 . . . . . **140** F6
Wensleydale Ave
Bebington CH62 . . . . **43** E5
Congleton CW12 . . . . . . **157** A5
Wensleydale Cl WA5 . . . . **14** F8
Wensley Dr SK7 . . . . **36** D7
Wensley Rd WA3 . . . . **3** E7
Wentworth Ave
Macclesfield SK11 . . . . . . **111** F6
Warrington WA1 . . . . **17** B7
Wentworth Cl
Northwich CW9 . . . . **104** E7
Widnes WA8 . . . . **13** A5
Wentworth Dr
Bebington CH63 . . . . **43** C5
Bramhall SK7 . . . . **36** A7
Kidsgrove ST7 . . . . **195** C3
Wentworth Gr CW7 . . . . **126** A2
Werburgh Cl WA13 . . . . . **19** C8
WERETON **209** C1
Wereton Rd ST7 . . . . **209** D1
WERVIN **96** A4
Wervin Rd CH2 . . . . **96** A3
Wesley Ave
Alsager ST7 . . . . **193** D4
Haydock WA11 . . . . **1** F7
[2] Sandbach CW11 . . . . . **175** B6
Wesley Cl
Nantwich CW5 . . . . **204** E5
Neston CH64 . . . . **66** D8
Wesley Ct
Congleton CW12 . . . . . . **156** D2
Winsford CW7 . . . . **126** F1
Wesley Gdns [7] ST7 . . . **195** A2
Wesley Pl
Crewe CW2 . . . . **190** D2
[4] Northwich CW9 . . . . . **104** A8
Wesley St ST7 . . . . **210** A1
Wessex Cl
Shavington CW2 . . . . **206** C3
Warrington WA1 . . . . **17** E7
Wessex Dr CW9 . . . . **104** C6
Westage La CW9 . . . . **79** B8
West Ave
Crewe CW1 . . . . **190** B4
Kidsgrove ST7 . . . . **194** C1
Middlewich CW10 . . . . . . **128** C2
Northwich CW9 . . . . **104** D7
Warrington, Stockton Heath
WA4 . . . . **16** C1
Warrington WA2 . . . . **16** B8
Warrington WA4 . . . . **207** B5
WEST BANK **23** A4
Alderley Edge SK9 . . . . **85** A8
Chester CH2 . . . . **118** C4
West Bank Dock Est
WA8 . . . . **22** E5
West Bank Prim Sch
WA8 . . . . **23** A4
West Bank St WA8 . . . . . . **87** B1
West Bank St WA8 . . . . . . **23** A5
West Bond St SK11 . . . . . **112** C7
Westbourne Ave CW1 . . . **190** A6
Westbourne Dr SK9 . . . . . **34** D1
Westbourne Ho
CW12 . . . . **156** B2
Westbourne Mews
CW12 . . . . **156** B2
Westbourne Rd
Blacon CH1 . . . . **118** A4
Warrington WA4 . . . . **26** B7
Westbrook Ave WA4 . . . . . **26** B7
Westbrook Cres WA5 . . . . . **7** B1
Westbrook Ctr WA5 . . . . . . **7** C2
Westbrook Dr SK10 . . . . . **87** C1
Westbrook Old Hall Prim
Sch WA5 . . . . **15** C8
Westbrook Rd WA8 . . . . . **75** B2
Westbrook Way WA5 . . . . . **7** B2
Westbury Cl
Crewe CW2 . . . . **206** C3
Middlewich CW10 . . . . . . **151** B8
Warrington WA4 . . . . **17** A8
Westbury Cl SK11 . . . . . . **112** A7
Westbury Dr SK11 . . . . . . **112** A7
Westbury Way CH4 . . . . . **140** F6

Westby Cl SK7 . . . . .36 A7
West Cheshire Coll
CH65 . . . . .70 B5
West Cheshire Coll
(Greenbank Ctr)
CH4 . . . . .141 D6
West Cheshire Coll
(Handbridge Ctr)
CH4 . . . . .141 D7
West Cl SK10 . . . . .87 F7
Westcliffe Ct WA8 . . . . . .13 B4
Westcliff Gdns WA4 . . . . .26 E3
Westdale Rd WA7 . . . . . . .17 A7
West Dr
Heswall CH60 . . . . .41 A7
Neston CH64 . . . . .66 E6
Warrington WA5 . . . . . . .15 B4
Winsford CW7 . . . . .127 A2
West Dudley St CW7 . . . .126 F1
West End CH3 . . . . .121 E7
West End Cotts CW12 . . .156 C2
West End Ct LL13 . . . . . .196 D8
West End Rd WA11 . . . . . .1 A6
West End Rd WA11 . . . . . .1 A6
Westenra Ave CH65 . . . . .69 F6
Westerham Cl SK10 . . . . .87 B2
Westerhope Way WA8 . . .12 F3
Westerings The CH62 . . . .43 C6
Western App CH2 . . . . . .118 E4
Western Ave
Blacon CH1 . . . . .117 D4
Macclesfield SK11 . . . . .112 C5
Macclesfield SK11 . . . . .112 D5
Milton Green CH3 . . . . . .165 C2
Nantwich CW5 . . . . .204 E3
Western Ct CH2 . . . . . . .118 E4
Western Dr SK11 . . . . . .112 C5
Western Pk CW11 . . . . . .191 F8
Westfield Ave ST7 . . . . .209 C2
Westfield Cl
Chester CH4 . . . . .141 B7
Winsford CW7 . . . . .149 C5
Westfield Cres WA7 . . . . .22 E1
Westfield Dr
Knutsford WA16 . . . . . . .56 E1
Willaston CW2 . . . . .205 E8
Westfield Gr CW8 . . . . . .77 F4
Westfield Mews WA7 . . . .22 F1
Westfield Prim Sch
WA7 . . . . .22 E1
Westfield Rd
Cheadle SK8 . . . . .34 F8
Mow Cop ST7 . . . . .195 C7
Northwich CW9 . . . . . . .104 B7
Runcorn WA7 . . . . .22 E1
Westfields WA15 . . . . . . .31 F8
Westfields Ave SK10 . . . .87 B1
Westfields Rise CW3 . . . .232 C1
Westford Rd WA4 . . . . . . .16 A1
Westgate
Widnes WA8 . . . . .22 B7
Wilmslow SK9 . . . . .59 C6
Westgate Ave CW7 . . . . .126 A1
Westgate Pk CW2 . . . . . .206 E2
West Gn CH5 . . . . .116 A6
West Gr
Alsager ST7 . . . . .193 E4
Heswall CH60 . . . . .40 F8
West Hall Ct WA16 . . . . . .29 C5
West Halton Hospl
WA7 . . . . .49 F6
Westhay Cres WA3 . . . . . .10 A5
WEST HEATH
Congleton 156 A4
Crewe 221 E8
West Heath Av WA13 . . . .18 C4
West Heath Sh Ctr
CW12 . . . . .156 A3
Westholme Cl
Congleton CW12 . . . . . .156 C3
Crewe CW2 . . . . .206 C8
Westholme St WA9 . . . . . .60 A2
Westhouse Cl CH63 . . . . .43 C5
West Hyde WA13 . . . . . . .18 C3
West La
Cuddington CW8 . . . . . .101 F3
High Legh WA16 . . . . . . .29 C6
Runcorn WA7 . . . . .49 F8
Westland Ct CW12 . . . . .156 C2
Westland Dr WA2 . . . . . . .8 E2
Westlands ST7 . . . . .209 F2
Westlands Cl CH64 . . . . . .41 F1
Westlands Rd CW10 . . . .128 B1
Westlands The CW12 . . . .156 C2
West Lorne St CH1 . . . . .237 A3
West Mains L24 . . . . .21 A3
Westmere Cl CW2 . . . . . .207 B5
Westmere Dr CW1 . . . . . .190 F2
Westminster Ave CH4 . . .141 B7
Westminster Cl
Middlewich CW10 . . . . . .128 B1
Warrington WA4 . . . . . . .17 C2
Widnes WA8 . . . . .22 B8
Westminster Ct CH2 . . . .118 F2
Westminster Dr
Bebington CH62 . . . . . . .43 D7
Cheadle SK8 . . . . .35 B6
Haydock WA11 . . . . .1 E7
Winsford CW7 . . . . .60 A4
Westminster Gn CH4 . . .141 D7
Westminster Gr
Ellesmere Port CH65 . . . .70 C6
Winsford CW7 . . . . .149 A8
Westminster Ind Pk
CH65 . . . . .69 F6
WESTMINSTER PARK
. . . . .141 B6

Westminster Pl [1]
WA1 . . . . .16 B5
Westminster Rd
Broughton CH4 . . . . . . .139 B3
Chester CH2 . . . . .118 F3
Ellesmere Port CH65 . . . .70 C6
Macclesfield SK10 . . . . . .87 C1
[4] Macclesfield SK10 . . .112 C8
Westminster St
Crewe CW2 . . . . .190 C2
[14] Macclesfield SK10 . .112 C8
Westminster Terr
CH4 . . . . .141 C7
Westmoreland Cl
WA14 . . . . .31 B8
Westmorland Ave
Talke ST7 . . . . .210 F7
Widnes WA8 . . . . .13 B1
Westmorland Cl SK10 . . .86 F2
Westmorland Rd M31 . . . .11 E2
Westmorland Terr
CW4 . . . . .130 B3
WESTON
Crewe 207 C5
Macclesfield 111 F8
Weston Cl
Middlewich CW10 . . . . . .151 C7
Northwich CW9 . . . . . . .103 F5
Weston Cres WA7 . . . . . . .49 A6
Weston Ct
Runcorn WA7 . . . . .48 F7
Shavington CW2 . . . . . .206 C5
Weston Ctr The CW1 . . . .190 E1
Weston Gr
Chester CH2 . . . . .118 E7
Halewood L26 . . . . .21 A6
Weston La CW2 . . . . . . .206 E5
WESTON POINT 48 D7
Weston Point Com Prim
Sch WA7 . . . . .48 E7
Weston Point Expressway
Runcorn, Rocksavage
WA7 . . . . .49 B5
Runcorn WA7 . . . . .22 E2
Runcorn, Weston WA7 . . .48 E6
Weston Prim Sch WA7 . . .49 A6
Weston Rd
Crewe CW1 . . . . .190 F1
Runcorn WA7 . . . . .48 E7
Weston CW1, CW2 . . . . .207 B7
Wilmslow SK9 . . . . .60 E6
Weston Sq SK11 . . . . . . .111 F7
Weston View WA7 . . . . . .49 D4
WESTON VILLAGE 48 F6
Weston Village Prim Sch
CW2 . . . . .207 C5
Westover Rd WA16 . . . . . .57 A1
West Park Ave SK12 . . . . .36 A4
West Park Dr [7] CH66 . . .94 F8
West Park Mus* SK10 . . .87 C1
West Quay Rd WA7 . . . . . .7 F3
West Rd
Congleton CW12 . . . . . .156 C3
Ellesmere Port CH65 . . . .70 C3
Runcorn WA7 . . . . .48 D7
Weaverham CW8 . . . . . . .77 B1
Westrees CW8 . . . . .101 D5
West Side Ave WA11 . . . . .1 A6
West St
Alderley Edge SK9 . . . . . .60 A1
Chester CH2 . . . . .237 C4
Congleton CW12 . . . . . .156 D3
Crewe CW1 . . . . .190 B5
Haslington CW1 . . . . . . .191 C5
Macclesfield SK11 . . . . .112 B8
Middlewich CW10 . . . . . .128 C1
Mount Pleasant ST7 . . . .195 B6
Warrington WA2 . . . . . . .16 B7
West Vale CH64 . . . . .66 E6
West View
Antrobus WA4 . . . . .53 A5
Ellesmere Port CH66 . . . .69 A8
Northwich CW9 . . . . . . .104 B8
Warrington WA4 . . . . . . .16 D3
West View Rd WA6 . . . . .101 A6
Westville Dr CW12 . . . . .156 A2
Westward Rd
Chester CH3 . . . . .142 B8
Wilmslow SK9 . . . . .59 F6
Westway CH60 . . . . .40 F6
West Way
Holmes Chapel CW4 . . . .130 B3
Sandbach CW11 . . . . . . .174 F4
Shavington CW2 . . . . . .206 D5
West Wing The CW10 . . .127 D5
Westwood WA3 . . . . .24 C1
Westwood Cl CW7 . . . . . .207 B1
Westwood Ct CH64 . . . . . .41 E2
Westwood Rd SK8 . . . . . .34 B8
WESTY 16 F5
Westy La WA4 . . . . .16 F4
West Gate La WA13 . . . . .19 E4
Wetheral Rd SK10 . . . . . .87 B2
Wetherby Cl
Chester CH1 . . . . .118 B2
Newton-le-W WA12 . . . . . .2 C5
Wetherby Way CH66 . . . .94 E8
Wetreins La SY14,
CH3 . . . . .197 D6
WETTENHALL 170 F7
WETTENHALL GREEN
. . . . .170 F6
Wettenhall Rd CW5 . . . .188 B4
Wetton La CW8 . . . . .76 E4
Wetton Way SK11 . . . . . .113 D2
Wexford Ave L24 . . . . . . .21 D2
Wexford Cl WA11 . . . . .1 D7
Weybourne Cl CH4 . . . . .140 E5

Weybridge Cl WA4 . . . . . .26 E7
Weybridge Dr SK10 . . . . .87 B3
Weygates Dr WA15 . . . . .32 C7
Weymouth Cl WA7 . . . . . .50 E6
Weymouth Rd WA5 . . . . . .6 F6
Whaddon Dr CH4 . . . . . .140 F4
WHALEY BRIDGE 65 D7
Whaley Bridge Prim Sch
SK23 . . . . .65 E7
Whaley Bridge Sta
SK23 . . . . .65 E8
Whaley St CH1 . . . . .117 A8
Whaley La SK23 . . . . .65 C8
Whalley Ave WA3 . . . . .5 C7
Whalley Dr CW6 . . . . . . .147 B3
Whalley Gr WA8 . . . . .13 D3
Whalley Hayes SK10 . . . .112 C8
Whalley Rd CW9 . . . . . . .104 A8
Whalley St WA1 . . . . .16 B4
Wharams Bank CW11 . . .176 F5
Wharburton Cl CW8 . . . .101 F2
Wharf St SK23 . . . . .65 E7
Wharfdale Ave CW11 . . . .173 B1
Wharfdale Cl WA5 . . . . . .15 A7
Wharfe Cl CW12 . . . . . . .156 F1
Wharfedale Rd WA7 . . . . .50 B6
Wharfedale Dr CH62 . . . .43 F5
Wharfedale Rd CW12 . . .157 A5
Wharfe La CH65 . . . . .70 A7
Wharf La CW12 . . . . .178 B3
Wharf Mill CW12 . . . . . .156 F1
Wharf La WA7 . . . . .24 E3
Wharf Rd
Collins Green WA12 . . . . . .1 E2
Whaley Bridge SK23 . . . . .65 E7
Wharfside Ct [6] WA4 . . .16 E1
Wharf St WA1 . . . . .16 C4
Wharf The
Chester CH1 . . . . .118 B1
Runcorn WA7 . . . . .50 F6
Wharmby Rd WA11 . . . . . .1 E6
WHARTON 127 A2
Wharton CE Jun Sch
CW7 . . . . .126 F1
Wharton Ct CH2 . . . . . . .118 F2
Wharton Gdns CW7 . . . .127 A3
Wharton Gn CW7 . . . . . .127 A4
WHARTON GREEN 127 B4
Wharton Hall CW7 . . . . .127 A3
Wharton Ind Est CW7 . . .126 F2
Wharton Park Rd
CW7 . . . . .126 F2
Wharton Rd CW7 . . . . . .127 A2
Wharton Ret Pk CW7 . . .126 F3
Whatcroft Cl WA7 . . . . . .49 D6
Whatcroft Hall La
CW9 . . . . .104 F1
Wheatcroft Cl WA16 . . . .15 C6
Wheatfield Cl
Barnton CW8 . . . . .78 A3
Ellesmere Port CH66 . . . .69 C3
Macclesfield SK10 . . . . . .87 C3
Wheatfield Rd WA8 . . . . .12 C5
Wheatland Rd CH60 . . . . .41 C7
Wheatlands WA7 . . . . . . .23 E1
Wheatley Ave CW1 . . . . .190 E6
Wheatley Rd CW1 . . . . . .190 E6
Wheat Moss SK11 . . . . . .84 B3
Wheatsheaf St SK23 . . . . .65 E6
Wheatsheaf La CW9 . . . . .53 B3
Wheatsheaf Rd SK23 . . . .65 E6
Wheelman Rd CW1 . . . . .190 A7
WHEELOCK 174 F4
Wheelock Cl
Alsager ST7 . . . . .193 A3
Handforth SK9 . . . . .34 D1
Kingsmead CW9 . . . . . . .103 F6
Wheelock St CW11 . . . . .175 A2
Wheelock Way [2]
CW7 . . . . .127 B1
WHEELOCK HEATH 192 A8
Wheelock Prim Sch
CW11 . . . . .175 A4
Wheelock St CW10 . . . . .128 C1
Wheelock Way [2]
ST7 . . . . .195 B2
Wheldon Cl CW10 . . . . . .128 E8
Wheldon Rd WA8 . . . . . . .21 F7
Wheldrake Cl CH66 . . . . .69 B5
Whernside WA8 . . . . .38 C3
Whetstone Hey CH66 . . . .69 D5
Whetstone Rd ST8 . . . . .179 C2
Wheycroft Mews
CW1 . . . . .190 C5
Whickham Cl WA8 . . . . . .12 F3
Whimbrel Ave WA12 . . . . .2 C3
Whimbrel Cl WA7 . . . . . . .49 F5
Whinchat Ave WA12 . . . . .2 C4
Whinchat Cl WA3 . . . . .3 E7
Whinchat Dr WA3 . . . . . . .9 F3
Whinfell Gr WA7 . . . . . . .49 F5
Whipcord La CH1 . . . . . .118 B2
Whirley Cl CW10 . . . . . . .151 C7
WHIRLEY GROVE 86 D3
Whirley La SK11 . . . . .85 F1
Whirley Prim Sch
SK10 . . . . .86 D1
Whirley Rd SK10 . . . . . . .86 C1
Whirlow Rd WA7 . . . . . . .206 B7
WHISTERFIELD 109 D3
Whisterfield La SK11 . . . .109 E3
Whiston Cl
Macclesfield SK11 . . . . .112 B4
Winsford CW7 . . . . .127 A4
Whiston Mews SK11 . . . .113 B4
Whiston St SK11 . . . . . . .112 C7
Whitbarrow Rd WA13 . . . .18 D4
WHITBY 70 A4

Whitby Ave
Chester CH2 . . . . .118 D5
Warrington WA7 . . . . .8 D2
Whitby Cl
Crewe CW1 . . . . .190 B8
Poynton SK12 . . . . .36 D4
WHITBYHEATH 70 B1
Whitby Heath Prim Sch
CH65 . . . . .70 B3
Whitby High Sch The
CH66 . . . . .70 A2
Whitby La CH1 . . . . .95 B6
Whitby Rd
Ellesmere Port CH65 . . . .70 C5
Runcorn WA7 . . . . .23 A1
Whitby's La CW7 . . . . . . .126 B1
WHITCHURCH 226 A1
Whitchurch Cl WA1 . . . . . .17 A8
Whitchurch Gr WA6 . . . . .73 D2
Whitchurch Rd ST5 . . . . .210 E2
Whitchurch Rd
Audlem CW3 . . . . .229 C3
Broxton CH3 . . . . .183 A3
Chester CH3 . . . . .119 B1
Christleton CH3 . . . . . . .142 E7
Edge Green SY14, CH3 . .199 B4
Handley CH3 . . . . .182 D8
Milton Green CH3 . . . . . .165 C4
Newhall CW5, SY13 . . . .228 B3
Royal's Green CW3,
SY13 . . . . .228 A2
Sound CW5 . . . . .217 E3
Waverton CH3 . . . . .143 B6
Whitchurch Way WA7 . . . .49 D7
White Ave CW2 . . . . .189 F4
Whitebarn Rd SK9 . . . . . .85 B8
Whitebeam Ave [5]
CH66 . . . . .69 F1
Whitebeam Cl
Newcastle-u-Lyme
ST5 . . . . .210 D1
Runcorn WA7 . . . . .24 C1
Whitebeam Row CW8 . . .102 E7
White Bear Yd [13]
WA16 . . . . .57 A2
White Broom WA13 . . . . .19 B4
White Clover Sq WA13 . . .19 A2
Whitecroft Ct SK10 . . . . .87 E2
Whitecroft Heath Rd
SK11 . . . . .109 B3
Whitecroft Rd CH66 . . . . .69 E2
Whitecroft Villas M31 . . . .11 E2
Whitecross Rd WA5 . . . . .15 E6
Whitefield WA13 . . . . .19 A4
Whitefield Ave WA12 . . . . .2 A2
Whitefield Cl
Golborne WA3 . . . . .3 A8
Lymm WA13 . . . . .19 A5
Whitefield Ct WA3 . . . . . . .4 F2
Whitefield Gr WA13 . . . . .19 A4
Whitefield Rd WA4 . . . . . .26 B8
Whitefields CH2 . . . . .72 B3
White Friars CH1 . . . . . .237 A2
Whitefriars Wlk [2]
M22 . . . . .33 D8
WHITEGATE 126 A7
Whitegate Ave WA3 . . . . . .4 F2
Whitegate CE Prim Sch
CW8 . . . . .125 F7
Whitegate Cl CW10 . . . . .151 C6
Whitegate Fields
LL13 . . . . .180 D1
Whitegate La CW11 . . . . .121 E7
Whitegate Rd CW7 . . . . .173 F3
Whitegates CW12 . . . . . .179 D4
Whitegates Cl CH64 . . . . .42 E1
Whitegates Cres CH64 . . .42 E1
Whitegates Ho CW7 . . . .189 E2
Whitehall Ave ST7 . . . . . .194 F2
Whitehall Cl
Barnton CW8 . . . . .78 A4
Wilmslow SK9 . . . . .60 A6
Whitehall Cl [3] CW5 . . .204 D5
Whitehall Dr CW8 . . . . . .103 C5
Whitehall La CW6 . . . . . .124 E1
White Hall La CW11 . . . .151 E1
Whitehall Pl [5] WA6 . . . .74 B8
White Hart Gdns CW8 . . .102 F4
White Hart La CW7 . . . . .205 E8
Whitehaven La CW5 . . . .203 A7
Whitehaven Rd SK7 . . . . .35 C5
WHITE HILL 195 B2
Whitehill Rd ST7 . . . . . . .195 B2
White House Cl WA11 . . . . .1 B6
White House Dr WA15 . . .32 B8
Whitehouse Dr WA1 . . . . .17 E7
Whitehouse Expressway
WA7 . . . . .50 B5
Whitehouse Ind Est
WA7 . . . . .50 E4
Whitehouse La
Nantwich CW5 . . . . .204 F7
Partington WA14 . . . . . . .20 D8
Plumley WA16 . . . . .80 F5
Whitehouse Rd WA16 . . . .30 B3
White La CH3 . . . . .142 D8
Whiteleas Rd SK23 . . . . . .65 D3
Whiteleggs La WA13 . . . . .19 B1
Whiteleys Ct CW9 . . . . . .104 D7
White Lodge Cl CH62 . . . .43 D5
White Lodge Mews
CW8 . . . . .102 A3
Whitemere Ct CH65 . . . . .70 C7
WHITEMOOR 179 D6
Whitemore Rd CW10 . . . .151 C6
White Park Cl CW10 . . . .128 D1
Whiteridge Rd ST7 . . . . .195 B2
Whitesands Rd WA13 . . . .18 C4

Whitesides Rd WA11 . . . . .1 B6
Whites La CW2 . . . . .207 B6
Whites Mdw CH3 . . . . . .142 A7
Whitesmead Cl SK12 . . . .38 D5
White St
Macclesfield SK11 . . . . .112 D6
Warrington, Stockton Heath
WA4 . . . . .16 C1
Warrington WA1 . . . . . . .16 A5
Widnes WA8 . . . . .23 A5
Whitethorn Ave WA5 . . . .14 F5
Whitethorn Way ST5 . . . .210 E1
Whitethroat Wlk WA3 . . . .9 F3
Whitewell Cl CW5 . . . . . .204 F5
Whitewood La SY14 . . . .212 D7
Whitfield Ave WA1 . . . . . .16 F7
Whitfield Dr SK11 . . . . . .112 B4
Whitfield Gr WA11 . . . . . .1 A5
Whitfield Rd ST7 . . . . . . .195 B2
Whitfields The SK10 . . . . .87 A1
Whitley Ave
Barnton CW8 . . . . .78 B3
Warrington WA4 . . . . . . .17 A4
Whitley Cl
Middlewich CW10 . . . . . .151 B7
Runcorn WA7 . . . . .48 F8
Whitley Dr CW8 . . . . . . .103 A4
Whitley La CW9 . . . . .55 B8
WHITLEY REED 53 D8
Whitley Village Sch
WA4 . . . . .52 D4
Whitlow Ave CW5 . . . . . .204 F4
Whitlow La CW9 . . . . . . .126 F8
Whitney Croft SK10 . . . . .113 A8
Whitson Cl WA16 . . . . . . .29 C4
Whitstable Pk WA8 . . . . . .12 E4
Whittaker Av WA2 . . . . . . .8 D2
Whittaker Cl CW1 . . . . . .190 A7
Whittington Gdns
CW9 . . . . .104 A2
Whittle Ave
Haydock WA11 . . . . .1 A5
Warrington WA5 . . . . . . .15 A7
Whittle Cl CW5 . . . . .116 A3
Whittle Hall La WA3 . . . . .10 A5
Whittlewood Cl WA3 . . . . .10 A5
Whitton Dr CH2 . . . . . . .118 E5
Whitwell Cl WA3 . . . . .9 E3
Whitworth St WA3 . . . . . . .9 E3
Wicker La
Altrincham WA15 . . . . . . .32 C8
Guilden Sutton CH3 . . . .120 A4
Wicklow Cl CH66 . . . . . . .69 A6
Wickson La CH3, CW6 . . .167 D3
Wicketead Ct CW5 . . . . .205 A4
Wicksten Dr WA7 . . . . . . .23 C2
Widdale Cl WA5 . . . . .14 F7
Widgeon Cl SK12 . . . . . . .36 B4
Widgeons Covert CH63 . . .41 F5
WIDNES 22 E7
Widnes Rd
Cuerdley Cross WA5,
WA8 . . . . .13 F2
Warrington WA5 . . . . . . .14 C3
Widnes WA8 . . . . .23 B8
Widnes Sta WA8 . . . . . . .13 A3
Wiend The CH2 . . . . .118 D4
Wight Cl CH65 . . . . .70 C1
Wightman Ave WA12 . . . . .2 C5
Wigmore Cl WA3 . . . . . . .10 A6
Wigsey La WA13 . . . . .19 A7
WIGSHAW 4 D2
Wigshaw La WA3 . . . . .4 D3
Wigwam Cl SK12 . . . . . . .36 C4
Wilbraham Cl
Acton CW5 . . . . .204 A7
Mickle Trafford CW2 . . . .119 F8
Wilbraham Rd
Acton CW5 . . . . .204 A7
Congleton CW12 . . . . . .156 F3
Weaverham CW8 . . . . . . .77 E1
Wilbrahams Way ST7 . . .193 A3
Wilbraham's Wlk ST7 . . .209 D2
Wilcock Rd WA11 . . . . . . .2 B8
Wilcote Cl WA8 . . . . .13 C4
Wilcott Dr SK9 . . . . .59 F4
Wild Arum Cl [8] WA3 . . . .3 E8
WILDBOARCLOUGH 137 E6
Wilderhope Cl CW9 . . . .106 C7
WILDERSPOOL 16 C2
Wilderspool Cswy
WA4 . . . . .16 C3
Wild Goose Ave ST7 . . . .195 D3
Wilding Ave [2] WA7 . . . . .23 B2
Wilding Bsns Pk CH3 . . . .119 C4
Wildings Old La WA3 . . . . .9 A8
Wilding St CW1 . . . . .190 E4
Wildmoor La CH3 . . . . . . .97 D1
Wildwood Gr WA1 . . . . . .17 B7
WILKESLEY 233 F7
Wilkins La SK9 . . . . .33 E5
Wilkinson Ave WA16 . . . .16 F6
Wilkinson Cl WA8 . . . . . . .23 A5
Wilkinson Ct CW7 . . . . . .149 B6
Wilkinson Ct N CH66 . . . .70 C5
Wilkinson St
Ellesmere Port CH65 . . . .70 C6
Warrington WA2 . . . . . . .16 B7
Wilkinson Street Mews [1]
CH65 . . . . .70 C6
Wilkinson Way CW7 . . . .149 B7
Willan Rd CH1 . . . . .117 D4
WILLASTON
Ellesmere Port 68 A8

WILLASTON continued
Nantwich 205 D8
Willaston CE Prim Sch
CH64 ....67 F8
Willaston Dr L26 ....21 A6
Willaston Farm CH64 ....67 F8
Willaston Green Mews
CH64 ....67 F8
Willaston Hall Gdns
CW5 ....205 C6
Willaston Prim Sch
CW5 ....205 D6
Willaston Rd CH63,
CH64 ....42 D4
Willaston Way 8 SK9...34 D5
Willbank La CW5 ....202 D5
Willerby Cl 1 SK10.....112 C8
Willeymoor La SY13 ...225 D8
William Barker Ct 10
CW11 ....175 B6
William Beamont Com
High Sch WA2 ....8 C1
William Ct CH64 ....41 F2
William Foden Cl
CW11 ....174 D7
William Johnson Gdns
CH65 ....70 C6
William Penn Cl WA5 ...14 E5
William Rd ST7 ....195 A2
Williams Ave WA12 ......2 C5
Williams Cl CH2 ....118 C4
Williamson Cres SK23...65 D8
Williamson Dr CW5 ....204 C5
Williamson Rd SK23 ....65 D8
William St
Chester CH1 ....237 B3
Chester, Hoole Park
CH2 ....118 F3
Congleton CW12 ....157 A4
Macclesfield SK10 .....112 F8
6 Northwich CW9 .....104 B8
Widnes WA8 ....13 C1
Winsford CW7 ....126 C1
William Stockton Com Sch
CH65 ....70 B5
Williams Way
Frodsham WA6 ....74 A8
Henbury SK11 ....111 C8
Willington Ave CH62 ....43 E3
Willington Cnr CW6 ....122 E2
Willington La
Duddon CW6 ....145 E7
Kelsall CW6 ....122 D4
Willington Rd
Duddon CW6 ....145 B7
Kelsall CW6 ....122 C2
Willis St WA1 ....16 D6
Willmer Cres ST7 ......195 B6
Willotts Hill Rd ST5....210 D1
Willoughby Cl WA5 ......7 C1
Willow Ave
Newton-le-W WA12......2 E4
6 Widnes WA8 ....13 B2
Willoway Rd CH3 ....119 B2
Willow Bank
Cheadle SK8 ....35 A6
Helsby WA6 ....73 D2
Nantwich CW5 ....204 F6
Willowbank Dr SK10 ....88 C8
Willow Bank East WA12..2 F4
Willowbrook CH5 ....116 B4
Willowbrow Rd CH63,
CH64 ....42 D3
Willow Cl
Chester CH2 ....118 D8
Lymm WA13 ....18 E4
Newcastle-u-Lyme ST5 .210 D1
Paddockhill WA16 ....59 B5
Poynton SK12 ....36 E3
Runcorn WA7 ....49 C7
Winsford CW7 ....126 D3
Willow Cres
Chester CH2 ....119 A4
Crewe CW2 ....189 F2
Moore WA4 ....25 A7
Warrington WA1 ....17 E8
Willowcroft Way ST7...195 E4
Willow Ct
Alsager ST7 ....193 E4
Connah's Quay CH5......91 D1
Higher Kinnerton CH4 ..161 A7
Macclesfield SK10 ....87 B2
Middlewich CW10 ....128 C2
Nantwich CW5 ....204 F7
Newton-le-W WA12......2 D4
Warrington WA2 ....7 F3
Winsford CW7 ....127 B2
Willowdale WA12 ....2 E3
Willowdale Way CH66 ...94 F8
Willow Dr
Blacon CH1 ....117 D5
Bunbury CW6 ....185 E8
Handforth SK9 ....34 D3
Sandbach CW11 ....175 E7
Warrington WA4 ....16 E1
Willow Gn
Knutsford WA16 ....56 F3
Weaverham CW8 ....102 D8
Willow Gr
Barnton CW8 ....78 B4
Chester CH2 ....119 B4
Ellesmere Port CH66....95 A8
Elton CH2 ....72 A3
WILLOW GREEN 77 B5
Willow Green La CW8...77 B5

Willow Hayes CH3 .....121 F7
Willowherb Cl CH3 ....142 A6
Willow La
Goostrey CW4 ....107 E1
Thornton Hough CH63,
CH64 ....42 D3
Warrington WA4 ....26 E4
Willow Lea CH1 ....94 F2
Willowmead Dr SK10 ...87 A5
Willow Rd
Chester CH4 ....140 F6
Haydock WA11............1 F7
High Lane SK6 ....37 F7
Newton-le-W WA12......2 E4
Partington M31 ....11 E2
Willows SK9 ....59 F6
Willows Cl CW2 ....206 B7
Willow Sq CW7 ....127 A2
Willow St CW12 ....156 E3
Willows The
Frodsham WA6 ....74 C8
Higher Wincham CW9 ...79 F6
Newton-le-W WA12......2 D4
2 Northwich CW9 .....103 E6
Partington M31 ....11 F3
Sandbach CW11 ....175 B7
Warrington WA5 ....14 F5
Willow Tree Ct WA8....13 D2
Willow Tree Gr ST17 ..193 F7
Willow Way
Bramhall SK7 ....35 D7
Broughton CH4 ....139 B3
Prestbury SK10 ....87 A5
Willow Wood Com Jun
Sch CW7 ....127 B2
Willow Wood Inf Sch
CW7 ....127 A2
Wilmere La WA8 ....13 A6
Wilmot Ave WA5 ....14 F6
Wilmot Dr WA3 ....2 F7
WILMSLOW 60 C5
Wilmslow Ave CH66.....69 E5
Wilmslow Cres WA4 ....17 D4
Wilmslow Ct WA3 ....34 D3
Wilmslow Dr CH66......69 E5
Wilmslow Grange Prim
Sch SK9 ....34 C4
Wilmslow High Sch
SK9 ....60 B6
Wilmslow Old Rd
Mottram St Andrew
SK10 ....61 A2
Wythenshawe M90 ......33 A6
WILMSLOW PARK 60 D7
Wilmslow Pk N SK9.....60 C7
Wilmslow Pk S SK9.....60 C7
Wilmslow Prep Sch
SK9 ....60 B7
Wilmslow Rd
Adlington SK10 ....61 D6
Alderley Edge SK9 ......60 A2
Gatley SK8 ....34 D7
Gatley SK8, SK9 ....34 C6
Handforth SK9 ....34 C6
Mottram St Andrew,
Greendale SK10 ....86 D8
Mottram St Andrew
SK10 ....61 A3
Woodford SK7 ....35 C1
Wythenshawe M90, SK9,
WA15 ....32 F5
Wilmslow Sta SK9 ......60 C7
Wilmslow Wlk 13
SK11 ....112 E7
Wilsbury Grange
CW8 ....103 A5
Wilsden Rd WA8 ....12 B1
Wilshaw Terr CH63 .....42 B6
Wilson Cl
Warrington WA4 ....17 D3
4 Widnes WA8 ....13 D1
Wilson Cres CW9 ....80 B3
Wilson Dr CW9 ....126 F7
Wilson Patten St WA1 ..16 A4
Wilsons La CH65 ....70 A3
Wilson St
Warrington, Bewsey
WA5 ....16 A3
Warrington, Birchwood
WA3 ....9 E5
Wilton Ave SK8 ....34 C7
Wilton Cl CW9 ....103 E4
Wilton Cres
Alderley Edge SK9 ......59 F2
Macclesfield SK11 .....111 E6
Wilton Dr WA15 ....32 C8
Wilton La WA3 ....4 B5
Wiltshire Cl
Macclesfield SK10 ....86 E2
Warrington WA1 ....17 D6
Wiltshire Dr CW12 ....156 E4
Wiltshire Rd M31 ....11 E2
Wiltshire Wlk SK10 .....86 F2
Wilwick La SK11 ....111 F7
Wimberry Dr ST5 ......210 D1
WIMBOLDSLEY 150 F4
Wimboldsley Com Prim
Sch CW10 ....150 F4
WIMBOLDS TRAFFORD
.................................96 F6
WINCHAM 79 C3
Wincham Ave CW9 ......79 D3
Wincham Bsns Pk
CW9 ....79 D3
Wincham Com Prim Sch
CW9 ....79 D3
Wincham La CW9........79 D3

Wincham Park (Witton
Albion FC) CW9 ....79 C2
Wincham Way
Ellesmere Port CH65....70 D4
Warrington WA5 ....15 C5
Winchester Cl
Shavington CW2 ....206 B3
Warrington WA5 ....15 E4
Wilmslow SK9 ....59 E5
Winchester Ct CW2 ...207 E3
Winchester Dr SK10 ...111 F8
Winchester Ho
11 Chester CH1........237 C3
12 Macclesfield SK10 ..111 F8
Winchester Sq CH4 ...128 C8
Winchester Sq CH4 ...140 F5
WINCLE 160 A7
Wincle Ave SK4..........36 F2
Wincle CE Prim Sch
SK11 ....136 F1
Windermere Ave
Chester CH2 ....119 A6
Warrington WA2 ....8 D3
Warrington WA8 ....13 B4
Windermere Ct CH64 ..66 F7
Windermere Dr
Alderley Edge SK9 ......59 F1
Congleton CW12 ....156 A2
Windermere Rd
Crewe CW2 ....189 E2
Ellesmere Port CH65....70 C2
Handforth SK9 ....34 C4
Haydock WA11............1 B6
High Lane SK6 ....37 E8
Winsford CW7 ....126 C2
Windermere St WA8 ....13 B4
Windfield Gdns CH66 ...69 D7
Windings The CW10 ...128 B2
Windle Ct
Neston CH64 ....41 E2
Warrington WA3 ....9 C4
WINDLE HILL 67 C7
Windlehurst Rd SK6 ....37 D7
Windlehurst Rd SK12 ...37 D8
Windmill Cl
Buerton CW3 ....230 E4
Warrington WA4 ....26 C6
Windmill Ctr The WA8 ..23 B8
Windmill Dr CW3 ......229 F3
WINDMILL HILL 24 C1
Windmill Hill Ave W
WA7 ....24 D1
Windmill Hill Ave N
WA7 ....24 D3
Windmill Hill Ave S
WA7 ....24 D2
Windmill Hill Ave E
WA7 ....24 C2
Windmill Hill Prim Sch
WA7 ....24 C2
Windmill La
Bollington SK10 ....88 B6
Christleton CH3 ....142 D8
Hankelow CW3 ....230 F4
Preston on t h WA4.....51 A6
Warrington, Penketh
WA5 ....14 E5
Warrington WA4 ....26 C6
Windmill Rise CH2.....118 D7
Windmill St
Macclesfield SK11 .....112 E6
Runcorn WA7 ....23 B2
Windscale Rd WA2 ......9 A2
Windsor Ave
Crewe CW1 ....190 B6
Nantwich CW5 ....204 F3
Newton-le-W WA12......2 D2
Tarporley CW6 ....146 D1
Wilmslow SK9 ....59 F7
Windsor Cl
Bollington SK10 ....87 E6
Cuddington CW8 ....101 F4
Poynton SK12 ....36 D4
Windsor Ct
Chester CH1 ....237 B1
11 Warrington WA4 ....16 E1
Windsor Dr
Alsager ST7 ....192 F4
Altrincham, Bowdon
WA14 ....20 F1
Broughton CH4 ....139 A3
Ellesmere Port CH65....70 A3
Faddiley CW5 ....202 E7
Haydock WA11............2 A7
Helsby WA6 ....73 B2
Warrington WA4 ....17 B2
Winsford CW7 ....149 C5
Windsor Gr
Cheadle SK8 ....34 F8
Runcorn WA7 ....49 B8
Windsor Ho
8 Northwich CW8 .....103 C5
Talke ST7 ....210 D6
Windsor Pl CW12 .....156 F2
Windsor Rd
Chester CH4 ....140 F6
Golborne WA3 ....3 C8
Widnes WA8 ....13 A4
Wilmslow SK9 ....59 F7
Windsor Sq SK11 ......112 D4
Windsor St WA5 ....15 E6
Windsor Way WA16....56 F2
Windways CH66 ....69 D7
Windy Bank Ave WA3 ...3 E8
WINDYHARBOUR 109 C1
Winfield Way WA8 ......23 B8
Winfrith Rd WA2 ....9 A2
Wingate Rd CH62 ....43 E5

Wingfield Ave SK9 ......59 E6
Wingfield Dr SK9 ....59 E6
Wingfield Pl CW7 ......149 B6
Winghay Rd ST7 ....195 B2
Winifred St WA2 ....16 C7
Winkwell Dr CH4 ....141 A5
Winlowe 18 SK11 ....112 E7
Winmarth Dr WA15 .....32 D7
Winmarleigh St WA1 ...16 A4
WINNINGTON 78 D1
Winnington Ave CW8 .103 C8
Winnington Ct 13
CW8 ....103 F8
Winnington La CW8 .....78 D1
Winnington Park Com
Prim Sch CW8 ....103 D7
Winnington St
Northwich CW8 ....103 F8
Winsford CW7 ....126 E1
Winnows The WA7......23 D1
Winscombe Dr CW9 ...119 C2
Winsford Rd SK7 ....36 E8
WINSFORD 126 E2
Winsford Cl WA11 ....1 F7
Winsford Cross Sh Ctr
CW7 ....126 D1
Winsford Dr WA5 ....6 E7
Winsford Gr CH66 ......69 C3
Winsford High Street Com
Sch CW7 ....126 D1
Winsford Ind Est
CW7 ....127 C3
Winsford Rd CW7 ......170 F6
Winsford Sta CW7 .....127 C1
Winsford Way CH1 ....117 F2
Winslow Cl WA7 ....50 D8
Winstanley Cl WA5 .....15 C5
Winstanley Ho WA6....56 F2
Winstanley Ind Est WA2..8 B1
Winstanley Rd CH64 ...66 E5
Winston Ave
Alsager ST7 ....193 C5
Newton-le-W WA12......2 C3
St Helens WA9 ....1 B2
Winston Ct CH2 ....119 A5
Winterbottom La
WA16 ....55 E8
Winterford La CW6 ....147 B2
Winter Gr WA9 ....1 B3
Wintergreen Wlk 3
M31 ....11 F3
Winterlea Dr L26 ....21 A6
WINTERLEY 191 F7
Winterside Cl ST5 .....210 D1
Winterton Way SK11 ..112 D3
Winton Ave WA7.........24 D1
Winton Rd WA3 ....3 A6
WINWICK 8 A6
Winwick CE Prim Sch
WA2 ....8 B6
Winwick La WA3 ....3 E3
Winwick Link Rd WA2,
WA3 ....8 A5
Winwick Park Ave WA2 ..8 A5
WINWICK QUAY 8 A3
Winwick Rd
Newton-le-W WA12......2 F1
Warrington WA2 ....8 A4
Winwick St WA2 ....16 B6
Winwick View WA5 ......1 D1
Wirksmoor Rd SK22 ...39 B7
Wirral Cl WA3 ....4 E4
Wirral Cres CH64 ....66 F5
Wirral Ctry Pk* CH64....67 C7
Wirral Metropolitan Coll
CH62 ....44 A7
WIRSWALL 226 A5
Wirswall Rd SY13 .....226 C8
Wisdom Wlk CH1 ......174 D7
Wisenholme Cl WA7 ...49 E5
WISTASTON 205 D8
Wistaston Ave CW2 ...189 F2
WISTASTON GREEN ...189 D2
Wistaston Green Cl
CW2 ....189 E2
Wistaston Green Prim Sch
CW2 ....189 E2
Wistaston Green Rd
CW2 ....189 E2
Wistaston Rd
Crewe CW2 ....190 C3
Wistaston CW5 ....205 E6
Wistaston Road Bsns Ctr
CW2 ....190 B4
Wistaston Westfield Prim
Sch CW2 ....205 E8
Wisterdale Cl CW2 ....206 A7
Wisteria Way WA9 ......6 A7
Witham Cl CW2 ....206 A8
Witham Way ST8 ......179 E1
Withens Cl CW8 ....102 D8
Withenshaw La SK11..136 E5
Withens La CW8 ....102 D8
Withers Ave WA2 ....16 D8
Wither's La
High Legh, Primrose Hill
WA16 ....28 C6
High Legh, Rowlinson's Green
WA16 ....28 B4
Witherwin Ave WA4 ....26 F7
Withington Ave WA3 ....5 A3
Withington Cl
Northwich CW9 ....104 A6
Sandbach CW11 ....175 C7
WITHINGTON GREEN
...............................108 E3

Withinlee Rd SK10......86 D6
Withins Rd
Culcheth WA3 ....4 F3
Haydock WA11............1 F8
Within Way L24 ....21 E1
Withnall Dr CW2 ....206 A4
Withy Cl WA6 ....74 C8
Withycombe Rd WA5 ..14 E4
Withy Croft CH3 ....142 B7
Withyfold Dr SK10 ......87 E1
Witney Gdns WA4 ......26 E6
Witney La SY14 ....213 D8
Wittenham Ho SK9 .....34 D2
Wittering La CH60 ......40 D7
Witterings The CH64 ...41 E1
Witton Church Walk CE
Prim Sch CW9 ....104 A8
Witton St CW9 ....79 A1
Witton Wlk 5 CW9 ....103 F8
Witt Rd WA8 ....23 A7
Wivern Pl WA7 ....23 B3
Wizard Country Pk
SK10 ....85 D6
Wobbs La SY13 ....225 C5
Woburn Ave WA12 ......2 D2
Woburn Dr
Haydock WA11............1 F7
Macclesfield SK10 ......87 C2
Northwich CW9 ....103 E5
Woburn Ct SK12 ....36 F4
Woburn Dr
Chester CH2 ....118 F7
Congleton CW12 ....179 B8
Cronton WA8 ....12 D6
Woburn Rd WA2 ....8 A4
Woking Rd SK8 ....35 A7
Wolfe Cl
Grappenhall Heys WA4 .27 A8
Knutsford WA16 ....57 C3
Wolstanholme Cl
CW12 ....156 F1
WOLVERHAM 70 D4
Wolverham Prim Sch
CH65 ....70 D4
Wolverham Rd CH65....70 D3
Wolverton Dr
Handforth SK9 ....34 D1
Runcorn WA7 ....24 D1
Wolvesey Pl CW7 .....149 B6
Woodacre Gr CH66 .....69 F8
Woodacre Rd CH66 ....69 F8
Woodacres St SK9 ......59 F6
Woodale Cl WA5 ....14 E7
Woodall Ave CH4 ......140 E6
Woodall Dr WA7 ....23 B1
Woodbank Ave CW3 ..229 A2
WOODBANK 93 F6
Woodbank SK9 ....60 A2
Woodbank Cl CW2 ....206 A7
Woodbank La CH1 ......93 D5
Woodbank Rd
Ellesmere Port CH65....70 B2
Warrington WA5 ....15 A4
Woodbine Ave M44 ....11 D4
Woodbine Cl WA3 ......19 B4
Woodbourne Rd SK22..39 A5
Woodbridge Cl WA4 ....26 E4
Woodbrook SK23 ....65 E8
Woodbrook Cl SK23 ...65 E7
Woodbrook Rd SK9 ....60 C1
Woodburn Dr CH60 ....40 F6
Woodchurch La CH66 ..69 E6
Woodclose CH66 ....44 A1
Woodcock's Well CE Prim
Sch ST7 ....195 C6
Woodcote Ave CH65 ...70 B1
Woodcote Cl WA7 ....8 D1
Woodcote Pl CW11 ...191 F8
Woodcotes The CH66...43 D6
Woodcote View WA5 ...34 F1
Woodcott Ave CW7 ...126 B2
Woodcott Cl WA7 .....206 E2
Woodcott Gr 8 SK9 ....34 E1
Woodcotthill La CW5 .217 B3
Woodcroft ST7 ....210 A1
Woodcroft Gdns WA4 ..26 F6
Wood Dr ST7 ....193 A4
WOODEND 38 E8
Woodend WA7 ....50 E7
Woodend Cl CW10 ....151 C6
Wood End Ct WA8 ......13 D2
Woodend La
Hollins Green WA3......10 D2
Mobberley WA16 ....58 E8
Wood End La CH64 ....206 B4
Woodend Rd CH65 .....69 F6
Woodfall Cl CH64 ....67 A6
Woodfall Gr CH64 ......67 A6
Woodfall La CH64 ......67 A6
Woodfall Prim Sch
CH64 ....67 A6
Wood Farm CW7 ......189 B4
Woodfield Ave CH4 ...139 A3
Woodfield Gr CH2 .....119 A5
Woodfield Ho CH2 .....119 A5
Woodfield Prim Sch
CH2 ....119 A5
Woodfield Rd
Cheadle SK8 ....35 B7
Ellesmere Port CH65....70 C5
Woodfield Rd N 2
CH65 ....70 C5
Woodfields CH3 ....142 E7
Woodfin Croft SK11....84 A3
WOODFORD 35 E2

Woodford Aerodrome
SK7 . . . . .36 A1
Woodford Ave WA3 . . . . .3 D7
Woodford Cl
Crewe CW2 . . . . .189 F2
Helsby WA6 . . . . .73 B2
Runcorn WA7 . . . . .49 B6
Warrington WA4 . . . . .17 C3
Woodford Court Ind Est
CW7 . . . . .149 A8
Woodford Ct CW7 . . . . .149 A7
Woodford La
Prestbury SK10 . . . . .61 D7
Winsford CW7 . . . . .149 B8
Woodford La W CW7 . . .149 A7
Woodford Lo SK12 . . . . .36 C4
Woodford Lodge High Sch
CW7 . . . . .149 A7
Woodford Mews SK9 . . .34 D4
Woodford Park Ind Est
CW7 . . . . .148 F8
Woodford Rd
Bramhall SK7 . . . . .35 E4
Poynton SK12 . . . . .36 B6
Wilmslow SK9 . . . . .61 B8
Woodgate Ave ST7 . . . . .194 A5
Wood Gdns SK9 . . . . .60 B2
Woodgreen La CW5 . . . .171 D5
Woodhall Cl
Bramhall SK7 . . . . .35 E3
Warrington WA5 . . . . .15 A8
Woodhall Rd ST7 . . . . . .195 C3
Woodham Cl CW8 . . . . . .103 C5
Woodham Gr CH64 . . . . .66 F5
Woodhatch Rd WA7 . . . .50 B5
Wood Heath Way
CH62 . . . . .44 A7
WOODHEY GREEN 202 B6
Woodhey Hall La
CW5 . . . . .202 B6
Woodhey La CW5 . . . . . .202 C5
Woodhouse Cl WA3 . . . . .9 F3
WOODHOUSE-END 135 C8
Woodhouse End Rd
SK11 . . . . .135 C8
WOODHOUSE GREEN
. . . . .158 D2
Woodhouse La
Biddulph ST8 . . . . .179 F2
Buerton CW3 . . . . .235 D8
Partington WA14 . . . . .20 C4
Warren SK11 . . . . .111 E1
Wythenshawe M90 . . . . . . .33 D7
Woodhouse Mid Sch
ST8 . . . . .179 E2
Woodhouse Rd M22 . . . .33 D8
WOODHOUSES 73 E4
Woodhouses Pk WA6 . . .73 F5
Wood La
Bradwall Green CW10,
CW11 . . . . .152 E3
Broughton CH4 . . . . .139 B4
Burton CH64 . . . . .67 C2
Duddon CW6 . . . . .145 E7
Goostrey CW4 . . . . .107 C1
Neston CH64 . . . . .41 D2
Partington M31 . . . . .11 C1
Runcorn, Brookvale WA7 . . .50 C6
Runcorn WA7 . . . . .49 F4
Sutton Weaver WA7 . . . . . . .49 F4
Tattenhall CH3 . . . . .167 A1
Warrington WA4 . . . . .26 E8
Weaverham CW8 . . . . .102 E8
Wilmslow WA16 . . . . .32 D1
Wood La E SK10 . . . . .63 B8
Wood La N
Fourlane-ends SK10 . . . . . . .63 B8
Wardsend SK10 . . . . .37 B1
Woodlan Ct CW6 . . . . . .146 B6
Woodland Ave
Crewe CW1 . . . . .190 F4
Lymm WA13 . . . . .19 A2
Nantwich CW5 . . . . .205 A5
Newton-le-W WA12 . . . . . . .2 F3
Widnes WA8 . . . . .12 F1
Woodland Bank CH2 . . .96 F1
Woodland Cl SK11 . . . . .84 A3
Woodland Ct ST7 . . . . . .193 D4
Woodland Dr WA13 . . . . .19 A2
Woodland End SK11 . . . .84 A3
Woodland Gdns CW7 . . .190 D6
Woodland Rd
Ellesmere Port CH65 . . . . . .70 B2
Rode Heath ST7 . . . . .193 E8
Woodlands CW8 . . . . . . .103 B5
Woodlands Ave
Chester CH1 . . . . .118 B4
Congleton CW12 . . . . .156 D4
Kidsgrove ST7 . . . . .194 D1
Woodlands Cl
Cheadle SK8 . . . . .35 A8
Cotebrook CW6 . . . . .147 A8
Neston CH64 . . . . .66 D8
Woodlands Cres WA16 . .29 C4
Woodlands Ct
Alderley Edge SK9 . . . . .85 A8
15 Knutsford WA16 . . . . . .57 B2
Woodlands Cvn Pk
WA16 . . . . .106 E3
Woodlands Dr
Chester CH2 . . . . .118 E4
Chorlton CW2 . . . . .207 C3
Goostrey CW4 . . . . .107 E1
Knutsford WA16 . . . . .57 B3

Warrington WA4 . . . . .17 D3
Woodlands Gr CW8 . . . . .77 F3
Woodlands Ind Est
WA12 . . . . .2 C6
Woodlands Inf Sch
CH66 . . . . .69 F2
Woodlands Jun Sch
CH66 . . . . .69 F2
Woodlands La CH3 . . . .119 A2
Woodlands Pk
Congleton CW12 . . . . .156 C3
Newton-le-W WA12 . . . . . . .2 C6
Woodlands Rd
Chester CH4 . . . . .141 A7
Handforth SK9 . . . . .34 E3
High Lane SK12 . . . . .38 A6
Huntington CH3 . . . . .142 A6
Macclesfield SK11 . . . . . . .112 C6
Neston CH64 . . . . .66 D8
New Mills SK22 . . . . .39 A8
Northwich CW8 . . . . .103 C5
Wilmslow SK9 . . . . .33 F1
Woodlands Rd E 1
CW8 . . . . .103 C5
Woodlands The
Higher Wincham CW9 . . . . .80 A6
Kidsgrove ST7 . . . . .194 E3
Winnington CW8 . . . . .78 E1
Woodlands Way CW6 . .146 D2
Woodland View
Ellesmere Port CH66 . . . . . .69 E7
Horwich End SK23 . . . . .65 F2
Woodland Wlk
Bebington CH62 . . . . .43 C8
Runcorn WA7 . . . . .24 A1
WOOD LANE 210 A1
Wood Lane Prim Sch
ST7 . . . . .210 A1
Woodlark Cl CW7 . . . . . .150 A8
Wood La S SK10 . . . . .63 B7
Wood La W SK10 . . . . .63 A8
Woodlea Ave CH2 . . . . . .118 F7
Woodlea Cl CH62 . . . . . . .43 D5
Woodlea Ct CW8 . . . . . . .103 D7
Woodlea Dr SK10 . . . . . . .87 E8
Woodleigh Ct SK9 . . . . . .60 A2
Woodley Fold WA5 . . . . .14 F4
Wood Meml Prim Sch
CH4 . . . . .140 F6
Woodnoth Dr CW2 . . . . .206 C5
Wood Orchard La
CW3 . . . . .230 A2
Woodpecker Cl WA3 . . . . .9 F4
Woodpecker Dr
Northwich CW9 . . . . .103 F4
Packmoor ST7 . . . . .195 E1
Woodridge WA7 . . . . . . .24 C1
Woodrow Ct 4 WA8 . . . . .15 C7
Woodrow Way
Irlam M44 . . . . .11 F8
Newcastle-u-Lyme ST5 . . . .210 F1
Woodruff Cl ST7 . . . . . . .195 F1
Woodruff Wlk 7 M31 . . . .11 F3
Wood's Cl WA16 . . . . .82 F6
Woods Ct WA12 . . . . .2 A3
Woodsfin La CH3 . . . . . .183 F7
Woods Gr SK8 . . . . .35 B7
WOODSHUTTS 194 F1
Woodshutt's St ST7 . . . .194 E1
WOODSIDE 99 C2
Woodside
Ellesmere Port CH65 . . . . . .70 C2
Knutsford WA16 . . . . .57 B1
Lawton-gate ST7 . . . . .194 E4
Poynton SK12 . . . . .36 F4
Siddington SK11 . . . . .110 A3
Woodside Ave
Alsager ST7 . . . . .193 E4
Crewe CW2 . . . . .189 F2
Frodsham WA6 . . . . .74 D7
Warrington WA5 . . . . .15 A1
Woodside Ct CH2 . . . . . .118 C4
Woodside Dr
High Lane SK6 . . . . .37 F7
Sandbach CW11 . . . . .175 C6
Woodside La
Crewe CW2 . . . . .189 F1
Lymm WA13 . . . . .19 B1
Poynton SK12 . . . . .36 E4
Woodside Prim Sch
WA7 . . . . .49 D7
Woodside Rd
Blacon CH1 . . . . .117 C5
Haydock WA11 . . . . .1 E7
Warrington WA5 . . . . .14 F6
Woodside St SK22 . . . . . .39 B6
Woodside Terr CW9 . . . .104 B4
Wood's La SK8 . . . . .35 B7
Wood's La CW8 . . . . .101 C5
Woodsome Cl CH65 . . . . .70 B1
Woodsome Dr CH65 . . . . .70 B1
Wood Sorrel Way WA3 . . .3 E8
Woods Rd M44 . . . . .11 F8
Wood St
Audley ST7 . . . . .209 E3
Congleton CW12 . . . . .156 D3
Crewe CW2 . . . . .190 D2
Golborne WA3 . . . . .3 A8
Macclesfield SK11 . . . . . . .112 D7
Mow Cop ST7 . . . . .195 D7
New Mills SK22 . . . . .39 B7
Sandycroft CH5 . . . . .116 A2
Warrington WA1 . . . . .16 B5
Widnes WA8 . . . . .13 C1

Woodstock Ave
Cheadle SK8 . . . . .35 A7
Newton-le-W WA12 . . . . . . .2 D2
Woodstock Ct SK10 . . . . .87 A2
Woodstock Dr CW10 . . . .151 E5
Woodstock Gdns WA4 . . .26 F6
Woodstock Gr WA8 . . . . .12 D2
Woodthorn Cl WA4 . . . . .24 F4
Woodvale Cl WA2 . . . . .8 E1
Woodvale Rd
Ellesmere Port CH66 . . . . . .69 D6
Knutsford WA16 . . . . .82 A8
Wood View ST7 . . . . .210 A1
Woodview Cres WA8 . . . .22 A8
Woodview Rd WA8 . . . . . .22 A8
Woodville Pl WA8 . . . . . . .12 D1
Woodwards Cotts
CH64 . . . . .66 E7
Woodward St CW8 . . . . . .77 D1
Woodward Wlk CH3 . . . .121 C3
WOODWORTH GREEN
. . . . .186 B8
Woodyear Rd CW1 . . . . . .43 E7
Woolacombe Cl WA4 . . . .16 D2
Woolaston Dr ST7 . . . . . .193 D3
Woolden Rd M44, WA3 . . .11 B8
WOOLFALL 230 C6
Woollam Dr CH66 . . . . . . .69 D7
Woolley Ave SK12 . . . . . . .36 D2
Woolley Cl WA6 . . . . .49 D2
Woolmer Cl WA3 . . . . .9 F4
WOOLSTANWOOD 189 E3
WOOLSTON 17 C8
Woolston Ave CW12 . . . .157 A2
Woolston CE Prim Sch
WA1 . . . . .17 D8
Woolston Com High Sch
WA1 . . . . .17 B7
Woolston Com Prim Sch
WA1 . . . . .17 C7
Woolston Grange Ave
Warrington WA1 . . . . .9 D1
Warrington, Woolston
WA1 . . . . .17 F8
Woolston Hall WA1 . . . . .17 D7
Woolston Rd WA11 . . . . . . .1 C7
Woolston St CH66 . . . . . . .69 F8
WOORE 232 B1
Woore Prim Sch CW3 . . .232 C1
Woore Rd CW3 . . . . .230 D3
Worcester Cl
Talke ST7 . . . . .210 D7
Warrington WA5 . . . . .15 C5
Worcester Pl CH1 . . . . . .118 A4
Worcester St CH65 . . . . . .70 C6
Worcester Wlk 6
CH65 . . . . .70 C6
Wordsworth Ave
Warrington WA4 . . . . .16 B2
Widnes WA8 . . . . .22 F8
Wordsworth Cl
Crewe CW2 . . . . .189 F1
7 Sandbach CW11 . . . . .174 D6
Wordsworth Cres
CH1 . . . . .118 A5
Wordsworth Dr CW1 . . . .190 F4
Wordsworth Mdw SK10 . .86 F1
Wordsworth Mews
CH1 . . . . .118 A5
Wordsworth Sq CH1 . . . .118 A5
Wordsworth Way
Alsager ST7 . . . . .193 D4
Ellesmere Port CH66 . . . . . .69 E1
Works Cotts WA7 . . . . . . .49 E3
Works La CW9 . . . . .79 E1
World Freight Terminal
M90 . . . . .32 F7
World Way M90 . . . . .33 B8
WORLESTON 188 F5
Worleston Ct CW10 . . . . .151 C6
Worley Ct CH3 . . . . .183 A8
Worrall St CW12 . . . . . . .156 D3
Worsborough Ave
WA5 . . . . .15 B5
Worsley Ave
Saughall CH1 . . . . .117 A8
Warrington WA4 . . . . .16 F4
Worsley Dr CW12 . . . . . . .157 B1
Worsley Rd WA4 . . . . .16 B1
Worsley St
Golborne WA3 . . . . .3 A8
Warrington WA5 . . . . .15 F7
Worth Ct SK12 . . . . .36 D2
WORTHENBURY 211 A1
Worthing St CW9 . . . . . . .104 C8
Worthington Ave 9
M31 . . . . .11 F3
Worthington Cl
Henbury SK11 . . . . .111 C8
Nantwich CW5 . . . . .205 A5
Runcorn WA7 . . . . .50 A7
Worthington Ct CH2 . . . .118 D4
Worth Prim Sch SK12 . . . . .36 F2
Wrekin Ho 8 CW8 . . . . .103 C5
Wrekin Way CH4 . . . . . . .140 F6
Wren Ave CW4 . . . . .129 C2
Wrenbury CI ST5 . . . . . . .210 D1
WRENBURY 216 F4
Wrenbury Dr 3 CW9 . . .103 E5
WRENBURY FRITH 216 C6
Wrenbury Frith CW5 . . . .216 B7
Wrenbury Gn CW5 . . . . . .216 E4

Wrenbury Hall Dr
CW5 . . . . .217 A5
WRENBURY HEATH 217 B5
Wrenbury Heath Rd
CW5 . . . . .217 D5
Wrenbury Ind Est
CW5 . . . . .217 A3
Wrenbury Prim Sch
CW5 . . . . .216 F4
Wrenbury Rd
Aston CW5 . . . . .217 B3
Chorley Bank SY14 . . . . . . .201 D1
Marbury SY13 . . . . .226 E8
Nantwich CW5 . . . . .216 B1
Wrenbury Sta CW5 . . . . . .217 A3
Wren Cl
Macclesfield SK10 . . . . .87 A1
Runcorn WA7 . . . . .50 A6
Warrington WA3 . . . . .9 F4
Wrenmere Cl CW11 . . . . .174 E8
Wrenshot La WA16 . . . . . .29 D4
Wrexham Cl
Biddulph ST8 . . . . .179 D1
Warrington WA5 . . . . .7 E1
Wrexham Rd
Bickerton SY14 . . . . .200 A8
Bulkeley SY14, CW6 . . . . . .184 E1
Burland CW5 . . . . .203 C8
Chester CH4 . . . . .141 B4
Faddiley CW5, CW6 . . . . . .202 D6
Holt LL13 . . . . .196 B7
Malpas SY14 . . . . .213 B5
Pulford CH4 . . . . .162 E5
Roughhill CH4 . . . . .140 F1
Worthenbury SY14 . . . . . . .211 C1
Wright Ave CW9 . . . . . . .104 D6
Wright Cres WA8 . . . . . . .23 A5
Wright Ct CW5 . . . . .204 F5
Wright Lo 6 CW5 . . . . . .204 F5
WRIGHT'S GREEN 27 A6
Wrights La WA5 . . . . .13 F2
Wright's La
Burtonwood WA5 . . . . .6 F3
Sandbach CW11 . . . . .175 D6
Wright St SY14 . . . . .194 D1
Wright Tree Villas
M44 . . . . .11 D5
Wrigley La SK10 . . . . .86 B3
Wrigley Rd WA11 . . . . .1 E6
Wrinehill Rd CW5 . . . . . .220 E7
Wroxham Cl
Chester CH2 . . . . .237 B4
Helsby WA6 . . . . .73 B4
Macclesfield SK10 . . . . .87 E3
Warrington WA5 . . . . .14 E6
Wr Twr (Mus)* CH1 . . . . . .118 B2
Wr Twr Rd CH64 . . . . .41 E1
Wr Twr St CH1 . . . . .237 A3
Wrynose Rd CH62 . . . . . . .43 E8
Wybersley Rd SK6 . . . . . . .38 A8
WYBUNBURY 220 A8
Wybunbury Delves CE
Prim Sch CW5 . . . . .220 B7
Wybunbury La CW5 . . . . .205 E3
Wybunbury Rd
Willaston CW5 . . . . .205 D4
Wybunbury CW5 . . . . .220 B7
Wyche Ave CW5 . . . . .204 E6
Wyche Cl CW9 . . . . .104 E6
Wyche La CW6 . . . . .185 F8
Wychelm Rd M31 . . . . . . .11 F3
Wyche Prim Sch CW5 . . .204 E6
Wyche Rd CW5 . . . . .185 F8
Wych House Bank
CW5 . . . . .204 D5
Wych-House La
CW10 . . . . .128 C1
Wych La SK10 . . . . .62 D5
Wychwood Ave WA13 . . . .18 C3
Wychwood Pk CW2 . . . . .207 C2
Wycliffe Ave SK9 . . . . .60 A7
Wycliffe Ct CH2 . . . . .119 A2
Wycliffe Rd
Ellesmere Port CH65 . . . . . .69 F3
Haydock WA11 . . . . .1 E7
Wyedale CH65 . . . . .70 B3
Wyedale Rd WA11 . . . . .1 E6
Wyncroft Cl
Ellesmere Port CH65 . . . . . .70 B3
Widnes WA8 . . . . .22 C8
Wyncroft Ct CW8 . . . . . . .77 C1
Wyncroft Rd WA8 . . . . . . .22 C7
Wyndham Cl
Bramhall SK7 . . . . .35 E7
Northwich CW9 . . . . .103 F5
Wyndham Cres CH66 . . . .69 E2
Wyndham Rd CH1 . . . . . .117 C4
Wynd The CW6 . . . . .122 C4
Wynfield Ave M22 . . . . . . .33 F7
Wyngate Rd WA15 . . . . . . .31 F8
Wynnstay Rd CW4 . . . . . .139 C4
Wynter Cl SY14 . . . . .198 B3
Wynter La SY14 . . . . .198 B3
Wythburn Gr WA7 . . . . . .49 E5
Wythens Rd SK8 . . . . .34 B8
Wythin St WA6 . . . . .168 D1

Yarrow Cl CH4 . . . . .139 C3
Yarwood Cl CW8 . . . . . . .103 F7
Yarwoodheath La
WA14 . . . . .30 E7
YATEHOUSE GREEN . . .128 D6
Yatehouse La CW10 . . . . .128 D7
Yates Cl WA5 . . . . .15 C5
Yates Rd
New Mills SK22 . . . . .39 C7
Thornton-le-M CH2 . . . . . . .71 E1
Yates St CW1 . . . . .190 C2
Y Berllan Geirios/Cherry
Orch LL13 . . . . .196 D8
Yeald Brow WA13 . . . . . . .18 B3
Yeardsley Ave SK23 . . . . .39 D3
Yeardsley Gn SK23 . . . . . .65 D8
Yeardsley La SK23 . . . . . .39 D3
Yearsleys La WA6 . . . . . .101 A5
Yeld La CW6 . . . . .122 E8
Yeoman Way CH66 . . . . . .69 F1
Yeovil Cl WA1 . . . . .17 C8
Yerburgh St CH2 . . . . . . .118 D4
Yewdale Dr CH66 . . . . .69 F1
Yewlands CH3 . . . . .118 D5
Yewlands Dr WA16 . . . . . .57 C2
Yew Tree Ave WA12 . . . . . .2 A4
Yew Tree Ave / Lon yr
Ywen LL13 . . . . .116 F7
Yew Tree Bank CW5 . . . .145 B5
Yewtree Cl CH64 . . . . .66 F7
Yew Tree Cl
Broughton CH4 . . . . .139 C3
Bulkeley SY14 . . . . .184 D2
Little Budworth CW6 . . . . .147 F7
Lymm WA13 . . . . .18 E4
Macclesfield SK11 . . . . . . .112 A6
Middlewich CW10 . . . . . . .128 B2
Prestbury SK10 . . . . .87 B7
Thornton-le-M CH2 . . . . . . .71 E1
Wilmslow SK9 . . . . .60 D7
Yew Tree Ct
Alsager ST7 . . . . .193 E2
6 Heswall CH60 . . . . .41 A8
Wimboldsley CW10 . . . . . .150 F3
Yew Tree Dr
Barnton CW8 . . . . .78 B3
Nantwich CW5 . . . . .204 D5
Yew Tree Farm Trad Est
WA11 . . . . .2 A8
Yew Tree La
Appleton Thorn WA4 . . . . . .27 C5
Astbury CW12 . . . . .178 C3
Bridgemere CW5 . . . . .232 A6
Crewe CW5 . . . . .205 D3
Yew Tree Park Rd SK8 . . .35 B6
Yewtree Rd WA16 . . . . . . .80 F3
Yew Tree Rd
Wardsend SK10 . . . . .37 B1
Wistaston CW2 . . . . .206 A8
Yew Tree Way
Golborne WA3 . . . . .3 B7
Prestbury SK10 . . . . .87 C6
Yew Wlk 1 M31 . . . . .11 E2
Yonne The CH1 . . . . .237 A2
York Ave
Culcheth WA3 . . . . .4 F2
Warrington WA5 . . . . .14 E7
York Cl
Biddulph ST8 . . . . .179 C2
Talke ST7 . . . . .210 D7
York Cres SK9 . . . . .60 D8
York Pl WA7 . . . . .23 A2
York Rd
Connah's Quay CH5 . . . . . . .91 C1
Ellesmere Port CH65 . . . . . .70 C5
Irlam M44 . . . . .11 D5
Warrington WA4 . . . . .17 A2
Widnes WA8 . . . . .22 C8
Yorkshire Rd M31 . . . . . . .11 E2
York St
Chester CH1 . . . . .237 B3
Macclesfield SK10 . . . . . . .112 E8
Runcorn WA7 . . . . .23 A2
Warrington WA4 . . . . .16 C4
Yorston Lodge Sch
WA16 . . . . .56 F1
Ysgol Borderbrook
SY14 . . . . .222 F5
Ystad Ddiwdiannol
Wrecsam/Wrexham Ind
Est LL13 . . . . .196 A1

Z

Zan Dr CW11 . . . . .175 A3
Zan Ind Pk CW11 . . . . . .175 A3
Zara Ct WA11 . . . . .1 C7
Zinnia Dr M44 . . . . .11 E8
Zion St 9 CW8 . . . . .103 E7

Y

Yardley Ave WA5 . . . . .15 F8
Yarmouth Rd WA5 . . . . . .14 E6

PHILIP'S MAPS
the Gold Standard for drivers

◆ **Philip's street atlases cover every county
in England, Wales, Northern Ireland and
much of Scotland**

◆ Every named street is shown, including alleys,
lanes and walkways

◆ Thousands of additional features marked: stations,
public buildings, car parks, places of interest

◆ Route-planning maps to get you close to your
destination

◆ Postcodes on the maps and in the index

◆ Widely used by the emergency services,
transport companies and local authorities

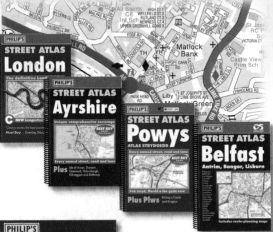

For national mapping, choose
Philip's Navigator Britain
the most detailed road atlas available of
England, Wales and Scotland. Hailed by
Auto Express as 'the ultimate road atlas',
the atlas shows every road and lane in
Britain.

Street atlases currently available

England
Bedfordshire
Berkshire
Birmingham and West Midlands
Bristol and Bath
Buckinghamshire
Cambridgeshire
Cheshire
Cornwall
Cumbria
Derbyshire
Devon
Dorset
County Durham and Teesside
Essex
North Essex
South Essex
Gloucestershire
Hampshire
North Hampshire
South Hampshire
Herefordshire Monmouthshire
Hertfordshire
Isle of Wight
Kent
East Kent
West Kent
Lancashire
Leicestershire and Rutland
Lincolnshire
London
Greater Manchester
Merseyside
Norfolk
Northamptonshire
Northumberland
Nottinghamshire
Oxfordshire
Shropshire
Somerset
Staffordshire
Suffolk
Surrey
East Sussex
West Sussex
Tyne and Wear
Warwickshire
Birmingham and West Midlands
Wiltshire and Swindon
Worcestershire
East Yorkshire Northern Lincolnshire
North Yorkshire
South Yorkshire
West Yorkshire

Wales
Anglesey, Conwy and Gwynedd
Cardiff, Swansea and The Valleys
Carmarthenshire, Pembrokeshire and Swansea
Ceredigion and South Gwynedd
Denbighshire, Flintshire, Wrexham
Herefordshire Monmouthshire
Powys

Scotland
Aberdeenshire
Ayrshire
Dumfries and Galloway
Edinburgh and East Central Scotland
Fife and Tayside
Glasgow and West Central Scotland
Inverness and Moray
Lanarkshire
Scottish Borders

Northern Ireland
County Antrim and County Londonderry
County Armagh and County Down
Belfast
County Tyrone and County Fermanagh

How to order
Philip's maps and atlases are available from bookshops,
motorway services and petrol stations. You can order direct
from the publisher by phoning **0207 531 8473** or
online at **www.philips-maps.co.uk**
For bulk orders only, e-mail philips@philips-maps.co.uk